EUROPEAN INVESTMENT IN GREECE IN THE NINETEENTH CENTURY

Banking historiography often does not sufficiently take into account bankers' deliberations of their decision making, but rather limits investigation to considerations of profit maximisation. This book shows that the decision-making processes of nineteenth-century bankers contemplating high-risk financial markets like Greece are just as complex as present-day investment decisions.

The book, now published in English after a first German edition, offers in-depth studies of decision making in concrete historical situations, considering political and economic circumstances and also the individual background of the actors concerned, including a reflection on the influence of cultural movements such as Philhellenism. Employing methodological inspirations from the field of behavioural finance, the book analyses a broad range of published and unpublished English, French, Greek, German and Swiss sources on European investment in Greece between 1821 and the Balkan wars. Additionally, rich insights into Greek economic history, the economic integration of the country into Europe and long-lasting European stereotypes of Southern Europe and Greece are provided; this furthers understanding of the historical background of the Greek financial crisis after 2009.

In combining the perspectives of financial, economic, political and cultural history, this book is primarily significant for students of various fields of historiography. Due to its strong awareness of methodological questions, it is also of great interest to academic historians. In addition, the strong public interest in the Greek financial crisis after 2009 and its consequences for Europe will, thirdly, attract the interest of a broader public.

Korinna Schönhärl is a Senior Researcher for Contemporary, Social and Economic History at Goethe University Frankfurt, Germany.

FINANCIAL HISTORY

Edited by Farley Grubb and Anne L. Murphy

MONEY, POLITICS AND POWER
Banking and Public Finance in Wartime England, 1694–1696
Richard A. Kleer

REGULATION OF THE LONDON STOCK EXCHANGE
Share Trading, Fraud and Reform 1914–1945
Chris Swinson

MONETARY PLURALITY IN LOCAL, REGIONAL AND GLOBAL ECONOMIES
Edited by Georgina M. Gómez

SHARE TRADING, FRAUD AND THE CRASH OF 1929
A Biography of Clarence Hatry
Chris Swinson

THE ORIGINS OF MODERN BANKING IN SPAIN
Monetary Plurality and Local Monopolies
Edited by Carles Sudrià and Yolanda Blasco-Martel

EUROPEAN INVESTMENT IN GREECE IN THE NINETEENTH CENTURY
A Behavioural Approach to Financial History
Korinna Schönhärl

For more information about this series, please visit www.routledge.com/series/FINHIS

EUROPEAN INVESTMENT IN GREECE IN THE NINETEENTH CENTURY

A Behavioural Approach to Financial History

Korinna Schönhärl

Routledge
Taylor & Francis Group
LONDON AND NEW YORK

First published in English 2021
by Routledge
2 Park Square, Milton Park, Abingdon, Oxon OX14 4RN

and by Routledge
605 Third Avenue, New York, NY 10017

First issued in paperback 2022

Routledge is an imprint of the Taylor & Francis Group, an informa business

Translated by Katharine Thomas. The translation of this work was funded by Geisteswissenschaften International – Translation Funding for Work in the Humanities and Social Sciences from Germany, a joint initiative of the Fritz Thyssen Foundation, the German Federal Foreign Office, the collection society VG Wort and the Börsenverein des Deutschen Buchhandels (German Publishers & Booksellers Association).

Original in German: Korinna Schönhärl: *Finanziers in Sehnsuchtsräumen. Europäische Banken und Griechenland im 19. Jahrhundert* (Schriftenreihe der Historischen Kommission bei der Bayerischen Akademie der Wissenschaften, Vol. 98), Vandenhoeck & Ruprecht, Göttingen 2017.

British Library Cataloguing-in-Publication Data
A catalogue record for this book is available from the British Library

Library of Congress Cataloging-in-Publication Data
Names: Schönhärl, Korinna, author.
Title: European investment in Greece in the nineteenth century : a behavioural approach to financial history / Korinna Schönhärl.
Other titles: Finanziers in Sehnsuchtsräumen. English
Description: 1 Edition. | New York : Routledge, 2020. |
Series: Financial history | Includes bibliographical references and index.
Identifiers: LCCN 2020025336 (print) | LCCN 2020025337 (ebook)
Subjects: LCSH: Finance—Greece—History—19th century. | Finance—Europe—History—19th century. | Banks and banking—Greece—History—19th century. | Banks and banking—Europe—History—19th century.
Classification: LCC HG186.G8 S3613 2020 (print) | LCC HG186.G8 (ebook) | DDC 332.67/34049509034—dc23
LC record available at https://lccn.loc.gov/2020025336
LC ebook record available at https://lccn.loc.gov/2020025337

ISBN: 978-0-367-25210-6 (hbk)
ISBN: 978-0-367-55350-0 (pbk)
ISBN: 978-0-429-28653-7 (ebk)

DOI: 10.4324/9780429286537

The Open Access version of this book was funded by Paderborn University.

For Product Safety Concerns and Information please contact our EU representative:
GPSR@taylorandfrancis.com
Taylor & Francis
Verlag GmbH, Kaufingerstraße 24, 80331 München, Germany

FOR CHRISTIAN

CONTENTS

PREFACE TO THE ENGLISH TRANSLATION

In August 2018, Greece was released from the Third Economic Adjustment Programme. This does not mean that the Greek government and economy are no longer closely supervised by the international lenders, but at the moment no new funds are under negotiation. And Greece is therefore no longer attracting the immediate attention of the international press, except in the context of African refugees on the 'Balkan Route'. Even the parliamentary elections in July 2019 were only briefly commented upon in the international press, although they led to the removal from office of prime minister Tsipras from the left-wing populist Syriza and to the forming of a conservative government. Greece is no longer the focus of European interest, notwithstanding the fact that the repercussions of the crisis continue to affect the economic and social life of the country. The negative Greek narratives that dominated much of the press coverage in the years after 2009, and that are traced back to the nineteenth century in this book, have thus moved out of the limelight – until the next Greece crisis, the historian would suspect.

It is therefore all the more important that in the calm after the storm, the fruits of this research should be made accessible to a broader, English-reading public, also in Greece. In April 2019, this piece of research was awarded a special prize by the trust 'Geisteswissenschaften International' (a joint initiative of the Fritz Thyssen Foundation, the German Federal Foreign Office, the collection society VG Wort and the Börsenverein des Deutschen Buchhandels [German Publishers & Booksellers Association]), who provided the necessary funds for the translation as prize money. Katharine Thomas could therefore translate the book, and my particular thanks go to her for her precise and empathic work and the smooth cooperation. I thank my student assistants Nasrin Düll and Nadya Melina Ramirez Lugo for adapting the citations to comply with the Routledge standards.

In the meantime, I have taken up a point that the book only touches upon in passing: the question of tax morale, which international observers suggested was disastrous in nineteenth-century Greece. Little has changed with this external opinion, and it also corresponds with the Greek self-description.

Remarkably, in Greece, it is totally acceptable to argue that inadequate tax payment behaviour is a regrettable legacy of Ottoman rule, which ended in 1830. In contrast in Western Europe, no serious political discussion could include the suggestion that inadequate tax payment behaviour, for instance in Germany or France, could be traced back to the Napoleonic wars and that this made it so difficult to improve. Why do people talk so differently about paying taxes in different countries and why have the related norms developed in such diverse ways? This is the research question I am pursuing in the context of the Heisenberg programme of the German Research Foundation at Goethe University Frankfurt, with West Germany, Spain and the USA in the second half of the twentieth century as case studies. The fundamental question thus continues to accompany me: we talk about the economy, how does it change in and through this discourse?

Frankfurt, in February 2020
Korinna Schönhärl

Part I

INTRODUCTION

INVESTMENTS BY EUROPEAN BANKERS IN GREECE IN THE NINETEENTH CENTURY

The burden and blessing of an ancient heritage in precarious financial situations

'Swindlers in the Euro-Family. Is Greece cheating us of our Money?' demanded the front page of the German news magazine *Fokus* on 22 February 2010.[1] This headline was illustrated with the famous statue of Aphrodite, the so-called Venus de Milo, an image of Greek antiquity that is firmly rooted in European visual memory and is today housed in the Louvre in Paris. Although the right hand is missing in the original, the Fokus added an arm with a raised middle finger. A dirty Greek flag was wrapped around the figure's hips (Figure I.1). Greece took the magazine to court for this so-called Greece-bashing. The case was heard in Athens and ended with an acquittal, but the damage to German-Greek relations was undeniable.[2]

Admittedly, it has long been common to illustrate headlines about Greece with images and symbols of antiquity, such as the Acropolis of Athens, even if usually without the obscene alienation effects. Greek politics and, in particular, the Greek financial crisis inevitably lead West European reporters to illustrate current events with images related to Greece's great past. This contrasts to, for instance, the situation with Ireland and Iceland where nobody would think of drawing on historical references. Even in the case of Italy, comparable historical images are seldom used. With Greece, it seems that the Europeans think automatically of antiquity (Klemm 2015, 352). Reporting on the financial crisis in Greece seems almost impossible without recourse to ancient history, which forms a glossy backdrop that further accentuates the severity of the contemporary situation. Between 2010 and 2012, reports in German media about the 'broke Greeks' were correspondingly negative, at times even defamatory (Bickes et al. 2015). Six months of this negative reporting, particularly prevalent in the *Fokus* and the *Bild*, were enough to fully activate the negative images of Greece (ibid., 347).[3] However, justifying a financial rescue policy for the crisis-stricken country seems similarly to require reference to its function as the cradle of Western civilisation and democracy, as seen in the poem

DOI: 10.4324/9780429286537-2

Figure I.1 Fokus, Cover, 22.2.2010.

by the famous German poet Günther Grass (Grass 2012).[4] It is equally rare for France to produce an unprejudiced view of Greece sine ira et studio (Basch 1995, 500), and in Great Britain, Greece is also 'an emotional word' (Holland/Markides 2006, 1). Throughout Europe, it is apparently impossible to think about or comment on Greece's finances without referring to antiquity. In contrast, Greece's Byzantine history is never used for comparison, despite the fact that in its latter days, it offered manifold examples of nepotism, corruption and state decline. In West European imagination, however, this era is hardly ever linked to Greece. The Greeks themselves occasionally utilise images of antiquity to their advantage. Thus at his first visit to the French president in Paris, the Greek prime minister Alexis Tsipras, who has held the position since January 2015, announced his delight at being in a country that had taken on the baton of democracy from Greece, thus audaciously building a bridge between the Acropolis and the Storming of the Bastille, as the *Süddeutsche Zeitung* commented (Cáceres/Wernicke 2015). However, there are comparable examples of extensive laments about the 'misfortune of being a Greek' and constantly being confronted with exaggerated expectations from abroad (Dimou 2012).

While the use of such comparisons with antiquity may seem particularly original to certain contemporary journalists, they can be traced back to before the founding of the modern Greek state in 1830. In the 1820s, Greek freedom fighters were in London and Paris promoting their cause in the hope of gaining financial support for their struggle for independence from the Ottoman Empire. They too used ancient Greek heritage and the hope for its renaissance as important arguments to persuade Philhellenes to provide investment. This linking of the spheres of culture and finance was to continue, as will be seen, far beyond the phase of great European Philhellenism at the time of the Greek Revolution, and can be traced throughout the entire nineteenth century. Greek thus became an 'imagined market'[5] for many West Europeans, an assimilation that drew together and intermingled many different periods, modifying the receiving culture while constituting the reference culture.[6]

This renders Greece particularly attractive for a cultural-historical investigation of the perception of financial markets by bankers, the mental dispositions underlying their actions and their cultural roots. A further advantage is the starting point provided by the especially convenient 'zero hour' of the founding of the Greek state in 1830 (Loules 1986, 409).[7] It is notable that despite three state bankruptcies (in 1827, 1843 and 1893[8]), Greece developed into an accepted investment market for European bankers in the course of the long nineteenth century, even if the country only accounted for 0.15% of world trade in 1913. It seems exaggerated to speak of Greece as an 'El Dorado'; the term 'emerging country' seems more applicable (Bonin 2013, 12, 42, 70). Before the Balkan Wars, Greece had no problems obtaining credit at reasonable conditions on the European exchanges, and numerous direct investments streamed into the country. The majority of European bankers now perceived Greece as a potential financial market, albeit a risky one.[9] The two Balkan Wars, starting in 1912, significantly changed business activities and banking in the region, and thus mark the end of the research period. In terms of the political history of Greece, the Goudi coup of 1909 and the subsequent coming to power of Eleftherios Venizelos in 1910 similarly heralded a new era, so that it seems reasonable to end the study period here. How, then, did Greece develop into a promising financial market in the perception of foreign bankers in the period from the Greek Revolution until the Balkan Wars?[10] This starting point leads on to interesting questions of financial and banking history: How did bankers make investment decisions in the nineteenth century?[11] How and via which paths did bankers access relevant information about interesting markets? How did they interpret this information? What forms of risk management did they develop and maintain, and how did they establish trust in the international context of globalising finance? The small size and limited economic importance of Greece in worldwide terms limit its comparability with other investment markets. However, pronounced contrasts in Western European perceptions of the country render it particularly interesting with regard to the cultural dimension of financial transfers. As images of Greece were and are so contradictory and powerful, the Greek example is especially suitable for an investigation of the multifacetedness of investment decisions.

Financial business in Greece was led by banks from Switzerland, France, Great Britain, Bavaria and – after 1871 – the German Empire; this sets the geographical framework for the investors. In terms of the area of investments, research is limited to the territory of the Greek state, which slowly increased in size throughout the nineteenth century. This excludes the area that was added to Greece after the Balkan Wars, as this was knowledge the actors could not previously be aware of, except possibly in the form of the 'Megali idea' (the notion of a large Greek state) that may have encouraged them to speculate on territorial expansion.[12]

Is Greece a risk?

'Classic' banking history would tend to focus on profit rates and risk premiums when answering this question. Traditional accounts of banking history assume that nineteenth-century bankers adopted a utility maximisation approach to investment projects and assessed the potential profits in order to decide whether to accept or reject a specific project. Other motives usually attract little attention. The aim of this cultural-historical investigation is to move beyond this approach and to consider the entire spectrum of motives that influenced bankers' investment decisions. Rather than assuming that bankers carefully conceived and followed some master plan, pursuing geostrategic axes across the Mediterranean for instance, the focus is on situative constellations of decision making.[13] Profits, on which all banking houses depend, are not neglected here. However, the analysis also includes bankers' statements preserved in the archives where they speak of additional and/or sometimes completely different kinds of motivation: their burning Philhellenism, their emotional enthusiasm for Greek antiquity, their drive to further their own reputation or improve their political relations, their fear of the competition, their dependence on once-chosen paths, their imperial fervour, to mention but a few. In banking history research, such findings, reflections and explanations tend to be dismissed as hollow, legitimating phrases, as 'obvious pure ideology' (Reitmayer 1999, 207, tr. by K.S.). However, findings from behavioural psychology and historical emotions research suggest that such statements should be taken seriously: they play an important role in the self-perceptions of financial market actors and significantly influence their decision making through various justification mechanisms.

This work thus adopts a meta-meta perspective (Gillespie 2008): observing the European bankers while they observed Greece. How did the bankers make their decisions, e.g. how did they differentiate between danger and risk, between investment and speculation, between trust and control? What risk strategies did they have and how did these strategies change over time?[14] The explicit focus is on bankers and not on other investors such as private individuals, who are much more difficult to trace in the sources and whose inclusion would require not only qualitative, but also quantitative methods. Most attention is paid to the long-term investments of bankers in industry, in the banking sector and in Greek state bonds, particularly project financing (Gourvish 2008), where it is much more difficult to determine potential risk in advance than is the case, for instance, with the granting of credit. Even today, it is not possible to measure the so-called operative risk of such project finance; due to the many incalculable factors involved, it can at best be estimated in terms of categories (Hughes 2007, 27f.). How did the bankers deal with this operative risk? The aim of this research is to analyse their decision-making processes with reference to Greece, combining the approaches of banking history and cultural history.

What types of bankers are we dealing with? In the nineteenth century, European banking was in a phase of profound change. The so-called merchant banks of the early modern period dealt with exchange and finance business as just *one* branch of their activities alongside trade, but around the end of the eighteenth century, banks developed that focused, sometimes exclusively, on financial matters (Chapman 1984). These were initially only private banks run by one family or individual. In the course of the nineteenth century, the face of the international capital markets and thus the banks then changed fundamentally. While at the beginning of the century government bonds offered the highest profits, by the end of the century industrial finance played a decisive role (Cottrell 1980).

At the same time, other new business formats developed as members of the European middle classes looked for investment opportunities for their savings. In Great Britain, the founding of joint-stock banks was permitted from 1825 (Cassis 1990, 74f.; Kynaston 1994, 40), and they then spread across the continent in the following decades (ibid., 2012, 69).[15] This form of organisation allowed the public to invest even smaller sums in large projects and thus promoted capital accumulation, which was most necessary for industrial growth. This development brought new challenges for bankers as the new financial products required specialised, trained salespeople and involved new bureaucratic and administrative tasks. Hired managers took over the business of these banks and, in the context of corporate governance, were required to report to supervisory boards and shareholders at regular intervals, legitimising their actions. This led to a professionalisation of the field (Litterer 1986; Burhop 2007; Kurgan-van Hentenryk 2008; Feldman 2008, 292; Dahlem 2009; Wylegala 2017), to the development of systems of experts in specific legal constellations with honed information-processing abilities (Berghoff 2004, 68). The various interests of the investors and managers needed to be communicated in order to ensure the viability of joint-stock banks, and the increasing bureaucratisation that ensued could also lead to a division of responsibilities (Baecker 2008, 153). There is controversy in the research field as to whether nineteenth-century managers of joint-stock banks were more willing to take risks than family bankers because they were not risking their own capital,[16] or whether they were actually more risk-averse because they bore responsibility for the money entrusted to them by shareholders (Schönhärl 2017b). In principle, both shared the same criteria of risk evaluation (Pohle-Fraser 1999, 108). It should, however, be emphasised that banking behaviour and the practices of risk management were deeply influenced by culture and could therefore vary greatly from country to country and from financial metropolis to financial metropolis (Cassis 1994; Feldman 2008, 291; Dilley 2009; Williamson 2010).[17]

With the increasingly international focus, techniques of risk management became evermore significant in the banks, who, at times following their industrial customers, ventured beyond their familiar and pragmatically manageable world of experience (Schütz/Luckmann 2003, 33; Tarrade 2012), in some cases into the Mediterranean area, in some cases into South America or Asia. The capital markets are also said to have experienced a first wave of globalisation in the nineteenth century, although a strong focus on Europe remained evident.[18] The banking houses that followed this development[19] were faced with uncertainties that required an offensive, risk-oriented course of action, but they also had to hedge these risks (Berghoff 2004, 71). To this end, some of the banks developed international networks. The Rothschild family is a well-known example. The sons ran branches in Frankfurt, Naples, London, Paris and Vienna, and supported one another in raising investment funds and in crises (Ferguson 2002). Many interconnections through marriage and strong loyalty relations safeguarded family businesses of this kind.[20] However, such networks were based not only on family, but could also include compatriots in the diaspora. Thus in the nineteenth century, the merchant bankers who originated from the Greek island of Chios developed a dense network of bases that covered the whole of Europe, enabling trusting cooperation and flat hierarchies (Dertilis 1995;

Harlaftis 2005; Minoglou 2002a, 2005; Christ et al. 2015). Religious communities could also form the basis of such networks (Δρίτσα [Dritsa] 1998, 304–344).

When talking about the risk management of banks, it is first necessary to define the term 'risk', a concept that has recently attracted growing interest among historians (Asmussen et al. 2014; Itzen 2016; Mohun 2016; Brakensiek et al. 2017). The earliest attempts at finding a definition date back to the 1920s (Knight 1921). Risk can be defined as the possibility that certain actions will lead to damage or losses. Risks thus refer not to the unpleasant circumstances of an uncertain world, but rather to the results of decisions made by economic actors (Hahn 1998, 49; Baecker 2008). Risks can always be linked to an actor's decisions, in contrast to external dangers that actors cannot influence.[21] Depending on how a particular situation is interpreted, it can thus be perceived as either risky or dangerous (Hahn 1998). While economic logic dictates the avoidance of dangers that cannot be influenced, risks arising from decisions may be sought out if profitable. Economic actors can derive profit from the contingency of future developments by receiving payment for assuming the risks (risk premium) (ibid., 49). This is particularly true for banks: they assume responsibility for compensating the time differences that constantly occur in the economy (Luhmann 2009, 8) and thus deal with promises of payment for a contingent future (Baecker 2008, VIf.). They secure the safety of payments through continued rescheduling and handle different types of risks, e.g. risk of fraud, risk of insolvency, risk of illiquidity and risk of default. Generally speaking, the banks run the risk that they may not be able to maintain the ability to meet their obligations (ibid., 108–112).

Banks are thus constantly faced with the decision to accept or reject risks. Indeed, their business is unimaginable without risk. The most important aim for bankers is (and was) not to be taken in by an illusion of security, because this would damage the chances of identifying and allocating risks.

> The only security that can be won in this situation is found by consciously engaging with risk structures that consist of a network of sufficient actors who are able to reveal, understand and, using their own resources, master that part of the risk that they assume.
>
> (Baecker 2008, V, tr. by K.S.)[22]

Nonetheless, bankers are often required to portray themselves to the public and policymakers as risk-averse because it 'is only by visibly maintaining the impression of risk aversion, and thus creating a fiction of security, that banks can act undisturbed by governmental and other public interference' (Pohle-Fraser 1999, 2). This leads to an unrealistic public image, such that 'banks' risk aversion has become a sort of doctrinal opinion' (ibid., 48).

Once risks have been identified, the next step is to develop methods for dealing with them. Through their risk management, the banks attempt to position themselves as profitably as possible in relation to the options for risk assumption in the market (Baecker 2008, 125). Risk management is undertaken on three levels: firstly, through observation of the market to identify profitable business opportunities; secondly, through risk management within the organisation to regulate the conditions of risk assumption and thirdly, through the design of financial instruments to split risks (ibid., 126). The latter includes the transformation or sharing of risks (unbundling of risks) (ibid., 135), e.g. by distributing risks among a number of partners.

This investigation thus explores the techniques used by nineteenth-century European banks to filter the noise of their environment in relation to Greece and to reduce the complexity of their decision-making situation. Which past experiences did banks draw upon (ibid., 36)?[23] Which paths and what methods did they choose to try to gain information, including the use of technological innovations (Müller 2016)? Which information-gathering practices were viewed as acceptable in banking circles (Simmel 2013, 278)? How did they deal with the constant information gaps and nonetheless take decisions? It should be noted here that the banks did not just passively receive information, but rather actively generated it themselves (Pohle-Fraser 1999, 373). Overcoming information asymmetries, including those that exist with customers ('brokerage'), is a core concern of the banking business (Battilossi 2008, 75–96, 78). It was thus essential that the banks possessed precise knowledge about the Greek market and the other actors involved, and an in-depth study of risk-management techniques in the private sector, as called for by Hartmut Berghoff, thus promises new findings and insights on industrialisation and globalisation (2004, 66).

Complete knowledge of one's counterpart that would allow a prognosis of his or her actions is as impossible in economic relations as in other forms of social interaction. Such actions are always contingent (Simmel 2013, 268, 274).[24] In the economic context, new institutional economics has established that increased control over a business partner is linked to increased transaction costs, whether these are caused through gathering information, monitoring or auditing (Berghoff 1999).

Such transaction costs can only be reduced if business partners, while fully aware of the risks (Ripperger 2005, 37f.),[25] decide to trust one another (Berghoff 1999, 59). Trust can be defined as a 'mechanism for stabilising uncertain expectations and reducing the associated complexity of human action' (Ripperger 2005, 9, tr. by K.S.). Trust should be clearly distinguished from hope because trust always involves awareness of the risk involved. Thus, 'trust reflects contingency, hope eliminates contingency' (Luhmann 2009, 29, tr. by K.S.). The recognition that economic action is not possible without a basis of trust can be traced back to the beginnings of sociology, e.g. in Georg Simmel's study of the nature of money (Simmel 1900).

> Trust as the hypothesis for future behaviour, which is certain enough thereby to ground practical action, is, as hypothesis, a middle position between knowledge and ignorance of others. Someone who knows all need not *trust*, someone who knows nothing cannot reasonably trust at all.
>
> (Simmel 2009, 315)

In recent decades, political sciences (e.g. Hartmann/Offe 2001), sociology, anthropology and economics have developed completely different notions of the phenomenon of 'trust' without arriving at a consensus concerning its genesis or, indeed, even attempting to do so (Fukuyama 1995, 493).[26] Ute Frevert's attempt to operationalise trust, or confidence, for historical analysis suffers from the lack of a clear, analytical definition.[27] She describes the nineteenth century as the 'century of trust' but simultaneously views the term as 'attractive, but vague and dubious' (Frevert 2003a, 43, 65, tr. by K.S.). Others are more concrete, e.g. Marek Korczynski distinguishes between trust in governance structures, trust in personal relations in line with Mark Granovetter, knowledge of the internal norms of the other party and system trust (Korczynski 2000, 5). However, this still does not allow the term to be operationalised.

This investigation therefore employs the understanding of 'trust' developed by Tanja Ripperger, who draws on the approach of new institutional economics. Trust or confidence between business partners is not viewed as an end in itself or as a moral value, but as an important competitive factor that can help to sink transaction costs (Ripperger 2005, 262).[28] Francis Fukuyama argues similarly, linking the high performance of certain industrial societies such as Japan or Germany to the social trust inherent to them. He suggests that these high-trust preconditions are important for economic success, although they are derived from non-economic areas of life (Fukuyama 1995, 150).[29]

When information is incomplete, the role played by trust in the principal-agent relationship is particularly vital. The principal intentionally decides to overcome information gaps concerning the intentions of the agent by extrapolating from existing information, for instance, by trusting his or her assessment or by generalising from previous experience with the same group (Ripperger 2005, 133). In the end, however, trust is a voluntary act and any reasons given to explain it serve only to legitimise a decision that cannot be based on pure rationality (Luhmann 2009, 31). Demanding or providing detailed factual information or evidence contradicts the nature of trust (ibid., 37). The principal actually achieves more with an irreversible investment, for instance, a contract or a risky advance payment. If this is not exploited by the agent, then this forms the starting point of trusting collaboration (Ripperger 2005, 131). As this collaboration is further consolidated, it becomes easier to do without means of control and safeguards against opportunistic behaviour and 'moral hazard' (ibid., 268).

When considering transaction cost theory, it is nonetheless important not to lose sight of the fact that bankers are 'businesspeople of flesh and blood, who rely more on experience and feelings, on everyday influences and ethical norms than on calculations of transaction costs' (Berghoff 1999, 174, tr. by K.S.). Decisions concerning trust are also influenced by the emotions of the moment. This makes it problematic to retrospectively classify bankers either as responsible and honest merchants or as speculators, depending on whether their business deals were successful or not, an approach that is often taken in banking history. Analysis should rather focus on the state of knowledge of the bankers at the time of their decision making (Pohle-Fraser 1999, 45–48).[30]

The question thus arises as to how the Greek financial market and its actors were able to win the trust of the West European bankers. Here, it is necessary to consider what factors were favourable for the development of trust in the nineteenth century generally and within the group of bankers in particular (Fukuyama 1995, 480). It seems likely that assessment of the potential business partner may have been much more important in developing a trusting relationship than the project itself, as can indeed still be the case in contemporary banking (Baecker 2008, 114). Mechanisms of fostering trust and building confidence in the nineteenth century have, for instance, been researched by David Sunderland (2007), who investigated the development of social capital in English society with regard to the use of clothing, language and objects and the role played by gifts, reputation and interactions with peers in the context of visits to the theatre, museums or art galleries.[31] The focus here is thus on symbols that demonstrate trustworthiness and generate social capital (Luhmann 2009, 36).[32] Newer approaches have moved away from viewing reputation as monolithic and think of it rather as multiple in nature and even as contradictory for different audiences; in all cases, reputation is understood as mediated (Olegario/McKenna 2013). Morten Reitmayer (1999) has investigated questions of social profile and habitus in German banking circles,[33] while for British circles, there are many relevant references to this field in the work of Youssef Cassis (1991, 53–71, 1995, 2015), David Kynaston (1994), Susie J. Pak (2013a, 2013b) and Christopher Kobrak (2013), as well as in the research of Lucy Newton (2000). Here, the focus is primarily on strategies of fostering and maintaining reputation as part of a generalised aspiration to social capital which could multiply an actor's potential impact (Ripperger 2005, 225f.).[34] It should be noted here that no firm or country was able to completely control its external image as this was influenced by many unmanageable factors (Olegario/McKenna 2013). Philanthropy research also provides interesting findings on the significance of social capital in the context of charitable activities such as donating and collecting among the middle classes, as was intensively practised by the Philhellene movement (Ostrower 1995; Adam 2009; Adam et al. 2009). Approaches from the field of postcolonial studies draw attention to the role of intermediaries like brokers in the development of trust and reputation and the initiation of business deals.[35] The term is clearly much more widely conceived here than is usual in banking history.[36]

Decision making in banks: notions from behavioural finance

Trust was, however, only *one* alternative for the bankers. The range of motives underlying the investment decisions of bankers was much greater than may be captured by transaction cost theory, notions of social capital or philanthropy research, especially as monocausal approaches should be avoided.[37] How then is it possible to grasp the entire spectrum of possible reasons for an investment decision (Samakovitis 2012)? Findings from behavioural psychology are helpful here. Choice theory intensively researches factors relevant to decision taking and 'has uncovered substantial and systematic regularities in how people make decisions' (Allingham 2002; LeBoeuf/Shafir 2012, 301). The need to supplement the rational choice model was recognised decades ago as it became clear that the notion of rational utility maximisation was unable to supply answers to questions concerning the different levels of success of national economies or the phased nature of financial market volatility (Fukuyama 1995, 351). The assumption that individuals always choose the most profitable alternative has lost ground vis-à-vis more differentiated models and the idea of 'bounded rationality' (Gigerenzer/Selten 2001a). These findings from behavioural and cognitive psychology are applied to the financial sphere by behavioural finance in an attempt to provide explanations for the decisions actually made by those active in the market (Daxhammer/Facsar 2012, 75). This also allows consideration of discrepancies between the reasons underlying a particular decision and the way that decision is justified in public.[38] The approaches can be operationalised for banking history and used to highlight interesting questions and open up new perspectives, even if it is clearly not possible to test the modern theories with historical material.

Behavioural finance views the perception of risks as the process 'by which an individual is in search of preeminent clarification of sensory information so that he or she can make a final judgement based on their level of expertise and past experience' (Ricciardi 2008b, 86). Risks are perceived very differently by different individuals, and it is this subjectively perceived risk, which may differ greatly from 'reality', that is decisive in a decision-making situation (ibid., 87f.).[39] Attempts to quantify risks are thus doomed to failure (Tanner 2005, 129). 'Essentially, perceived risk is a person's opinion (viewpoint) of the likelihood of risk (the potential of exposure to loss, danger or harm) associated with engaging in a specific activity' (Ricciardi 2008b, 88). It follows that the perception of risk can be understood as a highly individual method of organising and interpreting the sensations through which a person makes sense of his or her surroundings. Joseph A. Litterer describes perception as a process with two external factors: an overwhelming amount of information that caves in on the individual on the one hand, and the past experiences and values of that person on the other hand.[40] He goes on to describe three internal factors influencing the perception of the decision maker: selectivity, interpretation and closure. Selectivity refers to the conscious and unconscious choices of specific pieces of information as a mechanism to reduce information overload, which is necessary due to the limited capacities of human minds. Interpretation describes the way in which the same stimulus can be differently perceived by different actors, depending on their past experiences and values. Closure recognises people's preference for a complete and comprehensive image of a decision-making situation that makes sense in the context of the actor's experience. In order to construct such an image, any missing information may be supplemented to create consistency and contradictory information may be neglected to avoid cognitive dissonance. The risk perception created by this mechanism serves as a basis for the pending decision (Litterer 1973, 89f.).[41] In this way, events and sequences of events can be organised into meaningful stories that structure human memories and can significantly influence economic behaviour (Akerlof/Shiller 2009, 84–92).

> We are confident when a story we tell ourselves comes easily to mind, with no contradiction and no competing scenario. [...] The associative machine is set to suppress doubt and to evoke ideas and information that are compatible with the currently dominant story.
> (Kahneman 2011, 239)

Thus, it is clearly impossible to speak of a dominant strategy of utility maximisation. Although the preferences of actors on the financial market are viewed as stable by classical finance research, behavioural finance investigations suggest that they are actually multifaceted and changeable, and often only emerge in the course of the decision-making process. Such preferences can be egoistic or altruistic or a mixture of the two. Investors often strive to satisfy their expectations rather than to maximise their profits. They thus do not pursue the optimal solution, but are satisfied with the first option that meets the goals they have set themselves. They are seldom aware of the consequences of their actions and the entire range of alternatives available in the contingent future. Decisions are directed by the so-called heuristics, which can be described as rules of thumb that are firmly anchored in the mind (Daxhammer/Fascar 2012, 78) or as 'mental shortcuts or strategies derived from our past experience that get us where we need to go quickly, but at the cost of sending us in the wrong direction' (Ricciardi 2008b, 96). They allow market actors to remain functional in widely varied economic situations and are a quick and efficient way of coping with information overload. It would be misleading to suggest that heuristics are per se irrational, as they can lead to the fulfilment of personal goals – indeed, they often make it possible to actually arrive at the point of taking a decision in complex situations (Daxhammer/Fascar 2012, 78). Prospect theory focuses particularly on such mechanisms of decision making in uncertain conditions and thus explains decisions that are extremely inconsistent with a neoclassical, rational evaluation of probabilities and expected utility (ibid., 175).[42] Decision makers tend to prefer to utilise easily accessible, clearly presented and fresh information rather than complicated or old information; they see easily imaginable scenarios as more probable than those that are difficult to envision or remember; and they trust familiar sources of information more than unknown sources (availability heuristic). They feel more secure in situations that they believe they can control than in ones where they are forced to remain passive (perceived control); they tend to overly trust in their own abilities and knowledge (overconfidence) (Glaser/Weber 2010, 241–258); they view the avoidance of losses as more important than the achieving of gain (loss aversion); they make selective decisions by continuing to invest in non-profitable businesses to achieve turnaround and success after all (sunk-cost effect) (Daxhammer/Fascar 2012, 226). They tend to interpret new situations in the light of past situations, even if this is inappropriate (representativeness) (Taffler 2010). They allow themselves to be influenced by the presentation of a decision-making situation, e.g. through the use of particular vocabulary (framing); they overrate their first impression of a situation or retain references that were adopted earlier without incorporating newer information (anchoring); they privilege familiar data over unfamiliar (familiarity bias (Foad 2010), when concretely related to the home region then home bias (Tesar/Werner 1995)); they blindly trust experts (expert knowledge); they make decisions based on emotions, affects or intuition (affects/feeling) (Ricciardi 2008b, 95–105); they join in or follow the actions of other market actors, at times even ignoring their own information (herding) (Forbes 2009, 221–238; Daxhammer/Fascar 2012, 98–101, 192–194). Or they focus on fictional pictures of the future that are imagined in narratives, theories or discourses (Beckert 2013, 2016). As well as such individual factors, cultural factors can influence the long-term willingness of a specific group to take risks (Ricciardi 2008b; 105; Dilley 2017) and can also affect assessments of financial markets in particular countries (Williamson 2010, 631). Overall, it can be said that many decisions are actually made because they feel right, because of gut instinct (Akerlof/Shiller 2009, 33).[43]

This decision-making model is in no way compatible with the neoclassical capital market theory that sees all information about market activities as being captured by the pricing mechanisms of an efficient market (Ricciardi 2008a). Indeed, such a notion fails to satisfactorily account for the pronounced price fluctuations on the financial markets (Akerlof/Shiller 2009, 190). It assumes that investors make purely rational decisions based only on prices. This is not the case today and it was not the case in the nineteenth century. Numerous studies in the field of behavioural finance have rather shown that the rationality of actors on the financial markets is limited; they are 'remarkably illogical regarding their money, finances, and investments' (Ricciardi 2008b, 91). It may be helpful to think in terms of a 'homo oeconomicus humanus' who is often influenced by cognitive and emotional factors (Daxhammer/Fascar 2012, 77). His or her preferences may be based on selfishness, but also on altruism or morality, or on a mixture. Interesting results have been gained from research on green and ethical investment, which excludes products linked to animal testing, the weapons trade, environmental pollution or other morally questionable investment fields. Researchers have demonstrated that while those who practise ethical investment are certainly interested in profits, they are also keen to maintain a consistent lifestyle with all the associated moral implications (Cullis et al. 1992; Lewis/Mackenzie 2000).[44] They are examples 'of people putting their money where their morals are, bringing their values systems in line with their economic behaviour' (Lewis/Mackenzie 2000, 6). Of relevance here is the idea held by many investors that the 'nice guys' will make higher profits in the long run because ethically correct firms will come to dominate the market (ibid., 36). At the same time, many investors hope that the markets and the world will be morally improved by their actions and want to preserve their moral integrity, even if they are not necessarily on the left wing of the political spectrum (ibid., 49). Albert O. Hirschman described voice-and-exit strategies of this sort as early as 1970 (Hirschman 1970). Many investors are willing to accept reduced profits or even losses in this cause, even though their portfolios seldom consist only of ethnical investments. 'The raison d'être for our participants is putting their moral commitments into practice' (Lewis/Mackenzie 2000, 68). The origin of the money also plays a role for investors, i.e. whether it is inherited or independently earned.

It is, of course, impossible to simply apply psychological and finance models developed in the second half of the twentieth century to actors of the nineteenth century, as the existence of anthropological constants cannot be assumed. The historical context differs in many ways. For instance, especially at the beginning of the nineteenth century, it cannot be assumed that all actors had equal access to a range of information and thus simply needed to differentiate between the relevant and irrelevant. It was rather the case that networks of sources needed to be painstakingly established and maintained, as the example of the house of Rothschild demonstrates (Liedtke 2006). Heuristics should therefore be understood as culturally influenced and rooted in time and space (Gigerenzer/Selten 2001b, 9). However, the aim here is not to test modern models with historical data, but rather to open up new perspectives and stimulate inspiring questions that widen our view of the way in which European bankers of the nineteenth century made their investment decisions.[45] Furthermore, this approach allows a coherent narrative to be developed and tie together the case studies. In contrast to the dominant image of the classical economy, the picture of the economy that emerges is open to emotions, an aspect that has attracted a great deal of historical interest in recent years.[46] Furthermore, ethical perspectives also receive attention. For instance in Amitai Etzioni's new social economy, people are viewed not only as individuals, but also as members of communities which they support by prioritising the interests of the community over their own interests and accepting social and ethical obligations (Etzioni 1988, X; Reese-Schäfer 2001, 83). The focus is not only on various possibly moral preferences; rather, markets are more generally understood as not being completely regulated by prices. Consideration of power is also integrated into this approach (Etzioni 1988, 217–236; Reese-Schäfer 2001, 85–87).[47] Albert O. Hirschmann also emphasises the ability of market actors to reflect on their preferences on a moral level and to develop meta-preferences (Hirschmann 1970, 227f.).

In this investigation, the Greek financial market of the nineteenth century is thus not understood as efficient and solely controlled by prices, but rather as constructed in the heads of the bankers with all their preferences and emotions. The primary focus is on how the perception of this financial market occurred.[48] What information was available to the bankers? What did they select as being relevant and how did they interpret it based on their past experiences and their value systems? Which information did they supplement in order to render their impressions meaningful and to form closed images and visions of the future? What stories about Greece did they tell? These questions offer numerous points of access for banking and cultural-historical approaches. The biographies and careers of the actors are investigated in terms of their experiences, their 'biographically determined planning hierarchy' (Schütz/Luckmann 2003, 50, tr. by K.S.), the decisions that they make and the financial practices that they use, but also in terms of any relationships to Greece that may exist. Their value systems are analysed against the background of financial practices and banking norms typical of the time. The images of Greece that were meaningfully constructed through the so-called closure are reconstructed in the context of the reception of Greece among their contemporaries. The questions inspired by the behavioural finance approach thus make it possible to investigate the decisions of European bankers in the light of their perceptions of Greece, moving beyond financial topics to connect banking and cultural history (Löffler 2010). Banks can be understood as 'socially-constructed and historically-specific institutions whose functions and performance are dramatically shaped by the social structure, the cultural environment, and the legal and political set-up' (Battilossi 2008, 77). The intention is to free banking from some of its reputation as a 'cold and impersonal discipline' (Green 2008b, 14) and to render the history of banking more compatible with general history. Whether the historical findings contribute towards the process of risk management in modern-day banks remains an open question.[49]

Structure of the book

The main part of this book consists of nine case studies that shed light on the central investment projects of foreign financiers. They cover the most important fields of European investment activity in Greece: government bonds, investments in banks and direct investments in the economy. The choice of case studies was also influenced by the available sources, the conditio sine qua non for an in-depth analysis. In the selected cases, the sources allowed the detailed investigation of the decision-making situations and the risk management of the bankers involved – the only way for a historian to achieve reliable results on this individualised micro-level.

The first case study begins with the Greek Revolution and deals with the earliest Greek loans issued on the London Stock Exchange in 1824/1825 with the support of the London Philhellenic Committee. Chapter 2 then turns the spotlight on a key actor, Jean Gabriel Eynard, a great friend to Greece resident in Geneva. His activities are traced in detail up to the founding of the Greek National Bank (ETE) in 1841, which he initiated. The centre of attention is thus the continuation of Philhellene commitment in a phase when Western Europe was characterised by great disillusionment about the realities of the Greek situation. The third chapter considers another case of sustained devotion to Greece, focusing on the von Eichthal family, whose members were based in Munich and Paris, and their financial and cultural activities in Greece from the 1830s until the 1870s. This chapter hence presents a longer term view of several decades.

Convinced Philhellenes did not, however, play much of a role in the project considered in Chapter 4, even if antiquity was relevant. The case study concerns the development of the silver and lead mines of Lavrion in the middle of the 1860s, financed by French investors, and links back to the traditional mines of antiquity on which the wealth of Athens was once based.

The political context of such investments is considered in the following chapter. The fifth case study is concerned with the new phase of Greek foreign loans from 1879 to 1893, when within a few years more foreign capital flowed into the country than ever before. Of particular interest here is the German banker Gerson von Bleichröder, Otto von Bismarck's house banker, and the reasons for his commitment to Greece.

Chapter 6 examines the building of the Canal of Corinth, pursued at the same time but in a completely different field and initiated by France. The canal was intended to complete a project begun in antiquity to allow ships to avoid sailing around the Peloponnesus and facilitate trade in the Mediterranean.

This consideration of infrastructure is followed by an investigation of agriculture, more precisely the draining of the Copais marsh. This occurred at the same time as the two preceding projects and also has deep historical roots, as the draining of the marsh was first undertaken in Mycenaean times, allowing the fertile land to be cultivated.

The phase of new debt that attracted these large international investments to the country was followed by Greece's bankruptcy in 1893, which forced the country to accept an international financial commission in 1898. The role played by this commission in rekindling international trust in Greece forms the focus of the eighth chapter. Chapter 9 also considers the regaining of trust, this time through investigation of an early twentieth-century currant trading company, which aimed to optimise sales of this important export on the international markets.

Although the chronological order is not consistent, taking second place to the thematic focuses, the case studies nonetheless provide an overview of the overall development of the Greece economy in the nineteenth century. The fields that were touched by foreign investment also represent the most important pillars of Greek economic development: state finance, the property trade, mining, infrastructure (railway and canal construction), agriculture and trade. Simultaneously, the research traces 90 years of banking history. This was a time in which banking changed significantly; the financial markets at the beginning of the twentieth century differed greatly from those of the 1820s, both in terms of actors and of mechanisms. Although these changes are not the focus of attention here, they are often of relevance in explaining the institutional context of the investment decisions.

State of research

This research is able to draw on previous work in manifold regards. While a focus on questions of risk management is rare in banking history investigations (Hollow 2013, 2017), perhaps linked to the fact that the practice of identifying risk structures in banks is not straightforward (Baecker 2008, 138), the promising potential of this perspective has certainly been recognised.[50] Of particular note is the (unpublished) work of Monika Pohle-Fraser, who investigates risk management of German and French banks in the nineteenth century. Repeated reference is made to this research in the course of the discussion (Pohle-Fraser 1999). In addition to the work on habitus and social capital mentioned earlier, the 'human factor in banking' has received attention in newer banking history research (Green/Pohle-Fraser 2008; Demont 2011),[51] with its importance being acknowledged at least since the 1950s:

> In order to understand banking history it is indispensible to see the banker embedded in his familial, social and political context, which in part determines his professional activities.
>
> (Gille 1959, 271, tr. by K.S.)

Furthermore, studies of foreign investment exist for all the countries considered here (Great Britain, France, Germany and Switzerland). These are helpful in demonstrating the scale of the Greek investments and analysing the market as a whole, and also because they frequently pursue the question of the relationship between banking and politics as well.[52] In the case of the Ottoman Empire, a number of investigations focus on investments from various countries in a specific region (Clay 2000; Eldem 2005; Cottrell 2008a, 2008b; Geyikdağı 2011).[53]

There is a great deal of research on direct investments in the Greek economy[54] which presents their institutional and legal frameworks (Pepelasis 2011). This is also the case for the political history of modern Greece in the phase of nation state building and 'modernisation'.[55] Greek banking history is similarly well researched (Dertilis 1988; Κωστής, [Kostis]/Τσοκόπουλου [Tsokopulos] 1988; Pepelasis 2009).[56] This is particularly true for a number of banks such as the Ionian Bank (IOB) which was founded on the Ionian Islands in 1863 and became a Greek bank when the islands became part of the Greek state. The history of this bank is so well researched that it is only occasionally touched upon here, particularly as it was founded in the British era rather than the Greek (Cottrell 2007; Δερτιλής [Dertilis] 1980). In recent years, intensive research has also been directed towards Greek diaspora bankers throughout the world, in particular in the European metropolises and in Constantinople (Chatziioannou/Harlaftis 2002; Minoglou 2002a; Ioannides/Minoglou 2004; McCabe et al. 2005; Tziobas 2009; Calapodis 2010; Chatziioannou 2010; Sifneos 2011; Lyons/Mandaville 2012; Elo/Minto-Coy 2019). Even though this group of bankers is not the focus of the present investigation, this body of work provides interesting information about networks and individual brokers.

Numerous studies from the beginning of the twentieth century right up to recent years tackle the foreign loans taken out by Greece (Ανδρεάδης, 61T61T[Andreadis] 1904, 1925, 2010; Levandis 1944; Wynne 1951; Kofas 1981; Ηλιαδάκης [Iliadakis] 2011; Tsoulfidis/Zouboulakis 2016, Ψαλιδόπουλος [Psalidopoulos], 2019). There are even several publications on foreign direct investment in Greece (Γιαννίτσης [Giangitsis] 1977; Pepelasis/Varvaritis 2016), although some of these are strongly rooted in the Greek socialist research tradition and thus assume a Marxist standpoint that assesses all foreign investment negatively (Δραγούμης [Dragoumis] 1901; Στεφανίδης [Stefanidis] 1930; Μπελογιάννης, [Belogiannis] 1998).[57] All these investigations adopt a Greek perspective on the foreign investments rather than that of the financier investing. This is also true of studies of the individual projects considered here: the silver mines of Lavrion (Δερμάτης [Dermatis] 2003), the Canal of Corinth (Παπαγιαννοπούλου [Papagiannopoulos] 1989), the draining of Lake Copais (Papadopoulos 1993), the construction of the railways (Παπαγιαννάκης [Papayiannakis] 1982) and the currant trade (Πιζάνιας [Pizanias] 1988; Franghiadis 1990). Only Hubert Bonin's work on

French investments in Greece since the mid-1880s selects an alternative perspective and focuses on the bankers concerned. However, Bonin pays little attention to the cultural-historical dimension of the topic or to the processes of decision making, concentrating instead on the business and geostrategic interests of the banks and the French state in the Mediterranean area. His focus is on the development of business relationships between French and Greek banks in the last decades of the nineteenth and twentieth centuries (Bonin 2013).[58]

Turning to the cultural-historical dimension of the topic, the reception of Greece in Europe, extensive research has been directed towards Philhellenism at the time of the Greek struggle for independence in all the countries considered here (Penn 1936a, 1936b; Dimakis 1968; Dünki 1984; Quack-Eustathiades 1984; Hauser 1990; Noe 1994; Ruge/Konstantinou 1994; Heydenreuter 1995a, 1995b; Irmscher 1998; Landfester/Lessenich 2006; Βακαλόπουλος [Vakalopoulos] 2008; Prévélakis 2008; Barau 2009; Klein 2009; Maufroy 2011; Mazurel 2013; Meyer-Eisenhut 2013). Much less attention has been paid to the period after Greek independence until the First World War, but there are nonetheless several profound investigations for this period (Clarke 1989; Basch 1995; Tourraix 2000; Konstantinou 2008; Mylona 2014).[59] A great deal of research has been conducted into travel literature about Greece (Angelomatis-Tsougarakis 1990; Meid 2012; Mylona 2014). There are also a number of publications concerned with the reception of the Balkans in Europe, following the postcolonial tradition of Edward Said (1978). Marija Todorova (1997) sees the region as a bridge between the perceived 'other' of the Orient and the 'self' of Europe,[60] a hypothesis that proves extremely applicable to a nineteenth-century discussion about and in Greece concerning whether the country was now part of the 'West' or the 'East'.[61] Just as Todorova describes for the Balkans as a whole, certain contemporaries presented Greece as a peripheral part of the 'self', suggesting that its otherness and deviations endangered the order and certainties of the 'self'. In this way, Greece was said to be strongly influenced by the Orient but lacking its fairylike charm (Basch 1995, 30). The construction of such images clearly reveals the way in which new information may be made to fit with well-known images by ignoring details that are not compatible with the existing construct, as described by behavioural psychology. Furthermore, the social learning of images saves individuals the costs of learning or experimenting themselves (Henrich 2001).

However, Greece can be understood as part of the European 'South', which has also been the object of research in recent years. Benjamin Schenk and Martina Winkler base their investigations on the concept of 'mental maps', cognitive maps in people's heads that connect a region to a set of associations (Schenk/Winkler 2007b, 8). The South seems to appear as a place of sunshine and mild climate with a rich history and tradition, simple ways of life and relaxation (ibid.). Since the nineteenth and twentieth centuries, these pictures have been joined by images of economic backwardness, corruption, political chaos and criminality (ibid., 12). In the light of these reflections and discussion concerning the term 'historical region', a lively research landscape has developed on the history of the Mediterranean (Bourguet et al. 1998; Berndt/Pütz 2007; Troebst 2007; Borutta/Lemmes 2013; see also Consiglio et al. 2012; Dabag et al. 2014; Lichtenberger/Rüden 2014), also tackling, at times critically, Fernand Braudel's famous study of the Mediterranean from 1949 (Braudel 1949; Borutta 2016).

Sources

Unpublished sources on the history of foreign investments in Greece are found in the archives of the French, British and German banks which were involved. They are generally easily accessible for research purposes. The political archives in England, France, Germany and Greece also hold illuminating material on the investment activities of the domestic banks abroad, in particular the files of the foreign offices; this is, of course, also true of the Greek state archive. It was also possible to view the estates of individual politicians and bankers in special archives, e.g. the estate of the Swiss banker Jean-Gabriel Eynard in the Bibliothèque de Genève, the estate of the Greek prime minister Charilaos Trikoupis in the Hellenic Literary and Historical Archive (ELIA) and the bequests of the London Greek Committees (LGC) in the Athens National Library. The archives of the Greek national bank (ETE) also deserve explicit mention as they hold a plethora of materials (Λιάτα [Liata] 1980). The bank archives contain not only correspondence between the bankers and between bankers and politicians, but also balance sheets, statements, syndicate lists, reports and assessments that shed light on the individual investment projects. The Crédit Lyonnais (CL) archive even holds a report by an envoy of the bank about his two-month trip to Greece and a short description of all the Greek banks and their creditworthiness, an extremely interesting document with regard to information procurement and risk management.[62] In individual cases, handbooks for nineteenth-century bankers were also used to better understand the general practices of risk management (Rae 1850, 34ff.).

In addition to unpublished sources, there is also a wealth of published material. Memoranda, collections of documents or pamphlets of great use to the historian tended to be published particularly in cases characterised by conflict between the investors and the Greek government or Greek partners, for instance concerning the mines of Lavrion (Cordella 1864; Serpieri 1871a). Both the Philhellenes and, in the second half of the nineteenth century, various other interest groups published extracts of their work or correspondence for publicity purposes (Comité de Genève en faveur des Grecs 1826a, 1826b; N.N. (Ioannis Gennadios) 1878). Other printed sources include numerous descriptions, travel reports, memoirs and economic reports about Greece (Cheston 1887a; Théry 1905) and the documents published by the foreign offices (Bourne et al. 1987; Gaschke 2006).

An additional important source is contemporary newspaper coverage about Greece, particularly financial journalism, published in the international press, which underwent intensification and diversification during the research period (Taylor 2013; Schwarz 2016). Thematically catalogued compendiums of press cuttings on Greece collected by some of the banks and by the foreign offices were of some use here.

Notes

1 Tr. by K.S.
2 The term Greece-bashing, which describes the aggressive reporting on Greece found in much of the German media since 2010, is defined in Bickes et al. (2015, 326). At the first peak of the financial crisis, even the well-reputed Frankfurter Allgemeine Zeitung included extensive quotes from the work of the Frenchman Edmond About, one of the most vehement nineteenth-century critics of Greece. The paper's editors apparently saw no problem in transferring About's complaints concerning the shortcomings of the Greek financial administration to the present-day situation; see About (2012). On the court case, see Riehl (2012).
3 However, negative German stereotypes were simultaneously activated in Greece, where certain media sweepingly defamed the Germans as Nazis; see Tzogopoulos (2013, 5); Simitis (2014).
4 Concerning the debate about this poem, see N.N. (2012).
5 This term is inspired by Beckert (2013), who speaks of 'imagined futures'.
6 Due to this two-way interaction, Bergemann et al. speak of the transformation of antiquity as 'allelopoiese'; see Bergemann et al. (2011, 39).
7 The term 'zero hour' is used here in the sense that there was hardly any foreign investment in the corresponding area of the Ottoman Empire before the Greek state was founded.
8 It is nonetheless overstated to suggest that from 1800 (when the state did not even exist) until long after the Second World War, Greece found itself almost continually in arrears with payments; see Reinhart (2010, 29).
9 This conclusion is found, e.g. in a dossier on Greece entitled 'Finanzielles Arbeitsfeld Griechenland' by Karleugen Wehrli-Thielen from Zürich dated 12.5.1918 and held by DB, P11623.
10 This question is very different from that addressed by Hubert Bonin as to why and how the banks 'made' Greece a market; see Bonin (2013, 21).
11 On this question concerning firms in general, see also Plumpe (2016).
12 This contrasts with Bonin, who includes Saloniki and other nodes of the Greek diaspora in his investigation because, he argues, they were regions 'which it [Greece] was destined to acquire' (Bonin 2013, 355).
13 In contrast to ibid., 25–27.
14 The term risk strategies refers to patterns of behaviour that are always activated when a relevant problem emerges; see Kahneman (2011, 340).
15 Crédit mobilier was founded in France in 1852; see Fargette (2013).
16 With reference to modern family businesses, these are the findings of Naldi et al. (2007, 43).
17 For current national differences, see Willinger et al. (2003).

18 On historical research on globalisation, see e.g. O'Rourke/Williamson (1999); Osterhammel (2004); Torp (2004). A good overview of the latest trends of global history is provided by Kramper (2009); Barth (2014c).
19 It must, however, be noted that the majority of banks continued to operate on a national or even regional scale.
20 In family businesses, the individuals often identify so strongly with the group that they put the interests of the group before their own; see Fukuyama (1995, 156).
21 This definition differs clearly from the economic definition that follows the work of Frank Knight, who viewed risk as a definable value that can be measured with the help of mathematical probability calculations, while uncertainty is immeasurable and cannot be expressed as a probability; see Akerlof/Shiller (2009, 205).
22 See similarly Ripperger (2005, 19f.).
23 See also the volumes arising from the post-graduate programme 'Vorsorge, Voraussicht, Vorhersage: Kontingenzbewältigung durch Zukunftshandeln' held at University Duisburg-Essen with its publications (Becker et al. 2016; Bernhardt et al. 2016, 2017).
24 See also Tönnies (1887).
25 If the partners are not aware of the risks, then Ripperger refers to confidence (Zuversicht) rather than trust (Vertrauen).
26 A categorisation is also attempted by Marková et al. (2008).
27 Frevert (2002); a comprehensive history of the term trust is found in Frevert (2003a, 14–30). See also Frevert (2003b).
28 Also see with regard to financial centres Tanner (2014).
29 Akerlof draws on John Maynard Keynes' multiplier and hence suggests that there is even a trust multiplier that influences the behaviour of economic actors; see Akerlof/Shiller (2009, 33–39).
30 See also Priemel (2013).
31 For Jewish circles in Germany, see Lässig (2004); Schiif (2005).
32 Helpful indications are also provided in the handbook: Barnett/Pollock (2012).
33 See also Lässig (2008).
34 A profound overview of research on social capital is provided by Felis-Rota (2011).
35 'Intermediaries such as credit reporting firms and financial newspapers emerged precisely in order to bridge the gaps that exist between firms and the groups that have a stake in, but no direct knowledge of, those firms. [...] Rather than simply transmit images of a corporation to an undifferentiated public, intermediaries and networks confer reputations and make them meaningful to specific audiences. We can go even further and posit that without intermediaries and networks, the reputations of firms and individuals would not exist' (Olegario/McKenna 2013, 652). See also Engerman/Davis (2003); Schaffer et al. (2009); Jobs/Mackenthun (2013a).
36 See e.g. Krooss/Blyn (1971).
37 This is called for by Berghoff (1999, 175). The article deals with chances and deficits of transaction cost theory.
38 This is the central question in Pohle-Fraser (1999). See also Knake (2017).
39 However, Baker/Nofsinger (2010) 'Answers to Chapter Discussion Questions' define risk differently as known and calculable, while anything that cannot be calculated is termed uncertainty. See also **24 n.21** in this book.
40 See for this whole section: Litterer (1973, 106–132).
41 The model seems particularly compatible with the ideas of Alfred Schütz and Thomas Luckmann on lifeworlds (2003). They assume that actors always attempt to integrate new experiences from beyond their familiar lifeworld in their

familiar wealth of knowledge and experience. This is only questioned when new experiences cannot be integrated, a process that ends as soon as a new interpretation leads to the creation of congruence; see ibid., 37–41.

42 See also Altman (2010).

43 Game theory has made some interesting findings on the willingness of financial market actors to cooperate and the development of trust, but is not further discussed here; see Fukuyama (1995, 485).

44 An example of such investment funds being religiously based: Lainer-Vos (2013).

45 An attempt to apply prospect theory to the share markets is made by Barberis et al. (2001).

46 See e.g. Trepp (2001); Ciompi/Endert (2011); Frevert/Schmidt (2011).

47 Etzioni also influenced Amartya Sen with his social economy; see Reese-Schäfer (2001, 91).

48 A methodological focus on actor-network theory would be of little use in addressing this core question. In order to shed light on the Greek financial market, it would be necessary to analyse *all* the actors involved, in particular also on the Greek side. This is only undertaken here in exceptional cases. Attention is rather focused on the perspective of the investing West Europeans.

49 'To achieve this predictive capability, risk managers require a source of historical loss event data that has relevant exposure information and casual factors attached to each loss event' (Hughes 2007, 42). This refers to the internal data of banks. It may be worth considering, however, whether it can also be applied to banking historical research.

50 'This suggests that cross-country comparison of how risk-taking by bankers was disciplined will loom large in the future research agenda' (Battilossi 2008, 91). See also Colvin (2015).

51 There are also many indications in the work of Youssef Cassis, e.g. Cassis 1994; Kynaston 1994; Cassis et al. 1995; Cassis 2002.

52 For example, Jenks 1927; Cameron 1961; Cassis 1990; Schaefer 1995; Dilley 2009, 2012; Esteves 2011. However: 'The question of power and finance has been a perennial theme in imperial historiography' (Attard/Dilley 2013, 3).

53 A similar approach to the Italian financial market is found in a very concise form in Hertner (1991). An African region is the focus in Barton (2016).

54 Κατσούλης [Katsoulis] et al. (1985); Δερτιλής [Dertilis] (2009); Καλαφάτης [Kalafatis] et al. (2011); Τσουλφίδης [Tsoulfidis] (2009); Αγριαντώνη [Agriantoni] (2010). For agriculture e.g. Πετμεζάς [Petmezas] (2003).

55 To name but a few examples of overviews: Petropulos 1968; Zelepos 2002; Koliopoulos/Veremis 2010. On the formation of modern statehood generally in the nineteenth century: Maier (2012).

56 There are also numerous studies of individual Greek banks, particularly the National Bank ETE, which are considered in more detail below.

57 The ideological stance of many Greek historians is described by Δερτιλής [Dertilis] (2009, 594).

58 See also Schönhärl (2014b).

59 With a stronger focus on politics, see also Holland/Markides (2006).

60 See also Kaser (2002); Born/Lemmen (2014); Brehl (2016).

61 On the term 'West', see also Bavaj/Steber (2016).

62 Voyage de M. Guicciardi en Grèce, 1891, CL 62 AH 78, Grèce Affaires industrielles 1876–1891. Similar lists about business partners were made by the house of Oppenheim; see Pohle-Fraser (1999, 281).

Part II

FOREIGN INVESTMENT IN GREECE IN THE NINETEENTH CENTURY – NINE CASE STUDIES

1

PHILANTHROPY AS A MARKETING STRATEGY

Loans for Greece during her struggle for independence in 1824/1825

Greece in her struggle for independence

In 1821, the Greeks began to fight for their independence from the Ottoman Empire (Vlachopoulou 2017). The Serbs had revolted against the Ottoman rule in 1804–1813 (Jelavich/Jelavich 1986, 26–37), making the Greek rebellion the second attempt by Balkan people to free themselves from the Ottoman Empire. Preparations for the revolution had been going on among the Greek diaspora for at least three decades (Turczynski 2003, 34–82; St. Clair 2008; Koliopoulos/Veremis 2010, 16). In 1814, the so-called Philiki Heteria was founded in Odessa, a 'Society of Friends' that took up the cause of Greek independence and aimed to trigger a general Balkan revolution, supported by Russia (Jelavich/Jelavich 1986, 39f.).[1] The 1821 uprising began in Moldavia and Wallachia, where it was quickly suppressed. The independence fighters had more success on the Peloponnese and in January 1822, the revolutionaries drew up the first Greek constitution in Epidaurus, based on liberal Western models, and formed a provisional government (Jelavich/Jelavich 1986, 45). Despite a massive internal conflict, at times resembling civil war, the Greeks managed to hold their position until 1825 when the Sultan entrusted the Pasha of Egypt, Mohammed Ali, to lead a campaign against them.

The Greek revolution was greatly welcomed in many parts of Europe (Ruge/Konstantinou 1994). Intellectuals from all countries wrote newspaper articles and books (Gunnar 1994) about the repression of the Greeks and the atrocities conducted by the Turks; Philhellenic committees and associations were formed in innumerable cities all over the continent and even in North America, and collected considerable sums of money for the struggle for independence. Governments were put under pressure to support the Greeks, and volunteers were equipped to fight alongside the 'heroes'. The classical humanist education enjoyed by many of the middle classes stimulated enthusiasm for Ancient Greece and played an important role in this Philhellene movement (Konstantinou 1998). Many intellectuals and politicians saw 'in the modern Greeks the direct descendants of their schoolbook heroes' (Jelavich/Jelavich 1986, 48), and the appropriation and construction

DOI: 10.4324/9780429286537-4

of Greek antiquity as a reference culture were highly relevant for the further development of personal identity. In Victorian England, for instance, enthusiasm for Ancient Greece equalled or even exceeded that for Ancient Rome (Turner 1989). In many parts of Europe, Philhellenism was also a protected space in which liberal opinions could be freely formulated and networks of liberal clubs and societies developed. In this way, enthusiasm for Greek matters spread beyond classically educated circles to include members of the lower classes (Hauser 1990). The Philhellene movement thus had a genuine political character. In England, for example, it was associated with the liberal Whigs and radicals, who used the activities related to Greece to enhance their position vis-à-vis the conservative Tory government (Potter 2004; Barau 2009, 168ff.; Klein 2009). In France and in Switzerland, members of the association tended similarly to be moderate liberals, active in the opposition (Klein 2009, 182–209).[2] In the German countries, the political implications also played an important role (Quack-Eustathiades 1984; Spaenle 1990; Institute for Balkan Studies, Thessaloniki 1986). Many Philhellenes were prepared to support the Greeks in their struggle for independence, usually by financing the rebels. This outside assistance was warmly welcomed.

The first London loan of 1824

While the Greek freedom fighters initially attempted to fund their struggle by drawing on their own resources, voluntary donations[3] and the local capital market, it soon became clear that additional finance would be necessary and that an internal loan was insufficient (Kofas 1981, 1). The provisional government was forced to recognise 'that it was almost impossible to achieve their goal without foreign support'.[4] Offers of loans arrived quickly from abroad, although they were mostly of dubious and fairly untrustworthy origin and with such poor conditions that even the desperate freedom fighters were unwilling to accept them. Nonetheless, the first foreign loan of 102,000 Augsburg guilders (153,000 francs) was obtained as early as November 1821 on the basis of a guarantee from rich Greek merchants in the diaspora (Ανδρεάδης [Andreadis] 1904, 11). However, when the revolutionaries wanted to borrow more money abroad in the spring of 1822, difficulties arose: within the Austrian sphere of influence, restorative tendencies under Metternich made it impossible to find support for the unpredictable Greek revolution (Levandis 1944, 2ff.). An offer came from the Knights of Malta, who had been driven from that island in 1798, but this was linked to territorial claims in case of Greek success.[5] However, these negotiations were abandoned once it became clear that the Knights were unable to find any suitable bankers to support the loan in France, allied as the country was with Greece's enemy Egypt (Ibid., 7f.). Others were interested though. Greek sympathisers in Darmstadt believed the prospects for a loan in Germany to be positive, and the Zurich committee also saw opportunities in Switzerland.[6] In the meantime, however, attempts elsewhere met with success. Having gained independence from the colonial powers of Spain and Portugal and been recognised as independent states by Great Britain, the new states of Latin America were in great need of money, a situation that triggered a huge speculative bubble on the London Stock Exchange (Dawson 1990, 6f.).[7] In the following years, over 150 million British pounds were invested in South America, particularly in mining (Haupert 1997, 511). The overheating of the London market so encouraged risk taking that fraudsters were even able to market bogus securities, for instance, for the country of Poyais, which actually never came into existence (Dawson 1990, 60f.; Clavel 2018).

This was the situation when, at the beginning of 1823, the provisional Greek government sent a Greek merchant from Livorno, Andreas Louriotis (Λιγνάδης [Lignadis] 1970),[8] to raise money in the European financial centres. Initially, Louriotis had no success in London, Paris and Rome, but – perhaps in Spain – he made contact with a supporter of the Spanish revolution, Edward Blaquiere,[9] who was also enthusiastic about the Greek struggle and was instrumental in the founding of a Philhellene committee in London in March 1823 (Kofas 1981, 4). Blaquiere introduced Louriotis to John Bowring,[10] a merchant and literary scholar who had helped found a Philhellene committee in Madrid in 1821[11] and now became Secretary of the London Greek Committee (LGC). Many prominent Whig parliamentarians were among the founding members of the committee, e.g. Francis Burdett (Baer 2004), John Cam Hobhouse[12] and Joseph Hume,[13] to name but a few. The philosophers Jeremy Bentham and Lord Byron were also involved. For them, Philhellenism was one way of realising their broadly based liberal aims, which ranged from the abolition of slavery to penal reform (Klein 2009, 177f.). Contributions were also received from Tory supporters, although they kept their distance from the committee, which thus consisted only of members of the opposition, although this seems to have been unintentional (Rosen 2004b).[14] Shortly after its establishment, the committee sent Blaquiere to Greece to investigate the situation there. The journey was successful: not only could Blaquiere persuade the provisional Greek government to authorise a loan in London, his enthusiastic report on the economic opportunities in the country led to Greece being seen as a promising market for financial transactions in London circles, despite spirited contradiction from pro-Turkish voices (Blaquiere 1823).[15] In response to an invitation from the Philhellene committee in 1824, the Greek government sent Andreas Louriotis, Ioannis Orlandos[16] and John Zaimes[17] to London to finalise a loan. To the annoyance of the British king, who was anxious to maintain a neutral position, the foreign minister George Canning was present to receive the deputies (Levandis 1944, 14ff.).[18] Thanks to the good offices of the LGC, particularly those of its secretary John Bowring, the deal was then closed on 21 February 1824 with the relatively insignificant banking house of Loughnan Son and O'Brien (ibid.).[19] Alternative offers from Goldschmidt et Cie, Rougemont, Behrendos & Cie and John Smith were declined with full confidence in the advice of the Philhellenes.[20] The Greeks were initially very grateful to the Philhellenes as they were not convinced it would have been possible to gain the trust of the bankers without their help.[21] And the Philhellenes were relieved that the deal was concluded, even if the deputies 'carried on their discussions with our capitalists as if they were trading for old clothes with the Jews of Mayfair'.[22] Clearly, the Philhellenes acted as brokers here and contributed to the creation of the necessary basis of trust. The sources in this case do not, however, allow detailed insights into the risk perception of the bankers.

The nominal value of the loan totalled £800,000, floated at a rate of 59 of the face value and an interest rate of 5%.[23] In comparison with some of the Latin American loans of the same year, this was a rather small sum: £1.68 million (5%) went to Brazil, 1 million (6%) to Argentina, 4.75 million (6%) to Columbia, 3.2 (5%) to Mexico and 750,000 (6%) to Peru. The issuing rate for Greece was much poorer than for South America:[24] In cooperation with Thomas Wilson & Co., the house of Rothschild issued the loan for Brazil at a rate of 75, while a loan for Naples of £2.5 million was even issued at 91.5. With a rate of 59, Greece was almost at the bottom of the list, followed only by Mexico with 58.[25]

Investors at this time could choose between 624 joint-stock companies on the London Stock Exchange (Chatziioannou 2013, 40). Despite this strong competition, the Greek loan, promoted in flowery prose,[26] was oversubscribed within a few days; the rate rose briefly from 59 to 63 (Bartle 1962, 62ff.). But the Greek deputies were still bitterly disappointed by the result. They clearly had failed to realise exactly what a rate of 59 meant: of the nominal value of £800,000, only £472,000 was realised. After deducting all other costs,[27] the Greek government was actually left with only £336,000 at their disposal. From 1826, they were supposed to repurchase the bonds at current market prices, but not above 100, and to continue to do so as long as bonds were in circulation.[28] This sinking fund should have required 1% of the loan sum annually. The 'discretionary' repurchase of the bonds would thus have depended on their price: the cheaper they were, the more quickly the government could have repurchased them. If a par value price had been sustained (i.e. 100), then a repurchase according to these modalities would have taken 98 years.[29] The low rate made sense: if the revolution ended in victory, then the speculators could make a large profit, and this imagined future was of key significance. Greece guaranteed the loan repayments with her national estates,[30] customs revenues, and fishing and salt rights, but the speculative nature of the loan was undeniable. There was no fixed repurchase price for the end of the loan period, as was otherwise usual for loans at the time. Accordingly, the British ambassador in Patras judged that this loan was not an opportunity for serious capital investment but rather for speculation.[31]

Another problem also bothered the Greeks considerably. Not unusually in such a case, the money was not paid directly to the Greek deputies or to the provisional government, which was not internationally recognised (Levandis 1944, 19f.). The Greeks had clearly recognised this difficulty in advance as they attempted to replace the term 'for the use of the Greek government'[32] in the contract with the expression 'at the direction of the Greek government'.[33] The bankers, for their part, were keen to minimise their risks by involving three British commissioners to administer the payments: the two liberal parliamentarians and Philhellenes Edward Ellice[34] and Joseph Hume, and the father of the banker, Andrew Loughnan senior.[35] The Greek deputies firmly believed that Ellice and Hume were 'parties with no other interests other than the well-being of Greece'.[36] However, tensions soon emerged between the Greek deputies, who had no access to the money, and the commissioners, who repeatedly delayed the payments.[37] The commissioners felt that the Greek government was insufficiently prepared and were not convinced that the Greeks would ever be able to pay the interest.[38]

The situation worsened when in March the price fell to 54 (Bartle 1962, 64).[39] After the death of Lord Byron in Mesolonghi in May 1824, the bonds dropped still further, and Leicester Stanhope's pessimistic reports from Greece[40] later led to a further slump.[41] The Greek deputies believed that the Philhellenes had a moral obligation to intervene to support the price and complained bitterly that they failed to do so. The deputies clearly did not realise that the low price was actually an advantage for Greece because the bonds had to be repurchased at current market rates. This was not the only part of the terms and conditions which the two merchants obviously misjudged; perhaps the complicated English hindered their understanding of the various clauses of the agreement. They were also concerned about the risk carried by the bank, which had guaranteed the investors a price of 59, and were troubled by the notion that the Loughnan Bank could collapse as a consequence of the slump in prices.[42] However, the bank had actually passed on the entire risk of falling prices to the investors: they only guaranteed that the rate would not be below 59 *on the first day* of the issue; no other guarantee was given in the convention, and would in any case have been economically nonsensical.[43] The bank risked 'only' its reputation as an issuing house. The Greek deputies either misunderstood key points of the convention, thus suffering under information asymmetries typical of principal-agent relations,[44] or they deliberately played the fool.

Two completely contradictory images of Greece as an investment market collided here: while the deputies interpreted the loan primarily as philanthropic help for Greece, the bankers and Philhellenes were chiefly motivated by the prospect of profit. They wanted to earn money from the new market, which was rendered so promising by the enthusiasm for Greece displayed by the public, and were keen to externalise the risk as far as possible. Even in April 1824, Orlando and Louriotis noted disappointedly '"all that glitters is not gold"; self-interest seems to know how to hide under a cloak of philanthropic principles, liberalism and the protection of Greece and the Hellenes'.[45] They accused their business partners of instrumentalising a very real Philhellenism to disguise economic interests. Where both aims collided, the profit interest took priority. The Greeks communicated their disappointment:

> Yes, your Eminence, there are hidden motives behind all that and these motives are not at all of the sort to simply contribute and exclusively serve honour to contribute towards the well-being of our country; it is more a matter of enriching oneself at others' expense, but under honourable colours.[46]

The Greek deputies complained not only about the lack of intervention by the bankers to support the price of the bonds. They also had the impression that the commissioners repeatedly constructed new arguments to delay the payments. They linked this behaviour to the personal interests of the financiers:

> Would not the reputation of the Englishmen in England suffer if it were to be read that the cold calculations of four or five men, possessors of Greek state bonds, plunged into nothing and, even worse, into more barbaric slavery, a people who had risen up and prepared to constitute a free nation?[47]

The Greeks were so annoyed that they considered annulling the contract.[48] John Bowring, the Secretary of the Greek Committee, was particularly vehemently criticised, especially after he admitted at a committee meeting that his Philhellene tendencies were of little significance to him: 'where there is a question of interest, neither philanthropy nor patriotism nor independence play a role'.[49] Bowring and Ellice had invested large amounts in the Greek bonds and began to panic as the price fell. As investors, they carried the entire risk of the sinking prices. In June 1824, the Greeks accused Bowring of intriguing to prevent further payments because he was afraid of a Greek defeat.[50] Bowring was a protégé of the philosopher and friend of Greece Jeremy Bentham, who thus also became involved in the dispute (Bartle 1962, 62f.).[51] The London Philhellene committee soon judged the loan and its subsequent development to be a failure, and consequently dissolved in 1824, despite its successes with collecting donations (Klein 2009, 64f.).[52] The disappointment was mutual. It appeared that both parties had held misleading notions about the motivation of the other.[53] The Loughnan Bank was scarcely involved in these controversies and seems to have complied strictly with the instructions of the commissioners. No information concerning the subsequent history of the bank can be ascertained.

It should be added that even the limited amount of money that finally arrived in Greece did little to support the Greeks in their struggle for independence against the Ottomans. Despite this powerful enemy, the country had entered a phase of civil war. It seems likely that the finance provided was invested in the violent conflicts between the various Greek parties: the elite property owners and village chiefs from the Peloponnesus, the so-called Kotzampasides, the military elite of irregular soldiers on the continent, and the sea merchants on the Aegean islands, who shared the enlightened ideas of Western Europe.[54] Although the figures provided vary, the research makes clear that only very small sums were utilised for their original purpose (Kofas 1981, 10).[55]

The second London loan of 1825

It was only 1825 when the Greeks decided to attempt to cover their growing financial requirements with another foreign loan. The provisional Greek government – made up of the party of island Greeks under Kondouriotis – again sent Orlando, Zaimes and Louriotis to negotiate. Orlando and Zaimis travelled to London once more, which is somewhat surprising after the Greeks' sobering experiences in Great Britain. Indeed, when the possibility of a second loan was first discussed, the deputies implied that the Philhellenes and Bowring in particular were only interested in organising money to support the bonds from the first loan in the hope that this time the Greek government would send more amenable deputies to London.[56] However, the provisional government decided in favour of the experienced negotiators. Perhaps the Greeks assumed that the ever-growing speculation bubble on the London Stock Exchange would create a lower level of risk awareness there than, for instance, in Paris.[57] The desire to further Great Britain's involvement in Greek affairs also played a role (Levandis 1944, 16). And even though the LGC no longer existed (Klein 2009, 64f.),[58] several of its members continued to work for the Greek cause: Leicester Stanhope, the radical Parliamentarian John Cam Hobhouse and Edward Ellice were still in contact with the Greeks (Bartle 1962, 68). Furthermore, the deputies were now familiar with the rules of the game in London. However, this time the Greeks simultaneously investigated opportunities in France: the third deputy Louriotis did not join the delegation to London, but went to Paris.[59]

In the end though, it was the negotiations in London that were again successful. On 7 February 1825, the contract with the prominent London bank Jacob and Samson Ricardo was signed. The nominal value of the loan was £2 million. The issue rate was even lower than that of the year before, 55.1 (the Greek government had not authorised the deputies to go below 55), i.e. the capital expected to be raised from the loan amounted to only £1,110,000. In the first two years, an annual interest payment of 5% was due, thus totalling a dividend of 10%. £200,000 was thus reserved as interest and £20,000 (i.e. 1%) for the amortisation. From the following year, like with the first loan, the Greek government was to make 1%, i.e. £20,000, available annually for the repurchase of the bonds at current market prices. 'The whole of the National Property of Greece [...] until the whole amount of capital, which such Obligations represent, shall be discharged' guaranteed the loan prospectus (see Figure II.1.1). This vague guarantee shows that this was once again a highly speculative bond where the investor and not the banker carried the risk of future price trends. The bankers' commission was £60,000 (a relatively modest 3%), with another 2% to pay on the dividends, i.e. on the costs of the investors. According to these stipulations in the convention, a sum of £830,000 was to be made available to the provisional Greek government (Λουριώτης [Louriotis]/Ορλάνδος [Orlandos], 1839, 121–130, here 123).[60]

The floating of the loan was initially a great success: it was four and a half times oversubscribed (Levandis 1944, 18). As far as the administration of the money was concerned, the Greek deputies had learnt from their earlier experience: this time, the convention stated that the money was to be 'at the disposal and subject to the order of the said Ioannis Orlandos, Ioannis Zaimis and Andreas Louriotis or any two of them on account of the Greek Government'.[61] The money was to be paid out to the provisional government in nine monthly rates between February and October 1825.[62] To this end, a commission was immediately formed, consisting of Hobhouse, Ellice and Burdett, Philhellenes with whom the Greeks had not yet had negative experiences (Ibid., 19). This commission sent three deputies to Zante[63] to undertake the payments. The bankers also pursued other strategies to minimise their risks: the convention recorded their right 'to put an end to this contract at any time after the payment of the three first instalments and the payments then made by them on account of this Loan shall be thereupon considered as forfeited'.[64]

Despite these attempts at advanced risk management, a conflict quickly arose surrounding the question of intervention in support of the bond price. The convention recorded that the bankers should reserve £250,000 from the instalments to the issuers in order to repurchase bonds from the first loan at market rates, although not at a higher price than 60. If possible, the entire stock should be repurchased in this way within a year – given the low market price a perfectly realistic option, which would have been most advantageous for the Greek government (Λουριώτης [Louriotis]/Ορλάνδος [Orlandos] 1839, 124f.). However, the news of the fall of the long besieged Greek city of Mesolonghi, which developed into a European media event, then led to a rapid drop in the value of the bonds of the second loan: in April 1825, they fell to 15.[65] Suddenly, the deputies were under pressure from all sides not to send the money from the second loan to Greece, but to use it for more intervention purchases. Louriotis even claimed that the bankers had extorted him and his colleagues only to send more money to Greece if they also released large sums to repurchase bonds (Louriotis 1827, 12f., FN). Although the

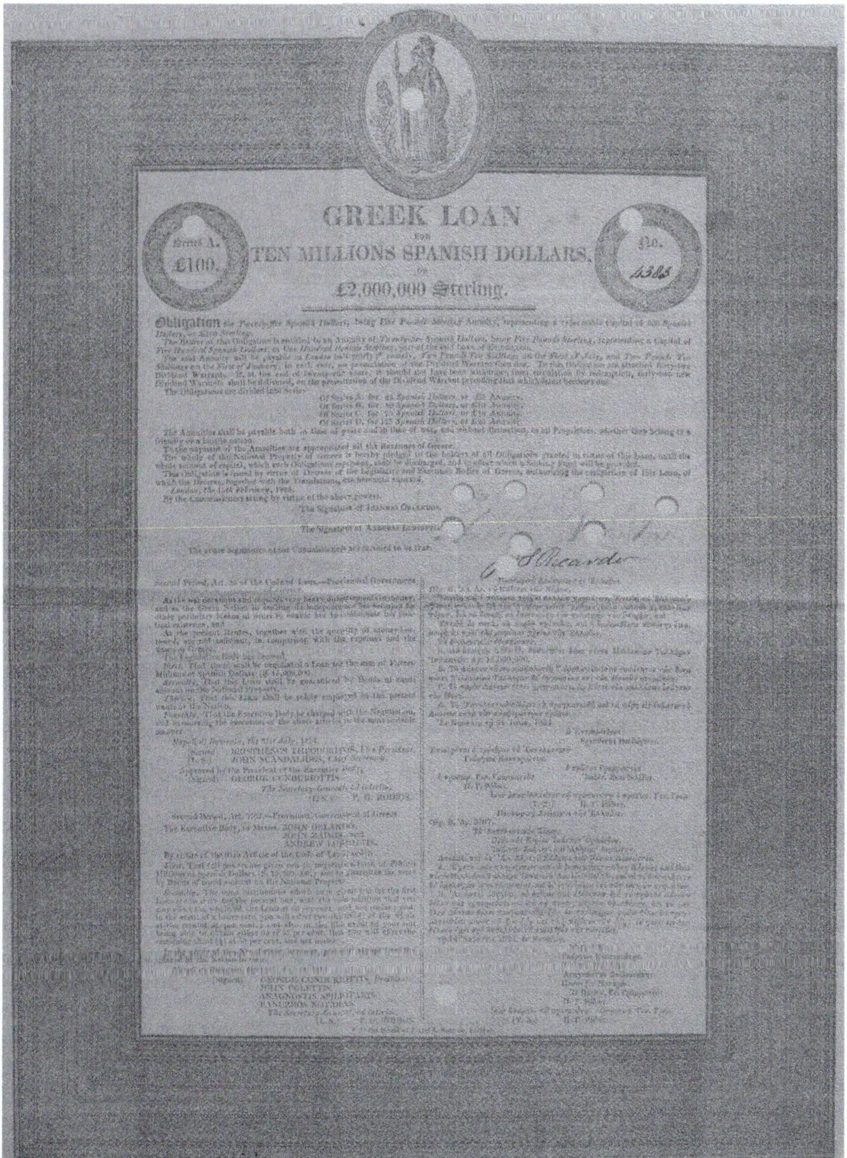
Series A.
£100.
GREEK LOAN
FOR
TEN MILLIONS SPANISH DOLLARS,
OR
£2,000,000 Sterling.
No.

Figure II.1.1 Loan Prospectus: Greek Loan for Ten Million Spanish Dollars or £2,000,000 Sterling.

bankers later vehemently denied any attempt to bring pressure to bear, evidence of such activities is clearly found in their letters.[66] They must have been concerned here with the bonds they held themselves and with their reputation as an issuing house, which required protection. £200,000 was lost through these purchases in the open market.

But even with the money that was actually available for the struggle for independence, well-known problems quickly emerged.[67] The bankers used all the delaying tactics possible to avoid supplying the local freedom fighters with money, because they did not know its intended purpose and doubted it would be used efficiently. Instead, they decided, initially with the agreement of the deputies, that a major proportion of the money should remain under their control and be spent in London, on military equipment to be transferred to Greece, a strategy intended to minimise the danger of misuse. The main desire was to purchase ships to fight against the Egyptian fleet. But as apparently no suitable ships were available for sale, the building of new ships was commissioned (Ανδρεάδης [Andreadis] 1904, 41–46). Orlando and Louriotis seemed at first to be in favour of this course of action. However, the construction of the frigates did not proceed as planned, but was repeatedly delayed. This made the Greeks nervous and, at the end of 1825, the provisional government displayed its mistrust of the two deputies by sending another one, named Spaniolakis (Bartle 1962, 68). He arrived in London at a bad time, economically speaking, as the speculation bubble had burst in November of that year (Kynaston 1994, 35–50; Haupert, 1997, 512).[68] Acquiring more money for Greece to speed up the construction of the frigates, as Hobhouse had suggested, was therefore no longer possible, certainly not with the incomplete ships as a guarantee, as the Ricardos categorically declared: 'We are ourselves such large holders of the Bonds & have lost so much by them that we cannot risk any more'.[69] Their appetite for risk concerning Greece was exhausted. The bankers broke off contact with Louriotis, pointing out that he was no longer authorised by the Greek government and that they would now only deal with the new deputy Spaniolakis.[70] At this point, Orlando and Louriotis, now most familiar with the game rules of the London financial world, appealed to the public and provoked a scandal.[71]

The media scandal of the defrauded freedom fighters

The public showdown began in November 1825 and January 1826 when Count Palma, a friend of Louriotis from his time in Spain and a passionate liberal, published letters entitled *Greece Vindicated* in the Morning Chronicle and the Morning Post, fiercely attacking the creditors and bankers.[72] *The Times* picked up on his accusations and in July 1826 began to report on the failure of the Greek loan. The conservative paper apparently welcomed the opportunity to turn public opinion against the strengthened

Whig opposition (Rosen 1992, 287).[73] Under the conditions of social modernisation that emerged from the industrial revolution, the ongoing disputes between the liberal Whigs and the conservative Tories reflected growing tensions between industry and landowners. What could provide better material for an anti-liberal campaign than a situation in which liberal Philhellenes, including a number of Whig parliamentarians, had disgraced themselves and behaved hypocritically? Bowring, at the time commissioned by Bentham to edit the Westminster Review, used this platform for his rejoinders (Bowring 1826), escalating the scandal.

Through the controversy, it became clear that some of the money had indeed been embezzled or at least wasted. Firstly, a commission of £60,000 had been paid during the negotiation process. This was completely usual when a loan was issued on the stock exchange; that the Ricardos charged for their services was nothing special. However, Greek business was considered by the public to be a philanthropic matter to which different norms should be applied than to normal business transactions. People could reluctantly accept that the bankers charged commission, despite the discordant note this struck, considering the philanthropic rhetoric in the prospectus. But the situation with the Philhellenes, who claimed to be acting altruistically for the good of the Greeks, was viewed somewhat differently: did they also keep some of the money that the freedom fighters needed so urgently? After much back and forth, it emerged that the Ricardo brothers had kept £22,000 of the commission for themselves, with money also going to the Philhellenes Easthope (£10,000), Lloyd (£6,500) and Ellice (£14,000). Bowring was also accused of having received several hundred pounds from Ricardo in return for brokering the second loan, although he never admitted that this was the case (Bartle 1962, 72).[74] And even the Greek deputies were said to have received £7,500, although Louriotis always vehemently denied this.[75] In public opinion, however, these payments to allegedly selfless persons claiming to fight for the freedom of Greece constituted the first part of the scandal.

The second part of the scandal was that the Philhellenes had tried to pass on their speculative losses to the Greek committee and the provisional government. Hume, for instance, had purchased bonds to the value of £10,000. As the prices sank, he panicked and sold them at a loss of £1,300, and then invoiced the Greek deputies and the Greek nation for this sum. In addition, he added another £54 as interest accrued over the time that elapsed until he was reimbursed. According to *The Times*, he persuaded the Greeks to comply with his demands through 'mobbing'.[76] It seems that John Bowring, who bought bonds worth £25,000, behaved in a similar fashion. When the price fell by 16%, he pressured the Greek deputies to relieve him of his bonds with a reduction of only 10% instead of 16%, in recognition of his past commitment to Greece. When the price rose again, and this time above the initial level, he declared the sale to be void and demanded his bonds be returned. In the end, he persuaded the deputies to reimburse the entire £25,000 that he originally invested.[77] Furthermore, it emerged that he had received a commission payment of £10,000 or £11,000 from Loughnan, O'Brien, Ellice and Company for the first loan (Kofas 1981, 7). The two Philhellenes were clearly unwilling to carry the same speculative risk as all the other investors, but wanted to outsource their risk to the Greeks. The public was not willing to accept this kind of risk management at the expense of Greece.

The third reason for indignation was that even the resting money was not used expediently. The Ricardos commissioned the British engineer Alexander Galloway with the construction of the frigates on the advice of Lord Cochrane, who was to lead an expedition to Greece.[78] But the ships were not completed, and the same was true of an additional one that had been commissioned in Marseille – a centre of the Greek diaspora in the Mediterranean area (Πάρη [Pari] 2008) – and one of the two that had been ordered in far-off New York.[79] Better to send the money across the Atlantic than to pay it out to the Greeks seemed to be the position of the bankers. It is not possible to determine whether the Greek deputies were informed about or had consented to these mandates, e.g. the contract with Galloway. When the scandal broke, they denied that this had been the case and accused the Ricardos of having acted on their own authority (Louriotis 1827).[80] The Ricardos, however, claimed that they had consulted the deputies and the Philhellenes in the commission at each step of the process.[81] Be that as it may, the Ricardos paid Galloway £392,000 for the construction of the frigates. The Greek deputies were repeatedly assured that the boats would be complete and set sail within a few weeks, but this never came to pass. Instead, Galloway continued to present invoices, which the Ricardos paid even after the Greek deputies had expressly asked that the payments be stopped.[82]

In September 1826, the British bondholders met to discuss and resolve the public accusations, hoping in this way to encourage the price of the Greek bonds to recover.[83] A commission was formed, consisting of David Hume, Leicester Stanhope and John Bowring – with the latter setting the fox to keep the geese. The delay in completing the ships remained a mystery. A conspiracy theory suggested that the engineer Galloway had deliberately delayed the completion of the frigates because his son was employed by the Egyptian enemy, but this could not be proved.[84] The only thing that seemed clear was the result: from the £2 million loan, only £182,000 in cash, £60,000 in the form of goods and £33,000 as accepted bills of exchange actually arrived in Greece (Kofas 1981, 13f.; Dawson, 1990, 132).[85] All those involved agreed that this was a truly shameful yield but they failed to produce a convincing explanation or to allocate responsibility. This seems equally impossible in retrospect.

The falling prices of the Greek bonds – in July 1826, they had dropped to 10 or 11 (Dawson 1990, 127) – encouraged *The Times* to further excesses:

'The Greek cause has been betrayed. It has been betrayed in England'.[86] The newspaper raised the affair to the level of a national scandal.[87] On 8 November 1826, the paper published a satirical poem in which the ghost of Miltiades appeared to a Philhellene and follower of Jeremy Bentham in a dream and asked him in the name of liberty to help Greece. The second verse proclaims:

> The Benthamite, yawning, left his bed –
> Away to the Stock Exchange he sped,
> And he found the scrip of Greece so high
> That it fired his blood, it flush'd his eye,
> And oh, 'twas a sight for the Ghost to see,
> For there never was Greek more Greek than he!
> And still, as the premium higher went,
> His ecstasy rose – so much *per cent.*
> (As we see in a glass, that tells the weather,
> The heat and the *silver* rise together),
> And Liberty sung from the patriot's lip,
> While a voice from his pocket whispered 'Scrip!'[88]

Unsurprisingly, the Benthamite, torn between his liberal worldview and his profit interests, immediately forgets his love of liberty when the price falls and is only concerned with saving his own skin. The poem thus suggests that when a love of liberty and self-interest become mutually exclusive, liberal hypocrites quickly reveal their true colours: a sole focus on maximising profit. Hereby the newspaper clearly takes up a position hostile towards the mercantile middle class in the party-political dispute in Great Britain. The poem fittingly concludes with Miltiades returning to the ferry across the Styx having uttered the scathing words:

> Of Liberty's foes the worst are they
> Who turn to a trade her cause divine,
> And gamble for gold on Freedom's shrine![89]

The Times not only cursed all the British parties involved,[90] but also promised that their reputations would be permanently ruined if it were not otherwise possible to prosecute them for their immoral behaviour[91]:

> But no man who means in future to appear upon the stage of public life, can ever suffer a transaction, in which his credit or honour are concerned, to subside without affording the fullest explanation of his conduct. Such a transaction will revive again and again in the general remembrance so long as he lives and attracts notice.[92]

Risk perception and risk management of the banking house of Ricardo

As has become clear, the high risk of the Greek loans was never a secret. So why did the bankers decide to take this risk? Did they learn nothing from the failure of the first issue?[93] How did they attempt to manage the risks?

Based on our behavioural finance model, it is important to first assess the information available to the bankers before they signed the contract. There is no evidence that they actively sought information from or about Greece. Communication seems to have revolved primarily around the Philhellenes. Certainly, the bankers failed to consult varied and independent sources to thoroughly investigate the creditworthiness of their customer – not that this was actually a common practice at the time (Chatziioannou, 2013, 53). However, the Ricardos certainly must have been fully aware that the bonds from the first loan were weak and that there had been disputes with the Greek deputies.

How then did the bankers interpret the scant information available to them, and according to what set of values? Jacob (1780–1834) and Samson Ricardo (1792–1862) were the younger brothers of the famous economist David Ricardo (1772–1823), one of the best-known liberal economists in London, who had gained his fortune through his activities on the stock exchange (Ricardo 1973). Like David, Jacob began his career as an assistant to his father, Abraham Israel Ricardo, in 1802 and followed the usual family career path to become a stockbroker. From 1806 to 1833, Jacob was a very successful member of the London Stock Exchange, even becoming president in 1820. He and his brother Samson (about whom little information is known) conducted their financial activities primarily in France. It could be supposed that the two younger Ricardos shared the liberal attitude of their brother David and that their political enthusiasm for Greece's struggle for independence led to their involvement in financing the Greeks, even if there is no indication that the Ricardo banking house was a family bank.[94] However, closer scrutiny of the situation dismisses this suggestion: the Ricardos were one of the London banking houses that in July 1823 planned to apply for a bond issue to the French government who required money to suppress the so-called Trienio Liberal. This revolt of Spanish liberals against their monarchy began in 1820 and was a genuinely liberal uprising against the restorative politics of the restored Bourbons. Under the officer Rafael del Riego, the revolt was initially successful and in March 1820 Ferdinand VII was forced to restore the liberal constitution (Barceló/Schmidt 2005, 268f.). However, at the Congress of Verona in the autumn of 1822, the other members of the Holy Alliance gave France free rein to intervene in Spain to counter the revolution, which led to the moderate and radical liberals being militarily defeated by 1823. The Spanish revolutionaries had hoped for support from Great Britain, as had been forthcoming in 1808 in the fight against

Napoleon, but Britain adhered to the principle of solidarity among the Great Powers to stabilise the balance of power in Europe and remained neutral (Fahrmeir 2010, 183).[95] Public opinion in England was, however, clearly on the side of the Spanish liberals,[96] and David Ricardo also actively supported the Spanish revolutionaries.[97] In contrast, this was far from the case with his brothers who were flirting with the idea of financing the fight *against* the liberals. They were harshly criticised by the press for this intention. Thus, *The Times* reported that several banking houses which had previously done business with France 'have refused, in the most decided manner, to take any share in this transaction, on account of the iniquitous purpose to which the money is to be applied'.[98] The newspaper noted disdainfully that only the London branch of Rothschilds was to cooperate with the banker Montefiore to support their French branch, while the Ricardo brothers were similarly preparing a listing on the stock exchange with the Paris bank of Mieville & Co.[99] In his eulogy for David Ricardo, who died on 11 September 1823, the economist Jean-Baptiste Say even felt it necessary to declare that David certainly would not have wanted to be involved in these business activities of his brothers (Ricardo 1973). Indeed, after the defeat of the Spanish revolution, David had turned to the Greek struggle, as had many supporters of Spanish liberalism. As a good friend of Jeremy Bentham and a convinced Whig, shortly before his death, David had actually been a founding member of the LGC (Penn, 1936b, 647).[100] Such liberal commitment was foreign to his brothers. Clearly, they only dropped their plans to participate in the French loan due to the public pressure that had been brought to bear: they were not one of the banking houses that finally submitted an offer to the French government on 10 July.[101] Perhaps the damage that such a bond issue would have done to their reputation in the liberal City was too high.

It is obvious that the two Ricardos did not share the liberal views of their older brother David. What remains unclear is whether they were simply politically indifferent or whether they actually wanted to support the restorative politics of the French monarchy, and also whether these differing political positions led to conflict in the family.[102] Perhaps the two brothers hoped to be able to compensate for the lost French transaction with the Greek bond issue, and also to repair their reputation in liberal circles. In any case, we can exclude the possibility that Jacob and Samson Ricardo were ideologically motivated to participate in the 1825 bond issue in terms of wishing to support the Greeks in their struggle for independence at all costs. However, they were undoubtedly attracted by the notion of a bond issue that could be easily sold to idealists close to the height of a speculation bubble. It is not possible to determine if the Ricardos actively sought out the opportunity to float the loan or if the Philhellenes first approached them.

As far as management of the risks is concerned, as mentioned earlier, the bank had contractually ensured the right to back out after the third payment instalment, although this never occurred despite all the problems.

The risk of falling prices remained, as with the 1824 loan, solely the responsibility of the investors. In this way, the bank's position was fairly secure and so it was unnecessary to find a partner to share the risk, as it became a common practice for bond issues in the second half of the nineteenth century. However, it seems that the bankers retained a significant proportion of the bonds for themselves, even though they could initially have sold them all. There is every reason to believe that their intention was to push up the prices, which would have improved their reputation as an issuing bank, if it had resulted in their customers profiting from high speculative gains. Large losses for the investors, however, would have negatively impacted on their reputation. While these bond purchases stabilised the prices, however, they also exposed the Ricardos to the effects of declining prices and thus subjected them to the risks assumed by the other investors.

Letters from Greece that were intercepted by the British Secret Intelligence Service[103] made clear that the bankers also attempted to profit from the loan in other ways. At the beginning of May 1825, a few months after the contract had been finalised, informants from Greece reported that the Ricardos had dispatched Count Gamba as an agent who was to get close to West Europeans transacting business in the country.[104] Shortly afterwards, other sources reported that Greek contracts for military equipment for 4,000 men had been acquired by British manufacturers who were to be paid by Ricardo in the course of the last instalment of the loan. The other half went to French businesses.[105] This evidence leaves little doubt that the Ricardos were also concerned to secure Greek armament orders for British firms, either for themselves or for their customers in the arms industry.[106] Therefore, they did not abandon the bond issue, although the contract would have allowed them to do so, but this could have led to the loss of the Greek armaments contracts. The Ricardos thus primarily viewed Greece as a promising market in which they wanted to gain a foothold. If the conflict should be prolonged or independence gained, then more contracts could be expected, which certainly fuelled the bankers' interest in the success of the freedom fighters. Their disappointment in the incompetence of the engineers they commissioned with the building of the frigates was correspondingly great and obviously honest.[107] Thus after the defeat of Mesolonghi, which seemed to seriously endanger the entire struggle for independence, they wrote to Ellice that it was 'painful to think that this melancholy catastrophe might have been prevented had better arrangements been made relative to the ill fated expedition'.[108]

The use of colonial images of Greece to justify her disenfranchisement

The bankers thus particularly wanted to sell weapons to Greece. The risks for them were, firstly, that the Greeks might be defeated in their struggle for independence and, secondly, that other arms suppliers might win the contracts. The bankers had to prevent this if they or their customers were to profit. They therefore tried to stop the Greeks from freely disposing of the money by assuming control of expenditure themselves. The Ricardos consequently did not treat the provisional Greek government as a true principal to whom they related as agents; they rather deprived the government of the right to make its own decisions.[109]

To legitimate this behaviour, the bankers used arguments related to 'authoritarian' British liberalism, as used by the Philhellenes Hume and Bowring, and also by Stanhope who had just returned from India: they described Greece from a colonial perspective as the oriental, the 'other' (Todorova 1997, 23), and denied that the Greeks were capable of self-government. In an authoritarian manner, the Philhellenes demonstrated their conviction that they knew best about how the Greeks should spend their money. Although such arguments were bitterly opposed by the Greeks, who attempted to defend their right to self-determination, they were largely (even if not entirely)[110] accepted among the Philhellene group. So, for instance, Jeremy Bentham, Bowring's mentor, persisted in supporting his protégé, making him the editor of his posthumous work despite all the accusations against him and although Bowring's standing with other European liberals was ruined.[111]

The bankers thus adopted the authoritarian-liberal pattern of legitimation to justify their actions. However, unlike the Philhellenes, they aimed not only to earn money through speculation, or at least to avoid losing money, but also hoped to profit from the armaments trade. They clearly failed to recognise that this moral argumentation exposed them to a certain risk: if they declared the Greeks to be incompetent and awarded the contracts themselves, then they also assumed responsibility for the orderly discharge of the contracts in line with the requirements of the struggle for independence. Louriotis pointed this out in no uncertain terms: the bankers, with the Philhellenes, had boasted of having assumed the burden of this difficult undertaking, and thus they also bore responsibility for its miscarriage (Louriotis 1827, 38). As the bankers did not prevent the failure of the shipbuilding project, in Louriotis' eyes, they lost all moral right to use Philhellenism as a legitimising strategy:

> Most assuredly, I have seen nothing in your conduct, from the first to the last of what you aptly call the ill-fated loan, which would warrant me in asserting that you would abandon one iota of your own interest for the good of my country.[112]

The Greeks explicitly accused the bankers of moral hazard and demanded that they themselves should finally be given control of all the available finance.[113] But the bankers nonetheless continued to cling to their legitimation strategy and now denied that the Greek government was in a position to act as a true principal[114]:

> We have not, in this business, acted as your agents, or as commission merchants to the Greek government; we have, in the interest of your country, and conjointly with some other gentlemen, friends to your cause, imposed upon ourselves the chief burthen of a difficult undertaking. To the sacrifice of our own interest in the neglect of our other avocations, we have been gratuitously and strenuously employed in forwarding the object.[115]

They presented the failure as a chain of unfortunate circumstances. Their good intentions raised them above every suspicion, the bankers argued.[116] Consequently, they regarded themselves as being under attack in the press campaign by people 'who know nothing about the matter'.[117] In *The Times*, they publicly denied ever having spent any money without instructions from the Greek deputies and rejected the notion that they could be held legally responsible for the failures[118]:

> Much has been said about Stock Brokers fitting out steam vessels – but were it known that these said Stock Brokers had been called to sit upon a court martial it would excite still many a surprise.[119]

They emphasised that the losses they incurred supporting the bonds by far exceeded their commission, which clearly showed that they had not put their own interests above those of the issuing country.[120] But they did not mention their interests in the armaments trade. Instead, they accused the deputies of corruption. In particular, they blamed Louriotis' 'own delinquencies' and 'knavery' and suggested that he was using the campaign to disguise his own mistakes.[121] Furthermore, the Ricardos tried to shift responsibility for the failure to the Philhellenes, as they had agreed with all the decisions.[122] While attempting to save any money that could be saved from the shipbuilding catastrophe, they therefore repeatedly requested the Philhellenes' approval[123]:

> We consider that we are fully entitled to call upon you for counsel in the present emergency, & we regret that up to this period we have not had more of your advice & assistance – You will perhaps tell us in reply that you never took upon yourselves the conduct of any part of the undertaking – we admit it but at the same time you must acknowledge that we also never undertook to execute the various tasks which the repeated delays & unexampled difficulties have given rise to we neither recommended nor approved the original plan but the chief burthen of the undertaking has devolved upon us & we have spared neither our time nor our effort to forward it. The event has been most disastrous, but we feel confident that you will acquit us of having been at all instrumental to this unfortunate result.[124]

However, the Philhellenes denied all responsibility: they had not been involved in commissioning Galloway, they had no authority to influence matters in any way and they never had possessed any such authority.[125] They did not want to be drawn into the unsuccessful principal-agent relationship, even though many of them shared the authoritarian-liberal image of Greece.

The press campaign certainly targeted the Philhellenes, but the bankers also came in for a dose of indignation. They were accused of dressing up moral hazard and deceiving their clients to further their own interests. This accusation weighed heavily and damaged the reputation of the bank in the long term, probably more than the collapse of the Greek bonds that the bank had issued, which ranked as part of the general stock market crash. It is thus certainly no coincidence that Jacob's oldest son John Lewis, who was continuing the family tradition as a stockbroker, no longer used the first names of his father or uncle for his business, even though Jacob died a rich man in 1834, leaving his children a large inheritance.[126] The family remained in contact with the FO in the cause of Greece until at least 1846 as representatives of the Committee of Greek bondholders.[127]

The provisional Greek government proved just as unreliable with the bonds as their financiers. The loans were only serviced until 1827, just as long as the necessary money could be taken from the ongoing loan instalments. Subsequently, the chaos of the war made it impossible to raise any more finance, even after 1827 when the Greeks won the Battle of Navarino with the help of the British, French and Russians. For the first time, Greece halted payments to foreign creditors, which led to them being excluded from the international stock exchanges for further loans. The London Philhellenes demanded that the provisional government should finally produce a reliable repayment plan, but this seemed unrealistic, given the conditions of civil strife and conflict in the completely devastated country.[128] Even after the Great Powers recognised Greece as an independent state in 1830, the foreign debts remained outstanding. The governments supported creditors in the negotiations. However, the British government repeatedly made clear that the bonds were transactions of a 'purely private nature', in which they had no wish to be involved.[129] The diplomatic pressure was thus not excessive. The first Greek president Ioannis Kapodistrias could not reach an agreement with the creditors, and neither could King Otto with his Bavarian regency, imposed upon the country by the Great Powers in 1832 after independence had been achieved (Ανδρεάδης [Andreadis] 1904, 54–57; Levandis 1944, 25).

The bonds, which by this time had become purely speculative, had been largely bought up by Dutch investors at the time when the Dutch Prince Leopold was a candidate for the Greek throne (Loukos 1986, 447), and repeatedly appeared in the form of payment demands in the files of the foreign offices well into the second half of the century.[130] Attempts to reach an agreement between Greece and the creditors regularly failed until 1878, when a settlement was made in the run-up to the Berlin Congress and Greece was readmitted to the European Stock Exchanges.[131] The repayments then continued until 1930, more than 100 years after the bonds had been issued (Δερτιλής [Dertilis] 2009, 591). And for much longer, the Greeks continued to relativise and frame their first bankruptcy with references to the despicable way they had been treated by the creditors of the 1824/1825 loans.

Conclusion

When issuing the Greek loan of 1825, the Ricardo brothers relied particularly on information that they received from the LGC, apparently without bothering to actively seek additional information. They failed to recognise how the Greek freedom fighters perceived themselves and wished to be perceived by others: as an independent nation and equal and autonomous business partners and principals. At the same time, the Greeks assumed that the liberal uprising of their people against the Ottomans deserved the disinterested support and help of liberal actors in Western Europe. They believed that this philanthropic attitude would rank above the 'rules of the game' of the London Stock Exchange and thus expected special treatment.

However, the Ricardo brothers, who did not rank among the dedicated friends of Greece or liberal activists, were primarily concerned with their own interests: firstly, a bond issue that could be readily marketed to the enthusiastic Philhellenes in the speculative bubble of the London Stock Exchange; and, secondly, acquiring armament contracts for themselves or their customers from the arms industry. In order to secure these contracts and to minimise the risk of the Greeks spending the money elsewhere, they not only awarded arms contracts where they saw fit, but also put the Greek deputies under immense pressure to intervene to support the price of the bonds. They legitimised their actions with a very different image of Greece, one that was greatly influenced by colonial traditions and that was shared by a number of the Philhellenes: the country was viewed as backward, needy and undiscerning of its own requirements, and was seen as part of the 'other' of the Orient. The bankers did not recognise this disorganised, corrupt Greece as an autonomous principal or fully fledged business partner, and they consequently did not regard themselves as agents who were bound to instructions. The feeling of perceived control thus generated led to the illusion that they could direct events themselves (Ricciardi 2008b, 102), a circumstance that seems to have been of decisive importance for the risk perception of the bankers. However, this denial of Greek autonomy proved to be an ineffective risk-management instrument.

Apparently, the bankers suffered considerable losses with the bonds that they retained for themselves. They may, however, have profited from the armament transactions linked to the loan. Nonetheless, the damage done to their reputation as an issuing house was probably a severe blow, as the

Greeks denounced their moral hazard and mismanagement in an extensive press campaign. However, for over 50 years, the image of the Greek financial market was dominated by the defaulted loans, which were not serviced after 1827 until repayment terms were finally agreed in 1878 (Chatziioannou 2013, 53).

Notes

1 The background of the revolution itself is covered in detail by Κορδάτος [Kordatos] 1957–1959. On the Philhellenic movement at the Congress of Vienna, see Kerschbaumer/Schönhärl (2013).

2 Klein undertakes a detailed analysis of the individual committees and the political opinions of their members; for the situation in France, also see Amandry (1983); Barau (2009).

3 Exact calculations of the extent of the voluntary donations given by Greeks abroad and Philhellenes are found in Kofas (1981, 2), and Ανδρεάδης [Andreadis] (1904).

4 Mavrokordatos from Tripolitza to Bowring from LGC, 2/14.7.1823, LGC 5, tr. by K.S.

5 As well as Rhodes, the late medieval seat of the Grand Masters of the Knights Hospitaller or Knights of Malta, the Maltese demanded two more islands as soon as Greece was liberated; see Dawson (1990, 64).

6 See Stanhope to Bowring, 6.10.1823, from Rastadt, in LGC 3; Stanhope to Bowring, 10.10.1823, from Bern, ibid.

7 For the development of the international money market in the 1820s in general, see Pan-Montojo (2019).

8 Biographical information on Andreas Louriotis is extremely rare. He was a merchant in the Mediterranean area and was also involved in international business; see Chatziioannou (2002, 36).

9 The Irish naval officer Edward Blaquiere (1779–1832), who came from a Huguenot family, fought in the Napoleonic wars. In May 1820, he travelled to Spain to support the Spanish revolutionary movement. Blaquiere was a dedicated liberal whose detailed reports were decisive in mobilising support for the Spanish freedom fighters among the general public in England. He was also responsible for disseminating the writings of Jeremy Bentham among the Spanish revolutionaries, see Rosen (2004a); Brennecke (2010, 90).

10 Blaquiere also brought Bowring into contact with the philosopher Jeremy Bentham, who became his mentor. Bentham made his protégé editor of the Westminister Review in 1823, much to the displeasure of, e.g. the Mill family. Later, Bowring also edited Bentham's posthumous work; see Bartle (1963, 28, 30).

11 Count Palma, an exiled Italian, founded the Madrid association; see ibid., 61. On the work and history of the committee, see Rosen (2004b).

12 In 1809, Hobhouse accompanied Lord Byron on his journey through Spain, Portugal and to the Ottoman Empire, including Greece. He was an admirer of Napoleon and a successful Whig; see Cochran (2004). His account of his travels: Hobhouse (1813).

13 From humble beginnings, Joseph Hume worked his way up through the East India Company and was one of the best connected leaders of the radical liberals in Britain; see Chancellor (2004).

14 On Philhellenism in England and particularly on the London committee, see also Penn (1936a, 1936b); Dakin (1955).

15 Blaquiere's report was criticised as being the product of complete ignorance, even by the Greeks, by the banker Sina from Vienna; see Sina to Bowring, 8.9.1823, LCG 5. On Sina (or: Schinas), see **87 n.90** and **134 n.51** in this book.
16 There is very little information available about Orlando. He came from Hydra and was involved in the provisional Greek government after 1823 (see Chatziioannou 2013, 35). After his time as a deputy, he became an administrative civil servant in Hydra; see Orlando to Napier, 7.9.1828 from Hydra, BL Add 49113, 131.
17 Ιωάννης Ζαΐμης [Ioannis Zaimes] is mentioned in John (2004).
18 Canning was one of the enthusiastic supporters of the Greek cause, although his position prevented him from active involvement. During his time as a foreign minister from 1822 to 1827, the activities of the Philhellenes were tolerated if not actually promoted; see Beales (2004).
19 In the contract, the bankers involved are named as Andrew Loughnan, Andrew Loughnan junior and Andrew Meagher O'Brien; the name of the bank is cited as Loughnan Son and O'Brien; see Λουριώτης [Louriotis]/Ορλάνδος [Orlandos] (1839, 113–120). Elsewhere, the bank is referred to as A. Laughman and Co; see Statistical Society of London (1878, 313). The few surviving letters from and to the Loughnan Bank are not particularly instructive. Whether the 'Ellice' mentioned in some of the secondary literature (Loughnan, O'Brien, Ellice and Company) is identical to the Philhellene Edward Ellice is unclear but would explain why the Philhellenes selected this particular bank.
20 Dalleggio (1949, 24), tr. by K.S. The alternative offers are mentioned in Orlando and Louriottis to LGC, 13.6.1824, LGC 8. The banking house of Baring is also said to have been interested.
21 Orlando and Louriotis to the Metropolitan Ignatius, 30.3.1824, in: Dalleggio (1949, 54ff.).
22 Bowring to Lord Byron, 13.2.1824, LGC 11.
23 Convention, in: Λουριώτης [Louriotis]/Ορλάνδος [Orlandos] (1839, 113–120), here 115. A rate below par (100) was quite common. The risk premium was reflected in the rate rather than in the level of interest: the lower the rate, the higher the chances of profit.
24 Orlando and Louriotis pointed out to the Metropolitan Ignatius that the circumstances were much worse than those in Columbia, Spain or Mexico, and that the contract thus comprised the best conditions possible; see Orlando and Louriotis to the Metropolitan Ignatius, 30.3.1824, in: Dalleggio (1949, 54ff.). There are nonetheless remarkable similarities between the Greek and the Mexican loans; see Salvucci (2009, 22ff.).
25 Statistical Society of London (1878, 313). A rate of 59.5 is cited for Greece here.
26 'After a struggle of three years, distinguished by a series of triumphant success, the independence of the Greek Nation has been established, and there is every probability of its speedy recognition by the different Powers of Europe. The Public, therefore, will not be surprised that the Senate of Greece should have determined to raise a Loan, to assist in bringing that pending contest to a just and happy conclusion'. Prospectus of the loan, BL Add. 49113.
27 The bankers reserved £16,000 for a sinking fund and two years interest at 5%, which was to be paid out every six months, thus £80,000. The bankers' commission was a one-off 5% of the nominal value, i.e. an additional £40,000.
28 For the repurchase, the Greek government was from 1826 to expend 1% annually (i.e. £8,000).
29 The figures cited in the secondary literature vary greatly, e.g. in Dawson (1990, 132), and Kofas (1981, 9), who calculates that only £298,700 was received by the Greek

government. The figures cited here are drawn only from the original text of the convention; see Convention in: Λουριώτης [Louriotis]/Ορλάνδος [Orlandos] (1839, 113–120). The repurchase modalities are not discussed in the secondary literature.

30 This concerns the real estate that was formerly held by the Ottoman regime and was supposed to be transferred to Greek control with independence. From 1831, decades of dispute about the final distribution of this land characterised Greek domestic politics, as will be discussed later (see **106, 113f, 256 and 332** in this book).

31 Much of the secondary literature shares this opinion; see, e.g. Levandis (1944, 15).

32 Louriottis and Orlando to Bowring, 13.3.1824, in LGK 6, tr. by K.S.

33 Ibid, tr. by K.S.

34 Edward Ellice's business interests focused on the USA and Canada. He also pursued a political career among the Whigs; see Millar (2004).

35 Prospectus of the loan in BL Add 39113, 4. Also Bartle (1962, 62). Kofas, however, wrongly names Lord Byron, Thomas Gordon and – as a provisional member – Leicester Stanhope as commissioners; see Kofas (1981, 7). These three were supposed to later supervise the payments. Only after pressure was brought to bear by the Greeks was one of their compatriots, Lazaros Koundouriotes, subsequently included in the second commission; see Orlando and Louriotis to Lord Byron, 18.3.1824, in: Dalleggio (1949, 48f.). Byron had already advanced the Greeks £4,000; see Orlando and Louriotis to Lord Byron, 6.4.1824, in: ibid., 56f. The contract ibid., 66.

36 Orlando and Louriottis to LGC, 13.6.1824, LGC 8, tr. by K.S.

37 Orlando and Louriotis to Hobhouse, 4.10.1824, BL Add. 36460, 332.

38 Stanhope to Murdock, 14.5.1824, from Zante, LGC 8.

39 An overview of the price trends is found in Flandreau/Flores (2009).

40 Stanhope earned his great reputation as an admiral in India. In 1823, he travelled on behalf of the committee to Greece. In light of his colonial experience however, he did not trust the Greeks to be independently responsible for the development of their own country. He worked on developing a school system and the press, and on reconciling the different parties of the Greek civil war, aiming to prevent those around Alexandros Mavrokordatos taking sole possession of the money raised in England. Canning summoned him back to England because he was not promoting British interests in Greece, which focused primarily on Mavrokordatos; see Baigent (2004).

41 Orlando and Louriotis to the Metropolitan Ignatius, 27.7.1824, in: Dalleggio (1949, 105); Orlando and Louriotis to Blaquiere, 3.8.1824, in: ibid., 114f.

42 Orlando and Louriotis to the Metropolitan Ignatius, 26.4.1824, in: ibid., 68f.

43 'And the said Loughnan Son and O'Brien are not to sell or dispose of the said obligations or any of them at a lower price than fifty nine pounds per cent'. Convention of the loan in: Λουριώτης [Louriotis]/Ορλάνδος [Orlandos] (1839, 113–120), here 115.

44 This is the hypothesis of Chatziioannou (2013, 55).

45 Orlando and Louriotis to the Metropolitan Ignatius, 26.4.1824, in: Dalleggio (1949, 68f.), tr. by K.S.

46 Orlando and Louriotis to the Metropolitan Ignatius, 26.4.1824, in: ibid., 68f., tr. by K.S.

47 Orlando and Louriotis to Sir Francis Burdett, 20.7.1824, in: ibid., 104, tr. by K.S.

48 Orlando and Louriotis to the Metropolitan Ignatius, 27.7.1824, in: ibid., 105; Orlando and Louriotis to Blaquiere, 3.8.1824, in: ibid., 114f.

49 Orlando and Louriotis to the Metropolitan Ignatius, 11.6.1824, in: Bartle (1962, 84ff.), tr. by K.S. The Greeks nonetheless rejected the resignation of Bowring as Secretary of the LGC, see Orlando and Louriottis to Bowring, 25.6.1824, LGC 8.

50 Orlando and Louriotis to Mavrokordatos, 1.6.1824, in: Dalleggio (1949, 81ff.). The deputies accused him early on of only being interested in increasing his own prosperity; see Orlando and Louriotis to the Metropolitan Ignatius, 11.6.1824, in: ibid., 84ff.
51 Bentham's letters to the LGC in LGC 6.
52 Klein makes clear that the negative assessment of research on English Philhellenism refers only to the involvement of the LGC in the loan, while all other aid for Greece is ignored, even though some such initiatives were most successful; see Klein (2009, 172ff.).
53 'With regards to the Deputies I consider it perfect loss of time to have any more to do with them as all our labour for the two past years in behalf of Greece is considered comparatively useless by their conduct. Whatever are their advices I know not, but every attempt on the part of the Greek Co. or myself to get them to do anything on our advice proves fruitless [...]'. Hume to Napier, 15.9.1824, in BL 49113, 32.
54 The group around Mavrokordatos, Kondouriotis, Zaimes and Kolletis, who made up the provisional government, received the loan. A clear overview of the parties is provided by Zelepos (2014, 40–46); Jelavich/Jelavich (1986, 45f.). See also Yannoulopoulos (1981).
55 A larger proportion of the money was invested in preserving the fleet from the Ottomans than previously assumed, argues: Λιγνάδης [Lignadis] (1970, 393–398).
56 Orlando and Louriotis to the Metropolitan Ignatius, 11.6.1824, in: Dalleggio (1949, 84ff.).
57 Others made use of this situation as well. Thus in 1824, there were also plans for a loan to Cyprus, which was not supported by the LGC, but was actually floated; see LGC 5, 6.
58 Klein emphasises this early date of dissolution. In contrast, Kofas writes that the committee again acted as a broker for the second loan. According to Klein, Kofas can only be referring here to individual members; see Kofas (1981, 14). Rosen dates the end of the committee to 1826; see Rosen (2004b).
59 The negotiations in Paris are referred to below; **57–60** in this book.
60 The figures in the secondary literature vary once more; see Kofas (1981, 13), who calculates £811,200.
61 Convention, in: Λουριώτης [Louriotis]/Ορλάνδος [Orlandos] (1839, 121–126), here 122.
62 Ibid.
63 The island today known as Zakynthos, which then belonged to the British Empire and was only relinquished to Greece in 1863.
64 Convention, in Λουριώτης [Louriotis]/Ορλάνδος [Orlandos] (1839, 121–126), here 122.
65 Orlando and Louriotis to Eynard, 14.4.1825, in: Dalleggio (1949, 139f.).
66 Jacob and Samson Ricardo to Orlando and Louriotis, 9.6.1825, in: Λουριώτης [Louriotis]/Ορλάνδος [Orlandos] (1839, 197f.). Here, the Ricardos explicitly advised the deputies to make intervention purchases and protested that they themselves had bought so many bonds that they were unable to intervene any more. Later, they denied this pressure; see Jacob and Samson Ricardo to Hobhouse, 11.8.1825, BL Add. 36461, 215. According to the Ricardos' report to the Philhellene Hobhouse, many more bondholders suggested to the deputies that a third or a quarter of the bonds should be withdrawn from the market in order to stabilise the prices, supposedly without the involvement of the bankers; the deputies yielded to the demands.
67 'The loan of £40,000 just arrived appears to have very slender instructions to accompany it. Mr. Ricardo merely tells the Master that he is first to ascertain

the existence of the Government and then deliver the money to Conduriotti and to consult Gamba in any difficulty. The former is at Hydra, and I have no doubt, were we not here, that the Fleet would come and help themselves'. Captain S. B. Pechell to Frederick Adam, 21.7.1825 from Nafplio (Napoli di Romania on the Peloponnesus), in: Dakin (1955, 110f.).

68 Although the acute crisis in December could be considered as over, the complete recovery of the British economy took until 1830.

69 Samson and Jacob Ricardo to Hobhouse, 23.11.1825, BL Add. 36461, 305. The bankers also advised against a hasty sale of the half-finished frigates at a poor price in London or America. The deputies, under pressure from Greece, saw this as a way to raise money.

70 Jacob and Samson Ricardo to Louriotis, 23.9.1826, in: ibid., 81.

71 '[We]... faithfully discharged our duty' claimed the Ricardos; they were not concerned about information from the public or the Greek government (Ricardos to Louriotis and Orlando, 5.6.1826, in: Louriotis 1827, 56f.). Later though the bankers warned decisively against going public (Ricardos to Louriotis, 16.9.1826, in: ibid., 75ff.). On the game rules of the media scandal, see Burkhardt (2006).

72 First printed in the *Morning Chronicle* of 23.11.1825 and 30.11.1825 and in the *Morning Post* of 10., 11. and 12.01.1826; in the same year, the fictitious letters were also published as a book: Palma (1826a). Palma himself was convinced that the publication had been delayed by intrigues, which explained his moving from one newspaper to another; see ibid., 297–284. Later, he published the sequels Palma (1826b) and Palma (1827).

73 However, *The Times* defended itself against the notion that political interests had motivated its investigation of the parliamentarians involved, stating that it was concerned only to clarify the situation; see *The Times*, 4.11.1826, in: N. N. (Gennadios) (1878, 30f.).

74 Bowring seems to have been the 'friend of Greece' who Louriotis claimed had received money, Bartle (1962, 70).

75 The Money Market, in: *The Times*, 28.10.1826; Louriotis to *The Times*, in: *The Times*, 30.10.1826.

76 See *The Times*, 4.11.1826, in: N. N. (Gennadios) (1878, 30ff.). *The Times* gave Hume credit for not denying that he had behaved in this way, unlike others involved, and for declaring himself willing to repay the money if two gentlemen should demand that he do so; see *The Times*, 15.11.1826, in: ibid., 42ff.

77 *The Times*, 28.10.1826, in: ibid., 24ff.

78 On the expedition plans Klein (2009), 111f; the naval officer Lord Cochrane earned his reputation in the Napoleonic wars. Between 1813 and 1816, he organised the fleets of Chile, Peru and Brazil in their struggles for independence from Spain. Later, he was won for the Greek cause; see Lambert (2004). However, he was also involved in a stock market scandal at the end of the Napoleonic era; see Dale (2006).

79 The ship in Marseille was never built due to the reservations of the French government; the money went back to the Ricardos; one of the ships in New York was completed, at a much inflated price; see Dakin (1955, 113–127). A detailed account of both is found in Chatziioannou (2013, 49f.).

80 Louriotis published his version of the occurrences here with many original letters from all those involved. The contract with Galloway signed by the Ricardos is also included: Louriotis (1827, 34).

81 Jacob and Samson Ricardo to Louriotis and Orlando, 5.6.1826, in: ibid., 56f. Translated into Greek in Λουριώτης [Louriotis]/Ορλάνδος [Orlandos] (1839, 322).

82 Louriotis to the Ricardos, 21.8.1826, in: Louriotis (1827, 63). Chatziioannou demonstrates that the equipping of the ships was to have been particularly

innovative; however, these technical innovations did not proceed as planned, but rather completely disrupted the timetable for construction; see Chatziioannou (2013, 48).

83 Responsibilities were again not clearly allocated. Thus, Hobhouse wrote to the Ricardos, explaining that a detailed examination of their accounts was 'no part of my duty – nor do I exactly know what my duty is' (Hobhouse to the Ricardos, 14.11.1826, BL Add. 36463, 26).

84 On 10.8.1825, in a letter to Hobhouse, the deputies expressed their suspicions that the Ricardos were agents of the Pasha, BL Add. 36461, 206.

85 The figures differ slightly from one another in these two sources; Kofas states that the final sum for Greece was £232,558.

86 *The Times*, 26.10.1826, in: N. N. (Gennadios) (1878, 23). This collection of articles from *The Times*, which was immensely protective of Greece, first appeared in 1878 when Greece was again looking to access the London Exchange. The editor was anonymous but the motivation for the publication is obvious: it was intended to demonstrate how badly Greece had been treated 50 years earlier, and thus to increase the chances of re-admittance to the Exchange. In the digital library Anemi, the collection is held under the name of the Greek ambassador to London, Ioannis Gennadios.

87 *The Times*, 28.10.1826, in: N. N. (Gennadios) (1878, 29).

88 *The Times*, 8.11.1826, in: N. N. (Gennadios) (1878, 33f.).

89 Ibid., 3f.

90 'But after the scandalous manner in which the Greeks have been plundered by a gang of humble knaves in this country, we do not know why that injured and unhappy people should not seek refuge in Royal protectors. May the money of which they have been robbed bring a curse upon those who possess it! May no Englishman ever repeat their names but with a shudder!' *The Times*, 28.11.1826.

91 In his analysis of the behaviour of the Philhellenes, especially John Bowring's, Frederick Rosen largely agrees with the interpretation of *The Times*: there were certainly good intentions, but the lovers of Greece were not willing to carry the entire risk of their financial activities: 'If Hume and Bowring were only concerned with their own personal advantage, they might very well not have supported the Greek cause of the Greek loan at all, given the information about conditions in Greece that they possessed' (Rosen 1992, 296).

92 *The Times,* 8.11.1826.

93 On the question of whether the banks were capable of learning, see Pohle-Frase (1999, 43ff.). She concludes that in the nineteenth century, it was the 'young' banks rather than the 'mature' banks that conceded they underwent such learning processes with the corresponding mistakes.

94 This is a false assumption made by Dale (2006, 46).

95 See for more detail: **78** in this book.

96 A comprehensive investigation of the reception of the Spanish revolution in London is provided by Brennecke (2010).

97 On 12 June, he was present at a meeting of supporters of the Spanish uprising in the London Tavern; see Ricardo 1973; the text refers here to the *Edinburgh Annual Register* (1823, 255). It was, however, not possible to verify this. *Cobbett's Political Register* dates the meeting to 13 June; see Cobbett (1823). John Cam Hobhouse and Joseph Hume were also on the relief committee organised by the meeting, figures that reappear later in the Philhellene movement; see Brennecke (2010, 108f.). A footnote here also displays an imprint of the petition from the friends of Spain discussed at the meeting, FN 104.

98 *The Times*, 7.6.1823.

99 Ibid.

100 David Ricardo is also named as having donated £20, a relatively large sum, in the first list kept by the London Greek Committee; see the list of donations from May 1824, LGC 1. In the minutes of a meeting of the committee in the Crown and Anker Tavern from 15.3.1823, David Ricardo is named as one of its first members. His interest in Greece may also have been heightened by a pupil of John Soane, the young architect George Basevi, who travelled in the country between 1816 and 1819; see Weatherall (1976, 86). He worked not only for David, but also for David's brothers Samson and Jacob. Basevi was related to the Vaudois banker William Haldimand in London, who in 1825, in turn, generously provided his nephew Marcet with £500 for an excursion to Greece commissioned by the Geneva Philhellenes; see Rothpletz (1899, 15) and John (2004). See also **84 n.36** in this book.

101 *The Times*, 12.7.1823. In the end, the Rothschilds were accepted for the lucrative bond issue.

102 The only two letters between David and Jacob that are available suggest that the two brothers had a good relationship but make no mention of political topics and were written more than ten years before the events of 1824. The letters are undated but the editor locates them in the period between 1807 and 1810. Jacob thanks David for material support which David had also promised him for the future; see Ricardo (1973).

103 These letters provide insights into the British government's knowledge of Greek matters and are published in Dakin (1955).

104 George Vitales to de Rumigny, 11.5.1825, in: ibid., 72f. However, Dakin is not completely certain whether the agent mentioned here is really Gamba, who is then later mentioned in connection to Ricardo.

105 George Vitales to de Rumigny, 15.–17.5.1825, in: ibid., 81. General Roche confirms the splitting of the contracts between the British and the French in a letter to the Parisian Comité de la souscription en faveur des Grecs from 13.5.1825, in: ibid., 76.

106 This idea is also supported, without evidence, by Dalleggio (1949, 26) and Levandis (1944, 20).

107 Jacob and Samson Ricardo to Hobhouse, 3.10.1826, BL Add. 36462, 358. However, Hobhouse believed that Galloway could never be prosecuted for his failure; as he wrote to the Ricardos, 14.11.1826, BL Add. 36463, 26.

108 Jacob and Samson Ricardo to Ellice, 22.5.1826, BL Add. 36462, 187.

109 Their great mistrust of the deputies and their openly expressed fears that the deputies were only interested in private gain are, e.g. found in a letter from Jacob and Samson Ricardo to Hobhouse, 11.2.1826, BL Add. 36461, 470.

110 This was not true of all Philhellenes: the Greek freedom fighters had, for instance, the full support of Blaquiere for their demands for financial autonomy. See his letters with the urgent request for prompt payment of the loan on Zante without further formalities, which only wasted valuable time, in LGC 8, e.g. Blaquiere to Stanhope, 24.5.1824, ibid.; other letters with urgent requests for prompt payment from the early summer of 1824 are in LGC 10.

111 Bentham's own motivation for his involvement in Greece was apparently the wish to see his liberal theories about the organisation of the state put into practice and thus to prove the quality of his arguments; see Rosen (1992, 298).

112 Louriotis to the Ricardos, 21.9.1826, in: Louriotis (1827, 38). Louriotis had the letter printed in *The Times*, 25.10.1826.

113 Louriotis, Orlando and Spaniolakis to the Ricardos, 7.2.1826, BL Add. 36461, 454.

114 Chatziioannou describes the relationship between the provisional government and the London bankers as a principal-agent relationship; see Chatziioannou

(2013, esp. 37). However, the bankers clearly did not want to accept their role as agents.

115 Jacob and Samson Ricardo to Louriotis and Orlando, 26.4.1826, in: Louriotis (1827, 36ff.). Emphasis by Louriotis.

116 Jacob and Samson Ricardo to Louriotis, 16.9.1826, in: ibid., 75–78; Greek translation in: Λουριώτης [Louriotis]/Ορλάνδος [Orlandos] (1839, 227–339).

117 Jacob and Samson Ricardo to Hobhouse, 3.10.1826, BL Add. 36462, 358.

118 Jacob and Samson Ricardo to *The Times*, no date, in: *The Times*, 28.10.1826. In mid-October, the Ricardos had actually promised to cooperate if suitable men were commissioned to undertake the investigation; see Jacob and Samson Ricardo 'to the President and Members of the Committee of the National Assembly of Greece', in: Λουριώτης [Louriotis]/Ορλάνδος [Orlandos] (1839, 93).

119 Jacob and Samson Ricardo to Hobhouse, 31.10.1826, in BL Add. 36462, 375.

120 Jacob and Samson Ricardo to *The Times*, no date, in: *The Times*, 28.10.1826.

121 Ibid.

122 Jacob and Samson Ricardo to Louriotis and Orlando, 26.4.1826, in: Louriotis (1827, 36ff.); Jacob and Samson Ricardo to Hobhouse, 18.2.1826, BL Add. 36461, 494. There were urgent issues related to the frigates to be discussed with Hobhouse, Ellice and Burdett. 'There is more responsibility attached to us in this affair than we like to incur without the sanction of all the parties who originated it & without their being made fully acquainted with all the proceedings'. In other letters, the Ricardos repeatedly asked Hobhouse for advice about how they should proceed in certain conflicts.

123 Hobhouse to Jacob and Samson Ricardo, 12.2.1827, draft, BL Add. 36463, 272.

124 Jacob and Samson Ricardo to Hobhouse, Burdett and Ellice, 14.2.1827, BL Add. 36463, 273. There is uncertainty about the reading of the word 'effort'.

125 Draft letter from Hobhouse, Ellice and Burdett to the Ricardos, 16.2.1817, BL Add. 36463, 284.

126 The death of Jacob Ricardo was followed by conflict among the heirs, as documented in the NA. The court heard evidence from Samson Ricardo to confirm the financial circumstances of his brother: in 1824 ca. £146,000, in 1826 ca. £142,000 and in 1831/1832 about £141,000. The deceased was apparently unaware that at his death his fortune had grown to £195,000 and had therefore failed to make sufficient provision for the legacy. It cannot be determined whether there is any link here to the Greek loan. (The first session of Trinity Term 1834. Ricardo-v-Ricardo Jacob Ricardo, NA PROB 37/895.)

127 FO, Addington, to S. Ricardo, 22.4.1846, in: Parliamentary Papers Bd. LXIX: Correspondence between British and foreign powers and communications between the British government to claimants, relative to loans made by British subjects, 1823–1847, No. 82.

128 'You are aware that all the national property of Greece is pledged for the payment of the Capital & interest of the Loan'. Bowring and Hobhouse, Draft from 31.7.1824, LGC 9.

129 FO, J. Backhouse, to A. Loughnan, 25.3.1830, in: Parliamentary Papers Bd. LXIX, 1823–1847, No. 72.

130 On the development of prices, see Δερτιλής [Dertilis] (2009, 588f.).

131 See **187** in this book.

2

LIBERALISM IN RESTORATION TIMES

The banker Jean-Gabriel Eynard as the founder of the Greek National Bank (1841)

A competing offer from Paris (1825)

The decision in favour of the Ricardos as the issuing bank proved even more annoying for the Greek deputies in retrospect, as there had been a competing offer from Paris – a much less significant financial centre than London but one whose importance was growing (Cassis 2007, 57). Were the risk perceptions and management of the bankers in Paris similar to or comparable with those of the London bankers?

In January 1825, Louriotis arrived in Paris to conduct negotiations at the same time as discussions were being held in London. The Philhellene association of Paris initially acted as intermediaries,[1] but the negotiations failed to get off the ground. The Parisian haute banque reacted with reserve, probably at least in part because the Paris capital market was less accustomed to foreign loan issues than the London market, and was still suffering from the aftermath of the Napoleonic wars (Levandis 1944, 17).[2] What was needed was a 'very rich man, very intelligent, an intimate friend of Count Capo d'Istria [who was later the first Greek President, K. S.], who will be more committed to your loan than anyone else'.[3] This figure was found in Jean-Gabriel Eynard, a Genevan banker of French origin (see Figure II.2.1).

Like many of the Genevan bankers, Eynard had excellent connections to the Parisian capital market.[4] These were urgently required in the difficult question of the Greek loan. Even the Delessert banking house, whose owner Benjamin Delessert was himself a member of the Paris Greek Committee and a good friend of Eynard (Dimakis 1966, 29),[5] was unwilling to bear the risk of the loan alone, although Delessert was interested in the issue. Delessert's old business partner Hottinguer similarly kept a low profile.[6] Eynard complained about the extreme risk adversity of the bankers, which he was unable to influence with ideological arguments: 'I have seen that, despite their sincere attachment to the Greek cause, these men do not have enough courage to conclude a contract'.[7] Eynard persevered, turning to the banking house of André & Cottier – Dominique André was the treasurer of the Société de la Morale Chrétienne, of which the Parisian Greek Committee

DOI: 10.4324/9780429286537-5

Figure II.2.1 Jean-Gabriel Eynard, Portrait by Horace Vernet, 1831.

was a part (Dimakis 1966, 29).[8] But André was unwilling to issue the loan alone, nor did he wish to act as the head of a consortium. Eynard had to continue his endeavours. In a letter to his uncle Pictet Turrettini, he noted the precise words of the negotiations with André & Cottier:

> 'You receive an opportunity that is useful for Greece and a good speculation.' 'We share your opinion but we would rather be associated with a bank that is appropriate.' After a long discussion, I said to them: 'Fine! I will bring in the house of my nephew M. G. Odier to issue the loan with you.' 'We gladly agree if you support him.' 'It goes without saying that I will support him.' 'In that case we have no difficulty in concluding the contract.'[9]

The philanthropic argument is certainly used here, but does not bear enough weight to persuade the bankers. A splitting of the risk was required. The situation changed dramatically when the highly regarded Eynard and his nephew Gabriel Odier[10] assumed leadership of the consortium. When Eynard informed Louriotis – who was not present at these negotiations – of his success, Louriotis replied euphorically, thanking Eynard in French, Greek and Italian, and immediately left for London to inform his colleagues. Eynard was very pleased with the results, as he confided to his uncle Pictet Turrettini.[11] He reported in detail on the conditions of the loan: 15 million francs (£600,000), with the option for the bankers to double this sum to 30 million (£1.2 million). The price of issue was 59, with 5% interest for two years, making a total of 10%. Eynard concluded that although the creditors would not get their money back at a price above 54, this was an attractive deal for both the philanthropists and the speculators.[12] Louriotis later provided the details of the terms of the loan in a printed 'Apology'. The conditions described here, which Louriotis had received from André & Cottier, were slightly different to those named by Eynard in the letter to his uncle. Here, the sum mentioned is 10 million francs (£400,000), to which a further 10 million could have been added in October of the same year if the bankers so wished. The issue price was 59, which would have given real capital of 5,900,000 francs (£236,000). With the nominal value of 10 million, the 5% interest, to be paid every six months, would amount to 1 million francs (£40,000) for two years, 500,000 francs (£20,000) were for the amortisation, 50,000 francs (£2,000) were to cover the costs of the issue for the bank and another 500,000 francs (£20,000) were to be used for commission – this amounts to 5%, an average amount. Thus, 3,850,000 francs (£154,000) would have been paid out in monthly instalments until August 1825. An annual sum of 10,000 francs (£400) was to allow the bonds to be bought back at market prices from 1827, so that all the bonds could be repurchased within 36 years (Λουριώτης [Louriotis]/Ορλάνδος [Orlandos] 1839, 127).[13] In a letter to his uncle, Eynard clarified the situation:

> I believe the loan to be exceptionally useful for the Greeks as they can provide it with moral value for the other powers, and I believe it also to be advantageous for the subscribers who take a chance on their success.[14]

The loan was said to demonstrate France's trust in Greece and was therefore of great moral importance. Eynard was reassured that this interpretation was also prevalent in the Parisian salons.[15] In the following days, he was happily able to inform his uncle that news of the deal in Paris had triggered a boom in the old 1824 Greek papers in London, which had now risen by 4–5%.[16] In Paris, Eynard commented, all political parties would greet the loan favourably,[17] and there were considerable opportunities for profit for the investors if Greece won her independence, which was thought to be very likely.

However, the planned loan was never issued. On 11 February, the Parisian Greek Committee received the news that, on the very same day as Louriotis, the Greek deputies in London had agreed a loan with the banking house of Ricardo, an agreement that prevented any further loans with other banks for the coming year.[18] Orlando wrote apologetically to Paris, explaining that Louriotis had informed London that there was no chance of reaching an agreement in Paris, and Ricardo had confirmed this assessment. The London contract had therefore been finalised.[19] This version of the story suggests that by the time Louriotis arrived in London, the Greeks could no longer choose freely between the two offers, even though the conditions discussed in London were clearly less favourable: the London emission price was 55.5, compared to the Paris price of 59, while the interest and other conditions were very similar. In retrospect, Louriotis described the process somewhat differently. When he arrived in London, he was confronted by Edward Ellice and his colleague Orlando with a contract that 'was about to be signed'.[20] According to this report, the contract that prohibited any other loans for the duration of one year[21] had not been signed before he arrived in the city. Because of the poorer conditions and many other reservations, he, Louriotis, expressed misgivings but Ellice called in the Ricardo brothers who presented an 'agreement which, after considerable discussions upon several points, was signed'. His report contains no more detailed explanation of why he signed the poorer contract rather than the Parisian one despite his reservations.[22] *The Times* later suspected that Edward Ellice had pressed the Greeks to choose the London contract, on which he was commissioned, over the more favourable Parisian one.[23] When Eynard heard that his offer, organised under difficult conditions, had not been accepted, he conjectured that Ricardos' representative in Paris had sent a message to London informing the Ricardos about the competing offer and so made them willing to contract. The Greek negotiators had clearly understood how to play one rival finance group off against another (Levandis 1944, 16f.; Kofas 1981, 13). But why did they decide to accept the poorer offer? It seems unlikely that the deputies really just allowed themselves to be pressured by their 'friends', despite their previous negative experience with those same friends, especially after they had displayed such skilful tactics. The scales may have been tipped by the wish to bind Great Britain more closely to Greece and her struggle for independence, or simply by the sum on offer: in London, £2,000,000 was being made available, while in Paris, it was only 10,000,000 or 15,000,000 francs, £400,000 or £600,000, a considerably smaller amount even with the prospect of doubling it later (Levandis 1944, 17). Another reason may have been the fear that the French parliament could refuse to authorise the bonds.[24]

Eynard was in any case far from being aggrieved about these developments:

> The moral and financial goal has been reached, because the Greeks can rightly say that they have raised as much money as they wanted and that they themselves rejected it. Here I concluded a loan that decided the London loan, and the result is that after I was willing to risk a large sum to serve the Greek cause I can retire from the game without risking anything but having provided the same service; confess that this is a fortunate proceeding; The French, after they had the spirit of a shopkeeper and cut a sorry figure to the Greek deputies, fulfilled their intention by signing the loan, and they received thanks upon thanks; thus everything is progressing in the best possible way in the world for the Greek cause and I have actually done both the French and the Greeks a service; I say that quite openly and that is bad; but as the whole world will not allow me to say that, I tell you about the case without wanting to hide it from any false modesty, because basically I have had much much [sic!] luck in the whole affair, which came just at that moment when it miscarried – and really nothing was there to tie it together again.[25]

He would have been willing to take the high risk of the loan. But if someone else would do so, then he was satisfied to retreat and congratulated himself on having indirectly helped to achieve it. Any expected profits played a very subordinate role for Eynard, and his outrage about developments in London was correspondingly restrained. After the scandal was later uncovered, Eynard demanded comprehensive elucidation in an article in *The Times* in order to restore Greece's reputation.[26] He concluded with an appeal to 'philanthropy and English generosity'.[27]

Eynard's fundraising for the struggle for independence

It seems as though profit maximisation was not of utmost importance for Eynard. In order to test this hypothesis and to assess the loan offer accurately, it is necessary to look at Eynard's other efforts to help Greece. After 1824, the banker developed a wide range of activities in an endeavour to support the Greeks. Thus on 4 September 1825, he was involved in the re-establishment of the Genevan Greek Committee, and in the following years, he became one of the most important promoters and organisers of the Philhellenic movement in Europe (Rothpletz 1899, 18).[28] The banker did not hesitate to use his own private financial resources: in the first year alone, he denoted 6,000 francs to the Genevan Greek Committee (ibid.), while the Paris Committee, which he joined during his stays in Paris,[29] even received 25,000 francs (of which 6,000 was intended to safeguard correspondence with Greece from the French and Austrian censorships) (ibid.). In parallel, he joined other like-minded persons in Geneva to imaginatively organise the collection of further donations for Greece.[30] Donations were collected in private circles, in ateliers, in academies and in the army; works by Philhellene artists were sold; charity performances took place in theatres and lotteries were set up.[31] Many similarities to modern philanthropic fundraising methods may be seen here. Additionally, Eynard developed a system of weekly collections among labourers, the so-called souscription hebdomadaire en faveur de Grecs, which brought in considerable returns due to its broad distribution.[32] By September 1825, 55–60,000 francs were thus collected for Greek affairs in Geneva.[33] The Genevans were so active that they soon took over the leading position of the Zurich association, initially to administer donations from the whole of Switzerland and later from the whole of Europe. The banker Eynard was expressly mentioned in the statement of accounts as being competent and trustworthy in these transactions.[34] The money was primarily used for the purchase of weapons for the Greek freedom fighters (although no accurate information on suppliers is available), for the construction of warships and to support Greek refuges in Switzerland.[35] Two commissioners were also dispatched to Greece to provide a point of contact with the provisional Greek government and to report on the situation (Rothpletz 1899, 15).[36]

Eynard undertook other activities in response to the aforementioned conquest of Mesolonghi by the Ottoman-Egyptian fleet under the command of Ibrahim Pascha, the son of Mehmed Ali. In light of the first beleaguering of the strategically important city by the Ottomans in 1822/1823, the renewed attack on Mesolonghi in 1825/1826 developed great symbolic significance for the Greek struggle for independence. Detailed and usually very biased reports in the European media (Schwarz 2016, 125f.) emphasised Greek heroism on the one hand and Ottoman atrocities on the other hand, and led to many donations being made to the Philhellene associations.[37] Eynard himself donated 12,000 francs, perhaps even 15,000, to secure the supply of the entrapped inhabitants (Rothpletz 1899, 28).[38] He also organised the difficult and dangerous transport of food goods through longstanding business partners in the Levantine, who at times waived the commissions they would have been entitled to (Rothpletz 1899, 28, 33). When, despite all these efforts, the city finally fell to the Ottomans on 23 April 1826, Eynard donated a further 5,000 francs to buy the freedom of the enslaved inhabitants (ibid., 40). The list of his donations and contributions continues: here, 800 francs for Princess Hantzery, née Mavrokordatos, who had fled from Constantinople and was in search of somewhere to stay in Europe with her children (ibid., 37); there, 3,000 francs for the Munich Greek association, which admitted Eynard as a member in 1826 (ibid., 48).[39] When in the same year a brig for the British admiral Thomas Cochrane was built to support the Greeks, Eynard donated 50,000 francs (ibid., 51).[40] In April 1827, his friend Ioannis Kapodistrias (a friendship that is further discussed below[41]) was elected as the first Greek president at the third Greek National Assembly in Troezen, and in May, Kapodistrias arranged for Eynard to be made an honorary Greek citizen. The banker then did everything in his power to support the new president: he made an advance of £10,000[42] and then in the same year offered Kapodistrias another 100,000 francs to buy back the Greek bonds of 1824 and 1825, suggesting that their low price – caused by the ongoing failure to pay interest on the bonds – represented a splendid occasion to do so.[43] Although Kapodistrias did not take up this offer, in November 1827, Eynard calculated that the total sum of his advancements for Greece was a proud 71,550 francs,[44] which did not stop him from offering further finance and donations.[45]

The Philhellenes' support of the Greek struggle for independence was not wasted: in 1827, a British-Russian-French fleet defeated the Turkish-Egyptian fleet at Navarino.[46] After the subsequent Russian-Ottoman war, the Sublime Porte was forced to recognise Greece's independence in the Treaty of Adrianople from September 1829. As soon as the Great Powers had agreed to guarantee a 60-million-franc loan to the future ruler of Greece (at this time, it was planned that this should be Prince Leopold von Sachsen Coburg-Gotha, but after long negotiations with Eynard in 1830 he rejected the offer[47]), Eynard intervened again and provided an advance of 1.5 million francs on this loan, which took some time to organise (Rothpletz 1899, 91; Historical Archives National Bank of Greece 1999, 20).[48]

His untiring interventions for Greece were not limited to financial donations and transactions. Of much greater importance was his social and political network, which he was willing to use for the benefit of the country. Eynard wrote thousands of letters to the organisers of other European Philhellene committees, to the monarchs of the continent, to diplomats, ambassadors and politicians, urging them to become active in the Greek cause (Chapuisat 1924). He also repeatedly tried to encourage his banking colleagues to make donations and investments.[49] He travelled to Paris and London to take part in direct talks with decision makers relevant for Greece (Rothpletz 1899, 75ff.), especially concerning payment of the three instalments of the 1832 guaranteed loan,[50] and composed memorandums for the French deputies.[51]

Support of nation building

When Greece was accepted by the Great Powers as an independent state in 1829, the Philhellene committees ceased their activities all over Europe[52]: Greece no longer seemed to need their support. Soon afterwards, the Philhellenes displayed great disillusionment with the contemporary Greeks, who failed to live up to the idealised image of their ancient ancestors that the European intellectuals had constructed. The work of Jacob Philipp Fallmerayer can paradigmatically represent this disappointment. As early as

1830, he argued that the ancient Greeks were extinct and that their successors were descended from Slavic and Albanian immigrants:

> The Hellenic lineage is eradicated in Europe. Physical beauty, sunward flight of the spirit, harmony and simplicity of the customs, art, racetrack, city, village, splendour of pillars and temple, yes even the name has disappeared from the surface of the Greek continent. [...] Because not a drop of genuine and unmixed Hellenic blood flows in the veins of the Christian population of today's Greece.[53]

Eynard was not swayed by such polemic. He continued his commitment and did his upmost to help Greece start towards a good economic and political future. 'To be useful for Greece'[54] was the motto that guided the following years of his life. This involved significant donations and advances. In 1827, Eynard revealed to his correspondent Kapodistrias that he wanted to put the profits from the speculation with Greek bonds in a new agricultural fund.[55] In 1830 and 1831, he provided the cash-strapped treasury with a further 550,000 francs as an advance on the guaranteed loan. He then provided another 500,000 francs in 1847, which the government urgently needed to pay the interest on the bonds from 1832 (Historical Archives National Bank of Greece 1999, 22). He also helped to finance the uprising against the Ottomans on the island of Crete (ibid., 21).

Furthermore, the banker was involved in genuinely philanthropic activities, like the building of a school on Aegina in 1829, other schools and educational facilities, and a hospital in Athens in 1836–1842 (Chapuisat 1952, 125; Turczynski 2003, 199). In 1842, he allowed himself to be elected the president of an association encouraging the education of the people (Société pour l'encouragement de l'instruction du people) (Historical Archives National Bank of Greece 1999, 21)[56] and donated 500 drachmas to the society on this occasion. He was moreover concerned with the education of young Greeks in Europe.[57]

Eynard was also involved in promoting the transfer of know-how in various fields. He made himself useful as a financial advisor for the young king. With French funding, he organised – the first time in response to a request from Kapodistrias – the dispatch of a financial specialist to advise the Greek government, Arthemond Regny, a friend from the days of the Napoleonic wars who had first visited Greece in 1821 (Vacalopoulos 1977; Ασανάκη [Asanaki] 1989; Βακαλόπουλος [Vakalopoulos] 2008, 457–480).[58] In addition, Eynard sympathised with the idea of a Swiss colony intended to take agricultural knowledge and capable colonists from Switzerland to Greece.[59] His attempt to introduce seed potatoes to Greece appears typical of his Enlightenment attitude. He provided exact instructions for the cultivation of the potatoes in a letter to Kapodistrias.[60] In order to ensure the continued support of the European public and to justify his own activities,

Eynard published many letters concerning the work of the Philhellene committees, incidentally revealing his great understanding of media impact.[61]

Even after his friend Johannes Kapodistrias was murdered by political opponents on 9 October 1831, Eynard continued his activities for Greece; he apparently felt bound by a promise that he had given Kapodistrias (Koukkou 1994b, 110).[62] He supported the choice of Otto, the second son of Ludwig I of Bavaria, as the King of Greece.[63] In 1832, Otto I arrived in Greece and initially established the seat of government in Nafplio (Friedrich 2015). The Bavarian civil servants who accompanied him were to prove extremely problematic for Eynard. In particular, he accused the head of the regency of the underage king, Joseph Ludwig Graf Armansperg,[64] of being completely occupied with private intrigues and family matters, and of carelessly neglecting state affairs (Chapuisat 1924, 45–49).[65] Eynard's confidant Regny, who was involved in a running battle with the ministers concerning the improvement of Greek finances, described his problems with the Bavarians in numerous letters to Eynard, as did the French ambassador Marie de Lagrené.[66] Eynard thus came to believe that the Athens 'Bavarokratie' was totally unsuited to tackling the economic and political problems faced by the country.[67] He was also disappointed in King Otto, seeing him as good-willed but indecisive, and resenting the fact that the king implemented very few of his financial recommendations; indeed, he actually failed to respond to many of Eynard's suggestions.[68]

The conflicts came starkly to light in 1834, when the banker demanded the refund of an advance of 200,000 francs, which he had conceded three years earlier. This occasion reveals something of the conditions governing this advance. Eynard pointed out that the money had been emergency assistance to Greece, entailing considerable personal financial disadvantage: the bonds that he had sold for a price of 81 in order to be able to advance Greece the necessary money were worth 103 two years later, which represented a loss of 50,000 francs. At least he received the saltworks of Thermitis as a guarantee for his invested capital.[69] On 1 June 1833, he informed Armansperg that the French Chamber of Deputies had agreed to the payment of the first two instalments of the 60-million loan (40 million francs) and that the money could thus shortly be expected; he therefore asked for his advance from 1831 to be refunded.[70] But Armansperg did not even reply. Eynard waited half a year before he complained that Armansperg treated him 'like an ordinary creditor who asks for a favour and whom one can dare to leave without any answer'.[71] How could he receive so little attention after all that he had done for Greece? 'For a long time she has been for me my only thought, and I feel a little bit like a lover left by his beloved darling'.[72] Still waiting for an answer, Eynard in March 1834 wrote more forcibly that he felt his honour was seriously damaged by being neglected like this. He had been informed that the saltworks of Thermitis had now been given as a guarantee to the three Great Powers for the 60-million loan. He had therefore sent copies of all letters directly to Munich to Ludwig I of Bavaria to inform him of the activities of his son's government. He was also thinking of appealing to Rothschilds, who were to pay out the new instalment of the large loan, and to get his money back from them.[73] Eynard pointed out his deep confusion: why was he being treated like this, despite having anyway converted most of his advances for Greece into donations, and despite the time and effort that he had invested in the welfare of the country in the last nine years, quite apart from financial donations? He was gradually coming to believe Talleyrand, who had insisted, 'governments have no memory'.[74] Armansperg left replying until June, and even then the answer was such as to 'incense even the patience of the calmest of men'.[75] Despite their protests to the contrary, the governing council had still not dealt with the matter, declared Eynard. Even if Greece should decide not to refund any other creditors, they should not deal with him in this way:

> Greece could decide not to refund any old debt, but this decision cannot concern me; the honour, the dignity, the etiquette, the interest of Greece, her credit of the future demand all the same that I am refunded with respect to that loan, because my last advancement was made only under this condition.[76]

How could they behave so dishonourably, especially when it was clear that they would need to borrow money at reasonable rates of interest in the future? Nonetheless, his love of Greece was so great that he had no wish to damage the country.[77]

The letters reveal how deeply the affair touched Eynard, both as a banker and as a Philhellene. On the one hand, it concerned his very special relationship to the country: he viewed himself as Greece's benefactor. On the other hand, he talks of 'confiance', a keyword in many of his letters. Monika Pohle-Fraser discovered the key role played by trust and confidence in international banking business before 1850, when the 'reputation approach' was the most natural form of risk perception.[78] The personal credibility of the business partner was much more important than specific projects. Repaying credits was thus a question of personal honour and a failure to service debts could lead to the loss of rights such as the right to vote. Relatives therefore often stepped in to make repayments and preserve the good name of the family (Pohle-Fraser 1999, 70–99).[79] When Eynard threatened Armansperg with publicising the matter at Rothschilds and in political circles, he was threatening him with the loss of his good name in the financial world and beyond,[80] by far the worst threat that the financier could make.

Even though Eynard finally received the repayment,[81] in subsequent years, he avoided working with this government more than was absolutely necessary. Various orders and decorations did nothing to change his attitude.[82] When Armansperg was replaced by Ignaz von Rudhardt in March

1837 (Petropulos 1968, 229; 270ff.),[83] it seemed that Eynard's relations with the Bavarian regency could improve, as he had great expectations of Rudhardt, particularly concerning the founding of a national bank.[84] However, when Regny (now on his third mission to Greece) communicated that Armansperg's entourage would remain in office and Rudhardt then quickly resigned from his position in December 1837, Eynard's hopes were disappointed (Chapuisat 1924, 49–56).

These problems did not prevent him from working intensively to develop Greece's economy. The most important cornerstone of his endeavours was the founding of a national bank[85] in 1841, remarkably early when considered in international comparison.[86] The Swiss banker was the driving force behind this project, which Kapodistrias had already attempted to pursue and which was of great urgency due to the continued lack of capital in Greece: before the founding of the bank, interest rates of between 20% and 30% had to be paid for credit (Loukos 1986, 438).[87] In 1828, Eynard had, together with King Ludwig of Bavaria and Kapodistrias, provided 100,000 francs for the project (Historical Archives National Bank of Greece 1999, 25).[88] But the founding of the bank, not yet in the form of a joint-stock bank (Christophorou 1926, 7), failed and the money went to the Greek treasury, without the investors seeing any part of it again (Loukos 1986, 439).[89] After 1832, the Greek regency then failed in an attempt to found the bank with capital from the 60-million loan (ibid., 439). Two Englishmen were equally unsuccessful in their 1831 plans to found the bank, as was the British banking house of J. Wright & Co in 1834, although here the main concern was with the repayment of the 1824/1825 loan. To this end, it was suggested that Greek national goods could be sold to London customers. Wright persevered but despite further negotiations with the head of the Bavarian regency von Armansperg, he was unable to reach a satisfactory conclusion; similarly unsuccessful were the Vienna diaspora banker Sina[90] and the London diaspora banking house Ralli,[91] which wanted to found the bank with capital from Greece and the diaspora. Dutch investors, who also wanted to use the profits of the bank to repay the revolution loans, experienced the same fate. Christos Loukos suggests that the repeated failures were linked to protests within Greece (especially from the group of Greek bankers who had previously controlled the market) against the sell-out of the country's finances to foreigners, and to diplomatic intrigues and international rivalries. Thus, the Russians refused to agree to British suggestions and the French, British and Austrians similarly begrudged one another success in the matter. Loukos records a total of 13 failed attempts to found a national bank between 1831 and 1840 (Loukos 1986, 29).[92] There was certainly no lack of foreign interest and the relevant international circles clearly thought that there was a high chance of success for such a credit institute. Eynard himself was involved in two of these attempts. At the beginning of 1838, he proposed a discount bank with issuing rights and capital of between two and four million drachmas. Eynard was competing here with a proposal for a mortgage bank without issuing rights from the British consulate of Smyrna Werry, and his suggestion failed to gain acceptance; despite the support of King Otto, he was accused by Greek moneylenders of pursuing purely speculative interests (Loukos 1986, 444). In British diplomatic circles, Eynard was said to be a French or even, thanks to his friendship with Kapodistrias, a Russian agent. He therefore made another attempt, this time working with the banking house of Wright to allay British concerns; the proposed bank was actually intended to have its seat in London (ibid., 445). However, the bankruptcy of the Wright banking house inevitably led to the failure of this proposal. His advantage over his competitors in the end was that by 1840 Eynard's partners de Regny and Georgios Stavros had already given Greek business partners 300,000 francs of credit from Eynard's capital at interest rates of 8% (Historical Archives National Bank of Greece 2001, 17). A bank founded in 1839 by the Augsburg banker Julius Hösslin was also incorporated in the new banking house.[93] These activities were institutionalised with the passing of the law on the founding of the National Bank of Greece (ETE) in March 1841.[94] It began its work in January 1842.

The first credit institute of the country was conceived as a joint-stock universal bank with capital of 5 million drachmas; it was able to conduct the whole range of banking business and intended to serve the economic development of the country.[95] The ETE was designed as a shareholder company with 5,000 shares, each of 1,000 drachmas. This modern ownership structure, which in this form had only been practised in Great Britain for 15 years, allowed the risk to be split and carried on many shoulders. With 300 shares, Eynard became the third biggest shareholder after the Greek government with 1,000 shares and the Greek banker Nikolaos Zosimas with 500. Ludwig I of Bavaria bought 200 shares (Historical Archives National Bank of Greece 1999, 32 FN 6).[96] In 1842, a total of 901 shares were held by 25 shareholders from Western Europe, 1,091 by the Greek state, 1,499 by 79 diaspora Greeks and 696 by 61 Greek investors (Pizanias 1986, 458). Without an additional advancement of 250,000 drachmas by Eynard, the Greek state would not have been able to buy its shares.[97] Again proving his awareness of publicity, Eynard persuaded the banking house of Rothschild to buy 50 shares and to permit a further 50, which he purchased himself, to run under their name, thus allowing the bank to profit from the reputation of the financial global player.[98] He also promoted the institute intensively among his colleagues throughout the whole of Europe.[99]

The discount business of the ETE was conducted at a fixed discount rate of 8% and limited to a fifth of the total capital; the focus of the bank's activities was thus on mortgage and Lombard credits, which accounted for four-fifths of the capital with a mortgage rate of 10% (Christophorou 1926, 6, 12). The bank had the sole right to issue paper money. The statute allowed three-quarters of the money in circulation to be covered by mortgage credit, only a quarter needed to be covered by metal reserves. This is somewhat surprising, as it is extremely unlikely that mortgages can be realised in the short term – one reason that the 1844 Bank Charter Act in Great Britain prescribed the 100% gold-backing of all bank notes.[100] In 1842, the bank statute was then rewritten: the discount business was strengthened, the mortgage business weakened and the revolving loan business was introduced (ibid., 15).

Both Eynard and Nikolaos Zosimas were elected as 'honourable administrators' of the bank and conscientiously performed these duties. With the support of the Rothschilds, Eynard was able to install his trusted partner in Athens Georgios Stavros[101] as the first governor of the bank,[102] an important element in his risk management. He conducted an immense correspondence with this first governor, addressing questions concerning accounts, business and personnel, the volume of money in circulation, the printing of banknotes and risk calculations. He also advised on the political positioning of the bank vis-à-vis the government, Greek bankers and foreign ambassadors, etc.[103]

Eynard's involvement in the ETE was actually quite lucrative: the bank proved a success story. This had been predicted by contemporaries like the Bavarian consulate and the English businessman Strong in Athens, who promoted the institute with Ludwig I of Bavaria, describing it as a 'safe and promising capital investment'.[104] For his part, Ludwig had advertisements and notices of the bank's dividends published in a prominent Munich newspaper, the Münchner Politischen Zeitung.[105] Even in just the first year of its existence, 1842, the bank was able to pay its shareholders a dividend of 7% and this continued to improve in subsequent years.[106] In 1848, political unrest throughout Europe triggered fears that there would be a run on the bank and led to temporary restrictions on convertibility,[107] after which the dividends nonetheless stood at 3.5%.[108] In 1849, they were back to 8.5%, in 1851 9.25% and in 1862 they were even at 11.5%.[109] It is hardly surprising that both Ludwig I and Eynard remained shareholders of the bank until the end of their lives. Eynard even left his shares to his family, dividing the 410 which he held at the time of his death between his heirs.[110] Although explicitly under no obligation to do so, they kept most of the shares[111] and passed them on in the family.[112] The bank was obviously viewed as a lucrative and safe investment among members of family.

Eynard profited not only from his shares in the ETE, but also through speculation with the Greek state bonds, as mentioned earlier. In addition, he invested in silk mills and the production of potash and paper (Κατηφόρη [Katifori] 1984, 150–152). Unfortunately, it is impossible to draw up a final balance for his activities in Greece: did he really put more money in donations and failed investments than he earned elsewhere with business in Greece? On the contrary, it may well be that he actually lost very little money and perhaps even earned a profit. If so, it was thanks to his excellent network and comprehensive information. This would explain why the time and energy that he spent on Greek affairs was more important to him personally than the invested or lost capital. The repeated setbacks did not leave him untouched. In 1839, he complained that he was really discouraged but that after 14 years he could not simply give up: 'After I have moved heaven and earth I am often like an ant who thinks it can perform a miracle by moving a fragment of wood that is twenty times bigger than it' (Chapuisat 1952, 162, tr. by K.S.). He persevered. In 1843, when Greece suspended all its diplomatic missions for reasons of economy, he offered to represent the country at the European courts free of charge. A formal office would be necessary, he explained, because the old Philhellenes were gradually dying out and he could therefore no longer resort to his informal networks.[113] Although the Greek revolution of 1843 rendered these plans obsolete, he continued to care for his 'second fatherland'[114] until the end of his life, even after 1848 when, now aged over 70, he increasingly retreated from the public sphere and, encouraged by his wife, turned to the study of religious texts (Chapuisat 1952, 199). Eynard remained unswayed by the so-called Don-Pacifico affair which in 1850, along with other diplomatic intrigues, damaged British-Greek relations just as badly as the reputation of King Otto.[115] Thus, for instance, after the Crimean War in 1856, he advocated mild treatment of Greece (Historical Archives National Bank of Greece 1999, 22). His popularity in Greece was so high that after King Otto was expelled and a new king was to be elected in March 1863, Eynard received numerous votes (even without being a candidate and having died in Geneva on 5 February 1863 at the age of 87) (Ibid.). In 1866, a memorial for him was built in Athens (Turczynski 2003, 435).

Eynard as a liberal

In Greek research, Eynard's untiring and diverse commitment to Greece remains unquestioned – Philhellenism is viewed as a widespread and to a certain extent natural phenomenon. If Eynard's biography is considered however, his love of Greece seems somewhat unlikely. Why did he choose Greece as the object of his endeavours? And why did he persist in his commitment to the country despite all the setbacks which he experienced? His wife commented:

> Gabriel has such perseverance and such commitment to the cause that he serves, and he goes so straight along his path to serve it, that it could be said that he does not want to see what could discourage him. He goes along his path regardless and does not express his thoughts as though they could make him see what he does not want to see, for fear that he must recognise that he will soon not be able to defend himself against the internal factions and English politics

> that work against him (the fault of King Otto and the lack of exact information that reaches his absolutist throne). Gabriel believes he can fight against this by writing for some length of time to the king about the dangers he courts through his lack of experience and his gullibility, which lead him to believe a party that clearly does not want the actual progress of the whole country.[116]

What was the background of experience and values against which Eynard interpreted the comprehensive information that he gathered from and about Greece? And how did he manage to blend out or simply ignore the discouraging information?

Jean-Gabriel Eynard was not among the classically educated Philhellenes who had learnt their Homer in the cradle. The Huguenot banking family originated from the Dauphiné, which they were forced to leave after the Edict of Nantes was revoked in 1685 (Rothpletz 1899, 9). The Eynard family then lived in Geneva until the time of Jean-Gabriel's grandfather Jean-Louis Eynard de Trémolières, who was known as an 'advocate of the poor', thanks to his social commitment (ibid., tr. by K.S.). It was Eynard's father Gabriel-Antoine who first returned to France, to Lyon, where he was a banker. The relationship to Switzerland nonetheless remained strong. Gabriel-Antoine's second marriage was to Marie-Madeleine Meuricoffre, the daughter of a wealthy Thurgau merchant. Jean-Gabriel was born on 29 December 1775 as the second of three children. There is little information about his childhood. He grew up in Lyon in Calvinist surroundings and was trained in trade and book-keeping by his father. Eynard was fond of theatre. There is no mention of him attending a higher education establishment (Historical Archives National Bank of Greece, 13) and it seems extremely unlikely that he did so as he later confessed to a lack of Latin.[117] He did speak Greek,[118] but this seems to have been Modern Greek learnt from friends rather than Ancient Greek, especially as he never used the written language in his letters.

In 1793, aged 17, Eynard collected his first military experience defending Lyon, which was considered a stronghold of Girondins and royalists, against the troops of the French National Convention. After the city's conquest, he escaped to Switzerland dressed as a woman (Rothpletz 1899, 10; Historical Archives National Bank of Greece 1999, 13). The entire family settled in Rolle near Geneva, where in 1790 Jean-Gabriel's sister Louise-Elisabeth (Lisette) had married into the Gaulis family, who were important merchants. Family relations were of great significance for Eynard's economic advancement. In 1795, he and his brother Jacques joined with an old employee of their father to found the trading house Eynard Frères et Schmidt in Genoa. They traded very successfully with olive oil and other foods, pigments and fabrics and were also, as was usual at the time, involved in financial transactions (Historical Archives National Bank of Greece 1999, 13).

The Napoleonic wars soon called the young Frenchman back to arms and in 1800 he fought with Napoleon to defend beleaguered Genoa against the British. Eynard's talent for organisation seems to have made an impression as he was entrusted with supplying the entrapped inhabitants during the period of worst starvation (Rothpletz 1899, 10). When, 26 years later, he organised the defence and supply of Mesolonghi, he was able to draw on a store of profound experience. After Genoa finally surrendered on 4 June 1800, Eynard moved on to Milan and finally, with the help of the merchants Sebastiani, to Livorno, where he again worked as a merchant banker (Historical Archives National Bank of Greece 1999, 14).[119] The numerous letters to his brother and father give an impression of the type of business in which Eynard was involved.[120] In 1802, in a masterpiece of finance, he granted a loan to Louis II of Parma, who was in severe financial distress: as Parma had been allocated to Napoleonic France, Louis was granted the newly created Kingdom of Etruria as compensation and urgently required a loan of 1.45 million livres in order to establish his rule. The merchants of Livorno refused to supply the new ruler and Eynard served as the only underwriter of the loan, which earned interest of 6%, a very good rate (Rothpletz 1899, 10; Historical Archives National Bank of Greece 1999, 14).[121] The transaction also had other consequences: on 11 July 1803, Jean-Gabriel congratulated himself and his brother on having finally achieved a monopoly of tobacco in Etruria, something he had worked patiently on for five years. He predicted an annual profit from this business of 160,000 livres.[122] Some contemporaries later suggested that part of his fortune had been gained under dubious circumstances during the wars.[123]

Eynard did not remain in Livorno for long and in 1803, having previously left the trading house he had operated with his brother,[124] he moved on to Florence (Historical Archives National Bank of Greece 1999, 14). The banker seems to have quickly established himself here, as in the following year he was sent as a legate of Tuscany to Paris, and later then to Milan, to represent the interests of the enlightened model state.[125] When in 1807 Élisa Bonaparte, Napoleon's sister, became the Grand Duchess of Tuscany, now formally annexed by France, she continued to promote Eynard, making him her close confident and financial advisor.[126] She twice proposed that he marry one of her court ladies, which would have involved the financier remaining permanently at her court (Chapuisat 1952, 35ff.).[127] Whether because court life did not suit him or thanks to his political far-sightedness (after the removal of Napoleon from power, Élisa returned to insignificance, having ruled for less than five years in Tuscany) (Pesendorfer 1988, 158),[128] Eynard chose a different path and in 1808 married Anne Charlotte-Adelaïde Lullin de Châteauvieux from a long-established and influential Genevan family. At the same time, he became a citizen of Rolle.[129] The marriage linked him to the important Genevan families of Pictet, Turrettini and de Rochemont.[130] For the banker, this represented a decision against the brilliant Tuscan court and for the Calvinistic and enlightened city, proud in its tradition of the rational philosophers Voltaire and Rousseau. However, despite his time in Italy, until his 33rd year, Eynard obviously never came into any close contact with Greece or Philhellene ideas.

How did this contact come into being? In the second half of the eighteenth century, Geneva, an independent city until 1793, had become something of a 'laboratory of revolution', catalysed by a discussion of the writings of Jean-Jacques Rousseau, a famous son of the city.[131] In 1798, after the victorious spread of the French revolution, Geneva had then been integrated into France (Hartmann 2002, 141ff.). In the meanwhile, submitting to pressure from France, in April 1798, the Swiss cantons had joined together to form the centrally ruled 'Helvetic Republic' with Napoleon as the First Consul. The country had kept only a pro forma autonomy, which led to some resistance: 1802 even saw a civil war between the federalists and the unitaires. Napoleon had taken advantage of the opportunity and created a 'Swiss Confederation' in which the republican element was greatly reduced. This arrangement had at least given the country 'a peaceful decade in the shadow of French hegemonic power' (Maissen 2011, 173, tr. by K.S.). With the collapse of the Napoleonic Empire, however, Switzerland's future seemed uncertain. Was it possible to return to the estate-based constitution and the rule of the old elites? Would the boundaries of the cantons as established by Napoleon remain? Opinions differed greatly and civil unrest threatened. However, the allies were concerned that Switzerland should remain peaceful to allow the passage of their troops in the battle against Napoleon. In 1813, this led to Tsar Alexander sending his diplomat to negotiate in Switzerland[132]: Johannes Kapodistrias, a Greek from the Ionian Islands in Russian service, later a close friend of Jean-Gabriel Eynard's and from 1827 the first president of the Greek state.[133]

The Tsar had been educated by the Swiss scholar, freemason and leading republican, Frédéric-César de La Harpe, who had prejudiced him in favour of his country of origin.[134] Alexander chose Kapodistrias as his envoy because of his republican attitude.[135] The Greek was, however, accompanied by the Austrian envoy Baron of Lebzeltern, who should strengthen the patrician structures in Switzerland in the service of the Habsburgs. It is not possible to enter into the many difficulties and complexities of the negotiations here.[136] The fact remains that shortly after the 'Battle of the Nations' at Leipzig in 1813, Switzerland declared her neutrality and allowed the passage of the allied troops, even if the path to the new federal treaty remained a stony one and many of the old cantons returned to the ways of legal inequality and rule by the patricians (Maissen 2011, 181ff.). Geneva joined Switzerland as a new canton with a de facto strongly restorative and counter-revolutionary constitution[137] and in 1814 Kapodistrias was awarded honorary citizenship in recognition of his diplomatic services (Koukkou 1994a, 109). In the following 'twenty-seven years of happiness' until 1841, the city prospered and was largely free of political unrest (Hartmann 2002, 149, tr. by K.S.).

It seems that during his visit to Switzerland, Kapodistrias met Eynard in Geneva (Historical Archives National Bank of Greece 1999, 17). The second meeting between the two then occurred after the end of the Napoleonic rule of the city when the banker was sent to the Congress of Vienna as the secretary to the city's two legates, his uncle by marriage Pictet de Rochemont and François d'Ivernois.[138] The aim was to negotiate a land bridge between Geneva and the other Swiss cantons.[139]

In his diary,[140] Eynard noted his daily routine, the process of negotiations and his communications with the potentates, often recording the exact wording and characteristics of the monarchs. The book is an invaluable source concerning his political position. The dazzling figure of Napoleon is omnipresent, in anecdotes about his life, his performance and his mistakes in both political and military terms.[141] Napoleon fascinated Eynard, like many of his contemporaries. On the one hand, he admired the great general's energy, determination and decisiveness, also viewing him as the 'strong man' who channelled the chaos of the French revolution. On the other hand, Eynard was disgusted by the exorbitance of Napoleon's power policy, which from a certain time he practised for its own sake without considering the welfare of his subjects, and which appeared to be callous and merciless (Sauvigny/Potin 2010). Eynard recognised many virtues of the good ruler in Napoleon but saw him as being perverted by his ruthless and irrational hunger for power.[142] However, he considered the Emperor to be legalised by the blood of his people, much more than the Bourbons, who based their power on bought bayonets.[143] Throughout his diary, Eynard criticised the monarchs in Vienna for lacking the habitus of rulers and for having no sense of responsibility at all, dancing and tippling like common men instead of concentrating on the important negotiations.

Eynard complained that Napoleon's pure power policy had irrevocably taken over European politics. He deeply regretted that politics no longer served an idea but only to preserve the power of the monarchs. He continually reduced his expectations of the congress:

> In short, the most powerful will hold on to what they have without concerning themselves with political equilibrium and the rights of petitioners, and all the rulers will go home and declare that the law of the strongest is the best. This law will give the poor people who live in Europe many hard nuts to crack.[144]

Eynard was incensed by the underdeveloped sense of responsibility the monarchs displayed towards the people entrusted to them. Between the lines of his diary, his consternation with the situation clearly emerges as he describes the way in which the rulers failed to tackle the difficult diplomatic problems which were to be negotiated, how they lacked self-control and spent their time dancing late into the night, drinking, hunting and clearly thinking only of their own pleasure, while the resources of their people were sapped by financing the waiting armies.[145] This frivolous jog trot stood in contrast to Eynard's rational conception of good government. With the aid of his descriptions, it is possible to paradigmatically follow the shift in the concept 'state' that occurred in the years after 1750,[146] as the responsibility of the monarchs for the well-being of their subjects became evermore central to the legitimation of rule (Foucault 2003, III, 800, 806f.). '[G]overnment has as its purpose not the act of government itself, but the welfare of the population, the improvement of its condition, the increase of its wealth, longevity, health, and so on' (Foucault 2000, III, 816f.). As portrayed by Jean-Jacques Rousseau's *Économie politique,* the good organisation of the economy played a key role here (Foucault 2003, III, 804). Eynard was convinced that even the most difficult problems of state leadership could be solved to the benefit of the subjects of the state by rational organisation and determination. He liked to refer to Tuscany, where he himself had contributed to the governing of the state, as the perfect example of such an approach.[147] When seen in this light, even the restructuring and improvement of Austrian finances appeared to the banker to be an attractive task.[148] Eynard believed in the dream of Enlightenment, in the feasibility of good government: in his opinion, the failure of this programme could only be due to insufficient commitment or the lacking ability of those responsible.

During the negotiations, Eynard met like-minded, liberal[149] contemporaries, especially in the Genevan committee who were striving to find a solution for the new Swiss canton (Eynard 1923, 120, 128, 181): his uncle Charles Pictet de Rochemont, editor of the 'Bibliothèque britannique' and later a member of the Greek Committee of Geneva; Ioannis Kapodistrias, from Eynard's perspective the ideal diplomat; Carlo Andrea Pozzo di Borgo, a Corsican who was an enemy of Napoleon's and a Russian diplomat in Paris, who in later years also became a close friend of Eynard[150]; Emmerich Joseph Duke of Dalberg, who came from Baden and was the legate of France at the congress, brother of the former Prince Primate of the Confederation of the Rhine Carl Theodor and from 1826 onwards member of the Paris Comité de publications en faveur de Grecs[151]; the British foreign minister and later promoter of Greek independence Georg Canning (Fry 1998); the Prussian minister and reformer Karl vom und zum Stein.[152] Madame de Staël,[153] whose salon Eynard later frequented, also campaigned for Geneva (Chapuisat 1952, 53f.). They were all united in their aversion to Napoleon, whether this had always been the case, like with vom Stein and di Borgo, or had developed over time after a phase of agreement or even cooperation with the Emperor, like with Kapodistrias, von Dalberg and Eynard himself. In the following years, Eynard contacted all these politicians in the cause of Greece; there was no need to argue his case as the network he had formed in Vienna was perfectly suited to advocate Greek interests because its members all shared the liberal 'esprit de Genève' (ibid., 113).

Eynard also became acquainted with other important political actors of his time: the foreign ministers of Britain Castlereagh (Stewart 1998), of France Talleyrand (N.N. 1990, 698ff.; Wilms 2011) and of Austria Metternich (Aretin 1994, 236–243), Tsar Alexander of Russia (Palmer 1994),[154] the French heir to the throne Charles,[155] the Austrian Emperor Franz II Joseph (N. N. 1956b, 348f.)[156] and King Ludwig I of Bavaria, to name just a few examples. Accompanied by his wife Anna,[157] Eynard met these powerful individuals at dinners and receptions, at balls and during sledge rides. By the time he left Vienna, before the 100-day return of Napoleon,[158] he had become part of the European diplomatic elite, a point of intersection in the fine-meshed political network. Here, his ability as a financial expert was particularly valued. In 1816, Ferdinand von Habsburg, restored as Grand Duke of Tuscany, drew on the banker's help, just as his predecessor Èlisa had done, in order to reorganise the finances of the territory, a task that led to Eynard being awarded the Order of Joseph (Rothpletz 1899, 10; N.N. 1956a). In 1820, he was even made a privy councillor of Tuscany and became a member of the Florentine nobility (ibid., 12). In his chosen home of Geneva, the 'citizen of the world'[159] was active in many fields. By 1814, he had already been elected to the Conseil représentatif, the legislative body of the city, where he was a member of the minority opposition.[160] As he was at the core of the liberal movement in the canton, however, advancement to the Conseil d'État was denied the banker, as was the case with most of his like-minded contemporaries.[161] Instead, he was involved in the new world of liberal associations in the city, e.g. the Reading Association (Société de Lecture),[162] the Art Association (Société des Arts),[163] the History and Archaeology Association (Société d'Histoire et d'Archéologie) and the Genevan Association for Public Utility (Société genevoise d'utilité publique); here, he gathered experience with the organisation of public philanthropy.[164] Eynard now increasingly displayed his wealth and influence to the outside world: from 1817 to 1821, he built his splendid neo-classical 'Megaron' in Geneva and also bought property in Florence, Rome and Paris (Historical Archives National Bank of Greece 1999, 17).[165] From his base in Geneva or from his country seat in Beaulieu, he maintained the contacts he had made in Vienna, as the vast correspondence that he left after his death reveals. He also travelled extensively throughout Europe in search of personal contacts, e.g. during his regular trips to Paris. Other congresses were also held, for instance, from September to November 1818 in Aachen, which Eynard again attended with his wife Anna, representing the interests of both Tuscany and Geneva[166] at a time when restorative political tendencies were increasingly ascendant (Fehrenbach 2001, 134). However, Eynard displayed no special interest in Greece at this time.[167] He met Kapodistrias, but their discussion focused on Switzerland and Geneva.[168] In Eynard's diary from 1821, the

Greeks are only mentioned in passing, as the victims of the Janissary riots in the Ottoman Empire.[169] He hardly mentioned the link between the Greek wish for freedom and independence from the 'Ottoman yoke' and the issues of humanity with which he was so concerned, only noting that a civilised Europe could not tolerate the massacre of thousands of Christians simply to maintain the balance of power.[170] The Greek uprising began in Wallachia in March 1821 (Turczynski 2003, 117), but Eynard only mentions it in April 1882 as the reason for the concentration of Ottoman troops there, which he thought made a war with Russia less likely.[171] It is thus hardly astonishing that Eynard was not involved in the founding of the first Philhellene committee in Geneva in 1822 and is similarly not listed as having donated to the cause (Hauser 1990, 109).[172]

From liberal to Philhellene

Between 1821 and 1824, certain influences disposed Eynard to turn towards Greece. At this time, the banker closely scrutinised the development of French domestic politics. He had watched with horror as Napoleon's failed attempt to regain power (Müchler 2014) was followed by acts of cruel revenge by the royalists of southern France against the supporters of Napoleon, particularly the Protestant citizens of Languedoc (Haupt et al. 2006, 287).[173] In the so-called Terreur blanche, lynch rule dominated and more than 2,000 people were killed (Schmale 2000, 205).[174] Eynard, who himself came from a Huguenot family driven from France in the seventeenth century, sided with the victims (Chapuisat 1952, 66, 76ff.).[175] But he was not only interested in religious questions: in 1814, the Bourbon Ludwig XVIII returned to the throne as the king by God's grace. He had indicated a readiness to compromise with the powers from the Napoleonic era and the constitutional charter thus included significant achievements from the revolution, e.g. the judicial and administrative reform and the sale of national estates. The nobility was nonetheless able to regain its strong position in both the upper and the lower houses of parliament and in the administration and state bureaucracy. However, despite the fact that voting rights were restricted by age and property, the ultras, the absolute supporters of the monarchy, lost an increasing amount of ground in the subsequent years, while the liberals and liberal democrats were able to gain new mandates (Schunck 1994; Schmale 2000; Haupt et al. 2006; Fahrmeir 2010).

The assassination of the French heir to the throne, the Duke of Berry, in 1820 triggered a swing to conservative politics for the monarchy. The ultra-royalists now won power and influence in close symbiosis with the counter-revolutionary Catholic Church. Eynard shared the anti-clerical resentments of much of the population, especially directed against the Jesuit Order, which had been re-established in 1814.[176] He perceived the Jesuits as 'an enormous power and [...] the true masters of France'.[177] In 1824,

Karl X then came to the throne. He was widely regarded as belonging to the group of ultras and reactionaries and his rule was characterised by the erosion of basic rights. The restitution of expropriated goods to returning emigrants gained particular significance and led to a slump in the value of French bonds, a development which also caused Eynard to suffer significant losses.[178] After 1830, Eynard became a confidant of the 'Citizen King' Louis-Philippe, with whom he held many discussions about Greek affairs (Chapuisat 1952, 140, 149, 172, 183). The king shared Eynard's love of modern daguerreotypes and therefore allowed him to take some of the entire royal family, occasions which Eynard then used to put in a good word for Greece (ibid., 168).

In addition to his concern for French domestic politics, Eynard was also interested in the revolutionary movements that were reawakening in southern Europe during the 1820s (Fahrmeir 1985; Schunck 1994; Barceló/Schmidt 2005). The Great Powers had agreed in 1820 that if a country was affected by a revolution, then military force could be used to restore a monarchy, and in 1821 Austria made use of this ruling in the case of Naples (Schunck 1994, 231). Meanwhile in Spain in 1820, the officer Rafael del Riego led an uprising against the restored regime; this Trienio liberal was initially successful and in March 1820 Ferdinand VII was forced to reinstate the liberal constitution (Barceló/Schmidt 2005, 268f.). The news of this success travelled fast and led to uprisings in Portugal, Sicily and Sardinia-Piedmont.[179] At the Congress of Verona in autumn 1822, France was then given permission to intervene against the revolution in Spain, leading to the military defeat of both the moderate and radical liberals by 1823.[180] Eynard discussed these developments with his friends, e.g. Pozzo di Borgo in Paris,[181] and he followed reports of the uprisings closely in the newspapers, cutting out many articles and sticking them in his diary, particularly from the *Constitutionell* and the *Courrier Français*. In an article from 25 October 1823, he heavily underlined the following sentences:

> But one of the most valuable fruits that can be gathered from this war in Spain, as this has become inevitable, is the certain discredit that is being increasingly attached to the ideas of *absolutist rulership*, even in the sentiments of those who were able to love it until now; that is the popularity that the monarchical system gets day by day, where the force necessary for action is regulated through *laws that form themselves*, as made possible by the fundamental law of the state. Absolute rulership, if it is not already judged by the numerous examples that history gives of its consequences, could now be judged by the causes and disasters of the war in Spain. *Absolute rulership creates the misfortune of the kings and likewise the suffering of the people.[…] Constitutional rulership,* in contrast, secures for the kings, in preserving the people from oppression, all blessings

> for the good that occurs without them needing to fear that they will be blamed for the bad.[182]

Eynard perceived close links between the various revolutionary groups, as demonstrated by the fact that he sent his uncle a newspaper article about the arrest of members of the revolutionary Association of Riego (Société de Riego) in the same post as he sent a notice concerning the founding of the Paris Greek Committee.[183]

All these events needed to be discussed with an equally involved interlocutor: in 1822, Ioannis Kapodistrias was suspended from the Russian diplomatic service.[184] He then wanted to return to his homeland, the Ionian Islands, but they were under British rule and Kapodistrias was refused permission from London to travel there; apparently, it was feared that his presence so close to the uprising could cause an uncontrollable escalation in the Greek struggle for independence. Kapodistrias therefore sought an alternative place of residence, somewhere from which he could support his compatriots, which was as unaffected as possible by censorship,[185] with a peaceful atmosphere, ideally in the centre of Europe in easy reach of the capital cities. He chose Geneva, where he was welcomed to Eynard's home as an honorary citizen and highly esteemed friend. The banker even built a small house named Fleur d'eau built in the garden of his country seat for him (Chapuisat 1952, 125). For Eynard, Kapodistrias became the key to the strange Greek world, an intermediary between the cultures. He merged the banker's liberal ideas with Philhellenism, opening up a new field of action. Like-minded Greeks gathered around Kapodistrias and stayed with Eynard while they visited, e.g. the former Hospodars of Wallachia and Moldavia, Alexandros Mavrokordatos and Mihail II Soutzos, not to mention the Greek students (Vakalopolos 1994, 242). Eynard's house developed into a planning centre of the Greek liberation movement (Rothpletz 1899, 11). The more the European monarchs oppressed their subjects, the more Eynard found himself on the side of the radical liberal movement supporting the Greeks. A conversation that he held with Metternich on 26 March 1825 in Paris[186] shows how his activities were perceived. In a relaxed but nonetheless very distinct manner, Metternich requested that the banker persuade the refugees lodging with him to leave Geneva, as their stay could lead to problems for Switzerland. Eynard assured him that there was no plot of any sort. Metternich though insisted that plans against Italy were being hatched in Geneva and that he was better informed about these matters than the Swiss police. 'I wish for the wellbeing of Switzerland more than anyone else; but not that she disturb her neighbours, and not that she tolerate people within her borders who try to disturb the peace in Italy'.[187] He complained of being accused of tyranny by the European public although all he wanted was to ensure peace in Italy and Austria, to which Eynard laughingly responded, 'You are regarded as the most extreme person in Europe'.[188] Continuing in a joking tone, Metternich suggested that the living conditions in Italy under the Austrian rule were much better than they had ever been under the French rule; much was being done for education and for industry. Eynard introduced Tuscany as a contrary example, where people loved their sovereignty due to the good and liberal government. This was rejected by Metternich: the country was simply fortunate in terms of nature and history; it was not possible to compare it.

Eynard regretted the inflexibility in Metternich's behaviour which could not adapt to the changed situation: 'Metternich wants to do anything to not allow any change, but everything wants to change – and surely the events will be stronger than him'.[189] In light of the barely disguised but in the end powerless threats of the Austrian, it is not surprising that Eynard perceived the Holy Alliance to be a 'deplorable system' that permitted neither freedom nor humanity nor progress (Rothpletz 1899, 12f., tr. by K.S.), and aligned himself even more strongly with the demands of his Greek friends. Indeed, at a time of 'liberal defeats', Eynard turned to the only revolution of the 1820s that proved successful, thanks to the fact that it could be integrated into the system of the Holy Alliance (Fahrmeir 2010, 197).[190] The Greek revolution marked the transition from the restrictive 1820s to the more reformist 1830s. The banker saw an opportunity to put his notions of good government into practice under an able politician. That it was Greece where he seemed able to realise his liberal hopes was in Eynard's case due to biographical chance, triggered by his friendship with the first president of the country. In a way that Schmale described as typical, Eynard believed it was 'to a certain extent immaterial whether France called itself empire, monarchy, citizen's kingship or republic and then empire again, in the practice of government this made little difference' (Schmale 2000, 203, tr. by K.S.). Exactly in this manner, the form of government of the newly founded Greek state was not particularly important to Eynard. 'May it become a monarchy or republic, if only I do not have to see it as a desert or a grave'.[191] What he really cared about was good governmental practice and well-structured institutions that were suited to further the economic and political well-being of the population (Boldt 1978, 38).[192] This was the background of values against which Eynard interpreted all the information he received from Greece. He used his financial resources to realise his ideals, behaviour which can be compared to that of 'ethical and green' investors at the end of the twentieth century who, like Eynard, were most concerned with 'putting their money where their morals are, bringing their values systems in line with their economic behaviour' (Lewis 2000, 6; Schönhärl 2019a). Like these modern investors, the Swiss banker also differentiated between different sources of income in deciding how to invest his money, for instance, using profits from his speculation with Greek bonds to the benefit of Greece[193] – behaviour that would be meaningless for the homo oeconomicus.

If his liberal programme failed to function, then Eynard directed sharp and direct criticism towards the political actors, no matter whether they were democratically legitimised presidents or monarchs. Thus in a letter to Kapodistrias, he quotes a message that has reached him via a friend: 'Compte Capodistrias is generally accused of inaction, even of indecision and, it pains me to say, a certain slackness'.[194] He used the same tone later to criticise King Otto, who he similarly accused of a lack of decisiveness and lethargy. Eynard told him that he needed to fundamentally change his working style and use good institutions to quieten the calls for a constitution.

> I do not desire a constitution, but institutions that are vigorous enough and positive enough to entirely replace the word constitution. Greece can and should not remain an absolutist monarchy, particularly because the sovereign does not have the necessary talent to govern in this manner.[195]

Eynard did not hesitate to repeatedly urge Otto to initiate reforms. The 1843 revolution finally forced the king to accept a constitution and dismiss all the Bavarians from his government, steps which Eynard then viewed as positive because the constitution was moderate rather than radical.

> If Greece and your Majesty honestly and loyally reach an understanding I foresee the best future for your kingdom, sire, but should imprudent counsel urge your Majesty to do everything to win back the position you have lost, – a little through your own fault, as I cannot restrain from telling you – I do not know how to beg your Majesty enough to reject these insinuations that could lose Greece and your Majesty, because if the troubles completely disorganise Greece then is it not possible to foresee that the disastrous events could cause the Great Powers to destroy what they have created?[196]

The banker openly pointed out mistakes of government to the king, arguing that they had caused the uprising. He regarded the revolution as justified because of these mistakes. His unswerving objective in all his efforts was to aid Greece to catch up with West European development.[197]

Conclusion

In complete contrast to the London bankers who issued the 1825 loan, Jean-Gabriel Eynard was exceptionally well informed about Greece. He maintained a dense network of correspondents in the country itself and abroad and thus also protected himself from loss in his diverse projects. When it came to interpreting the information thus gained, Eynard was a man of conviction, an ardent liberal who turned to the only successful revolution in

Europe in restoration times, the Greek revolution. His confidence in the Greek cause, to which he had no humanistic connection, was provided by his friend Ioannis Kapodistrias, the first president of Greece, whom he admired as an able diplomat and politician. Kapodistrias awakened Eynard to Greece both as a nation state and as a new market. He was the intermediary who inextricably united the two spheres of liberalism and Philhellenism, opening up a field of action for Eynard's political convictions: Greece as the 'Piedmont of the Orient' (Basch 1995, 36).[198] Eynard understood Greece as an opportunity to put his liberal convictions into practice, also using investment – a strategy reminiscent of ethical investment funds at the end of the twentieth century. He was willing to accept high risks and low profits because he was not concerned with personal benefits but with the long-term development of his 'promised land'. His aim was to prove that with a liberal government and good institutions, the experiment of an independent nation state in restoration Europe could be successful, and to this end he wanted to invest his money. In terms of risk management, he ensured that he distributed the risks between various projects and, with the founding of the ETE, between a number of partners.

In this context, Eynard simply blended out any discouraging information. His Philhellenism survived Kapodistrias' murder and the onerous conflicts with the Bavarian regency in Nafplio. For decades, he devoted himself to Greece with a range of activities, including donations and advance payments, campaigns and discussions in diplomatic circles, financial advice and investments. The fact that Eynard did not once travel to Greece in the 40 years of his lived Philhellenism[199] seems only partly linked to a fear that he might be co-opted by the political parties, and perhaps served rather to protect his idealistic image of Greece from being confronted with the reality of the country. The sobering nature of such a confrontation is demonstrated by the experiences of the von Eichthal family, discussed in the following chapter.

Notes

1 Orlando had informed the association of Louriotis' arrival in January 1825; see Orlando to the members of the association Lasteyrie, Lameth, Ternaux, La Borde and Didot on 10.1.1825, in Dalleggio (1949, 131f.). For more details on the history of the association, see Dimakis (1966, 27–48).

2 Levandis demonstrates that in addition France was more interested than Great Britain in cooperating with the Ottoman Empire and especially with Egypt; also see Cassis (2007, 57f.).

3 A. de Staël to André Louriotis in February 1825, in Dalleggio (1949, 132), tr. by K.S. De Staël expressly advises Louriotis to remain in Paris until Eynard's arrival, because he would be able to get the loan underway.

4 Generally on the Swiss capital market, see Guex/Mazbouri (2010).

5 On François Delessert and his bank, see Stoskopf (2002a). The Paris Committee also had many politically active members from the circle of moderate liberals

and a striking number of Protestants were involved; see Klein (2009, 185ff.). According to Klein, the committee was founded on the occasion of Louriotis' first visit to Paris in search of a loan in 1824; see ibid.

6 Eynard to Turrettini, undated, BGE, MS suppl. 1871. On Jean-Henri Hottinguer and his bank, one of the most respected houses of the Parisian haute banque; see Stoskopf (2002a, 213–217).

7 Eynard to Turrettini, undated, BGE MS suppl. 1871, tr. by K.S.

8 In 1808, the founder of the bank, Dominique André, appointed his nephew François Cottier to a position in the bank; see Stoskopf (2002a, 66–70), here 66. The roots of the André family are in Geneva, which explains the good contacts to Eynard.

9 Eynard to Turrettini, undated, BGE MS suppl. 1871, tr. by K.S.

10 Gabriel Odier was the son of Charles David Odier, repeatedly a Genevan syndic, and Eynard's sister Caroline; see Hubler (2011). However, there was no direct link to the banking house Lombart Bonna & Cie, after 1830 Lombard Odier & Cie. The banker giving his name here was Charles Edouard Odier, a cousin of Gabriel. He was a founding member of the Comité de la souscription en faveur des Grecs in 1823; see Dimakis (1966, 29); Chaponnière Meyer (1998, 95) and Chapuisat (1952, 25).

11 Eynard to Turrettini, BGE MS suppl. 1871.

12 Eynard to Turrettini, 5.2.1825, ibid. This view was shared by the Greek deputies in London; see Orlando and Louriotis to Monsieur le Président et à MM. les Membres du Comité Grec à Paris, in Dalleggio (1949, 134).

13 Somewhat differently the secondary literature speaks of 10 million francs, nowhere is a possible doubling of the sum mentioned. The interest is said to have stood at 5%, the amortisation at 1%, the issue price was 50%; see Kofas (1981, 13). Further self-justification by the Greek deputies is found in Ορλάνδος [Orlandos] (1841); Σπανιολάκης [Spaniolakis] (1839/1840).

14 Eynard to Turrettini, 5.2.1825, evening, BGE MS suppl. 1871, tr. by K.S.

15 Ibid. Eynard enjoyed the situation whereby he could follow the discussion without being identified as pulling the strings of the loan: 'It is very amusing to find oneself incognito in a discussion of which one is the cause' (Ibid., tr. by K.S.).

16 Eynard to Turrettini, 9.2.1825, BGE MS suppl. 1871.

17 It is almost unimaginable that this was true of the ultra-royalists. On the internal political categorisation of the Parisian Philhellenes, see Klein (2009, 184ff.).

18 Orlando and Louriotis to André & Cottier and Gabriel Odier, 11. and 15.2.1825, in Dalleggio (1949, 133).

19 Ibid.

20 Louriotis to *The Times*, in *The Times*, 30.10.1826.

21 It was indeed the case that for 1825 the contract prohibited other loans with an issue price of less than 60; see Convention in Λουριώτης [Louriotis]/Ορλάνδος [Orlandos] (1839, 121–126), here 124. The Ricardos were correspondingly indignant when they caught the Greek government negotiating for another loan in April 1825; see Jacob and Samson Ricardo to Orlando and Louriotis, 26.4.1825, in ibid., 194f.

22 Louriotis to *The Times*, in *The Times*, 30.10.1826.

23 *The Times*, 4.11.1826, in N. N. (Gennadios) (1880, 30–33).

24 Apparently, the chamber refused to approve the papers for André-Cottier-Odier because they were unfamiliar; see Le Bret (2012, 69). This cannot, however, refer to the loan of 1825, as it never reached the French parliament.

25 Eynard to Turrettini, 14.2.1825, BGE MS suppl. 1871, tr. by K.S.

26 The Money Market, in *The Times*, 27.9.1826, in N. N. (Gennadios, Ioannis) (1880, 16f.).

27 Eynard to *The Times*, 13.9.1826, in *The Times*, 27.9.1826, in ibid., 17f.
28 The certificate of the re-establishment of the Société de Genéve en faveur des Grecs and its calls for donations over the following years are found in BGE MS suppl. 1891.
29 See the at times very frustrated reports of the meetings of the illustrious committee. Thus, the Duc de Broglie asked Eynard at a Parisian reception on 3.2.1825: 'And your committee, how is it going?' – 'Like all committees: we talk a lot, we utter beautiful sentences, we decide nothing'. – 'But you are a gathering of the best heads of France!' – 'Yes, we discuss a lot; there are all possible philanthropic ideas among us; but some want to hurry to Greece's help by sending books and money to develop industry and education; others want to collect voluntary donations, without a loan, and nobody arrives at the goal'. BGE MS suppl. 1871, tr. by K.S.
30 An overview of the methods of fundraising for philanthropic projects, including an international comparison for the nineteenth century is found in Adam et al. (2009).
31 Compte des recettes et dépenses du comité établi à Genève en faveur des Grecs, depuis le 4 de Septembre 1825, jusqu'au 31 décembre 1826, BGE MS suppl. 1891.
32 The exact instructions from 27.11.1826 in BGE MS suppl. 1891; also see Le Comité établi à Genève en faveur des Grecs (1826).
33 Historical Archives National Bank of Greece (1999, 18).
34 Compte des recettes et dépenses du comité établi à Genève en faveur des Grecs, depuis le 4 de Septembre 1825, jusqu'au 31 décembre 1826, BGE MS suppl. 1891.
35 See ibid. In 1823, there were 163 Greek refugees in the city; see Chapuisat (1952, 106).
36 For this task, Eynard proposed the young Marcet, a nephew of his Vaudois colleague William Haldimand in London, and also William Romilly, a son of the British legal scholar and Member of Parliament Samuel Romilly – the former was a particularly good choice as Marcet was generously supported with £500 by his uncle. Eynard provided 5,000 francs, which helped relieve pressure on the finances of the committee (see **55 n.100** in this book).
37 The wave of sympathy which engulfed the whole of Europe during the beleaguering of the city and which represented a second phase of enthusiasm for Greece is impressively described by Hauser (1990, 98–101). He calculates that in 1826–1828 donations amounting to about 360,000fl were made in the territory of the German Confederation; this is almost six times the donations collected in 1821–1824 (about 60,000fl). Hauser conducts exact calculations of donations, not only in southern Germany.
38 The higher amount is given in Historical Archives National Bank of Greece (1999, 18).
39 Eynard is immortalised as a benefactor of Greece in an inscription at Königsplatz in Munich.
40 As Rothpletz has drawn up a comprehensive list of all Eynard's donations, it is unnecessary to do likewise here.
41 See **79ff.** in this book.
42 Eynard to Kapodistrias, 17.8.1827, in Θεοτόκης [Theotokis] (1929, 23). He also managed to ensure that an advance of £95,000 made by the banking house of Ricardo could remain in place.
43 Eynard to Kapodistrias, 20.8.1827, in ibid., 25. Kapodistrias did not accept this offer.
44 Eynard to Kapodistrias, 1.11.1827, in ibid., 48.

45 For example, in November 1827 as aid for foreign officers in Greece, see Rothpletz (1899, 81).
46 The battle did not occur by chance nor was it unsought, as older research suggested. It was rather the culmination of developments whereby the Great Powers manoeuvred one another into positions from which they could not retreat; see Schulz (2011). This is also indicated by Gall (1982, 8).
47 The banker actually did conduct the negotiations with Leopold. They are recorded in his dairy, 20.4.–21.5.1830: Grecs, prince Léopold de Cobourg. In a 'Note très confidentielle au Prince Léopold sur la Grèce', Eynard summarised Leopold's reasons for rejecting the offer, BGE MS Supp. 1871. See also Foreign Office (1830).
48 In 1825, Baron von Rothschild also donated 6,000 francs to support the struggle for independence; see Chapuisat (1952, 118). For more details on the 60-million loan, see **116–119** in this book.
49 For example, Kapodistrias to Eynard, 5.3.1826, in Θεοτόκης [Theotokis] 1929, 7f.; Eynard to Kapodistrias, 1.10.1827 in ibid., 37.
50 In the negotiations on the second and third instalments of the loan, the Great Powers used Greece as a match ball in their various conflicts; see Krauss (1987).
51 For example, in December 1830, see Chapuisat (1952, 132).
52 On 31.5.1830, the committee in Geneva published its final accounts and a word of thanks for the donations and support given over the eight years of its existence. The efforts were said to have been successful and Switzerland was an example for the whole of Europe; see Dernier compte des recettes de dépenses du comité établi à Genève en faveur des Grecs depuis le 1er Janvier 1827 jusqu'au 31 Mai 1830, BGE MS suppl. 1891.
53 Fallmerayer (1830, 1, IIIf.), tr. by K.S. Fallmerayer triggered a wave of indignation among the Philhellenes and educated Greeks with his work.
54 For example, in Eynard to Stavros, 17.6.1843, in Εθνική Τράπεζα της Ελλάδος [National Bank of Greece] 1923, 6, tr. by K.S.
55 Eynard to Kapodistrias, 26.11.1827, in Θεοτόκης [Theotokis] 1929, 54f.
56 Also see Eynard to Stavros, 7.3.1841, in Εθνική Τράπεζα της Ελλάδος [National Bank of Greece] 1923, 24.
57 For more details on Eynard's activities for the Greek school system, see Batardon (2006).
58 After Regny's death in 1841, Lemaitre was sent to Athens, again following Eynard's suggestion; see Vacalopoulos (1979). An earlier mention of Regny is found in a letter from Eynard to his brother Jacques from 19.9.1796, BGE MS suppl. 1840.
59 Eynard to Kapodistrias, 18.8.1828, in Θεοτόκης [Theotokis] (1929, 130); on the founding of the Société de colonisation Suisse en Grèce, see Vakalopulos (1994, 246); the idea of founding a Genevan colony had already been suggested, although in Waterford in Ireland, by François d'Ivernois when the leaders of the 1782 revolution had to leave the city. Colonies of this sort were then actually founded in Brussels and in Constance, the former by the Odier family; see Hartmann (2003, 276). Eynard's approach was thus neither totally original nor absurd. See also Mitsou (2016).
60 Letters from Eynard to Kapodistrias, 16.12.1827, in Θεοτόκης [Theotokis] 1929, 63f.; 2.1.1828, 69f.; 29.3.1828, 75f.; this detail is of interest because potatoes played an important role in the development of agriculture in the mountainous regions of Switzerland at the end of the eighteenth century; see Maissen (2011, 141, 145). Clearly, Eynard was trying to transfer this successful approach to Greece.
61 As a member of the Geneva committee, Eynard made a total of three such publications: Comité de Genève en faveur des Grecs (1826a); Comité de Genève en

faveur des Grecs (1826b) and the most comprehensive volume: Plusieurs membres de l'ancien comité grec de Paris (1831).

62 Eynard's respectful elegy for Kapodistrias is found in Ferrari (1980, 178–180).

63 Numerous letters to Otto are printed in Chapuisat (1924); other letters in BGE MS suppl. 1888.

64 A very different assessment is found in Armansperg (1976).

65 Also see a detailed account of the conflict described below in Κατηφόρη [Katifori] (1984).

66 Several letters are also found in Chapuisat (1924). Others are scattered through BGE.

67 There is a controversial discussion concerning the fitness of the Bavarian regency and King Otto and their mistakes, e.g. Πετρόπουλος [Petropulos] (1985/1986); Messinesis/Ritthaler (1966); Kotsowilis (2007); Kotsowilis (2004). Publications on Bavarian history usually only refer to Bavarian sources, e.g. in Baumstark (1999); the standard works – in addition to the short chapter in Spindler (1974, 168–173) – thus continue to be Seidl (1981) and Seidl (1981). An edition of the protocols of the Bavarian regency, drawn up in German, by Rainald Becker and Emanuel Lechenmayr (Kommission für bayerische Landesgeschichte) is in preparation.

68 Even if Eynard never directly mentioned this in his letters, it can be assumed that he did not approve of the Greek military expenditure which totalled ca. 60% of total expenditure between 1833 and 1838; see Dertilis (2006, 401).

69 Eynard to Armansperg, 1.6.1833, a copy, BHSA III, Estate Armansperg, 36.

70 Ibid.

71 Ibid, tr. by K.S.

72 Ibid, tr. by K.S.

73 Although Eynard often described Rothschilds to others as his partners and cooperated with them, he also at times viewed them as competitors and scoffed that the Rothschild father had the aura of an old butcher (9.7.1823), according to Chapuisat (1952, 108).

74 Eynard to Armansperg, 20.3.1834, a copy, BHSA III, NL Armansperg, 36, tr. by K.S.

75 Ibid, tr. by K.S.

76 Ibid, tr. by K.S.

77 Ibid.

78 Chiapello and Walter speak of an 'actuarial convention'; see Chiapello/Walter (2016).

79 To compare Pohle-Fraser's approach with the Convention Theory, also see Knake (2017).

80 Eynard to Armansperg, 22.3.1834, a copy, BHSA III, NL Armansperg, 36.

81 The first half of the 100,000 francs in May 1835; see Κατηφόρη [Katifori] (1984, 146).

82 For example, on 17.7.1837 the Grand Cross of the Saviour (Großkreuz des Retters), which Otto personally gave him (although not until 1862) at his country seat of Beaulieu near Rolle in Switzerland; see Historical Archives National Bank of Greece (1999, 20). In 1843, he also received the Order of St. Anna from Tsar Nicholas in recognition of his services to Greece, ibid., 22. He became a member of the Legion of Honour in 1838; see Chapuisat (1952, 149).

83 The spelling in the sources varies between Rudhart and Rudhardt, also in the secondary literature. In March 1837, Rudhardt repaid Eynard the rest of the capital he had lent to Greece with interest, 124,000 francs; see Κατηφόρη [Katifori] (1984, 148).

84 Rudhardt to Eynard, three letters in 1837, BGE MS Suppl. 1887.

85 The bank organised a large exhibition in honour of its founder in 1999; see Ιστορικό Αρχείο [Historical Archives National Bank of Greece] (1999). A chronological biography and comprehensive bibliography are provided in Historical Archives National Bank of Greece (1999). There is even a video with information about Eynard; see Seni et al. (1994).

86 The Swiss national bank, for instance, was not founded until 1906; see Landmann (1906).

87 For more details on the credit relations of Greece before and shortly after the revolution, see Pizanias (1986, 447–476). He mentions interest rates of between 15 and 45%.

88 Half came apparently from Eynard; see Eynard and Kapodistrias, 16.4.1828, in Θεοτόκης [Theotokis] (1929, 87). For more details on the founding of this first bank and the introduction of the phoenix as the first Greek currency, see Loules (1986).

89 A table giving an overview of the failed attempts to found the bank in ibid., 449.

90 Simon Georg Sina (1753–1822). On the banking house of Sina, the most important Greek banking house in the Austrian diaspora, which grew rich primarily thanks to the cotton trade, see Λάιος [Laios] 1972; Lanier (1998). See also **50 n.15, 134 n.51** in this book.

91 On the widely spread Ralli family, see Chatziioannou (2010, 226–228, 233, 237).

92 For details on the founding of the bank and the failed attempts, see Ζωγράφος [Zografos] (1925).

93 This descendent of the Hösslin family, who had their roots in Augsburg, was born in Triest (1802–1849) and in 1839 was responsible for founding the first bank in Greece in the Western sense; see Hösslin (1990, 27–31). In 1841, Hösslin was a member of the committee that prepared the start of trading of the ETE; see Ιστορικό Αρχείο [Historical Archives National Bank] 2001, 17. I thank Günter Schneider for the reference to Julius Hösslin.

94 The history of the Greek National Bank has been recorded in detail, see, e.g. [Valaoritis] (1902); Eulambio (1924); Christophorou (1926); Εθνική Τράπεζα της Ελλάδος [National Bank of Greece] (1966); Στασινόπουλος [Stasinopoulos] (1966); Thomadakis (1985); Βαλαωρίτης [Valaoritis] (1902); Κωστής [Kostis] (2003); Παγουλάτος [Pagoulatos] (2006).

95 Comparable to a modern development bank whose task is 'the financing of long-term investment projects of significance to development policy'. Such credit institutes are especially active in the so-called 'developing countries', 'as they lack an efficient capital market and capital creation is therefore insufficient due to low mobilisation of domestic savings'; see Klein/Schöning (2015), tr. by K.S.

96 In 1843, Eynard sold 100 shares but kept the transaction secret so as not to damage the reputation of the bank; see Eynard to Stavros, 16.9.1843, in Εθνική Τράπεζα της Ελλάδος [National Bank of Greece] (1923, 122). A total of 3,043 shares were initially sold; see Eulambio (1924, 5).

97 In letters to Stavros from 16.11.1841 and 25.11.1841, he names this sum as a loan to the Greek government at an interest rate of 8%; see Εθνική Τράπεζα της Ελλάδος [National Bank of Greece] (1923, 4–12); later, he conceded that Stavros should set the interest himself 'as you believe to be fair', tr. by K.S.

98 Eynard to Stavros, 27.1.1842, in ibid., 16.

99 Eynard to Stavros, 6.8.1843, in ibid., 114; Eynard also tried to win the reputation of the Baring banking house for Greece when he wanted to promote it as the driving force for the rescheduling; see Eynard to Kapodistrias, 26.8.1827, in Θεοτόκης [Theotokis] (1929, 28ff.). Concerning Barings, see Austin (2007).

100 Bank of England (1844).

101 After spending his youth in Ioannia, Georgios Stavros (1788–1869) travelled throughout Europe, also to St. Petersburg where he met Kapodistrias and became a member of the Philiki Heteria, the 'Society of Friends'. His acquaintance with Eynard may have begun in Livorno. During the struggle for independence and under Kapodistrias, Stavros held various state offices. From 1841 until his death, he remained the governor of the ETE (see Μεσσηνέζης [Messinesis] 1956; Βαβαρέτος [Vavaretos] 1967; Ιστορικό Αρχείο [Historical Archives National Bank] 2001).

102 'The first director Stavros, who was unanimously elected, was previously director of the bank of M. Eynard, and guaranteed the National Bank the confidence of this capitalist and the Misters Rothschild. His election was termed by both a conditio sine qua non for their shares in the bank – Vranes, also elected almost unanimously [as second director], is a well-reputed civilian who owns large estates in Hungary. It is hoped that his election will win over the banker Sina in Vienna for the local bank'. Report of the Bavarian ambassador Franz Gabriel Count of Bray in Athens to Ludwig I from 30.11.1841 on the first general meeting of the National Bank (to which he sent embassy secretary Faber rather than attending in person due to his lack of knowledge of the Greek language), BHSA III, MA 84431, tr. by K.S.

103 The French correspondence is published in Εθνική Τράπεζα της Ελλάδος [National Bank of Greece] 1923.

104 Strong to Ludwig I, 27.4.1841, BHSA III, MA 84431, tr. by K.S.

105 Letters from Ludwig I to Bray, the first from 14.6.1842, BHSA III, MA 84431. The printing of the dividends in the *Münchner Politische Zeitung* on e.g. 23.8.1842, No 201; 20.8.1845, No 196; 23.3.1846, No 70; 17.4.1847, No 92; 7.12.1847, No 213.

106 Bray to Ludwig I, 20.7.1842, BHSA III, MA 84431. Ludwig always had the dividends settled via his court banker von Eichthal.

107 Perglas to Ludwig I, 5.5.1848, BHSA III, MA 84431. In this context, the ambassador also reported to Ludwig about accusations against the bank's director Stavros, who was said to privilege personal friends when granting credit; see Perglas to Ludwig, 22.4.1848, BHSA III, MA 84431. Ludwig was unlikely to have been particularly moved by the news from Athens at this time, as he was fighting the revolution that had induced him to abdicate on 20.3.1848; see Büttner (2001, 313).

108 Perglas to Ludwig I, 23.7.1848, BHSA III, MA 84431.

109 Perglas to Ludwig I, 30.7.1849, 31.1.1851; Hompesch to Ludwig I, 20.1.1862, BHSA III, MA 84431. This may have been some small comfort to Ludwig, who after his abdication was forced by the Bavarian parliament to settle from his appanage the outstanding loan of 1.9 million guilders (2.85 million francs) that he had granted Greece during his reign, and who urgently required money to complete the neoclassic buildings on Königsplatz in Munich; see Seidl (1981, 157–273); Raff (1995). For more details on the Bavarian loan, see Ανδρεάδης [Andreadis] (1904, 105–113) and on their repayment in 1881 after pressure was brought to bear by Bismarck Ioannidou-Bitsiadou (1993). See also **213 n.108** in this book.

110 102 to his niece Anna Charlotte Adelaide Eynard; 102 to his wife Anna Eynard Lullin; 103 to Gabriel Alfred Eynard and 103 to his nephew Charles Francois Adolphe Eynard; see Notary Demole from Geneva to Stavros, 26./28.3.1863, in Letters of the shareholders to the Greek National Bank, ETE AISVIMetoxeoiYA'F2YF1.

111 Jean-Jacques Eynard to Stavros, 23.2.1863, ETE A1S6Y1F2YF2.

112 In 1868, Jean-Jacques Eynard counted up; at the time, he himself held 25 shares, Madame Eynard Hottenroth 53 and Cerrini Eynard 25; see his letter to Stavros,

15.1.1868, ETE A1S6Y1F2YF2. In 1869, he reported that the shares of Madame Eynard-Lullin, Eynard's widow, had been transferred to Charles Wodemar Eynard; Jean-Jacques Eynard to Stavros, 11.4.1869, ETE A1S6Y1F2YF2.

113 Eynard to Otto, 23.9.1843, in Chapuisat (1952, 204–208).

114 Diary Voyage à Aix-la-Chapelle 1818, BGE MS Suppl. 1863.

115 The Jewish merchant Don Pacifico lost his fortune during anti-Semitic riots in Greece in 1847. As a British citizen, he demanded diplomatic aid and in 1850 Great Britain under Lord Palmerston responded to his demands for compensation with a two-month blockade of the harbour of Piraeus. The incident, which must be seen in the context of the territorial disputes between Greece and Great Britain related to part of the Ionian Islands occupied by Great Britain, caused international uproar, in addition to other diplomatic incidents this year, e.g. the George Finlay affair; see Hannell (1989); Hicks (2004); Taylor (2008). Apparently, the trigger for the anti-Semitic riots was Rothschilds' intervention in the settlement of Greek debts; see Basch (1995, 90).

116 Note from Anna Eynard Lullin from 17.5.1841, BGE MS suppl. 1888, cited in Chapuisat (1952, 70ff.), tr. by K.S.

117 Thus in a discussion with the pope, he was unable to understand the Latin quotes: 'I am not a very strong Latinist, I don't understand them'. Chapuisat (1952, 135), tr. by K.S.

118 At least in 1846, see Chapuisat (1952, 180). As early as 1839, Ioannis Kolettis wrote to him in Greek; see Kolettis to Eynard, 28.9.1839, Academy of Athens, *Kolettis Papers*, online at http://psifiakaarxeia.academyofathens.gr/en/rec.asp?id=66548 [6.5.15].

119 The early friendly relationship to Sebastiani is also emphasised by Chapuisat (1952, 24).

120 For the correspondence with his brother Jacques about the bank's business, see BGE MS suppl. 1840.

121 The contract is in BGE MS suppl. 1844.

122 Eynard to Jacques Eynard, 11.7.1803, BGE MS suppl. 1845.

123 'He was the treasurer, trésorier, of Napoleon and he supposedly cheated him and in that position laid up his riches. I even heard that if Napoleon had ruled and lived longer, then Eynard would no longer live. I don't presume to judge this, but I believe that envy and exaggeration combine to belittle this now certainly worthy and respectable man'. Jäger (1838, 205), tr. by K.S. Rothpletz indignantly defends Eynard against such accusations: 'Envy and malice declared his riches to be ill-gotten. There is no reason whatsoever for the absurd allegations'. Rothpletz (1899, 10), tr. by K.S.

124 This seems to have been amicably agreed as correspondence between the two brothers continued in a friendly manner.

125 In the Habsburg secundogeniture, the brother of the reformist Emperor Joseph II, Pietro Leopoldo (the later Emperor Leopold II), introduced between 1765 and 1790 far-reaching enlightened reforms and moulded Tuscany in the liberal spirit; see Pesendorfer (1988, 119). His son Ferdinand, who became a ruler in 1790, continued this tradition until 1800 when he was removed from power by Napoleon as a consequence of the Treaty of Lunéville. Between 1801 and 1807, Tuscany was transformed into the Kingdom of Etruria and allocated to the heir to the throne of Palma, Ludwig, a nephew of the Spanish King Charles IV, as recompense for the loss of the duchies of Parma and Piacenza; see ibid., 53ff., 143f., 164f. Eynard's activities for Tuscany thus began under Ludwig.

126 Ibid., 154. Eynard also maintained close relations to Napoleon's brother Lucien; see Eynard (1914b, V).

127 Chapuisat (1952, 35ff.). The literature discusses whether the girl who Eynard later adopted was Élisa's daughter and perhaps also his, the connection thus possibly being not purely of a business nature; see Chapuisat (1952, 201f., FN 3).

128 Pesendorfer (1988, 158). In 1814, Ferdinand III could return to Tuscany where he ruled until his death. Despite joining the Holy Alliance, he allowed significant elements of the Napoleonic reforms to remain and strived to achieve a synthesis between old Tuscan and modern French legislation, providing Tuscany with the reputation of being an enlightened example; see ibid., 165. Many liberal revolutionaries fled to Tuscany during restoration times and the duchy supported Greece's struggle for independence. After 1824, Ferdinand's son Leopold III continued the liberal politics of his father, although the scope for this within the Holy Alliance was minimal; see ibid., 165–167.

129 Her very emphatic biography: Alville (1955); see also Rothpletz (1899, 10). The Lullin family had acquired citizenship in Geneva even before the reformation and were thus among the old established families; between 1760 and 1792, they sent three councillors to the Small Council; see Hartmann (2002, 243f.).

130 The latter two only acquired citizenship in the seventeenth and eighteenth centuries, but had nonetheless sent councillors to the Small Council of the city; see ibid., 245.

131 See for the following section Im Hof (2007); Maissen (2011).

132 A compilation of the most important sources on this mission with a detailed commentary is provided by Bouvier-Bron (1984).

133 The Greek research has intensively studied the first president of the country, e.g. Πανδής [Pandis] (2008); Σπανός [Spanos] (2008); Τούντα-Φεργάδη [Tounta-Fergadi] (2009); Βακαλόπουλος [Vakalopoulos] (2009). An English summary of his biography: Koukkou (1994a).

134 Maissen (2011, 158); Eynard's correspondence with Le Harpe is in BGE MS suppl. 1898. At the Vienna Congress, the dilemma posed for Alexander by his liberal education became clear, noted Eynard. Thus, the Tsar supported the restoration of Poland as an independent nation, but under his rule; this was only possible if Prussia was compensated by the relinquishment of Saxony; see Eynard (1923, 221).

135 In his autobiography from 1826, Kapodistrias reports the following words from Tsar Alexander:

> You love the republicans and I love them too. Now it is about saving one who has been subjected to French despotism and has been reserved for the fate of the free cities of Germany, of Geneva and Venice. It is Switzerland that we speak of. On the evening before crossing the Rhine with her armies, the allied sovereigns must secure the affection of this loyal and combative nation, help it to became itself again, and restore it to a state in which it can contribute, with us, to the great work of restoring the European system, as the rulers of the German Confederation have done.

Quoted from Bouvier-Bron (1984, 19), tr. by K.S. Perhaps Kapodistrias was able to understand the federal system of Switzerland particularly well, thanks to his origins on the Ionian Islands; see ibid., 279.

136 For detailed source citations and explanation, see Bouvier-Bron (1984).

137 As early as September 1814, the Swiss Diet agreed in principle to the incorporation of Geneva as the 22nd canton. However, because of negotiations concerning the boundaries of the territory, the treaty of unification was not signed until 19 May 1815, after the Congresses of Vienna and Paris; see Hartmann (2002, 148, 151f.).

138 For Pictet de Rochemont's autobiography, see Pictet (1892); the correspondence between the two legates from Geneva during the negotiations is found in Pictet et al. (1914). François d'Ivernois had been one of the leaders of the Genevan

revolution in 1782, but after the outbreak of the French revolution had made his opposition to France clear; see Hartmann (2002, 158).

139 This demand was complicated by the regions in question being primarily Catholic. Only once Napoleon returned for the '100 days' was Switzerland able to achieve extensions of territory; see Maissen (2011, 179).

140 Eynard (1914a); in German translation: Eynard (1923). See on Philhellenism at the Vienna Congress Kerschbaumer/Schönhärl (2013).

141 It can be assumed that Eynard met Napoleon I personally in 1807 when he accompanied Élisa, Grand Duchess of Tuscany, to negotiations with her brother in Venice; see Chapuisat (1952, 34).

142 On the great disappointment of many European intellectuals about Napoleon being crowned emperor in 1804, see Sauvigny/Potin (2010).

143 Diary Voyage à Aix-la-Chapelle 1818, from 21.10.1818, BGE MS Suppl. 1863.

144 Eynard (1923, 69), tr. by K.S.

145 Ibid., 77.

146 Already in 1757 Johann Heinrich Gottlob von Justi saw the 'common happiness of the subjects and the entire state' as the final goal of government (tr. by K.S.). The enlightened monarchs Friedrich the Great and Joseph II saw themselves as the first servants of their states; see Boldt (1978, 1–154).

147 For example in talks with Castelreagh, when Eynard reported that starvation was still prevalent in Piedmont while people in Tuscany lived in safety, see Diary Voyage à Aix-la-Chapelle 1818, BGE MS Suppl. 1863; e.g. in a letter to King Otto, 25.8.1842, in Chapuisat (1924, 140–143).

148 Ibid., 213.

149 Although the word 'liberal' was not yet clearly defined in political terms, it was already among the most useful and meaningful words that could be taken to describe a well-meaning and reformist government; see Vierhaus (1978, 753). It was first used by Napoleon on 18 Brumaire 1799 to portray the goals of the Directoire, ibid., 749f. Eynard's ideas initially targeted a governmental liberalism rooted in the tradition of enlightened absolutism and supported by the bureaucracy. Such a notion of liberalism had long been championed by the educated classes in Germany, who had great expectations of the liberality of governments. Eynard was so disappointed by the Congress of Vienna, however, that he moved towards a more radical position within the liberal movement; see ibid., 755. On the concept of liberalism, also see Leonhard (2001).

150 On the complicated relationship between Carlo Andrea Pozzo di Borgo (1764–1842) and Napoleon, see McErlean (1996). Pozzo di Borgo also kept a diary about the 100 days: Pozzo DiBorgo (1961). His relationship to vom Stein has been researched by Ouvaroff (1846), and his correspondence with the Russian diplomat Nesselrode is documented in Pozzo Di Borgo/Nesselrode (1890).

151 Emmerich Joseph Duke of Dalberg (1773–1833); see Knudsen (1987, 490f.); see also Dimakis (1966, 34).

152 Heinrich Friedrich Karl vom und zum Stein (1757–1831) cannot be found as a later correspondent of Eynard, probably because he retreated into private life following his disappointment at the Vienna Congress; see Stern (1893, 614–641). Stein's commitment to Greece, also in cooperation with von Gagern and Dalberg, is demonstrated in his letters to Kapodistrias; see Dieterich (1928).

153 Madame de Staël was linked to the Pictet family in Geneva and the Neckar family in Paris in a close-knit family network; see Hartmann (2002, 295).

154 Eynard's description of Alexander is in Eynard (1923, 220–223).

155 From 1824 Charles X of France (1757–1836), see Sauvigny (1959, 536–543).

156 Eynard's description of Franz II in Eynard (1923, 223f.).

157 After a miscarriage, the marriage remained childless; see Chapuisat (1952, 39). Anna accompanied her husband on many of his travels; see Alville (1955).
158 His diary during the 100-day return of Napoleon: Eynard (1914b). Eynard argues in favour of Switzerland being strictly neutral; see ibid., 143–152.
159 On the problematisation of the term, see Theile (2000); Zons (2000).
160 The importance of marrying the daughter of an old Genevan family in order to be elected to political office is shown by Hartmann (2002, 257). The Conseil représentatif was created in 1814 as a legislative body with 250 members. Voting rights were strictly controlled by census and did not permit the political participation of all citizens. 'According to the new constitution, wealth, chance and privilege represented the criteria which determined the right of political participation'. ibid., 149f., tr. by K.S.; see also 157.
161 Ibid., 532f.
162 Eynard was one of the founding members of this elite society in 1818; see Crue/ Brocher (1919).
163 This society had been founded in the Ancien Régime and represented a stronghold of conservative and restorative thinking, so Eynard's membership is surprising; see Hartmann (2002, 530).
164 On the world of associations in Switzerland, see Maissen (2011, 184).
165 On Eynard's building activities, see Corboz (1975); Eynard (1986).
166 His diary of the Aachen Congress as a copy in BGE MS suppl. 1863. The Eynards were greeted everywhere as old friends; the atmosphere was relaxed. Thus, Lord Castlereagh asked about the other representative of Geneva at the Vienna Congress, who was not in Aachen: What was d'Ivernois now doing? To the amusement of all participants, Eynard replied: 'But he is making children with his wife'. (Diary, as a copy, from 20.8.1818, BGE MS Suppl. 1863, tr. by K. S.).
167 Chapuisat suggests that Eynard already displayed a special love of Greece in 1822, but provides no proof; see Chapuisat (1952, 103ff.).
168 Kapodistrias repeatedly reaffirmed his love of Switzerland and his pride in his honorary Genevan citizenship, even if he did not believe he could solve the concrete problems of the city in Aachen, because the congress was not concerned with such small issues. Eynard had presented the desire of the Genevan Catholics to be placed under a Swiss bishop rather than a Savoy one; see Diary Voyage à Aix-la-Chapelle 1818, from 20.8.1818, evening, BGE MS Suppl. 1863.
169 Diary from 19.8.1821, BGE MS suppl. 1870.
170 Diary from 12.9.1821, BGE MS suppl. 1870.
171 Diary from 29.4.1822, BGE MS suppl. 1870.
172 Elsewhere, it is claimed that he was already involved in the founding of this first association; see Historical Archives National Bank of Greece (1999, 17). However, his name is not found in the files before 1825; see Documents concernant la constitution du Comité de Secours, avec des lettres des souscripteurs, BGE MS suppl. 1891. Eynard is only listed among the donators after the re-establishment of the committee on 10.8.1825. On the founding of the first Philhellene committee in 1822, see Vakalopolos (1994, 242).
173 On religious tensions in France, see Schneider (2011).
174 Eynard's description of the Terreur blanche in Eynard (1914b, 239f.); also 267f.
175 After the attempted assassination of Louis-Philippe in 1846, Eynard also came to the defence of the Protestants; see ibid., 184f.
176 Fear of a Jesuit conspiracy, which had been widespread in Europe at the beginning of the eighteenth century, experienced something of a renaissance among liberals after the Vienna Congress; see Défourneaux (1965).

177 Eynard to Turrettini, 7.2.1825, 20.2.1825, BGE MS Suppl. 1871, tr. by K.S.
178 Eynard did not believe that the bonds would rise again quickly, as predicted to him by Baron von Rothschild, but sold them with great losses; see Eynard to Turrettini, 20.2.1825, BGE MS Suppl. 1871.
179 The strength of links between the revolutionary movements and the extent to which, e.g. the revolutionaries in Piedmont identified with the Greek struggle for independence has been investigated by Boaglio (1994).
180 The Ricardo brothers wanted to participate in a loan to France for this purpose; **42** in this book.
181 Diary from 15.4.1822, BGE MS Suppl. 1870.
182 Diary from 25.10.182, BGE MS Suppl. 1870, tr. by K.S. With glued in newspaper article, apparently from the *Constitutionell*. The italics mark Eynard's underlining.
183 Eynard to Turrettini, 20.2.1825, MS Suppl. 1871.
184 In 1821, Kapodistrias attended the Congress of Laibach in the service of the Tsar and clearly distanced himself from the leader of the Greek uprising in Wallachia, Alexander Ypsilantis; see Fahrmeir (2010, 199). It is unclear whether he went on leave at his own request in the middle of 1822 or the Tsar dismissed him. Koukkou (1994a, 109) argues for Kapodistrias. Chapuisat (1952, 15), however, talks of an intervention by Metternich which led to Kapodistrias' dismissal. Whichever may be the case, it seems that the Greek had markedly lost favour with the Tsar before he left his service; see Ferrari (1980, 27f.). In his memoirs from 1826, Kapodistrias explains that he could no longer support the politics of the Tsar with regard to his homeland and that the parting had been amicable; see ibid., 156–170.
185 Switzerland joined the Holy Alliance in 1817 but the suppression of liberal tendencies was in practice comparatively mild; see Im Hof (2007, 99).
186 Diary from 26.3.1825, in Paris, BG MS Suppl. 1871. The secondary literature suggests that Metternich found Eynard a particularly boring person but this cannot be deduced from the conversations in the diary; see Rothpletz (1899, 55).
187 Eynard to Turrettini, 19.3.1825, BGE MS Suppl. 1871, tr. by K.S.
188 Ibid, tr. by K.S.
189 Ibid, tr. by K.S.
190 'There is good reason to view Greek independence as a triumph of the Vienna order. The shift of power in the eastern Mediterranean compensated Russia for the strengthened position of France and Austria and so preserved the European balance of power'. Fahrmeir (2010, 204), tr. by K.S.
191 Cited without a reference in Rothpletz (1899, 55), tr. by K.S.
192 Here on Hegel (1821, 27).
193 Eynard to Kapodistrias, 26.11.1827, in Θεοτόκης [Theotokis] (1929, 54f.).
194 Ibid., 147, tr. by K.S.
195 Eynard to Lemaitre, 27.5.1843, in Chapuisat (1952, 188f.), tr. by K.S.
196 Eynard to King Otto, 6.10.1843, in ibid., 209ff., tr. by K.S.
197 An idea that became dominant in development theory in the twentieth century; see Gerschenkron (1966).
198 The term expresses the hope of many European intellectuals that Greece could become a model of liberal reform policies, similar to Piedmont.
199 As was equally the case with Winckelmann, Lessing and Goethe, see Jenkyns (1980, 13).

3

BANKING BUSINESS BETWEEN SAINT-SIMONISM AND PHILOLOGY

The Bavarian-French d'Eichthal family

Bankers as intermediaries between the cultures

Perception of the risks connected to a new financial centre is a multi-layered process whereby bankers select a limited amount of information as being significant and interpret it to compile a meaningful image. Personal preferences and experience play a great role here, as seen with Eynard.[1] The greater the cultural distance between the familiar setting and the unknown market, the more important the role of intermediaries in the process of risk perception. Intermediaries tend to be individuals with knowledge of both cultures and languages, due to, e.g. their place of origin, time spent elsewhere as a prisoner or refugee, missionary activities or trading (Jobs/Mackenthun 2013b, 7). In the case of Eynard, Kapodistrias acted as an intermediary promoting transculturation between the cultures – a term from postcolonial studies.[2] In the ambiguous and uncertain field of contact between different cultures, such intermediaries or agents try to encourage understanding between the different spheres in which they move with the aim of improving their own living conditions, the living conditions of their peers or the living conditions of humanity as a whole (ibid., 14, 20). Within a framework of norms, social expectations and rules, some of these intermediaries manage a balancing act that allows them to develop practices and strategies for the development of their own identity and simultaneously trigger change (ibid., 14). Alternatively, the term 'transformation' is used to refer to 'complete processes of change [...] that occur between a field of reference and a field of reception'. An 'agent' selects certain aspects whereby the act of appropriation not only modifies the reception culture, but also constructs the reference culture (Bergemann 2011, 39, tr. by K.S.). In exactly this way, the politician Kapodistrias introduced Greece to Eynard as a new state and a new market. The question of how financial specialists actually carried out the functions of intermediaries remains. What did their transculturation look like in practice and could it extend beyond the financial sphere? What images of Greece did they transport? The von Eichthal family, who were active in Greece from the 1820s, serve as a case study through which to examine

DOI: 10.4324/9780429286537-6

the role of brokers in bankers' decision making. In 1833, a son of the Paris branch of the family, Gustave d'Eichthal, travelled to Greece and attempted to establish himself there. Although he failed in this endeavour and soon returned to Paris, his correspondence with his father Louis (1780–1840), his uncle Simon (1787–1854) and his brother Adolphe (1805–1895) represents a unique body of sources that sheds light on the investment decisions of three bankers from the same family but from two different cohorts.[3]

The Eichthals as an international family bank

Gustave d'Eichthal was born in 1804 as the eldest son of Louis d'Eichthal. Louis (or Ludwig) came from Munich, where during the Napoleonic wars his father Aaron Seeligmann, who was from Palatinate, had become *Hoffaktor* of the Wittelsbacher and a confidant of their leading minister Prince Montgelas (Hummert 1927).[4] For his merits in this period, Aaron was ennobled in 1814 and took the name von Eichthal, five years before he converted to Catholicism (Hohenlohe-Schillingsfürst 1953, 115–125). All of his five sons became bankers or financial specialists, while his five daughters were all married to men with similar occupations. The family was divided among a number of different cities. Simon, the youngest (see Figure II.3.1), remained in Munich and in 1824 succeeded his father as *Hoffaktor* (Düring-Ulmenstein 1987). In 1835, he was one of the founders of the Bayerischen Hypotheken- und Wechselbank (Bayerische Hypotheken- und Wechselbank 1935, 20ff.), and was involved in railway construction in Bavaria. Bernhard, the least successful of the brothers, died at a young age in 1830 in Rome. Arnold founded a banking house in Augsburg, which collapsed in the crisis of 1837/1838 (Le Bret 2012, 32). David became the Grand Ducal *Hofagent* in Karlsruhe and found success in the salt trade and in the production of sugar. In 1797, Ludwig (see Figure II.3.2) was sent to Paris at the age of 17 to undertake an internship and then settled in France. Initially, he lived in Nancy, where he married Fleurette Lévy, the daughter of a Jewish banker.[5] His two sons Gustave (1804–1886; see Figure II.3.3) and Adolphe (1805–1895; see Figure II.3.4) were born in the city before the family moved to Paris in 1812. In 1817, Louis was then able to found his own banking house, which organised the transfer of French reparations of 70 million francs to Bavaria after the Congress of Vienna (Hummert 1927). Louis specialised in trading with foreign bonds on the exchange, but also traded with insurance bonds and industry papers (Le Bret 2012, 68). The bank soon rose to the ranks of the Paris haute banque (Stoskopf 2002a, 158–162). In the same year of 1817, twins were born into the family, although only the daughter Anette survived and was later a correspondent of Gustave.

When the family moved to Paris, Louis' sons were eight and nine years old. Both the foreign background of their father and their religion were

Figure II.3.1 Simon von Eichthal, portrait by Joseph Heigel 1824.

Figure II.3.2 Louis d'Eichthal, portrait by Joseph Stieler 1845.

Figure II.3.3 Gustave d'Eichthal, portrait by Edmond Fechner 1827.

Figure II.3.4 Adolphe d'Eichthal, portrait by Edmond Fechner 1827.

obstacles to their integration. However, their father did all he could to ensure the social advancement of his children. In 1817, he had them both christened into the Roman Catholic Church and sent them to school at the Lycée Henri IV, one of the best-regarded and most expensive schools in Paris, where Gustave excelled (Ratcliffe 1977b, 118). Their father's dream was to see his sons study at the École Polytechnique, where they could master the scientific knowledge of their day and become engineers, contributing to the technical progress of humanity. The choice of such a profession not only reflected a dominant belief in progress typical of the era, but would also have been an additional step in the family's integration, turning away from 'Jewish' money market trading and towards 'ideologically neutral' engineering and sciences.

The relationship between the generations was far from easy. Gustave later described his father as tyrannising the house with his dominant and imperious nature (Le Bret 2012, 30). As a man of business, his father had no understanding of the rather contemplative character of his eldest son, who loved discussion and debate. Adolphe, the younger son, resembled his father more closely and was sometimes able to mediate between the two. The biographer Herve Le Bret describes the relationship between the brothers as symbiotic but also conflict-prone, suggesting that while Adolphe lived in the dimension of space, Gustave lived in that of time (ibid., 58f.). They valued one another tremendously and, despite their considerable and at times serious disputes, always remained in close contact.

To prepare Adolphe for the entrance exam to the École Polytechnique, in 1822 Louis d'Eichthal appointed Auguste Comte as a tutor to teach his son mathematics (ibid., 94). Gustave joined the lessons and the tutor, six years his senior, became his mentor and close friend. Gustave also supported the philosopher financially. In 1824, he was sent to Berlin to study and used the opportunity to disseminate Comte's positivistic philosophy in Germany, as well as to familiarise himself with contemporary German philosophy. He stayed with the Mendelssohn-Bartholdy family,[6] business partners and friends of his father, which led him into the intellectual society of Berlin salons. In 1825, his father then sent him to the Netherlands to learn about the coffee, sugar and grain trade, but Gustave was already sure that he had no wish to become a banker (Le Bret 2012, 107). The next stage in his training was England, where he travelled in the company of Adolphe – seeking to escape the despotism of his father, as Le Bret writes, but also to learn about the modern financial instruments of the London City, e.g. the savings banks (ibid., 134). The two brothers used their stay to study English society and all the consequences of industrialisation, similarly to Tocqueville five years later (Tocqueville 1835). They visited factories, mines, docks, the first railways, workers' housing and schools in many parts of the country; attended parliamentary debates, learnt about modern credit techniques and built up their networks. Adolphe completed an internship with Heath & Co. and was delighted with the financial centre of London. Gustave's diary, addressed to his father, reveals his enthusiasm for the industrial developments but also clearly shows that he was aware of the dark side of industrialisation, the social question (Ratcliffe 1977a). His most formative encounter was with John Stuart Mill, two years younger than him, who became a lifelong friend and correspondent.[7] The relationship to Comte suffered from Gustave's experiences abroad. He became convinced that an industrialised society could not manage without religion, a conviction that was clearly opposed to the positivism of his teacher, who believed the economy alone to be decisive. When he returned to the continent in 1829, after almost nine months in England, Gustave published a memorandum about the organisation of public credit in France, drawing on his English experiences (D'Eichthal 1829). His core thesis was that state debt should not be completely paid off, as the public debate in France demanded, but that the long-term borrowing of the state from its citizens was of benefit to all concerned. Many of his father's colleagues reacted positively to this publication, and the Saint-Simonians became aware of Gustave's activities (Le Bret 2012, 113, 135–138). Even before his time abroad, there had been points of contact with this group. One of Saint-Simon's students, Olinde Rodrigues, was a good friend of Gustave, and the fathers of the two young men were also close.[8] Furthermore, between 1817 and 1824, Auguste Comte was Saint-Simon's private secretary, overlapping with the time when he taught the d'Eichthals. Although the collaboration between Saint-Simon and Comte ended acrimoniously, Comte introduced Gustave to Saint-Simon shortly before the latter's death in 1825.[9] Comte later wrote articles for the Saint-Simonian journal *Le Producteur*, before he finally broke completely with the group in 1826. Comte was deeply disappointed when his student then joined the Saint-Simonians, and this created an unbridgeable breach between the two men. All contact between them ceased, despite Gustave's attempts to justify his decision (Le Bret 2012, 119f.).

Through the crisis-ridden time before and after the July revolution in France, the Saint-Simonian programme proved most attractive to the offspring of the Paris business elite, particularly so in banking circles.[10] The founding father of the movement, Claude Henri de Rouvroy, Comte de Saint-Simon (1760–1825), was a successful military and business man before he dedicated himself to philosophy.[11] He propagated a radical change of society at the transition from feudalism to industrialisation,[12] envisioning society as a community of workers of the hand and the spirit. This society was to be led by its most competent members according to principles of economic efficiency, thus by industrialists, bankers, scientists and also artists, but not by idlers who lived off their capital. Based on principles of equality, the necessary competence for leadership would be demonstrated only by individual abilities and actions, not by birth or place of origin. All available capital should be placed in the hands of the most able specialists to be used for the benefit of society;

this would involve the abolition of inheritance rights. Entrepreneurism and technical and scientific progress should help create a harmonious society and, in particular, improve the life of the lower classes. The banks were given the task of systematically managing the economy and investment through the granting of credit. Saint-Simon's decidedly pacifist construct included women within the principle of equality and granted them sexual freedom and divorce rights. The foundation of the new social order was to be shared religious values based on altruism and esteem for science.[13]

After Saint-Simon's death in 1825, his students Barthélemy Prosper Enfantin and Saint-Amand Bazard led the movement and continued to develop the doctrine. Under their dual leadership, the Saint-Simonian teachings became evermore mystified and evolved towards a 'Nouveau Christianisme', with the group increasingly resembling a sect. There were schisms and controversy within the movement, e.g. about their attitude towards the July revolution of 1830 (Régnier 2010, 23f.). After Bazard and Enfantin had been accused of inciting the masses in this context, the latter retreated to a ruined estate in Ménilmontant on the edge of Paris. Here, he and about forty of his followers, including Gustave d'Eichthal, lived in a celibate, quasi-monastic community (ibid., 25f.). Examination of the sources leads Ratcliffe to deduce that there was a sexual dimension to Gustave's devoted veneration of Enfantin.[14] The court case brought against the Saint-Simonians in 1832 gave them the chance to justify themselves. Gustave d'Eichthal used the opportunity to explain the fascination of the doctrine for members of his 'romantic' generation, who after the end of the Napoleonic wars had lacked possibilities to develop their strength and energy (Le Bret 2012, 212).[15] Enfantin and Bazard were given prison sentences, but were soon pardoned.

For Gustave, the affiliation to the community had serious consequences. He placed his entire private fortune at the disposal of the group when he became a member. His contributions totalled 150,000 francs, of which only 60,000 francs were returned in 1840 (ibid., 205, 210). As the son of a banker, in September 1831, he also became responsible for administering the finances of the movement. Furthermore, he contributed towards the development of the doctrine in a number of publications, for instance, in 'Lettre à un banquier' in the weekly Saint-Simonian newspaper *L'Organisateur*. His arguments underline the necessity of society having a canon of values and have similarities with those of modern sociologists like Francis Fukuyama. Religion is said to be indispensable 'because there is no node of industry without an association and no association without trust and no trust without *religion*'.[16] Taking this functional approach, Gustave advocated the necessity of new institutions to provide a basis of trust. The – morally purified – bankers were to take on an important role in this centrally managed economy by systematically granting credits. Gustave did not limit his activities to these publications; he also sought personal contacts, e.g. on missionary trips to Germany in July 1830 (during the July revolution) and to England from December 1831 to March 1832, where John Stuart Mill supported him (Le Bret 2012, 166f.). Moreover, he wrote numerous effusive letters to his friends, his father and his brother, trying to persuade them of the value of the doctrine and convince them to join the movement. As far as the family was concerned, these attempts failed, although Adolphe and even Louis had some sympathy for the Saint-Simonian ideas, thanks to their high estimation of Olinde Rodrigues; they particularly valued the proposals for new practices within the banking profession (ibid., 202). However, Adolphe rejected the notions of abolishing inheritance rights, socialising the means of production and cutting interest charged on loans, arguing that they were immoral and ridiculous. Their father had the impression that his eldest son was completely losing his head. As the community developed increasingly into a sect and news of its internal power struggles reached Paris, the family viewed Gustave's involvement as evermore detrimental for the reputation of the bank (ibid., 173). Appeals for loans to help the financially struggling community were correspondingly rejected by the d'Eichthals (ibid., 206). All members of the family tried to bring Gustave back to the family circle but this was only possible shortly before the start of the court case in November 1832 and led to him suffering a nervous breakdown because he felt like a traitor (Ratcliffe 1977b, 140).

Why Greece?

Most of the Saint-Simonians chose to find their way abroad after the court case. This was encouraged by the fact that the international dimension of Saint-Simonian teaching gave these stays abroad a purpose. As a space of encounter between the Orient and the Occident, the Mediterranean was of particular interest. In 1932, Michel Chevalier presented his 'Système de la Méditerranée' (1832) in a series of four articles published in the Saint-Simonian newspaper *Le Globe*. He envisioned using the equivalent of the military expenditure of the European nations over 12 years to construct a network of railways. This would connect the entire continent from Spain and southern France to St. Petersburg and Asia, via Frankfurt, southern Germany and Vienna to Thessaloniki and Constantinople. People would thus have the opportunity to get to know and value each other, and to cooperate in academia (Chevalier imagined a student from Göttingen who within 24 hours could visit the Louvre and the Jardin de Plantes in Paris). The economy would be stimulated and the prosperity of all regions would improve. In this plan for world peace, he envisioned a place for the powerful and for the artists, for the engineers and the industrialists, for the traders, the workers and the poor, and indeed for the bankers. It is thus hardly surprising that numerous Saint-Simonians chose Mediterranean countries within the French sphere of influence as their place of exile. Prosper Enfantin, for instance, pardoned in 1833 by Louis Philippe after nine months of imprisonment, turned to Egypt where he worked under Mohammed Ali developing plans for the building of the Suez Canal. His companions helped to found a polytechnic school in Boulac and a hospital in Kasr-Al-Aïny, trained Egyptian officers and took many positions in the country's administration (Régnier 2010, 26–30). In the 1840s, Enfantin then turned his attention to French Algeria (ibid., 31).

Chevalier only mentioned Greece briefly in his articles: 'It is Greece, the poetic Greece, the civilised Greece, the pleasant and fertile Greece, where the Orient and the Occident were as often uprooted as they were torn into tatters'.[17] Why did Gustave nonetheless choose to go there? Of course, the small, newly created state attracted a great deal of attention in France, not only from the Philhellenes, but also from the government. This is demonstrated, for example, by the despatch of an official state-funded scientific expedition to Greece in 1828–1833, which was tasked with gathering knowledge in the fields of art, architecture, classical studies, geology, zoology and botany.[18] Nevertheless, no previous mention of Greece is found in Gustave's drawings, letters or writings. This is all the more astounding as he had indeed come into contact with Philhellenism at various instances. Not only was Gustave's close schoolfriend Gustave de Gérando active in the Société de la morale chrétienne in Paris, which organised French help for Greece (Le Bret 2012, 87), but since 1828 Adolphe d'Eichthal had been one of its administrators (Stoskopf 2002a, 161). Gustave would also certainly have been confronted by the topic when he visited the salon of Rahel Varnhagen von Ense in Berlin, whose husband rhapsodised over the Greek struggle for independence, following all the news that came out of Greece with great emotional involvement.[19] Gustave must also have witnessed debates about Greece in England in 1828/1829, even if *The Times* scandal about the Greek loans of 1824/1825 occurred two years earlier. John Stuart Mill, who distanced himself from the Benthamites at this time, may have spoken to d'Eichthal about this episode of Greek loans, embarrassing as it was for Bentham.[20] But when reporting on encounters with Francis Burdett and John Hobhouse, Gustave did not even mention their involvement in the Greek cause.[21] Despite his classical education, it seems that before 1832, the Greek struggle for independence held no significance for Gustave – in contrast to his mother who had always been passionate about Ancient Greece.[22]

Where did the idea of a journey to Greece come from? One trail leads to the Munich branch of the family, Gustave's uncle Simon von Eichthal. Since the death of his father Aaron in 1824, Simon had been head of the Munich banking house and had taken over the position of *Hoffaktor* at the Munich court. He became involved in the Munich Philhellene association early on.[23] In contrast to the situation in most European cities, in Munich, Philhellenism was not to be understood as a liberal opposition to absolutist rulership (Tornow 1977, 178f.).[24] Here, it was rather the case that support for Greece stemmed from Crown Prince Ludwig, from 1825 Ludwig I of Bavaria, who desired the involvement of the Munich dignitaries (Krauss 1987, 279f.; Spaenle 1990). Both liberal and conservative powers were active within Ludwig's Philhellenism (Spaenle 1990, 86). It is therefore difficult to say whether Simon joined the association due to enthusiasm for the cause or rather for reasons of opportunism. Several of his letters to the Bavarian General Heideck (Seewald 2009) from the years 1826 to 1829, when the general was in Greece supporting the freedom fighters, have survived. In the at times humorous letters, Eichthal avoids all mention of politics so as not to provide the censor with any reason to intervene, as he himself wrote.[25] He often mentioned the prestige this exchange of letters with Heideck brought him in Munich society and with the king.[26] Moreover, he undertook practical action to support the struggle for independence, organising funding for Heideck through the Munich Philhellene Association[27] and ensuring that he was supplied with money via business partners in southern Italy and on the Ionian Islands. He chuckled over Heideck's idealistic expectations of receiving free help from the local bankers:

> But you are not right to complain about the deduction [made by a banking house in Ancona from a transfer from Munich K.S.], because what should we bankers live well from if we do not fleece gentlemen like you. At other times you well understand the art of allowing the Courants from our sacks to wander into your own. After all, we are still polite and use no violence and only plunder with our wits.[28]

In his replies, Heydeck reported in detail on the country and the people, the botany and the agriculture, the condition of the ships and the state of the roads,[29] the adventures of the journey, military actions and the difficulties besetting the cooperation between the Bavarian and Greek troops. He also sent full statements concerning the way in which the donated money had been spent.[30] Many of his letters from Greece were printed in the Bavarian press (Spaenle 1990, 178).

When Otto I, the second son of Ludwig I, came to the Greek throne in 1832, Simon von Eichthal was given the task of organising the finances of the fledgling king: he became his *Hoffaktor* and thus in practice took on the role of a finance minister. Particularly important was the issuing of the loan of 60 million francs guaranteed by the Great Powers, which required the involvement of a reputed issuing house. Simon tackled his new tasks with great energy. Not only did he plan to send his son Rudolf (1810–1854) to Greece (Le Bret 2012, 218),[31] but his brother Arnold from Augsburg also sent his son Wilhelm (born 1805) to Nafplio as royal legation councillor (Hohenlohe-Schillingsfürst 1953, 117).[32] Simultaneously, Adolphe d'Eichthal successfully applied to be the consul general of Greece in Paris. This multiple deployment of the entire family demonstrates how interested the von Eichthals were in the new market. Given the dynamic context of banking in the 1830s, this is hardly surprising; for instance, the Rothschilds were also working to further extend their European network at this time.[33]

The idea to also send Gustave to Greece may well have come from Adolphe, who first advised his brother to travel to the country in December 1832, shortly after Gustave had left Ménilmontant. Once Gustave was there, Adolphe suggested, then Simon should obtain a request from the Bavarian regency to the French foreign minister de Broglie asking that Gustave be included in the French legation in Athens. King Otto would certainly welcome the presence of a member of the family who was so loyal to the Wittelsbachers in Munich. Such a position could, Adolphe suggested, represent the first steps of a diplomatic career.[34] Louis therefore asked his brother Simon in Munich to use his good connections to the king's court to organise a post for Gustave in the new Greek administration in Nafplio (Le Bret 2012, 218). This should in no way be interpreted as the exclusion or banishment of Gustave from the family circle: 'Being gone was not a position outside, but inside the family' (Sabean/Teuscher 2011, 6).[35] At the beginning of 1833, the plans became more concrete and Louis and Adolphe considered whether Gustave could be sent to Nafplio as the bearer of the contract for the loan between Greece and the Great Powers, an idea that Simon was not keen to take up.[36] He pointed out that he should not misuse his position to sponsor his relatives and advance them into state posts. This had only been possible in the case of his nephew Wilhelm because Wilhelm was working without payment. Simon suggested adopting a more indirect approach for Gustave.[37] This did nothing to dampen Adolphe's enthusiasm for his brother's trip to Greece. He believed that the ancient people were reawakening to new life so there was room for all kinds of activities, even if Gustave's past made an official position difficult at the moment. The infrastructure needed development, as did the agriculture and the military, so Gustave would be able to choose between numerous fields of occupation. Adolphe also named two areas of business in the new market that seemed particularly lucrative. Firstly, with increasing stability, a bank would certainly be of use and could profit from and support the rapid development of the country. Secondly, Gustave should get to know the country well enough to identify areas where land values could be expected to increase quickly.[38] Adolphe was also interested in military contracts.[39] He proudly reported on his forthcoming nomination as the consul general, affirmed his intention to pursue activities in Greece that would be to his advantage but also to the advantage of the country, and seemed convinced that Greece had a promising economic future. Even though he could not himself undertake a journey there, in his position as the consul general and from respect to Uncle Simon, he wanted to advance Greek affairs 'with the same zeal as if they affected me myself'.[40] His brother should send him all available information about the country, its inhabitants, its imports and exports, land ownership and other 'fruitful matters'. 'Make this journey your work'. It would also be important to make many contacts in both business and political circles, and Gustave should spare no effort to achieve this: 'Make yourself a courtier, both for yourself and for us'.[41] Personal relationships were indispensible, especially in such an under-established economic market that was so dependent on politics.[42] Adolphe's hopes were also coloured by thoughts of the competition; the young Rothschild from London was on his way to Greece to investigate new business opportunities there: 'Ensure to get there first and to place us favourably'.[43] Although Adolphe would dearly like to embrace his brother again, Gustave should this time see his project through to the end and not return home without some success.[44] He should find a way to establish himself and stay as long as necessary.[45]

The notion of the journey being something of a probation for the 'black sheep' Gustave, and an opportunity for his rehabilitation, was much more important for the older generation than for Adolphe. Gustave's uncle Arnold from Augsburg wrote to Louis, who forwarded the letter to Gustave with no further comment:

> As far, dear friend, as your son is concerned, I believe that no cure could be as appropriate for him as the travel cure that he is now undertaking. I have very little doubt that after he has pinned back the ears of several bakers in Constantinople, because of the bread being too light, and on classical Greek ground has acquainted himself with the present-day inhabitants, who run around as naked and dirty as their dogs, only covered with more fleas, then he will, even without taking into account the experiences that await him in Egypt, become convinced that France is after all a country where a free-minded man can live without having the duty imposed on him of having to shoot himself to death.[46]

Thus while his brother focused on hopes of tapping into a new, promising market,[47] his father's generation was more concerned with 'grounding' the idealistic Gustave, using deterrence to bring him back to the proper path. The father and son left in Paris did not always have the same agenda or the same ideas about Greece. The older generation of von Eichthals viewed the Greeks as uncivilised, primitive, crude, brutal and without exception unkempt, as Todorova suggests is typical of West European perceptions of the Balkans (Todorova 1997, 32). There was no question of doubting their own cultural superiority here; it was self-evidently taken for granted. Which of the two images of Greece would dominate interpretations in decision-making situations was greatly dependent on Gustave's reports and experiences.

While their motives may have differed, both generations in Paris and in Munich did their utmost to ensure the success of the journey, drawing on all possible relationships within their networks.[48] Simon contacted the – rather sceptical – Joseph von Armansperg, head of the regency, and the Duke of

Dalberg,[49] Adolphe several times arranged to meet the Greek ambassador Mihail II Soutzos and his wife, and similarly the foreign minister Victor de Broglie.[50] Louis organised letters of recommendation from the British embassy in Paris, from Salomon Rothschild in Naples and from Georg Simon von Sina in Vienna.[51] Letters of credit were sent to finance the journey.

Could Gustave have rejected the suggestion of his family and rebelled against the authority of his father? His financial circumstances alone made this extremely difficult, especially after the failure of his expensive experiment with Saint-Simonism.[52] After his arrival, Gustave interpreted his journey as follows:

> It was necessary that the seizure of power by Otto there in a way positioned my family, and that, on the other hand, my passion for running after the good and the beautiful has prevented me from settling anywhere else until now. Here I therefore hope to find united the well-being of the family and everything else.[53]

Gustave's friend and another enthusiastic Philhellene Saint-Hilaire later suggested that visiting Greece was Gustave's own decision, but this retrospective interpretation seems somewhat unlikely (Queux Saint-Hilaire 1887, 9).

Gustave d'Eichthal's visit to Greece (1833–1835)

In October 1833, Gustave arrived full of energy, ideas and dreams in Nafplio and began to provide the family with detailed information about the country and its people.[54] Even though his cousin Rudolf did not accompany him after all, in Nafplio, he had the support of another cousin, Wilhelm, who was one of those Bavarians 'who most strongly believed in the future of Greece'.[55] Gustave had heard of the deficiencies of the Bavarian regency when in Corfu, on British territory,[56] but he nonetheless planned to enter into their service either as an officer or in the administration. Based largely on negative experiences during his travels, he described the Greeks as stubborn, proud and focused on their own advantage, characteristics that – if directed appropriately – qualified them for greatness.[57] From the very start of his travels, he therefore pursued the notion of attracting West European colonists to Greece in order to dilute the intractability of the locals, following the example here of Saint-Simon who concerned himself for many years with the sale of Spanish national estates (Régnier 2010, 15). The colonisation project seems to have been the only one that Gustave pursued and developed on his own initiative, without receiving the suggestion from Paris.[58]

He did not stay long in Nafplio before continuing his journey to Athens, motivated by a wish to see the country.[59] On the way, he fell seriously ill with dysentery. By February 1834, he was back in Nafplio, convinced of the stability and liberality of the Bavarian regency and the prosperity of the country: 'The longer one stays on this earth, the more one has to admire it, be in love with it; this expression is the only fitting one'.[60] Gustave satisfied the desire of his family for information about the economy, although he did require some prompting from his father, who forbade him to send letters that were only about ruined antiquities.[61] Instead, Gustave provided detailed descriptions of business activities, e.g. about the large quantities of land in and around Athens that were being bought by a group of Frenchmen who wanted to establish a model farm. He believed that continued purchases of this sort would lead to a boom in land prices around Athens,[62] and gathered information about land for sale which he promised to send to Paris. He also reported on changes in the legal system, e.g. in penal law.[63] In letters to his friends, his tone was more lyrical: the country would need cities, theatres and concert halls as well as streets, harbours and ships: 'All this I imagine dancing before my eyes'.[64]

After almost half a year, Gustave then seemed to find a way to translate his ideas into reality and set up the Office for Political Economy (Bureau d'economie politique) within the ministry of the interior. Here, he was joined by the temperamental French republican Alexandre de Roujoux, who like Gustave was an ex-pupil of the Lycée Henri IV, was associated with the French legation and mastered the local language, and also by the experienced Greek merchant and freedom fighter Nikolaos Poniropoulos.[65] Friedrich Thiersch had called for the establishment of such an institute in an exposé about Greece published a year earlier (Thiersch 1833; Psalidopoulos/Mata 2002; Scholler 2008; Baloglou 2009, 170; Psalidopoulos/Theocarakis 2011). The Francophile minister of the interior, Ioannis Kolettis, was patron of the office, which was primarily intended to focus on the statistical documentation of the country and organise colonisation. Gustave hoped to act as a successful intermediary between the two worlds. He explained to his family that the Greeks were clever in business matters and finance and would certainly adopt any industrial improvements from Europe that could enhance the value of their country.[66] The local Greeks were certain to accept industrial colonies in particular, and probably agricultural ones too as long as the redistribution of the national estates was satisfactorily organised. The colonies remained his favourite project. Gustave read around the subject and sent both the Bavarian regency and his brother and friends suggestions concerning the choice and organisation of colonists from England, France and Germany. 'You can promise your friends who are willing to colonize a beautiful sky and a liberal government; the Greek citizenship; freedom of faith; absence of peerage, a law, excellent customs, an extraordinary fertile soil, etc'.[67] D'Eichthal regarded the absence of a feudal system and religious freedom as brilliant conditions for attracting colonists. He could imagine all kinds of property rights,[68] from purchasing land to various long concessions. Messenia and Elis seemed to be particularly appropriate, thanks to their proximity to Europe, the beauty of the coasts, the richness of the woodland and their fertility. Other nations might beat the French to it, Gustave argued with concern. The new British Poor Laws had triggered a wave of emigration which he believed could lead to the areas being British and Austrian if France did not become actively involved. This project seemed at last to have given him a task and a goal, and an identity as an intermediary in the Saint-Simonian sense. He expressly presented it as a 'soft glimmer for the future' in the series of Saint-Simonian initiatives in Egypt, Great Britain and America.[69] In May, he was officially named as a member of the Office for Political Economy. The only downside seemed to be the conflictive and complicated politics of the Great Powers and their local representatives, especially the British envoy, and the intrigues surrounding the regency.[70]

He eagerly began work, drawing up a draft law to distribute the national estates among the veterans of the struggle for independence, which he regarded as a conditio sine qua non for establishing colonies. He discovered that the ownership structures in many regions were completely unclear, and proposed to the regency that a cadastre should be compiled, planning to bring order to the country through the use of modern technical and scientific methods. This would provide a basis upon which the first permits could be granted to the local municipalities and the poor in the coming spring, while the remainder of the land could be auctioned off once the king reached his majority, with consideration of the interested parties from Britain, Germany, France and Italy.[71] The draft legislation was submitted, but was initially delayed. It failed to correspond with the interests of the regency or with those of the Great Powers, who had been given the national estates as guarantee for the loan of 60 million francs. At least now Jean Gabriel Eynard's trusted friend Françäis Arthemond de Regny had taken up his position as financial advisor to the government and strictly monitored any sales of land, which until then had been seriously undervalued (Ratcliffe 1977b, 144).

Just a few months later, Gustave's hopes of making an effective contribution in Greece were shattered. His Saint-Simonian past was the official reason for his removal from office. In 1834, a revolt against the regency erupted on the Peloponnese, which can be viewed as the climax of the power struggle between the leader of the regency von Armansperg and the minister of the interior Kolettis (Petropulos 1968, 218–233).[72] Then in August, three impecunious Saint-Simonians arrived in Nafplio and turned to Gustave for help. In October, Kolettis received two official letters from the regency, strictly forbidding all Saint-Simonian activities in Greece and demanding that the minister discharge d'Eichthal from his position.[73] Kolettis insisted that both d'Eichthal and the new arrivals were completely harmless and denied any risk of conspiracy. Initially, he also allowed Gustave to remain in office.[74] Gustave then entered into discussions with von Armansperg,[75] who proclaimed that he was unsatisfied with the achievements of the office, which had only managed to produce one draft version of legislation. Gustave reacted with annoyance and displayed little diplomacy. He tried to explain to the other member of the regency Ägid von Kobel, with whom he had a better understanding, that establishing colonies before the national estates were distributed among the local population would be completely irresponsible as the colonists would only be exposed to the locals' envy, hunger and poverty.[76] Was dissatisfaction with the work of the office the real reason for Gustave's dismissal? He himself remained puzzled, but it seems likely that d'Eichthal was a victim of power struggles at the court of Nafplio (Petropulos 1985/1986, 212–217). The only information that Gustave received from von Kobel was that his dismissal had not been ordered from Munich. Even a royal audience failed to clarify the situation as the king actually urged Gustave's departure because there were so many foreigners looking for accommodation in Nafplio.[77] Gustave wanted to resign but Kolettis encouraged him to remain in the position of state counsellor, to take some holiday and journey through the provinces of Livandie and Phtoiotide on the Peloponnesus. Gustave agreed to this suggestion, commencing his journey at a very unfavourable time of year (Queux Saint-Hilaire 1887, 40f.). At least he was travelling in a district where Kolettis' family and dependents, from whom he could hope for support, owned a great deal of land.[78]

At the beginning of November, Gustave went first to Athens, from where he began his journey, accompanied by a servant and three horses. In his diary, he focused particularly on his 'sociological' interest in the real estate of the country, with which he had been so theoretically concerned in recent months. He found property ownership taking completely different forms in different eparchies and municipalities.[79] In some places, the Ottoman rulers had totally abolished all private property so that in Thebes even the houses belonged to the national estates. In many places, such circumstances prevented effective agriculture.[80] Where the land was still privately owned, like in the area around Lake Copais, property was mostly fragmented as a result of the inheritance traditions.[81] Elsewhere, property rights had been so completely disordered during the revolution that they were now completely obscure and the municipalities had lost their urgently needed common land.[82] The ownership structures of the monasteries also required regulation.[83] While rich Greeks from abroad demanded that the monastic land should be immediately expropriated and the monks evicted, local Greeks were appalled at the authoritarian abolition of certain monasteries, a step that not even the Turks had dared to take during their centuries of rule.[84] Gustave recommended that whatever decision was reached, the land should continue to be cultivated by the present, competent tenants.

Naturally, he continued to pursue the idea of colonisation, but his initial euphoria quickly vanished. The Greeks, he had to concede, were – in spite of their hospitality to travellers – quite hostile to immigrants.[85] He was shocked by the poverty and the poor treatment dealt out by the Greeks to the refugees from Thessaly.[86] How would they behave towards settlers from foreign countries with different beliefs when there was not even a chance of close marriage ties? The dignitaries and landowners with whom he discussed this topic assessed the possibilities of success very differently. Some believed that founding colonies would be difficult but should be attempted, particularly where there was a lack of labour. Others believed that the native Greeks would react to such a project with brute force, turning against the colonists.[87] D'Eichthal summed up the situation negatively, 'Concerning this last point, I do not have, for my part, the courage to call one single colonist to Greece before a national assembly is pronounced'.[88]

Instead, he recommended local improvements, e.g. using the taxation system to improve agriculture and the economy. At present, he argued, taxation privileged livestock farming over arable farming. This meant that livestock farming was increasing to such an extent that in many places, there was a shortage of grazing and severe tension between the Greek population and the nomadic Vlachs.[89] Arable farming, however, could be greatly intensified, e.g. through reducing taxes which in some cases amounted to 25%, by using fertiliser or by alternating crops instead of leaving land fallow.[90] Gustave demonstrated that he was also acquainted with the latest state of scientific knowledge concerning agriculture. He pointed out that monthly interest rates of 2% (so 24% per year) were much too high for investment in innovative cultivation techniques, so only rich landowners were able to experiment, e.g. by growing cotton.[91] D'Eichthal discussed founding a bank to help alleviate this state of affairs with local dignitaries.[92]

Although he was familiar with the misery of the working-class areas of London and Manchester, he was nonetheless affected by the poverty he encountered in many places.[93] On his journey through the bitter winter cold, he described the paltry huts in which many Greeks lived, and the high rate of child mortality. Instead of medical care, it was normal for the bible to be read aloud by the fathers.[94] He heard repeatedly of deserters from the Bavarian forces or the Greek troops who received no pay, lived a vagabond existence and starved.[95] He frequently described the authorities as corrupt,[96] the harbours and roads as being in a catastrophic condition. Although there had once been manufactories, e.g. of textiles, these had disappeared and the farmers had to import their clothes, their grain and their cattle from abroad, while there were hardly any goods to export.[97] However, there were local landowners who ruled over their subjects in an almost feudal fashion and were not sparing of pomp.[98] D'Eichthal proposed that, adopting the practices of Western Europe, a survey should be conducted to document the state of the eparchies.[99] What he gathered on his travels could be no more than an initial impression.

Gustave also used the time on his travels to learn Greek, which he was then able to speak fluently by the end of his journey.[100] He thought about retreating to a small, picturesque estate somewhere in Greece, perhaps with his colleague and friend Roujoux.[101] However, abandoning these plans he returned to Athens, now the seat of government, at the beginning of January 1835.

In June 1835, Otto I achieved his majority and took over the government. To Gustave's disappointment, he named von Armansperg as his chancellor, apparently pressured to do so by his father from Munich and the British diplomats (Petropulos 1968, 232). This represented a victory for the English and Russian parties against Kolettis, who was supported by the French and who d'Eichthal regarded as embodying progress.[102] Kolettis was requested by von Armansperg to resign as minister of the interior and in 1835 was sent to Paris as ambassador (Krauss 1987, 309). The fall of his patron meant that Gustave had little choice other than to leave for home, having made a farewell visit to the king (Queux Saint-Hilaire 1887, 71). Officially, he had still not been dismissed and was only on leave, but he never returned to Greece.[103] In contrast, Saint-Simonian ideas continued to survive in the country (Baloglou 2009).

Investment ideas in the family

The reports about Greece sent by Gustave d'Eichthal were the basis upon which his father and his brother in Paris developed their investment ideas for this new market. After returning from England in 1830, Adolphe d'Eichthal had become a part-owner of his father's bank. The relationship between the two partners was not easy; they were both quick-tempered. Louis regarded some of Adolphe's investments as worthless, for instance in mining, but allowed his son to go ahead regardless.[104] In 1834, Adolphe married Louisa de La Rüe, the daughter of a Protestant Geneva banker and granddaughter of the London banker Heath with whom he had completed his internship. She brought 125,000 francs as dowry into the marriage and thus decisively strengthened Adolphe's position in his father's bank. Adolphe himself brought 200,000 francs to the marriage (Stoskopf 2002a, 161).[105] In 1835, a daughter was born, the first of three children, who they named Louisa. Adolphe, whose business in France was ever more successful, had clearly established himself as a banker and member of the bourgeoisie in Paris.

How did the two Paris bankers react to Gustave's information from Greece? What risks and opportunities did they see, where did their perceptions diverge and how did they justify and legitimate their decisions? What role did Simon play in Munich, as the *Hoffaktor* of Otto in Greece, who was entrusted with handling the 60-million loan?

Initially, Louis and Adolphe were delighted about Gustave's development and plans. Adolphe euphorically predicted that Gustave's professional expertise would bring him an important position in the ministry and city council.[106] Louis, who was always fascinated by exact science, greeted the establishment of the Office for Political Economy with warm words[107] and saw his son as being well on the way to becoming a state counsellor[108] and a 'positive man of action'.[109] However, he also reacted most sensitively when he had the impression that Gustave was developing new 'hollow ideas'[110] and drifting into lyricism[111] – he remembered negative experiences with such enthusiastic 'framings' from decision-making situations in Gustave's Saint-Simonian time. Louis then relentlessly presented Gustave with the image of his younger brother who was busy with wedding preparations, and assured him that the family was also looking for a good match for Gustave. He should finally also embark on 'something rational' and justify his father's belief in him.[112] Alongside such hard words however, Louis was also extremely concerned about his son's health, warned him against overworking and advised him to make frequent trips into the country to relax, and told him to buy a horse to spare himself.[113] From affection for his son, the old banker even supported some of Gustave's Saint-Simonian friends in Paris.[114]

The father and son in Paris were interested in various investment opportunities in Greece. Louis often mentioned the construction of a canal through to the Isthmus of Corinth. In connection with the plans of the regency to move the seat of government from Nafplio to Athens, he reasoned that Corinth, economically speaking, had much more to recommend it, even if the reconstruction of the ruins of Athens would bring more glory.[115] Louis consistently tried to exclude enthusiasm for antiquity as an argument for economic decisions. The idea of a trading centre on the Isthmus was also publicly discussed in Greece (Baloglou 2009, 169). Louis recommended that Gustave keep an eye open for possible land purchases in the surroundings of Corinth, as property here could increase in value with the building of the canal. Gustave should gather information about the prospects of such a canal, even if a permit from the chamber[116] would certainly not be easy to come by.[117] The reason why Louis then abandoned this idea seems to have had little to do with Greece: at the beginning of 1834, he reported that the d'Eichthal banking house was so preoccupied with the Paris-St. Germain Railway Construction Company, initiated by Adolphe, that there was no capacity for further infrastructure projects in Greece.[118] Behavioural finance would talk here of a home bias (Tesar/Werner 1995): investments in his own geographical surroundings seemed much more promising to Louis than ones in unknown and remote locations. Gustave had in any case not reacted to the suggestions and had delivered no relevant information on a possible canal.

Adolphe's interest was in establishing a steamship company from Greece to Constantinople and Egypt on the one hand, and to Italy and France on the other, as he reported to Gustave as early as May 1833.[119] Parisian competitors were also interested in the project, so haste seemed called for.[120] Even before his brother's arrival, Adolphe was working on his plans and sent them to von Armansperg.[121] This was an expensive project which could not be initiated without generous funding from the Greek government.

He tasked Gustave with discovering how things stood with von Armansperg, and commented that a timely trade agreement between Greece and France would improve the prospects.[122] At the beginning of 1834, Adolphe gathered more detailed information in Marseille and Genoa, even though it seemed unlikely that any decision would be made by the regency before the next winter.[123] Gustave clearly passed on his brother's enquiries to the regency,[124] but it seems the matter was not further pursued because no reaction was forthcoming from the Bavarian regency who seemed thoroughly disinterested. The founding of a shipping line in 1837 then apparently had nothing to do with the d'Eichthals.[125]

Adolphe's early suggestion concerning the purchase of land was one of the most intensively discussed projects, particularly as Gustave was very active here and gathered detailed information. Louis also reiterated his interest in the topic. However, Simon in Munich held a very different opinion, as proven by extracts from Simon's letters that Louis copied for Gustave. Simon claimed that he had followed developments in Greece for ten years and had friends there who were extremely well-informed about the situation. He planned no great investments as the country lacked resources.[126] While he admitted that there was a chance of earning 15–20% in real estate speculations in Greece, he suggested that there was neither the manpower nor the equipment to cultivate the ground.[127] Simon portrayed himself as risk-adverse in this assessment, a self-image that was frequently evoked by bankers in the nineteenth century (Pohle-Fraser 1999, 100ff.). Nonetheless, he felt himself bound by family loyalty:

> If however you would like to undertake something in Greece, and wish me to participate with a modest sum I would not refuse you so as to give you proof of my liking and the interest I take in your son Gustave.[128]

Louis did not allow his brother's opinion to completely dampen his interest in land speculation. He emphasised that even if this was perhaps not the moment to embark on the project, such information could be of great use later.[129] As for many of those active on the financial markets, the behaviour of competitors was important for Louis, and he was therefore very interested in Gustave's reports concerning the investments of other bankers.[130] The competitors seemed more willing to take a risk than his brother in Munich. Thus, Louis discovered that the Baring banking house in London supposedly wanted to invest £100,000 in a company to buy Greek land.[131] And Sophie de Marbois-Lebrun, Duchess of Plaisance, a Philhellene of French origin, bought great estates around Athens.[132] If Gustave wanted to participate in a joint-stock company in this field, then, Louis emphasised, he should do so only in the company of first-class houses and keep speculators and the holders of the old Greek bonds from 1824/1825 at a distance.[133] Louis believed that it was not impossible to find investors with an interest in Greek stocks, and that public interest in reminiscing about antiquity played a role here. He cautioned, however, that the path from basic interest to an actual investment was a long one, as they were currently discovering in the search for investors in the railway project in France.[134] Sometimes, his tone became sharper: it was very doubtful that the City of London or the Paris exchange would put their trust or capital in his business as long as Gustave had not proved himself. 'I think that you are once again creating a sweet illusion for yourself. I do not believe that you can get a foothold in the world with this project. More positive and more serious acts are necessary'.[135] Gustave should engage with the local and foreign capitalists to find better projects.[136] Louis moved from one extreme to the other, was sometimes influenced by Simon as the self-declared expert, but at other times wanted to copy the investment behaviour of other bankers who seemed to be more risk-oriented. It is striking that he always referred to the opinions of others rather than developing and maintaining his own point of view. Adolphe, who was later to be the founder of the French mortgage bank (Le Bret 2012, 419–426), remained optimistic for longer than his father. He continued to encourage Gustave to address real estate issues.[137] When the situation in Greece had stabilised (and only then), it would be possible to think about buying an estate. Their father had already invested a great deal of money in Gustave, but his business was so successful that he would be able to provide their sister Anette with a good dowry and at the same time provide Gustave with money for a project in Greece.[138] Closely linked to this project were Gustave's plans to produce a cadastre from his position in the Office for Political Economy.[139] Although the family welcomed his activities in this institution, Louis advised him to be cautious concerning the cadastre: the classification of land was certainly not simple in practice, and a cadastre that was used as a basis for distributing the estates could damage French interests[140] – after all, the national estates were the guarantee for the 60-million-franc loan.[141] Perhaps Adolphe was also referring to the fact that after the land had been reliably classified, the scope for speculation, as the d'Eichthals planned, would inevitably be curtailed. The family reacted positively to Gustave's draft legislation on the distribution of the national estates, but they also heard from Munich that it had been neglected by the regency for months.[142] Then in June 1835, a law was passed that at least regulated the acquisition of land by small farmers (Πετρόπουλος [Petropulos] 1985/1986, 236ff.).

For Gustave himself, the cadastre was only part of the preparations for his plan to bring colonists from Western Europe to Greece – the primary idea on which his activities as an intermediary were focused. The plan, certainly inspired by French experience in Algeria, was not wholly illusionary, but had already been discussed under Kapodistrias (Baloglou 2009, 170). In June 1834, the project of a military colony was given a legal anchor (Maurer 1968, 99). Louis regarded these plans very sceptically, referring explicitly to

Uncle Simon who did not want to be involved in the establishment of colonies and without whom Louis was also unwilling to participate.[143] He nonetheless offered his advice about how such a project should be organised: the length of time for which the government would make no claims on the colonists (in the form of taxes or fees) was of decisive importance. Gustave argued geostrategically that France could be overtaken by Great Britain and thus lose influence, but Louis rejected this: if there were going to be colonies, then it would be better to get the first colonists from England or Russia rather than from France.[144] There would then still be enough room for the French, especially as they were usually the better colonists.[145] Adolphe was also far from encouraging on the subject of colonisation, suggesting that his brother was overly optimistic. Such a step would only be possible after a thorough statistical cadastre had been completed.[146] He reported that his information suggested that the inhabitants of Provence or Languedoc were most unlikely to allow themselves to be persuaded to migrate to Greece, and advised Gustave to concentrate instead on the Greeks abroad who could be expected to return home with much capital once stability was assured.[147] The Paris bankers regarded the Greek diaspora as having a moral responsibility to get involved in Greek affairs: Louis found it obvious that bankers with Greek roots or new links to Greece via marriage should show financial commitment to the country.[148] When Gustave failed with both his cadastre and the distribution of the national estates, Adolphe comforted him that in the tight financial situation, others would certainly make use of Gustave's work and further develop it.[149] On the issue of colonisation, the interests of the intermediary and the bankers diverged. While Gustave was concerned with the philanthropically motivated improvement of the country in cultural and economic terms and planned to achieve this with foreign colonists and by strengthening French influence in Greece, the family was not at all interested in these Saint-Simonian geopolitics. Louis and Adolphe focused solely on the profit opportunities of the individual projects. They interpreted Gustave's lyrical arguments as unrealistic, a view that was also coloured by their past experience with the young man.

Closely connected to the question of property rights and investments in agriculture was the establishment of a bank, something Adolphe planned before Gustave's departure and that was also being pursued by a number of other financiers.[150] Louis again allowed himself to be guided by Simon, who viewed the idea somewhat negatively: of course, the foundation of the first Greek bank could represent splendid business, but due to the climate, poor living conditions and Russian intrigues against all kinds of liberal institutions, a very reliable and strong character would be needed for this job – it was unnecessary to point out that this last criterion disqualified Gustave.[151] Simon was reluctant to lead the business himself as his own sons were still too young to deputise for him in Munich. Louis copied the letter for Gustave (like he copied Gustave's letters for Simon)[152] and added: 'I think my dear friend that this letter will fix your ideas about what remains for you to do in Greece in all manners [...]'.[153] Gustave should soon leave the country, e.g. in the direction of England – and this at the end of 1833, just after Gustave had arrived in Greece! Neither Louis' nor Simon's opinions were particularly consistent, however.[154] In later letters, Louis held forth about the possibility of founding a bank in Nafplio. Pioneers were always given great opportunities, even if they also faced high risks. Decisive for his about-turn was again the behaviour of the competition: via Simon, the Rothschilds had communicated their interest in Gustave's trip to Greece, and they could prove helpful.[155] Adolphe remained, at least during the first year, much more positive in his assessment and much more ready to take risks, even though he thought it unlikely that he would himself travel: 'Your descriptions, your enthusiasm make me also fall in love with Greece'.[156] He repeatedly emphasised his great interest in Gustave's descriptions of the country and the people and his pleasure in having the opportunity to thus learn so much about a country that was completely unknown in Europe, even though Europeans had been concerned with it for 15 years.[157] Adolphe would have welcomed an extension of Greece towards Constantinople, where the state could have played an independent and respected role and helped to secure freedom in Europe, and he firmly believed that the Mediterranean area would soon regain its old significance.[158] At least in his general thoughts, Adolphe clearly picked up on Gustave's geostrategic reflections.

It was not until Gustave reported on his travels through the countryside from November 1834 that Adolphe's assessment changed, as he expressed in a long letter to his brother. He initially blamed the unstable political situation both domestic and foreign: the state of European-Bavarian Greece as described by Gustave was most unfortunate, its continued existence was not certain and the accession of the young king to government could lead to further crises. He also argued that there was a lack of institutions: the founding of a mortgage bank for agriculture was not possible as long as the property rights were so confused.

> It would therefore be imprudent to commence with any business of any importance and as this is our conviction you can believe that we could not commit our friends to do what seems too risky for us.[159]

His third line of argument was thus concerned with the moral responsibility of the banker for his customers and partners: if the risks were too high for him, he could not recommend the investment to anyone else. But also in a wider context, it was 'certainly very difficult to find bankers or speculators disposed to risk their capital'.[160] But these arguments did not suffice for Adolphe; he returned to the philanthropic Saint-Simonian level to justify his refusal, arguing that the purchase of land by foreigners for their own use was not of benefit to Greece. Rather than have some administrator placed on an estate who has to import everything, it would be more sensible to organise the import of cattle, seeds and materials, and then to make these imports available to the local inhabitants at good conditions. Finally, Adolphe argued by referring to the situation of the d'Eichthal bank: while the last two years had not been bad, it was nonetheless not in a position to tie up great amounts of capital in Greece.[161] The d'Eichthals were not able to throw 20,000 francs out of the window.[162] Adolphe concluded his risk analysis: Greece was too far away and too little known to risk investment there. 'Do not therefore count on financial cooperation until a new order, unless the face of affairs in Greece changes greatly'.[163] This way of closing a process of risk perception is almost too paradigmatic. From the plethora of information gathered from the intermediary and other sources, only those few pieces are selected that can be put together to create a coherent and clear picture. Past experience with Gustave played a significant role in this interpretation, but references to Simon's expert knowledge, the fear of loss and a lack of control also influenced the interpretation. All elements were combined to create a familiar picture: Greece as a chaotic Oriental country, which was too far away and too unknown for Western-style banking to be practised there. Precisely in the sense of a home bias, such investments in an unknown, far-off place were not an option for Adolphe.

The chronology of events makes it clear that it was not just the reports from their intermediary that caused the image of Greece to be actualised in a negative fashion. Gustave arrived in Greece in October 1833 and in December, Simon announced his withdrawal from all investment plans, even though he had initially supported Gustave's journey to Greece. The question arises as to why Simon experienced such a change of heart. In order to understand this, it is necessary to consider whether Simon and the rest of the von Eichthal family had other experiences and learning processes related to business in Greece, other than the reports from Gustave. In fact, the first large project that the new Athens *Hoffaktor* Simon von Eichthal promoted proved extremely complicated: the organisation of the guaranteed loan of 60 million francs at the time when Otto took office (Schönhärl 2019b).

Digression: the Rothschilds and the guaranteed loan of 1833

The guaranteed loan of 1833 was issued by the house of Rothschild, which with Baring was one of the best-regarded banking houses of the era (Cassis 2007, 48). Finding an issuing house with such a good reputation was of eminent importance for the sale and success of the bonds, as its reputation would reflect on the loan issued (Flandreau/Flores 2009; Lehmann 2011). How was the young country able to persuade Rothschilds to participate? The business relationship was initiated by an intermediary: the Bavarian regency commissioned Simon von Eichthal to find a suitable banking house for the issue of the loan in either Paris or London, as he was unable to manage the loan by himself. In mid-1832, von Eichthal therefore approached Rothschilds. They were hesitant. The internal communication in the house of Rothschild gives detailed insights into the reasons for this initial hesitation and the factors that contributed to Rothschilds' risk management.

There was interest in the business from the beginning of negotiations in 1832, but the Rothschilds wanted to beat down the price. James de Rothschild (Paris) felt that 80 was an appropriate price for a Greek loan, one that involved no risk.[164] A higher price would hinder the issue and the price of 92 proposed by von Eichthal seemed ridiculous to James. James believed that he had a good bargaining position and played for time but von Eichthal had other ideas. To Rothschild's complete surprise, he concluded a contract with the Spanish banker Alexandre Marie Aguado[165] for the issuing of the agreed 40 million francs, at a price of 94, payable in 12 instalments, with a commission of 2.5%.[166] Aguado then approached James de Rothschild to offer a participation in the loan.[167] Furthermore, a competitor from London, Wilson, was prepared to take James' place in the deal.[168] James was extremely angry about the 'renegade' von Eichthal and his apparent intrigues: 'It is absolutely disgraceful how these people wreck the business'. At the same time, he tried to downplay the significance of the affair, commenting '[Anyway] we won't make our fortune from it'.[169] He did not want to be forced into making a hurried decision (if only because it would appear 'very stupid'), and certainly not without hearing the opinions of his brothers in London and Frankfurt.[170] He asked the family to reply quickly and emphasised the good chances of the bonds at the London exchange, even if they seemed to be overpriced for Paris. James was clearly not wholly positive, but also mentioned his doubts. The Rothschilds were certainly reluctant to act in a project where they seemed to be merely filling a prepared place in a deal negotiated elsewhere, as this would not benefit their reputation as a first-class issuing house. It was therefore particularly important to James de Rothschild that Aguado should promise not to publicise his role in the issue. The loan should appear under the name of Rothschild.[171] If the deal were to be closed, then James planned elaborate risk management: he wanted to use a lawyer to draw up the bonds so the Great Powers would be fully responsible for servicing them. A legally watertight guarantee of this sort was an important part of his risk management, and it was even more important because an international guarantee of this sort was without precedent.[172] The price continued to be of concern: even if it was not more than 89.5 after all the discounts, this was still too high. James did not want to risk getting involved without the agreement of his brother in London and continued to string along his negotiation partners. James was convinced that Aguado and von Eichthal would concede him time for decision making: he was completely aware of the significance of the Rothschild name at the London Stock Exchange, which he saw as strengthening his position.[173]

To James' great annoyance, the newspapers were then informed about the deal between Greece and Aguado, so that the Spanish banker was not able to remain completely in the background. Immediately, James told his brother that he was willing to withdraw from the transaction, after all it was not 'such a brilliant deal'.[174] This interpretation of the business was underscored by his negative impression of those he was negotiating with: Aguado was trying to intensify his networks in liberal political circles and wanted only to improve his reputation with the deal, while von Eichthal was primarily interested in profits even if he 'really plays the part of the Gentleman'.[175] Eichthal seems to have played the Philhellenic card intensively in his role as the Greek negotiator: he accused James of being 'difficult and hard' and of describing Greece as a 'worthless [place]'.[176]

Amschel Mayer Rothschild in Frankfurt was not convinced by the conditions that James described. Firstly, the planned price of 90 or even 89 was too high, compared with similar state loans which were offered much more cheaply, even though Greece had not yet caught the 'light of life'.[177] Secondly, von Eichthal had behaved badly in dropping the Rothschilds suddenly after half a year of negotiations and then signing a contract with Aguado; this had seriously damaged confidence in von Eichthal, as Amschel Mayer pointed out. Aguado might feign generosity but the real reason for his offer was that he was not up to issuing the loan alone and desired to split the risk. Thirdly, the Rothschild bank was rich and big enough with enough bonds in the portfolio so that there was no urgent need to step into this business with so many doubtful parameters, for example, the question of what the 'guarantee' of the Great Powers meant in reality (indeed, the guarantee of the Powers would certainly improve the loan's conditions; see Schönhärl 2019b). The options for controlling the loan seemed insufficient. It would be quite different 'if you alone [were] in charge of the deal', as Amschel argued.[178] The message from Frankfurt was clear: 'I am therefore not in favour of us entering the business in this way'.[179] The reply from James' brother Nathan in London was also negative. But by the time his letter reached James, it was too late: James, despite all his previous utterances, had already promised to accept Aguado's offer (or so he said) and could no longer withdraw: 'Heartiest congratulations'.[180] All James could now do was to legitimise his actions towards his elder brother in London. He argued that Nathan's son Nathaniel Rothschild[181] had strongly advised him to take a lead in this business, and that was what he had done, despite his dislike of chasing up other people. At least his quick decision had meant that the London banker Wilson was fobbed off with a participation of only five million francs, although he had travelled personally to Paris. Wilson had even been willing to buy James' share of the deal for 100,000 francs, an offer which James had refused, although he thought that Nathan would perhaps have accepted it.

> If however, Wilson would then have returned, and played the part of the 'man of importance' in front of the Conference, by claiming

> that he had helped the Greeks, you would then have become very cross, my dear Nathan.[182]

James was loath to lose this prestige to any competitor. Accordingly, the contract with Aguado stipulated that the loan should be issued only under the name of Rothschild frères, while the result, whether profit or loss, should be equally divided between the two banking houses.[183] The question of prestige was most important. The Russian legate in Paris, Carlo Andrea Pozzo di Borgo (a friend of Eynard's) and the whole of the French ministry had asked him to take on the lead of the consortium, suggesting that such a big international loan could not take place without participation of the house of Rothschild![184] Avoiding a loss of prestige even justified cooperating with the 'renegade' von Eichthal. James penalised von Eichthal however, by conceding him a participation of only one million francs instead of the five million he had asked for. James also mentioned the profit of a 'handsome sum' of 40,000 francs. Furthermore, he pointed out the opportunities to profit from business with Turkey, which was to receive part of the sum in reparation for the recent war, and with Greece: '[F]undamentally the Greeks are [Gentlemen] and with [Gentlemen] there is money to be earned, just as with Spain'.[185] Disagreements with von Eichthal concerning the payments of dividends provided a possibility for James to withdraw, which he did not take advantage of.[186] Rather, he now pointed out his happiness about the conclusion of the contract to Amschel Mayer, mentioning the strong demand in London, and called the Greek loan an 'excellent affair'.[187] Expectations concerning the prestigious nature of the deal had completely changed James' interpretation. On 12 January 1833, James signed the contract with von Eichthal as the Greek negotiator – alone and without Aguado: the price for the 40 million francs approved thus far by the conference was fixed at 94, with an interest rate of 5%. Greece had to form a sinking fund of 1% of the entire sum, and the refund was planned at par within a period of 36 years. All real estate and income of the Greek state including the import duties were named as guarantees. The issuing house received commission of 1%. The Rothschilds secured the option for the third instalment of the emission.[188] The issue indeed proved to be a good deal: in February, the papers started on the Paris exchange at a price of 103.[189]

The von Eichthals and the Greek business

From a Greek perspective, Simon's handling of the matter was clever and successful. He had put pressure on the Rothschilds by approaching their competitors, circumnavigated their delaying tactics, finally won the renowned issuing house for the deal and nonetheless achieved a very high price. Greece could not have hoped for more successful representation of its interests. Simon's work for Greece was, however, far from finalised. From

December 1832 until July 1833, he was primarily in Paris to deal with the politically complicated negotiations about the loan; during this time, he lived with his brother's family.[190] This also affected his nephew: although Adolphe believed his uncle to be a brilliant man, he found it strenuous to entertain him every evening.[191] His sister Anette recorded with some glee that Simon reprimanded her father Louis for his continuous smoking,[192] but she was nonetheless getting 'a little tired' of him.[193] Adolphe was required not only to entertain his uncle. The future consul general was charged with gathering up all the signatures for the guarantor powers (all three of the Great Powers had to sign all three series of the total loan individually) and with completing the bonds, an extremely tedious task, as he complained.[194] The difficulties were not at an end with the successful issuing of the first two instalments. The third instalment was at the centre of a long, drawn-out diplomatic tug of war in which Simon von Eichthal continued to act as the financial representative of Greece (Heine 1836). By the end of 1833, it must have been clear to him that Greece was slipping into a most unfortunate state. The country was becoming a match ball for the interests of the Great Powers without being able to gain any scope for independent action. It was 1839 before Russia allowed the third instalment to be paid out (Driault/Lhéritier 1929; Krauss 1987, 302–327). Simon could do nothing in the interim but wait, although he communicated the variable, often gloomy prospects of the third instalment to the family. If it could not be paid out, Louis argued, then this would have a very negative effect on the plans to found colonies and a trade committee.[195] Rumours about the catastrophic Greek financial situation multiplied; apparently, even the king admitted to having absolutely no more uncommitted funds and no orderly record of revenue and expenditure, and to knowing about the squandering of the money lent thus far:[196] 'imagine the impact on the creditworthiness of Greece if that was made public'.[197] The Greek royal couple had to embark on begging tours to their parents and parents-in-law in Europe (Krauss 1987, 323f.). The impact on the views of the West European bankers was inevitable: 'Greece was looked upon as part of the barbarous East and capital, which was non-existent in the country, was terrified at the idea of emigrating there from the West' (Eulambio 1924, 4).[198]

But it was not only the politicians who were involved in severe disputes; cooperation between the bankers was also difficult, particularly after their rather disharmonious start. Of the first 40 million francs, 11 were destined to be paid directly to Turkey as compensation.[199] As discussed, James de Rothschild had hoped for additional gains from these transfers. The contract contained detailed stipulations on which parts of these 11 million, divided in ten portions, had to be transferred when, explicitly without any further allowance.[200] The Greek government was committed to amortising enough security papers in time to provide the Rothschilds with the necessary sum.[201] In summer 1834, five million francs of these Ottoman claims were still open, and the Rothschilds suddenly diminished payments to the Sublime Porte. The sources unfortunately do not clarify whether this was because the Greek government was in arrears with the amortisation, whether there was a link to the delay in the third instalment of the guaranteed loan or whether there were other reasons.[202] From von Eichthal's perspective at least, the Greek government had done nothing wrong. The Sublime Porte was nonetheless most displeased and refused to receive the Greek ambassador.[203] The Eichthals, in cooperation with the Greek diplomats in Paris, Constantin Caradja and Mihail II Soutzos, tried to pressurise the Rothschilds to continue payments at once. Simon von Eichthal's son Charles even verbally threatened James de Rothschild, saying that he would withdraw his commissariat for Greece if all the necessary monies were not immediately transferred to Turkey. James de Rothschild was so furious that he answered unmistakably that if this happened, he would completely destroy the credit of Greece on the financial markets and would unsettle all of von Eichthal's business affairs.[204] Charles von Eichthal was very upset by this blustering threat, which so contrasted with the smooth and gentile surface of banking business, and, incensed, named James 'King of Jerusalem'.[205] Charles believed Rothschild to be obsessed by the wish to monopolise the international emission markets and afraid of his competitors, concerned that 'a small flake of snow leads to a threatening and dangerous landslide which is difficult to hold back'.[206] The conflict was even taken into the public sphere.[207] James de Rothschild finally gave in and resumed the transfer of the money, perhaps thanks to the intervention of Sina from Vienna.[208] Representing Greece's interests, the von Eichthals were again able to bring the banking house Rothschild to reason. In the long run, the relationship of at least the French part of the Eichthal family to the Rothschilds was not even seriously damaged by the dispute, as demonstrated in the following years by the continued cooperation between Adolphe and the Rothschild brothers concerning railway construction in France. For the von Eichthals, however, Greece had again proved an extremely complicated client.

At the same time, Adolphe's expectations of the position as the Greek consul general in Paris remained unfulfilled. The official bestowal of the title from Athens was much delayed and the title that he had originally aspired to, that of 'agent général', was never forthcoming. At the beginning of 1834, he still had not received the certificate of appointment as the consul general, despite his repeated enquiries. He asked his brother in Nafplio to deal with the issue because he did not want to annoy von Armansperg with any more written requests. With great humility, Gustave should assure the head of the regency that whether with or without the title, Adolphe would use every opportunity to serve the country.[209] Even before he received the official title, however, Adolphe was given diverse tasks by Nafplio. Thus, he handled the minting of the new Greek currency in Munich and Paris

(Μπρέγιαννη [Bregianni] 2011, 109–113), a task that proved much more complicated than expected and in his opinion bore no relation to the commission of a quarter per cent that he received in return for his efforts.[210] Furthermore, he was not given any other lucrative Greek business as compensation. His wish that the Greek government should finally entrust the Paris banking house of d'Eichthal with a larger sum of money, thus entering into a bond of trust with a risky advance, remained unfulfilled. And even if this had been forthcoming, through clenched teeth, Adolphe admitted to Gustave that without Simon the risk of independent Greek investments would have been too high. To his annoyance, he remained dependent on his sceptical uncle, who at times even failed to provide him with anything like adequate information.[211] One reason for Adolphe's rather limited appetite for risk may have been that, like Eynard and other bankers of the time, he found the Greek regency thoroughly unreliable.[212] There were occasions when his Uncle Simon received no response from the Greek king to his enquiries, even to the most urgent of them.[213] And furthermore, Adolphe himself repeatedly made purchases in Paris for Greece, e.g. a new royal dinner service, and ended up footing the bill himself despite his complaints.[214] Such negative experiences left their mark. It was also impossible to talk of increased stabilisation in the country: the d'Eichthal family heard about the international dealings concerning Greece and the disputes within the regency not only from Gustave, but also from Simon's diverse informants and from the newspapers. It became ever clearer how serious the problems were. Even Simon now believed the strong Bavarian interests in Greece to be unfortunate and condemned the on-going intrigues,[215] although if he continued to value von Armansperg.[216] Louis correspondingly counselled Gustave on repeated occasions not to rely on the French party, but to take advice from Simon, to align himself with the wishes of the Greek and Bavarian kings, and to remain close to von Armansperg.[217] He reiterated this advice even more vehemently as the situation within the regency became increasingly tense and its reorganisation was imminent.[218] At a certain point, however, Simon and Louis' annoyance at their poor treatment by the regency began to dominate.[219] In August 1834, Louis finally freed Gustave from his responsibility to represent the interests of the family with the regency. It was now more important that Gustave maintain his independence, which meant that his father was no longer necessarily advising him to join von Armansperg and his party. If the young king should prove to have character, then Gustave should abide by him. Nonetheless, he suggested that Gustave should avoid writing negatively to Simon about von Armansperg because this would only annoy his uncle without convincing him.[220] When the rift between Gustave and von Armansperg occurred, the Paris family believed the accusation of Saint-Simonism to be an excuse – that Gustave's past was his weak spot had always been clear.[221] Decisive for the rift was rather Gustave's critical attitude towards von Armansperg, which the minister could not forgive.[222]

The letters from the family sound understanding rather than reproachful; the escalation seems not to have come as a surprise.

With the collapse of the plans for Gustave's career in the Greek administration, the question of his future returned. Adolphe advised Gustave to stay in Greece despite all the problems, if he could find a useful occupation there.[223] He should not allow himself to become involved in the intrigues, make a clear plan of his goals and follow this plan unswervingly with an eye to his future career, so as to earn himself a place in public service. When he returned, this could then be the basis for a position in French politics – Adolphe was thinking here, for instance, of a seat in the Chamber of Deputies, which he believed would not be difficult to achieve.[224] When it became clear that Gustave was coming home, the problem of his future plans was even more intensively addressed. Those who had remained in Paris could not imagine taking Gustave as a partner into the bank. Did Adolphe view him as a competitor, even though he himself was successfully established as his father's successor?[225] Gustave was also not convinced about a future as a banker.[226] What did he want to do with his life? The family habit of distributing unsolicited advice about ways of life, as Adolphe expressed it, led to serious disputes between father and son and between the two brothers.[227] Gustave's future plans had not gained any clearer contours from his detour to Greece.

What had become clear, however, was that the d'Eichthals did not regard Greece in the mid-1830s as an attractive financial or investment market. The interpretation of the country was rather dominated by the image of an Oriental and chaotic Greece, which made the risk of investment appear too high. This was the perception of all three bankers, who may have differed from one another in their rhetoric but not in their conclusions. In the end, none of them invested. The intermediary returned to France without having achieved anything. His numerous ideas to benefit the state of Greece through the use of modern science, e.g. statistics, geology and agricultural technology, and through the acquisition of foreign capital were put on ice.

From intermediary to Hellenist

Gustave d'Eichthal did not surrender his newly found identity as an intermediary between the worlds. Soon after his return, he wrote the essay 'Les deux mondes', in which he compared the two worlds of the Orient and the Occident, and presented the centuries of conflict between them (D'Eichthal 1836).[228] Gustave differentiated between these two so different worlds with a clarity that would have delighted Edward Said (1978),[229] reducing the Orient almost entirely to its otherness (Todorova 1977, 23).[230] He emphasised that the Orient was characterised by the importance of beauty, repose and a complete lack of providing for the future, in contrast to people in the scientifically oriented Occident.[231] The banker's son suggested that

Orientals were like birds that do not sow but reap, while the Occident was dominated by technical progress, acceleration, efficiency and managing any uncertainty and risk in the future. However, Gustave d'Eichthal was explicit about not considering these characteristics as a value judgement: he contrasted the continuous progress of occidental industrialisation to the apparent standstill of medieval times and the regression of the Orient, suggesting that they were justified like rest after work (D'Eichthal 1836, 71f.).[232] Both ways of life were essential and both required the other as a complement of itself. Gustave called for a transculturation of both worlds, a mutual influencing of one another in terms of culture and way of life. He thus preempted the thoughts formulated by Fernando Ortiz a good 100 years later (Ortiz 1940; Ortiz et al. 1947). In contrast to Ortiz, however, Gustave d'Eichthal was not concerned with describing the zone of contact between two different 'strong' cultures in an imperial context. He rather demanded the programmatic emancipation of the Orient and its recognition as an equal partner by the Occident. In his book, he dedicated an entire chapter to his Greek experiences, remaining optimistic: he predicted that the country had a future as a great free port that could bring together the trade from East and West as 'the first benefactor of the people and nations'.[233] The country was thus portrayed as a bridge between East and West and as being 'between different levels of development', just as Todorova records is typical of the West European image of the Balkans. Greece is described here as 'half-developed, semi-colonial, half-civilised, half-oriental' (Todorova 1977, 34ff., tr. by K.S.). Gustave saw the mistakes of the Bavarian regency as stemming from a failure to take the Oriental character of Greece seriously and from not having attempted to achieve a balance between the worlds. The regency rather simply transferred the institutions of the Occident to Greece, where they did not belong. It would have been better, Gustave argued, to give the local institutions more scope and freedom instead of subjecting everything to dysfunctional central control. He criticised the regency harshly, mentioning von Armansperg by name,[234] and also condemned the irresponsible politics of the Great Powers who misused Greece as a match ball in the struggle around their interests (D'Eichthal 1936, 129). D'Eichthal campaigned intensively for the Greeks, describing their intelligence and morality as being in no way inferior to that of the Occident and the majority of the population as being characterised by their love of freedom, diligence and frugality (ibid., 132). He furthermore accredited Austria with a decisive role as an intermediary: like its double-headed eagle, the country had always turned its gaze in both directions (ibid., 76ff.).

'Les deux mondes' constitutes the starting point for Gustave's existence as an independent intellectual, as Hervet Le Bret extensively describes.[235] In the following years, he wrote about the emancipation of the Jews[236] and of women (D'Eichthal 1852), about the union of Europe and the preservation of peace (idem 1840), about the world religions (idem 1863a) and about ethnology (idem 1847), to mention but a few of his topics. He concerned himself intensively with French Algeria (idem 1839), which he visited in 1838/1839, also to maintain certain Saint-Simonian contacts. The topic of Greece was initially not prevalent in his writing, although he continued to be in friendly contact with some of the acquaintances from his time in Greece, e.g. Karl von Abel and Alexandre Roujoux[237] and with some of the Greeks (Queux Saint-Hilaire 1887, 76). Gustave also continued to try to actively attract French capital to Greece. In 1842, Gustave, encouraged by his former superior Kolettis, who had been the Greek ambassador in Paris since 1835, sent a group of engineers from the highly repudiated Ponts et Chausses, led by Françoise Clément Sauvage, to Boeotia to evaluate the drainage of Lake Copais, a large marsh district which he himself was familiar with.[238] Kapodistrias and Otto I had already drawn on scientific expertise to assess the chances of this project, but Gustave d'Eichthal's approach obviously was the first time that banking circles used expert opinions for a decision-making process in Greece.[239] He considered founding a joint-stock company for this enterprise. But Sauvage concluded that the draining of the area by a joint-stock company, which required timely profits, would not be lucrative; the project required the involvement of government who could achieve profits over a longer period (Sauvage 1868). D'Eichthal accepted this expert opinion. He presented the detailed plan that the engineer had produced to the Greek government in order to enable the import of French engineering to Greece, even if he could not finance it. Nothing is known about the reactions of his brother Adolphe to this project, without whose support and capital Gustave would not have been able to establish such a company (Le Bret 2012, 511).[240] In 1880, the Compagnie française pour le dessèchement et l'exploitation du Lac Copaïs (CFC) was finally founded to drain the marshland, but apparently without the involvement of the d'Eichthals. Gustave also commissioned the engineer Sauvage to draw up a plan to extend the passage between the island of Euboea and the mainland, as was implemented in the 1860s and opened up the straits for traffic to Thessaloniki and Constantinople (Yéméniz 1865, 866).[241] Sauvage also assessed the mineral deposits on Milos (Κυρίτση/Μάλλης [Kiritsis/Mallis] 2005, 217). Gustave seems to have invested a great deal of money in these scientific reports, even though he then initiated none of the projects. He did invest in Greek state bonds: in 1844, he held 58.[242] When in 1863 the new king took office and the Greek government sought new foreign loans, Gustave in 1867 tried to persuade his brother's business partners, the Péreire brothers, to support such a loan, which then failed to materialise for over ten years.[243] With the international loan proving impossible at the time, in 1875, he purchased 37 bonds for an internal Greek loan of 26 million drachmas from the year of 1874.[244] And when in 1882 the Société internationale du Canal Maritime de Corinthe (SICC) began to build the Canal of Corinth, a project already contemplated by Louis d'Eichthal at the beginning of the 1830s,

Gustave bought 100 shares from the building society (Le Bret 2012, 513).[245] This was perhaps to be even more expected as he had since college times been friends with Ferdinand de Lesseps, the great canal builder of Suez, who lent his name to the Corinth project (Queux Saint-Hilaire 1887, 6).

Gustave clearly invested in Greece as far as he was able, but what about his brother Adolphe, the banker? While Gustave was occupied as a scholar and author, Adolphe was pursuing a successful career in the Paris haute banque. His marriage to Louisa de La Rüe brought him important contacts not only in England and Switzerland, but also in French politics.[246] The bank cooperated with the Rothschilds and the banking house of Laffitte in issuing numerous foreign loans on the Paris exchange (Le Bret 2012, 307f.). In addition as early as 1819, Adolphe invested in insurance, especially in maritime and fire insurance, and in the development of saving banks (ibid., 309–313), and he was one of the pioneers of French railway construction, e.g. with the Paris-St. Germain line which was opened in 1838. Especially with his railway investments, Adolphe often cooperated successfully with the Saint-Simonian colleagues of his brother, who in the meanwhile had secured important positions in the French business and political worlds, e.g. with the Péreire brothers, Chevalier and Enfantin. He made a decisive contribution to the development of the French concession system (ibid., 314–322). Adolphe's railway activities were not restricted to France, but extended also to Austria, Switzerland and Russia (Cameron 1961, 219, 231, 277). As early as 1839 when he was only 34 years of age, he was elected as one of the regents of the Banque de France, an office that the Rothschilds had strived for years to achieve without success (Le Bret 2012, 327–331). After the death of his father in 1840, he was the only proprietor of the bank until 1843 when D'Eichthal & Cie took on a new partner.[247] In 1846, Adolphe was elected to the French parliament.[248] Although he had to surrender both the office in the Banque de France and that in parliament as a result of the disastrous consequences of the 1848 revolution for his banking house, and despite his initial outrage about Louis Napoleon's coup,[249] he quickly managed to establish himself in the Second Empire. In 1852, he played a significant role in the founding of Crédit Mobilier, remaining a director until 1862; this was one of the first French joint-stock banks in which the Pereire brothers implemented part of the Saint-Simonian banking programme (Le Bret 2012, 387–412). From 1851 to 1854, Adolphe was also a city councillor in Paris (Faure 1970). In 1863, he was a member of 11 supervisory boards, demonstrating the importance of the d'Eichthal bank within the Parisian finance world. He campaigned for the strengthening of the Banque National and the absolute necessity of free trade. Furthermore, Adolphe d'Eichthal was philanthropically active, as a patron of the arts and a promoter of science (Le Bret 2012, 354, 530–532). Le Bret suggests that the start of the Third Republic in 1870 marked the climax of Adolphe's career, and in 1890, his bank occupied a very respectable 15th place among the Parisian haute banque (ibid., 477, 548). Contact between the two brothers remained very close; together, they maintained and used their far-flung networks in all spheres of French and European societies.

At times, Adolphe took high risks and invested abroad, for instance, in a Spanish railway project and the canalisation of the Ebro (ibid., 392). This was, however, not true for Greece. Astonishingly, Adolphe was not even among the founders of the Greek National Bank, established in 1841 by Jean Gabriel Eynard, although as the Greek consul general his involvement would seem predestined. Was Adolphe's perception of Greece so set in stone that not even the propaganda of his Swiss colleague could soften it? Or was the relationship to Eynard in some way strained? Before, during and after Gustave's travels, there seems to have been almost no connection between the d'Eichthals and the Genevan banker. Naturally, there were isolated points of contact: thus, Eynard handled the donations of the Bavarian Philhellene Association for Simon von Eichthal in the 1820s, because Eynard coordinated the Philhellene activities of the whole of Europe. Part of the money sent to Gustave on his travels was also transferred via Eynard.[250] Furthermore, the Parisian family was in contact with Eynard's confidant de Regny before he travelled to Greece on behalf of France. De Regny was repeatedly mentioned in correspondence, even if not in connection with Eynard.[251] The Eichthals socialised with Eynard's nephew Charles Odier and his family, as well as with André & Cottier, so it seems certain that they were informed about Eynard's activities.[252] But there was no direct correspondence between the Parisian d'Eichthals and Eynard, and the d'Eichthals did not participate in the founding of the ETE. However, in a letter to the governor of the ETE Stavros from 1847, Adolphe actually describes the Genevan banker as 'our common friend'.[253] The sources do not reveal whether the two banking houses regarded one another as competitors or whether there were other reasons for their lack of cooperation. Adolphe d'Eichthal was in any case certainly in professional contact with the ETE and had an account there,[254] although there was no intensive cooperation. With regard to Greece, Adolphe remained very cautious and seems to have made no investments. He surrendered his position as the Greek general consul in Paris at the beginning of the 1860s.[255] The papers wrongly suggested that Adolphe was responsible for the plans to drain Lake Copais, when in fact it was his brother Gustave who organised and paid for this draft of the project.[256] It was Adolphe's son of the same name Adolphe d'Eichthal (1841–1909) who, after a fusion with the Banque Mirabaud (Le Bret 2012, 550) in 1895, was involved in the founding of the Banque de l'Union Parisienne (1904), a joint-stock bank that was more intensively involved in business in Greece (Stoskopf 2002a, 159), e.g. in the raisin trade.[257] The banking houses Delessert and Hottinguer, old friends from Saint-Simonian times, or at least their sons, were also involved (Salomon-Delatour 1962, 25).

Judged in terms of the investment behaviour of his brother, Gustave's role as a financial broker must be declared a failure. He was unable to persuade his brother to invest in Greece, and until the 1870s, there was overall scarcely any French investment in the country. But what about the process of transculturation in other fields? The mutual influencing of Orient and Occident had been Gustave's goal. How did peripheral Greece affect imperial France? In 1864, almost 30 years after his journey to the country, Gustave published a short piece entitled 'De l'usage pratique de la langue grecque', promoting Ancient Greek as the world's common language and triggering a spirited public discussion in France and in Europe (D'Eichthal 1887).[258] His essay was published both in French and in Modern Greek with the translation being undertaken by Markos Renieri, the vice-governor of the National Bank of Greece where Gustave was a customer.[259] In 1842, Renieri had already published 'What is Greece? East or West?' (Ρενιέρης [Renieri]/Γεννηματάς [Gennimatas] 1998),[260] in which he picked up on many aspects of d'Eichthal's 'Deux Mondes' without directly citing him. Renieri clearly defined Greece as part of the West and categorised the 'Eastern' elements as belonging to periods of decline and decay (ibid., 98).[261] It was thus not surprising that d'Eichthal's new writing attracted attention. The publication was well-timed. Firstly, the 1866–1868 uprising in Crete against the Ottomans had excited the minds of many intellectuals in Paris.[262] Secondly, in the run-up to the World Exhibition of 1867, ideas like an international postal system and international currency[263] were being intensively discussed – so why not a common world language? Gustave argued that Greek was the language that every educated person learnt, that could be traced back to the origins of humanity and that touched upon all fields of the spirit (Queux Saint-Hilaire 1887, 77–81). He suggested replacing the Greek pronunciation developed by Erasmus with the 'Oriental', an idea that found support from the ministry of education and the Académie Française (ibid., 86–94). This discussion should be viewed against the background of the development of classical studies and the move from Philhellenism to Hellenism in France: the image of antiquity held by scholars of the time was changing (Bergemann 2011, 46). The 'transformation from the romantic and literary veneration' of Greek antiquity 'to the methods of German philology' that occurred between 1840 and 1860 had also run its course in France (Vidal-Naquet 1996, 170); in discussion of the important question of pronunciation, it thus seemed important not to again be pre-empted by the Germans.[264] Even though the new pronunciation failed to become standard, Gustave persevered. Together with the classics scholars Charles Brunet de Presle, Professor of Modern Greek at the École des langues orientales vivantes (Vaucelles 1956), and Charles Beulé, Professor of Archaeology at the Sorbonne (Prevost 1954), both of whom were active in creating good publicity for Greece, in June 1867, Gustave d'Eichthal founded the Association pour l'encouragement des études grecques en France (Queux Saint-Hilaire 1887, 94ff.; Prevost 1954; Basch 1995, 139–144) – in the same year as Greece proudly attended the World Exhibition in Paris and presented 100 journals that were regularly published in Greek (Basch 1995, 138). Gustave proclaimed that among the Philhellenes, 'an entire harmony of ideas and sentiments' dominated. 'We always have in common what may be called the religion of Greece; the same admiration, although not exclusive, for its past, the same confidence in its future'.[265] Gustave attempted to combine the study and veneration of antiquity with interest in modern Greece, as the former was much more compatible with French traditions (Basch 1995, 141).[266] Against the backdrop of tensions in French society, 'La Grèce imaginaire' continued to serve as a screen on which to project very different notions about the ideal society, and Athens in particular was viewed as the 'ideological location of modern liberalism' (Loraux/Vidal-Naquet 1979, 209, 217, tr. by K.S.).[267] With the help of the Greek ambassador (and later prime minister) Theodoros Delyannis and Markos Renieri, it was possible to gain the support of important individuals like the diplomat Achille-Léon Victor de Broglie and Théobald Piscatory for the association. The list of participants (a total of 600 members and supporters) constitutes a who's-who of the Second French Republic.[268] Gustave was the treasurer of the society and edited the yearbook, in which he regularly published articles on Greek philosophy, language and culture, as indeed he did in other journals.[269] Especially during the bleak period of German occupation in 1871 – which Gustave d'Eichthal spent in England – the association was a comfort to its members: 'Everything therefore contributed to maintaining this great image of Greece in front of us, to attach its remembrance to the preoccupations of our life for us'.[270] As his mediation between modern Greece and France had been unsuccessful, Gustave had moved antiquity to centre stage, 'whereby the act of appropriation not only modifies the culture of reception but in particular also constructs the culture of reference'.[271] The experiences of his travels in Greece 40 years earlier seemed to fade in contrast to this image of antiquity, which acted as a projection screen for his dreams and hopes. In this way, d'Eichthal paradigmatically represents numerous French and European intellectuals in the mid-nineteenth century (Loraux/Vidal-Naquet 1979). Many of them viewed Greece rather as 'a model than an object of direct knowledge' (idem 1996, 174): this reception of antiquity was primarily concerned with improving their own culture in the course of constructing the culture of reference. Ernest Renan's poem 'Prière sur l'Acropole' from 1876 is one example of this development (Basch 1995, 170; Vidal-Naquet 1996, 174).[272] The founding of the École Française d'Athènes in 1846 with a focus on archaeology was another official expression of French interest in antiquity, and in the following decades, this institution housed most of the prominent French travellers to Greece (Basch 1995, 20). The establishment of the school was to be understood as a demonstration towards Great Britain; the British School of Archaeology in Athens was then founded in 1879 (Bowen 1989, 177).

While the reception of antiquity flourished, perceptions of 'la Grèce moderne' became evermore negative. Certain Western travelogues provided positive descriptions (Leconte 1847) but a negative image of modern Greece had become firmly established, one which was dominated by 'laughter, derision, mockery' (Basch 1995, 25, tr. by K.S.). This tendency was strengthened by Great Britain's alienation from Greece, caused by Britain's determination that Crete should remain under the Ottoman rule (ibid., 45). The nadir was reached in 1854 with the publication of Edmond About's work (About 1854), which sharply pilloried Greece for its lack of tax morale, its insufficient concept of government and its high level of indebtedness, and which received much attention in France and internationally.[273] Three years later, About continued his attack with his 'King of the Mountains' (About 1857),[274] and his work proved much more popular than the diverse replies (Basch 1995, 78–128). About deliberately excluded the positively connoted Ancient Greece and promoted a tendency for the image of antiquity to become increasingly divorced from that of contemporary Greece (ibid., 92, 126). It was thus logical that the promotion of the capital transfer to Greece, which began at the end of the 1870s, consistently drew on the antique Hellene traditions to explain and justify French investment.[275] Only this link to antiquity had the potential to 'ennoble' contemporary Greece and its profane economic affairs in the eyes of the elite (Bergemann et al. 2011, 46).

Conclusion

At the beginning of the 1830s, the von Eichthal family showed lively interest in Greece as a new investment market and sent, among other members of the family, the Saint-Simonian Gustave to the country to gather information and develop contacts, but also to prove himself personally. At the same time, Gustave's brother Adolphe became the Greek consul general in Paris and their Uncle Simon was *Hoffaktor* at the royal court in Athens. A dense, carefully maintained network provided the von Eichthals with information about Greece. When making recommendations for the improvement of the Greek institutions, Gustave, drawing on his excellent education, recommended the use of statistical methods, geology and agricultural technology and the creation of a cadastre. He was also the first banker to commission reports from renowned engineers about possible investment projects, making use of scientific expertise in the process of risk assessment.

The correspondence within the family clearly records factors relevant to their risk perception. Principally sceptical of Gustave's enthusiastic and lyrical 'framing' of the situation, the family carefully followed the actions of competitors who were prepared to take risks, anxious not to be pre-empted; this corresponds with the notion of 'herding'. However, much weight was given to the judgement of the Munich Simon von Eichthal, whose negative experiences with the Bavarian regency and the issuing of the 60-million loan led him to advise urgently against further involvement. While Gustave's father Louis moved between these two extremes, his brother Adolphe remained willing to invest for a considerable time. He only changed his mind when Gustave, after being politically sidelined, began to report negatively on conditions in the country. Adolphe's closure of the decision-making process involved reducing his image of Greece to that of an Oriental, chaotic and foreign country. In this way, he could easily justify his decision to his brother. The Eichthals did not invest in Greece but, in line with the home bias, concentrated on more familiar markets.

After his return to Paris, Gustave, who had clearly failed as a broker in the financial field, bought Greek bonds as far as his means allowed but never managed to persuade his brother to make any significant investment. Some of the large infrastructure projects planned by Gustave and those he commissioned were implemented in later years, but without the involvement of the d'Eichthal bank. Gustave found much more success as a cultural broker. On the basis of his experiences in Greece, he argued about the relationship between Orient and Occident, attempting to reconcile the two, and successfully promoted Ancient Greek and philological studies, thus supporting the reception of Greek antiquity in France. This successful transculturation was, however, between France and *Ancient* Greece (Schönhärl 2020). In contrast, once the enthusiasm for the Greek struggle for independence had dissipated, the image of the contemporary country remained bleak into the 1860s.

The Rothschilds, however, participated in the issuing of the loan to Greece in 1832 primarily for reasons related to their reputation as a leading international issuing house, which they wished to protect from their competitors. Simon von Eichthal cleverly used this fear of competition to improve the conditions for Greece. The Rothschilds secured themselves against risks by ensuring that the guarantee of the loan by the Great Powers was legally watertight.

Notes

1 See Chapter II. 2 of this book.

2 This term is based on the work of Fernando Ortiz, who demonstrates that even in the imperial context it is not possible to speak of the assimilation of one culture by another. When two cultures collide, both of them experience change (see Jobs/Mackenthun 2013b, 8f.). Even in cases where violence is used, the process is one of mutual transformations with the 'stronger' culture also being changed. It is, however, difficult to provide evidence for this process because the influence of the centre on the periphery is easier to prove than the other way around. The latter is often only captured in archival remains (see ibid., 11). The term is used here purely descriptively and not in the sense of a critical evaluation as is often the case in postcolonial studies.

3 These sources also stimulate a desire to research the investment behaviour of different generations of bankers. It would be most interesting to investigate the extent to which generation-specific investment behaviour can be detected (see Jureit 2006). However, the sample of bankers per generation investigated in this project is too small to allow generalisations to be deduced. It remains to note the impression that investment behaviour within one generation can at times

differ more than between different generations, as shown by a comparison of the d'Eichthal family with Jean Gabriel Eynard.

4 See also a very anti-Semitic essay by Weckerle (1941/1942). A detailed family tree commissioned by Baron von Houwald aus Lüggen, Neuhaus, from 27.8.1941 is in the Bundesarchiv in Berlin, BAR R1 128.

5 A detailed account of the history of the mother's family is found in Le Bret (2012, 43–62).

6 When a young man Abraham Mendelssohn completed his internship along with Louis d'Eichthal in Paris at Worms de Romilly (see Ratcliffe 1977b, 115). According to Ratcliffe, Gustave not only stayed with the Mendelssohns, but also completed an internship in the Mendelssohn banking house (see ibid., 134). There are interesting connections between the d'Eichthal and Mendelssohn families in various fields (e.g. also in musical areas [see Le Bret 2012, 102]). The Mendelssohn family was interested in diverse projects in Greece, even if they never took a leading role. In 1870–1874, the historian of the family Carl Mendelssohn-Bartholdy published his two-volume history of modern Greece: Mendelssohn Bartholdy (2004; 1st ed. 1874). He also travelled to Greece (see Löschburg 1998). A precise evaluation of the Mendelssohn archive with a focus on the relationships to Greece should be the subject of future research.

7 Gustave's son Eugène edited the correspondence (see D'Eichthal 1898).

8 Isaac Rodrigues was the third internee along with Louis d'Eichthal and Mendelssohn in 1787 at Worms de Romilly in Paris (see Ratcliffe 1977b, 115).

9 Le Bret and Ratcliffe describe the order of events differently. According to Ratcliffe, the meeting between Gustave and Saint Simon took place in 1823 (see Ratcliffe 1976, 490).

10 For sources on the role of banks as envisioned by the movement, see Jacoud (2010).

11 Saint-Simon gave up his title in the revolution (see Régnier 2010, 13–15).

12 The following very concise summary draws particularly on Salomon-Delatour (1962), also on Picon (2002) and Musso (2006).

13 'Saint-Simon is a character from the early 19th century, a seigneur who fights the nobility, a decadent who advocates progress, a maker of programmes and projects who founds a school and stages propaganda like a journalist, an idealist who organises industry, the messiah of a church that makes science the dogma of the new beliefs, the prophet of the proletariat who thinks of socialism as philanthropy, he thus stands between eras as Seigneur Sans-Culotte' (Salomon-Delatour 1962, 12, tr. by K.S.).

14 Ratcliffe (1976).

15 Le Bret (2012, 212). This case thus involves the concept of generations being reflected upon by those involved. Otherwise, the term is used here analytically (see Jureit 2010). Gustave feels himself to be part of this collective, whose needs he communicates to society as a whole.

16 D'Eichthal (1830). Emphasis in the original. The original letter was addressed to Francois Cottier, a partner of Dominique André, Jean Gabriel Eynard's nephew (see Le Bret 2012, 176, tr. by K.S.).

17 Chevalier (1832), tr. by K.S.

18 On the instructions of the French government, the scientists and artists accompanied the military corps who remained in Greece after the Battle of Navarino until 1833. Their findings were published in the series Expedition scientifique de Morée in the two sections 'Beaux-Arts' (3 volumes) and 'Sciences Physiques' (3 volumes) between 1831 and 1838. This was an 'affair of national prestige' (Brifaud 1998, 292, tr. by K.S.).

19 A synopsis of Varnhagen van Enses' Philhellenic statements in letters and especially in his Prussian diaries is found in Dieterich (1929). On Gustave's visits see Le Bret (2012, 238).

20 The reception of Plato and Ancient Greece played an important role in Mill's consideration of Bentham's works (see Pappé 1979). Commonalities and differences between the Benthamite and Saint-Simonian monetary theories are discussed by Bellet (2011). Even at the end of the eighteenth century, there was much interest in utilitarianism among many later Saint-Simonians, e.g. Etienne Delessert.

21 Diary of 26 May 1828, in: D'Eichthal (1977, 28–33).

22 Gustave d'Eichthal to Henriette, 8.10.1883 from Corinth, quoted from D'Eichthal (1887, 11).

23 See, for instance, his signature under a call for donations by the Munich Philhellene Committee of 1826, printed in: Heydenreuter (1995a, 64–66).

24 In 1821, Thiersch was forbidden to set up such an association in Munich, a prohibition instigated by Prussia and Austria, but after Ludwig took office in 1825, the association was founded after all.

25 'This is the sixth letter that I write to you, how it is possible that you have only received one I don't know probably the whales responsible have swallowed them. I abstain in my letters from everything political and even the Turks could have been permitted to read them'. Simon von Eichthal to Heydeck, Munich, 30.7.1827, STABI Heydeckiana II. 1a.

26 Simon von Eichthal to Heydeck, Munich, 11.4.1827, STABI Heydeckiana II. 1a, tr. by K.S.

27 The payment was settled, as could be expected, via Jean Gabriel Eynard; see Simon von Eichthal to Heydeck, Munich, 11.4.1827, STABI Heydeckiana II. 1a.

28 Simon von Eichthal to Heydeck, Munich, 10.10. 1826, STABI Heydeckiana II. 1a, tr. by K.S. There is uncertainty about the reading of the word 'Courants', German 'Couranten', which seems to have been a vernacular expression.

29 'On this occasion I write of the streets in Hellas, which resemble our mountain paths and which cross rivers and streams without bridges without planks, becoming impassable in rainy weather – hence the war in this country is so difficult and hardly European. There is no trace of wagons or wheels to find and in Hellas a calèche would be like a warship on Maximiliansplatz in Munich – an object of curiosity, not of use'. Heydeck to von Eichthal, STABI Heydeckiana II.2b, tr. by K.S.

30 Heydeck to Simon von Eichthal, STABI Heydeckiana II.2b.

31 However, Rudolf never made the journey.

32 From 1834, Wilhelm then moved on to Constantinople but remained in close correspondence with Gustave; see Wilhelm von Eichthal to Gustave d'Eichthal, 14./26.8.1834, BDA MS 13747, 135. Wilhelm's year of death is unknown but he died in New York.

33 The way in which the von Eichthals organised for members of the family to be geographically distributed is a common characteristic of international families (see Sabean/Teuscher 2011, 4f; Derix 2012).

34 Adolphe d'Eichthal to Gustave d'Eichthal, 28.12.1832, BDA MS 13747, 37.

35 The authors quote here Antenhofer's paper in the same volume but give the quote a more general meaning.

36 Adolphe d'Eichthal to Gustave d'Eichthal, 18.1.1833, BDA MS 13747, 43.

37 Planat de la Faye (husband of Frédérique d'Eichthal, a niece of Simon and Louis') to Adolphe d'Eichthal, 24.7.1833, BDA MS 13747, 90.

38 Adolphe d'Eichthal to Gustave d'Eichthal, in June 1833, BDA MS 13747, 85.

39 Adolphe d'Eichthal to Gustave d'Eichthal, 6.10.1833, BDA MS 13748, 40; Adolphe d'Eichthal to Gustave d'Eichthal, 28.2.1834, BDA MS 13748, 47.
40 Adolphe d'Eichthal to Gustave d'Eichthal, 6.10.1833, BDA MS 13748, 40, tr. by K.S.
41 Adolphe d'Eichthal to Gusvate d'Eichthal, 23.8.1833, BDA MS 13747, 103, tr. by K.S.
42 Adolphe d'Eichthal to Gustave d'Eichthal, 6.10.1833, BDA MS 13748, 40.
43 Adolphe d'Eichthal to Gustave d'Eichthal, 23.8.1833, BDA MS 13747, 103, tr. by K.S. In September 1833, Nathaniel von Rothschild actually did travel to Athens in order to complete negotiations with the Greek government – he rather than Gustave thus delivered the documents. However, even just from the Ionian Islands, Nathaniel had the very discouraging impression that the people were undemanding and lacked social ambition, and the climate was unhealthy. Business people there reported to him about the 'horrors of a long stay at such a place'. He therefore did not wish to remain in Nafplio longer than was absolutely necessary; see Nathaniel von Rothschild to his parents from Zante, 4.9.1833, RAL T7/2.
44 Adolphe d'Eichthal to Gustave d'Eichthal, 23.8.1833, BDA MS 13747, 103.
45 Adolphe d'Eichthal to Gustave d'Eichthal, 12.11.1833, BDA MS 13748, 42.
46 Arnold von Eichthal to Louis d'Eichthal, 19.8.1833, BDA MS 13747, 100, tr. by K.S.
47 It is thus not surprising that Adolphe expressly asked Gustave to send important letters to him personally and not to their father, and to keep some information, e.g. about Gustave's health problems, secret from their parents. See Adolphe d'Eichthal to Gustave d'Eichthal, 23.8.1833, BDA MS 13747, 103; Adolphe d'Eichthal to Gustave d'Eichthal, 11.12.1833, BDA MS 13748, 43.
48 Louis d'Eichthal to Gustave d'Eichthal, 24.7.1833, BDA MS 13747, 89.
49 Louis d'Eichthal to Gustave d'Eichthal, 8.4.1833, BDA MS 13747, 68.
50 Adolphe d'Eichthal to Gustave d'Eichthal, 6.10.1833, BDA MS 13748, 40.
51 Louis d'Eichthal to Gustave d'Eichthal, 5.8.1833, BDA MS 13747, 93. The Sina banking house was later one of the most significant Greek foreign banks (see Vlasto 1885, 266). Sina was active in the London Greek Committee from the time of its founding; see his extensive correspondence in LGC.
52 The assertion and practices of patriarchal power in international families are considered in the edited volume Johnson (2011).
53 Gustave d'Eichthal, 5.10.1833, from Corfu to unknown, cited from Queux Saint-Hilaire (1887, 10), tr. by K.S. Emphasis in the original.
54 His letters from Greece were edited and published twice in the nineteenth century. First, the Greek D. Vikelas in 1886–1892 published a selection translated into Greek in two Greek journals: Βικέλας [Vikelas] (1886); Βικέλας, [Vikelas] (1887/1892); later, these were brought together in D'Eichthal (1974). Second, Gustave's friend Saint Hilaire included certain passages in his essay about Gustave d'Eichthal's service in Greece (see Queux Saint-Hilaire 1887). The selections differ from one another in places. For instance, Vikelas included longer passages about the intrigues of Great Britain which Saint Hilaire did not. The answering letters from the family are in BDA.
55 Louis to Gustave from Munich, 9.10.1833, BDA MS 13748, tr. by K.S.
56 Gustave d'Eichthal, 5.10.1833, from Corfu to unknown, cited from Queux Saint-Hilaire (1887, 10).
57 Gustave d'Eichthal, 8.10.1833, from Corfu to his mother, cited from ibid., 15.
58 On the transfer of such concepts from Western Europe to the Balkans, see Daskalov/Mishkova (2014).
59 His letters from Athens have not survived (see Queux Saint-Hilaire 1887, 18).

60 Gustave to the family, 7.2.1834, in: ibid., 19–24, tr. by K.S.
61 Louis d'Eichthal to Gustave d'Eichthal, 3.12.1833, BDA MS 13748, 4.
62 Gustave to the family, 7.2.1834, in: Queux Saint-Hilaire (1887, 19–24).
63 Ibid.
64 Gustave d'Eichthal to Duveyrier, 17.3.1834, in: ibid., 24–28, tr. by K.S.
65 As a member of the regency, Georg Friedrich Maurer declared that the office was founded to finally make progress with the many fields of work that had lain dormant under Joseph von Armansperg, e.g. the question of colonisation. He described d'Eichthal and de Roujoux as 'quick-witted and active men' (see Maurer 1968, 99, tr. by K.S.). After the failure of this attempt, a new Greek Office for Political Economy was only founded in 1886; see 1893–1894 [C. 6855–56] FO 1893. Annual Series. No. 1169. Diplomatic and Consular Reports on Trade and Finance. Greece. Report by Mr. E. F. G. Law on the Present Economical and Financial Position in Greece, in: UK Parliamentary Papers, https://parlipapers-proquest-com.proxy.ub.uni-frankfurt.de/parlipapers/docview/t70.d75.1893-071122_0091?accountid=10957 [07.02.2020], 2. The French ambassador had high hopes of the office; see Baron Rouen to MAE, 23.6.1834, AEE, P10500.
66 Gustave d'Eichthal to Duveyrier, 17.3.1834, in: Queux Saint-Hilaire (1887, 24–28).
67 Ibid., tr. by K.S.
68 Property rights are understood as the rights of disposal of a resource. 'The constitution and culture of a social system is manifested in its institutions or the structure and allocation of property rights'. They can be explicitly enforced judicially or implicitly enforced through terminating cooperation or other social sanctions. Ripperger (2005, 26ff.).
69 Gustave d'Eichthal to Duveyrier, 17.3.1834, in: Queux Saint-Hilaire (1887, 24–28), tr. by K.S.
70 A comprehensive description of the foreign parties, their leaders and the intrigues surrounding the Bavarian regency is found in a letter from Gustave d'Eichthal to unknown, 5.8.1834, in: D'Eichthal (1974, 46–59).
71 Gustave d'Eichthal to unknown, 29.6.1834, in: Queux Saint-Hilaire (1887, 30f.).
72 Kolettis profited politically from the revolt, which was suppressed within six weeks, so that Petropulos suspected him of having failed to prevent it or even of having organised it (see Petropulos 1968, 223).
73 Bavarian regency Armansperg, Kobel, Heideck to the minister of the interior Kolettis, 19.9./1.10.1834 and 26.9.1834, in: D'Eichthal (1974, 104, 107).
74 Kolettis to the regency, 20.9./2.10.1834, in: ibid., 104–106.
75 Gustave d'Eichthal to Louis d'Eichthal, 19.10.1834, in: Queux Saint-Hilaire (1887, 36f.).
76 Gustave d'Eichthal to Louis d'Eichthal, 8./20.10.1834, in: ibid., 38.
77 Gustave d'Eichthal to Louis d'Eichthal, 19.10.1834, in: D'Eichthal (1974, 108–110).
78 Gustave d'Eichthal to Roujoux, 16/28.12.1834, in: ibid., 75–80.
79 Diary of Gustave d'Eichthal, 3.12.1834, in ibid., Queux Saint-Hilaire (1887, 52–55).
80 Diary of Gustave d'Eichthal, 11.11.1834, in ibid., 41f.
81 Diary of Gustave d'Eichthal, 20.11.1834, in ibid., 43.
82 Diary of Gustave d'Eichthal, 22–24.11.1834, in ibid., 43–46.
83 Ibid.
84 Diary of Gustave d'Eichthal, 28.12./9.1.1835, in ibid., 68–70.
85 Diary of Gustave d'Eichthal, 3.12.1834, in ibid., 52–55.
86 Gustave d'Eichthal to Roujoux, 16./28.12.1834, in: ibid., 58–62.
87 Gustave d'Eichthal to Roujoux, 1.1.1835, in: ibid., 63–67.

88 Ibid., 66, tr. by K.S.
89 Gustave estimated the number of nomadic Vlachs in the region to amount to about 2,000–3,000 families who kept about 200,000 head of cattle. See Diary of Gustave d'Eichthal, 26.11.1834, in: ibid., 47–50. On observation of the Vlachs in Greece by foreign travellers before 1821, see Angelomatis-Tsougarakis (1990, 207–211).
90 Diary of Gustave d'Eichthal, 3.12.1834, in: Queux Saint-Hilaire (1887, 52–55).
91 Diary of Gustave d'Eichthal, 11.11.1834, in ibid., 41f.
92 Diary of Gustave d'Eichthal, 15.–18.12.1834, in ibid., 63.
93 Diary of Gustave d'Eichthal, 11.11.1834, in ibid., 41f.
94 Diary of Gustave d'Eichthal, 28.12./9.1.1835, in ibid., 68–70.
95 Gustave d'Eichthal to Roujoux, 1.1.1835, in ibid., 63–67.
96 Diary of Gustave d'Eichthal, 3.12.1834, in ibid., 52–55.
97 Gustave d'Eichthal to Roujoux, 1.1.1835, in ibid., 63–67.
98 Gustave d'Eichthal to Roujoux, 16./28.12.1834, in D'Eichthal (1974, 75–80).
99 Gustave d'Eichthal to Roujoux, 16./28.12.1834, in Queux Saint-Hilaire (1887, 58–62); Gustave d'Eichthal to Roujoux, 1.1.1835, in ibid., 63–67.
100 Gustave d'Eichthal to Roujoux, 16./28.12.1834, in ibid., 58–62.
101 Gustave d'Eichthal to Roujoux, 1.1.1835, in ibid., 63–67.
102 Gustave d'Eichthal to unknown, 20.5./1.6.1835, in: D'Eichthal (1974, 86–90).
103 Gustave d'Eichthal to the Greek ministry of the interior, 13.10.1835, BDA MS 13759.
104 Louis d'Eichthal to Gustave d'Eichthal, 3.7.1834, BDA MS 13748, 21.
105 Adolphe converted to Protestantism for his wife.
106 Adolphe d'Eichthal to Gustave d'Eichthal, 19.1.1834, BDA MS 13748, 46.
107 Louis d'Eichthal to Gustave d'Eichthal, 17.4.1834, BDA MS 13748, 18.
108 Adolphe d'Eichthal to Gustave d'Eichthal, 19.1.1834, BDA MS 13748, 46.
109 Louis d'Eichthal to Gustave d'Eichthal, 13.8.1834, BDA MS 13748, 24, tr. by K.S.
110 Ibid., tr. by K.S.
111 This also included Gustave's ideas about the possibility of self-government for the Greeks, which Louis viewed as totally unrealistic. Louis d'Eichthal to Gustave d'Eichthal, 27.1.1834, continued, 3.2.1834, BDA MS 13748, 11.
112 Louis d'Eichthal to Gustave d'Eichthal, 4.4.1834, BDA MS 13748, 13, tr. by K.S.
113 Louis d'Eichthal to Gustave d'Eichthal, 17.4.1834, BDA MS 13748, 18.
114 Louis d'Eichthal to Gustave, 3.12.1833, BDA MS 13748, 4; Louis d'Eichthal to Gustave d'Eichthal, 13.8.1834, BDA MS 13748, 24. Adolphe also reported on important positions that the Saint-Simonians rightly took on under the 'Citizen King' Louis-Philippe; see Adolphe d'Eichthal to Gustave d'Eichthal, 19.1.1834, BDA MS 13748, 46.
115 Louis d'Eichthal to Gustave d'Eichthal, 3.12.1833, BDA MS 13748, 4.
116 The reference here seems to be to the French chamber and permission to found a joint-stock company.
117 Louis d'Eichthal to Gustave d'Eichthal, 3.12.1833, BDA MS 13748, 4.
118 Louis d'Eichthal to Gustave d'Eichthal, 21.1.1834, BDA MS 13748, 9 (see also Soulié 2013).
119 Louis d'Eichthal to Gustave d'Eichthal, 15.5.1833, BDA MS 13747, 76. 1855–1861. Adolphe d'Eichthal was then first president of the Compagnie générale maritime (see Stoskopf 2002a, 160).
120 Louis to Gustave from Paris, 28.8.1833, BDA MS 13748. The concern that the competition could pre-empt the von Eichthals appears repeatedly in the correspondence. Thus, Louis explicitly demands that Gustave should use his letters to let Uncle Simon in Munich know that his presence in Greece was very

necessary to prevent the competition from pre-empting them; see Louis d'Eichthal to Gustave d'Eichthal, 3.12.1833, BDA MS 13748, 4.

121 Adolphe d'Eichthal to Gustave d'Eichthal, 6.10.1833, BDA MS 13748, 40.
122 Ibid.
123 Adolphe d'Eichthal to Gustave d'Eichthal, 28.2.1834, BDA MS 13748, 47.
124 Gustave d'Eichthal to the regency, 9.4.1834, BDA MS 13759, 7.
125 In 1837, Gustave's friend Roujoux was named Agent des paquebot à vapeur français en Grèce; see Gustave d'Eichthal to one of his aunts, April 1837, BDA MS 13759.
126 Simon von Eichthal to Gustave d'Eichthal, (apparently) copied by Louis d'Eichthal, 18.12.1833, BDA MS 13748, 6.
127 Ibid.
128 Simon von Eichthal to Gustave d'Eichthal, (apparently) copied by Louis d'Eichthal, 18.12.1833, BDA MS13748, 6, tr. by K.S.
129 Louis to Gustave, 3.12.1833, BDA MS 13748, 4.
130 'Investment decisions may be influenced by observing the decisions of others to the point that some individuals may ignore their own private information' (Seasholes 2010).
131 Louis d'Eichthal to Gustave d'Eichthal, 26.7.1834, BDA MS 13748, 23.
132 Adolphe d'Eichthal to Gustave d'Eichthal, 30.12.1832, BDA MS 13747, 38 (see also Codman 1965).
133 Louis d'Eichthal to Gustave d'Eichthal, 26.7.1834, BDA MS 13748, 23.
134 Louis d'Eichthal to Gustave d'Eichthal, 4.4.1834, BDA MS 13748, 13.
135 Louis d'Eichthal to Gustave d'Eichthal, 5.4.1834, BDA MS 13748, 14, tr. by K.S.
136 Ibid.
137 Adolphe d'Eichthal to Gustave d'Eichthal, 28.2.1834, BDA MS 13748, 47.
138 Adolphe d'Eichthal to Gustave d'Eichthal, 12.4.1835, BDA MS 13748, 62.
139 In queries to acquaintances in other parts of Greece, he combined these areas of interest, asking about ownership structures, the chances of acquiring land and colonisation, and so received information that he could use both for the family and his official activities; see Lenz to Gustave d'Eichthal, 12.7.1834, BDA MS 13747, 124.
140 Louis d'Eichthal to Gustave d'Eichthal, 26.7.1834, BDA MS 13748, 23.
141 The practice of demanding land as a guarantee for credits was common in banking in the nineteenth century (see Pohle-Fraser, 125–131, 165–189), although bankers were often rather reserved about demanding such guarantees as this could be interpreted as a sign of mistrust and damage the reputation of the borrower. In addition, the value that could actually be realised from such a guarantee was rarely equivalent to the calculated guarantee value (see Galassi/Newton 2001).
142 Louis d'Eichthal to Gustave d'Eichthal, 13.8.1834, BDA MS 13748, 24.
143 Louis to Gustave, 3.12.1833, BDA MS 13748, 4.
144 Louis d'Eichthal to Gustave d'Eichthal, 21.1.1834, BDA MS 13748, 9.
145 Louis d'Eichthal to Gustave d'Eichthal, 3.7.1834, BDA MS 13748, 21.
146 Adolphe d'Eichthal to Gustave d'Eichthal, 28.2.1834, BDA MS 13748, 47.
147 Adolphe d'Eichthal to Gustave d'Eichthal, 31.7.1834, BDA MS 13748, 53.
148 Louis d'Eichthal reported that both the Sina father and son in Vienna had recently married Greeks and could thus also do something for the country, e.g. by providing discounts and purchasing land; see Louis d'Eichthal to Gustave d'Eichthal, 11.5.1835, BDA MS 13748, 30.
149 Louis d'Eichthal to Gustave d'Eichthal, 11.5.1835, BDA MS 13748, 30.
150 On the founding of the national bank, **67–69** in this book. Julius von Hösslin, who came from an Augsburg merchant family, was undoubtedly well-acquainted

with the von Eichthals and in 1839 founded the first Western-type bank in Greece; **87 n.93** in this book.

151 Simon von Eichthal to Gustave d'Eichthal, (apparently) copied by Louis d'Eichthal, 18.12.1833, BDA MS 13748, 6.

152 Louis to Gustave, 3.12.1833, BDA MS 13748, 4.

153 Simon von Eichthal to Gustave d'Eichthal, (apparently) copied by Louis d'Eichthal, 18.12.1833, BDA MS 13748, 6, tr. by K.S.

154 Louis d'Eichthal to Gustave d'Eichthal, 17.4.1834, BDA MS 13748, 18.

155 Louis d'Eichthal to Gustave d'Eichthal, 21.1.1834, BDA MS 13748, 9.

156 Adolphe d'Eichthal to Gustave d'Eichthal, 28.2.1834, BDA MS 13748, 47, tr. by K.S.

157 Adolphe d'Eichthal to Gustave d'Eichthal, 10.3.1835, BDA MS 13748, 60.

158 Adolphe d'Eichthal to Gustave d'Eichthal, 12.4.1835, BDA MS 13748, 62.

159 Adolphe d'Eichthal to Gustave d'Eichthal, 10.3.1835, BDA MS 13748, 60, tr. by K.S.

160 Ibid., tr. by K.S.

161 Ibid.

162 Ibid., 63.

163 Ibid., 60, tr. by K.S.

164 James de Rothschild, Paris, to Nathan Rothschild, London, 20.12.1832, RAL XI/109J/J/32. The reference to these sources is found in Ferguson (2002, 650). The letters are partly written in Yiddish and the Rothschild archive provided a translation into English that was undertaken in the context of Ferguson's work. The archive explicitly points out that mistakes have since been found in some of the translations; it cannot be ruled out that such mistakes occur here.

165 Aguado originated from Seville and fought on France's side in Spain during the Napoleonic wars, after 1815, he embarked on a career as a banker in Paris and accumulated a significant fortune. He was also known as a patron of the arts (see Luis 2009; Simal 2019). In 1823, Aguado participated in the loans for the defeat of the Trieno liberal, but later attempted to make contacts in liberal Paris circles. From 1831, he was associated with the bank Jean-Chilon Ferrère-Laffittes, the nephew of Jacques Laffitte (ibid., 213; Monnier 2013). This explains why the name Ferrère-Laffitte appears in the contract for the Greek loan. The Paris banking house Blanc Colin was also named as a partner. André et Cottier (the bank of Eynard's nephew), which Luis names as head of the Paris syndicate (Luis 2009, 229), cannot be found in the contract or in the other correspondence.

166 After deduction of the previous interest payments and amortisations, the actual price was thus 89; see Lionel Rothschild, Paris, to his parents, London, RAL XI/109/27/1/54.

167 James de Rothschild, Paris, to Nathan Rothschild, London, 22.12.1832, RAL XI/109J/J/32A.

168 This may have been James Wilson from the merchant bank James Wilson & Co (see Edwards 2004).

169 James de Rothschild, Paris, to Nathan Rothschild, London, 22.12.1832, RAL XI/109J/J/32B.

170 James de Rothschild, Paris, to Nathan Rothschild, London, 22.12.1832, RAL XI/109J/J/32A; Lionel Rothschild, Paris, to his parents, London, 22.12.1832, RAL XI/109/27/1/54.

171 Ibid.

172 Ibid. In fact, the responsibilities and obligations of the guarantor powers were laid down in great detail in the contract.

173 Ibid.
174 James de Rothschild, Paris, to Nathan Rothschild, London, 25.12.1832, RAL XI/109J/J/32.
175 Ibid.
176 James de Rothschild, Paris, to Nathan Rothschild, London, 27.12.1832, RAL XI/109J/J/32.
177 In Amschel Mayer Rothschild, Frankfurt, to James de Rothschild, Paris, 25.12.1832, RAL XI/109/27/3/24, tr. by K.S. This was, however, also the case for the Latin American borrowers in the 1820s (see Clavel 2018).
178 Ibid., tr. by K.S.
179 Ibid., tr. by K.S. At the end of the month, James' brother Amschel in Frankfurt clearly changed his mind and advised James to act accordingly; see Lionel Rothschild, Paris, to his parents, London, 31.12.1832, RAL XI/109/27/1/62.
180 James de Rothschild, Paris, and Nathan de Rothschild, London, 27.12.1832, RAL XI/109J/J/32.
181 This refers to Nathan von Rothschild's son Nathaniel (1812–1870).
182 James de Rothschild, Paris, and Nathan de Rothschild, London, 27.12.1832, RAL XI/109J/J/32. This refers to the London Conference of the Powers negotiating the future of Greece in 1832, which in July 1832 concluded the Treaty of Constantinople which set the boundaries of the new kingdom of Greece.
183 Contract between James de Rothschild and Aguado, no date, ANMT, Fonds Rothschild, 32 AQ T35. This also applied to any profits from the payments to Turkey.
184 James de Rothschild, Paris, to Nathan Rothschild, London, 25.12.1832, RAL XI/109J/J/32. It remained only to settle whether they should wait for the agreement of the French parliament or use the present great enthusiasm for the project and issue immediately; see Lionel Rothschild, Paris, to his parents, London, 31.12.1832, RAL XI/109/27/1/62.
185 James de Rothschild, Paris, to Nathan de Rothschild, London, 27.12.1832, RAL XI/109J/J/32. On the role of Turkey, **120f.** in this book.
186 James de Rothschild and Aguado assumed a price of 94, which should have included the interest payments for six months, in 12 monthly rates. In contrast, Eichthal wanted a price of 94 and 12 monthly rates with interest on the entire sum but starting with the first payment. He declared that he was not authorised to agree to a different arrangement, so that Aguado finally had to give in; see James de Rothschild to Amschel Mayer Rothschild, Frankfurt, 24.12.1832, RAL XI 109/27/1/60. James, who had already predicted this, declared 'that after the manner in which he had conducted himself towards us, we could not do otherwise than continue sharing the risks with him' (Lionel Rothschild, Paris, to his parents, London, 31.12.1832, RAL XI/109/27/1/62). The sum that the Rothschilds had to pay to Greece was thus 37.6 million francs; see Contrat de l'Emprunt Grèce, 12.1.1833, ANMT, Fonds Rothschild, 32 AQ T3.
187 Lionel Rothschild, Paris, to his parents, London, 31.12.1832, RAL XI/109/27/1/62.
188 Contrat de l'Emprunt Grèce, 12.1.1833, ANMT, Fonds Rothschild, 32 AQ T3.
189 James de Rothschild to Amschel Mayer Rothschild, Frankfurt, 19.2.1833, RAL XI/109/20/2/3.
190 Louis d'Eichthal to Gustave d'Eichthal, 24.7.1833, BDA MS 13747, 89.
191 Adolphe d'Eichthal to Gustave d'Eichthal, 28.12.1832, BDA MS 13747, 37.
192 Anette d'Eichthal to Gustave d'Eichthal, 12.2.1833, BDA MS 13747, 51.
193 Anette d'Eichthal to Gustave d'Eichthal, 21.3.1833, BDA MS 13747, 62, tr. by K.S.
194 Adolphe d'Eichthal to Gustave d'Eichthal, 6.10.1833, BDA MS 13748, 40.
195 Louis d'Eichthal to Gustave d'Eichthal, 17.4.1834, BDA MS 13748, 18.

196 For details on how they were used, see Ανδρεάδης [Andreadis] (1904, 84–92).
197 Adolphe d'Eichthal to Gustave d'Eichthal, 21.11.1834, BDA MS 13748, 57, tr. by K.S.
198 Although this hypothesis is undermined by the insistent attempts to found a bank undertaken by Eynard and many of his colleagues throughout the 1830s. There were indeed bankers who were seriously interested in the Greek market in the long term; **67f.** of this book.
199 Adolphe d'Eichthal to Gustave d'Eichthal, 23.8.1833, BDA MS 13747, 103. The rest was intended for minting money and establishing a steam ship line, thus precisely the two projects with which the von Eichthals were most concerned. The sums named in the sources vary greatly.
200 '[S]ans aucune bonification d'intérêt'. Contrat de l'Emprunt Grèce, 12.1.1833, ANMT, Fonds Rothschild, 32 AQ T3.
201 Ibid.
202 See for further considerations Chatziioannou (2019).
203 Louis d'Eichthal to Gustave d'Eichthal, 3.7.1834, BDA MS 13748, 21. The letter refers to 800 francs being retained, although this seems a very small sum to trigger such disputes.
204 Charles von Eichthal to Adolphe d'Eichthal, Paris 18.7.1834, as a copy from Adolphe to Gustave, BDA MS 13748, 67, tr. by K.S.
205 Ibid., tr. by K.S.
206 Ibid., tr. by K.S.
207 Adolphe d'Eichthal to Gustave d'Eichthal, 28.7.1834, BDA MS 13748, 52.
208 Charles von Eichthal to Adolphe d'Eichthal, Paris 18.7.1834, as a copy from Adolphe to Gustave, BDA MS 13748/67.
209 Adolphe d'Eichthal to Gustave d'Eichthal, 19.1.1834, BDA MS 13748, 46.
210 Adolphe d'Eichthal to Gustave d'Eichthal, 12.11.1833, BDA MS 13748, 42.
211 Adolphe d'Eichthal to Gustave d'Eichthal, 19.1.1834, BDA MS 13748, 46.
212 Other bankers also had similarly negative experiences with the regency, e.g. Humann; see Adolphe d'Eichthal to Gustave d'Eichthal, 21.11.1834, BDA MS 13748, 57.
213 Louis to Gustave, 3.12.1833, BDA MS 13748, 4.
214 Greek legation in Paris to the Greek foreign ministry in Athens, 10/22.9.1835, GNA, foreign ministry 1832–1862, Fak. 042, GRGSA-CSA_PA0/008.00.
215 Louis to Gustave, 3.12.1833, BDA MS 13748, 4.
216 Simon von Eichthal to Gustave d'Eichthal, 16.6.1834, BDA MS 13748, 64.
217 Louis d'Eichthal to Gustave d'Eichthal, 20.1.1834, BDA MS 13748, 8.
218 Louis d'Eichthal to Gustave d'Eichthal, with an addition by Charles von Eichthal (the son of Simon), 28.6.1834, BDA MS 13748, 20.
219 Louis d'Eichthal to Gustave d'Eichthal, 11.7.1834, BDA MS 13748, 22.
220 Louis d'Eichthal to Gustave d'Eichthal, 13.8.1834, BDA MS 13748, 24.
221 Louis d'Eichthal to Gustave d'Eichthal, 21.1.1834, BDA MS 13748, 9.
222 Louis d'Eichthal to Gustave d'Eichthal, 20.11.1834, BDA MS 13748, 28.
223 Ibid., 56.
224 Adolphe d'Eichthal to Gustave d'Eichthal, 10.3.1835, BDA MS 13748, 60.
225 Networks of international families were often developed through unsuccessful sons being sent far away from home. The families continued to support them but '[t]he key point was to keep them away from the home town and competition for scarce familial goods' (Sabean/Teuscher 2011, 10f.). In the case of the d'Eichthals, it was at least the case that Adolphe was keen to finally settle the question of a profession for his brother.
226 Adolphe d'Eichthal to Gustave d'Eichthal, 16.8.1836, BDA MS 13748, 76.

227 Adolphe d'Eichthal to Gustave d'Eichthal, 25.9.1836, BDA MS 13748, 93.
228 Gustave's text was the (even in his opinion overly long) foreword to the translation in French of the book by Daniel Urquhart (1836). *Revue des deux mondes* is the title of the successful Saint-Simonian journal which is still published today.
229 D'Eichthal marked the dividing line between Orient and Occident on a map. Here, not only the aforementioned north-south axis was visible, but also an east-west axis connecting Constantinople and Paris in the shape of a possible shipping line (see Le Bret 2012, 230–233).
230 Many aspects of d'Eichthal's image of the Orient correspond in detail with the elements of Western 'Orientalism' described by Said (1978); see Todorova (1997, 31).
231 'He [the Oriental man] enjoys the present and pleases himself with a carefree attitude towards the future, dreading the prudence that sees misfortunes too far in advance, he has extreme trust in that kindness of Providence that never leaves its children in need, and equally extreme mistrust of the skill of man to foresee the harm that threatens him. Allah khèrim! Et bakaloum! [...] He [the Occidental man] loves to foresee the future, to foresee unfavourable fortunes; *he never leaves anything to chance that he can avoid through advice or foresight;* he believes that with his reason God gave man a second providence: *Help yourself and heaven will help you*'. D'Eichthal (1836, 27, 30f.), tr. by K.S. Emphasis in the original. Note the capitalisation of the word 'providence' in the first case but not in the second.
232 Todorova calls ideas like this a 'mystical flight to the Middle Ages' (Todorova 1977, 32).
233 D'Eichthal (1836, 125), tr. by K.S.
234 Gustave's criticism did not prevent his Uncle Simon from continuing to develop his links to the house of Armansperg: in 1847, his son Julius married von Armansperg's daughter Marie. Simon also received the Greek Order of Merit for his services (see Le Bret 2012, 37f.).
235 After the death of his father in 1840, Gustave was so financially secure that he could marry without having to take on a bread-and-butter job (see Le Bret 2012, 290).
236 Gustave d'Eichthal worked actively for the emancipation of the Jews in Austria and even met Metternich to talk to him about the topic. His idea was that the religious community should make a one-off payment and thus buy their way out of the special taxation regime (see Le Bret 2012, 234–242).
237 Karl von Abel to Gustave d'Eichthal, 7.10.1836, BDA MS 13748, 95; Gustave d'Eichthal to Abel, undated (1836–1837?), BDA MS 14393–14394 (Queux Saint-Hilaire 1887, 75). Roujoux was later the French consul in Athens and in 1841 was a member of the supervisory board of the ETE (see Ιστορικό Αρχείο [Historical Archives] 2001).
238 For a detailed account of the draining project, d'Eichthals' involvement and the engineer Sauvage, see **125** in this book.
239 On the growing importance of expert culture, see e.g. Fisch/Rudloff 2004; Kohlrausch et al. 2010; Vandendriessche et al. 2015. What bankers most feared from technical experts was their lack of business acumen and their possible bias (see Pohle-Fraser 1999, 189). On occasion, the experts were required to submit proof of loyalty to the bank (see ibid., 192).
240 See also **142 n.256** of this book.
241 It is unknown whether d'Eichthal here also cherished plans to make use of the project for his private business ends. Also see *L'Observateur d'Athènes*, 7.11.1853

and French legation Athens to MAE, 7.11.1858, AN F/12/2670. Here, the total costs were estimated at 120,000 drachmas.

242 Statement from the D'Eichthal banking house to Gustave d'Eichthal, 5.4.1844, BDA MS 13755; he obviously sold the bonds in 1846.

243 Archives Familiales Péreire, quoted in Le Bret (2012, 511f.). In his letter to Émile Péreire from 4.3.1867 quoted here, Gustave still argued in favour of an enlargement of Greek territory.

244 Gustave d'Eichthal to the governor of the ETE, 11.2.1875, ETE, XXIIB'B'3226. In December, he obtained three more bonds; see Gustave d'Eichthal to the governor of the ETE, 16.12.1876, ibid.

245 On the building of the Canal of Corinth, see Chapter II.6 in this book.

246 E.g. to Guizot, but also to Cavour in Italy (see Le Bret 2012, 282–286).

247 In 1843, the bank was reorganised into this one with Charles-Édouard Pasteur (see Stoskopf 2002a, 159).

248 In the constituency of Sarthe, Le Mans. Gustave had been an unsuccessful candidate in the same constituency five years earlier, but did not begrudge his brother's election victory (see Le Bret 2012, 333–348). Adolphe voted there with the conservative majority (see Faure 1970).

249 Information on his judgement about the situation is provided in his letters to the Baring-Bank in London from 1849–1870, BAL HC 7.27. His resignation as regent was initially not accepted, even though his bank had temporarily needed to halt payments (see Stoskopf 2002a, 159).

250 Louis d'Eichthal to Gustave d'Eichthal, 4.4.1834, BDA MS 13748, 13.

251 Louis d'Eichthal to Gustave d'Eichthal, 11.7.1834, BDA MS 13748, 22; Louis d'Eichthal to Gustave d'Eichthal, 13.8.1834, BDA MS 13748, 24.

252 Louis d'Eichthal to Gustave d'Eichthal, 17.4.1834, BDA MS 13748, 16; Anette d'Eichthal to Gustave d'Eichthal, 12.12.1832, ibid., 28; Adolphe d'Eichthal to Gustave d'Eichthal, 23.1.1833, ibid., 44.

253 Adolphe d'Eichthal to the governor of the ETE, 11.4.1847, ETE XXIIB'B'412, tr. by K.S.

254 The statement in ETE, XXIIB'B'511.

255 When exactly Adolphe surrendered this office and why is unknown. In 1867, it was taken on by Emil Erlanger, who is discussed further below (see **344–347** in this book). However, Erlanger did not follow Eichthal directly. There was at least one other consul general between them; see Emil Erlanger, Paris, to GA, 17.1.1867, GA 1867-37-2, Generalkonsulat Paris.

256 *L'Industrie. Journal des Chemins de Fer, du Crédit Foncier de France et de tous les grands Intérêts du Pays*, Vol. 14, No 38, 23.9.1865, 591, as a quote from *Le Temps*. On the later draining of Lake Copais with French and English capital, see Chapter II.7 in this book.

257 **339f.** in this book.

258 D'Eichthal (1887). In this volume, Gustave's son Eugene d'Eichthal re-published not only this memorandum by his father with the Modern Greek translation by Renieri, but also eight reactions to the piece by contemporaries, e.g. Mendelssohn Bartholdy (1865), and Littré (1865). The volume brings together all Gustave's writing on the subject of Greece.

259 From 1869 to 1890, Markos Renieri was governor of the ETE (see Ιστορικό Αρχείο [Historical Archives National Bank] 2001, 35–37).

260 The article was first printed in 1842 in the journal *Humanist (Ερανιστής)*.

261 Renieri distanced himself from Fallmerayer's ideas and asserted that Greece was in the process of extinguishing the last traces of the Byzantine era and like the needle of a magnet to find once again its orientation to the West.

262 On the uprising on Crete 1866–1868, see Basch (1995, 170); Holland/Markides (2006, 83).
263 The Latin monetary union was founded in 1865. Greece joined three years later. **325 n.106** in this book.
264 'Must it be hoped, if not for the sake of Greece then at least for love of ourselves as the French, that it is again the North from whence the light comes to us?' D'Eichthal (1887, 95), tr. by K.S.
265 D'Eichthal (1877, 6), tr. by K.S.
266 On the reception of antiquity in France and England, also in competition with one another, in the Early Modern period and into the eighteenth century, see Ferris (2000); Zabel (2016).
267 'Athens or the bourgeois history. Athens or the bourgeoisie in the face of their own doubts: republic or empire? Authoritarian empire? Liberal empire? Athens assumes all these images simultaneously…' (Loraux/Vidal-Naquet 1979, 222, tr. by K.S.).
268 Gustave d'Eichthal listed the members in D'Eichthal (1887, 29–33). Among them was Émile-Louis Burnouf, who in 1850 also published a piece on the draining of Lake Copais: Burnouf (1850). **261f.** in this book. On Burnouf, see Prevost (1956); Basch (1995, 140, 177–180). Burnouf later published other work on Greece (e.g. Burnouf 1887, 1896).
269 For example, D'Eichthal (1863b, 1881, 1887). An incomplete list of publications is found in Le Bret (2012).
270 D'Eichthal (1877, 70), tr. by K.S.
271 Bergemann et al. (2011, 39) would therefore describe Gustave as a 'broker' because he made such a choice.
272 Renan's published his famous 'Prière sur l'Acropole' in the Saint-Simonian journal *Revue des deux mondes*.
273 On the history of its reception, see Basch (1995, 78–128).
274 In 1902, an American translation was published (see Basch 1995, 104).
275 On the Greek state loans after 1878, see Chapter II. 5 in this book.

4

ANTIQUE MINES MOLTEN AGAIN

Lavrion

The largely negative reception of Greece in France around the middle of the century was also caused by the perception of political and economic stagnation of the country at this time. Under the rule of King Otto, it seemed to be impossible to generate an economic upturn and important political goals remained similarly distant. Due to the initial successes of the Russians in the Crimea War of 1853–1856, many Greeks cherished the hope that the Ottoman Empire would soon cease to exist, giving them an opportunity to realise the 'Megali idea', the dream of a great country embracing all the areas inhabited by Greeks around the Mediterranean (Zelepos 2002; Marinov/Vezenkov 2015). However, Greek uprisings in the Ottoman territories of Epirus and Thessaly led only to the French-British blockade of Piraeus and other harbours (1854–1857), which damaged the economy and clearly demonstrated the weak position of the childless King Otto and 'the limits of Greece's sovereignty' (Zelepos 2014, 61–65). The Great Powers legitimated their blockade with reference to the Greek debts of 1832, which the country had not serviced since the revolution of 1843 (Ηλιαδάκης [Iliadakis] 2011, 32–39). The expulsion of King Otto in 1861 was at least in part related to the humiliation that many Greeks felt at the gunboat diplomacy of the Great Powers.

In 1863, after a difficult search for a candidate,[1] Wilhelm von Sonderburg-Glücksburg, the son of the Danish King Christian IX, was chosen as George I, the new Greek King. Great Britain gave Greece the Ionian Islands as a coronation gift (Holland/Markides 2006, 46–80).[2] Except for a few manufactories, George's kingdom on the edge of Europe was almost untouched by industrialisation, although individual trading centres like Athens, Ermoupoli on Syros and Patras had experienced notable economic upturns (Αγριαντώνη [Agriantoni] 2010, 62–70). Further industrialisation was hindered by a lack of infrastructure and capital and the continued ineffectiveness of the administration. With the exception of the founding of the National Bank in 1841, no foreign capital had entered the country since the 60-million loan. 'Greece requires nothing so much as a good position on the Stock-Exchange of Europe', commented *The Times*.[3] And in fact the

DOI: 10.4324/9780429286537-7

country could have provided the international markets with interesting investment projects: flourishing trade, agricultural products and, in particular, natural resources. Greece not only had marble and emery, but also lead and silver deposits. The minerals represented an important resource for the expansion of industry: 'Mineral wealth is the backbone of any industrial society' (Gregory 2001, 166).[4] Greece's mineral resources thus seemed to be one option to accelerate the country's industrialisation and enable it to catch up with central Europe.

The metallurgy of silver mining

In the eighteenth century, metallurgy in Europe experienced a new upturn. From the middle of the century, old mines were reactivated in many countries, e.g. in Sweden, Bohemia and Spain. The use of modern steam-powered pumps accelerated this development. The demand from industrialisation was immense: for instance, lead was the basis for manufacturing gas and water pipes and was also used in the chemical industry for the production of sulphuric acid (Chastagnaret 2005, 269f.). Furthermore, the techniques used to process silver were revolutionised in the course of the nineteenth century. For thousands of years, silver had been gained from copper ore by smelting and cupellation. In the 1850s, the so-called Pattinson process made it possible to process silver from molten lead-silver alloy (Gregory 2001, 91), a technique that became widespread by 1870 (ibid., 91).

Demand for lead was very high in Great Britain, the pioneer of industrialisation. Up to about 1840, it was possible to meet this demand from domestic production, e.g. from deposits on the Isle of Man and in Cornwall (ibid., 92ff.). In 1838, the country accounted for about 40% of worldwide production (Fletcher 1991, 195). After this date, however, growing domestic demand caused Great Britain to become an importer of lead ore, which came particularly from the Levant (Chastagnaret 2005, 269f.). There were, of course, other rich deposits, e.g. in the USA (Gregory 2001, 78; Coulson 2012, 66ff., 101–103). For Europe, Marseille was the undisputed centre of the lead trade until the beginning of the 1860s, when the focus shifted increasingly towards the Atlantic. One of the centres of production was Spain, where the state monopoly on lead ore was abolished in 1817, leading to a strong increase in mining (Fletcher 1991, 196; Chastagnaret 2005, 269f.). Initially, this was undertaken by small, local companies with limited investment. From the 1850s, British financiers then played a central role in the development of the industry, alongside Belgian, French and German investors.[5] Spanish production soon outstripped the British, particularly because of its low prices (Coulson 2012, 131).[6]

The discovery and development of new mines was – and indeed continues to be – an extremely capital-intensive investment that requires long term commitment (Gregory, 2001, 167–169). The strongly fluctuating market prices of metal ore lead to high risks for investors. Moreover, at some point, the mines are exhausted and must be closed without the option of the infrastructure erected in and around them being transferred to another location. The dividends for investors must thus be high enough to cover repayment of the invested capital. This is seldom the case, so these days private investors usually keep their distance from mining companies: 'mining is not a legitimate field of investment for widows and orphans'.[7] In the 1870s, bankers were also well-aware of the difficulties of estimating the profits of a silver mine:

> The cost of *production* depends on so many causes: – on the accessibility of the mine; on the means of subsistence there; on the depth of the mine; on its position; on the character of the soil to be pierced; on there being enough water; on there not being too much water; on the cost of labour in the country; on the character and richness of the ore when gotten; on the percentage of gold, silver, or other metals which it may contain; on the skill of the miners; on the goodness of the machinery; on the cost of carriage of the ore, or of the silver itself, if the ore is of such a kind as can be smelted on the spot; on the cost of quicksilver for smelting purposes [...]; and on many other conditions differing in different times and places.
>
> (Gibbs 1876, 4, emphasis in the original)

However, fabulous profits can and could be made in the case of success (Gregory 2001, 171).

When developing a mine, it has always been important to consider the legal situation, which in the nineteenth century varied greatly from country to country. In England, the mineral rights belonged to the owner of the land on which the deposits were found; if the landowner refused to mine the deposits, then the rights could be transferred to someone else (ibid., 136). In contrast, on the continent, minerals generally belonged to the ruler of the country as part of the sovereign rights of the monarch; at best, the owner of the land's surface would be compensated for damage caused to the land. Thus in 1783, Carlos III of Spain declared all mines to be the property of the crown and levied a tax of 20% on their income. In France, the legal situation was different again. Here, the state controlled the mines without owning them. When deposits were found, the state gave the discoverer a concession and the landowner would be compensated (ibid.). International investors had to adapt to the differing conditions. In the nineteenth century, using the remnants of previous smelting processes, including those left from the era of antiquity, proved particularly lucrative, as this enabled the high investment costs to be reduced. With the new refining process, it became possible and lucrative to smelt the waste tips from the old mines and produce good profits with little effort, and certainly without having to mine new ore. Such methods were practised in Spain, southern France and Sardinia (Gironés/

Viejobueno 2001, 201; Coulson 2012, 31). Thus, the era of industrialisation saw ancient heritage being extremely practically appropriated and put to use by its heirs.

The mines of Lavrion

Under these circumstances, it was only a matter of time before the metallurgists remembered the ancient Greek silver and lead mines of Lavrion, located close to Athens. These mines had been described by many authors of antiquity (Καραγιάννης, [Karagiannis] 2011): they had provided the financial basis for the success of the ancient polis, and were used into the Roman era.[8] About 2,000 shafts had been sunk in the area, with depths of up to 300 metres (Coulson 2012, 22).[9] In the second century AD, Pausanias described the Lavrion mines as disused due to exhaustion, but perhaps their abandonment also had to do with finding richer deposits in Macedonia and Thrace (Coulson 2012, 22); thereafter, they only attracted the attention of travellers very sporadically.

This changed with Greece's independence. It seems that the first Greek president Kapodistrias investigated the mines to see if they could be further used (Κακαβογιάννης, [Kakavogiannis] 1998), but he did not want to leave their exploitation to foreign companies as the British ambassador seems to have suggested (ibid.). The Bavarian regency and King Otto also demonstrated interest in the mineral deposits, with Otto seeking expert advice by commissioning the mining engineer Karl Fiedler in 1835 with the investigation of the mines (Fiedler 1840). The secondary literature usually suggests that Fiedler advised against exploiting the mines and failed to recognise their value.[10] This is, however, inaccurate. Fiedler reported that the slag heaps had been investigated in many places to check whether re-smelting would be profitable, and he declared further research for underground deposits, especially of iron ore, to be desirable. He warned that the investment costs would be high but he wished every courageous entrepreneur who wanted to embark on the undertaking '*Good luck!* from the whole of his heart' (Fiedler 1840, 59, 74, 79).[11] The geologist Joseph Russegger also travelled to the mining area of Lavrion with a royal commission and reported that 'there should still be a great deal of mining hope available'. However, due to the large amount of capital necessary, he advised the government 'to either leave such undertakings to private industry, with whom the government, without squeezing them, probably is in any case hardly able to compete, or to wait for a more appropriate time' (Russegger 1848, 185f., tr. by K.S.). In the highly indebted kingdom, this more appropriate moment was not seen for the next 25 years.

It was the beginning of the 1860s before interest in the Lavrion mines reawakened. The Italian-French company Hilarion Roux et Cie tackled the business, but within only a few years came into serious conflict with the Greek government. The 'Lavrion affair' not only affected Greek domestic politics, contributing to the fall of a total of five governments between 1870 and 1873, but it also led to diplomatic imbroglios that some contemporaries saw as bringing Europe to the verge of war.[12] Georgios Dertilis believes that the history of the Lavrion affair is one of the most complex topics of modern Greek history, involving economic, political, diplomatic, legal and technological factors (Πρεβενά [Prevena] 2004, 574). Whether the instability of the political situation impacted the economy or whether the economic problems confounded the politics is a question that has been intensively discussed by historians of Greece (ibid., 578). For those interested in foreign investment, the Lavrion affair is equally fascinating; it led not only to the production of diverse political records in the archives of the foreign offices, but also to the publication of innumerable memorandums, justifications, collections of documents and articles. This compensates somewhat for the fact that the archives of Compagnie Française du Laurium, which operated in Lavrion until 1982, is currently closed to the public.[13] Rich secondary literature is also available: Greek historians have conducted detailed research to shed light on the Lavrion affair, considering the role of international diplomacy, Greek domestic politics, legal preconditions and technological aspects.[14] Here, the focus is on the significance of the mines and the affair for Greece. In the context of the present research, interest is directed rather towards the risk perception of the investors, their risk management and the effects of the investment on the images of Greece held by the European financial markets. In order to address these questions, it is necessary to first consider the actors who reactivated the Lavrion mines.

The actors

Andreas Kordellas

In December 1860, a young Greek mining engineer travelled to Lavrion, commissioned by Queen Amalia to inspect the antique Lavrion mines and assess their suitability for metallurgic exploitation. The use of scientific expertise in the evaluation of investment projects, as initiated by Gustave d'Eichthal in the 1840s, had by the 1860s become a firmly established part of risk assessment. Particularly in the field of mining, it was viewed as indispensable (Schleiff/Konečný 2013). Andreas Kordellas (1836–1909), who was born in 1836 in Asia Minor, was predestined for such a task. His father came from Ambelokipi in Thessaly and had moved to Smyrna to represent his family's trading house (Βοβολίνης [Vovolinis]/Βοβολίνης [Vovolinis] 1958–1963, B, 44).[15] Andreas attended the Protestant school there, accompanied members of the family on journeys to the Aegean Islands and completed various internships in the trading houses of family friends. At not quite 15 years of age, the boy was then sent to Grottau in Bohemia to his uncle Anastasios Kordellas, who lived in the midst of a flourishing Greek diaspora and traded with Macedonian cotton. The advice his uncle gave to Andreas clearly reveals Greek stereotypes about Western Europe: 'Andreas, look to it that you gather the blossoms from the Europeans like a busy bee, and not the dirt like the flies' (ibid., 45). From 1852 to 1855, Andreas attended the industrial school in Zittau, but he also educated himself by reading the classical Greek authors. After completing school, he studied at a well-known mining academy in Freiberg, graduating in 1858 as a mining engineer.[16] His uncle, who actually wanted him to become a doctor, had allowed himself to be persuaded that Greece required able engineers and technicians, and that modern science was in a position to bring progress. During and after his studies, Kordellas visited the most important mines in the German-speaking countries, especially in Prussia. He afterwards registered to study philosophy in Bonn, and then in Liège. Extensive travels through Europe also took him to France before he returned to Smyrna in 1860. The declared goal of the patriot educated in the diaspora was to initiate the exploitation of Greece's natural resources and thus to trigger industrialisation of the kingdom, where technical know-how was in short supply (Agriantoni 2011, 18). Kordellas was persuaded of the benefits of industrial development and believed it required foreign capital (Κορδέλλας [Kordellas] 1865, 4). On his arrival in Athens, he was welcomed by Queen Amalia and immediately received the commission to inspect the old mines of Lavrion.[17] It seemed that the expertise imported from Freiberg was greatly valued at court. In December, Kordellas accordingly inspected the old lead mines at Lavrion and the remains of the ancient mining activities. In his memoires, he portrayed himself, drawing on the title of the Greek hero of the revolution Rigas Velestinlis, as the 'new Anacharsis' on unexplored paths.[18] He described the labyrinth of ancient tunnels and imagined the thousands of workers who brought the riches of the earth into the light of day in antiquity. The so-called scoriae, the remnants of ancient smelting activities, seemed of particular interest to him, as they still contained rich deposits of metal that could be easily extracted using modern techniques. In his report for the ministry, written just a week later, he estimated these silver-lead scoriae to amount to 1.5 million cubic metres, and chemical analysis suggested that they were 0.725% metal. The scoriae were thus in no way inferior to those being exploited abroad. With the right people, it would take little effort to extract the lead and then the silver from the stone. If the state were not currently able to undertake such an endeavour, then Kordellas advised selling the scoriae for 5.4 drachmas per tonne.[19] He not only delivered his report to the ministry of the economy, but also gave a copy of it (Κορδέλλας [Kordellas] 1865, 10) to Theodor Erik Hermann von Heldreich (1822–1902), who since 1851 had been the director of the botanical gardens in Athens and who must have known the Lavrion region well from his extensive botanical travels through Greece (Βοβολίνης [Vovolinis]/Βοβολίνης [Vovolinis] 1958–1963, B, 50). It is obvious that Kordellas gave him the report in order for Heldreich to pass it on to interested industrialists and financiers in the West, perhaps even with the express request to do so. This notion is supported by the fact that Kordellas went to some trouble to publicise his findings in Europe, e.g. through publications in appropriate specialist journals. Thus in August 1864, he authored an article for the mining and metallurgy journal *Berg- und Huettenmaennischen Zeitung* on slagging in Lavrion. Here, he described how 'because of the incomplete smelting process of the ancient Greeks' the slag contained 'pieces of silver-bearing lead from the smallest of sizes up to one of a cubic centimetre'. In some places, he had been able to gather with his bare hands 'more than two pounds of pure deposited silver-bearing lead' from the kernels that sparkled in seawater 'like the stars in heaven'.[20] The first to react to Kordellas' report was an Italian: Jean Battista Serpieri.

Jean Battista Serpieri

Jean Battista (Gimbattista, Ioannis Baptista) Serpieri (1832–1887) was born on 23 March 1832 in Rimini as the son of the Catholic Enrico Serpieri (1809–1872), a fighter of the Italian Risorgimento. Enrico, who had studied medicine in Bologna and was a follower of Guiseppe Mazzini's liberal 'Giovani Italia',[21] had been sentenced to life imprisonment by the papal government in 1845 due to revolutionary activities, although he was pardoned a year later by pope Pius IX (N.N. s.t.c; Altgeld 2002, 273f.). This close friend of the national democrat Mazzini and the national liberal Camillo Benso di Cavour (Serpieri 1982, 8f.) passed on his political commitment to the eldest of his three sons. In 1848, at the age of 16, Jean Battista joined his father in defending Rome against French troops who wanted to maintain the status quo in Italy against the Risorgimento (Farina 2013, 24ff.). The family fought on all fronts for a liberal and united Italy. In 1849, the father Enrico Serpieri was a deputy in the constituent assembly of the democratic Roman republic proclaimed by Mazzini, which, despite the fierce resistance of Garibaldi, was soon defeated by Austrian, French, Spanish and Neapolitan troops (N.N. s.t.c; Altgeld 2002, 287). After the collapse of the republic, Enrico Serpieri was forced into exile. He fled with his family to liberal Sardinia-Piedmont, where Cavour became the prime minister in 1852 (Altgeld 2002, 258). After the failure of his political activities, Serpieri turned to business, embarking very successfully on metallurgy in Cagliari. He made most effective use of the scoriae left from the Sardinian mining of antiquity and the thirteenth and fourteenth centuries, by smelting them a second time. In 1862, his smelter thus produced over half of all Sardinian lead. Enrico was active in the chamber of commerce of Cagliari, the first president of the Banca di Cagliari, a member of the freemasons lodge Vittoria and an important philanthropist (Farina 2013, 27). He also remained politically active and in 1866 became a parliamentarian in the kingdom of Italy, demonstrating the extent of his continued links with the liberal movement (ibid.).

His son Jean Battista moved in exile to Genoa in 1850 and studied mathematics and engineering before working for a few years in his father's business on Sardinia (N.N. s.t.b). He then went to Marseille, the centre of Levantine lead trade and a gathering point for the Greek diaspora (Πάρη [Pari] 2008), where he completed an internship in the banking house Roux et Fraissinet, a leader in the lead trade. It can be assumed that his father organised this position for his son through his business partners. This extension of the family beyond the Italian peninsula, which later continued in the direction of Greece, may have reflected the wish of several democrats of the Italian Risorgimento for Italy to have more influence in the wider Mediterranean, as Clara Lovett has suggested (Lovett 1982, 232f.; Isabella 2009). Serpieri also worked for his employer in Paris, and like his father was an active freemason (Farina 2013, 31) and sympathised with the legacy of Saint-Simonianism.[22] In Marseille, he married the Frenchwoman Clemence Leboyl (N.N. s.t.b). Giorgios Dermatis describes Jean Battista Serpieri as a representative of homo oeconomicus, without defining this more precisely and without taking into account his liberal convictions (Δερμάτης [Dermatis] 2003, 78).

How did the family hear of the mines in Lavrion? Serpieri later told his engineer Alfred Huet, who worked in Lavrion from 1873, that in 1859 an Italian guest visited his father's mines on Sardinia and told them of similar antique scoriae in Attica near Athens, where he had hunted. Serpieri had organised for a crate of the Greek scoriae to be delivered to him, although he had then left this unopened for two years. A Greek cheese merchant who was travelling in Sardinia later also told the Serpieris about the scoriae in Attica, but even this failed to move them to open the crate (Huet 1879, 735).

In 1861, Serpieri then commissioned a Greek captain to transport a load of Sardinian scoriae to Marseille. In the presence of the Greek cheese merchant, the captain reported knowing of very similar material from Lavrion in Greece. Serpieri hence finally opened the crate of Greek scoriae and discovered rich deposits of the best quality (ibid.). The young Greek disappeared to apply as quickly as possible for a concession to exploit the deposits in Lavrion. Serpieri thus hurriedly sent his son Jean Battista, who lived in Marseille, to Greece with instructions to similarly apply for a concession (ibid., 736).

This story reveals elements of the risk perception of the Serpieri family. Firstly, it was largely by chance that the metallurgist Enrico came across the information from various travellers about the deposits in Lavrion. Secondly, he organised to view samples which he could subject to chemical analysis and thus to scientific testing. For two years, Enrico was then too preoccupied with other affairs to investigate the matter. It was the competitive situation with the young Greek, the fear that Lavrion could be snatched away from him, that finally triggered his action. The expansion of the lead trade at the beginning of the 1860s and the search for new sources of the material form the backdrop of the decision-making situation.

This version of the story is by no means the only one.[23] Andreas Kordellas' memoires suggest that the Serpieris drew even more intensively on scientific expertise to aid them in their decision: they possessed the report that he, Andreas Kordellas, had written for the ministry of the economy and had passed on to Theodor Heldreich. Serpieri told Kordellas that he had obtained this report from Heldreich before travelling to Athens (Βοβολίνης [Vovolinis]/Βοβολίνης [Vovolinis] 1958–1963, B, 50). But how did this contact occur? Did Heldreich come into direct contact with the Serpieris on his extensive botanical travels through Italy and Sicily in the early 1840s (Βοβολίνης [Vovolinis]/Βοβολίνης [Vovolinis] 1958–1963, A, 225–228; Dolezal 1969)? Elsewhere, another intermediary is named: Orazio Antinori (1811–1882), later an explorer of Africa. This supporter of the Risorgimento and comrade-in-arms of the Serpieris at the defence of Rome was said to have drawn the attention of the family to the lead mines at Lavrion (Farina 2013, 31).[24] This seems more likely. In 1849, Antinori initially fled to Athens from Rome, and would certainly have visited Lavrion on his exploratory travels in the area (N.N. s.t.a). It is possible that his interest in scientific travelogues brought him into contact with the botanist Heldreich at court in Athens. Heldreich, who was keen to fulfil Kordellas' request to look around for financiers interested in lead mining, would have welcomed Antinori's suggestion of his friends the Serpieris who were active in lead mining in Sardinia. This reconstruction does not contradict the first story recounted by Huet; the two accounts complement one another. The second version would, however, suggest even more strongly that at the beginning of the 1860s, scientific expertise was already a conditio sine qua non for a positive investment decision by the entrepreneurial family. Between the writing of the report and Serpieri's arrival in Athens in October 1863, more than two and a half years went by.

On his arrival, Serpieri discovered that a Greek had already applied for a concession for the Lavrion mines: Georgios Christodoulos Pachis from Artis in Epeiros, who lived on Sardinia and was the son of the Greek vice consul there (Δερμάτης [Dermatis] 2003, 74). Was this the 'Greek cheese merchant' who Serpieri later mentioned to his engineer Huet, perhaps ironically?[25] Pachis was in fact anything but a simple merchant; he was a merchant banker with international relationships and married to Emilia Skouses, a daughter of the influential banker Alexandros Skouses from Constantinople.[26] In August 1861, the Greek government, acting on a suggestion by Kordellas, had passed a law on mining, closely based on the equivalent French law from 1810 (Δερμάτης [Dermatis] 2003, 71). Only a few months later, in November 1861, Pachis applied for the concession to exploit the Lavrion mines,[27] although a decision was not forthcoming for some considerable time. In his petition, Pachis had emphasised his great competence in dealing with industrial methods and had declared his willingness to pay the tax laid out in the new regulations. However, while the site of the various deposits could not be exactly determined, it seemed clear that they were all on the territory of the deme of Lavrion. This led to the petition being passed back and forth between the ministry and the local authorities for two years, with Kordellas also expressing his opinion on several occasions (Βοβολίνης [Vovolinis]/Βοβολίνης [Vovolinis] 1958–1963, B, 49). In September 1863, the ministry of the economy commissioned Kordellas, shortly after he had been officially appointed a mining engineer in the service of the ministry, to undertake a thorough assessment of the petition (ibid.). The engineer saw two problems. Firstly, he regarded the property rights of the scoriae, the location of which was not exactly documented, as being totally unclear. Could the state award a concession if the scoriae were on territory belonging to the municipality of Keratea? Secondly, he rejected Pachis' plan to export the scoriae to Italy and to process them there, where he had the appropriate machinery, as this would prevent the development of a smelting industry in Greece.[28] In his final report at the beginning of October 1863, Kordellas advised the ministry not to grant Pachis a concession, even though Pachis had now secured the exploitation rights for the scoriae from the municipality of Keratea (Δερμάτης [Dermatis] 2003, 75). The scoriae were in state ownership and were not private property, Kordellas argued, and they should definitely be processed in Greece so that the corresponding industry could develop locally.[29]

Only a week later, on 10/22 October (according to the Julian/Gregorian calendar), as recorded in Kordellas' memoires, Jean Battista Serpieri appeared at the ministry of the economy to speak to him (Βοβολίνης [Vovolinis]/Βοβολίνης [Vovolinis] 1958–1963, B, 50). He told Kordellas about his interest in the scoriae and his commission from two Marseille trading houses, explained that he had already received Kordellas' report from Heldreich and declared that he wanted to develop the necessary industry for processing the scoriae in Greece. Kordellas offered him his full support (ibid.).

A few days later, on 14/26 October 1863, Serpieri submitted his first petition requesting a concession from the ministry of the economy.[30] He did this in the name of the two trading houses Bouquet et Serpieri and Roux et Fraissinet, who had a great deal of experience in Sardinia, Spain and other countries in the processing of the antique remains of old mines. Revealing his knowledge about internal Greek frictions, Serpieri asked whether the scoriae were the property of the state and whether the state wanted to negotiate about the concession, and requested a speedy reply.[31]

The petition showed that Serpieri had obviously come to Greece well prepared. Before his journey, he had brought together a group of investors who were willing to finance the enterprise and split the risks. Joining the Serpieri family in the group were the Marseille banker Bouquet, who had worked with Enrico Serpieri for a considerable time and who later took the part of a silent partner, and Serpieri's Marseille boss Hilarion Roux, who was the ideal partner in the Lavrion undertaking.

Hilarion Roux

Julien-Hilarion Roux (1819–1898) was born on 7 May 1819 in Marseille as the eldest of the three children of the businessman Joseph-Hilarion Roux and his wife Élizabeth-Rose, née Albanely, the daughter of a surgeon. In 1834, his father founded the company Fraissinet et Roux with another Marseille merchant and banker, whose name continued to be borne by the company even after his death in 1837. From 1831 to 1835, Hilarion attended the renowned school L'abbaye école de Sorèze where he joined numerous children from the Marseille bourgeoisie and learnt the classics (Richard 1999).

In the 1840s, Joseph-Hilarion Roux was one of the first ranks of Marseille bankers, not least because of his close ties to the house of Rothschild, which he represented. Roux conducted grain speculation for the Rothschilds and was involved in railway construction (Lyon – Avignon, Avignon – Marseille), but also represented the Rothschilds in Spain and was interested in business in Algeria (ibid.). Moreover, he was active in the Marseille chamber of commerce. His son Hilarion was sent to Spain to monitor the granting of commercial loans for the Rothschilds. From Alicante, he quickly moved on to Carthagène/Cartagena, perhaps because there already was a Rothschilds correspondent in Alicante or because in Carthagène, there was more demand for capital for industry finance and the banker wanted to be close to his customers (Chastagnaret 2005, 274). In 1844, he married the Spanish María Piedad Aguirre Aldayturriaga, the daughter of a retired naval officer, which encouraged him to settle in the region (Perceval/López-Morell 2009, 191). His two brothers-in-law became important business partners.

Lead extraction was the leading branch of the region and the focus of Roux's activities. In the 1820s, the Marseille trading houses were already involved in the export of silver and lead from Andalusia, at a time when mining there was a purely local undertaking (Chastagnaret 2005, 272). Legal restrictions on the extent of concessions had led to production being fragmented between numerous very small companies (Perceval/López-Morell 2009, 191). From the 1840s, the market and production underwent considerable transformation. Metallurgic processing grew in the regions of Almagrera and Carthagène, where silver was now also extracted and the smelting works were extended. Investors from elsewhere in Spain (Chastagnaret 2005, 272) and from Great Britain, Belgium, France and Germany were now also involved in financing the mining and processing of the metals.[32] Thus, for instance, the Rothschilds owned two Spanish smelting works, the Alicantina and the Británica companies (Perceval/López-Morell 2009, 190). Hilarion Roux also procured and speculated with the shares from numerous smelting companies and mines (ibid.). Many companies used the technique of remelting the waste from antique mines in order to extract the considerable quantity of minerals still contained within it. Large-scale facilities also developed; for example, the Marseille merchant banker Isidore Brun founded the San Isidoro mine on the east coast of the bay of Chathagène, in Escombreras (Chastagnaret 2005, 273).[33]

Hilarion Roux granted Brun a loan of 60,000 francs in February 1843, which was to be repaid in deliveries of silver-bearing lead. In 1846, Brun found himself unable to service the loan and the mine therefore fell into Roux's hands. As a buyer could not be found for the large enterprise, even though it was equipped with the most modern machinery in the region, the Marseille banker was forced to run it himself (Chastagnaret 2005, 275). Roux thus developed from banker to metal merchant and finally to metallurgic entrepreneur and his contact to the Rothschilds weakened as he focused less on banking (Perceval/López-Morell 2009, 193). Roux appointed his father-in-law and two brothers-in-law to manage the mine, which 20 years later was still the largest producer of silver-bearing lead in the region (Richard 1999).

Roux himself, whom Richard describes as 'catholique de tendance orléaniste' (ibid., 272), in the meanwhile returned to Marseille, the centre of the silver and lead trade. In December 1851, he joined his father and other relatives to found Roux et Fraissinet et Cie, becoming head of the company after his father's death in 1857. The challenge for the banker was to construct and manage a multi-polar, complex economic space (Chastagnaret 2005, 276). In addition to trading with lead and silver, the company was active in many branches and strongly diversified its portfolio (ibid., 277). Its second-most important activity was the arms trade but Roux et Fraissinet et Cie was also involved in trading with latex and silk, in insurance and in diverse trading companies, e.g. with Africa (Richard 1999). In 1881, Roux also founded a company for the trading of dynamite. Furthermore, he was a founder of the Société marseillaise de Crédit and continued to act as Rothschilds' local correspondent (Chastagnaret 2005, 282).

The silver and lead trade remained the most important business of the company. It was to Roux's advantage that he was not just firmly rooted in Marseille, but also, thanks to his mine, in the producing region of Carthagène. Consequently, the gradual shift of trading in silver and lead away from the Mediterranean towards to Atlantic and northern Europe at the beginning of the 1860s hit him less severely than his competitors. The growth in demand for silver and lead, especially from Great Britain, seemed rather to call for an extension of production. Roux thus ran mines not only in France, Spain, Italy and Belgium, but also in Algeria, Nicaragua and Costa Rica (Richard 1999). For the 1870s, Chastagnaret describes Roux as the 'most important industrialist in the lead trade in the Mediterranean and without doubt even in Europe' (Chastagnaret 2005, 286f., tr. by K.S.). As he demonstrates, the extension of Roux's field of business does not seem to have followed a fixed plan, but rather developed in response to the opportunities that presented themselves (ibid., 277). When seen in the context of his other fields of activity, Greece was certainly not particularly exotic for Roux.

The lack of a private record (ibid., 271) makes it impossible to follow Roux's decision-making process in the sources. It can be assumed that his employee Jean Battista Serpieri spoke to him about the Lavrion mines sometime between the beginning of 1861 and the beginning of 1863, and provided him with his information: the positive report by Kordellas, who had studied at the renowned mining school in Freiberg; the results of the chemical tests carried out by his father in Sardinia and the reports from Antiori, Heldreich and the Greek sailors. Clearly, Roux welcomed the opportunity to work with antique remains very similar to those in Carthagène and thus to transfer his know-how to a new region and gain goods for the expanding market. Cooperation with the wealthy and experienced Enrico Serpieri from Sardinia was probably also attractive, particularly as he knew Serpieri's son as a reliable and knowledgeable employee. In any case, when Serpieri left for Greece, he had in some way procured Roux's agreement to participate, and could thus name Roux et Fraissinet as his business partners in his first petition. For Serpieri, the involvement of the 'lead king' Roux brought not only capital and know-how, but also benefited the reputation of his company significantly. It is not particularly surprising that the merchant banker participating in the venture was already involved in the lead-mining business, as at the beginning of the 1860s, industry finance was still viewed as very risky, an image which it could only gradually escape in the second half of the nineteenth century (Pohle-Fraser 1999, 104).

The founding of the first Lavrion company

Only a few days after Serpieri's first petition, the minister for the economy sent Kordellas and the French engineer Viallet to Lavrion to determine the exact position of the scoriae. On 24 October, their report was submitted.[34] Kordellas estimated the size of the silver- and lead-bearing scoriae to be 1,674 cubic metres with a lead and silver content of between 6% and 10%. The Keratea municipality claimed ownership of the scoriae but the property rights were unclear and seemed to be based largely on common law. The municipality was willing to relinquish their claim to the Marseille company in return for limited compensation. Kordellas was warmly in favour of this concession and believed that it would promote local industry and national wealth.[35] However, negotiations between the central government and the local authorities proved most complicated (Βοβολίνης [Vovolinis]/Βοβολίνης [Vovolinis] 1958–1963, B, 51). Serpieri thus submitted a second petition on 12 November, offering a one-off payment of 50,000 drachmas (45,000 francs) for the exclusive exploitation rights, plus an annual payment of 2,000 drachmas (1,800 francs) for each year of use (Κεκροπούλου [Kekropoulou] 2007, 19). Only a week later, the minister for the economy again sent Kordellas with two colleagues to check up on the property rights and to draft a topographical map for this purpose.[36] The situation was complicated by the woodland.

A law from 1836 had declared all woodland to be state property if no title of ownership was submitted within the stipulated time limit. No such submission had been made in Keratea. However, there was also no land register that showed which areas had been covered by woodland in 1836 – had woodland perhaps been cleared in the interim? The government and the municipality held differing opinions about this issue and a court case between the two had been pending since 1861, when the new mining law had been passed (Riz 1872, 8). Kordellas and the colleague with whom he produced the report of 11 January 1864 declared that about two-thirds of the scoriae belonged to the state as no other title of ownership could be produced for them, and the remainder were the property of the municipality of Keratea.[37] While Kordellas then headed for Naxos to conduct other metallurgic investigations, another commission, this time consisting of legal specialists, assessed the question of ownership. The commission recommended allocating a double rate of taxation to the scoriae that were state property.[38]

Serpieri received no answer to either of his petitions because the government was not certain whether the scoriae were even their property and whether they could grant a concession on them, or whether they were actually the property of the municipality of Keratea (Serpieri 1871b, 11). As it became clear that no concession would be forthcoming through these channels in the foreseeable future, Serpieri sought another option: he attempted to find an agreement with Pachis, who had secured many years of exploitation rights of the scoriae from the municipality of Keratea. He co-opted his competitor, along with his property, as a partner in a new French company. Serpieri also planned to buy land from another property owner, Melis, for 245,000 francs (Serpieri 1871a, 4). The corresponding contracts were drawn up but the Italian nonetheless wanted to ensure that he received government approval.

On 14 April 1864, his representative Theodor Heldreich submitted a new petition to the ministry in Serpieri's name (N. N.: s.t.d., 34f.).[39] Heldreich declared that the antique scoriae were not subject to the mining legislation because they were the product of human work and therefore belonged to the person who owned the land on which they were located (Riz 1872, 7). The Marseille businessman and Pachis had together procured the land in question from the residents of Keratea. However, before the necessary investments were made, they wished to know if the state was in agreement with this contract or if it still intended to assert a claim to the scoriae; here, the question of the woodland was explicitly addressed. Heldreich emphasised the anticipated 'increase in common wealth' that could be expected from the undertaking.[40] This new venture by the businessmen reveals how clearly they were aware of the uncertainty of the property rights. They tried to protect themselves in all possible ways.

This time Serpieri received an answer from the finance minister: the question of ownership had not yet been finally resolved.[41] However, the state was extremely interested in a speedy commencement of work and Serpieri was therefore assured that no claim to the named scoriae fields would be made, with the exception of a field close to Ergastiraki. Otherwise, the company could begin work and required no further permit (Serpieri 1981b, 4). Serpieri was still not satisfied. On 19/31 April, he wrote another letter to the ministry, this time having it conveyed by the French ambassador. He explicitly mentioned that the extent of afforestation of the scoriae in the past was unclear and that the scoriae around Ergastiraki were particularly important for his plans. Did the treasury nonetheless make no claim? For the scoriae field near Ergastiraki, where the extent of past woodland was in dispute, Serpieri offered to deposit a guarantee of 10,000 drachmas in case any relevant ownership rights should emerge from the court case between Keratea and the government (ibid., 7f.).[42] In a letter dated 25 May, also conveyed via the French ambassador, the ministry then declared their agreement to the guarantee and repeated that the treasury made no claim to the scoriae fields requested and endorsed the commencement of work (Κορδέλλας [Kordellas] 1865, 12; Serpieri 1871b, 4). With regard to the legal situation, the investors clearly pursued careful risk management. As Serpieri later asserted to the French government, in this unclear state of affairs, he had tried to secure his position in all ways possible: firstly, he regarded himself as having (re) discovered the deposits, secondly, he had acquired the land in question and thirdly, he had received a concession from the ministry. As the 'discoverer, owner of the land and concessionaire',[43] he believed that he was protected from any competing legal claims. This emphasis on legal protection was a new element in the risk management of the investors.

The businessmen reacted promptly. Serpieri now bought the scoriae concerned from Melis, the municipality of Keratea and the monastery Pentelis, a purchase that was marked with a public celebration for the local population (Δερμάτης [Dermatis] 2003, 90). Moreover, on 28 April (clearly before the notice from the ministry can possibly have arrived), the Marseille notary Fortoule Taxil signed a preliminary contract for the founding of the company Hilarion Roux et Cie. Just two days later, on 30 April, the limited partnership was registered in Marseille, with the aim of exploiting, trading and re-smelting the scoriae in Greece.[44] The partners involved were Hilarion Roux, Georgios Pachis, Enrico and Jean Battista Serpieri and their Marseille partners Ioannes and Mazrikios Bouquet. With the exception of the latter two, all the partners brought to the new company all the Lavrion scoriae in their possession. The company was intended to have capital of 600,000 francs at its disposal, although it had not yet been decided who would contribute how much.[45] Interest was calculated at 6% a year. Roux acted as the president with far-reaching rights: he was to receive 10% of the profits as salary and could name a director, stipulate the period of existence of the company and change its purpose. The president was to be allowed to use up to 25% of the profits a year for new investment. In addition, Jean Battista Serpieri and Georgios Pachis were to receive 6,000 francs annually. Of the remaining net profit, one half was to be split between the partners: 30% for Pachis, 15% for Serpieri et Bouquet and 5% for Roux. These allocations were not explained further but may have been equivalent to the amount of scoriae each partner contributed to the company. The preliminary contract again explicitly mentioned that Pachis was accredited with having discovered the scoriae. The other half of the net profit was to be divided between the partners in accordance with the capital invested.[46] It seems clear that the Marseille diaspora bankers Theodoros and Pavlos Rodokanakis were taken on board at a later date. As they provided a quarter of the capital (150,000 francs) (Κορδέλλας [Kordellas] 1865, 12), it can be supposed that the other three partners also contributed a quarter, although this cannot be proven.[47]

The statutes discussed here tellingly reveal the risk management of the bankers. At the time of founding the company, Roux risked very little. He had acquired only a small proportion of the scoriae, about 10%, while Pachis contributed 60% and Serpieri 30% – these two thus carried a much greater risk. Roux probably provided only a quarter of the capital, 150,000 francs. Nonetheless, his reputation as a mine owner and important lead merchant meant that the company bore his name and that he occupied the influential and profitable position of president, while Serpieri was named only an administrator.[48] Roux indisputably held the position of power in the company, even though he initially invested very little. Pachis, the local but least experienced partner, was only to 'be available in Athens' as an administrator, as the preliminary contract vaguely phrased it. His rights within the organisation were minimal. Roux's risk management is impressive: he managed to use his social capital so that he otherwise contributed little of monetary value but could nonetheless secure the decision-making rights.

A few weeks later, in May, Hilarion Roux came to Athens himself, and then travelled with Kordellas to Lavrion. Kordellas was impressed not only by Roux's rhetorical talents, but also by his unshakeable calm and composure and his geological and metallurgic knowledge. Serpieri joined them in Lavrion. Equipped with carriers, blankets and provisions, the three men headed off to view the scoriae in the Greek wilderness. At night, they secured their camp with fires to fend off the wolves. In the midst of the almost impassable terrain, they planned the exact location of the factory, the workers' quarters, the streets and even the station for an envisaged railway, as Kordellas remembered (Βοβολίνης [Vovolinis]/Βοβολίνης [Vovolinis] 1958–1963, B, 52). The building work was quickly started and in July Serpieri brought his wife to Athens. The Italian was already planning beyond Lavrion. Still in 1864, Jean Battista Serpieri's brother, Attilo Serpieri, accompanied Kordellas on his travels to the Greek islands and to Asia Minor – the engineer had taken leave from the ministry and was carrying out explorations financed by Hilarion Roux et Cie (Κορδέλλας [Kordellas] 1865, 12; Δερμιάτης [Dermatis] 2003, 93). During his time in Athens, Attilo also stayed in Kordellas' house (Βοβολίνης [Vovolinis]/Βοβολίνης [Vovolinis]

1958–1963, B, 53). The cooperation between science and capital seemed to open up promising opportunities.

The ownership dispute between the municipality of Keratea and the Greek state was still pending in court. On 19 January 1865, Kordellas submitted another report on the unresolved issues to the ministry of the economy.[49] In it, he admitted that the law of 1861 limited private ownership of mines and declared metal deposits to be national property. However, he also stated that the legislator was undoubtedly thinking about the benefit of the state; here, his line of argument led him as far back as Xenophon. Hindering the industrialisation of the country was certainly not pursuant to the law, he argued (ibid.).

As early as April 1865, the first specialists and engineers arrived in Lavrion from Carthagène (ibid., 54). It was an international workforce consisting of Spaniards, Italians, Albanians and Belgians, as well as Greeks, some of whom came from the Greek islands and from the Ottoman Empire.[50] Modern workers' quarters were erected where workers could live with their families in keeping with the hygiene standards of the time (Agriantoni 1994).[51] Roux and Serpieri appointed Andreas Kordellas as the head engineer, who therefore resigned from his position in the ministry of the economy, expressly referring to the great national significance of the mining project for the industrialisation and welfare of the country. The ministry accepted his resignation and replied, agreeing with Kordellas' assessment of the young company (Βοβολίνης [Vovolinis]/Βοβολίνης [Vovolinis] 1958–1963, B, 56). In May 1865, just a year after the site had been surveyed, the factory could be inaugurated with the blessing of the Orthodox Church and began its work with great success (ibid., 55). The high expectations were not disappointed[52]: in the 18 smelting ovens that had been imported from France, 30–35 tonnes of scoriae were smelted every day, as Kordellas depicted in the frontispiece of his 1869 publication entitled 'Le Laurium' (see Figure II.4.1). The washing equipment from Belgium had 90 horsepower. It was thus possible to extract 9,000–10,000 tonnes of lead with about 2 kg of silver per tonne annually, which was equivalent to half of the entire production of France. The company made no delay in developing serviceable infrastructure in the region (Ledoux 1872, 566f.).[53]

Occident and Orient from the perspective of Andreas Kordellas

In advance of their decision making, the investors thus gathered diverse information from travellers, engineers and chemists, and through their own impressions. They interpreted this information against the background of their many years of rich experience in the lead and silver business. But what were the values framing their actions? What images of Greece dominated their minds? The lack of ego documents prevents the reconstruction of this

Figure II.4.1 The smelting ovens of Lavrion, illustration from 1869.

early phase in the cases of Serpieri and Roux, but the situation is different with regard to Andreas Kordellas, their chief engineer. In 1865, a number of newspapers started a campaign around the scoriae, providing an occasion that sheds light on Kordellas' thinking. The papers accused foreign capitalists of having snatched the scoriae, the heritage of splendid antiquity, from the clueless Greeks and to now be skimming off the profits. The reports wrongly suggested that the scientists dispatched by Otto to investigate the scoriae had failed to recognise the potential of the old mines,[54] and similarly claims were made that nobody else in Greece had appreciated the possibilities. One calculation indicated that if the profits were divided among the Greeks, then every family would receive a payment of 100 drachmas.[55] Andreas Kordellas was hurt by these comments and felt misunderstood by the accusations that he was letting himself be bought by foreigners and thus selling out the country while continuing to be paid by the ministry of the economy. In his memorandum 'On the scoriae and the metallurgic industrialisation of Greece' from 1865, the engineer argued his case in detail. He not only protested against the notion that he received two salaries at the same time (Κορδέλλας [Kordellas] 1865, 10–14), but also emphasised that he and other engineers had fully informed the ministry about the value of the scoriae. Furthermore, he noted that the ministry had expressly recognised that it was his love for his country which had motivated him to pursue metallurgy, the 'main source of the people's wealth', within a private company. Here, Kordellas recorded an explicit statement of faith in industrialisation that would have done credit to any Saint-Simonian. Greece would only be able to master the great political challenges of the East by adopting Western science, work ethics and free trade (ibid., 4). The Greeks should not build walls to the West which would cause Europe to perceive it as lying even behind China or Japan, but should try to do everything possible to bring foreign capital into the country. Without capital and the appropriate know-how, it would not be possible to make use of Greece's national treasures to benefit the common wealth (ibid., 10–14). Kordellas estimated the company's profits, after deducting all costs and investments, at between 10% and 12% a year (ibid., 21). And even if the fantastic sums publicised in the Greek press were accurate, they would not justify expropriation: in a state under the rule of law, this would be no better than robbery. He described great potential for regional and national development and emphasised that the profits were justified in light of the risks that the investors took (ibid., 30).

In his memorandum, Andreas Kordellas differentiated between West and East in the same dichotomous fashion as Gustave d'Eichthal, although he clearly viewed Greece as part of the Orient and not as something in-between the two as Gustave did. Kordellas' concern was to mediate between the worlds. Greece should profit from superior Western science and engineering, which should be brought to the country through foreign investments that would then encourage Greek development. Kordellas censured his country harshly, questioning the centralisation of the administration and criticising the policies of the ministry of the economy, which he claimed employed many incompetent members of staff and had failed to react not only to his reports on Lavrion, but also to those of competent Greek colleagues who were posted away or dismissed when they demanded that action should be taken (ibid., 12). He also condemned the attitude of many of his compatriots who would rather have Greece resemble an empty desert than allow foreign investors the opportunity to make a profit. He did not deny the intelligence, determination and diligence of the Greek workers, but suggested that they were also irritable, unaccustomed to regular work, unwilling to cooperate and demanded high wages. Shirking and indolence had smothered all entrepreneurship in the country, and the aim now was simply to deprive hardworking businessmen of their well-deserved profits (ibid., 28f.).

Kordellas, as a Greek who was born and grew up in the West, presented the 'Oriental' image of Greece that he believed the investors encountered. Using their mother tongue, he tried to confront his compatriots with the foreign perspective and to galvanise them so they did not live up to these stereotypes but rather presented the investors with a different Greece, the 'emerging market', which he believed was the only path to prosperity for his country. He constructed his identity as an intermediary from his ambition to show the foreigners this new, attractive Greece. In his memoirs, he described his hard and strenuous work in the factory and office. Proving himself worthy of the esteem of the foreign investors, who had entrusted him with the first industrial works of his home country, was a question of honour for Kordellas (Βοβολίνης [Vovolinis]/Βοβολίνης [Vovolinis] 1958–1963, B, 56). Naturally, he also referred to other development projects in his writing: infrastructural improvements, the plans for draining Lake Copais, the building of the Canal of Corinth. When discussing the mining of the various mineral deposits in Greece, he emphasised that all that glitters is not gold and urged potential investors to make use of the scientific expertise of his colleagues (Cordella 1869/1871, III). He implied that there may well be further underground deposits at Lavrion, which the ancients had not known about but which thorough investigations could find – he portrayed the mines as still having great potential (ibid., 77f.).

In his French writings, Kordellas also activated images of Ancient Greece. He described the ancient mines of Lavrion in great detail, drawing confidently on classical authors like Homer, Xenophon and Pausanias, and also on contemporary research from classical studies (ibid., 17). The mines had been the foundation of the riches of ancient Athens and continued to be used by the Romans. He described the ancient practices of extracting metals, which had also been undertaken by private citizens with state concessions, and portrayed the working and living conditions of the slaves (ibid., 28–30, 80–93). Pausanias was the first to have described the mines as exhausted and abandoned, after being in use for over 700 years (ibid., 19–21). Kordellas dedicated one chapter of his work to the archaeological findings around Lavrion that had emerged in the course of the mining and smelting, and he quoted extensively from the inscriptions that had been discovered (ibid., 33–41). He concluded by directly linking the new scientific research he was recommending with Ancient Greece: 'These investigative shafts could be dug very economically by incorporating the ancient shafts and the rubble from this blind shaft would most advantageously find a place in the empty spaces of the ancient works' (ibid., 111, tr. by K.S.). Here, Kordellas endeavoured to connect the images of Ancient and Modern Greece and thus to ennoble the business activities, presenting them as the antithesis of the images of Oriental Greece that would only have deterred potential investors.

Successful mining business

The company was extraordinarily successful. Technical progress facilitated the work. In 1866, underground springs were found in the arid region and, following an Italian example, a horse-drawn tram was established (Βοβολίνης [Vovolinis]/Βοβολίνης [Vovolinis] 1958–1963, B, 57–60), which then in 1869 was replaced by steam-powered operations. A 150-metre-long quay was erected for ships of up to 1.6 tonnes and about 30 km of new roads were built.[56] A hospital was also constructed for the free use of the 1,500 workers (Cordella 1869/1871, 24f.). In Ergastiraki, a veritable town developed. The company learnt to accommodate itself to the somewhat difficult security situation, dealing, for instance, with demands for protection money from a local gang leader in Attica, Kytzos, who had excellent relationships with the Athens business world and politicians. Ledoux, the source from which *The Times* drew its information, reported that Kytzos had been killed in an armed fight with representatives of the company but had then been immediately replaced by an even worse gang leader (Ledoux 1872, 567).[57] However, the secondary literature has an alternative version whereby Serpieri managed to negotiate with Kytzos so the money demanded was reduced by half and at the same time the gang agreed to protect the factory (Κεκροπούλου, [Kekropoulou] 2007, 339f.; Farina 2013, 32f.). Both stories show that there was clearly not a state monopoly on the use of force in Attica and that the state was not in the position to effectively protect the investments being made. The institutional framework seems to have been most unstable. This did not hinder success: the amount of lead won was continually increased. In 1866, lead to the value of 2,481,429 drachmas was extracted; by 1870, this had risen to 4,860,900 drachmas and by 1873 to 5,031,600 drachmas (Moraïtinis 1877, 335). The capital of the company, which had started with 500,000 francs, had increased sevenfold by 1867 to 3.5 million francs (Δερτιλής [Dertilis] 2009, 510). In a country where the total revenue of the state was only just over 27 million drachmas in 1866 (almost 24 million francs or £950,000) (Καλαφάτης [Kalafatis] et al. 2011, 3, 126), this was an immense amount of money, which became the object of covetous desires.

The Lavrion affairs

The first Lavrion affair

The first discord concerning taxes arose in December 1865, when it was clear that the company was enjoying considerable success and had applied for permission to export the first 400 tonnes of silver and lead. The export was allowed but only after Serpieri provided his personal guarantee and pledged the estate of the company in Lavrion, which had to declare its willingness to respect future tax legislation.[58] In April 1867,[59] the government issued a new law on taxing lead and the scoriae of Lavrion.[60] They were acting under immense pressure from nationalist parliamentarians who took exception to the concession being awarded to foreigners and complained about the selling out of national resources; the law was an attempt to placate the indignant voters (Κεκροπούλου [Kekropoulou] 2007, XI). The government was simultaneously fighting a number of battles. They were involved in intense negotiations with the English banking house of Bischoffsheim and Goldschmidt about repayment of the old loans from 1824/1825. Furthermore, the unification of the Ionian Islands with Greece in 1863 had brought with it the problem of integrating the IOB, which had previously held the privilege of issuing bank notes there, into the Greek financial sector (Δερτιλής [Dertilis] 2009, 512).[61] All three fields were highly sensitive domestic and international political terrain, ridden with patriotic ideas and criticism of capitalism (ibid., 572–576).

The 1867 law established that profits from privately owned scoriae were to be taxed at 10%. For scoriae owned by the state, an additional levy of 20% was charged, leading to a total tax rate of 30%.[62] This was a hard blow for the company: most of the Lavrion scoriae were now claimed as state property. In December 1867, the court of appeal in Athens had awarded part of the territory in question to the government rather than the municipality of Keratea,[63] and the treasury now demanded a tax payment of 30% of the value of the scoriae located on this land. The company protested vehemently and referred to the ministerial letter from 1864 that declared that the state made no claim to the scoriae. This decision by the ministry of finance had not been based on a mistake or deceit by the applicant.[64] The state should be bound by the commitment made by its minister of finance. This was a position that was supported by the French and Italian embassies, to which Hilarion Roux et Cie appealed, much to the displeasure of the Greek government.[65] The Greek minister of finance countered with the claim that the state had only wanted to ensure that there was no obstacle to work commencing, but had waited for the end of the case with the municipality of Keratea before definitively stipulating any rights (Sotiropoulos 1871, 10). The argument was continued in court, where the company won in the first instance but lost at the Athens court of appeal in 1871.[66] The court recognised the property rights of the state over most of the scoriae, sentenced the company to paying the 30% taxation, retrospectively to 1868, plus 12% interest, a total sum of almost two million drachmas.[67] Serpieri protested against the procedure itself, which involved the taxation being applied to the processed scoriae rather than to the net profit of the company, but his protest was dismissed (Riz 1872, 12).[68] At least the company had obtained a concession for the use of the scoriae after the law had come into force. They thus had the right to extract silver- and sulphur-bearing lead in an area of 10,791 stremmata[69] or, according to a second version, of 14,500 stremmata.[70] However, they were no longer alone in their exploitation of Greek mineral deposits. Despite the new law, their success in Greece had triggered a 'gold rush' (Δερτιλής [Dertilis] 2009, 508). After 1869, the ministry of the interior received 1,086 petitions for concessions for mining companies in various parts of the country and granted 360 of these (Pepelasis 1959, 182). The correspondent of *The Times* spoke of a 'Laurium bubble'.[71]

The second Lavrion affair

The lost court case of 1871 was not the climax of the conflicts between Hilarion Roux et Cie and the government concerning the scoriae. At the end of 1868, the company had begun with the smelting of other ancient remains near Kamariza and Sinterini, which Serpieri had bought from the prefect of Attica and Boeotia for two drachmas a tonne (Sotiropoulos 1871, 11). These remains were not scoriae and thus not the remains of antique smelting works, but were ecvolades, waste heaps of stone that had been removed from the mines in antiquity but had never been processed because they contained too little metal.[72] As soon as they heard of these activities, the ministry of the economy forbade the company from using the materials because they did not result from past human work. Serpieri argued in response that the ecvolades were included in his 1867 concession because they should be understood as being part of the mine (Sotiropoulos 1871, 12). The Greek government did not agree with this interpretation, but sent a commission who estimated that net profits of almost 130 million drachmas could be achieved from the ecvolades (Dücker 1873, 9). In March 1871, the minister of the economy Deligiorges submitted a draft law on the ecvolades,[73] which were then declared to be state property.[74] The concession granted to Hilarion Roux et Cie in 1867 was said to include only the scoriae but not the ecvolades. A concession to use the ecvolades could be obtained in return for 60% of the net profits (Riz 1872, 19ff.). To prevent the company from continuing to process the ecvolades, the factory in Lavrion was occupied by government troops and work was stopped (Serpieri 1872, 2; N.N. s.t.d, 12ff.). Under these conditions, it was anyway completely impossible to continue the work, because the scoriae and ecvolades were not sorted separately but had been mixed, and indeed it was necessary to mix them for processing, just as was done in Sardinia and Spain (ibid., 12ff.). The negotiations continued against the background of the increasingly vehement agitation of many Greek newspapers against the foreign investors (Σαλίμπα [Salimba] 2005, 50). Serpieri was reviled as a schemer, adventurer, exploiter and robber. He was accused of complicity in the sudden death of his servant and of black-market dealings with ancient relics (ibid., 52). The discourse became evermore acerbic and polemic. In his cabinet speech, Deligiorges, now prime minister, described Hilarion Roux et Cie as a 'company of speculators' and accused them of fomenting opinion against Greece throughout the whole of Europe (Serpieri 1872, 3).[75] Serpieri countered (ibid.)[76] by arguing that the law retrospectively declared the ecvolades to be state property even though the company had applied for and been granted a concession to process them in April 1864 (ibid., 34ff.). The government responded by indicating the option of legal procedures in the Greek courts. This route was not favoured by the company, not least because of their experiences with the first court case about the scoriae. A court, as Serpieri expressed it, could only judge according to the pertinent legislation and this was what had been retrospectively changed, so a legal case would not be able to help them win their rights. The company's perception of the situation clearly did not include the existence of so-called 'post-conflict justice institutions', such as a reliable legal system, which would have given foreign investors confidence in the reliability of the local economy.[77] Serpieri appealed instead to the Italian and French embassies, requesting diplomatic support and calling for an international court or commission of arbitration. This was decidedly rejected by the Greek government because they viewed it not only as questioning the impartiality and quality of the Greek legal system, but also as an attack on Greek independence. Neither Italy nor France would ever agree to such an international court of arbitration to settle disputes with foreign entrepreneurs within their own borders, and the Greek government claimed the same rights (Riz 1872, 26).[78] Like any other government, they could change their laws as they pleased.[79] Furthermore, the 1871 law had not changed the legal situation but merely clarified it.[80]

Both Italy and France were willing to support their nationals in this situation.[81] The dispute kept European diplomatic circles on tenterhooks for two years at a time when the continent was trying to regain some equilibrium after the German-French war. Diverse reports investigated the legal situation in Greece and compared mining rights in France, England, the Ottoman Empire, Bavaria, Prussia, antique Greece and Rome, coming to diverse conclusions (N. N., Mémoire affaire du Laurium, question des Ecvoladés, s.t., 46).[82] Simultaneously, the Lavrion affair massively destabilised Greek domestic politics, with five governments coming to power just between 1870 and 1873 (Δερτιλής [Dertilis] 1980, 228f.).[83] The new king tried to consolidate his own position, which was unbeneficial to the stability of the government (Μπάλογλου [Baloglou] 1988a, 204; Κεκροπούλου [Kekropoulou] 2007, XI; Δερτιλής [Dertilis] 2009, 519–529). He saw the Lavrion affair as not only affecting foreign perceptions of the country's finances, but also of his reputation,[84] and the attitude of the politicians to Lavrion was highly relevant to his decisions about who should be charged with forming a government (Δερτιλής [Dertilis] 2009, 512).[85] For perceptions of Greece as an emerging financial market, the affair had far-reaching consequences.

Mining the depths of images of Greece

No unanimous decision about whose position in the Lavrion affair could best be justified was ever made, either by contemporaries or by historical research. Greek historians have conducted detailed investigations of Serpieri's petitions and the ministerial replies (was the word 'mines' or 'scoriae' or 'ecvolades' used, and when and in what context) and of the legal basis of the conflict (e.g. Μπάλογλου [Baloglou] 1988a, 199). The reason for Serpieri's disappointment is clear however: in Lavrion, he wanted to re-smelt the remains of antique mines exactly as his father did in Sardinia and Roux did in Spain. Neither of them had encountered problems with property rights. The investors assumed that the same conditions would also apply in Greece – in the terminology of behavioural finance, this is a case of representativeness, i.e. transferring familiar conditions to a new, actually different situation. This transfer proved to be a mistake, as was the notion that in Greece the company could influence domestic legislation on foreign investment as was common in Spain (Puig/Castro 2009, 532). It was consequently inevitable that the investors would be disappointed.

The question of right or wrong is of less interest in the present context than the European discourse about the Lavrion affair and the images of Greece that were reactivated, constructed and transported in this discourse. Jean Battista Serpieri published all the relevant documents from the interactions between the company and the Greek government, the first time with the subtitle 'a spoliation' (Serpieri 1871a). The administrator of Hilarion Roux et Cie felt that he had been unfairly dealt with by the Greek authorities, who he believed had allowed themselves to be influenced by the dissatisfied public: 'the ignorant masses deplore seeing the national riches handed over as prey to the grasping speculation of foreigners'.[86] He denied that the government had only discovered the value of the scoriae in 1869 and had granted the concession unknowingly (ibid., VI). He repeatedly questioned the independence of the Greek justice system. He followed this first publication with numerous other collections of documents that countered the Greek government's representation of the situation. In his published writings, Serpieri left others to draw their own conclusions: 'I leave it to those who wish to dedicate themselves to an impartial examination of this affair to take care to say on which side they find dishonesty'.[87] When writing to the French government, however, he expressed himself more openly, displaying his indignation that old laws were being 'exhumed' to justify claims that the state had not considered for 30 years. In a civilised country, it would not be possible that before a final court decision, the treasury should initiate an armed occupation of a company and transform a factory into a besieged camp.[88]

> We ask them to allow us to practise our industry freely, otherwise we will sadly find it necessary to completely cease all our work and make them responsible for the resulting losses.[89]

He claimed 'that the Greek government bitterly fights using all the means possible to despoil us of our property; and that their manoeuvres tend towards the complete annihilation of our company'.[90] Serpieri particularly denounced the political instability: the politicians simply ignored all the decisions that their predecessors had made and sacrificed justice to the nationalist idea.[91] This was his legitimation for appealing to international diplomacy. In order to gain support, Serpieri elevated the conflict to a fundamental national level by interpreting Greek behaviour as 'the attempt to refuse France all fair influence in the Orient and to show that we are no longer feared and thus no longer respected'.[92] In line with Todorova's findings, Greece was portrayed here as a transitional and peripheral state, endangering itself but thereby also endangering the order of the centre by not respecting its leadership (Todorova 1997, 36). As part of the Balkans, rather than being understood as the other, Greece was understood as the incomplete self. The Italian and French diplomats affiliated themselves with Serpieri's reading and offered their entire diplomatic arsenal to protect the company. The affair reached an impasse, despite offers of mediation from Austria and Russia.[93]

The parties attempted to attract as many influential voices to their side as possible.[94] The diplomatic arguments were therefore also conducted in public, where the difficulties of the company were generalised and portrayed as problems affecting the Greek finance market in general: 'The result of the conflict between Roux and Co. and the Greek Government will probably be accepted as deciding how far foreign capital can be safely invested in the country'.[95] For instance, at the very beginning of the dispute, the British ambassador Ellis confirmed Serpieri's representation of the atmosphere in Greece being generally hostile to investment:

> [T]he existence of any portion of the precious metal has so excited the cupidity of all classes, that there is a cry for getting rid of the company by means of high export duties, and a foreign speculation is treated as necessarily injurious to native interests.[96]

This hostility was primarily blamed on the distorted reporting of the Greek press.[97] The success of the foreigners and their great accomplishments for the entire region went equally unrecognised by the Greek government, claimed *The Times*.[98] Harsh criticism was directed towards the resulting aversion to investments of foreign capital, displayed by the Greek public sphere.[99]

> A State like the Hellenic Kingdom, which must depend for its political and commercial prosperity on the good offices and the trade of foreign countries, ought carefully to avoid the reputation of envious hostility to the employment of foreign capital in permanent investments in the country.[100]

French travellers like Henry d'Ideville came to similar conclusions:

> Mr Roux and his English [sic!] and Italian partners have erected a veritable town on this dry coast. But it must be added that since the day on which our brave Frenchmen set foot in Greece there has been no barrier, no harassment, no threat of blackmail which the Greek government and its subordinate agents has not used to wear down Mr Roux and his company.[101]

Foreign diplomats in Athens emphasised that this was not an individual case. When foreigners were successful with their business in Greece, they were accused of enriching themselves at the expense of the Greeks, and political agitators would goad the labour force to demand vastly inflated wages until the investors gave up and left their factories in ruins behind them.[102] D'Ideville asked with great moral indignation if 'it is not to be feared that, as in the tale, the hen on the golden eggs will soon be cut open?'[103] A popular example of the economic irrationality of the Greek position was the Don Pacifico affair of 1850 when Great Britain undertook a two-month blockade of the harbour of Piraeus because Greece denied a British merchant his 'rights'.[104] The message was clear: investors could not expect to receive fair, rational treatment of Western standards in Greece. That popular slanderer of Greece Edmond About naturally used the opportunity to exult about the negative predictions for Greek investment he had made 18 years earlier and to demand that another warship should be sent to Piraeus (About 1872).[105]

In order to generalise about and denounce the ostensible hostility of the Greeks to investment, the West European newspapers used familiar negative images of Greece, with *The Times* focusing particularly on the disparities between Orient and Occident: 'The whole affair, as we understand it, reduces itself to the old dog-in-the-manger quarrel between semi-savage life and superior civilization'.[106] This contrasting of Orient and Occident could be taken further:

> An indolent, ignorant race is set down by *providence* in the midst of every imaginable blessing of soil and climate; it pines in want and wretchedness in districts which to assiduous labour (!) yielded once, and would yield again, inexhaustible wealth, it dies of wasting fevers amid dismal swamps which were two thousand years ago Elysian fields; it perishes from drought at the foot of mountain ridges the snows of which could supply perennial moisture; finally, it treads on ground pregnant with riches, blind to the actual heaps of glittering ore already dug up by their predecessors, and which are mere samples of the treasures that industry and enterprise would bring to light. But let only an intelligent and active stranger appear on the spot, and attempt on his own behalf and on that of the natives

> that which these latter could never have achieved for themselves, and no sooner has the field or the forest, the vineyard, the canal, or the mine, been turned to the purposes for which a bountiful Nature intended it, than the unreasoning indigenous race is lashed into a fury of envy and covetousness; it declares itself defrauded to the full extent to which the stranger, and itself with him, has been benefited, and it gives itself no rest till, either by sheer violence or by fraud and chicane and arrant breach of faith, it tears from its benefactor's hands the reward to which his industry is entitled.[107]

French publications also contrasted the Western civilising mission with the Oriental sloppiness that resists it. Here, the newly developed town of Ergastiraki was acclaimed as

> an industrial town enlivened by all the movement and all the modern activity, a rare sight in these regions of the Orient where the masters of laziness and *far niente* reign. Eight years sufficed to work this metamorphosis; it is entirely due to the patient energy of the foreigners who have brought their capital, their experience and their practical skills to this forgotten country.'[108]

Voices that attempted to legitimise the Greek position, e.g. in letters to the papers, were marginalised.[109] The old Saint-Simonians tried to use the attention attracted by the Lavrion affair to praise Greece as 'the avant-garde of civilisation and the most advanced and vigilant sentry of Europe in the Orient', to celebrate the University of Athens for bringing the light of Europe to the Orient[110] and to deplore the widespread mistrust of Greece.[111] But they were fighting their last stand. Even friends of Greece had to admit that the country would have done better to simply leave the company alone rather than damaging its reputation so thoroughly, no matter what the rights and wrongs of the situation were.[112] To defend Greece, its advocates highlighted the (undisputed) profit motive of the company and vilified the investors as glory-hunting 'speculators' (Dücker 1873, 18), or they resorted to references to national autonomy (Moraïtinis 1877, 333).[113] However, the negative images of Greek were so potent that commentators who viewed Greece positively had trouble countering them, especially Edmond About's 'unfortunate silhouettes' (Dücker 1873, 5, 19f.).[114] And even in some of the positive representations, the modern Greeks sometimes did not appear as implementers of progress, but rather as noble savages of impressive beauty and strength who guided the wanderer through the wild landscape 'like a wolf without worrying about the undergrowth and the brambles' (Ledoux 1872, 565, tr. by K.S.). This was hardly an image that suggested business partners on an equal footing.

The vast majority of the reporting remained highly negative and provided repeated opportunities for Greece to be categorised as part of the endangered Balkans or the backward Orient. Incidents such as the kidnapping and murder of one Italian and three British travellers near Marathon in 1870, which triggered a diplomatic crisis between Athens and London, strengthened this impression still further (Jenkins 1998)[115] as the agitated public blamed the unsuccessful rescue attempt on the inept handling of the negotiations by the Greek government.[116] The affair provided an occasion for numerous anti-Greek publications condemning the lawlessness and bandits said to stem from the tradition of the Palikars and deploring state passivity towards them (Basch 1995, 182f.).[117] The reportage clearly portrayed Greece as an Oriental country which, echoing the opinions of d'Eichthal, not only currently lacked state institutions, but was also failing to provide for the future. When the French Lavrion company was joined by two Greek Lavrion firms, the commentators correspondingly criticised their lack of planning and scientific research of mineral reserves, blaming this on the Greek national character: 'Gifted in the arts, they overly neglect the study of positive science and lack a spirit of practicality and organisation. They have an overabundance of lawyers and doctors but hardly any engineers' (Watbled 1883, 15–20, tr. by K.S.). Without foreigners, it was claimed, all the companies in Greece would fail, sooner or later.

Many of the newspaper articles and memoranda placed the Lavrion affair in the context of antiquity. At times, the comparison was presented negatively, using the background of Greece's ancient heritage to highlight the small-mindedness and unreasonableness of the Greeks of today, their inability to recognise the benefits and rules of the game of modern investment.[118] They were not nearly as astute as those described by Homer.[119] Elsewhere, the glorious past was conjured up in an attempt to persuade the Greeks to compromise (Ledoux 1872, 571). And pro-Greek representations also reflected on antiquity, suggesting that: 'We normally view Greek antiquity through classical memories and regret, with the poet, the age when, in majestic grace,/ Fair heaven amid the gods made earth her dwelling-place' (ibid., 552).[120] Often, the ancient ways of mining were described in detail and compared to modern methods in order to accentuate the evident progress, also in terms of the humane working conditions. The modern factories were described in their picturesque setting with a view over the wonderful islands of the Cyclades, surrounded by the sea ('the blue waves like shining pearls') and the ancient remains of the temple of Apollo on Cape Sounion.[121] Modern progress and antiquity were also combined in pictorial representations such as that in the *Illustrated London News* (see Figure II.4.2).

The modern industrial plant situated in the midst of meadows of roses and anemones with ancient remains attracted numerous admiring travellers (Cheston 1887a). Such voices were also heard in Germany: the engineer who was sent to assess the Lavrion mines by the German government proved to be a dedicated Philhellene who praised the great progress made by courageous and patriotic people: 'Admirers of the old classical Hellas are bound

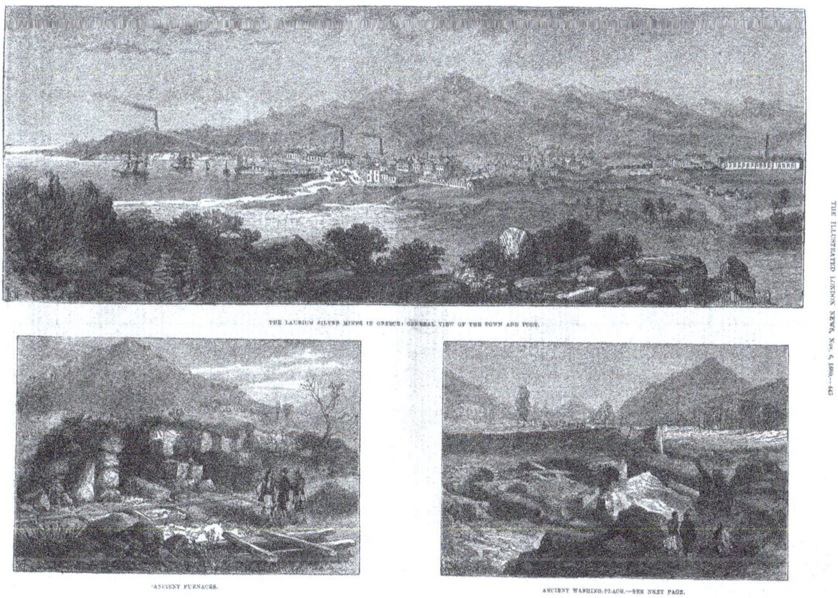

Figure II.4.2 The Laurium Mines in Greece. General View of the Town and Port; Ancient Furnaces; Ancient Washing Place, *The Illustrated London News*, 6.11.1880.

to be delighted by the sight of the stately buildings which are now again being constructed from the same Pentelic marble seen in the temple remains of the old Acropolis' (Dücker 1873, 19f., tr. by K.S.). International interest in the famous excavations in Mycenae (1874–1876) encouraged such enthusiasm for antiquity (Basch 1995, 228).

After the sale: lessons unlearnt?

Italian and French diplomacy searched for a consensual solution between Hilarion Roux et Cie and the unstable Greek governments, which in some cases were dissolved explicitly due to the Lavrion affair. Nonetheless, the Greeks did not waver on their course, even when French troops began manoeuvring in Greek waters, and in 1873 they even closed their embassies in Paris, London, Rome and St. Petersburg for a year (Basch 1995, 204). The state purchase of the company seemed an obvious step. The company offered to sell all property and concessions in Lavrion to the Greek state for a sum of 22 or 20 million drachmas. The Greeks offered only 11 million drachmas (Δερτιλής [Dertilis] 2009, 511). For months, it was impossible to reach an agreement (ibid., 519–526). Then in 1873, a solution seemed to be found: Andreas Syngros, a banker from Constantinople, presented Hilarion Roux et

Cie with an offer for 12.5 million drachmas (11.5 million francs), which had been well prepared in advance (Μπάλογλου [Baloglou 2009, 39).[122] Serpieri and Roux accepted the offer and sold the company in February 1873. At least the Lavrion works were now in Greek hands, even if the Greek newspapers quickly began a polemic against the diaspora banker Syngros because he did not reside in the country (Μπάλογλου [Baloglou] 1988a, 200).[123]

It could be supposed that after these experiences, the two investors Roux and Serpieri would turn their backs on the Greek investment market. Of course, despite all the difficulties, they had earned a great deal of money in Lavrion. By 1871, the total capital of Hilarion Roux et Cie amounted to 3.5 million drachmas; as they then sold the company for 12.5 million drachmas, their capital had increased 3.6-fold within nine years[124] – an impressive annual dividend of 40%. But the institutional framework for investment in Greece had proved unreliable. The investors, as they saw it, could not count on the state having a monopoly of force, or on a secure legal framework, or on the validity of contracts. Instead of concluding with large profits, the affair could have led to expropriation without compensation, and thus ended with the complete loss of the money invested. The risks had thus been extremely high. From the perspective of new institutional economics, withdrawing from this situation was the obvious decision.

Serpieri decided differently. On 1 March 1873, Andreas Syngros founded the Greek Metallurgic Company of Lavrion (Ελληνική Εταιρεία των Μεταλλουργείων Λαυρίου), with investors from the Greek diaspora in Constantinople, Odessa and London (Μπάλογλου [Baloglou] 1988a, 199; 1988b, 41).[125] The president of the company was Markos Renieri, translator of d'Eichthal's work on Greek as a world language six years earlier and now governor of the ETE. The company's capital amounted to 20 million drachmas, divided into 100,000 shares each of 200 drachmas (162 francs). This capital was to be paid in four instalments (Μπάλογλου [Baloglou] 1988b, 42). The legal framework seemed clear this time: the company was to pay 44% (instead of the initially proposed 53%) of its profits as taxation to the state (Μπάλογλου [Baloglou] 1988a, 211, 214; Σαλίμπα [Salimba] 2005, 53). It clearly cannot be said that the Greek state was being forced to give away its national assets without accruing any benefit (Κεκροπούλου [Kekropoulou] 2007, XII). Jean Battista Serpieri was a shareholder and co-founder of this new company, and was voted onto the supervisory board for seven years (Μπάλογλου [Baloglou] 1988a, 211).

The flotation of the new company represented the climax of a metal and banking bubble in Athens (ibid., 197). The shares were targeted by extensive speculation.[126] Potential investors stood in queues when the papers were issued (Μπάλογλου [Baloglou] 1988a, 212) and they were oversubscribed many times.[127] On 2 April 1873, the last day of issue, 350,000 shares were subscribed: 100,000 by Greek investors and 250,000 by investors from Constantinople, Egypt and England (Σαλίμπα [Salimba] 2005, 52). However, the shares then very quickly lost value, responding to various rumours on the stock exchange. Within three days, they fell to 154 drachmas (135 francs); after payment of the first instalment, the price fell to 50 drachmas and in November, it was then only 12 drachmas (ibid., 53). The crisis spread quickly and the entire Athens exchange rapidly collapsed to an unprecedented extent (Δερτιλής [Dertilis] 2009, 563ff.). The public were indignant, the investors felt cheated (Farina 2013, 43) and there were demands for Syngros and Serpieri to be called to account (Μπάλογλου [Baloglou] 1988a, 215). The next great Lavrion scandal had appeared.

Roux and Serpieri persevered undaunted. In 1875, they founded the Compagnie Française des Mines du Laurium (CFML) with a capital investment of 13.5 million francs. The company aimed to exploit other reserves in Lavrion and elsewhere in Greece.[128] Andreas Syngros was again involved. The development of infrastructure in the Lavrion region continued: in 1880, Ergastiraki was connected to the telegraph network and provided with electricity, and a little later the railway link to Athens was completed (Farina 2013, 44). The CFML remained in operation until 1982 (ibid., 26; Παπαστεφανάκη [Papastefanaki] 2005, 29).[129]

In terms of risk management, it seems clear that in all his Greek investments, Roux was concerned to spread his risks as broadly as possible.[130] He worked not only with a group of Marseille bankers, but also persuaded colleagues from Paris and Belgium to invest in his projects (Chastagnaret 2005, 284). This approach was less successful with the founding of the large Compagnie Française des Mines d'Escombrera-Bleyberg in 1877, in which he combined the Escombreras mines in Spain with the mines in Bleyberg in Belgium to form one company (ibid., 284). Of the 19,000 shares, he took 79% himself, equalling a value of 9.5 million francs (Perceval/López-Morell 2009, 200). In Marseille, the lead king built a factory to process the metals from Lavrion, Sardinia and the Maghreb (Chastagnaret 2005, 227). In cooperation with well-known engineers, he developed new procedures and so remained at the forefront of technical progress. At the same time, the focus of his activities moved away from mining and back to banking. Like his father, he was active in the Marseille chamber of commerce and administered the branches of the Banque de France (1865–1877). In 1875, he was ennobled by the Spanish King Alfonso XIII and given the title 'Marquis d'Escombreras'. However, the heart of his international business shifted increasingly to Paris (ibid., 285). 'Through his connections, the importance of his company, the extent of his horizons, Hilarion Roux became a businessman of international stature' (Richard 1999, 272, tr. by K.S.). Nonetheless, he was unable to survive the silver price crisis at the beginning of the 1880s (triggered not least by the suspension of bimetallism in many countries) (Perceval/López-Morell 2009, 201) combined with the general economic crisis, and in 1883 Roux et Cie filed for bankruptcy (Richard 1999). This inevitably also affected the

CFML, which could only avoid a similar fate through the resignation of the entire supervisory board.[131]

If Roux showed a great appetite for risk with regard to Greece, and indeed generally, Serpieri surpassed him by far. He was clearly not content with founding the CFML in 1875, although he still held 1,400 shares of the company in 1878, making him by far the largest shareholder.[132] Just five years later, he initiated the Société Anonyme des Mines de Seriphos et de Spiliazeza au Laurium, in which several banks from Constantinople, French investors and the Banque Ottomanne were involved and which was in operation until 1910. In 1882, he continued his activities with the Compagnie Française des Mines de Siphnos & Eubée, which focused on mineral deposits on Milos, Cynthus and Antiparos (Παπαστεφανάκη [Papastefanaki] 2005, 29).[133] His Greek projects extended beyond metallurgy. In 1887, he and Henri Foulon de Vaulx obtained a 30-year concession for the supply of water and light to Athens, which in 1889 led to the founding of the Société hellénique du gaz d'Athènes et autres villes in which his son Fernandos was also involved (Farina 2013, 48).[134] The industrialist also bought a palazzo in Athens, which continues to bear his name today, and developed a reputation as a patron of the arts (Farina 2013, 45).

Serpieri's investments were not only limited to Greece, but also concerned Italy. In 1881, the mining company of Montecatini in Italy was founded and he became its first president, in line with the strategy of the Italian government to promote the development of heavy industry in northern Italy in an attempt to counter the terrible effects of the agrarian crisis. In the 1880s, metallurgy virtually exploded (ibid., 47; Lill 2002, 325, 331).[135] The family also continued Enrico Serpieri's political engagement in Italy. Jean Battista's son Achilles (born in 1849) moved to Rome with Garibaldi in 1867 (N.N., s.t.b).[136] And in Rimini, in 1882 and again in 1891, Jean Battista himself stood for election to the Italian parliament as a moderate, constitutional liberal, but was both times defeated by candidates from the radical left (Mengozzi 1931–1937, 264; Lill 2002, 328f., 336).[137] Serpieri seems to have paid a great deal of money for positive reports and electoral advertising in the newspapers.[138]

Towards the end of his life, Serpieri chose to live in Italy rather than in Greece. Farina speculates that the bloody workers' protests that took place in Lavrion in 1896 deeply troubled the paternalist industrialist and led to his return to Italy (Farina 2013, 53–56). In Greek historiography, the way Serpieri is assessed varies, with some portrayals suggesting that he was a benefactor, while others view him as a capitalist exploiter. After his death in 1887 in Athens, a monument was erected for him in Ergastiraki; this was then vandalised in 1984 after a critical documentary was shown in Greek television. It was removed for safekeeping to the National Museum in Athens and could only be returned to Ergastiraki in 2006 (ibid., 56–60).

Conclusion

The two investors Hilarion Roux and Jean Battista Serpieri used various sources of information to assess the prospects of profit from the Lavrion mines: reports by travellers and those who knew the area, a scientific report by a well-reputed mining engineer, the results of chemical analyses of samples of rock and their own impressions of the site. Once they decided to make the investment, they employed cautious risk management. They attempted to safeguard their investment despite the uncertain property rights concerning the scoriae by purchasing the land from local owners, portraying themselves as the (re)discovers of the deposits and applying for a state concession. They hoped that in this way they could minimise the risks caused by the unreliable institutional conditions in Greece. At the same time, they split the risk between a number of dependable investors. The way in which the profits and influence within the company were allocated depended more on the reputation of those involved than the sum they invested. Thus, Hilarion Roux, the 'king of the lead trade', contributed a comparatively modest proportion of scoriae property rights but gave his name to the company and acted as the president.

Despite this diverse risk management, the company found itself in a serious conflict with the Greek government who, in response to nationalist sentiments in the country, attempted to force high taxes and levies on the investors. Once they lost in court, the investors demanded the support of their home countries, elevating the dispute to the diplomatic level. The foreign investors mistrusted the Greek legal system, causing indignation among the Greeks. The disagreement provided an occasion for extremely polarised images of Greece to be published in the international press. Often, this involved stereotypes of Orient and Occident being updated so that Greece, in line with Todorova's arguments, was usually perceived as a border region of the self, which due to its Oriental characteristics and uncontrollable nature was viewed as a threat to the existing order of the centre. Negative experiences were generalised to apply to the entire Greek economic area, which was denounced for its hostility to foreign investment. Both the anti-Greek and the pro-Greek reporting tended to use images of the ancient Lavrion mines to reflect on the current situation.

The investors themselves, who in the end were forced to sell their property to a Greek company, albeit at a good price, were obviously less impressed by the conflicts and institutional uncertainty than by the profits they earned. They continued to do business in Greece, even intensifying their activities in metallurgy and other fields, although they were slandered as exploiters by the Greek press and public. Their ongoing investment in Greece could, however, do nothing to alter the unfavourable effect of the Lavrion affair on perceptions of the Greek financial market among European investors.

Notes

1 On the possible role played by the London banking house Hambro & Son in the choice and election, **341f.** in this book.
2 The effects of Britain's support for Italian Risorgimento, against Austria, on the national disposition of the Ionian Islands were very considerable: 'British Protection in the Ionian Islands was irreparably broken' (ibid., 53).
3 London, Thursday, December 18, 1862, in: *The Times*, 18.12.1862.
4 On emery mining by the Englishman J. M. Evans, who represents another example of foreign investment, see Δερτιλής [Dertilis] (2009, 596f.).
5 Important French and German direct investment in Spain is investigated by Puig/Castro (2009).
6 Coulson (2012, 131). In the 1880s, only 14% of the world's production came from Spain; see Fletcher (1991, 195).
7 H. W. Gartrell, quoted from Gregory (2001, 170).
8 The classical studies literature on the mines of Lavrion is extensive; see N. N. (2006).
9 Legend has it that the holy Barbara, the patron saint of miners, found shelter in Lavrion before she was martyred; see Gregory (2001, 146).
10 The question of who was the first to recognise the value of the mines in the Modern Era was of great significance in the later Lavrion affair. The businessman Edouard Roux, brother of the first mine operator, was one of the first to claim that Fiedler (**147** in this book) and Russegger (see ibid.) failed to recognise their value (see E. Roux: The Mines of Laurium, in: *The Times*, 16.10.1872). Many other contemporaries were of the same opinion, e.g. Watbled (1883, 13). It seems likely that the incorrect information in the secondary literature stemmed from these pieces. The Greek engineer Andreas Kordellas, who was the first to thoroughly investigate the mines, certainly did not accuse the two German researchers of such a misjudgement; see Cordella (1869/1871).
11 Emphasis in the original, tr. by K.S.
12 Eastern Europe in the Vienna Exhibition, from Our Special Correspondent, 27.6.1873, in: *The Times*, 1.7.1873.
13 A collection of published sources is found in ELIA; see Μπαμπούνης [Babounis] (1988). The article also provides an overview of the material in the unusable archive of the CFC. For help with identifying and accessing relevant sources, I thank Giorgios N. Dermatis.
14 The metallurgy museum in Lavrion provides a comprehensive overview of the literature and the published sources on the topic of Lavrion online: courses.arch.ntua.gr/fsr/130595/1-2.pdf [24.10.2019].
15 The following information on Kordellas' biography is taken from this biographical dictionary if not otherwise indicated. The Vovolinis brothers quote broadly from Kordellas' memoires, which are based on the diaries that he kept for many years and today are stored in the Gennadios Library in Athens. Thanks to the comprehensiveness of the quotes, it was unnecessary to view the original.
16 The Freiberg mining academy was important in the transfer of technology, e.g. to Spain in the first half of the century; see Gironés/Viejobueno (2001, 201).
17 Apparently because the application from the Greek Pachis (who is the subject of further consideration below) had awakened the interest of the monarchy, see Κακαβογιάννης [Kakavogiannis] (1998, 445).
18 Diary from 19./20.12.1860, quoted from Βοβολίνης [Vovolinis]/ Βοβολίνης [Vovolinis] 1958–1963, B, 47. Rigas Velestinlis' book is entitled 'New Anacharsis' ('Νέος Ανάχαρσις') (Βελεστινλής [Velestinlis] 1797). In Greek mythology, Anacharsis

is a Skythian who attempts to introduce Greek beliefs and knowledge that he learnt on his Greek travels to his homeland, which leads to his murder by his brother King Saulios; see Erler (1882, 75); Herodot (2001, 4,46; 4,76f.).

19 Reports by Andreas Kordellas for the Greek ministry of the economy, quoted from Βοβολίνης [Vovolinis]/ Βοβολίνης [Vovolinis] (1958–1963, B, 47).

20 Cordella (1864), tr. by K.S. Before commencement of the French-Italian investment, Kordellas had also promoted Lavrion in the Greek newspapers; see Cordella (1869/1871, 23).

21 'Giovani Italia', founded in the context of the French July-Revolution of 1830, replaced the secret organisations that had been common in certain circles of the liberal Italian elite with an appeal to the masses and planned an uprising of the population against the existing restorative system. Mazzini's goal was a republican nation state of Italy; see Altgeld (2002, 274–276).

22 This is with reference to Dertilis: Κεκροπούλου [Kekropoulou] (2004, 338f.).

23 In another version in the secondary literature, recorded without mention of the sources, it is said that in 1859, a vessel travelling empty from Greece to Marseille took the debris on board as ballast. Serpieri immediately recognised the value of the samples and started his journey to Greece. Kakavogiannis regards this version purely as an attempt to justify Serpieri's involvement; see Κακαβογιάννης [Kakavogiannis] (1995, 443).

24 Farina refers to the special issue of the newspaper 'Italia, periodico politico e letterario Riminese', No 1 e 2, Rimini, Tipografia Danesi già Albertini (1882). It was printed during the election campaign in Rimini, where Serpieri was a candidate for a seat in the Italian parliament.

25 It is also reported that Pachis was a representative of the Roux and Serpieri company; see Κακαβογιάννης [Kakavogiannis] (1995, 443). Kakavogiannis tells several other variants of this version of the story, although his focus is on whether Serpieri should be accredited with having 'discovered' the mines. He himself suspects that Serpieri may have sent Pachis on an exploratory trip to Greece (ibid., 445). A discussion of the various stories is also found in Δερμάτης [Dermatis] (2003, 79–82).

26 Pachis' daughter Lauria later married Serpieri's son Fernandos.

27 The petition in Κορδέλλας [Kordellas] (1870, 7f.). Others were also interested in Greece's natural resources, e.g. in 1862, the London banker Vasiliow Mela acquired a concession for mining emery on Milos; see Παπαστεφανάκη [Papastefanaki] (2005, 28).

28 Statement by Andreas Kordellas concerning Georgios Pachis' petition from 13.4.1862, quoted from Βοβολίνης [Vovolinis]/Βοβολίνης [Vovolinis] (1958–1963, B, 49).

29 Report by Andreas Kordellas concerning the petition of Georgios Pachis, from 2.10.1863, quoted from ibid., 50. Huet reports that Serpieri later had the contracts the 'young Greek' had signed with the municipality of Keratea subjected to a judicial examination and annulled so that he could then draw up contracts with the municipality himself; see Huet (1879, 736). More details on Pachis' venture are found in Δερμάτης [Dermatis] (2003, 76–80).

30 Petition from Jean Battista Serpieri to the Greek ministry of the economy from 14./26.10.1863, quoted from Βοβολίνης [Vovolinis]/Βοβολίνης [Vovolinis] (1958–1963, B, 50).

31 Ibid.

32 For example, the mines Linares and Fortuna opened in 1852 and 1885 in Andalusia; see Coulson (2012, 131).

33 Other similar examples of credit transactions are discussed by Perceval/López-Morell (2009, 192).

34 Report by Andreas Kordellas on Sepieri's petition, 24.10.1863, quoted from Βοβολίνης [Vovolinis]/Βοβολίνης [Vovolinis] (1958–1963, B, 51).
35 Ibid.
36 A copy of this map, which shows the location of the scoriae and the woods, is found in Μαρκουλή-Μποντιώνη [Markouli-Bontioni] (2010), no page numbers. On the analysis of the historical maps which cannot be pursued in detail here, see Schneider (2012).
37 Report by Andreas Kordellas and T. Bouris from 11.1.1863, quoted from Βοβολίνης [Vovolinis]/Βοβολίνης [Vovolinis] (1958–1963, B, 51).
38 Ibid., 52.
39 The French translation later proved most contentious.
40 Heldreich à Monsieur le Ministre des Finances, 14.4.1864, in: Serpieri (1871a, 22ff.), tr. by K.S.
41 A detailed summary of the petitions and the negotiations is found in Κεκροπούλου [Kekropoulou] (2007, 18–21).
42 Serpieri à Monsieur le Vicomte d'Amelot Chargé d'Affaires de France en Grèce, 19./31.5.1864, in: Sotiropoulos (1871, III–V). Riz (1872, 11), talks of 6,000 drachmas. This account written at the highpoint of the Lavrion affair under the pseudonym of Riz by the Greek ambassador in Paris, Rangabe, deviates considerably from the account given by Vouvoulinis. Rangabe reports that the inexperienced finance minister Valvis had granted Heldreich's petition although it was not within his power to do so.
43 Serpieri to MAE, Duc Tacher de la Tagocie, Chargé d'Affaires de France à Athènes, 29.6.1871, AN, F12/6540, tr. by K.S.
44 Both documents in Κορδέλλας [Kordellas] (1866, 54–62). Copies of both were sent on 11.5.1864 to the Greek minister of the economy.
45 Also see Μαρκουλή-Μποντιώνη [Markouli-Bontioni] (2010, 30). Clearly, the distribution of the capital was laid out in a contract from 4.5.1864, the exact wording of which has not survived (see Hilarion Roux et Cie to the Greek consul general (in Marseille) from 7.5.1864, in: Κορδέλλας [Kordellas] 1866, 52).
46 Preliminary contract and charter, in ibid., 54–62.
47 Dermatis suggests that elsewhere an initial capital of one million francs was mentioned to the Greek government; see Δερμάτης [Dermatis] (2003, 89).
48 Preliminary contract, in: Κορδέλλας [Kordellas] (1870, 62).
49 Report by Andreas Kordellas, 19.1.1865, in: (Βοβολίνης [Vovolinis]/Βοβολίνης [Vovolinis] 1958–1963, B, 53f.).
50 On the development of the town of Lavrion, see Κεκροπούλου [Kekropoulou] (2007).
51 Agroantoni does not want to talk of social policy or philanthropy, but rather emphasises the functionality of the facilities.
52 See Greece (From our Own Correspondent), in: *The Times*, 27.10.1865.
53 Watbled (1883, 13) even wrote that this is the equivalent of almost all French production.
54 **178 n.10** in this book.
55 The Mines of Laurium, from our Own Correspondent in Athens, in: *The Times*, 16.10.72.
56 Watbled (1883, 13).
57 See also Mines of Laurium (From Our Special Correspondent), in: *The Times*, 9.10.1872.
58 Le Ministre de Finances Sotiropoulos to Serpieri, 30.11.1865, in: Sotiropoulos (1871, VIf.).
59 Why this law was passed so late is investigated by Πρεβενά [Prevena] (2004). She disputes the notion that this was due to the repeated government shake-ups and

unstable political situation and sees the Lavrion affair as rather being the cause of the domestic political problems; see ibid., 573.

60 Loi ΣΙΓ'sur l'impôt du plomb et des scories du Laurium, from 14.4.1867, in: Sotiropoulos (1871), IXf. The law was supposed to encourage foreign investors and attract domestic Greek savings to the benefit of metallurgy; see Gregory (2001, 135); Σαλίμπα [Salimba] (2005, 49).

61 On Greek domestic politics in 1871–1873, also see Δερτιλής [Dertilis] (1980).

62 La Cour d'Appel d'Athènes, printed in: Serpieri (1871b, 47–58, 53).

63 Ibid., 4, 9.

64 Conclusions de la Société Hilarion Roux et Cie contre le Fisc, 27.4.1871, printed in ibid., 32–46, 34.

65 Serpieri to Le Comte de Gobineau, Ministre plénipotentiaire de France à Athènes, 2.6.1868, AN, F12/6540; Le Ministre des Finances Simos (Athènes) au Ministre des Affaires étrangères (Athènes), 9.8.1868, in: Sotiropoulos (1871, XIf.). The important role played by the French diplomat Jules Ferry in the negotiations is emphasised by Δερτιλής [Dertilis] (1980, 84–87). On Ferry, also see Basch (1995, 198–204).

66 Extrait de l'Arrêt de la Cour d'appel d'Athènes sub No 720/32,362, rendu dans la séance du 14 Juin 1871, in: Sotiropoulos (1871, XIII–XVII); La Cour d'Appel d'Athènes, printed in: Serpieri (1871b, 47–58), here 48; Riz (1872); Βοβολίνης [Vovolinis]/Βοβολίνης [Vovolinis] (1958–1963, B, 57).

67 Conclusion du Fisc contre la Société Hilarion Roux et Cie devant la Cour d'appel d'Athènes, 15.4.1871, printed in: Serpieri (1871b, 19–23). 1,981,678 drachmas, equivalent to a sum of 1,883,500 francs; see Ledoux (1872, 570).

68 Riz (1872, 12); Serpieri (1871b, 17f.).

69 Stremma (plural: stremmata) is the Greek unit for measuring land. One stremma is equivalent to 1/10 hectare.

70 Concessions from 23.8.1867 and 31.12.1868; see N. N. s.t.d, 39. Also see Le Ministre des Finances (Athènes) au Ministre des Affaires étrangères (Athènes), 27.5./8.6.1871, in Sotiropoulos (1871, XXXVIIf.).

71 Laurium and Greece, from our Own Correspondent, Athens 8.2., *The Times*, 25.2.1873.

72 A detailed explanation of the differences between these products of the ancient mines is provided by Κακαβογιάννης [Kakavogiannis] (1998, 440f.). The term 'Ecvolades' comes from the antique Greek writer Strabo; see Dücker (1873, 9).

73 Projet de loi pour les 'Ecvolades' (Halden), NA FO 32–443.

74 Loi des Ecvolades, in Sotiropoulos (1871, XXXVII).

75 Speech by M. Deligeorges in cabinet from 26.4.1872, printed in Serpieri (1872), tr. by K.S.

76 The text comments on and counters Deligiorges' speech in cabinet.

77 See on this phenomenon in the second half of the twentieth century Appel/Loyle (2012).

78 The author argued that anyone who did not want to trust in foreign courts should not invest abroad.

79 Speech by M. Deligeorges in the cabinet, printed in Serpieri (1872, 5).

80 Ibid., 40.

81 The company also tried to gain British protection through the shareholder Naegely. Eskine, the English ambassador in Athens, went no further than submitting an unofficial warning to the government that the company should not be treated in a way that would deter other foreign capital; see British legation in Athens, Eskine, to the FO, Granville, 12.3.1871, NA FO 32–443.

82 This report, apparently originating in the French foreign ministry, came to the conclusion that the ecvolades were certainly included in the concession.

83 A list of the governments and prime ministers in Δερτιλής [Dertilis] (1980).
84 German legation, St. Petersburg, to the AA, Bismarck, 25.12.1871, R901-36209.
85 Δερτιλής [Dertilis] (2009, 512). Thus in December 1871, the king supported Voulgaris because he was the only politician who did not have a completely negative attitude towards the foreign firms in the Lavrion affair. In the spring of 1872, Voulgaris won the election.
86 Serpieri (1871a, IV), tr. by K.S.
87 Ibid., 18, tr. by K.S.
88 Serpieri to the French legation in Athens, 15.11.1870, AN F12/6540.
89 Ibid., tr. by K.S.
90 Serpieri to Le Ministre des Affaires étrangères, duc Tacher de la Tagocie, Chargé d'Affaires de France à Athènes, 29.6.1871, AN F12/6540, tr. by K.S.
91 Ibid.
92 Ibid., tr. by K.S.
93 Eastern Europe in the Vienna Exhibition, from Our Special Correspondent, 27.6.1873, in *The Times*, 1.7.1873.
94 Most memorandums expressively emphasised their neutrality in contrast to all other available sources. Serpieri provided a very friendly reception for travellers who could be expected to write influential reports; see Sandys (1887, 37).
95 From our Own Correspondent: Greece, in *The Times*, 6.7.1871.
96 Mr. Ellis (British ambassador in Athens): State of Greece, in: *The Times*, 23.4.1867. The Lavrion affair was the first occasion where British diplomacy developed a genuine interest in the Greek economy, argues Δερτιλής [Dertilis] (2009, 596).
97 From Our Own Correspondent: The New Greek Ministry, in *The Times*, 8.8.1872.
98 Our Own Correspondent in Paris, Greece, in *The Times*, 9.10.1872.
99 From Our Own Correspondent: Greece and the Eastern Question, in *The Times*, 15.12.1871.
100 From Our Own Correspondent: The Mines of Laurium, in *The Times*, 5.11.1872.
101 D'Ideville (1875), entry from 23.1.1867, 223, tr. by K.S.
102 Ibid., entry from 24.2.1867, 256f.
103 Ibid., tr. by K.S.
104 Our Own Correspondent in Paris: Greece, in: *The Times,* 9.10.1872. On the affair, **89 n.115** in this book.
105 About, seemingly the only one to do so, linked the defeat of France against Prussia in 1871 to the new courage of the Greeks proceeding against the French company; see ibid., 3f, 12. The two newspaper articles published here had appeared on 18.12.71 and on 8.3.1872 in *Le Soir.*
106 Our Own Correspondent in Paris: Greece, in: *The Times*, 9.10.1872.
107 Without title, Thanks to Our Paris Correspondent, in *The Times*, 9.10.1872. Emphasis in the original.
108 Ledoux (1872, 561), tr. by K.S.
109 'Un Grec': The Mines of Laurium, in *The Times*, 10.10.1872; and again in *The Times*, 17.10.1872. Hilarion Roux's brother countered this article in E. Roux: The Mines of Laurium, in *The Times*, 16.10.1872.
110 Riz (1872, 3), tr. by K.S.
111 Foreword by Saint-Hilaire, in Moraïtinis (1877, VII–XII, VIII).
112 From Our Own Correspondent: Public Works in Greece, in *The Times*, 17.10.1871.
113 Moraïtinis was the son of the president of the Athenian Areopagus; see Basch (1995, 209–216). On the business and private relationships between Moraïtinis

and Syngros, see Δερτιλής [Dertilis] (2009, 551). Dertilis suggests that Moraïtinis wrote and acted on behalf of Syngros.

114 If young Greeks were still able to be delighted by France despite his disparagements, this deserves quite particular recognition; see Riz 1872; Le Laurium, 2.

115 Dilessi murders, called after the church in which the hostages were held captive before their murder, also known as the Massacre of Oropos.

116 See, e.g. The Massacre in Greece, from Our Own Correspondent, in *The Times*, 6.5.1870.

117 The name Palikars was given to the freedom fighters who lived in the mountains during the Greek struggle for independence and who used highway robbery as one source of income.

118 Our Own Correspondent in Paris: Greece, in *The Times*, 9.10.1872.

119 The Mines of Laurium, by telegraph, From our Own Correspondent, Paris, 9.8.1873, *The Times*, 10.8.1873.

120 The poem is quoted from de Musset (1857, 1). The English translation is taken from de Musset (1908, 1).

121 Ledoux (1872, 563), tr. by K.S.

122 This Greek banker from Constantinople was one of the most influential and best connected of the nineteenth century. For a biographical introduction, see Συγγρός [Syngros] (1998, 1, 6–128). In 1872, Syngros had founded the Bank of Constantinople and the Credit Bank (Γενική Πιστωτική Τράπεζα), based on the example of the French Crédit Mobilier; see Δερτιλής [Dertilis] (1980, 15–20); in 1881, he co-founded the Epiro-Thessalien Bank. Syngros played a key role in procuring the Greek foreign loans between 1879 and 1893. On Syngros' preparation of the Lavrion deal, see Δερτιλής [Dertilis] (2009, 549ff.). Dertilis provides details of Syngros' political networks and his agitations. Dertilis views the Greek 'capitalist' as having had a very great influence on King George, Prime Minister Deligeorgis and Greek politics in general.

123 Diaspora Greeks were sometimes perceived by the public as Greek investors and sometimes as foreign ones; see Δερτιλής [Dertilis] (2009, 593).

124 Ibid., 511. Dertilis estimates that this price was equivalent to the true value. Chastagnaret (2005, 285), however, speaks of a doubling of the invested capital within seven years. His figures seem inaccurate.

125 On the later history of the Greek and French companies, also see Δερμάτης [Dermatis] (2011, 162–166).

126 Material Progress in Greece, from Our Own Correspondent, Athens, 1.11.1873, in *The Times*, 21.11.1873.

127 File 'Laurium Company' of the London Stock Exchange from 1890, GL App 412 26B. The files were created in 1890 when the company applied to register in London.

128 The statutes of the company, which was set up for 50 years, are found in the *Gazette des Tribunaux*, 14.10.1875. The capital was divided into 27,000 shares each of 500 francs.

129 In 1986, the Metallurgic Museum of Lavrion was founded; see Κακαβογιάννης [Kakavogiannis] (1988, 345).

130 This technique is described by Pohle-Fraser (1999, 119–123).

131 Newspaper notes (without further details) from 19.3.1884, CAEF B006871-1.

132 Liste des actionnaires ayant déposé des actions en vue de l'assemblé générale du 29 Juin 1878, CAEF B006871-1. Further down the list, Jean Battista Serpieri is found again with 1,500 shares. At the same point in time, Hilarion Roux only held 100 shares.

133 In the same volume, there are several short articles about the mining work on the individual islands, e.g. on Milos or Seriphos. This work was led by the German engineer Emil Grohmann.

134 The company had close credit relations to the BNP (Banque Natinonale de Paris et de Paribas), which is why their archive holds comprehensive material on the financial history of the Société hellénique du gaz d'Athènes et autres villes; see CEP 11-DFOM-221-717, especially A 359 Dossier 4.

135 Lill refers to a close alliance of political power [of the moderate left, K.S.] and organised capitalism with state subventions for large companies and monopolies; see ibid., 332.

136 This attempt to conquer the State of the Church was, like the first one in 1862, repelled by papal and French troops; see Altgeld (2002, 315).

137 In 1892, the Socialist Party was established in Italy.

138 In connection with his candidacy, there is a diatribe that accuses Serpieri of adultery, fraud, avarice and bribery of the press which must be seen as a blackmail attempt: Capizucchi 1884. I thank Katharina Tugend for help with the translation.

5

AT THE SERVICE OF THE CHANCELLOR

Bleichröder and the Greek loan of 1889[1]

Greece at the time of the Congress of Berlin

In terms of economic development, the 1870s saw Greece still needing to catch up. Some slight progress had been made with industrialisation: in 1867, there were only 22 factories and manufactories with a total of 300 hp; by 1880, there were 108 factories with 2,884 hp (Κατσούλης [Katsoulis] et al. 1985, 198).[2] (By way of comparison, in Prussia in 1840, there were 174 steam engines with 5,400 hp just in mining; by 1849, this figure had risen to 332 with 13,200 hp (Nipperdey 1998, 186)). By 1879, 153 joint-stock companies had been established in the whole of the Greek kingdom, almost half of them in the 1870s (Pepelasis 2011, 31). Nonetheless, Greece remained a primarily agricultural country. In 1890, 68% of the population were still employed in agriculture; only 6% were members of the industrial workforce (Κατσούλης [Katsoulis] et al. 1985, 198) (in 1875 in the German Empire, the equivalent figures were 50% in agriculture, 29% in industry and 21% in trade and services) (Kocka et al. 2001, 49). It was correspondingly important that the national estates taken over by the Ottomans were finally distributed among the rural population in 1871; this introduced private property relations to Greek agriculture for the first time.[3] However, the extensive subdivision of the land later proved problematic.[4]

Trade had traditionally been the most important branch of the Greek economy (Παπαθανασόπουλος [Papathanasopoulos] 1983). Not least thanks to the many Greeks in the European diaspora, trade relations in the Levant blossomed in the decades after the Crimea War. Shipping was profitable and contributed to growing capital accumulation and prosperity (Chatzis/Nikolaides 2000; Harlaftis 2005). In particular, Syros, Piraeus and Patras had been able to establish themselves as trade centres. In addition to the agricultural products, the natural resources of the country were also significant exports, such as emery from Naxos, silver and lead from Lavrion and marble. However, there were increasing imports, including grain, worsening the balance of foreign trade, which was nearly always negative. The banking sector had developed strongly: in 1873, there were only two banks, the ETE

DOI: 10.4324/9780429286537-8

and the IOB, but by 1883, there were four banks with considerably increased capital resources.[5]

In contrast to the other Balkan countries, whose independence was first recognised at the Congress of Berlin in 1878, Greece had been able to achieve positive economic development in the past decades, even if the growth was modest by Western standards. Furthermore, the country was strategically positioned near the Ottoman Empire. All these factors stimulated hope among European investors that Greece would experience rapid industrialisation. The Congress of Berlin was marked by political success and territorial expansion for the country, which gained Thessaly and parts of Epirus from the disintegrating Ottoman Empire. Greece took occupation of these areas in 1881 after further disputes about the positioning of borders (Geiss 1978, 97).[6] The incorporation of the region's 'granary' into the country promised increased agricultural production and encouraged many diaspora Greeks, who had suffered severe losses in the Egyptian financial crisis of 1875, to invest in their homeland or even to return (Vlasto 1885, 266f.). This was far from satisfying the 'Megali idea' of the Greeks (there had been hope of including Crete, the Aegean Island and parts of Anatolia in the Greek territory (Zelepos 2002; Biondich 2011, 47)) and tensions with the Ottoman Empire repeatedly triggered extremely costly military mobilisations. However, the Congress of Berlin seemed to provide at least a preliminary resolution to the acute Oriental question, which had for decades hung like the sword of Damocles over Europe threatening war. World peace and peace in the Balkans seemed at least temporarily secured (Keisinger 2008).

As far as images of Greece were concerned, the Hellenic ideals continued to be seen in, e.g. France in the 1870s and 1880s: 'the "Hellene dream" again became, more than ever, the "consoling refuge of the poets" and the travellers' (Basch 1995, 235, tr. by K.S.). These images were, however, almost exclusively related to Greek antiquity: 'Greece played no other role than that of an accessory, and that of an accessory only in the name of its glorious past' (ibid., 206, tr. by K.S.). There was considerably less influential literary work published about modern Greece than in the preceding decade, but more political or documentary writing in which images of the deceitful, backward Greece often displaced romantic ideals (ibid., 223). This was due to the disappointment of many travellers with the country: although Greece had been criticised for being part of the Orient for decades, many journalists and visitors now complained that the general modernisation, Europeanisation and 'Occidentalisation' of the country involved the decay of its original character: 'Greece was reproached for leaving the framework of the Orient after being criticised for years, if not for centuries, for its orientalisation!' (ibid., 206, tr. by K.S.). Although the Balkan identity of the country gradually receded as Greece grew closer to Europe (Todorova 1997, 30) – in October 1883, the Orient Express travelled from the Gare de l'Est in Paris to

Constantinople for the first time (Basch 1995, 223) – in many publications, the image of Greece as part of the Orient or as a peripheral Balkan region survived, but was now described as broken down and decaying (ibid., 174, 177). This ambiguous view of the Westernisation of the country contrasted with the purely positive evaluation of its economic development, as was usual in financial circles.

Another positive factor for potential investors was Greece's low level of debt (both domestic and foreign), which was primarily linked to the barring of the country from the international exchanges since 1827. Greek debts amounted to 186 million drachmas in 1877 (Δερτιλής [Dertilis] 2009, 604; Ψαλιδόπουλος [Psalidopoulos] 2019). In order to judge this figure and compare it both internationally and over time, it should be seen in relation to the nominal gross domestic product (Scherf 2011, 403), so that the government or public debt ratio can be calculated. In 1876, this ratio stood at 60% or 640% of annual tax revenue in Greece (Δερτιλής [Dertilis] 2009, 603), which was rather low when compared internationally: in 1871, the public debt ratio was 86% in Great Britain, in France, it was 81% in 1875, and in Spain in 1875, it was even 160% (Taylor s.t., 15), while in the German Empire, it was only 37% in 1880 (Ritschl 1996, 24). This shows Greece's strong economic growth in the previous decades: the debt from 1843 of 150 million drachmas had after all created a public debt ratio of 153%, 14 times the annual tax revenue (Δερτιλής [Dertilis] 2009, 203). The Greek government bonds were also seen as being relatively safe (ibid., 584).

Before the Congress of Berlin of 1878, Greece finally and significantly managed to reach an agreement with the creditors of the old debts from 1824/1825.[7] The settlement was masterminded by the Greek ambassador in London, Ioannis Gennadios, who was also responsible for the publication of extracts from the 1825 press reports mentioned earlier (N. N. (Gennadios) 1878; Gennadios 1880; Ανδρεάδης [Andreadis] 1904, 67–70; Chatziioannou 2002, 54).[8] It was relevant for the negotiations that the Great Powers wanted to adopt a softer approach to Greece than had hitherto been the case, as a 'reward' for Greece's neutrality in the Russian-Turkish war of 1875–1878 and were consequently willing to make compromises concerning the loan of 1832 (Dertilis 2006, 419).[9] This paved the way for Greece to be readmitted to the European exchanges and to take out new international loans. Greece thus joined the ranks of the new Balkan states, all of which required foreign credit to be able to carry out government functions and to develop state infrastructure, despite the fact that this involved them becoming dependent on their creditors (Biondich 2011, 50–63). The timing of the loan was exceptionally good from a European perspective. The world economic crisis of 1873 had weakened the rapid economic growth of the previous decades so that many countries were hit by deflation and stagnation in the following years.[10] However from autumn 1879, in France as in Germany (Schaefer 1995, 92f.), an upturn could be noted, which boosted activities on the exchanges. The crisis seemed to have bottomed out: 'The years 1878-1882 were certainly the period of the most intense speculation in France in the nineteenth century' (Caron 1979, 53). In this era of the gold standard, the London City also blossomed as never before (Obstfeld/Taylor 2004, 126f.). Papagiannopoulos speaks of the 'time of hens with golden eggs' (Παπαγιαννοπούλος [Papagiannopoulos] 1989, 43, tr. by K.S.). Interest on government bonds in Paris, London and Berlin was very low, so investors on the European exchanges were searching for investment opportunities with higher interest in other parts of the world (ibid., 294). From the 1870s, foreign state bonds were particularly popular in France where investors tended to be more conservative, especially as interest from the bonds was not subject to taxation and the repayments and interest payments were made in gold, which rendered the papers independent of dangerous exchange rate fluctuations (Levandis 1944, 56ff.). In France, a clear economic upturn was seen from 1883, while in Germany, the recovery strengthened from the mid-1880s. Similarly in Great Britain, foreign investments reached a new peak between 1886 and 1890 (Mathias 1969, 366). At the same time, from the beginning of the 1880s and particularly after the Baring crisis at the start of the 1890s, new strategies could be noted among the bankers. It had previously been the case that one bank had issued government bonds, using its reputation as guarantee, while the risk of unsellable bonds was carried by the state itself (Bramsen/Wain 1979, 330); individual banks thus usually acted as 'gatekeepers' for specific states which had little choice in the matter. After 1880, the growth in competition, also internationally, meant that the banks themselves had to take on the underwriting risk in order to gain the states as customers, because the states could choose from among a selection of issuing banks. They split this risk by forming 'underwriting groups' on the quiet or, increasingly, syndicates that jointly issued the bonds quite openly. This practice gained public acceptance after the Baring crisis as it seemed to help prevent bank failures. Syndicates, also international ones, became respectable (Mikkelsen 2014; ibid., 2017).

This was the situation, favourable in many ways, when in 1879 the Comptoir d'escompte de Paris (CEP), in cooperation with the Greek banker Andreas Syngros, issued the first new Greek loan on the Paris exchange. The French government exerted considerable pressure to ensure that the bonds were authorised despite the massive protests of Dutch and British investors who held bonds from the 1824/1825 loans and felt that they had not been adequately compensated.[11] The new loan was the starting point for a series of seven Greek loans between 1879 and 1893 (see Table II.5.1).

The nominal credit totalled 640 million francs overall, which completely changed the quite low level of indebtedness within only 15 years. If commissions, brokerage and insurance are deducted, then a net total of 464 million arrived in Greece. A certain proportion of this money had to be immediately used to service debts, which rose dramatically. By 1893, debt

Table II.5.1 Greece's new foreign debts, 1879–1893

Year	*Nominal value in million gold francs*	*Issue price*	*Realised sum in million gold francs*	*Nominal interest in %*	*Real interest in %*	*Guarantees*	*Issuing banks*
Jan. 79	60	73	44	6	8.18	Stamp duty	CEP, Bank syndicate (Syngros)
Dec. 80/81	120	74.6	89.52	5	6.7	Custom duties from Athens, Piraeus, Patras, Zante	Bank of Constantinople, CEP, Hambro
Jan. 84	100 instead of planned 170	69.8	69.78	5	7.15	Custom duties from Volo, Arta, Tsagezi; surpluses from the custom duties from Athens, Piraeus, Catacolo, Kephalonia, Kalamai	Bank of Egypt, Bank of Constantinople, BNP, CEP, Epiro-Thessalienbank, ETE, SG
May 87	135	67.4	90.99	4	5.95	Monopolies on salt, petroleum, matches, playing cards, cigarette papers, emery from Naxos; collected by the Société de Régie de Monopoles de Grèce	CEP and others
Feb. 89	155 (30 + 125)	68.125/72.75	111.375 (20,4375 + 90.9375)	4	5.87	None	First half: Hambro Second half: Bank of Constantinople, Bleichröder, Anthony Gibbs

(*Continued*)

Year	*Nominal value in million gold francs*	*Issue price*	*Realised sum in million gold francs*	*Nominal interest in %*	*Real interest in %*	*Guarantees*	*Issuing banks*
April 1890	60 instead of planned 89.9	52.95	52.95	5	5.66	Railway profits	Hambro, Credit bank (Γενική Πιστωτική Τράπεζα), Nationalbank für Deutschland
May 1893	9.739 instead of planned 100	65	5.5	5	8.8	None ('Funding Loan')	Bank of Constantinople, Epiro-Thessalien Bank, ETE, Hambro
Total	**639.739**	**Average 72.54**	**464.121**	**Average 4.86**	**Average 6.9**		

Table based on: Ηλιαδάκης [Iliadakis] 2011, 56. The figures differ slightly elsewhere, e.g. Levandis 1944, 56, 67–71, 77, or Χαριτάκης [Charitakis] 1933. An overview together with domestic loans is found in Παντελάκης [Pantelakis] 1995, 92–95. As the issue price, like with state loans, was usually below 100%, the realised sum was never as high as the nominal value. For the last two loans no purchasers could be found for a proportion of the bonds so the sum planned could not be issued in its entirety.

servicing had increased to the extent that it accounted for 33% of the entire state budget. From 1879 to 1893, Greece paid 470.4 million francs in interest, more than the sum that was newly borrowed, not including repayments of the principal (Ανδρεάδης [Andreadis] 1904; Levandis 1944, 72ff.).[12]

This begs the question as to why the foreign banks continued to issue bonds for Greece despite the obvious and continuous growth in the government debt ratio in excess of healthy limits. After all, the bankruptcy of the country would have a serious impact on the reputation of the issuing house. So why did the European banks continue to issue Greek bonds?

Risks of Greek bond issues

Andreas Andreadis, the 'Nestor' of Greek economic and social history, asked this question as early as 1925 (Ανδρεάδης [Andreadis] 2010, 164f.) and produced several convincing answers.

The large profits, e.g. commissions, played an important role. According to Andreadis, every new loan resulted in enormous short-term profits for the banks and middlemen involved, which helps to explain their efforts to organise more loans (Levandis 1944, 56ff.). Indeed, the average profits that the banks made from the Greek bonds were somewhat higher than those accruing from West European government bonds (Δερτιλής [Dertilis] 2009, 583f.), and in certain cases were very lucrative.[13] However, this cannot be taken to apply generally to all the bond issues, as will be seen later. Moreover, Andreadis emphasised the personal trust of Western politicians and financers towards the Greek prime minister, Charilaos Trikoupis,[14] who had spent part of his life in Paris and London and was therefore extremely well-connected in international diplomatic circles. Contemporaries accredited Trikoupis with playing an important role in the economic upturn of Greece:

> Untiring work, the most vigilant application to the study of his country's needs, the firm will to satisfy them, the energy and perseverance that guarantee the execution of reforms, the courage to resist his friends when public interests demand it and, what is even rarer, to sacrifice his own advantages, these are the qualities that Mr Tricoupis has deployed in his political career, which has lasted nearly twenty-five years.[15]

Tricoupis indeed argued very skilfully to explain why Greece needed foreign capital, also in foreign languages.[16] Firstly, the country would need money to acquire Thessaly, which was granted to Greece at the Congress of Berlin under the condition that Greece agreed to take over the proportion of the Ottoman foreign debt ascribed to this region. Secondly, Tricoupis argued that capital from abroad would enable the Greek government to convert internal Greek loans with interest of 8% or 9% into loans with much lower interest. This would unburden the state's finances considerably and render a balanced budget possible, the condition for the restoration of the convertibility of the drachma, which was very significant for international trade with Greece. Thirdly, Tricoupis planned to use the money to build up infrastructure like streets and railway lines and to industrialise Greece. This seemed highly necessary as in 1880 Greece had only one railway line of nine kilometres in length, which connected Athens with Piraeus (Παπαγιαννάκης [Papayiannakis] 1982).[17] Trikoupis' up-to-date arguments convinced not only foreign diplomats, but also investors.[18]

In order to finance his plans, in the 1880s, Trikoupis completely reorganised the customs and taxation system. In the past, the government had largely relied on indirect taxes, but Trikoupis now shifted to direct taxation, a measure that led to great inequalities, for instance, in the agricultural sector; while the big landowners of Thessaly tended to profit from the changes, the impact was particularly negative for livestock farmers (Αγγελόπουλος [Angelopoulos] 1933; Περάκης [Perakis] 2000; Συρμαλόγλου [Sirmaloglou] 2007). The tax revenue rose from 23.2 million drachmas (a per capita taxation of 15.22% of income) in 1869 to 86.2 million drachmas (37.63% per capita) in 1893 (Levandis 1944, 73). Customs policies were also restructured. Thus, the import duties for food and especially for wheat were fairly low in the 1860s but were increased fivefold by the reform of 1884. This trend continued in subsequent years and was in keeping with the protectionism displayed by many states in the 1880s. The aim was to promote domestic wheat production. At the same time, high custom duties were charged on imports of industrial goods that could also be produced in Greece, a policy intended to protect domestic production from foreign competition. The continuous fall in the value of the drachma against foreign currencies led to a further de facto increase in custom duties (Freris 1986, 21–24). However, the change in policy failed to achieve the intended effect: imports of wheat continued to increase and industrialisation remained sluggish. The tax revenue at least provided an important source of income for the treasury (ibid., 22).

In addition to Trikoupis' policies, Andreadis mentioned other reasons why the bankers lent to Greece. He suggested, for instance, a lack of information on the part of the bankers. This argument is less convincing, because there were many foreigners present in Greece who realised that only some of the borrowed capital was being employed for infrastructure, while much money was used for armaments and military purposes.[19] And there were certainly many foreigners in Athens, besides the official legates.[20] For instance, in the 1880s, France responded to a request from the Greeks by sending a so-called Mission française, a group of French engineers who worked for the government planning building projects and the extension of infrastructure.[21] These engineers reported regularly to Paris, as did the special envoys from France or Great Britain.[22] Some industrial enterprises like the German firm Krupp had their own deputies on-site to keep close contact to the military and politicians, and industrialists like Friedrich Alfred Krupp even travelled to Greece themselves.[23] Furthermore, certain bankers were well-connected in Greece with contacts not only to diplomats there and at home, but also with close ties to the Greek National Bank ETE, and some banks also sent their own envoys to Greece to get an idea of the local situation and to negotiate with local business partners.[24] Even the West European press reported extensively on Greece and its finances, as did economic specialists in memorandums (Théry 1905). Clearly, contemporaries had the opportunity to gain information on the Greek economy and finances if they so wished, much more so than in the first half of the century.[25]

So why did the financiers decide to invest part of their capital in the 'niche market'[26] of Greece? If they had merely been keen to spread and diversify their risks,[27] they could have found safer candidates. Other factors besides a hope for profit must have played a role. It is easier to explain the decision making of the banking houses that had close business ties and personal relationships to the country over decades, for example, the von Eichthals, Hambro or Erlanger. In these cases, there were strong path dependencies.[28] But what about complete newcomers to the Greek market like, e.g. the Bleichröder banking house, which only started to take an interest in Greece and to introduce Greek bonds to Germany in 1888,[29] and did not participate in the emission of a Greek loan until 1889, without ever having been particularly involved in the country before? There was little encouragement for such involvement in Germany: the Deutsche Bank, for instance, suggested that Greek investments were incompatible with intensive involvement in the Ottoman Empire.[30] So, in this context, why did Bleichröder enter into Greek business? In the following, the case of Bleichröder is investigated as an example of risk perception and management in the issuing of Greek bonds in the 1880s.

Bleichröder and the Greek 4% loan of 1889

In May 1889, Bleichröder, in cooperation with Anthony Gibbs & Sons and Hambro & Son, issued a tax-free consolidated gold loan with a nominal value of 125 million francs (£5 million or 100 million Reichmarks[31]) on the Berlin Stock Exchange. The nominal interest was 4%; the runtime was 30 years. The bonds were emitted at 400, 2,000 or 10,000 marks.[32] The issue rate in Berlin was 77 1/8, the real interest 5.5% per annum. This issue rate was clearly above the average of Greek bonds in the 1880s, which Schaefer calculates at 73 (Schaefer 1995, 321), although it was rather low compared with other state bonds, clearly marking the bonds as a high risk investment. The capital from the emission was bound for the conversion of four older Greek loans: the 6% loan from 1879, the 6% loan for the railway line Myli-Calamata from 1888, the 6% loan for the line Mesolonghi-Agrinio and the Greek internal loan from 1874.[33] This explains the involvement of Gibbs as in 1888 the bank had participated in the financing of the railway line from Myli to Calamata, the concession for which the Greek government had awarded to the Belgian Société Anonyme Internationale de Construction et d'Entreprise de Travaux Publics. The work on this project was in difficulties and Gibbs' aim was to acquire new capital for the completion of the project (Παντελάκης [Pantelakis] 1995, 56, 158). Strong path dependencies help explain the involvement of Hambro as this bank had been the gatekeeper for Greece on the international financial markets for decades and had emitted several Greek loans (Minoglou 2002b).[34] But Bleichröder's decision is less easy to explain because the bonds that he had introduced at the Berlin and Frankfurt Stock Exchanges in 1888 had no direct connection with the loan of 1889,[35] he had no other direct connection with Greece and he cannot be suspected of any sort of Philhellenism.

Bleichröder was born in 1822 in Berlin. His father was the Jewish banker Samuel Bleichröder and his grandfather was Gerson Jakob Bleichröder, who had moved to the city from Bleicherode in the Harz region (Schnee 1955). Samuel Bleichröder, who had founded a modest bills exchange and lottery business in 1803 (Landes 1963, 196), managed to establish himself as a Rothschilds' representative and informant in Berlin from 1828 or 1831, displacing the Mendelssohn banking house from this position. The literature suggests that this could have something to do with the conversion of the Mendelssohns to Christianity (Heilbrunn 1981, 288). The close relationship to the Rothschilds provided Bleichröder with a special position among the many successful Jewish bankers in Berlin (Mosse 1976, 69). Samuel's banking house was active in the market for government bonds and issued such bonds for Rothschilds in Berlin, but also ventured into innovative business fields involving railway and insurance companies and industrial credit (Landes 1963, 197).

There is very little information available about Gerson von Bleichröder's (see Figure II.5.1) youth. He may have attended the boys' school of the Berlin Jewish community (founded in 1826 to replace the Jewish independent school) (Simon 1988, XX), where German, French, Hebrew, business studies, arithmetic, accounting, writing and drawing were taught (Geiger 1988, 137f.). But even if he went to one of the many small private Jewish schools in the city, which about a quarter of Jewish children in Berlin attended (Külow 2014, 38), he would not have been educated in the classics. At the age of 17, in 1839, Gerson joined his father's business. In 1847, he became a partner and, after marrying Emma Guttenberg, the daughter of a banker from Breslau in 1851 (Stern 1988, 33) and Samuel's death in 1855, he became head of the company, in which his brother Julius also worked. In 1860, he then left the family business and set up his own banking house (ibid.).

Gerson Bleichröder inherited his father's position as a Rothschilds' agent, a connection which brought tremendous social capital and profitable involvement in numerous transactions. Furthermore, in 1859, the diplomat

Figure II.5.1 Gerson Bleichröder, painting by Emile Wauters, 1888.

Otto von Bismarck was posted from Frankfurt to be ambassador in St. Petersburg and asked Meyer Carl von Rothschild to recommend a reliable Jewish banker in Berlin who he could entrust with his financial affairs. Rothschild suggested Bleichröder (ibid., 44). This opened the door to the second level of Bleichröder's business success. Bismarck brought Bleichröder rich customers from the world of the court and politics, in increasing numbers as his own prestige grew over the years (Landes 1963, 198). Even more significantly, Bleichröder acted not only as Bismarck's private banker, but also served him in his official capacity: in 1865/1866, Bleichröder organised the finance to mobilise troops in the war against Austria without involving parliament; in 1871, he was instrumental in the designation and collection of French reparations; and Bismarck also obtained Bleichröder's advice and help when founding the Reichsbank and privatising the railways (ibid., 207). From 1859, Bleichröder also joined the Frankfurt Rothschilds, the Preußische Seehandlung (Prussian Maritime Trading Company), the Disconto-Gesellschaft, the Handelsgesellschaft, Sal. Oppenheim and several others as a member of the so-called Prussian consortium, which practically had a monopoly on Prussian (and later German) government bonds and served the financial needs of the monarchy (ibid., 199). Bismarck also valued Bleichröder's advice in political matters and the banker used his position and his close personal contact to the chancellor to extend his networks in the world of politics, diplomacy and journalism, developing relationships with important members of the AA and politicians in England and Russia (Heilbrunn 1981, 304). In 1866, he became a British general consul in Berlin. Bismarck used Bleichröder's contacts to convey political messages that he was unable to communicate through direct channels, e.g. via Bleichröder and the Rothschilds to Napoleon III (Landes 1963, 205f.). 'Over time Bleichröder came to see himself as a secret employee, a special advisor to the head of the Prussian government' (Stern 1988, 62, tr. by K.S.). In some cases, the banker provided his patron with very specific information, for instance, on the insubordinate German ambassador Harry von Arnim-Suckow, who, he organised, should be spied upon in 1873/1874 in Paris (Pöls 1970).[36] 'Bleichröder was a businessman through and through, but certainly saw himself as a little wheel in the system of European politics, one that made no decisions but was definitely important for the functioning of this system' (Heilbrunn 1981, 209, tr. by K.S.). However, the banker continued to develop his network in the financial world, particularly to the Rothschilds (Liedtke 2006, 238). The daily reports that he sent to Lionel von Rothschild in London about the Congress of Berlin of 1878 are a good example of this (Knight 1983, 226–234). Until the death of James d'Rothschild in 1868, the Paris banking house was the focus of his attention but afterwards he concentrated increasingly on the London Rothschilds (ibid., 207).

His services were honoured appropriately: e.g. with the Order of the Red Eagle, 4th class, in 1858 and the position of *Kommerzienrat* in 1865 (Mosse 1987, 90). In 1872, Bleichröder was the first non-baptised Jew to be elevated to the hereditary nobility and a year later, he purchased the feudal country seat of Gütergotz where Wilhelm I visited him four years later (Heilbrunn 1981, 293). Many more honours and awards followed, also from abroad (Schnee 1955). Bleichröder's blindness, which increasingly afflicted him through the 1870s, did not prevent him from continuing to extend his sphere of influence.

Bleichröder continued the business traditions of his family, for instance, issuing foreign bonds for countries on all continents except for Australia (Landes 1963, 199). But he was also entrepreneurially active, e.g. with the Silesian Laura foundry, and accumulated a considerable fortune, estimated at 23,333 thalers in 1861 but already amounting to 100,000 thalers by the end of the 1860s (Heilbrunn 1981, 291). His family was said to be worth about 70 million marks in 1911 and he was known as the richest man in Berlin (Liedtke 2006, 238).[37] He avoided risky investments, e.g. in the German colonies, as far as possible, restricting his involvement there to a minor role at most (ibid., 309), as in the case of the New Guinea consortium which he founded with Adolph von Hansemann in 1883/1884 but which only existed for five years (Wehler 1969, 393f.). Bleichröder had other reasons for carrying out colonial activities that 'could not be justified in business terms'; thus 'their only justification was the service that was herewith rendered to the German Empire' (Landes 1963, 206, also FN 206, tr. by K.S.).

Despite all his efforts however, as a Jew, Bleichröder encountered great hostility throughout his life, particularly because of his close relationship to Bismarck. He was viewed as a 'not really socially acceptable parvenu' who was not recognised as an equal even by those who gladly made use of his services (Liedtke 2006, 238, tr. by K.S.). This was demonstrated, for instance, by the anti-Semitic hostility of the court chaplain Stöcker in 1880 about which Bleichröder protested – without success (Stern 1988, 47). He nonetheless remained loyal to Judaism and was an assiduous visitor to the Berlin synagogue. He also worked to support Jews in various contexts, especially in Eastern Europe, e.g. in Rumania.[38] However, unlike many other Jews, including his brother Julius, the increasing tolerance of anti-Semitism by the German government did not lead him to turn to the left-wing liberals; he remained in the conservative camp: 'Bleichröder was a conservative, an interventionist and an anti-socialist' (Heilbrunn 1981, 296, tr. by K.S.).

Bleichröder gathered valuable experience on the Balkans. His activities in support of the Jewish population in Rumania were closely linked to the large railway-building project in the country, in which Bleichröder had joined the Disconto-Gesellschaft in 1873 in response to a request from Bismarck. The concessionaire Baruch Heinrich Strousberg had been unable to complete the project and had become hopelessly entangled in diplomatic problems between the German and Rumanian governments. The tough negotiations went on for years, causing the financiers a great deal of trouble and only negligible profits (Schulin 1976, 119; Stern 1988, 509–513, 540–544). At least, Bleichröder was simultaneously able to achieve several of the aims agreed in 1878 in Berlin concerning the equal legal rights of Jews in Rumania.

Bleichröder's Rumanian activities were not the start of involvement in the railways on the Balkans, although the banker was clearly interested in the Ottoman Empire (Clay 2000, 496, 505, 556f.). In 1882, he considered entering into the financing of the Orient railways on the Balkans when the concessionaire Maurice de Hirsch was having difficulties. However, Bismarck was concerned that he might be accused of sponsoring 'his' Jew in Constantinople and requested Bleichröder not to pursue the matter (Grunwald 1966, 47). In 1890, Hirsch then sold his shares to Deutsche Bank, which saw the Orient railway as an important step towards the project of a Bagdad railway (ibid.).

During these deliberations, in March 1889, Gibbs had already asked Bleichröder if he was interested in selling the Greek bonds of 1888 in Berlin for him, as he was issuing the second tranche of the 1888 loan (£277,200 of a total of £950,000).[39] Bleichröder had just gone through a difficult time in his relationship with Bismarck: in 1888, the chancellor had initiated a 'financial war' against Russia and prohibited Lombard credits on Russian bonds in Germany. Bleichröder, who was active in the Russian market, disapproved of this decision as he believed it only profited France and thus paved the way for the Russian-French alliance feared by the chancellor (Heilbrunn 1981, 311). At the beginning of 1889, Bismarck then moderated his anti-Russian position, so Bleichröder could again participate in Russian bond issues. Nonetheless, his plans to convert the old Russian debts led to his first serious conflict with the new Emperor Wilhelm II.

This was the situation when Gibbs approached von Bleichröder about Greece. As was normal in banking at the end of the 1880s, Gibbs was looking for partners with whom he could create a consortium for the Greek loan. Bleichröder refused because the business did not seem important enough to him, but he simultaneously dangled the possibility of his participation in a bigger loan.[40] In May, when Hambro and Gibbs issued the first tranche of the 4% loan of 1889 (30 million francs) and Gibbs was already preparing the emission of the second part, Bleichröder was therefore invited and participated in the emission with no further discussion.[41] Still in May, the prospect for the 4% loan of 1889 was authorised at the Berlin Stock Exchange (Börsen-Enquête-Kommission 1893, 26f.). Bleichröder also participated in a syndicate with capital of £1 million to stabilise the Greek bonds, together with Gibbs, the Bank of Constantinople with its branch in Athens and the ETE.[42] In June, Gibbs proposed that the still owing part of the loan should also be issued in Berlin, an offer which Bleichröder accepted as it promised high profits.[43] When Bleichröder expressed doubts in July because of the poor performance of the bonds already issued (which had sunk since May from 77½ to 74⅗), Gibbs reassured him: the reason for their poor performance was the Cretan crisis and the weak situation of the international money market in general, caused by the danger of war, bad relations between the German and the Russian Empires, the problems of French domestic policy and the fiasco of the conversion of Egyptian bonds.[44] Gibbs recommended not intervening to counter this depression, because in the long run, the political situation in the Orient would develop to the advantage of Greece in any case, even if events caused the bonds to drop in the short term.[45] He was clearly able to convince Bleichröder. The emission of the second instalment of the loan in London started in October.[46] Again, Bleichröder participated in the syndicate to stabilise prices in November with capital of £643,720.[47] However, he did not sell this second tranche (£1,200,000) in Berlin, but left this business to be carried out by the banking house of Markus & Volkmar in August 1890 (Börsen-Enquête-Kommission 1893, 28f.).

Bleichröder realised about 23 million francs with his part of the loan, a profit of 687,500 francs (550,000 marks), i.e. about 3%; the colleagues who sub-participated profited with $1^7/_8$%.[48] This result explicitly outperformed Bleichröder's expectations. Nonetheless, the profit was far from overwhelming when compared to his other activities: with certain German bonds, Bleichröder made profits of between 4% and 10%.[49] His Russian loans, e.g. the emission of the obligations of the Russian railways in 1889 with 175 million roubles in gold (700 million francs), of which Bleichröder took on $26\frac{11}{12}\%$ (about 188 million francs),[50] brought him profits of between 3% and 8% (Stern 1988, 619f.).[51] Comparison of the sums issued in Russia and Greece clearly shows that the southern European country – hardly surprisingly – was small business. Nonetheless, the invested sum was not insignificant even for a banker like Bleichröder, a major figure in the emission of foreign loans: Bleichröder's private fortune is estimated to have valued about 125 million francs at the end of his life (Schnee 1955).

At the end of 1889, Bleichröder held 15 million francs (£600,000) of the Greek loan of 1889 himself. These bonds had to be sold, but this was not a very difficult task. The Berlin Stock Exchange traders and the German public were very interested. This was caused partly by a big media event in Athens. On 27 October 1889, the Greek heir to the throne Constantine married Sophie of Prussia, the sister of new German Emperor Wilhelm II, despite Wilhelm's declared dislike of Greece, attracting a great deal of attention.[52] Bleichröder and Gibbs had rightly expected the Berlin Stock Exchange to react positively to this wedding.[53] Because the public did not really understand the political background of the marriage,[54] many investors interpreted it as a kind of guarantee by the house of Hohenzollern for the Greek royal dynasty, as would have been the case with a bourgeois marriage where the future in-laws would certainly have ensured that the suitor had economically sound prospects.[55] However, Wilhelm II and Otto von Bismarck were actually more interested in intervening in domestic Greek power struggles. They aimed to direct the party of Prince Constantine, who had been educated in Berlin and was seen as an admirer of Wilhelm, the so-called Small Court, onto a peaceful course towards the Ottoman Empire. This policy was motivated by the ever closer links between the German and the Ottoman economies (Loulos 2010, 141f.).[56] Wilhelm even travelled to Athens to attend his sister's marriage,[57] and subsequently used the opportunity for extended travel through the Ottoman Empire.[58]

Against this background, the Greek loan was popular among German small investors (although the minimum sums of investment were much higher in Germany than in London or Paris) (Finger 2016). Philhellenic motivation might have been significant in some cases: e.g. the investor Prof. Dr. Flach, chief editor of an unnamed newspaper and family father, referred in a letter written in 1894 to having signed bonds of the Greek loan for 2,500 francs, due to his attachment to the Greek nation, 'the language and destiny of which have shaped my life's studies'.[59]

Due to change in currency exchange rates, Bleichröder's profits from the Greek loan increased in early 1890 to 875,000 francs (700,000 marks), 3.8%.[60] One reason for this was that the papers reported positively on the Greek government's new budget which would close with a surplus.[61] From May to October 1890, the bonds sold so well in Berlin that Bleichröder was able to realise most of his stock, and he additionally sold some bonds for Gibbs.[62] This must have relieved the concerns of his clerk Benvenisti, who had obviously been greatly worried about the Greek loan when he commented, 'With God's help we will be freed also from this burden'.[63] It could hardly be made clearer that the bankers had not expected this positive development. In the light of these details, our question becomes even more puzzling: why did Bleichröder agree to get involved in this business, which did not promise extraordinarily high profits and was judged to be high risk? The available sources and the relatively reluctant and limited participation do not suggest that he considered Greece as an 'emerging market' where the risk was worth taking like, e.g. Rumania where he invested great sums (Stern 1988, 490–547). Neither can any direct influence of the house of Rothschild, Bleichröder's close cooperation partner, be proved.[64] Clearly, other factors must have played a role in Bleichröder's decision making. As Fritz Stern describes Bleichröder as a particularly politically oriented man,[65] well-connected in Berlin diplomatic circles, it seems worthwhile to search for further insights in the archives of the German Foreign Office (AA). What did German diplomats think about the chances and risks of investment in Greece? This question touches upon research concerning the relationship between banks and imperialism, a much explored field of economic history (Edelstein 1982; Davis/Huttenback 1986; Hertner 1990; Barth 1995a, 1995b; Schaefer 1995; Wiczlinski 2011).

The position of the German Foreign Office (AA)

Until the mid-1870s, German diplomats in Athens took a fairly negative view of the prospects of Greek infrastructure projects and industrialisation generally. This is well illustrated by the example of the railway, which was awaited in southern Europe with great excitement[66] because it had after all vastly accelerated industrialisation in central Europe (see, e.g. Roth 2005). The German diplomats remained sceptical, however. For instance, in the case of the railway line planned to run from Piraeus to Lamia and the Turkish frontier and thus connect the Greek railway network to the European one,[67] the German ambassador Hirschfeld judged that it was only 'the easily stimulated fantasy of the Greek' that led him to see on 'big international trade routes the wealth of two empires floating into his country'. Neither the hopes of the Greeks nor those of the international traders were fulfilled,[68] and in the mid-1880s, the German position remained reserved.[69] Accordingly, the diplomats did not regret the failure of German banks to commit themselves in Greece. This is hardly surprising given that, e.g. in 1885, when the Greeks mobilised their troops during the Serbo-Bulgarian War, Greece's budget deficit of 66 million francs again exceeded the regular state revenue of 63 million.[70] An additional reason for the German reservations was that Greece was totally unimportant in Bismarck's complicated policy of alliances. The only reason why the German chancellor had supported Greek claims against the Ottoman Empire at the Congress of Berlin in 1878 was their potential to prolong the Oriental question and thus to occupy the rivals Russia, Austria and the Ottoman Empire, distracting them from establishing alliances against the German Empire. In these plans, Greece, like the other Balkan states, was nothing more than a means to an end for Bismarck (Kosev 1982). The notion of Germany having reached saturation point in the Mediterranean, as propagated by Bismarck, was held by all German diplomats. Who wanted to invest money in a country like this? One could calmly continue to leave such business to others.

But this situation changed in the following years, as the German Empire further penetrated the economies of Southeast Europe (Gross 2015). Following its readmission to the European Stock Exchanges in 1878, the Greek state had started to build up its railway network intensively and to invite tenders for various railway projects.[71] By 1888, the railway network included the Volo-Larissa and Volo-Tricala-Kalambaka lines with 225 km and the Peloponnesus line with 365 km. Connections from Patras to Pyrgos and from Nafplio to Calamata were under construction.[72] Railway construction, which had proved to be an extraordinarily profitable business in Eastern Europe in previous decades, seemed to be taking off, no wonder that the investors were euphoric. Orders for the materials and construction were mostly given to firms abroad, because the necessary machinery and know-how were not to be found in Greece, like the necessary capital. The funding was in part organised by limited companies, which acquired the exploitation rights for several years and paid their shareholders dividends in line with profits.[73] In addition, the Greek state emitted loans abroad and paid subsidies for the construction of certain sections of track or engaged sub-contractors to build certain routes. There was an intense competition for the orders between various European consortia and firms.[74] However, this competition did not only concern railway construction. In a period of intensifying imperialism, Greece had also become an increasingly attractive trading partner for French and English firms, a development that the Germans observed closely.[75] British entrepreneurs even demanded that the FO systematically collect and make available information about smaller trading houses, as was usual in Germany and Austria, so that they could better judge the risk of giving long-term credit to their business partners.[76] The fear of competition led German diplomats in the 1880s to start to demand tariff agreements and trading deals with Greece so that German business should not be disadvantaged in the Greek market.

The German diplomats understood that the industrial orders were significantly influenced by the streams of capital to Greece. The successful tenders always came from firms from the countries where bankers had supplied finance for the construction or had issued the shares of the companies involved. The poor political situation of the country and its great dependence on foreign credit seem to have led to this link, which was not typical internationally. German competitors (the firm Krupp in particular had applied for several railway projects[77]) were rarely successful in acquiring big infrastructure projects; it was rather the French and Belgian firms that won the contracts. 'France, Belgium and England outrival us in this respect'.[78] The German diplomats found this unsurprising, because the French, Belgian and British banks had provided the necessary capital. If the Germans wanted to improve the situation for German firms, they would have to stimulate German investment in Greece:

> The success of this industry could be much greater if it were, like the Belgians, supported by national capital and the national entrepreneurial spirit. As far as this report can interest German investors, engineers and circles of entrepreneurs in these lucrative construction works more than has so far been the case, I would recommend forwarding it to the press.[79]

German trade representatives active in Greece agreed with this assessment: the reason for the lack of orders won by German companies was 'to be found in the lack of participation of German capital in large local ventures, because naturally the export industry of a country directly profits from the involvement of its capital in foreign ventures'.[80] The tone of the reports that regularly reached the German chancellor Otto von Bismarck was clear: to acquire further orders for German industry in Greece, the German bankers would ultimately have to show their commitment to the country.[81] The emerging Greek economy should persuade German investors of the opportunities for success.[82] The diplomats viewed the risks as being manageable or at least tolerable, although they did not completely ignore them:

> Not least, Greek bonds are as secure as and maybe even more secure than many other bonds traded at the Berlin Stock Exchange. One has to admit that this could change some day, but it may not. And businesses with high gains and no risks probably do not exist at all today anywhere.[83]

The diplomats now clearly regretted the reservations of German bankers towards Greece.[84] Their first cautious attempts were, however, not encouraging. In summer 1888, the Frankfurt-based bank Erlanger & Sons introduced bonds of £600,000 of the Greek 4% monopoly loan of 1887 in Frankfurt,[85] which were issued by the London branch of the bank, but the newspapers reacted with discrediting articles[86] arguing that the 'morality and conscientiousness of Greek borrowers' was probably even worse than that of the Turks, and the Greek state finances were wholly distressed. 'The fact that a Greek loan can be traded at the German stock exchanges is a very bad sign of the times!'[87]

Under these circumstances, it was hardly surprising that the bankers continued to have reservations. Every single order that came from Greece for a German firm despite the bankers' aloofness was celebrated by the diplomats as a leap of faith in German quality, e.g. in the case of Harkort from Duisburg who beat a Belgian competitor despite higher prices.[88] In fact, there were a number of individual orders for German companies despite the reluctance of German banks to follow industry to Greece. The chances for such material orders were especially high when Greek enterprises won the construction orders, because they were willing to shop in Germany. One example was the railway line between Pyrgos and Catacolo, where Krauss-Munich provided the necessary machinery and the Bochumer Verein the trucks. This was also the case for the Peloponnesus railway, where in addition the Gutehoffnungshütte produced the bridges. The railway construction between Patras and Pyrgos was executed by the Greek engineer team Vlangalis and Matsas who contracted orders of six million marks to Germany. The Attic railways, also constructed by a Greek company, imported tracks from Ruhrort and wagons from Esslingen.[89] The large orders received by the Krupp company for armaments were mentioned earlier. But these isolated contracts did not suffice in the eyes of the German diplomats, who saw greater opportunities. Attempts were made to draw the 'attention of German capitalists' towards all the possible projects for which the Germans could supply building materials, e.g. the development of water supplies for Athens and Piraeus in 1890.[90]

The diplomats were concerned with the trading advantages that financial involvement in Greece could provide for German business. Further negotiations concerning the construction of the abovementioned railway line between Athens, Larissa and the Ottoman frontier were thus of great interest for the industrialists. After several failed attempts[91] in 1888/1889, three different bids were on hand: two English consortia (Seligmann-Lafayette and Watson-Pierson) and one international group consisting of Comptoir d'Escompte, Länderbank Wien and Deutsche Bank had submitted proposals.[92] Deutsche Bank, which was otherwise not particularly interested in the Greek market, saw the construction of the Greek railways as a natural continuation of its commitment in the Ottoman Empire (where in the same year of 1888, it had been able to outrival Bleichröder in a tender for the concession of the Anatolia Railway) (Wiczlinski 2011, 260). But the situation was not easy for the German group. Thanks to the range of bids, the Greek government was able to tighten its conditions. Not only was the guarantee of interest reduced from 6% to 5%, but an obligation was also added whereby the winning firm was to be independently responsible for obtaining the Ottoman concession to connect the Greek line with the Ottoman one. If this connection was not completed, a high convention penalty would have to be paid to Greece by the consortium. The Germans counted on their good relationship with the Sublime Porte and Tricoupis seemed to be quite in favour of their tender, as he explained to the German ambassador.[93]

But the Deutsche Bank was not willing to accept further tightening of the conditions. In February 1889, the consortium refused the terms, which now seemed unprofitable, and withdrew its offer.[94] In March 1889, Comptoir d'Escompte collapsed, causing a total breakdown of the group in which Deutsche Bank participated. However, in the following months, the Greek government changed its mind and decided not to contract a concession with a guarantee of interest, but to lead the railway construction itself, giving orders to sub-contractors who could be paid, thanks to a new international loan. Deutsche Bank therefore picked up the project again and instructed its representative Alfred von Kaulla to negotiate in Constantinople.[95] German diplomats were anxious to foster these attempts, also in personal talks with Trikoupis.[96] The competitors, e.g. from Belgium, were denounced. It was quite deplorable, reported the Germans, that 'the Belgians are still not as discredited and in disfavour as would be advantageous for our interests'.[97] The diplomats repeatedly emphasised that only firms from countries that provided the necessary capital had any chance of winning the sought-after orders.

Was it this pressure from German diplomacy that led to Bleichröder's willingness to issue the loan for Greece? Did Bismarck pass on these wishes to him with the request that the ideas should be translated into action? In this case, the hopes of the German diplomats were not fulfilled. The order for the railway line to the Ottoman frontier, on which so many hopes were focused, was given in June 1889 to the English firm Godfrey, Eckerley and Liddeton (Παπαγιαννάκης [Papayiannakis] 1982, 129),[98] with financial support from the bank Seligmann-Brothers.[99] Due to its strong negotiating position, the Greek government could not be forced to negotiate a so-called tied loan, which would have bound it both to an investor and a constructor. Rather, it had finally invited tenders for the construction by offering a mileage allowance with the quite low price of 140,000 francs per km. The English company had accepted this and therefore emerged as the winner of this 'industrial competition'.[100] Against the background of growing national tensions, German diplomats interpreted this unprofitable English commitment as a long-term strategy: obviously, the English wanted to prepare for more lucrative projects later on, 'when the country will be covered with English industrial developments of all kinds and when the English engineers will have got to know the country better'.[101] The diplomats very much regretted that the Germans had not even submitted an offer in the last round (the price seems not to have been acceptable for the group associated with Deutsche Bank).

> For its own sake, the absence of German industry in this competition is to be much regretted. For a long period to come the German iron and mechanical industry will painfully experience English domination on the Greek market, a position which it had good opportunities to acquire itself. Under the given circumstances the

> best scenario will be that the funding of the project could produce profits for German banks, because it probably will be facilitated through a loan with participation of the Bleichröder bank.[102]

As has been previously demonstrated, even these profits were quite limited. Bleichröder so thoroughly failed to fulfil the hopes of the diplomats that it seems doubtful that he even attempted to do so. Firstly, he emitted the loan in cooperation with two English banks and in no way attempted a national solo act as the diplomats, concerned with nationalistic criteria, suggested. Secondly, he did not ensure that the use of the money was restricted to infrastructure projects. It was rather determined for the conversion of previous loans. One could at least have hoped that the loan would open doors for further German investment. But this hope also remained unfulfilled. Only the Nationalbank für Deutschland participated in 1890 in a Greek loan at 5% for the railway line between Piraeus and Larissa in cooperation with Hambro & Son, who, given the disastrous Greek financial situation, were willing to again issue a loan.[103] Further loans with German participation did not take place and German investment in Greece remained sporadic.[104]

The loan as a political instrument

Why though was Otto von Bismarck's confidant and house banker willing to issue the loan? Because Bleichröder and Bismarck conversed frequently face to face, sometimes even daily, their conversations are difficult to reconstruct – with Fritz Stern, we have to bewail the catastrophic consequences of oral communication for the historian. However, sources prove that Bleichröder later (after Bismarck's dismissal from office) did actually have links to Greece. Thus in 1892, the Greek banker Georgios Coronio, resident in Paris, reported to Trikoupis that Bleichröder would try to persuade his government to 'send a competent man as legate to Athens'.[105] Furthermore, Greek diplomats in London also received information on the plans and ideas of the German government from Bleichröder.[106] But what was the situation in 1889? An instructive source that helps address this question emerged from the wedding of Princess Sophie in Athens, to which the state secretary of the AA, Herbert von Bismarck, son of the chancellor, accompanied his Emperor.[107] In conversation with the German diplomat, the British delegate Sir Edmund Monson articulated his growing fears caused by the war propaganda of Greek prime minister Tricoupis towards the Ottoman Empire. This was triggered by the annexing of East Rumelia by Bulgaria in 1885, which contravened the Congress of Berlin but had nonetheless been accepted by the Great Powers (Geiss 1978, 102; Biondich 2011, 64f.). Greece had protested vehemently against this breach of contract by its competitor for the Ottoman legacy and had begun a massive military build-up; it had only been brought to reason by a demonstration of naval might by the Great Powers at Piraeus and Phaliron (Basch 1995, 237). The tension and threats nonetheless continued unabated. Monson hoped that a warning from Bismarck to the insubordinate Greek prime minister might prove more fruitful than his own words. After all, in 1881, before the international conference called to draw up borders with Turkey, Otto von Bismarck had managed to successfully pressure Greece to repay the house of Wittelbach for the remaining Bavarian loans that Ludwig I had granted his son Otto in the 1830s.[108] Trikoupis thus knew from his own experience that Bismarck was a negotiator who was well-versed in all the tricks of the trade. The young Bismarck left Monson in no doubt that the German Empire, in common with all the other Great Powers, would no longer patronise Greece if she entered into new conflicts. While it would worry him very much to leave sweet Princess Sophie in a country which so endangered itself, the marriage in no way caused any political liabilities: 'Germany would never move her little finger to save Greece from the expenses of her own folly'.[109] In a later discussion between Bismarck junior and Tricoupis, arranged by Monson, the German politician ruthlessly explained to the Greek prime minister that his aggressive policy not only strained the sympathies of the Great Powers, but also could be the 'cause of heavy financial prejudice to Greece'.[110] This formulation could, of course, address the high costs of an eventual war, and Monson perhaps understood it this way. But the passage can also be understood as a threat of a quite different sort: that Otto von Bismarck's banker Bleichröder could allow the Greek loan project to fail and severely damage Greek finances. The following events confirmed this interpretation. The situation between Greece and the Ottoman Empire did not escalate, and the Greek loan was issued a few months later. Bleichröder executed the emission – despite the pressure of German diplomacy, no other German banker could have been persuaded to undertake the project.[111]

Conclusion

Greek finances between 1879 and 1893 were characterised by new borrowing. But why were European bankers willing to issue bonds for Greece that exceeded the country's economic performance? The participation of Gerson von Bleichröder in the 4% loan of 1889 has served as an example. Von Bleichröder was extremely well-informed about the situation in Greece through his relationships to international banking circles, diplomats and the chancellor Bismarck. He did not expect to make much profit from the transaction and he judged the risks to be high. Why did he join the undertaking? It has been demonstrated that in this case political factors determined the interpretation of the decision-making situation. There is no evidence to support the notion that von Bleichröder was catering to the wishes of the German diplomats in Athens, who wanted to see more German capital in Greece at a time of increasing imperial competition. Similarly, the banker von Bleichröder was clearly unlikely to dance to the tune of German industry. However, it has been shown that the loans fulfilled a different function for the German chancellor and foreign minister Otto von Bismarck, von Bleichröder's business partner and patron: they served to put political pressure on Greece to adhere to a peaceful course of action which suited Germany. Bleichröder issued the loan primarily to please Bismarck, as a kind of political 'housekeeping'. In terms of the principal-agent theory, the costs and risks of the Greece loan for von Bleichröder can thus be understood as the so-called signalling costs that served to promote the agent to his principal (Ripperger 2005, 65) and were intended to make Bismarck aware of Bleichröder's importance and indispensability. To this end, Bleichröder was willing to take the financial risks and even to accept possibly damaging his reputation as an issuing house. However, he minimised the risks by acting in an international consortium and chose to issue the bonds at a favourable moment, taking advantage of the enthusiasm for Greece that flourished after the wedding of Princess Sophie.

Clearly, this finding cannot be simply generalised to apply to the risk perception and decision making linked with other loans issued between 1879 and 1893. It may well be that quite different motivations played a decisive role with other Greek loans. The Bleichröder loan nonetheless provides an avenue through which to explore the greatly changing world of international banking in the 1880s and 1890s, and allows banking practices to be revealed. It clearly demonstrates the importance of the political and diplomatic background to the financial activities of European banks in Greece. The following chapters explore whether the images of Greece held by the investors generally became less significant over time, as in the case of Bleichröder.

Notes

1 This chapter has been published in two forms: Schönhärl (2013a) and Schönhärl (2018). Some passages also draw on Psalidopoulos/Schönhärl (2013).
2 The figures differ slightly in Αγριαντώνη [Agriantoni] (2010).
3 On the great problems of distributing the national estates, see Mariadis (1966); MacGrew (1985; Karouzou [Καρούζου] (2018).
4 For more details, **256, 332**. in this book.
5 On the development of Greek banking, see Kostis (1988); Κωστής [Kostis]/Τσοκόπουλος [Tsokopulos] (1988).
6 How serious the situation was perceived to be is demonstrated by a telegram from the governor of the ETE Renieri to the Rothschild brothers in Paris from 4.2.1878, in which he asked them to obtain the protection of French troops for the ETE, see AAE, P 10592.
7 The government compensated the bondholders with new papers which were issued to the amount of £1.2 million; see Wynne (1951, 295); Ανδρεάδης [Andreadis] (1904, 72). **47f.** in this book.

8 The relevant correspondence between Gennadios and Trikoupis is in Τρίχα [Tricha] (1991, 21, 35, 94–96, 258, 306).
9 The final settlement of the 60-million-franc loan dragged on into the twentieth century: the Russian demands ceased with the October Revolution of 1917; in 1965, Greece reached a settlement with France agreeing a repayment of 169,195 francs which was then paid in the following year. It seems that no agreement was reached with Great Britain at this time and it is unclear whether and when such an agreement was found; see Ηλιαδάκης [Iliadakis] (2011, 37).
10 Although research has not termed the years 1873–1898 as a 'great depression' for quite some time, see Mathias (1969, 361). Mathias emphasises the continued increase in British national income and real wages at this time; see 364.
11 The documents of the CEP on the Greek loans have not survived. For more details on the relations of the bank to Greece, **220f**. in this book. On the intervention of the French government, see Cameron (1961, 509).
12 For details on the Greek national debt with the exact conditions of each internal and foreign loan, see Παντελάκης [Pantelakis] (1995).
13 In 1887, the Bethmann brothers received a dividend of 8% for an investment of £10,000 as part of a loan to the Greek government of over £200,000 with an option for a further £400,000; see Schaefer (1995, 322, FN 346).
14 On his biography, see Τρίχα [Tricha] (2009); Τρίχα [Tricha] (2016).
15 Vlasto (1885, 272), tr. by K.S. Vlasto also emphasised the importance of Trikoupis' father, who had made his name fighting for independence. Tricoupis the younger would be very popular with the younger generation, and the expatriate Greeks were said to trust him completely.
16 On the following, see Tricoupis (1887).
17 A survey map of the building projects of the coming decades is found in Παπαγιαννάκης [Papayiannakis] (1982, 160). Also see Jüttner (1882); Hertner (2008); Roth (2008b).
18 For more details, see Psalidopoulos/Schönhärl (2013).
19 Between 1866 and 1870, military expenditure accounted for about 27.7% of the budget, later, between 1883 and 1895, even 48.6%, while education accounted for about 3% (see Τσουκαλάς [Tsoukalas] 1981, 63). By way of comparison, in 1872, the defence budget in France accounted 38.7%, and in 1913 31% of the total budget (Jauffret 1992, 16).
20 See, e.g. Moral, Felix (civil engineer, formerly German trading association in Berlin, technical office in Athens): Geschäftsbericht für das Geschäftsjahr (1889/1890) und Mittheilungen von allgemeinem Interesse über die industriellen Verhältnisse Griechenlands, BAR R 901 1536. The department was founded in 1889; since 1882, there had been a German trading association in Berlin that was intended to create new markets for German industry in Greece and Turkey (see ibid., introduction). It maintained branches in all the important trading centres in Greece but its activities were judged by the German legation not to be particularly clever.
21 For example, the chief mechanic A. Gotteland; see Stefanos Dragoumis archive in the GE, envelope 53.3.
22 An example is the British special envoy Sir Edward Fitzgerald Law; **297, 301** in this book.
23 See the list of his interlocutors in Athens in November 1888 in the Krupp archive WA 4/1031. The reports of the agent Otto Dingler, who was responsible for deliveries to the Ottoman Empire and Greece, are found in WA 4/1484.
24 Thus, e.g. Monsieur Guicciardi travelled to Greece from May to August 1891, commissioned by the CL; see CL 62 AH 77.

25 Georgios Dertilis also emphasises the function of private Greek brokers who, due to the shortage of suitable personnel in the civil service, were sometimes entrusted with the brokering and organisation of the foreign loans, earning well from these activities. Δερτιλής [Dertilis] (2009, 583–612); Zelepos (2015, 71).
26 The term is taken from Bonin (2013).
27 This is suggested in ibid., 359.
28 On the concept, see Durlauf (2008, 318ff.); Jedwab et al. (2015).
29 In October 1888, Bleichröder, together with the Nationalbank für Deutschland, introduced parts of the loans of 1881 (110,635,000 francs, issue rate 82.0) and of 1884 (96,100,000 francs, issue rate 82.0) in Germany. In January 1889, part of the gold monopoly loan of 1887 (135,000,000 francs, issue rate 77.25) followed; see Börsen-Enquête-Kommission (1893, 24ff.). Also see Schaefer (1995, 322). However, Schaefer is wrong in one point: the bonds offered in May 1889 by Bleichröder and the Nationalbank für Deutschland at the Berlin Stock Exchange were not part of the conversion loan of 1887, but part of the 4% gold loan which is the main focus in this chapter.
30 Griechenland, no date, DB S3829.
31 By way of comparison: in 1889, the German portfolio investments abroad amounted to about 500 million marks; see ibid., 98.
32 Loan Agreement and Prospect, NBB Loan Agreements 64.
33 Loan Agreement and Prospect, NBB Loan Agreements 64.
34 For more details, **340–344** in this book.
35 See **209 n.29** in this book.
36 Not only did Bismarck view von Arnim-Suckow as a dangerous competitor, Arnim-Suckow had also supported a financial group that was in competition with Bleichröder; see Heilbrunn (1981, 299).
37 However, Schnee speaks of 100 million Marks; see Schnee (1955).
38 At the Congress of Berlin, Bleichröder played a significant role in the decision to give Jews equal legal rights in the young Rumanian state; see Iancu (1987). Also see Landes (1963, 199f.).
39 Gibbs to Bleichröder, 14.3.1889, MA MS 11.113-2-164, 471.
40 Gibbs to Bleichröder, 18.3.1889, MA MS 11.113-2-164, 479.
41 Gibbs to Bleichröder, 20.5.1889, MA MS 11.113-2-164, 503; 21.5.1889, 508; 22.5.1889, 514; 22.5.1889, 516. In London, the bonds were issued on 24 May; see Gibbs to Bleichröder, 24.5.1889, 533.
42 Gibbs to ETE, 5.6.1889, MA MS 11.113-2-164, 680. On the various types and functioning of syndicates in banking, see Tchernoff (1930).
43 Gibbs to Bleichröder, 29.6.1889, MA MS 11.113-2-165, 65. Gibbs believed the price might almost double.
44 Gibbs to Bleichröder, 27.7.1889, MA MS 11.113-2-165, 237.
45 Gibbs to Bleichröder, 2.8.1889, MA MS 11.113-2-165, 271–273.
46 Gibbs to Trikoupis, 25.9.1889, MA MS 11.113-2-165, 485.
47 Gibbs to Bleichröder, 12.11.1889, MA MS 11.113-2-165, 710.
48 Benvenisti from Berlin to Bleichröder, 30.12.1889, NBB VIII Imelmann.
49 In the German Empire, Bleichröder had also invested large sums in railway construction, the Laura foundry, the textile and petrol industry, and deep-sea fishing, to mention but a few examples. See the index to Bleichröder's estate in BAR.
50 Ibid., 241.
51 In the 1880s, the bank was also involved in Mexico and Rumania, in the Ottoman Empire, in Italy, Hungary and Egypt (see the index to Bleichröder's estate in BAR).
52 According to his mother Victoria, see Holland/Markides (2006, 93).

53 'It is said that the emperor and empress of Germany will travel to Athens to attend the wedding of their daughter with the Duke of Sparta: hopefully this journey will occur and its effect will be favourable'. Gibbs to Bleichröder, 18.6.1889, MA MS 11.113-2-164, 744, tr. by K.S.

54 The *Allgemeine Zeitung* (1.11.1889, quoting from the Italian *Riforma*) interpreted the marriage as the rapprochement of Greece with the Triple Alliance, suitable for strengthening stability in the Mediterranean area. The *Kreuzzeitung* (8.10.1889), however, suggested that although Greece had such intentions, the virulence of the Crete question counteracted them: Greece's wish to be united with Crete was in opposition to the position of the Ottoman Empire, and the German wish to improve relations between the Ottoman Empire and the Triple Alliance meant that there was no chance of a rapprochement between Germany and Greece. The presence of Wilhelm II at the wedding in Athens was said to be merely motivated by familial reasons. However, the alliance with a member of the Danish house of Sonderburg-Glücksburg, which had important dynastic connections throughout Europe, was approved of in dynastic terms. Schönpflug (2013, 96) interprets the marriage as strengthening the link between the Hohenzollerns and the British and Dutch royal families.

55 The influence of the financial press on investment behaviour is investigated by Radu (2017).

56 On the German-Greek relationship, also see Loulos (1986); Hildebrand (1996, 99); Τσακίρης [Tsakiris] (2000). Νικολοπούλου [Nikolopoulou] (2010), talks of the 'unmistakeable complexity of the construction' of Bismarck's system of alliances at this time, tr. by K.S.

57 When Sophie later converted to Orthodox Christianity, Wilhelm broke off all contact with her and for three years refused permission for her to travel to Germany; see Röhl (1987, 106f.).

58 This first journey to the Orient is only briefly mentioned in Richter 1997, who examines in detail the second.

59 Flach to Trikoupis, 17.4.1894, ELIA Estate Trikoupis, 16/106/d, tr. by K.S. After the bankruptcy of Greece, Flach asked Trikoupis for advice about how to avoid larger losses. This intention should be borne in mind when interpreting the source. No reply from the prime minister has survived. Numerous similar letters are found in ELIA Estate Trikoupis 22/1-14.

60 Benvenisti to Bleichröder, 1.1.1890, NBB VIII Imelmann.

61 Benvenisti to Bleichröder, 30.12.1889, NBB VIII Imelmann.

62 Gibbs to Bleichröder, 27.5.1890, MA MS 11.113-2-166, 82; 1.8.1890, 121.

63 Benvenisti to Bleichröder, 1.1.1890, NBB VIII Imelmann, tr. by K.S.

64 Bleichröder became established in Berlin largely thanks to his close relationship to Rothschilds. Since the 1850s, Rothschilds had competed with the Péreire brothers, whose business partners Hottinguer, Eichthal and Oppenheim were also active in Greece, so that it could be supposed that Bleichröder, commissioned by Rothschilds, was avoiding simply leaving the Greek market to the competition. There is, however, no such explanation indicated in his letters from 1889 held in the RAL in London (RAL XI/63/17), and equally no indication in the letters of the French Rothschilds in the ANMT (132 AQ 2 P 0582 and 0583). Research is hampered here by Bleichröder's somewhat illegible handwriting.

65 This may also be due to Stern having had no access to the sources in the London Rothschild-Archive, which are now available for research. Specific information on Greece is, however, very scarce.

66 On the building of the railways in Southeast Europe, see Rechberger (1960); Rechberger (1961); Jensen/Rosegger (1968); Plaschka et al (1993); Divall (2003).

67 For more details on the construction of this line, see Παπαγιαννάκης [Papayiannakis] (1982, 126–133). Also see Gournaris (1989).
68 Report 'Das Projekt einer Eisenbahn von Piräus über Lamia an die türkische Grenze', Athen 21.11.1875, as an attachment to a letter from the German legation to the AA from 21.11.1875, BAR R901-15278, tr. by K.S.
69 Thus, the German general consul Oberg wrote from Piraeus to the AA on 3.1.1884: 'I am not in a position to judge whether German participation in this undertaking is to be recommended…'. BAR R 901-15278, tr. by K.S. At this time, the Erlanger banking house in Frankfurt was particularly interested in the Piraeus-Larissa railway but did not request the services of the German embassy in Athens for the negotiations (German legation in Athens to AA, 10.11.1884, ibid.).
70 Most of this money was spent on armaments, as expected, also with the Krupp company, which received armament contracts worth 1,090,840 Reichsmarks from Greece in 1885; see KA, WA 4/1031.
71 For more details, see Psalidopoulos/Schönhärl (2013).
72 Georgii/Harr: Griechenlands Finanzen im Jahr 1888 und seine handelspolitischen Beziehungen zu Deutschland. Handwritten print, 11, BAR R 901-1539.
73 An overview of the routes, the share prices and the dividends paid is found in ibid. 14f. The delivery contracts won by German firms are also noted here, as are the countries from which the capital came.
74 The link between export of capital and the contracts won by the domestic economy is also emphasised by Feis (1974).
75 For France, see, e.g. Chambre française de commerce d'Athènes-Pirée, to the MAE, Paris, 3.5.1890, F12/6540. For Great Britain, see Greece, Piraeus, Report by Consul Merlin on the Trade and Commerce of Continental Greece for the Year 1879, in Diplomatic and consular reports from various countries, 1862–1914, 733–743, ETE AIIA19Book35–43.
76 Report of Consul Merlin on the Trade and Commerce of Continental Greece for the Year 1885, in: Parliamentary Papers, C. 4915.
77 The Krupp company was also involved in the memorandum by Georgii and Harr quoted **211 n.82** in this book as emphasised in the letter from the legation in Athens to AA from 27.12.1888. The letter aimed to increase the export of capital to Greece in order to better the opportunities for German exports. The main business of the Krupp company in Greece was arms export, which blossomed in the 1880s.
78 German legation in Athens to AA, 27.12.1888, BAR R 901-1539, tr. by K.S.
79 German legation in Athens to AA, 2.6.1889, BAR R 901-15279, tr. by K.S.
80 Moral, Felix: Geschäftsbericht für das Geschäftsjahr (1889/1890), BAR R 901-1536, no page numbers, tr. by K.S.
81 It is possible that the diplomats, who would have been familiar with the economic theory of their time, were also thinking of the theory of the gold standard and may have been assuming automatism in the foreign trade balance. This suggests that the capital export of a country automatically leads to the increased purchase of goods from this country, which would have then re-equalised the balance of payments; see Wiczlinski (2011, 101).
82 As argued by Georgii/Harr: Griechenlands Finanzen im Jahr 1888 und seine handelspolitischen Beziehungen zu Deutschland. Handwritten print, 14, BAR R 901-1539. The authors emphasise the brilliant opportunities for German industry: 'All the pre-conditions necessary to successfully cultivate a fruitful field of work are fulfilled, if only German capital also wanted to show an interest in Greece. The objective of these lines is to bring this about'. Tr. by K.S. On occasions, the diplomats pressured industrialists to increase their involvement in Greece even if

they were rather sceptical. Thus in 1888, the German legate LeMaitre tried to persuade a representative of the Krupp company, who in return explained the limits of Krupp's interests and doubted that his interlocutor was well-informed about matters concerning railway construction; see Abschriften der Berichte von Geh. Rat Jeneke über den Besuch beim deutschen Gesandten LeMaitre, 29.11.1888, KA WA 4/1031.

83 German legation in Athens to AA, 27.12.1888, BAR R 901-1539, tr. by K.S.

84 However, this caution is typical of bankers in the imperialist era, who seldom allowed themselves to be persuaded to select particular countries for investment based on political considerations concerning national interests. They relied, e.g. on international cooperation to spread risk and the internationally networked financial elite was characterised by 'financial pacifism', which scarcely accorded with political goals. See Wiczlinski (2011, 66). A contrasting example is found in Part II Chapter 6 of this book dealing with the building of the Canal of Corinth.

85 £600,000 from £5,400,000, issue rate 72.30; see Börsen-Enquête-Kommission (1893, 124f.).

86 German legation in Athens to AA, 12.10.1888, BAR R 901-1539; this report drew on the article cited **212 n.87** and Ein Protest, in: *Handelszeitung des Berliner Handelsblatt*, 10.7.1888.

87 Eine griechische Anleihe, in: *Der deutsche Ökonomist*, 14.7.1888, tr. by K.S.

88 German general consul Oberg in Patras to AA, 23.5.1889, BAR R 901-15279.

89 Georgii/Harr: Griechenlands Finanzen im Jahr 1888 und seine handelspolitischen Beziehungen zu Deutschland. Handwritten print, 14, BAR R 901-1539.

90 German legation in Athens to AA, 19.7.1890, BAR R 901-1536, tr. by K.S.

91 The negotiations intensified in 1875; in 1884, the Frankfurt branch of the Erlanger banking house expressed interest in the business; see German legation in Athens to AA, 10.11.1884, BAR R 901-15278.

92 German legation in Athens to AA, 14.2.1889, BAR R 901-15279. The US Bank J. & W. Seligman & Co. had no recognisable connection to the Seligmann/von Eichthal family. It was founded in 1846 by Joseph Seligman, son of a Jewish haberdasher from Baiersdorf near Nürnberg, in New York; see Birmingham (1967).

93 German legate Le Maistre to the AA, 14.2.1889, BAR R 901-15279.

94 German legation in Athens to AA, 14.2.1889, BAR R 3101-7401.

95 German legation in Athens to AA, 27.5.1889, BAR R 901-15279. Alfred von Kaulla was the director of the Württembergischen Vereinsbank and led the negotiations with Constantinople for the DB; see Wiczlinski (2011, 260). The corresponding documentation from 1900 is found in DB S 1283.

96 German legation in Athens to AA, 27.5.1889, BAR R 3101-7401. But Trikoupis was suddenly less interested in connecting up with the European network, emphasising how tired of negotiations with Turkey they were and stating an intention to concentrate initially on the Greek part.

97 German legation in Athens to AA, 27.5.1889, BAR R 3101-7401, tr. by K.S. There is uncertainty about the reading of the word 'interests' (in German: 'Interessen').

98 However, the company was unable to complete the building work due to technical problems and other difficulties. In 1893, the Greek government therefore requested a German adjudicator to mediate between the government and the company; see *Frankfurter Zeitung*, 13.7.1893, BAR R 901 15280. In 1898, the contract for the railway was to be granted again, and the DB displayed lively interest in constructing the track as a continuation of the Orient railway. Siemens even travelled to Athens; see *Vossische Zeitung*, 24.11.1889, BAR R 901-80106. In the end, the contract was awarded to the Eastern Railway Construction Syndicate and was financed by English and French investors, including Emil Erlanger; see *Frankfurter Zeitung*,

28.3.1900 in BAR R 901-80106. This group completed the railway line in 1908 although it was not possible to connect it to the Turkish network.

99 Seligmann transferred the deposit of £80,000 via Gibbs to the Greek government; see Gibbs to the Greek minister Gennadios, 7.8.1889, MA MS 11.113-2-165, 288.

100 German legation in Athens to AA, 27.6.1889, BAR R 3101-7401.

101 German legate, Tschirschky, to AA, 27.6.1889, BAR R 901 15279, tr. by K.S.

102 German legate, Tschirschky, to AA, 27.6.1889, BAR R 901 15279, tr. by K.S.

103 Nominal sum £3,595,000; issue rate $92^{5}/_{8}$. See Börsen-Enquête-Kommission (1893, 28f.). As the relevant documents on Greece are not preserved in the archive of the Nationalbank für Deutschland, it is not possible to reconstruct the reasons for this involvement. The DB were involved with a sub-participation of £54,000; see Griechenland (Übersichtsliste), DB S3829.

104 Another reason for the lack of investment may have been the anti-Jewish riots on Corfu from April 1891: the legate Ludwig Graf von Wesdehlen cited the riots as the reason why negotiations between the Greek government and Jewish financiers from Berlin were abruptly broken off; see German legation in Athens to AA, Caprivi, 3.6.1891, BAR R 901-1540. It is only possible to speculate whether Bleichröder was also affected.

105 Georgios Coronio continued, explaining that if the French government advised him to do so, then Bleichröder would willingly open up his counter for a Greek loan. Telegram from M. Coronio to Trikoupis, 8.10.1892, ELIA Estate Trikoupis, 16/64/g, tr. by K.S. In 1871, Coronio founded the company Syngros, Koronios & Sia in Constantinople with Andreas Syngros; see Συγγρός [Syngros] (1998, vol. 3, 3ff.).

106 The Greek legate Theotokis to Trikoupis, 18./30.3.1893, in ELIA Estate Trikoupis, 20/3/g.

107 Herbert von Bismarck pursued his father's 'pet Jew' 'with an unrelenting hate' after finding out the role Bleichröder played in preventing his marriage with Princess Elisabeth Carolath; see Heilbrunn (1981, 299, tr. by K. S.).

108 Greece paid the sum of 2.6 million francs to the house of Wittelsbach. The negotiations in Munich were led by Stephan Streit on the part of the Greeks; see Ioannidou-Bitsiadou (1993); the German ambassador von Radowitz also describes them in his memoires: the money was used to finance the wedding between Prince Ludwig Ferdinand and the Infanta Paz of Spain. This enabled Bismarck 'to demonstrate ad oculos to the Bavarian court the practical advantage of the newly emerged power of the German emperor in foreign relations'. Holborn (1967, 157), tr. by K.S. **88 n.109** in this book.

109 British legate in Athens, Monson, to FO, Salisbury, 28.10.1889, NA FO 286–393.

110 British legate in Athens, Monson, to FO, Salisbury, 31.10.1889, NA FO 286–393.

111 This informal influencing of the bankers by politicians would fit very well with the way in which Herbert Feis described the relationship between the two spheres in the German Empire. He contrasts this type of manipulation to the behaviour of the FO, which, at least officially, did little to influence the investment activities of the banks, and with that of the French, who directly attempted to lay down rules for the banks; see Feis (1930, 85f.).

6

PARIS AS THE NEW ATHENS

The Canal of Corinth 1882–1893

Through the Isthmus of Corinth: plans for a canal between the continent and the Peloponnesus

The Congress of Berlin in 1878 signalled not only a new phase in state loans. The following years also saw a flood of private investment entering the country. The trend of the time was for large-scale infrastructure projects. In addition to the construction of the railways mentioned earlier, canal-building experienced a renaissance, even if it was decades since the height of 'canal mania', a term coined in Great Britain. At the end of the eighteenth century, 'a wild enthusiasm for a new and exciting mode of transport that was to carry the world to a Utopia, based on industry and trade' (Burton 1993, 9) had allowed British shareholders to earn astronomical sums with certain canals. For example in the 1770s in Birmingham, the value of canal stocks increased tenfold within only a few months (ibid., 10), and 45 new canals were built in Britain just between 1792 and 1794 (ibid., 12). In a debate in the House of Commons, an MP expressed a hope that his grandchildren would be born with webbed fingers and live off fish, because by then there would be no dry land left on the entire island (ibid., 14.). Investors in the construction of these canals were industrialists interested in important transport routes, but also speculators looking for quick profits. Their hopes were not always fulfilled and the estimated costs of construction were often exceeded (ibid., 17–44, 147).

The successful completion of the Suez Canal by Ferdinand de Lesseps in 1869 (Bonin 2010) then fanned the flames of enthusiasm for large maritime canal projects among international investors. One such example is the Kiel Canal connecting the North Sea and the Baltic, which the German government was keen to build for reasons of military strategy (Morazé/Allen 1976, 360f.). In the case of Greece, one glance back to the times of antiquity was enough to identify a promising canal project: the Isthmus of Corinth where the first attempt to construct a canal dated back to the reign of Emperor Nero (Payne 1959, 45ff.). The project attracted little attention through the Ottoman era but shortly after the founding of the Greek state, President

DOI: 10.4324/9780429286537-9

Kapodistrias commissioned the French engineer Virlet d'Aoust, who had come to Greece as part of the French Morea expedition in 1828–1833,[1] to evaluate the ancient plans for the construction of a canal in Corinth (Glasemann 2010, 3). In 1832, a Greek engineer continued d'Aoust's preliminary work, conducting surveys and producing cost estimates amounting to 12 million francs. As in the case of Lavrion, King Otto then displayed an interest in the Corinth plans: he sent the Bavarian mining commissioner Gustav Fiedler not only to Lavrion, but also to Corinth. Fiedler recommended the building of such a canal, or at least of a railway line across the isthmus (Fiedler 1840, 235–239). 'But it [the building work, K.S.] must never be undertaken by a foreign company if Greece should again become Hellas'.[2] Fiedler expected 'relatively speaking, not very large expenses' without being more concrete.[3] However, just like in Lavrion, no financial funds were found for the implementation of the project in the following decades. And in February 1858, the situation was further complicated by a severe earthquake in the region that completely destroyed the town of Corinth.

At the beginning of the 1860s, when work on the Suez Canal was already fully underway, French and Bavarian engineers developed new plans for Corinth which they presented at the Académie des Sciences de Paris, thus attracting international attention (Werner 1993, 40). Against this background, Ferdinand de Lesseps, promoter of the Suez Canal (and, incidentally, an old school friend of Gustave d'Eichthal, see Queux Saint-Hilaire 1887, 6),[4] applied to the Greek government for a preliminary concession for the building of the Canal of Corinth. The second concessionaire was the Hungarian István (Stephen) Türr, who had supported him in Suez. In the same year, as work began in Lavrion, this preliminary concession was actually granted. However, in contrast to proceedings at the ancient mines, no immediate action was taken in Corinth as the two concessionaires were fully employed in Egypt. It was not until 1869, shortly before the completion of the Suez Canal, that de Lesseps first visited the Isthmus of Corinth. He then apparently came to seriously doubt the importance of the shipping route and lost interest in the project.

The concessionaires were also completely preoccupied by another, much larger project. In 1876, the so-called 'Syndicate Türr' (Société Civile Internationale du Canal Interocéanique de Darien) was established with a capital of 300,000 francs. The aim of the group was to gain a concession for the building of the Panama Canal, which was to open a shipping lane between the two American sub-continents (Diesbach 1998, 296). Türr was the president of the syndicate in which many high-ranking individuals were involved, including his brother-in-law Lucien Napoléon-Bonaparte Wyse and, e.g. the banker Isaac Péreire. Financier of the syndicate was Jacques de Reinach, a Jewish banker from Germany who had co-founded the bank Kohn, De Reinach et Cie in Paris. The bank had achieved much success through trading in military equipment and speculating in French railway stocks (McCullough 1977, 60) and was involved in risky capital investments throughout the world, e.g. in Algeria, the Ottoman Empire, Persia, Eastern Europe, Indochina and South America, especially in the field of railways.[5] The syndicate employed the Hungarian engineer Béla Gerster who later also worked in Corinth.[6] De Lesseps was not officially involved (McCullough 1977, 60). In May 1876, the Société Civile Internationale du Canal Interocéanique de Darien obtained a provisional concession for the Panama Canal, after two extensive and at times discouraging excursions to the region (Mack 1944, 282). The concessionaires were Wyse and Türr, who were to pay the Columbian government 750,000 francs for building permission valid until 1882 (Glasemann 2010, 6). This never actually occurred as Wyse and Türr sold their concession to de Lesseps for 10 million francs (£2 million) in 1879 – the Türr syndicate thus realised a profit of 3,000% (McCullough 1977, 101). Payment for the concession was half in money and half in stocks in the newly founded Panama company (10,000 stocks). De Lesseps also surrendered his share of the 1864 concession for Corinth, which was then held by Türr alone (McCullough 1977, 101; Glasemann 2010, 6).[7]

De Lesseps now prevailed with his plan for the Panama Canal to be built without locks or tunnels, despite the opposition of Belá Gerster (ibid., 67). In 1879, de Lesseps then founded the Compagnie Universelle du Canal Interocéanique de Panama, after a voluble presentation at the annual meeting of the Société de Géographie in Paris. The company began work in Panama in January 1882. Two years later, Jacques de Reinach, who was simultaneously active in Corinth, became the main financier of the company. The three large canal projects Suez, Panama and Corinth were thus closely associated with one another through the individuals involved, both in terms of those initiating the projects and in terms of the financiers and engineers. Contemporaries viewed Corinth as the 'little sister' of the two larger projects (Παπαγιαννοπούλος [Papagiannopoulos] 1989, 164).

Türr now turned his whole attention to Corinth, the project 'of lesser importance, though significant' (Morazé/Allen 1976, 360f.) – he no longer lacked the necessary capital. In 1880, the governor of the ETE, Markos Renieri, a friend of Gustave d'Eichthal,[8] who Türr had known for almost 20 years, thanks to his diplomatic activities, interceded to ensure that the concession would be renewed (Glasemann 2010, 6).[9] In May 1881, Türr then received a 99-year concession to build the canal from the Greek government. Construction work was to begin within 18 months and to be completed by 1887. The engineer Béla Gerster, who Türr brought to Corinth, drafted three alternative routes, and Türr finally selected the ancient Nero route. The necessary land was to be expropriated by the Greek government. Türr now needed to follow the example of the Suez Canal company and the Panama company and set up a joint-stock company to finance the project.

The actors

In order to assess the risk perception of the bankers, this rough outline of the project must be supplemented by consideration of the actors involved. How trustworthy were they and what were their particular links to Greece?

István Türr

The promoter of the project was the Hungarian István Türr (1825–1908). He was born on 10 August 1825 in Baja in Hungary as the son of a hardware dealer.[10] He interrupted his studies in 1842 to join the Austrian Army, where he advanced to the rank of second lieutenant in the infantry regiment 'Erzherzog Franz Karl'. In January 1849, he then deserted, apparently because he wanted to join the troops of the Hungarian national movement in the 1848 revolution (Fornaro 2004, 11)[11] – although another report cites rumours that he deserted to avoid a disciplinary enquiry because of a breach of trust concerning money (Werner 1993, 41f.). After the bloody defeat of the revolution in Hungary, he travelled through Europe on the heels of revolutionary uprisings: Prussia, Baden, Turin, Bern, Paris, London, Constantinople and, especially, Italy where he came into contact with Giuseppe Mazzini and the Hungarian freedom fighter Lajos Kossuth, whose liberal movement he supported (ibid., 13). He spied among the Austrian troops in Italy for Mazzini (ibid., 41). There is no evidence as to whether he also went to Sardinia and met the Serpieris, who invested in the Lavrion mines in Greece 15 years later, but it is certainly not unlikely. In 1853, Türr was involved in a liberal revolt in Milan. His revolutionary attitude and opposition to the Habsburg monarchy in Austria may have been the reason that he was sentenced to death in absentia after his desertion, a punishment that was later commuted to lifelong banishment. Türr volunteered his services in the Crimea War and he also entered into British diplomatic service, undertaking long journeys in the Mediterranean in this context (Fornaro 2004, 16). In 1856 in Constantinople, the British envoy Stratford Canning introduced him to Ferdinand de Lesseps, who was acting as the consul in Cairo and Alexandria (ibid., 17). In 1859, Türr joined Garibaldi in the fight for an independent Italy against the Austrian rulers, became one of his trusted companions and was made a general (ibid., 20, 22). Türr built up a reputation as a champion of the suppressed peoples of Europe, although he was especially concerned with his homeland Hungary (Fornaro 2004, 21). He did not hesitate to combat resistance, even that of the suppressed themselves: in September 1860, acting as a general of Garibaldi, he unrelentingly quelled a revolt by farmers in Irpinia who were opposed to the Risorgimento (Werner 1993, 42).[12] After the founding of the Italian nation state in 1861, Türr was taken into the Italian army. Furthermore, he was entrusted with diplomatic tasks, e.g. he pursued the idea of a confederation of the people of the Danube region

(Confédération danubienne) and of a similar confederation of the Balkans (Confédération des Balkans) with its seat in Constantinople. The confederation 'for the defence and development of progress' was intended to respect the autonomy of each individual country and provide defence.[13] The 'man who is to some extent involved in all the battles of our times'[14] emphasised the right of all nations to independence in numerous newspaper articles in French, Hungarian and German.[15] He argued that the principle of nationality originated from France and had been sealed with French blood (Türr 1878c, 24). At the same time, Türr firmly believed in progress, civilisation and industrialisation, which should dispense with the need for violence in the nineteenth century: 'I am liberal; my whole life has been employed in trying to help the cause of liberalism and of progress to triumph'.[16] His plans for a Balkan confederation embracing the Rumanians, the Slavs and the Greeks (which finally came into being in the run-up to the first Balkan war in 1911) were well-received in Greece. Thus, Markos Renieri, who had been the Greek envoy in Constantinople since 1860 and the vice-governor of the ETE since 1861,[17] corresponded in 1861/1862 with Türr about the plans for a confederation, and King Otto also displayed an interest (Fornaro 2004, 123f., FN 83).[18] Türr repeatedly expressed his admiration of the Greek struggle for independence, praising the Greeks for being the first to shake off the yoke of the Ottomans and calling for Greece to be given all the territory to Thessaloniki (Türr 1878b, 8f.).[19] In the 1880s, he then pursued the idea of pan-European integration as a way for the old world to assert itself against America and China (Türr 1887, 21).

In 1861, Türr married Adeline Wyse-Bonaparte, the 22-year-old daughter of the ex-British envoy in Athens and granddaughter of Lucien Bonaparte, a brother of Napoleon I; although she lacked any fortune, she brought a great deal of family prestige to the marriage.[20] Then in 1863, Türr was dishonourably dismissed from the Italian army – accused of misappropriation of funds (Werner 1993, 42). Fornaro suggests that this was due to the many enemies that Türr had made with his tough approach to disciplinary problems in the military, and that envy motivated the move against him (Fornaro 2004, 40). Türr continued his diplomatic activities for Italy for several more years and worked, apparently simultaneously, on the Suez Canal with Ferdinand de Lesseps, albeit in a subordinate role (Diesbach 1998, 296).[21] In 1864, Türr, together with de Lesseps, applied for and received a preliminary concession for the Canal of Corinth. It seems likely that Renieri may have played a role here. In 1867, Türr returned to Hungary, able to do so after his 20-year banishment came to an end with the installation of the dual monarchy. There, he entered into the Hungarian diplomatic service (Werner 1993, 37f.).[22] He tackled infrastructure and canal projects and the promotion of trade in the Danube region (Fornaro 2004, 114f.) and propagandised the autonomy of the nations under a liberal Danube monarchy (Türr 1868, 15f.). From 1876, Türr dedicated himself to the Panama project and was able to successfully sell his concession to de Lesseps, as described earlier. In 1881, he then possessed the only concession for the building of the Canal of Corinth. In addition to the financial capital that he gained from the Panama business, he also brought with him the prestige of having been de Lesseps' partner in Suez and Panama, the expertise he had gained in canal planning in Hungary, an excellent network in international diplomatic circles and his reputation as a liberal freedom fighter and experienced diplomat married to a great-niece of the illustrious Emperor. Clearly, he was able to mask the stains in his past, especially the fact that he had twice been dishonourably discharged from military service, and appear as a trustworthy business partner with a good reputation. Türr turned to France, the homeland of his wife, to find investors for his Canal of Corinth.

The position of the French government

A key reason for this choice was the positive attitude of the French government towards this 'important work', which had been followed with great interest since the 1850s.[23] In the 1860s, the French foreign office (MAE) firmly believed in the desirability of extending French-Greek trading relations, e.g. by establishing trading houses. The wish to prevail against British competition played an important role here.[24] The harbour of Piraeus in particular was viewed as 'a very important trading point' for France.[25] It was hoped that a canal at Corinth could dispense with the dangerous circumnavigation of the Peloponnesus, a route which often ended with serious shipwrecks in winter. The project was thus seen as extremely beneficial for trade and agriculture in Greece. The costs were thought at this time to be in the range of 12 million francs, and seem to have been based on estimates made in the 1830s. The French vice-consul in Piraeus predicted wonderful profits for a joint-stock company founded to build the canal.[26] This enthusiasm continued into the early 1870s: the project was said to be very popular and linked to great hopes for the development of trade, especially with France.[27] France's interest in Greece and the development of its infrastructure intensified with the Congress of Berlin. As mentioned earlier,[28] in 1882 the French government responded to a request by the Greek prime minister and sent a French Mission for public works to Greece (Mission Française des travaux publiques), a team of three engineers who travelled through the country in search of promising infrastructure projects (Παπαγιαννοπούλος [Papagiannopoulos] 1983, 49). It goes without saying that, as in other countries, the French combined their technical advice and scientific expertise with promoting French industry, and attempted thereby to gain an advantage over the British competition. Although the Mission Française was somewhat controversial in Greece due to its high costs and the strength of French influence, it was able to continue operations under prime minister Delyannis from 1885, albeit on a smaller scale (ibid., 50). French influence on the infrastructural policy of the Greek government of this time should not be underestimated (ibid., 53). In this contest, the notion of the work at Corinth being carried out by a French company was most welcome, especially as other concessions for the mining of metals and quarrying had been granted to French companies in the vicinity of the Canal of Corinth (ibid., 43).

The comptoir d'Escompte (CEP)

It was thus understandable that Türr should attempt to found a joint-stock company for the building of the canal in France. But which bank should he approach? Türr decided in favour of the CEP. Its predecessor, the Comptoir national d'escompte de Paris (CNEP), had been set up in March 1848, when the consequences of the February revolution had undermined all confidence in the French banking system, which was consequently on the verge of collapse. A whole series of respected banking houses had ceased payments or been forced into bankruptcy (Stoskopf 2002b, 398).[29] The initiative to found the bank was made by Louis Garnier-Pagès, who had been the finance minister since March 1848. He worked with two fellow freemasons, an accountant and a small businessman, who were well-known for their resistance to the July Monarchy, and managed to create the option for discount banks (comptoirs d'escompte) to be established in all towns willing to support them (ibid., 401). The expert commission for the institution consisted not only of bankers, but also of numerous intellectuals who had nothing to do with banking (ibid., 403). The bank, which was based on the model of a deposit bank, introduced a series of innovations into the French banking system, some of which had been contemplated by the Saint-Simonians.[30] This was the first joint-stock bank to be founded without the approval of the state council. The capital, brought down to an initial investment of 1.6 million francs, was provided by three groups: a third by the French state, a third by the municipalities and a third by shareholders at the stock exchange (with a dividend of 5%), a model which was considered to be explicitly democratic (Stoskopf 2002b, 407).[31] Banking houses like Rothschilds, Fould and Fould-Oppenheim were also involved. The aim was to provide the ailing economy and trade with fresh money and to democratise the granting of credit. Even though many of the counters that were opened in 1848 could not be retained, the bank kept its republican character and made an important contribution to the recovery of the banking landscape (ibid., 410). After the coup of 1851, which very quickly re-established confidence in the French financial system, the bank extended its activities beyond the field of commercial credit, e.g. in 1854 with a subscription of shares for the newly founded Banque de l'Algérie (Cameron 1961, 127). In 1852, the founding of Crédit Mobilier by the Pereire brothers in the spirit of Saint-Simonism enriched the Paris banking world with another international banking house, demonstrating its recovery (Cassis 1990, 81–83). The CNEP was transmuted into the ordinary joint-stock

Comptoir d'Escompte de Paris (CEP) without a state guarantee in 1854 (Cameron 1961, 127; Cassis 1990, 80f.). The bank was especially active in the French colonies, but also in Shanghai and Calcutta. In 1870, the CEP had 100 million francs of capital and branches in London, Alexandria, Bombay, Hong Kong, Saigon and Yokohama (Cameron 1961, 126). Although the 1876 bankruptcy of Egypt hit the bank badly (Παπαγιαννοπούλος [Papagiannopoulos] 1989, 48), it continued to be interested in the Mediterranean region. The CEP had close links to Greece and had participated in the issue of the Greek state loans in 1879, 1881, 1884 and 1887.[32] Personal relationships played an important role here: the vice-director of the CEP, Antonios Dimitrios Vlasto, had been born in Greece and was a close friend of the influential banker Andreas Syngros from Constantinople, who had taken over the French-Italian Lavrion works with his Greek company (Παπαγιαννοπούλος [Papagiannopoulos] 1989, 41).[33] Syngros described Vlasto as being exceptionally well-connected in French political circles, but not in Athens or with prime minister Trikoupis, and suggested that Vlasto was the only Greek in the West who was able to influence the opinions of the Europeans (Συγγρός [Syngros] 1998, 152).[34] Indeed, in 1884, Vlasto compiled a brochure promoting the Greek financial market in the warmest colours, praising the 'powerful vitality' of the Greeks and, quoting Epaminondas, declaring them 'the makers of great things' also in the present times (Vlasto 1885, 289).[35] The CEP's interest in the extension of the Greek niche market was certainly due in part to Vlasto's influence. The bank had also participated (albeit with a small amount)[36] in the syndicate issuing the Panama shares in 1881, which had been led by the Banque franco-égyptienne in cooperation with Kohn-Reinach (McCullough 1977, 125; Brötel 1996, 36).[37] The investment shows the interest of the bank in canal projects at a time when French capital exports were increasing greatly (Cassis 2007, 122ff.).[38] It is thus unsurprising that Türr approached this Paris bank with a view to founding the Société Internationale du Canal maritime de Corinthe (SICC). It is open to speculation whether the contact was made via Markos Renieri from the ETE, who had business relations with the CEP.

Risk perception

István Türr first contacted the CEP in writing in April 1882, nearly a year after he had obtained the final concession from the Greek government.[39] The concise form of the letter makes it clear that oral negotiations must already have been held. He told the CEP of his intention to found a company to build and later operate the Canal of Corinth and requested the bank's patronage and the issue of the shares. The company, Türr wrote, should issue 60,000 shares of 500 francs each for a total capital of 30 million francs.[40] He offered 1 million francs as commission. This generous offer shows that Türr had learnt from de Lesseps' initial problems in Panama and knew how to gain the interest of the banks by offering them good opportunities for profit, thus ensuring a successful share issue. In addition to the commission, Türr offered the bank the prospect of half the so-called founder shares to which he was personally entitled according to the articles of incorporation; these entitled the holders to 20% of the expected profits.[41] No dividends were paid on the founder shares during the construction phase of the project, in contrast to the normal shares which had an interest rate of 5% during construction – on the very competitive French capital market this was intended to attract small investors for whom Greece was largely terra incognita (Παπαγιαννοπούλος [Papagiannopoulos] 1989, 39).[42] The bank was not made responsible for the costs of founding the company.[43] The only document attached to this letter is the expert report of the French engineer Guillaume-Vincent Dauzats, who had worked as the chef du service de travaux in Suez and was also involved in the planning for Panama.[44] This fitted with the now common banking practice of using technical reports as a basis for decision making; in some cases, banks even employed their own engineers; Rothschilds was one such example (Pohle-Fraser 1999, 51). Even though the bankers could rarely understand much of the detail of such reports, the use of specialist input was intended to prove that all possible care had been taken – especially in the event of the project failing when the decision would then need to be retrospectively justified (ibid., 133ff., 195f.). At a time when belief in the calculability of the world was increasing and when small investors were to be convinced of the low risks of investment, the bankers established 'a new fiction of security, expressed by involvement with and employment of scientists' (ibid., 368).[45] The aim was the 'delegation of risk evaluation to experts who could make use of the benefits of specialisation and scale as well as learning curve effects' (Berghoff 1999, 65, tr. by K.S.). From the bankers' perspective, the reputation of the specialists and the institution in which they had studied were much more important than their actual competence, which in any case the financiers were usually unable to judge.

> The project approach, that is, the procurement of primary information in the economic sense, such as balance-sheet data and technical reports, was often regarded by bankers as ineffective in relation to decisions they had to take for or against a piece of business.
>
> (Pohle-Fraser 1999, 251)

Rather than relying on information that they were unable to evaluate, the bankers typically resorted to 'second-order observations', appraising those who had produced the information and assessing their reputations (ibid.; Weiss 1982) – in the present case, Dauzats thus benefited from the reputation he had gained as the chief engineer of Suez. No consideration was taken of the fact that the geological, climatic and technical conditions varied greatly between different canal projects. The settings of these building projects were not characterised by their stability and did not provide consistent cues that would have given the experts an opportunity to develop reliable intuition based on their experience (Kahneman 2011, 327–240). In addition, the experts tended to repeatedly evaluate weakly predictive cues in the same way, which led to numerous misjudgements; they also did not recognise the limitations of their own experience (ibid., 241).

In the case of Corinth, the engineer Dauzats had not even viewed the site of the proposed canal, but had simply based his assessment on the calculations made by Béla Gerster and another petrophysical evaluation.[46] In a detailed and very technical report, he agreed completely with the fundamentals of Gerster's plans but proposed minor, cost-saving modifications, like, e.g. connecting up with the governmental telegraph line to Athens rather than erecting an independent one. He calculated the costs to total 24.6 million francs, and proposed that Gerster should be appointed the chief engineer of the project, praising his competence.[47] A map was included to additionally emphasise the way in which the trade routes from Brindisi and Messina to Athens would be shortened. There is no indication that the bank verified the report, commissioned a second opinion or indeed obtained any other information about Dauzats or Türr. Clearly, the bankers were not even aware of the unflattering articles published in the newspapers about Türr's dishonourable dismissals from the military (Wurzbach 1883).

Despite this thin information, the bank reacted quickly, probably influenced by the successful issue of the Panama shares in December 1880. In May 1882, the CEP wrote to various partners to invite them to join an underwriting syndicate. Many business partners in France, Switzerland and Italy immediately agreed, some taking on large numbers of shares[48] for which they expected to receive a commission of 5 francs per share (for Panama, the commission had been 20 francs). At this time of a general boom on the Paris exchange, it was expected to be a 'nice subscription', as the Lullin banking house in Geneva put it.[49] The negative responses to the CEP's request, like that from the CEP's own branch in Marseille, were always justified by reference to the situation on the local exchange and never expressed any scepticism about the project itself.[50] A total of 60,090 shares were subscribed by various banks, more than were actually available,[51] and this was before the public issue of the shares that began on 9 May 1882. The branches of the CEP undertook the sale in Paris, Lyon, Marseille, Nantes and London, while the banking house of Lullin was responsible in Geneva. In Italy, Crédit Mobilier dealt with the Canal of Corinth; in Constantinople and Smyrna, it was the Imperial Ottoman Bank. The bank of Rumania and the ETE in Athens were also involved (Παπαγιαννοπούλου [Papagiannopoulos] 1989, 38).[52] It was also possible to acquire shares in Odessa, Barcelona and Brussels. The CEP did its best to fan the flames of enthusiasm, putting out targeted newspaper articles to advertise the project.[53] On 12 May, after only three days, it was possible to dissolve the syndicate because all the shares had been disposed of.[54] The public subscription was apparently oversubscribed fivefold by more than 5,000 investors, a third of whom were in Greece.[55] In April 1882, only four months after building started in Panama and before the shares had even been issued, preliminary construction work began in Corinth.

Advertising strategies

The share issue was thus a complete success with the banks and the international public. How was this achieved? What were the unique selling points of the canal, also in terms of distinguishing it from Panama? Does consideration of this allow the bankers' process of risk perception to be reconstructed? Insights into the marketing strategy are provided not only by the prospectus for the issue, but also by the Bulletin of the SICC, which the company published for its shareholders from September 1882, following the example of the Suez company, as indeed the Panama company also did (see Figure II.6.1; Mack 1944, 302).

The bulletin aimed to gain the trust of the shareholders and other interested parties by allowing them

> to regularly follow the progress of work towards breaching the Isthmus of Corinth, keeping them in constant contact with the administration of the company and informed about all the important decisions that are taken.[56]

Readers' queries and letters from all over the world were also printed, as were the responses to this correspondence, and there was a detailed press review. The bulletin thus provided information to shareholders and the bankers involved and encouraged their active involvement. It also offers a good insight into the sales strategy of the company.

Economic benefits and opportunities for profit

Firstly, the company argued that the canal provided considerable economic benefits and opportunities for profit. Supporting their forecast with statistics, they predicted that 5,897,706 tonnes per year would be shipped along the canal.[57] Ships from the Adriatic Sea would shorten their journey by 342 km by using the canal, and were to be charged 1 franc per tonne. Ships from the Mediterranean would save 178 km and were to pay 50 centimes per tonne. A little map printed on the share (which was decorated with Corinthian columns) depicted these two routes (see Figure II.6.2).

A dividend of 5% was promised for the shares, which were issued in denominations of 500 francs, and this during the construction work rather than only after its completion.[58] A future dividend of 11% was forecasted

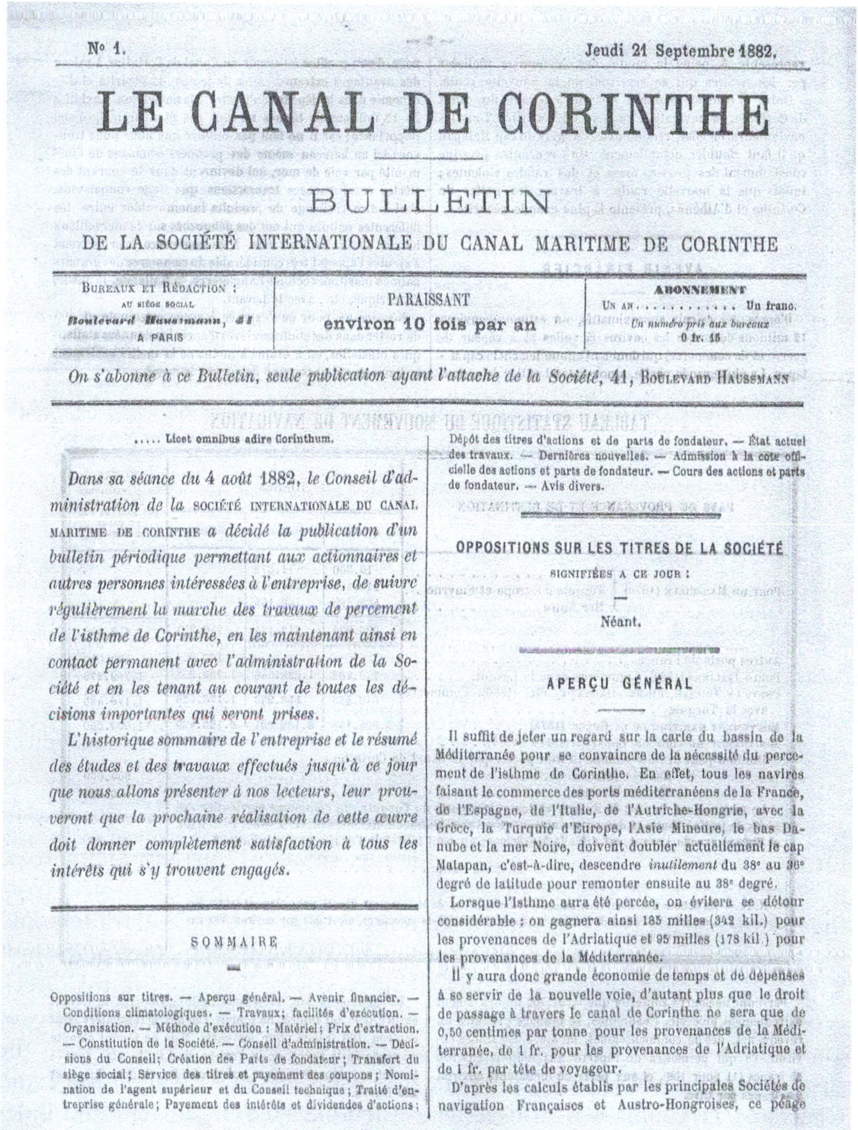

No 1. Jeudi 21 Septembre 1882.

LE CANAL DE CORINTHE

BULLETIN

DE LA SOCIÉTÉ INTERNATIONALE DU CANAL MARITIME DE CORINTHE

BUREAUX ET RÉDACTION : AU SIÈGE SOCIAL *Boulevard Haussmann, 41* A PARIS	PARAISSANT **environ 10 fois par an**	**ABONNEMENT** UN AN . . . . Un franc. *Un numéro pris aux bureaux* 0 fr. 15

On s'abonne à ce Bulletin, seule publication ayant l'attache de la Société, 41, BOULEVARD HAUSSMANN

. . . . . Licet omnibus adire Corinthum.

Dans sa séance du 4 août 1882, le Conseil d'administration de la SOCIÉTÉ INTERNATIONALE DU CANAL MARITIME DE CORINTHE *a décidé la publication d'un bulletin périodique permettant aux actionnaires et autres personnes intéressées à l'entreprise, de suivre régulièrement la marche des travaux de percement de l'isthme de Corinthe, en les maintenant ainsi en contact permanent avec l'administration de la Société et en les tenant au courant de toutes les décisions importantes qui seront prises.*

L'historique sommaire de l'entreprise et le résumé des études et des travaux effectués jusqu'à ce jour que nous allons présenter à nos lecteurs, leur prouveront que la prochaine réalisation de cette œuvre doit donner complètement satisfaction à tous les intérêts qui s'y trouvent engagés.

SOMMAIRE

Oppositions sur titres. — Aperçu général. — Avenir financier. — Conditions climatologiques. — Travaux; facilités d'exécution. — Organisation. — Méthode d'exécution : Matériel; Prix d'extraction. — Constitution de la Société. — Conseil d'administration. — Décisions du Conseil; Création des Parts de fondateur; Transfert du siège social; Service des titres et payement des coupons; Nomination de l'agent supérieur et du Conseil technique; Traité d'entreprise générale; Payement des intérêts et dividendes d'actions; Dépôt des titres d'actions et de parts de fondateur. — État actuel des travaux. — Dernières nouvelles. — Admission à la cote officielle des actions et parts de fondateur. — Cours des actions et parts de fondateur. — Avis divers.

OPPOSITIONS SUR LES TITRES DE LA SOCIÉTÉ

SIGNIFIÉES A CE JOUR :

Néant.

APERÇU GÉNÉRAL

Il suffit de jeter un regard sur la carte du bassin de la Méditerranée pour se convaincre de la nécessité du percement de l'isthme de Corinthe. En effet, tous les navires faisant le commerce des ports méditerranéens de la France, de l'Espagne, de l'Italie, de l'Autriche-Hongrie, avec la Grèce, la Turquie d'Europe, l'Asie Mineure, le bas Danube et la mer Noire, doivent doubler actuellement le cap Matapan, c'est-à-dire, descendre *inutilement* du 38° au 36° degré de latitude pour remonter ensuite au 38° degré.

Lorsque l'Isthme aura été percée, on évitera ce détour considérable ; on gagnera ainsi 185 milles (342 kil.) pour les provenances de l'Adriatique et 95 milles (178 kil.) pour les provenances de la Méditerranée.

Il y aura donc grande économie de temps et de dépenses à se servir de la nouvelle voie, d'autant plus que le droit de passage à travers le canal de Corinthe ne sera que de 0,50 centimes par tonne pour les provenances de la Méditerranée, de 1 fr. pour les provenances de l'Adriatique et de 1 fr. par tête de voyageur.

D'après les calculs établis par les principales Sociétés de navigation Françaises et Austro-Hongroises, ce péage

Figure II.6.1 Bulletin de la Société Internationale du Canal Maritime de Corinthe, No. 1, 21.9.1882.

Figure II.6.2 Société Internationale du Canal Maritime de Corinthe, Obligation au Porteur à cinq cents francs, 8.3.1888.

for the shares, and even 22% for the founder shares.[59] Furthermore, a fixed price was agreed by the construction company, protecting the project from the risk of soaring costs.[60] It was also thought that shipping and trade would increase in the region, a topic that formed one of the main focuses of the bulletin in the years to come.[61] Particular interest was displayed in the Greek economy and its 'extraordinary progress',[62] which was said to be worthy of amazement. Reports were published on the draining of Lake Copais,[63] the suspension of the forced exchange in 1885 was greeted with euphoria[64] and Charilaos Trikoupis was praised as a warm-hearted, intelligent and indefatigable prime minister for his promotion of the railways and infrastructure.[65] From this perspective, the canal project seemed essential to remove a serious barrier to the continued economic upswing of Greece, which was in a phase of economic take-off: 'That is the best praise for General Türr: he accomplished a sort of cosmic work, work which nature indicated just as trade demanded it'.[66] The personal support of King George I for the project was greatly emphasised: he not only opened the construction work on 10 April 1882, but also regularly visited the building site with his entire family and then had breakfast with the Türrs[67] in a family setting where the royal family could admire Madame Türr's extensive bird collection with two real ostriches.[68] When George was in Paris, he was willing to hold interviews with the SICC.[69] The king's approval of the progress of work was emphasised; indeed, 'all these illustrious visitors seem very satisfied with the state of the work'.[70]

Corinth as part of the series of large maritime projects

Secondly, the project was presented as being part of a series of large projects with the other two 'new paths of world trade' that the French had opened or wanted soon to open (Ilbert 2010, tr. by K.S.). Here, the reference to the Suez Canal, successfully completed in 1869, was central. Extracts of letters between Türr and de Lesseps were printed in the prospectus for the share issue. Türr wrote: 'Suez is finished. You are doing Panama. It is impossible to leave the Isthmus of Corinth as an obstacle to shipping'.[71] The encouraging answer that came from de Lesseps was also printed, as was the commission for Corinth which was given to the chief engineer of the Suez Canal Dauzats.[72] This created the impression of a globally active troop of canal builders who had a bird's eye view of obstacles to global shipping and took steps to responsibly and competently remove them. It is unclear whether Türr, who had played a somewhat subordinate role in Suez, was really motivated by the wish to emulate the Grand Français Ferdinand de Lesseps,[73] but the 'magic sound' of de Lesseps' name (Παπαγιαννοπούλου [Papagiannopoulos] 1989, 38) was constantly used in both the prospectus and the bulletin. De Lesseps was also willing to continue to support Türr. He was elected the honorary president of the SICC, which he wanted to assist with his experience and advice – a fact that was highlighted in bold print in the first SICC bulletin.[74] De Lesseps' visit to the building site in Corinth featured in detail in the bulletin, including coverage of the enthusiasm which greeted him on his travels.[75] Many references were made to the continuous increases in shipping on the Suez Canal, which were of advantage for the whole Mediterranean region, and the resulting growth in revenue.[76] Particular emphasis was given to the illustrious members of the SICC supervisory board who had also held such positions in Suez and Panama (Türr, Cousin and Oscar de Reinach).[77] Little diagrams compared the length and complexity of the work in Suez, Panama and Corinth, with the latter seeming mere child's play compared to the two 'big sisters' (see Figure II.6.3).

> The breaching of the Isthmus of Corinth is not of such grandiose importance as that of the Isthmuses of Suez and Panama. It is, nonetheless, one of the beautiful, the more useful and the more meritorious affirmations of what modern science can do, combined with capital and directed by a firm and tenacious will.[78]

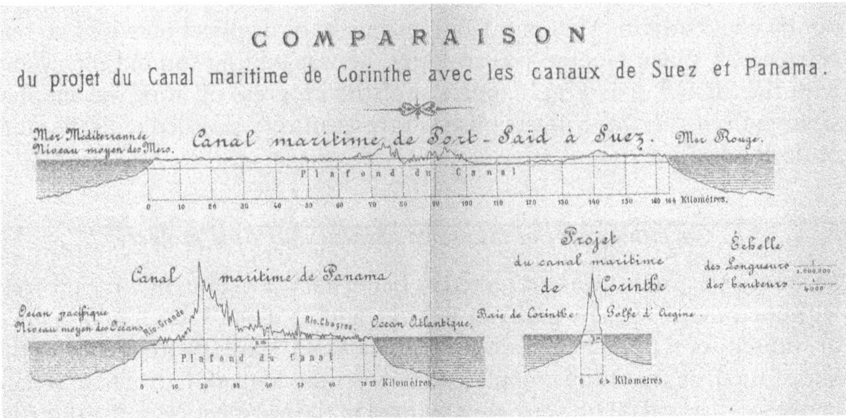

Figure II.6.3 Comparaison entre les canaux de Suez de Panama et de Corinthe, Prospectus May 1881.

The bulletin fuelled the ‘canal mania’ with reports of other canal projects elsewhere in the world: plans for a canal in St. Petersburg,[79] discussion about a project through the Isthmus of Perekop in Crimea[80] and another canal planned in southern Italy.[81] The laying of the foundation stone for the Kiel Canal in 1887 similarly did not pass without mention.[82] Optimising the world’s shipping routes seemed to be an indispensable part of the unstoppable advance of progress. In inter-banking business, having actively participated in the share issues for the Suez or Panama Canals was certainly a recommendation for inclusion in the Corinth deal.[83] Crises in the performance of the shares could also be justified with comparisons to the other canals: after all, the Suez shares had suffered for years before then celebrating great success, and clearly Panama was going through much the same process.[84] When the crisis affecting the Canal of Corinth became ever more serious after 1887, the bulletin explained the situation by referring to the problems in Panama, which were said to be causing a loss of confidence in canal projects throughout the world.[85]

Scientific expertise

The third key argument was based on engineering and scientific expertise. As demonstrated earlier, the technical knowledge and calculations, e.g. in Dauzats’ report, were almost incomprehensible to lay persons. They had to rely fully on the scientific experts.[86] This was facilitated by the reputations of the engineers: Dauzats as the successful chief engineer of Suez, Béla Gerstner as a leading figure in Panama.[87] In addition, other specialists were consulted, e.g. the geologist Augustin Franzenau, deputy professor of geology at the École Polytechnique in Paris, who conducted exploratory drillings in Corinth and who completely agreed with Gerster's findings. The building contractors also had an excellent reputation: the Société des ponts et travaux en fer (ancienne Joret et CP^{ie}) (N. N. 1910) had been founded in 1857 and was responsible for famous constructions like the steel bridge across the Quai d'Orsay, built for the World Exhibition of 1867.[88] Later, when the work encountered difficulties, Dominique Bazaine was appointed the new chief engineer of the company, a chief engineer of ponts et chaussées, former professor of the École nationale des ponts et chaussées and former chief engineer of the Compagnies des chemins de fer de Strasbourg à Bâle, Amiens à Boulogne, Paris à Lyon.[89] The engineers of the Mission Française in Greece, Rondel and Goteland, were also asked to contribute their expertise on a case-by-case basis.[90] And when the problems started to get the upper hand, then detailed scientific reports such as that by the engineer Fuchs sufficed to fill the columns of the bulletin, as there were now scarcely any success stories to be told.[91] The difficulties were blamed on an unexpected layer of marl. The question as to why none of the experts involved had spotted this hindrance was never posed.

Türr did all he could to establish the project in the geological and geographical discourse. At the Paris conference of the Sociéte Geologique in 1879, de Lesseps had received the 'blessing' of the scientific community for the Panama Canal – although most of the delegates had apparently been bribed. Türr likewise presented the Canal of Corinth to the 1881 Congrès géographique in Venice, where the attendees endorsed the project and congratulated Türr on it.[92] Equally worthy of mention is Türr's major speech in front of the Académie des sciences in 1881, likewise other speeches at scientific conferences in later years, e.g. at the Exposition Internationale des Sciences géographiques in 1884[93] and at the Congrès international de Navigation intérieure in 1886.[94] On these occasions, Türr managed to address the specialists and scientists appropriately but was also able to make the great significance of technical progress and modern engineering comprehensible for lay people: 'Towards the European Far East we find ourselves in the process of executing a work where modern science will again confirm its superiority through a success which the ancients had relinquished'.[95] The attempt to visualise and popularise the difficult scientific expertise runs through the sources as a common theme. Thus, relief images of the building site were repeatedly printed in the bulletin to document the progress of work, and in the SICC office, visitors could view the same images at a larger scale and in colour (see Figure II.6.4).[96]

Furthermore, three-dimensional models were displayed at the general meeting of shareholders and at the World Exhibition in 1889.[97] In 1883, the cartographer Charles Muret was commissioned to produce a detailed map of the region presenting the canal from various perspectives, including cross-sections and longitudinal views (see Figure II.6.5).

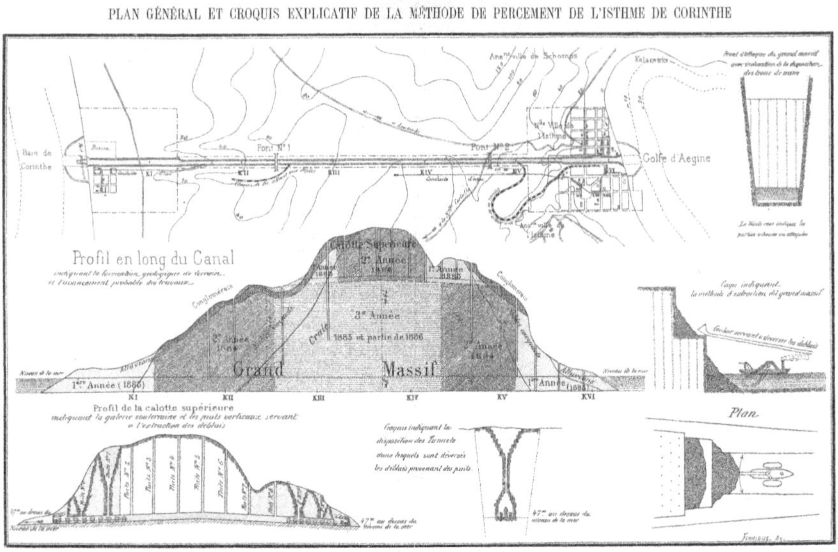

Figure II.6.4 Plan Général et croquis explicative de la méthode de percement de l'Isthme de Corinthe, June 1884.

The message conveyed by the visual material was very simple: it demonstrated perfect scientific planning and the great progress of the work. From 1886 onwards, detailed meteorological tables were included in the bulletin to document the state of the weather and the local working conditions.[98]

The scientific community thus helped to portray the project as spearheading progress, and Türr did not hesitate to use pathos. This was an 'enterprise destined to open a new path for progress and civilisation'.[99] The lack of modern technology was said to have prevented the completion of the canal in antiquity, a deficit that was now overcome.[100]

> Marco Polo has mapped out our mission, Gentlemen: it is to practise good in our endeavours, to bring our knowledge to the aid of all peoples less intelligent and less knowledgeable, and to help them: to bring all peoples closer together, and, as our presidents Ferdinand de Lesseps and the Prince of Téano have said, thus to banish the last relicts of barbarism on earth. The scholars divide the world in two realms: the natural and the animal. Let's force them to admit, Gentlemen, that there is, separate from the latter, also a human realm.[101]

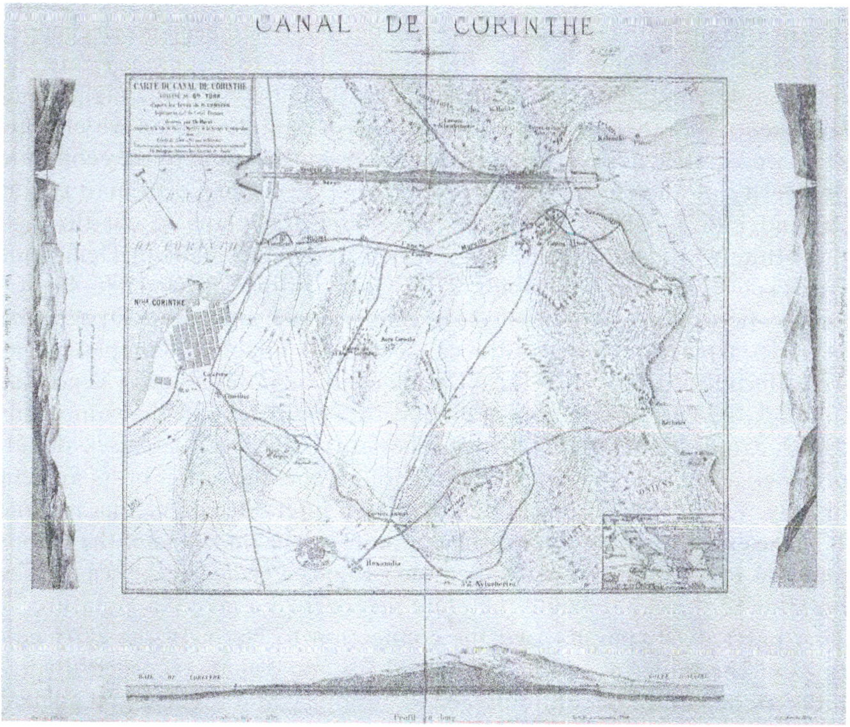

Figure II.6.5 Carte du Canal Corinthe de Charles Muret, 1883.

The notion of progress used here included not only technical and scientific developments, but also an advance of civilisation. The latter also played an important role in the bulletin, legitimating the project. Thus, engineer Bazait rejoiced about the fact that at the ends of the canal, where two years earlier there had been only empty desert, small towns were growing (Poseidonia at the Gulf of Corinth and Isthmia at the Gulf of Aegina) with water supplies for all the houses, hotels, restaurants, offices, workers' barracks, telegraphs, post offices, hospitals, two railway lines and a ferry port. The climatic conditions and the health of the workers were said to be so good that a stay at the canal could be compared with a stay at a sanatorium.[102] The construction of the canal thus appeared as a great work of progress but also as furthering peace among nations.[103]

Links to antiquity

The image thus created, fourthly, certainly did not neglect antiquity, and this was the unique selling point of the Greek project in comparison with the other two major canals: in Corinth, it was easy to make the connection to antiquity.[104] During the classical period, it had been much cheaper and safer to pull ships across the isthmus than to circumnavigate the route of 4,000 stadions around the peninsula. Between the eighth and sixth centuries, there was therefore a diolkos, a slideway, on which warships were pulled across the land, decisively contributing to the economic prosperity of ancient Corinth (Werner 1993, 12). The Corinthian tyrant Periander (628–585 BC) then developed the first plans to cut through the isthmus, and plans were also drawn up by the diadoch Demetrios Poliorketes (336–283 BC) (ibid., 27f.), Gaius Julius Caesar (100–44 BC) and Emperor Caligula (12–41 AD). Emperor Nero (37–68 AD) actually began construction work on the canal but was unable to complete it, as were Herodes Atticus (101–177 AD) and centuries later also the Venetians (ibid., 32f.). Türr thoroughly exploited this prehistory in the campaigns for his canal project. All of his speeches at the diverse congresses and all of his essays about the canal began with an epic depiction of its ancient history. Thus at the Congrès de navigation intérieure in Vienna in June 1886, he explained that the word Peloponnesus meant *island* of the Pelops and that Pindar himself had called the isthmus a *bridge* in the sea.[105] The building of the canal would therefore just correct a mistake of nature.[106] Türr particularly emphasised the connection to Nero. In the early editions of the bulletins, a section named 'Literary chat' recorded diverse links to the authors of antiquity, e.g. Pausanias, and reported on ancient plans and work, attributing Nero with a key role.[107] It almost appears that the choice of route for the canal was also influenced by the wish to emulate the Roman Emperor: Gerster, who was most familiar with the terrain, had proposed two alternative routes which were somewhat longer but avoided the high crest of the hill. However, Türr decided in favour of the direct Nero route and never failed to mention the link to the ancient Emperor. The argument that it was possible to profit from the scanty preliminary work undertaken by Nero seems to bear little weight in face of the quantities of earth that needed to be removed. Nonetheless, the SICC shares (Figure II.6.2) displayed two Corinthian columns framing the elevation plan and a miniature map of the shipping routes, decorated with a Pegasus and the helmeted head of Pallas Athena.[108] And the company bulletin was presented under the Latin motto 'Licet omnibus adire Corinthum'. It regularly included reports about life in ancient Corinth and at the Acrocorinth, illustrated with full-page, picturesque pen and ink drawings (Figure II.6.6).[109]

The ancient excavations were included on all the maps and the SICC supported the classical digs, for instance, by providing the Ecole française d'Athènes with workers.[110] Travel reports in the bulletin never failed to describe the ancient excavations.[111] In 1884, Béla Gerster even dedicated a complete publication to the ancient precursors of the canal (Gerster 1884).

Figure II.6.6 Acro-Corinthe et Ancienne Ville de Corinthe, 1882.

Numerous newspapers echoed these images of antiquity, including *La France industrielle* which rhapsodised:

> Corinth! What classical reminiscences this name calls up. Corinth, physically and morally located between Sparta, the puritanical capital of the Peloponnesus, and Athens, the graceful city of Attica! Corinth is like the core of Greece, like the soul of this little country, situated on this slender strip of earth that links the two parts of ancient Hellas, the homeland of our civilization.[112]

It was not until shortly before the bankruptcy of the company that some journalists reacted with irritation to the continuous references made to 'Themistocles or Epaminondas', which they viewed as being of little use in solving the problems.[113]

The national project

The enthusiasm for antiquity and technical and scientific progress could be linked with a fifth argument: French national pride and sense of mission as an advanced nation with a duty to further civilisation (Thomas 2011). The SICC was an explicitly international company and the SICC concessionaire was certainly not a Frenchman – despite the advantages of marriage to a relation of Napoleon. Nonetheless, the national significance of the project was thoroughly emphasised, along with the fact that the canal was not only 'good business', but also a 'great French work'.[114] Türr, born in Hungary and a naturalised Italian, did not hesitate to adopt this tone when he eulogised about the civilising aims of the undertaking: 'to bring our knowledge to the aid of all peoples less intelligent and less knowledgeable, and to help them'.[115] The Grande Nation was proud of its technical prowess:

> Our race, whose commercial genius is obstinately denied by certain sceptical interests, will nonetheless be the one which with a boldness consisting at least as much of generosity as of calculation, will in less than thirty years have opened three new routes for world trade.[116]

In the terminology of behavioural finance, this heuristic may be described as 'overconfidence', a feeling of superiority and of being invulnerable to risks, despite acknowledging the existence of those risks. Experts are particularly likely to display 'expert overconfidence behaviour' (Ricciardi 2008b, 98).[117] Of further relevance in the case of the Canal of Corinth was the imperial affront suffered by France with the Suez Canal. In 1875, the British prime minister Disraeli had, with the support of Rothschilds, organised a blitz operation which resulted in over half of the Suez company shares being held by the British (Davis 1983 151ff.), and this despite the fact that Great Britain had sought to obstruct the completion of the Suez Canal for decades. From 1875, this majority holding in the Suez Canal company secured British influence in Egypt, which then in 1882 helped considerably with the establishment of formal British imperialism in the region. This was a painful setback to French interests in the Mediterranean. The 1880s saw a growth in the imperial tensions between the two Great Powers.

Against this background, the French were anxious not to lose Greece to the competition, neither as an area of imperial influence nor as a market – which also explains the decision to send the Mission Française des travaux publiques to the country. On the one hand, the French insisted on the importance of modern ties between the two nations and emphasised the undying gratitude of the Greeks for France's help in the struggle for independence and the founding of the new Greek state 50 years previously.[118] On the other hand, of equal importance was the long-standing competition between France and Great Britain concerning the legacy of Greek antiquity, as had developed in the seventeenth century (Zabel 2016). The significance of this classical legacy was intensively discussed in both countries (Lecoq 2001). In Victorian times, classical studies, particularly Greek, were an important part of elite education in both countries, especially as current political affairs could be debated in this Greek guise (Turner 1989, 63f.).[119] In Great Britain, where tensions between the social classes were increasing in the course of industrialisation, deriving ideological support for the position of the elites played an important role (Bowen 1989, 161). From the mid-nineteenth century, much time and attention was thus given to ancient Greece in lessons at the exclusive public schools (ibid., 162). The history of the Attic Republic was perfectly suited for reflection on the English political system, and the Homeric epics could be compared to the battles of the Empire. 'Greek political and ethical thought could help to define elite civic life in a liberal democracy. [Aristotle and Plato] provided a philosophy for a political elite legitimated by merit and by moral and intellectual superiority' (Turner 1989, 77f.). Arguments against utilitarianism and scientific naturalism could also be derived from studies of ancient Greek texts, as especially encouraged by German idealism (ibid., 76). Victorian painting was equally influenced by Greek elements (Jenkyns 1989). Greece was viewed as a cultural model worthy of emulation.

The Third, still unstable, Republic of France was also greatly interested in the construction of ancient Athens as a society shaped by discussion and the involvement of its citizens, in decided contrast to the courtly life of the empire. The debates in the Assemblée nationale show the extent to which the discourse about modern Greece – e.g. with regard to trade relations – was intermingled with discourse about Greek antiquity, despite criticism of this by a number of speakers. Greek armaments contracts were thus discussed in the same breath as the division of finds from ancient digs.[120]

Was civilising the world in Attic style then the preserve of Great Britain or of France (Zabel 2016)? In this context, the Canal of Corinth, presented as part of the classical legacy, was a prestige object for France, not only from a technical, geo-strategic and economic perspective, but also in nationalistic and humanistic terms. This appropriation of antiquity not only modified the French receiving culture, but also constructed an image of the reference culture (Bergemann et al. 2011, 39). The genuine French character of the undertaking could therefore not be over-emphasised and the risky and problematic nature of the project, determined by its location in modern Greece, was 'ennobled' by the links to antiquity (ibid., 46). For the SICC, this meant that it was at times necessary to justify purchases of materials or machines that were not made in France.[121] It seemed clear that the resources for such a progressive project could not be found more cheaply or better than in France – overconfidence was apparent in every respect.[122]

A satire from the year 1893, entitled 'The Canal of Corinth', shows the close connection between the nationalist and the antique dimensions of the project. It is primarily concerned not with the building of the Canal of Corinth, but rather with the Panama Canal. De Lesseps had failed with this project in 1889 and the Panama company had filed for bankruptcy. It was not until three years later, however, that a media scandal resulted. This was not particularly concerned with the approximately 20,000 human lives that the building work had apparently cost (Greene 2009, 26). The scandal focused rather on dishonest financial dealings in the context of the Panama share issue, which involved corruption and bribery among French politicians (Mack 1944, 381–386; Mollier 1991). The financier de Reinach, who was not only the administrator of the Panama company, but also that of Corinth, had in April 1888 allegedly bribed more than 150 French MPs and senators in order to ensure approval of the lottery loan for Panama (Mack 358–360). De Reinach died in mysterious circumstances during the investigation. The scandal had widespread repercussions so that in December 1892, the French government was forced to resign (ibid., 381–386). In a court case held in 1893, several defendants were found guilty, including Charles de Lesseps, son of the great but now mentally deranged canal builder (ibid., 403). This was the context that inspired the satire 'Le percement de l′isthme de Corinthe' (dealing, despite its title, with the Panama Canal project), parts of which were printed in *Le voleur illustré*[123] (see Figure II.6.7; Durocher 1893).

It is quite clear that the caricatures were of Ferdinand de Lesseps, de Reinach and the politicians involved, and equally clear that the target of ridicule was the wastefulness and extravagance of the Panama company, as

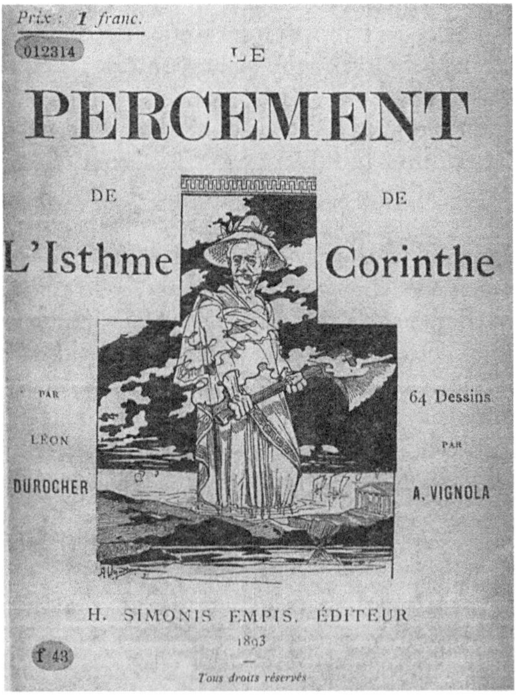

Figure II.6.7 Durocher: Le Percement de L'Isthme de Corinthe, 1893, Cover.

had been brought to light in 1892/1893.[124] A sense of distance is produced through the transfer of the situation to antiquity: the investing public is located in ancient Athens. The caricaturist thus utilises a common practice of the 1890s, speaking about Greece but at the same time referring to France (Basch 1995, 245).[125] This technique allows the equation of the Parisian financial and political elite with the elite of antiquity to be caricatured.

> The poor of Attica, whose imagination had already multiplied the resources a hundredfold, hurried to get their savings, which had previously been hidden in sterile wool stockings or at the back of unproductive cupboards. The rich used the opportunity to contribute to the glory of Athens by increasing their capital tenfold....
>
> (Durocher 1893, 13, tr. by K.S.)

The link to Athens enables an amusing form of caricature: the large-scale newspaper campaign initiated by de Lesseps at the beginning of work on the canal is justified by an uttering of the Oracle of Delphi, and newspapers critical of the canal are suspected of being paid by Sparta (ibid., 17). The methods of bribery employed by the banker 'Orimaroth' and his sudden death during the later investigation are portrayed in a detailed caricature, as are the French elite at the World Exhibition of 1889, a setting that is enriched with classical elements (ibid., 24; 28f.). An engineer called Xanthippe is finally sent to find the canal, but instead comes across a lavish party at the Acrocorinth where carefree theatricals are offered as entertainment:

> Danae, or the Republic of Athens, locks herself in a prison to protect herself from Jupiter the Corrupter. The god falls in golden rain through the bars of the gate and Jupiter the Corrupter executes the dance of millions (at the feet of Danae: the Republic of Athens yields, dazzled).
>
> (ibid., 20f., tr. by K.S.)

When Xanthippe returns to Athens and tells those responsible of his doubts about the technical feasibility of the canal, the construction of which he considers impossible, he is corrected: 'Impossible, is not Greek' (ibid., 26, tr. by K.S.). In the context of the satire is this actually a reference to 'Greek' or rather to 'French'? Both levels seem to overlap here. It seems unnecessary to say that the disastrous consequences that followed the bankruptcy are also described in flowery terms. The word Greek is finally forbidden and the Greeks are re-named 'Hellenes' (ibid., 51, tr. by K.S.).

Using flashbacks and strongly distorted, the satire shows how links to antiquity were combined with the pride of carrying out a large, international engineering project for the self-glorification of the imperial, Parisian elites in the financial and political circles of the Third Republic. This was not an exclusively French phenomenon: when the USA successfully revived the project of the Panama Canal after 1902, symbolism related to Hercules was frequently used, and the construction of the canal played an important role in promoting the self-assurance of the nation (Greene 2009, 2).

It is not possible to determine whether the decision making of the CEP bankers was actually influenced by the marketing strategies and legitimation of the SICC. It is, however, clear that the CEP bankers were involved in the design of the prospectus and approved of it, i.e. believed it would be promotionally effective. The interplay of the arguments used to promote the canal rendered it a promising investment project in which the bank gladly participated.

The difficult work

Work on the building site was delayed almost immediately and the goal of completing the canal by 1887 quickly appeared overambitious. This was due, firstly, to delays in the delivery of various machines and materials from abroad.[126] It took a great deal longer than anticipated until the arrival of large machines such as the digger 'Schimmelbusch',[127] two identical diggers 'Poseidonia' and 'Isthmia', the tugs 'General Türr' and 'Etincelle', the yacht 'Nero', the diamond drill 'Taverdon' and the grab dredger 'Priestmann'. Like in Panama (Mack 1944, 323), the expressive names provided orientation on the building site for readers of the bulletin, and their size and performance could trigger real storms of enthusiasm among observers.[128] Another problem was that the extent of the preliminary work had been completely underestimated: it was necessary to put up accommodation for the workers, to install the telegraph system, to build the two harbours and to construct the railway so that the excavated material could be removed.[129] Two years went by before Türr regarded the preliminary work as complete, in 1884.[130] At times, there was a lack of labour; between 800 and 2,100 workers were employed on the building site over the years, most of whom were Italian, Armenian and Montenegrin, while Greeks were usually only seasonal workers.[131] There were also unexpected technical problems with the rock strata, which caused the costs to explode.[132] In 1886, a deposit of marlstone was discovered, a serious problem because the engineers were afraid it would cause the canal to cave in when it was flushed out by the sea. Additional protective walls were therefore built, at great expense.[133] The soaring costs caused the SICC shares to plummet.[134] It was furthermore necessary to contract a new company to undertake this additional work because the original firm was uninterested.[135] As it was clearly impossible to complete the project punctually, King George extended the deadline for completion by two years, up to 1889.[136] The company had to issue bonds to provide supplementary capital.

The issue of 60,000 bonds of 500 francs each[137] is particularly interesting because at this point the bankers and their risk management are again visible in the sources. The bank estimated the interest for the bonds to total 990,000 francs, not including the costs of the issue, which meant a loss per bearer share of 50 francs, i.e. 10–20% of the current price.[138] However, it was the bank's task to justify this expensive decision to the shareholders. Why did the CEP agree to support the SICC once more? What was the risk management strategy of the bank?

Initially, the issue of additional bonds was favourable for the CEP. The bank obtained the bonds from the company at a price of 475 francs but they were issued for 490 francs so that the bank made a profit of 15 francs per bond sold, a respectable commission. However, this was not the decisive point. The CEP must also have been interested in preserving the company from bankruptcy: at the end of 1888, the SICC had debts of almost 9 million francs with the CEP, most of which had been advanced to pay for materials, etc.[139] The fear of losing this advanced money was, of course, one strong argument in favour of stabilising the SICC, which behavioural finance would call a case of loss aversion.

However, the decision called for additional legitimisation. This was provided by a report drawn up by the engineer Bazaine in 1886. Bazaine declared that the SICC would actually have completed the work without exceeding the originally estimated costs if the unexpected rock strata had not caused a problem.[140] He estimated the expenses incurred by the marlstone to amount to 5 million francs. Were these costs really unavoidable? The internal report of the bank casts doubt on this, despite the photographs (see Figures II.6.8 and II.6.9). Nonetheless, reliance was once again placed on the observations of the experts provided by the SICC. The company

Figure II.6.8 Building site of the Canal of Corinth (1)

Figure II.6.9 Building site of the Canal of Corinth (2).

established a commission consisting of 'competent engineers, both with geological knowledge and with experience of working at the sea'.[141] The positive report produced by the commission was made available to the bank and supplemented by optimistic forecasts concerning the number of ship passages that could be expected.[142] Increases in volumes of shipping would ensure that the project was still profitable.[143] Based on this information, the CEP decided to continue to support the construction of the canal, clearly still believing that it could be completed. Indeed, the bank had little choice in the matter. Severe reputational damage threatened if the SICC were allowed to go bankrupt, leaving their shareholders out in the cold, especially as many of the shareholders had become involved upon the advice and advertising of the bank. Dissatisfaction was in any case rife, given the massive fall in price of the shares.

It was beyond dispute that a syndicate needed to be formed to launch the bonds on the market, in order to stabilise the price. The organisation of the syndicate fell to the CEP and several partners were found to be willing to participate: Hentsch freres & Cie itself (1,192 bonds), brokered by Hentsch the Banque Fédérale in Switzerland,[144] and also Banque Paris & Paribas (1,000) and Crédit Mobilier (1,700), to name but a few examples.[145] No illusions were held about the dismal prospects of the issue, which explains why only one-third of the bonds, a total of 20,000, were offered to the public at the stock exchange; the rest remained meanwhile in the hands of the CEP. To make the bonds more attractive, on 8 March 1888, an issue price of 490 was selected at a nominal value of 500 francs.[146] Repayment should occur within 75 years, the interest was an attractive 6%, the real interest rate was 7.5% and that at a time of low interest on the Parisian stock exchange. The bonds were designed like the shares of 1882 with Corinthian columns, ancient pictograms, the elevation plan and the little map with the shipping routes (Figure II.6.2). The CEP undertook a great deal of publicity work: 122,705 francs were spent on encouraging conservative, provincial newspapers to report – ideally positively – on the bond issue.[147] However, the journalists were not all able to suppress their scepticism. Thus, the *Bulletin du Crédit* printed a detailed and very positive article about the economic and financial state of Greece[148] and reported in the same issue on the new bonds. In the latter article, the journalist seems to writhe between the wishes of his client and his own opinion. He expresses unease about the unclear role of the CEP in the issue. The syndicate was said to be an extremely lucrative deal for the members of the supervisory board, for which the CEP bore moral responsibility. In addition, he argued, it had recently been revealed that the SICC had made mistakes; this was not a good basis upon which to ask the public for another 30 million francs. However, the article emphasised the extremely high interest rate and made clear that despite the difficulties encountered, the construction work could still be smoothly and quickly completed. And in any case the integrity and competence of the CEP director, Denfert-Rocherau, earned complete confidence.[149] The *Finance Nouvelle* also failed to hide its scepticism, reproving the unexpected increase in costs and casting doubt on the economic viability of the building work. In this context, the reader was also made aware of the unreliability of the scientific evaluation:

> It is better to lend on hypothecary credits than on hypotheses. The subscribers lend only on hypotheses and when those hypotheses prove to be miscalculations they can blame nobody but themselves. The prudent capitalist will wait before engaging in this area until the matter has left the period of uncertainty.[150]

Sceptical voices were also heard in Germany where it was suggested that the shipping companies would baulk at the fees and instead prefer to navigate around the Peloponnesus.[151] Other newspapers showed a greater tendency to cater to the wishes of the CEP and praised the bonds because of their fixed interest.[152] With the help of the syndicate, it was at least possible to dispose of this first third.

Nonetheless, in December 1888, the company found itself unable to pay the promised share dividends (Glasemann 2010, 10). By the beginning of 1889, it was becoming clear that there was insufficient money despite the bond issue and in banking circles scepticism grew. Lullin, a colleague from Geneva, bluntly asked Denfert-Rocherau about possible options in the event of the project failing. In response, Denfert-Rocherau tried to explain the unfortunate situation by referring to Panama: 'The misfortune of Panama has rebounded on the Corinthian obligations', he wrote to Lullin. 'Thanks to sincere promotion we have started stable sales and we hope that the public will be interested in this value'. Nothing stood in the way of completing the canal, he suggested, especially as Türr was already negotiating with various governments about additional funding.[153] The consent of the French national assembly to the lottery loan for Panama (achieved through bribery, as later became clear) was seen as offering encouragement for Corinth.[154]

Then in March, the CEP itself collapsed, although the canal project apparently played a very minor role here (Hautcoeur 2014). At this time, the SICC had about 1.5 million francs of debt with the bank, in addition to the 40,000 unsold bonds. Matters were twice as bad for the SICC because its building company, the Société de construction et d'exploitation, which was closely connected to the CEP, also went bankrupt.[155] It was necessary to use troops to prevent rioting by the workers at the building site,[156] and the company's shares hit rock bottom. With the collapse of the bank, it was no longer possible for the company to maintain an illusion of prosperity (Pohle-Fraser 1999, 307). The bulletin refrained from printing the usual table of current prices, mentioning them only in the text: the bonds were now at 110; the shares stood at 65. Türr attempted to obtain additional finance or at least an interest guarantee from the Powers concerned.[157] In his speech to the general meeting, he not only again used images of antiquity,[158] but also compared Corinth to the other canals: Suez had finally cost 500 instead of 200 million francs; the estimates for Panama had totalled 600 but costs were already at 1,400.[159] In Corinth, 41,072,120.03 francs had been spent thus far, and he would find the means to bring the project to completion.[160] However, Türr's hopes of help from the Greek government were illusionary: the concession stipulated that the building site and all the materials on it would become the property of the Greek state if the contract was not fulfilled (i.e. the canal not punctually completed). So why should Greece help Türr?[161] The Greeks could simply play for time, especially as the European governments displayed reservations about the project.[162] In Berlin, Türr was not received by Bismarck, and even moral support was denied to him, not least because he was accused of having drifted too far into 'French waters' in recent years.[163] Türr's idea of organising an international conference to rescue the canal also failed.[164] As the German legation in Athens reported:

> Since the Greeks are much too shrewd business people not to recognise that it would mean acting against their own interests, [...] making sacrifices to gain a fruit the enjoyment of which must be shared with others, when one is as good as certain that with no effort it will fall into one's lap as exclusive property.[165]

The Athens newspapers saw the situation as an opportunity to make the canal a purely Greek affair, which would be of particular strategic advantage.[166] In February 1890, the SICC was forced into bankruptcy.

Rescue attempts after the bankruptcy

It initially looked as though the shareholders of the SICC would lose all their invested capital. However, in Greece, not least due to the intervention of King George, an initiative emerged to rescue the project. No investors could be found for the SICC, but the establishment of a new company was possible. Andreas Syngros joined with de Reinach (as yet unaffected by the Panama scandal) and Vlasto from the CEP to make the attempt, and also took the ETE and the Epiro-Thessalien-Bank on board. Once again, as nine years previously in Lavrion, it was Andreas Syngros who was willing to pick up the remains of European investment, after he had for a while (at least pro forma) supported Türr.[167] Scientific expertise continued to be of importance: Syngros again commissioned Béla Gerster to inspect the building site,[168] and similarly Quellenec, the engineer of the Mission française in Athens.[169] This expertise provided a basis for the founding of a new Greek company in April: the Société Hellénique Canal de Corinthe (SHCC) with capital resources of 5 million francs. Zafirios Matsas, later director of the BA, acted as the director of the company. On 5 July of the same year, the SHCC issued 40,000 bonds.[170] The prospectus sparkled with guarantees: the new company had acquired all the materials from the old; the building contractors had agreed a fixed price, so unexpected increases in costs were no longer possible; with capital of 20 million drachmas, the Epiro-Thessalien-Bank guaranteed interest payments to creditors (also during the 2½-year building period until 1893) and the ongoing payments to the contractors.[171] The prospectus again contained a map and a diagram illustrating the state of work: four-fifths of the earth had already been removed.[172] The profits were to be divided and three-quarters of the surplus was to go to the old international company, so the old shareholders could expect up to 8% interest and growing profits, an agreement that the receivers of the SICC saw as very advantageous.[173] The shareholders of the old company did not always share this opinion, as a protest published in 1890 makes clear (Jean 1890). Türr also felt that he had been badly treated.[174]

The French foreign ministry had no reservations about the shares of the new company being launched on the Paris stock exchange.[175] The CEP, which had itself just been rescued, organised a syndicate for the issue of the shares and bonds of the new company.[176] The renewed involvement of the bank shows the depth of commitment felt to the customers who had been persuaded to buy the SICC shares. Old Greek investors such as Emil Erlanger joined the syndicate, as did diaspora Greeks from Marseille.[177] The vice-director of the CEP Vlasto also bought 600 bonds for 71,400 francs. The guaranteed interest had the desired effect: a total of 18,700 bonds worth 2,225,300 francs were subscribed in advance; in the public issue, 22,500 were then disposed of,[178] securing a commission payment of 168,750 francs for the CEP. Some of the French newspapers contributed to the success of the issue by praising the safe dividends, guaranteed as they were by a prestigious Greek bank.[179] Elsewhere, however, sharp warnings were issued against the new shares: the rock strata were said to be unsuitable and the revenues doubtful; in short, the whole affair was 'dubious and mediocre'. How, asked some of the newspapers, could the new CEP simply continue the dubious business of the old?[180]

The relationship between the shareholders in the old company and those in the new company, whose headquarters was in Athens, was tense.[181] Lebandy, de Reinach and Vlasto belonged to a Parisian committee that Athens was required to consult.[182] In July 1890, Vlasto was named the vice-president of the SHCC after Stefan Streit, the governor of the ETE, resigned from this office.[183] The company purchased the buildings that had already been erected and the machinery of the old company from the Greek state (Glasemann 2010, 13). In July 1890, it was possible to resume work and the opening was planned for August 1893. There were conflicts about whether, e.g. more Frenchmen should be brought into the country to administer the finished canal or whether it could just as well be managed by a Greek.[184] Work progressed well nonetheless.

The opening ceremony was held on 6/25 July 1893 (according to the Julian/Gregorian calendar) in the presence of Türr and the king, whose yacht 'Sphaktiria' was the first to ship through the canal. However, the successful exploitation of the canal was delayed[185] due to structural defects: parts of the walls repeatedly collapsed because they were too steep. Many shipping lines therefore chose to travel around the Peloponnesus. The circumnavigation had become less of a challenge than in the past, thanks to improvements in the technical equipment on the ships. The estimates of the number of ships that would use the canal thus proved to be exaggerated, which was not uncommon with international canal projects (Ratcliffe 1985, 117ff.). It proved necessary to inform the bondholders as early as 1894 that the coupons could not be paid due to the insufficient provision of funds.[186] In May 1894, Vlasto resigned from the Paris committee because of French-Greek tensions.[187] In 1906, a group of Greeks attempted to effect a hostile takeover of the company and to sell the canal at a knock-down price. The French reacted furiously and formed a Comité de Défense to fend off these plans.[188] The canal again became the object of intense speculation, although this is not relevant to the present discussion. In 1907, the company was re-founded as the Nouvelle Société Anonyme du Canal de Corinthe with the intention to modernise and restore the canal.[189] The necessity for continuous repair work devoured money and continued to haunt the company into the 1920s, so hardly any dividends could be paid. After the devastation of the Second World War, the canal was again made navigable. In 1980, after the 99-year concession had expired, the company became the state-owned Corinth Canal Company, Athens, and in 2001 it was privatised.[190]

Conclusion

Why did the CEP become the house bank and issuing bank of the SICC, which in 1882 began to build the Canal of Corinth? The bank possessed little information about the project. However, the bankers' unconditional belief in progress and expertise prevented them from questioning the only report available and from thoroughly scrutinising the promoter. In light of the reputation of those involved, the bankers relied on superficial scientific expertise which tended to legitimate decisions rather than serve as a basis for making those decisions. The available information was interpreted against the background of the experience and values of the bank: thanks to a strong interest in the Mediterranean and a Greek vice-president, the CEP was happy to engage in Greece, especially as the French government had geo-strategic and imperial motives for supporting such business. The republican and Saint-Simonian tradition of the CEP also favoured the support of an infrastructure project led by the liberal freedom fighter Türr.

The 'overconfidence' of the bank was further fed by nationalistic emotions in this era of growing imperial tension. The canal project could be viewed as part of a series of large maritime projects, which after the completion of the Suez Canal delighted the French public and investors. The project was presented as a French national task and part of the civilising mission of the country. This was then tied to an argument that represented a unique selling point for Corinth in comparison to the other canals: the link to Greek antiquity. The special Greek-French relationship of modern times was used to support the project, as was the claim that republican France was the spiritual successor of ancient Athens in the face of competition from Great Britain. The link to antiquity 'ennobled' the project and distracted from the risky financial environment of the modern Greek market. This heuristic led to the risks being underestimated. Despite establishing a consortium to spread the risk, the CEP, as the house bank of the SICC, bore the largest share of risk itself, particularly in terms of its reputation as an issuing house.

The discovery of unexpected rock strata was one reason why the project could not be completed in French hands; other contributing factors included the bankruptcy of the CEP, the failure of the Panama project and the slump on the Paris exchange after 1883. A Greek company then managed to finish the canal in 1893. However, it seems clear that the CEP's reliance on the 'reputation approach' to scientific expertise and nationalistic hubris failed to lead to success – the canal made very little profit even after completion.

Notes

1 On the Morea Expedition, see **132 n.18** in this book. After the expedition, a geological book was published which was co-authored by d'Aoust: Boblaye/d'Aoust 1833. His report on the Canal of Corinth was published in 1881 (see D'Aoust 1881).

2 Fiedler (1840, 238), tr. by K.S.
3 Ibid., 239, tr. by K.S. The lawyer and researcher of Albania, Johann Georg von Hahn (1811–1869), who was born in Frankfurt and worked in the Greek judiciary in 1834–1843, also promoted the plans to construct the canal; see Hahn 1879.
4 **126** in this book.
5 An extensive list of the business fields of the private bank *Kohn, Reinach et Cie* is found in Brötel (1996, 31–41).
6 Béla Gerster (1850–1923) studied engineering and architecture at the Technical University of Vienna and specialised in hydraulic engineering. In 1877, e.g. he worked on the Great Bačka Canal. From 1882 to 1889, he was the head engineer of the canal construction at Corinth (see Glasemann 2010, 19). Gerster later published a piece justifying his position. Gerster (1884).
7 No price is mentioned by Mack (1944, 300).
8 See **142 n.259** in the book.
9 Glasemann (2010, 6). Glasemann claims that Türr and Renieri first met in 1880 in Aachen. Fornaro uses letters from the Hungarian National Archive to show that Türr and Renieri corresponded at least since 1862 (see Fornaro 2004, 124f, FN 83). Also see **128, 142 n.259, n.264** in this book.
10 Detailed biographical information making extensive use of newspaper reports from the 1880s but very biased against Türr is found in Wurzbach (1883). Wurzbach suggests that the family had German roots. A romantic, novelistic story of Türr's life up to 1866 in two volumes is found in Schwarz (1868).
11 Fornaro refers here to an unpublished biography by Türr's sister Stefania.
12 Fornaro praises Türr's decisive intervention (see Fornaro 2004, 26).
13 Fornaro (2004, 45), tr. by K.S. On the idea of the confederation: Progetto Klapka di una confederazione danubiana, in: La Comunità Internazionale, V, no. 4, Ottobre (1950, 18–21), cited from: Commissione per la pubblicazione dei documenti diplomatici (1959), I documenti diplomatici italiani. Prima serie, No. 253, 293–295.
14 Türr (1868, 3), tr. by K.S.
15 A list of publications is found in Fornaro (2004, 255f.).
16 Türr (1878a, 25), tr. by K.S.
17 Ιστορικό Αρχείο της Εθνικής Τράπεζας [Historical Archives National Bank of Greece] (2014, 14f.).
18 **246 n.9** in this book and Il Generale Türr a Vittorio Emanuele II., 28.3.1862, in: Commissione per la pubblicazione dei documenti diplomatici (1959), No. 202, 253. A telegram from Renieri in Athens is also printed here. The idea of a Slavic-Greek confederation with its headquarters in Constantinople continued to be mentioned in the newspapers up to 20 years later (see Vlasto 1885, 288).
19 In contrast, Türr denied the past prosperity and future opportunities of the multi-ethnic Austrian-Hungarian Empire and the Ottoman Empire. 'As long as there are different languages, the universal monarchy will remain the most impossible, the most unrealisable of all dreams' (Türr 1878b, 14, tr. by K.S.).
20 Lucien Bonaparte was friends with Jean Gabriel Eynard; see **89 n.126** in this book.
21 Türr is not mentioned in Bonin (2010). In Fornaro (2004), a decidedly political biography, less than two pages are dedicated to the Canal of Corinth (123f.); the focus is rather on Türr as a freedom fighter and diplomat. From the perspective of the Canal of Corinth, this seems distorted; after all, Türr dedicated several years of his life to the project. Fornaro fails to mention Türr's work in Suez at all, and only mentions his involvement in Panama in passing.

22 A particular focus was on restricting Russian influence (see Fornaro 2004, 87–100). Türr seems subsequently to have distanced himself from Garibaldi. Thus in 1868, he condemned the attack on Rome (see Türr 1868, 9, FN).
23 MAE, Direction des consulats et affaires commerciales au Ministère de l'Agriculture et du Commerce, 4.3.1854, AN F 12 2670, tr. by K.S.
24 Note statistique sur le commerce de la Grèce, no date but apparently early 1860s, AN F12 2670.
25 Extract from a report about Piraeus, 19.9.1863, from Consul Varieux to the MAE, as a copy, 20.10.1863, AN F 12 2670, tr. by K.S.
26 Report by the French vice-consul from Piraeus Varieux to the MAE, 30.10.1862, as a copy, AN F 12 2670.
27 Report by the French vice-consul from Patras to the MAE, 12.3.1870, as a copy 18.8.1870, AN F 12 2670.
28 **192f.** in this book.
29 The banking house d'Eichthal was also affected; **126** in this book.
30 The Péreire brothers had already attempted to found a joint-stock bank of this sort in 1830 (see Cameron 1961, 126).
31 Capitalisation of up to 20 million francs was authorised.
32 The relevant source material on these issues has not survived in the archive of the CEP.
33 On the joint business conducted by these two, see Ηλιαδάκης [Iliadakis] (2011, 78–85).
34 On Vlasto, who is usually mentioned in connection with the bankers of Constantinople, see Βοβολίνης [Vovolinis] (1958–1963, Γ, 400α; E, 444a).
35 Vlasto (1885, 264), tr. by K.S. Vlasto emphasised the role of the so-called 'Homogènes', the Greeks abroad. 'They are usually shipowners, traders or bankers. Many belong to the oldest families of the country and represent with their traditions, with their trading habits, that which remains of the most Hellene of the old reserves of Greek civilisation'. After 1875 (financial catastrophe in Egypt and the Ottoman Empire), these Greeks increasingly invested in their old homeland and some returned to live there. They were also said to hold the majority of Greek foreign debts. Vlasto mentioned the acquisition of Thessaly and the abilities of Trikoupis as reasons for the recovery. He praised the industrial and agricultural upturn of the country but conceded that there were considerable problems in the administration, although he claimed Trikoupis would deal with these (276f.). He argued that Trikoupis attracted the attention of Europe to Greece and its prospects (280). Vlasto emphasised the cultural splendour of Ancient Greece and the severe decline that began under Alexander the Great, but also claimed that Greece was now on its way up again (287).
36 The CEP is not explicitly mentioned in Bonin's list (see Bonin 2006, 280).
37 Also involved were Société Générale, Banque de Paris et des Pays-Bas, CL, Crédit Industriel et Commercial, Société des Dépôts et Comptes Courants, Banque d'Escompte de Paris, Séligmann Frères (see Loizillon 2013, 51).
38 Between 1875 and 1913, the amount of French capital invested abroad tripled.
39 Kohn Reinach & Cie, Türr, to Compoir d'Escompte, 13.4.1882, CEP DS 070.
40 Türr to Compoir d'Escompte, 13.4.1882, CEP DS 070.
41 There were similar founder shares in the Panama company as well (see Mack 1944, 311).
42 French state bonds had an interest rate of only 4%.
43 Türr to Comptoir d'Escompte, 20.4.1882, CEP DS 070.
44 An obituary in N. N. 1885.
45 See in general: Porter (1995); Smith (1990).

46 Dauzats to Türr, 5.12.1881, CEP DS070.
47 Ibid.
48 Gérod to Compoir d'Escompte 1.5.1882, CEP DS 069; Lullin to Comptoir d'Ecscompte 21.4.1882, ibid.; Banque de Crédit Industriel de Grèce, 21./3.5.1888, CEP DS 070; Banque de Crédit Industriel de Grèce, 21./3.5.1888, ibid.; Kohn Reinach & Cie to Comptoir d'Escompte, 6.5.1882, ibid.
49 Lullin to Comptoir d'Escompte, 5.5.1882, CEP DS 069, tr. by K.S. Travelling to Corinth for the start of work was though too much for Lullin.
50 For instance Aterio Rostard to Deufert, 29.4.1882, CEP DS 069. In this case, the refusal was said to be due to the fact that all locally available resources in Marseille had just been put into recently issued local bonds so no capital was available. Furthermore, Marseille had not fully recovered from the last crisis. As both the Greek national loans were traded at the Marseille exchange, it was also expected that the Greek 'colony' would not have any further interest in Greek papers, as communicated by a representative of the group. In the end, Marseille participated after all.
51 The following, among many others, participated in the syndicate: the ETE (who took 1,200 and 40 founder shares), Crédit Industriel à Athenès (5,300 and 110), Oscar de Reinach (1,020 and 34), Hentsch Lutsches & Cie (300 and 100), G. Victor (1,500 and 50), LB Wyse (1,500 and 50), Banque d'Escompte de Paris (1,800 and 60), Hottinguer (540 and 18), Kohn, Reinach & Cie (3,000 and 100), Banque de Paris & des Pays Bay (6,000 and 200), Lullin & Cie (1,500 and 50), Hoskier (150 and 5), Banque Franco Egyptienne (2,820 and 94), Heine (990, number of founder shares illegible), CEP (9,300, number of founder shares illegible). See List of subscribers, no date, CEP DS 70. Also see Bonin (2014b, 45, 47).
52 Concerning the role of ETE and other Greek bankers see Ζακυνθινού-Ξάνθη, M. [Zakinthinou-Xanthi, M.] et al. (2018). Here, rich graphic material is provided.
53 See the proofs of various newspaper articles with corrections CEP DS 069.
54 Comptoir d'escompte, Form dated 12.5.1882, CEP DS 069.
55 Bulletin de la SICC, No 1, 21.9.1882, 5. Greeks abroad and in Greece subscribed to shares worth 12 million francs (see Glasemann 2010, 8). The shareholder structure seems to have soon shifted however: in 1883, 60,000 shares were distributed among just 3,270 shareholders. 30,500 shares were now held in France, 15,600 in Switzerland, only 5,300 in Greece, 3,000 in Rumania, 2,000 in Italy, 500 each in Turkey, Germany, Belgium and Spain, and 1,600 in various other countries; see Bulletin de la SICC, No 9, 15.11.1883, 2. It is not possible to determine the number of Greeks abroad holding shares from these figures. At this time, it seems that a few large shareholders dominated the company: at the 1883 general meeting in Paris were, e.g. only 233 shareholders (ca. 7%) but they controlled more than 26,429 shares (44%). Bulletin de la SICC, No 9, 15.11.1883, 2.
56 Bulletin de la SICC, No 1, 21.9.1882, 1, tr. by K.S. In the first year, the annual subscription cost one franc; the costs were then increased to two francs in France and three francs abroad.
57 Bulletin de la SICC, No 1, 21.9.1882, 2.
58 Prospectus for the Canal Maritime de Corinthe, CEP DS 069. It was very unlikely that the bonds would be suitable for small investors.
59 Bulletin de la SICC, No 1, 21.9.1882, 1. These calculations were carried out by the 'principales Sociétés de navigation Françaises et Austro-Hongroises' and thus totally reliable.
60 Contemporaries were well aware of the explosion of costs in Suez, as shown by, e.g. the report by the German envoy Gutschmid to the AA, von Bismarck,

23.6.1881, BAR R 901-951 AA. The information sent to the AA was then published in *Norddeutsche Allgemeine Zeitung*, 5.7.1881.

61 Bulletin de la SICC, No 3, 10.1.1883, 6; No 8, 29.9.1883, 3; No 31, 15.11.1886, 4; No 13, 15.5.1884, 1.

62 Bulletin de la SICC, No 17, 5.12.1884, 4, tr. by K.S.

63 Bulletin de la SICC, No 32, 31.12.1886, 3.

64 Bulletin de la SICC, No 18, 14.2.1885, 2f.

65 *Le Petit Journal*, cited from Bulletin de la SICC, No 8, 29.9.1883, 3.

66 *Le Moniteur des Intérêts maritimes*, cited from Bulletin de la SICC, No 8, 29.9.1883, 4, tr. by K.S.

67 Bulletin de la SICC, No 46, 30.6.1888, 2.

68 Ibid.

69 Bulletin de la SICC, No 1, 21.9.1882, 5; No 6, 16.6.1883, 4.

70 Bulletin de la SICC, No 14, 30.6.1884, 4, tr. by K.S.

71 Türr to de Lesseps, May 1881, in: Prospectus de Société Internationale canal maritime de Corithe, Emission de 60,000 Actions de 500 francs, CEP DS 070, tr. by K.S.

72 De Lesseps to Türr, no date, and Dauzats to Türr, 5.12.1881, in: Prospectus de Société Internationale canal maritime de Corithe, Emission de 60.000 Actions de 500 francs, CEP DS 070.

73 According to Papagiannopoulos, Türr had the ambition to emulate de Lesseps. But Papagiannopoulos believes that Türr demonstrated neither de Lesseps' diplomatic skill nor his excellent contacts in political and financial circles, even if he possessed a keen awareness of French interests. The significance of the canal for Greece was said to have been of less importance for Türr (see Παπαγιαννοπούλου [Papagiannopoulos] 1989, 44).

74 Bulletin de la SICC, No 1, 21.9.1882, 5.

75 *Revue économique et financière*, cited from Bulletin de la SICC, No 5, 21.4.1883, 3.

76 Report of General Fiquet, in: Bulletin de la SICC, No 2, 18.11.1882, 3.

77 The supervisory board brought together financial competence, engineering and shipping expertise, and relationships to Greece (e.g. Renieri as the governor of the ETE and the Athens banker Skouses). To underscore their seriousness, the SICC choose a building on Boulevard Haussmann (number 41) for their headquarters, the traditional address for a Parisian haute banque; see Bulletin de la SICC, No 1, 21.9.1882, 5.

78 Mayer, Il Canale di Corinto, 1884, quoted from: Bulletin de la SICC, No 15, 15.8.1884, 3, tr. by K.S.

79 Bulletin de la SICC, No 17, 5.12.1884, 4.

80 Bulletin de la SICC, No 33, 15.2.1887, 2, 4.

81 Bulletin de la SICC, No 41, 31.12.1887.

82 Bulletin de la SICC, No 36, 8.6.1887, 2.

83 Thus, the Banque d'Alsace et de Lorraine registered much too late with the CEP to be included in the syndicate. They nonetheless hoped to be able to participate as they had so enthusiastically issued the shares for Suez and Panama. Banque d'Alsace et de Lorraine to Comptoir d'Escompte, 4.5.1882, CEP DS 069.

84 Bulletin de la SICC, No 2, 18.11.1882, 6.

85 See, e.g. *Allgemeine Zeitung*, 29.12.1888, BAR R 901-9531 AA.

86 The importance of expert cultures for the establishment of cultures of trust in the nineteenth century is emphasised by Berghoff 2004, **66f.** Also see **141 n.239** in this book.

87 Bulletin de la SICC, No 1, 21.9.1882, 5.

88 For a collection of photographs of bridges, halls, etc., built by the company since 1869 in France and abroad, see N. N. 1910.
89 Bulletin de la SICC, No 18, 14.2.1885, 2.
90 Bulletin de la SICC, No 6, 16.6.1883, 4.
91 Bulletin de la SICC, No 39, 7.10.1887, 1.
92 This was also mentioned in the German press, e.g. *Norddeutsche Allgemeine Zeitung* 21.5.1882. Reference was made to Türr's marriage to Wyse-Bonaparte.
93 Bulletin de la SICC, No 14, 30.6.1884, 1.
94 Bulletin de la SICC, No 38, 12.8.1887, 1f.
95 Bulletin de la SICC, No 8, 29.9.1883, 3, tr. by K.S.
96 Bulletin de la SICC, No 28, 30.6.1886.
97 Bulletin de la SICC, No 46, 30.6.1888, 2. See more generally: Kraemer et al. (1985), Ingenieurkunst auf der Pariser Weltausstellung.
98 Bulletin de la SICC, No 27, 15.5.1886, 46.
99 Anonymous newspaper article, no date, CEP DS 070, tr. by K.S.
100 A quote from a speech made at a conference by Alexandre R. de Dorn in the Oriental museum in Vienna; see Bulletin de la SICC, No 29, 16.8.1886, 2.
101 Speech by Türr at the Congrès géographique Venise, 1881, cited from Bulletin de la SICC, No 27, 15.5.1886, 4, tr. by K.S.
102 Bulletin de la SICC, No 17, 5.12.1884, 3.
103 Bulletin de la SICC, No 34, 21.3.1887, 3.
104 For example, in a report from the vice-consul from Piraeus, Varieux, to the MAE, 30.10.1862, as a copy, AN F 12 2670.
105 Bulletin de la SICC, No 29, 16.8.1886, 2.
106 Moniteur des intérêts maritimes, cited from: Bulletin de la SICC, No 10, 29.12.1883, 3.
107 Bulletin de la SICC, No 4, 24.2.1883, tr. by K.S.
108 The graphic design of the bond certificate of 1888 (Figure II.6.2) is identical to that of the first share from 1882. This is printed in Glasemann (2010, 26).
109 Correspondance Bleue, 28.12.1882, cited from Bulletin de la SICC, No 3, 10.1.1883, 5.
110 They thus brought to light, e.g. the entrance gates to the Isthmian Games and inscriptions from Justinian times; see Bulletin de la SICC, No 5, 21.4.1883, 1.
111 Engel, Eduard: Un printemps en Grèce, first printed in a leading Berlin newspaper which is not named, and then as a monograph (Engel 1887), translated into French by Eugène Remy, in: Bulletin de la SICC, No 30, 30.9.1886.
112 A. de Lorquin, Le canal de Corinthe, in: *France Industrielle*, 12.7.1886, cited from Bulletin de la SICC, No 29, 6, tr. by K.S.
113 La Grèce, in: Le Bulletin du Crédit, 11.3.1888, CEP DS 069, tr. by K.S.
114 *Revue économique et financière*, cited from Bulletin de la SICC, No 5, 21.4.1883, 3, tr. by K.S.
115 Speech by General Türr at the Congrès géographique Venise, 1881, cited from Bulletin de la SICC, No 27, 15.5.1886, 4, tr. by K.S. The perspective also penetrated the semantics, for instance, when readers were presented with figures showing that the proposed canal was only 6,342 metres long, just twice the length of the Champs-Elysées; see the report by General Fiquet in Bulletin de la SICC, No 2, 18.11.1882, 3.
116 *Moniteur des intérêts maritimes*, cited from: Bulletin de la SICC, No 10, 29.12.1883, 3, tr. by K.S.
117 Ricciardi suggests that the reason for this is a 'failure to contemplate the way human mistakes influence technological systems, the notion of overconfidence in scientific knowledge, inattentiveness to how technological systems perform

together as a whole, and failure to predict how people respond to safety procedures'.
118 Report by General Fiquet, in: Bulletin de la SICC, No 2, 18.11.1882, 3.
119 The use of the Roman republic as a reference in discussions of the British political system had lost popularity in Britain following the experiences of French and American republicanism (see Jenkyns 1980, 163–174; Turner 1989, 69).
120 Suite de la 1er délibération sur le projet de loi portant approbation de la convention provisoire de commerce entre la France et la Grèce, in: Chambre des Députés. Compte rendu in extenso – 38. Séance du 13 décembre 1888, in: Journal officiel du 14 décembre 1888, 2923ff.
121 Bulletin de la SICC, No 50, 31.12.1888, 3.
122 Many aspects of this image of Greece are found in Leconte (1847, 1–12).
123 *Le voleur illustré*, 25.5.1893.
124 Παπαγιαννοπούλου [Papagiannopoulos] (1989, 59) replicates the title page of Durocher. However, she wrongly identifies Ferdinand de Lesseps as George I of Greece and misses the satire's direction against Panama.
125 Basch demonstrates the use of this technique in writings by Émile Faguet.
126 Bulletin de la SICC, No 2, 18.11.1882, 6.
127 Named after Julius Schimmelbusch, a German pioneer of metallurgy (1826–1881).
128 Ferdinand de Lesseps to General Türr, quoted from: Bulletin de la SICC, No 11, 15.2.1884, 2.
129 Bulletin de la SICC, No 3, 10.1.1883, 1.
130 Bulletin de la SICC, No 14, 30.6.1884, 3.
131 Bulletin de la SICC, No 23, 15.10.1885, 2.
132 Bulletin de la SICC, No 21, 30.6.1885, 4.
133 Bulletin de la SICC, No 28, 30.6.1886, 5.
134 Bulletin de la SICC, No 34, 21.3.1887, 2.
135 Bulletin de la SICC, No 49, 22.11.1888, 2.
136 Bulletin de la SICC, No 35, 4.5.1887, 2.
137 Banque d'épargne et de crédit to Comptoir d'Escompte, no date, CEP DS 068.
138 SICC, Note sur le transit futur du Canal de Corinthe, CEP DS 068.
139 SICC, Situation, CEP DS 068.
140 SICC, Situation 1.1.1887, CEP DS 068.
141 Ibid., tr. by K.S.
142 Ibid.
143 Report by Engineer Bazaine, in: Bulletin de la SICC, No 36, 8.6.1887, supplement.
144 Banque Fédérale to Comptoir d'Escompte 2.3.1888, CEP DS 068.
145 List of subscribers from 8.3.1888, CEP D 068.
146 At CEP, ETE, Société Générale de Crédit mobilier Italien, Banque de Crédit Italien, MM Delloye et Cie, MM Morpurgo et Parente, Banque de Roumanie, see Prospectus SICC, Souscription publique à 60.000 Obligations 6% de 500 francs, CEP DS 068.
147 Lavigerie to CEP, Denfert-Rochereau, 1.3.1888, CEP D 068. *Lavigerie, L'Echo de la Bourse, Economie Financière, Gazette, Pays Financier, Eclaireur, Journal de Bruxelles, Courrier de Bruxelles, Soir, Chronique, Réforme, Etoile, Moniteur des Intérêts Matériels, Cote libre, Le Rapide, Capitaliste Belge, Agence Havas, Indépendance Belge, Opinion, Écho de Bruxelles, Semaine Industrielle* and *Moniteur du Commerce* were in this group.
148 Corinthe et le comptoir d'escompte, in: *Le Bulletin du Crédit*, 11.3.1888, CEP CS 068.

149 Ibid.
150 Le canal de Corinthe, in: *Finance Nouvelle*, 1.3.1888, CEP CS 068, tr. by K.S.
151 *Berliner Börsen Zeitung*, 6.9.1888.
152 However, it must have been clear that the shareholders would now receive about 30 francs less per year because this amount would go to the holders of the bonds – the calculation was thus kinder than that of the CEP; see L'émission du canal de Corinthe, in: *Le Figaro*, 3.3.1888, CEP CS 068.
153 Denfert to Lullin, 18.1.1889, CEP CS 068, tr. by K.S.
154 Note 'Corinthe', January 1889, CEP D 068.
155 Türr's report at the general meeting, in: Bulletin de la SICC, No 55, 17.7.1889, 1. After the SICC had managed, with the help of an advance, to pay the last coupon, the shares immediately rose back to 130, the bonds to 300. Παπαγιαννοπούλου [Papagiannopoulos] (1989, 40) estimates fairly correctly the spending thus far to total 42 million, while Werner (1993, 51) speaks only of 35 million.
156 German legate in Athens to AA, von Bismarck, 12.3.1889, R 901-9531 AA.
157 Bulletin de la SICC, No 55, 17.7.1889, 2.
158 Ibid., 3.
159 Türr to Renieri, 10/22.6.1889, in: Bulletin de la SICC, No 55, 17.7.1889, 3f.
160 Bulletin de la SICC, No 56, 1.8.1889.
161 This observation was also made by the German legation in Athens; see German legate Le Maistre to AA, von Bismarck, 14.1.1889, R 901-9531 AA.
162 'Whether our shipping has sufficiently great interest in the accomplishment of the aforesaid canal project to justify the provision of a state contribution for the same, I do not want to presume to decide. Only in relation to the person of General Türr I would like, in view of the imminent visit of the same to Berlin, to dutifully recall that the political sympathies of the same are indeed with the French side and that he at times finds himself obliged to provide a French law gazette published here, the Messager d'Athènes, with articles that are not friendly to Germany and Your Serene Highness. The erstwhile leader of insurgents is married to a Miss Wise-Bonaparte, a sister of the notorious erstwhile Mmd. Ratozzi, but is otherwise a man of quite good manners and very well regarded'. German legate, Le Maistre, to AA, von Bismarck, 8.3.1889, R 901-9531 AA, tr. by K.S. Türr actually did sharply criticise the German Empire about the partitioning of Poland and the annexation of Alsace-Lorraine (see Türr 1878a, 27, 30).
163 AA to Oberregierungsrath von Rottenburg, 24.3.1889, R 901-9531 AA, tr. by K.S.
164 German legation in Athens, Le Maistre, to AA, von Bismarck, 11.6.1889, R 901-9531 AA.
165 German legation in Athens, von Tschirschky, to AA, von Bismarck, 1.7.1889, R 901-9531 AA, tr. by K.S.
166 The *Messanger d'Athènes* and *L'Ephéméris*, cited in: Bulletin de la SICC, No 56, 1.8.1889, 1f.
167 Syngros to Antoine, 22./4.8.1889, CEP DS 073.
168 Report by B. Gerster to A. Syngros, 5.3.1891, as a copy, ETE A1S25YA'F29. Gester was in favour of additional protection for the walls of the canal and recommended starting the preparations for operating the canal punctually.
169 Prospectus SHCC, Emission de 46.667 Obligations 6% de 1ère Hypothèque, CEP DS 070. Engineers could rarely be held accountable for malpractice (see Pohle-Fraser 1999, 194). On the Mission française, **192f**. in this book.
170 Glasemann (2010) claims 10,000 bonds each of 500 francs, 12.
171 Prospectus SHCC, Emission de 46.667 Obligations 6% de 1ère Hypothèque, CEP DS 070. In another version, the ETE was named as providing the guarantee for

the interest payments; see Announcement of the emission by CEP, 23.6.1890, ETE A1S25YA'F29.
172 Prospectus SHCC, Emission de 46.667 Obligations 6% de 1ère Hypothèque, CEP DS 070.
173 Liquidateur Philis to CEP, 23.6.1890, CEP DS 070, Folder: Rapports, prospectus, extraits de journaux.
174 Türr was to receive a severance payment of 800–900,000 francs in return for his agreement, and was to be permitted to keep his real estate and house in Corinth. Türr complained that Syngros later failed to remember this agreement; see Türr to CEP, 29.7.1892, CEP DS 073. In contrast, Glasemann suggested that Türr received a severance payment of 13 million gold francs, an astronomical sum (see Glasemann 2010, 13).
175 MAE to the French ministry of finance, 20.10.1890, CAEF B-0031223-3.
176 Acte de Syndicat. Obligations et actions de la SHCC, CEP DS 070.
177 On this banking house (see Paris 2001; Chatziioannou 2010, 236).
178 Emil Erlanger (with 800 bonds, i.e. 95,200 francs), Crédit Algerien (800 = 95,200), Banque Internationale (2000 = 238,000), Crédit Suisse (400 = 47,600), Seligmann (200 = 23,800), Zarifi London (800 = 95,200), Zafiropoulo (800 = 96,200), Kohn, Reinach & Cie (2000 = 238,000), Banque Hellénique de Crédit the same, Zafiropoulo Zarifi (200 = 238,000). Liste Syndicat Obligations Corinthe, CEP DS 070.
179 Le canal de Corinthe, in: *La revue économique et financière* 24/25.6.1890, CEP DS 070, file: Rapports, prospectus, extraits de journaux.
180 *Le Courrier d'Etat*, 18.7.1890, cited from *Le National,* ibid, tr. by K.S.
181 Philis to Comptoir d'Escompte, Vlasto, 20.9.1890, CEP DS 071.
182 Séance du Comité, Syndicat Corinthe, 5.1.1891, ETE A1S25YA'F29.
183 Comptoir d'Escompte, Vlasto to Syngros, 24.7.1890, CEP DS 071. Vlasto regretted that Streit gave up the office. See on Streit **320 n.6** in this book.
184 Vangelis to Andreas Syngros, 20.2.1893, CEP DS 073.
185 Letter of complaint from the shareholders, CEP 073.
186 Circular from the SHCC, 27.12.1894, CEP DS 073.
187 SHCC to Vlasto, 29./11.5.1894, CEP DS 073.
188 Procès-verbaux. Canal de Corinthe, réunion du 16 décembre 1905, CEP DS 195. The initiative was taken by a Mr Papanicolaou, who was supported by the BA. When asked, the director Ioannis Pesmazoglou (**337–339** in this book) affirmed that he had withdrawn from that speculation; see Canal de Corinthe. Défense des intérêts français, 12.2.1906, ETE A1S25YA'F29.
189 Note sur la question du canal de Corinthe, no date, ETEA1S25YA'F29.
190 Glasemann (2010, 16).

7

GROUNDED IN A MARSH

The Lake Copais Company

Agriculture and land improvement in the nineteenth century

Another project into which foreign investment flowed in the 1880s was intended to improve Greek agriculture. On 6 October 1886, John Cockburn Francis Lee, engineer and substantial investor from London, signed a contract with the Compagnie française pour le dessèchement et l'exploitation du Lac Copaïs (CFC). This contract involved the transfer of the concession held by the French company, founded in 1880, to drain and exploit Lake Copais in Boeotia, where the land was known to be uncommonly fertile.[1] Lee paid £500,000 for the concession, almost £100,000 more than the French company had spent thus far. His own British company had capital totalling £1 million, which was intended to cover not only the purchase of the concession, but also the costs of drainage and the cultivation of the farming land thus gained. The area was to be transformed from a malaria-ridden marsh, annually inundated by large-scale flooding, into a blossoming garden, to the benefit of Greece and the West European investors.

The project was the only large-scale agricultural undertaking on the Balkans funded by foreign investors in the nineteenth century (Lampe/Jackson 1982, 187; Glasemann 2010, 14). Agriculture was of fundamental economic importance for the societies of Southeast and Central Europe at the time: 'the world was a world of farmers' (Osterhammel 2010, 314, tr. by K.S.). The nineteenth century brought not only the industrial revolution, but also an 'agricultural revolution' with fundamental structural transformations spread over many decades.[2] In many regions of the world, the century saw the emancipation of the peasants, usually involving uprisings and revolts. Agricultural methods became generally more scientific, e.g. through the use of guano fertilisers, artificial fertilisers, special crop rotation techniques and improved irrigation systems. This led to increased productivity, and the growing population created a ready market for the goods. Estimated agricultural production increased worldwide by 1.06% annually in the period between 1870 and 1913, although per capita production grew more slowly. Simultaneously, the product range was diversified and tropical products

DOI: 10.4324/9780429286537-10

like coffee, cocoa, palm oil and cotton became more important (ibid., 315f.; Beckert 2015). Until the end of the century, there continued to be failed harvests and famines in many regions, e.g. in India (Tauger 2011, 104). At the same time, agricultural production focused increasingly on market requirements, as so-called 'capitalist farming' developed (ibid., 81, 84). Europeans attempted to transform tradition farming systems in the colonies in Asia and Africa by introducing European agricultural methods, often forcibly and without consideration of local needs, drawing the regions into a Eurocentric world trade system (ibid., 81). Private, often globally active companies played a key role in the processing and trading of agricultural products. Modern transportation allowed the globalisation of agricultural trading on a worldwide market where competition was ubiquitous (ibid., 90; Engel 2013). Thus at the end of the 1870s, competition from the USA was largely responsible for the falling grain prices, leading to the introduction of protective tariffs in many European countries, e.g. in Germany, France and Italy (Tauger 2011, 91). The role of the state in the transformation of agriculture was not limited to regulating the conditions of foreign trade. Governments also intervened with regard to property rights and attempted to facilitate modernisation, e.g. by granting credit.[3] Nonetheless, strong price fluctuations repeatedly endangered the livelihoods of farmers, especially as their political weight was declining in comparison to that of other social groups.[4] At the same time, the romantic era saw the idealisation of rural life among the European elites, especially in England where the 'cultural ideals of a pre-industrial rural life' continued to be dominant (Osterhammel 2010, 316, tr. by K.S.; Tauger 2011, 92).

In England, the homeland of the investor Lee, agriculture changed as production became increasingly industrialised, e.g. with the abolition of the commons, often resulting in serious social conflicts as early as the seventeenth and eighteenth centuries (ibid., 86f.).[5] Landowners in England leased their land to tenants whose labourers then often lived below the poverty line (ibid., 87f.). Until 1846, the Corn Laws protected British producers from foreign competition, but after this date, the government upheld a commitment to free trade. In the 1870s, the British farmers therefore experienced strong competition and the grain prices fell (Jones 1976, 18f.).[6] The leaseholders of agricultural land managed to negotiate a reduction in the duties they paid and the range of products grown diversified. Between 1884 and 1891, when the Lake Copais Company (LCC) was founded, Britsh agriculture then showed signs of recovery (Hooper 1955, 15).

Bank loans were not commonly used to finance agriculture by leaseholders in nineteenth-century England, and neither was finance obtained on the stock exchange. This was because of the small size of farms in England and the rather low profit margins in comparison to industry (ibid., 17f.).[7] In contrast, the stock exchange played an important role in the financing of agricultural projects in the colonies. It is therefore not surprising that a British investor interested in agricultural projects should turn to a 'colonial' country like Greece, especially as the conditions there made land reclamation seem an attractive prospect. The growing Greek population was one factor which contributed to strong increases in agricultural production in the 1870s and 1880s,[8] but new property relations also played an important role. After decades of debate, in 1871, the national estates were finally distributed among the population; this concerned the areas that the Greek state had acquired from the Ottoman Empire or Ottoman landowners in 1830 (Karouzou [Καρούζου] 2018). The estates had previously been cultivated by smallholders, either as tenants with very expensive leases or without a legal basis through anarchical occupation (Petmezas 2013, 89). Now the government was forced to release the land to the farmers as private property because population growth demanded agricultural intensification and the cultivation of more land. In 1861, only 16.2% of the land was cultivated (Papadopoulos 1993, 78), which was not enough to feed the growing population. It was hoped that once the farming smallholders owned their land, they would carry out the necessary land improvements and increase yields. Furthermore, the smallholders were to be a primary element in support for the monarchy. The distribution process began in 1871 and continued for the next 40 years. In areas where the land was not part of the national estates, it was mostly already owned by smallholders, who on average cultivated an area of just 50–200 stremmata. Usually, land was equally divided between all the heirs on the death of the owner, which led to a continuous increase in the fragmentation of agricultural property (Lampe/Jackson 1982, 186). When land was leased, the system was one of sharecropping where contracts were usually drawn up for just one year. A lease of about 5% was charged. In addition, the farmers paid taxes of about 10%; in many places, their situation was precarious. It was therefore urgently necessary to create new fertile agricultural land in Greece. Unlike in France, Germany or England, however, little of the land was actually used for the cultivation of grain. Traditionally, much less grain was grown than was required. Large amounts were imported, which negatively influenced the Greek trade balance (ibid.). As a result, in the 1880s, in contrast to the countries named earlier, Greece profited greatly from the low prices for grain imports.[9] The country's own agriculture was at the time increasingly specialised and focused on luxury goods, especially raisins and currants, but also tobacco, dried fruits, citrus fruits and olive oil, ideal products for the families of farming smallholders to produce. The export of these products brought large profits: international trade constituted the engine of agricultural growth in Greece, and it was possible to significantly reduce the trade deficit (Petmezas 2013, 91f.).[10] The importance of agriculture grew against the background of the delayed and sluggish industrialisation of the 1870s to 1890s, even though the poor infrastructure conditions (railway construction was in its infancy) led to great regional discrepancies (ibid., 93). The growing significance of agriculture in Greece was strengthened by the devastation caused among the French vineyards by phylloxera, which meant that France needed to import large quantities of raisins.[11] Wine and grapes could be grown on less fertile ground but the other specialist crops required especially rich soils and in some cases irrigated land – just the sort that could be reclaimed from the marshland of Copais.

The idea of reclaiming land by draining marshes can be traced back to antiquity in many parts of the world and is seen throughout medieval times (Blackbourn 2007, 11). At all times, people have tried to win new estates by drainage. Conflicts were always an inevitable part of land improvement as the marshes were not unpeopled, even in their original state. Water levels changed through the seasons, allowing some areas of the marshes to be cultivated in the summer; the wet meadows provided emergency grazing in the hot summer months; and the residents fished the waters or used the reeds (ibid., 18f.).[12] 'The aim of the natural economy was not profit maximisation, it was rather the maintenance of a complex subsistence system [...] whereby consideration of ecological aspects to minimise economic risks played an important role' (Guderman 2000, 6, tr. by K.S.). From the start of the modern era, the marshes became subject to more intensive change, producing both winners and losers and increasing social tensions (ibid., 2). The investigation of the conflicts that developed in the context of this 'social appropriation of nature' is a significant aspect of more recent research on land improvement (ibid., 12), also in the only detailed study of Lake Copais by Papadopoulos (Papadopoulos 1993). Unfortunately, his thesis neglects to compare the social conflicts of Copais with those of land improvement projects in other regions and epochs. But this contextualisation is urgently required considering the long and regionally dispersed history of these techniques. Thus, the colonisation of the fens in Holland and in East Friesland dates back to the beginning of the early modern era (Blackbourn 2007, 179), in the sixteenth century, many wetlands were drained in Italy (Ciriacono 1995, 282) and the great era of land drainage in France saw about 15,000–25,000 hectares of marshland being drained between 1599 and 1650 (Morera 2011, 10). Nine of these projects have been investigated in detail by Raphaël Morera (ibid.). They were financed by private companies, often with inputs of Dutch capital and know-how; state involvement was limited to defining and guaranteeing a reliable legal framework for the projects. This allowed a large number of investors to participate and the risks to be widely spread. The profits earned by the investors are difficult to reconstruct but Morera estimates them at 5–18% on average, which was very high for the pre-industrial era (ibid., 218). 'In the modern epoch the exploitation of the earth constitutes the basis for wealth creation. The conquest of the marshes thus counted as one of the most lucrative activities of the seventeenth century' (ibid., 13, tr. by K.S.). Such companies were often run by members of the elite from the inner circles of the central government. They invested in land drainage to exploit the potential returns (ibid., 240). Their involvement guaranteed the stability of the business and the security of investments, but also led to the strengthening of central government (ibid., 237). All of the drainage projects were affected by conflicts between the investors and the residents of the marshland or the local elites. Such resistance had to be broken but could seldom be completely abolished – the projects always also involved the enforcement of power (ibid., 2; Blackbourn 2007, 14). Over time, the local urban elites became increasingly involved in the companies. The large amounts of capital required for further improvements, maintenance and renovation through the centuries meant that these new investments were urgently required (Morera 2011, 235). Thus between 1820 and 1850, 76 new companies were founded to drain marshlands in France; these companies were placed under the state supervision of the prefectures and their functions precisely regulated by the law. For the period between 1790 and 1915, Yannis Suire even speaks of a 'seduction, an ecstasy in response to the marshes that were rediscovered' (Suire 2006, 341, tr. by K.S.). Particularly in the 1880s, a new wave of development plans emerged (ibid., 348, 371). The idea of harnessing nature remained the same, but the tone changed 'from the sunny optimism of the enlightenment of the 18th century' to the 'unshakeable belief in science and progress of the 19th century' (Blackbourn 2007, 12, tr. by K.S.). Conflicts continued, e.g. between neighbouring settlements with their very different interests (Dessaux 1998, 326–327, 531–571). From the mid-nineteenth century, increased attempts were made in Northern Germany to find legal solutions to the conflicts rather than using force, as in the case of the fens in East Friesland. The rights of those affected by the projects were strengthened (Gudermann 2000, 482; Blackbourn 2007, 15). One reason for this was that the 'internal colonisation' in Prussia served to secure new state territory, e.g. after the annexing of Hannover in 1866 (ibid., 180). At this time, land improvement funds and a state cultural apparatus were established to support the intensive initiatives aimed at land improvement (ibid., 182). David Blackbourn describes how the financial situation of the fen projects in Northern Germany varied widely: while some projects flourished and supported a population of several thousands, in other areas the impoverished marsh farmers struggled to survive (Blackbourn 2007, 185). The leasing conditions (size of land parcels, cost of the lease, fees for extra services such as lock dues and the duration of contracts) played an important role, as did the quality of the peat and the canals. Until the mid-nineteenth century, most of the projects in Northern Germany were also financed by private companies (ibid., 185). Around the turn of the century, an increasing number of fen colonies then developed under the aegis of the state; lessons had been learnt from failed attempts in the past and the focus was now on smaller projects where technical uncertainties could be more easily mastered (Gudermann 2000, 484). In the USA, the state was also involved in drainage projects, both in the financing of developments and in forcing the participation of unwilling landowners in the name of the common good (Meyer 2004, 93).

In England, where the Copais investors originated,[13] a veritable euphoria surrounded land improvement from the 1840s, not least because mass production of the necessary materials sharply reduced the costs (Phillips 1989, 167).[14] The focus here was on improving wet and heavy soils through drainage, rather than on reclaiming land from marshes. The projects were usually financed by both owners and tenants. On the one hand, such large-scale projects were impossible without the participation of the aristocracy and the landowners used the plans to attract new tenants (ibid., 168). On the other hand, after the projects were completed, the installations continued to require intensive maintenance which could only be provided by the local farmers (ibid.). In 1849, the General Land Drainage Company was founded (after 1852: Lands Improvement Company) to provide loans for the development of agricultural enterprises and the improvement of land (Hooper 1955, 78).[15] This company was necessary because it was difficult to find private investors as the profits were much lower than those from investments in industry, although they were also safer in the long term.[16] The enthusiasm of the 1840s had already greatly abated by the 1870s.

Some of the large drainage projects attracted international attention, such as the draining of Lago Fucino in Italy. Like Lake Copais, Lago Fucino was enclosed by high mountains and had also been the object of various unsuccessful drainage attempts in antiquity (Linoli 2005, 168). Concrete plans for draining the lake emerged in the 1830s but it was initially impossible to raise finance. In 1850, the Roman banker Alessandro Torlonia (Felisini 2016) took over the project and its financing – a rather unusual approach as most land improvement schemes for large marsh areas in Europe were financed through capital transfer from abroad (Ciriacono 1995, 300). Torlonia was wont to say that either he would dry out the lake or the lake would dry out him – an indication of the manifold technical difficulties that needed to be overcome in the course of the work. By 1875, the lake had then completely disappeared. Torlona cultivated some of the reclaimed land himself and sold other sections at a high price, leading to severe social tensions with the local farmers.[17] Nonetheless, the project was judged to be a success, not least thanks to the way in which it was presented by the head engineer (Brisse/Rotrou 1876). It seems that the CFL in Greece later took over workers and engineers from the previous Italian project (Papadopoulos 1993, 131).

The marsh of Copais

Lake Copais lay in the heart of Boeotia, between the cities of Thebes, Livadia and Lamia (Papadopoulos 1997, 365; Λάμπρος [Lampros] 2000). The lake was surrounded by the high mountains of Parnassus, and fed by five rivers although only one of these, the River Melas, carried water all year round. The marshland of Copais covered about 25,000–26,000 hectares in the mid-nineteenth century, although the waterlogged area shrunk to about a third of this in the summer months. The humus layer was three to four metres deep and exceedingly fertile, thanks to the minerals which were leached out of the mountains and organic deposits in the water. There were, however, many roots and reeds that had to be cleared before cultivation could begin (Papadopoulos 1997, 365). The water rose to its highest point in early May before falling again, thanks to evaporation and runoff through the so-called katavothres, cave-like underground channels that led through the mountains towards the sea (CΓC 1884a, 3). Even in Mycenaean and classical times,[18] attempts had been made to facilitate the runoff and lower the water levels by enlarging the channels and building additional ones.[19] This was intended to make much of the lake area cultivable. Alexander the Great also planned work at Lake Copais.

The first West European travellers to the area after independence attested to the great potential of the region. Friedrich Thiersch, for instance, travelled around Greece[20] in 1831, visiting the ruins of Mantinea and ancient Orchomenus and reporting on the plateau in the mountains:

> Everywhere surrounded by mountains, there is only an underground outlet for the waters in the eastern corner. It is a gaping, now quite dry, rocky cavity in which one can enter and take about forty steps before it contracts into smaller openings. Some of these are silted up. With these obstructed drains, the water, which collects from all the mountains through the winter, therefore transforms a large part of the valley into a lake, which runs away too late in the summer for it to be possible to till the fields. It is characteristic of the poor husbandry of the Kapodistrias′ administration that people have not got round to, no not even thought of, cleaning and enlarging the holes through the dispatch of the silt, as occurred in earlier times, sometimes even under the Turks, in this way securing the most fruitful land for cultivation.[21]

Perhaps due to these lines, which were printed in the newspaper *Allgemeine Zeitung* (without the reference to Kapodistrias), King Otto[22] sent his representative Forchhammer to Boeotia, and in June 1834, Forchhammer reported back. He related the legends of residents of the surrounding villages and discussed whether the visible shafts and ditches in the rock were the result of human activities, which he strongly doubted. He advised cleaning the deposits and obstacles from the existing katavothres and, in the course of doing so, checking whether there had once been a channel under the reeds that could be dredged. Forchhammer closed by referring to the saga of the Sphinx and Oedipus and recommended the enlightened motto 'Help yourself and heaven will help you'.[23] Against the background of the disastrous financial state of Greece, no further activities materialised, but the painter Karl Rottmann included a drawing of Lake Copais in his collection for Munich (Papayannis 1992a, 165).[24]

Ten years later, in 1844, the idea of financing the project with foreign capital first emerged, thanks to Gustave d'Eichthal. He had visited the katavothres during his travels through Boeotia in 1834.[25] The serious flooding in winter and the prevalence of fever in summer led him to advise moving the town of Livadia. The marsh itself could, he suggested, best be used for rearing cattle or water buffalo.[26] Gustave's former superior in the Greek ministry of the interior, Ioannis Kolettis, had been the Greek ambassador in Paris since 1835, and he probably discussed the project with the banker's son.[27] D'Eichthal seized on the idea and provided finance for a group of engineers from the Ponts et Chaussées to travel to Boeotia.[28] They were led by the young French engineer Clément Sauvage, who remained in the area for a year and drew up an extremely detailed report (Sauvage 1868),[29] including calculations of the amount of water that needed to be diverted and the pressures involved, a description of the soil and information about the residents of the surrounding settlements, their property and way of life. He drew positive conclusions concerning the feasibility of the project, the fertility of the soil and the existing irrigation, and even believed that there was a possibility of exploiting water power. However, he calculated the costs of the project to total at least 6 million francs and did not believe it would yield the quick profits required by a private company. He also anticipated difficulties attracting enough labour and colonists into the area.

> Lastly, we conclude by repeating again that the draining of Lake Copais is the finest operation that a government can undertake; but a company, however strong it may be, cannot speculate on a distant future and the operation would be impractical for such a company unless it were supported by high subsidies.[30]

D'Eichthal therefore abandoned his plan to found a company in cooperation with the Greek banker Sina, who resided in Vienna (Μέλιος [Melios]/Παπαδόπουλος [Papadopoulos] 1988, 1163). Unfortunately, the sources provide no information about his brother's opinion of the project. Gustave, who continued to have close links to the country, forwarded the Greek government the report free of charge (Sauvage 1868, III).

Sauvage's plan brought the idea of draining the lake to France, but it was not endorsed from all sides.[31] In 1850, another traveller, Émile Burnouf, suggested that the lake in the heart of the region was 'the principal reservoir of fresh water of Oriental Greece'. The strong evaporation of the water meant that the lake provided the most fertile region of Boeotia with urgently required precipitation.

> [I]n the body of animals the heart is the centre from whence life spreads into all parts, likewise Lake Copais is for the valley of Boeotia the origin and principle of all fertility.'

Drying out the lake would kill this 'source of life.[32] This remarkably early ecological reflection was not, however, able to influence opinion significantly. In the following years, French interest in the Copais region was limited to archaeology (Pittakïs 1857, 51–55). However, in 1850, the Greek government provided finance to clean the katavothres for the first time and in the especially dry year of 1856, a team of Greek engineers tackled the work, although they were unable to complete it before the waters returned (Papadopoulos 1993, 98). Was artificial drainage the answer? The Englishman Webster initiated a venture in Copais in 1858 but it did not prosper, although the reasons for this are unclear.[33] Nonetheless, this attempt led to the idea becoming popular in England.[34] In 1863, George I became the king of Greece. In his homeland Denmark, there were centuries of experience with land improvement (Ciriacono 1995, 283). The government then started intensive attempts to acquire foreign capital, also for Lake Copais, especially targeting wealthy Greeks abroad: in 1863 (and again in 1868), the head of the department of public works in the ministry of the interior, E. Manitaky, republished Sauvage's report with an extensive introduction. Here, he emphasised that the attitude of the Greek government to foreign investors had been transformed and promoted the project, explaining not only that new technology had emerged in the last 14 years, but also that the infrastructure of the region had also been greatly developed and the American civil war had led to increases in the price of cotton. Manitaky argued that under these circumstances, Sauvage's opinion would be more positive and that the Frenchman would certainly now recommend that a private company should undertake the project (Sauvage 1868, VIf.). This new publication fell on fertile ground in France, as demonstrated two years later by an essay by Eugène Yéméniz in the Saint-Simonian, pro-Greece *Revue des deux mondes* (Πολυκανδριώτη [Polikandrioti] 2012) in which Yéméniz intensively promoted investment in Greece in general and in Copais in particular, also making reference to the preliminary work undertaken in antiquity (Yéméniz 1865).[35] The Greek opposition did not want to leave such an important project to foreigners but demanded that the government should carry it out themselves (Papadopoulos 1993, 101). The government nevertheless continued to promote the venture abroad, especially in Paris. In the same year, the newly elected Greek prime minister Koumoundouros signed a contract with the Italian-French entrepreneur Sarrazin Momferrier, which parliament then failed to ratify. Momferrier therefore withdrew from the agreement and in 1867 surrendered his rights to the Frenchman Henry Bonnaire, Knight of the Legion of Honour and former Inspecteur général des finances (ibid., 103). The Greek parliament passed the draft legislation for the draining of Lake Copais, but only with extensive modifications. It is unclear whether this was the reason for Bonnaire's withdrawal from the venture or whether he was unable to find investors (ibid.). In 1876, an attempt was made by Greek banks, led by the ETE, to tackle the project, but this too was unsuccessful. The report commissioned from the French engineer Revol failed to convince the relevant Greek banking houses of the profitability of the undertaking (ibid., 110f.).[36] The sources are insufficient for an analysis of the risk management or motives of the financiers involved. However, one feature emerges clearly: leaving antiquity aside, the history of the Greek and French plans to drain Lake Copais dated back almost 50 years before they were finally implemented in 1880. The sources for the CFC are little better, which explains the brevity of the following discussion before the second British company takes centre stage.

The Compagnie française pour le dessèchement et l'exploitation du Lac Copaïs (CFC)

The first company set up to drain Lake Copais went by a French name and had its headquarters in France, but half of those involved were members of the Greek diaspora. The first step was undertaken by the Greek banker John D. Vouros who, with Stefanos Skouloudis acting as an intermediary, was able to negotiate an agreement with the Greek government that was signed on 30 May 1880. In October of the same year, the CFC was formed in Paris and bought the rights from Vouros for 4.8 million francs. The company had a capital of 15 million francs in 30,000 shares of 500 francs each. The extent to which the project fitted with contemporary images of nature being improved by a cultivating human hand is clearly indicated by the design of the shares by the Belgian painter Gustave Fraipont (see Figure II.7.1).[37]

The presentation of an uncultivated natural landscape with a cultivated, agricultural landscape underneath shows how the development of the marshland was romanticised at a time when 'tourism vert' was emerging and local elites were beginning to approach the natural phenomena of their surroundings 'scientifically', for instance, with photography, botany, ornithology and poetry (Suire 2006, 345). Barren earth and wasteland thus became the 'raw material of far-reaching social utopias' (Gudermann 2000, 480, tr. by K.S.). The CFC aimed to drain and cultivate the marsh of Copais and all other Greek wetlands that could be acquired (CFC 1880, 3). The company secured the ownership rights for 8,000 hectares (80,000 Greek stremmata) of the Lake Copais area and the exploitation rights for 99 years for the remaining 24,000 hectares of the lake. The company also gained permission to construct buildings as required in the port of Larymna. A 300,000-franc guarantee was included in the purchase price, which Vouros had been obliged to deposit with the Greek government. The government also reserved the right to demand a bond for 1.7 million francs as an additional guarantee from

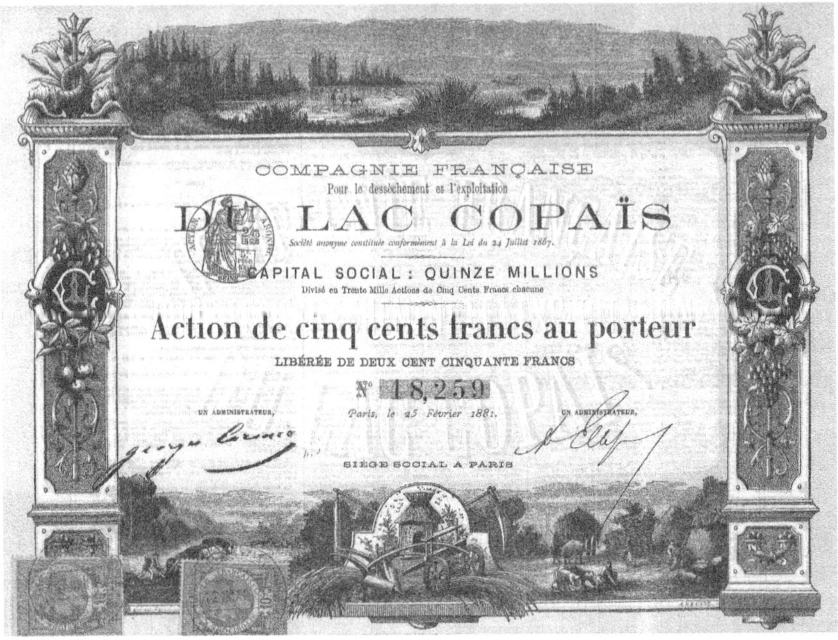

Figure II.7.1 Compagnie Française du Lac Copaïs. Action de cinq cents francs au porteur, 1881.

the company (Μέλιος [Melios]/Παπαδόπουλος [Papadopoulos] 1996, 3). The supervisory board of the CFC comprised an almost equal number of French and Greek members (CFC 1880, 9),[38] and included not only the president Markos Renieri, the governor of the ETE, but also Coronio and Georgios Athinogenis, the director of the Athens branch of the Bank of Constantinople and the brother-in-law of Stefanos Skouloudis. The latter became the administrator of the CFC (Papadopoulos 1993, 115).[39] There were a striking number of diaspora Greeks involved, reflecting increases in investments by this group in Greece at the time, motivated not least by growing competition in Egypt, Rumania, Russia and the Ottoman Empire (ibid., 112f.).

The company committed to using modern agricultural techniques to cultivate at least a third of the area (Papadopoulos 1993, 114).[40] However, there was a grace period of five months before a final building plan had to be submitted to the Greek government. This regulation was important because a year before completing the contract, an additional report was commissioned from the French engineers Moule and Tarrate. These experts suggested a different method of draining the lake to that proposed by Sauvage: the water was not to be drained through the mountain Ptoos but diverted from the large Lake Copais to the two smaller lakes Likiri and Paralimmi, which could then act as reservoirs for irrigating the reclaimed land (Μέλιος [Melios]/Παπαδόπουλος [Papadopoulos] 1996, 4). Three smaller canals were to merge into a large one that would then issue into the sea. The overall length of the canals was to be 80 km, while the tunnel leading to the sea would need to be 860-m long (CFC 1884a, 8). The costs for Moule's plan totalled 7.5 million franc, compared to the 6 million forecasted by Sauvage, but it was expected that the estate owned by the company would end up in the fertile part of the area and would thus be of greater value. The second model was thus selected. In 1882, the company commissioned an exact geographical map to illustrate the circumstances (see Figure II.7.2).

It was stipulated that the Greek government should carry out the necessary expropriations for the company, whereby compensation was to be paid in line with values before the beginning of the project.[41] Enormous profits were expected: an anonymous English memorandum from 1881 found in the company documents forecasted net profits of 5 million francs or 33%.[42]

However, the change of plan led to problems because to date only Sauvage's version had been accepted by the Greek parliament, not the new model. The necessary negotiations lasted two years as the opposition insisted on linking their acceptance of the new plans to numerous other modifications. Rapid changes of government complicated matters and various Greek interest groups collided in parliament, especially from the region affected.

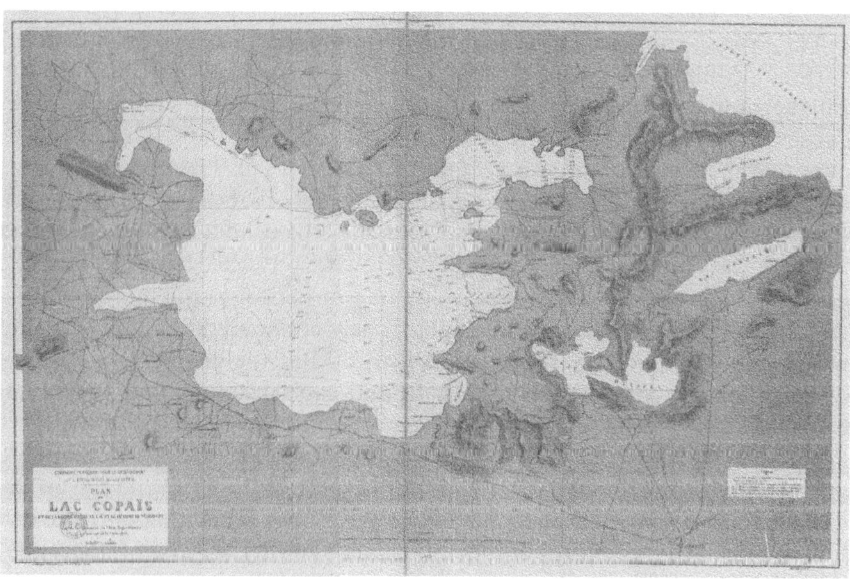

Figure II.7.2 Compagnie Française du Lac Copaïs: Plan du lac Copaïs et de la région entre le lac et le détroit de Négrepont, 1882.

The changed plans were positive for some local communities but catastrophic for others, depending on how the water levels would develop in the various districts (Papadopoulos 1993). While in the area of Lake Copais more land would be available for cultivation than originally planned, increases in the water levels of the two smaller lakes would lead to the flooding of existing farmland.[43] A fundamental problem was the unclear state of property rights: many local farmers regarded the areas that dried out in the summer as their property and not as belonging to the lake, which was officially part of the national estates. Several farmers could provide ownership titles from Ottoman times or from after 1871 when the national estates had been distributed, others invoked Common Law.[44] Together, all these claims were diametrically opposed to that of the CFC, which aspired to the entire area of the lake (Papadopoulos 1993, 120–125). As several of the large landowners of the region were also members of the Greek parliament, heated debates flared up. The local population had always favoured a cooperative solution in which they had a say, preferably without the interference of foreigners (Μέλιος [Melios] 1996, 3). It was September 1882 before a convention could be passed, and the disputes had not then been resolved, but had rather been passed on to the law courts. The company relinquished to the state an area of 15,000 stremmata, the location of which was not yet fixed; this was to be used to compensate legitimate property titles. In spring 1883, Ladislas Lerat, the contractor commissioned by the company, could begin with the work, which the convention stipulated should be completed by 1886 if the company were to avoid large contract penalties.

The French engineer Leon Pochet, who managed the work on site, faced various problems. Malaria incapacitated many workers (CFC 1884a, 10). Furthermore, there was dissatisfaction with the building contractors because of repeated delays. The case went to court and the CFC decided to continue the work on its own account (CFC 1884c, 3). The political unrest on the Balkans complicated the recruitment of workers as the Greeks were conscripted for military service and foreigners like the Italians were afraid to enter the country (CFC 1886/1887). However, Pochet believed that the hour was approaching 'when Lake Copais would be nothing more than the cultivated domain of Copais [...], laboriously conquered from nature, and which has no equal in Greece for fertility'.[45] But the problems were very difficult for the company to cope with and each delay created additional expenses.

The crucial issue was, in the end, not a technical one. A press campaign against Stephanos Skouloudis, the administrator of the CFC and the Greek ambassador to Spain, flared up in Greece. A number of newspapers regarded him as one of the 'vampires of the nation who, under the guise of honest patriots, would, if they could, put their country up for auction'.[46] Skouloudis was said to have abused his political power and persuaded the residents of his constituency to buy Copais shares at three times their actual value. He was accused of having sold 7,000 such shares in his constituency of Syra and 8,000 in Athens, although the project had no chance of success and was only intended to enrich his friends,[47] especially his brother-in-law Athinogenis of the Bank of Constantinople.[48] The Greek shareholders of the company were called upon to refuse the payment of further instalments.[49] Although not all the newspapers published such negative reports,[50] the campaign was enough for numerous shareholders to boycott further payments: many failed to provide the second half of the 500 francs. The company therefore ran out of money as it could not access all of the subscribed capital. In 1886, 1,080 shares, whose owners had refused to pay the instalments due, were annulled. The hope that the inauguration of the first large canal near Karditza, executed on time, could change the mood of the shareholders (CFC 1886, 12) was not fulfilled. But at least the inauguration was an opportunity for detailed press reports about the project.[51]

The inauguration of the canal as a media event

The majority of reports about the inauguration of the canal were published by the French specialist press. Thus, *Le Génie civil*, for instance, described the project in great detail, discussing many technical details and problems, and including all the plans and even the soil analyses.[52] *La Nature* compared the work with the aforementioned draining of Lago Fucino in Italy. Comparisons were also drawn with the gardens of Valencia and Malaga, the fertile plains of Lombardy and the oases of Algeria and Tunisia.[53] Much was made of the perfection of drainage techniques, which meant that such land reclamation projects were both safe and economical. At the same time, the work presented a good opportunity to further develop the technology.[54] It was expected that the project would be completed within three years.[55] Like *Le Génie civil*, most of the other magazines published photographs, sketches and plans of the work, which the company had made available to the press, thus actively encouraging the reporting. Almost all the publications emphasised the great cultural benefit that would accrue to the poor residents of the region, thanks to the reclamation and the combating of malaria.[56] However, few colonists were expected to come from Greece itself but rather from Italy as many Italians still emigrated to South America.[57] Most of the newspapers also used antiquity as an argument, citing the earliest attempts at draining the area from Mycenaean times and the era of Alexander the Great, both of which had failed. They argued that the technological advances of the present day now ensured the success of the undertaking.[58] Drawing on a statement given by the engineer Pochet, the hope was expressed that the Greek people would not forget this great feat of their French benefactors.[59] This instance of French aid for Greece was said not to be the only one: under the Trikoupis government, many tasks were being tackled with the help of French engineers and French capital, e.g. the construction of railways and roads.[60] Reference was also gladly made to the other large French project in Greece, the Canal of Corinth:

> Among the great projects that are attracting attention at the moment, two are located in Greece: the breaching of the Isthmus of Corinth and the draining of Copais; both are French projects. We insist upon this, to show once again that our race does not lack a spirit of enterprise.[61]

The strong position of the diaspora Greeks in the company was not mentioned in this context. The presence of the French ambassador and many French representatives at the celebrations was rather interpreted as evidence that this was a thoroughly French project. 'These important projects offer an opportunity to once again note a manifestation of French genius in the accomplishment of a project of great public interest'.[62] As had been the case with the Canal of Corinth, the land reclamation project was presented as part of the French mission to further civilisation. An entire province was to be rendered fertile and freed of disease through drainage and irrigation technology. Opponents of the venture in Greece who viewed it as a 'national disaster' were only mentioned in passing, if at all, and dismissed as 'leech-fishers'. They should rather submit to the 'divine law of work', because 'heaven will reward their efforts with rich harvests'.[63]

Even *The Times*, which had reported so negatively on Lavrion in the early 1870s, sent their Greece correspondent to the inauguration, who then composed a truly panegyric article. He described the region as a wide expanse of 'green-topped reeds, so famous in antiquity for their musical uses'[64] but went on to explain that even the ancient sagas recognised that such fever-ridden marshes harboured deadly danger, as demonstrated by Heracles' fight against the Lernaean hydra. The article continued with details of the ancient work undertaken by a 'mysterious race' in Copais, who in the time of Homer achieved 'an accuracy of calculation not surpassable by modern appliances'. The Mycenaean were unsuccessful because, like Alexander the Great, they lacked dynamite and steam power, but the author understood the present-day engineers as 'modern successor[s] to those mythical engineers'.[65] He described the great significance of the project, which was to affect an area twice as large as that of Lago Fucino in Italy, praised the fact that it seemed likely that the work would remain within budget and concluded with a reference to the Canal of Corinth, which he also lauded as a profitable venture.[66] Just three days later, the author continued with a second part of the article:

> Greece enjoys a geographical situation unrivalled, now as formerly, for participation in the commerce of the Mediterranean and the East. All that is needed for the restoration to it of much of the trade it once nearly monopolized is the co-operation of its citizens with

> the world's merchant fleets, which will be glad to pay them toll, if they prepare themselves to receive it.[67]

The author then elegantly linked this notion of contemporary economic cooperation back to his starting point, arguing that this internationally financed project would bring many incomparable archaeological treasures to light. The Greek government should allow foreigners to access these finds, making them 'available for study and enjoyment, as Greeks should be to the foreign skill and zeal which are endeavouring to recover for them the natural advantages they have long forgotten how to use'.[68]

Scientific expertise as the basis for decision making

This enthusiastic reporting did not, however, help the CFC. The defaulting shareholders could not be brought to reason and a painful gap in the budget resulted. It became clear that the available capital was insufficient to complete the planned drainage work, not to mention the necessary reclamation and cultivation of the land and the development of infrastructure. Additional capital was urgently required. In light of experience to date with the shareholders, there was, however, considerable reluctance to issue more shares or bonds in Paris and/or Athens. Interested parties were to be found in London though. In September 1886, just three months after the opening of the Canal of Karditza, a proposal from the British financier John Cockburn Francis Lee reached the CFC, clearly based on preliminary talks.[69] Lee proposed giving the CFC £500,000 for the concession and, with the agreement of the Greek government, taking over all the plans, assessments and maps. He wanted to establish a joint-stock company under British law with a capital of £1 million. There would thus be enough capital available to complete the canals, for which Pochet had budgeted £120,000, and for further developments with planned costs of £60,000.[70]

Lee's offer was not unprepared. He and his lawyer Charles Cheston had systematically and meticulously gathered information about the project. Lee had sent Robert Castle to Boeotia to gain an impression of the undertaking and the area – Castle had been recommended to Lee by the shipping entrepreneur James Caird.[71] He was given a detailed catalogue of questions to work on and tapped into all possible sources of information.[72] He travelled to Athens, where he gathered general information about agriculture in Greece and about the Copais area in particular from the British legation and the British general consulate.[73] He then inspected the site and talked to both employees of the CFC and residents of the neighbouring villages.[74] Castle's report opened with a description of the geographical situation and the transport connections to the Greek markets,[75] and moved on to present the state of work.[76] He believed that the Canal of Karditza, which was already complete, was actually sufficient to gradually drain the lake.[77] It was inaugurated nine days before the deadline set by the Greek government so as to avoid the payment of penalties. Nonetheless, Castle argued, a declaration should be obtained from the Greek government that expressly recognised the opening of the canal as the conclusion of work. Castle referred all legal questions related to Greek law to another expert,[78] Professor Damaschinos, professor of commercial law in Athens, who had been recommended by the British ambassador.[79] Castle included an English translation of this assessment with his report. Damaschinos declared that it was unlikely that the company would be expropriated because of delays in the progress of work. However, he alluded to the penalty for non-completion of 50,000 drachmas, which redoubled annually, and also pointed out the right of the Greek government to demand a bond of 1.7 million drachmas from the company. Damaschinos regarded obtaining a mortgage as unproblematic as the farmers had no particular rights in such a case. It was necessary, though, that at least a third of the land was cultivated using modern agricultural methods.[80]

Castle also organised for a scientific evaluation of the soil, despite previous investigations by Sauvage and Moule. He ordered the French engineers to take 14 soil samples and sent them to the laboratory of the Ecole Nationale Supérieure de Chimie in Paris. The results seemed exaggeratedly positive so he had new samples taken from locations which he stipulated precisely on a map, and had the samples examined by a laboratory in London, G. W. Wigner & R. H. Harland. The previous findings were confirmed: the soil was so rich in mineral and organic materials that it was even more fertile than the famous Russian 'black earth'.[81] Castle included both analyses with his report. The layer of humus was between two and five yards (1.8–4.4 m) thick, but thinner in the east of the region, precisely where the property of the CFC was situated. Castle described the climate and weather of the area,[82] and emphasised the range of goods that could be cultivated: from tobacco, corn, wheat, millet, lentils, beans, rice, sesame, onions, melons, grapes and cereals to green vegetables and roots. Horses, cattle, sheep, goats and pigs could also be reared.[83]

In line with the catalogue of questions he had been given, Castle also obtained information about the duties and taxes that the farmers rather than the landowners had to pay to the state.[84] At the time, 2,500 acres were said to be under cultivation and 3,000 were used as pastureland. The income from the leases for the previous year totalled £2,800. This could not be increased because of the extreme risk of fever from the standing water on the remaining land. As Castle pointed out, if workers were hastily sent there and thus endangered, then the reputation of the company could be damaged in the long term.[85] In realistic terms, it would be five years before all the land could be brought under cultivation. He listed a series of tasks required to develop the area: new roads (the existing ones were said to be wholly insufficient), smaller canals to divert the rainwater and irrigation systems. The recruitment of tenants from Asia Minor or southern Italy would, in Castle's opinion, be unproblematic.[86] If all the land was cultivated, then the leases should generate an income of about £70,000 a year (for £1 million of capital, this was the equivalent of 7% interest), or a market value of £871,875. This figure was calculated from the land prices of the area without including possible increases in value resulting from a railway or the use of water power, which could transform the town of Anthedon into an industrial centre.[87] Castle expressly pointed out the speculative value of the property but emphasised the uncertainty of all forecasts. For a mortgage of £300,000, as Lee had in mind, the property was certainly an outstanding guarantee.[88]

Castle's report, even with the legal and chemical evaluations it included, was not enough for Lee. Unlike the investors in the Canal of Corinth, he did not rely on the reputation of the experts involved, but had the scientific standard of findings assessed by another specialist. To this end, he sent the engineer P. A. Fraser from the renowned engineering firm Livesey & Son to Boeotia.[89] Before travelling to Lake Copais, Fraser studied all the plans and maps in Paris. Once in situ, he investigated the area in the company of a French engineer who was employed in Copais, at times using a canoe, and described it as a vast landscape of reeds growing to between eight and ten feet in height. Fraser related an incident that had occurred at the opening of the Canal of Karditza, but which was not reported in any of the newspapers. After just a few hours, one of the provisional dams had burst due to excessive water pressure and an uncontrolled torrent of water had shot through the canal.[90] The problems had, however, been solved and would not recur. Fraser believed the CFC documentation to be completely plausible and reliable and judged that the engineering work had been carried out with care and accuracy. He checked Pochet's cost estimates point for point and corrected them in several places. For instance, he suggested that more machines would be required because they were much more reliable than the manual labourers who usually only stayed for six months and were also vulnerable to fever. Costs for administration and engineering also needed to be budgeted, and 5.5% should be allowed for unexpected work. Fraser judged the undertaking to be technically unchallenging but calculated the costs to total at least 3,750,000 francs (£150,000).[91] Overall, he concluded: 'the whole project is one which seems to me a most promising one'.[92]

Risk management through contracts

After the risks had been assessed by scientific experts, the next task was to manage them. Action was urgently required with regard to the takeover, as the annulment of the 10,972 shares belonging to the defaulting shareholders meant the capital of the French company had shrunk to 9.5 million francs. The Paris financial crisis may well have also played a role in encouraging many shareholders not to meet their obligations (CFC 1886/1887, 3). In October 1886, the supervisory board therefore signed a preliminary contract with Lee, initially without the approval of the shareholders. In advance, the French company had also obtained comprehensive juridical advice.[93] At the time of signing the preliminary contract, Lee had not yet received the reports discussed earlier.[94] However, the first contract, when compared to later versions, already clearly shows that Lee earnestly wished to limit his risk and attempted to create ironclad safeguards.

In the preliminary contract, the capital was calculated generously:[95] £1 million in 100,000 shares at £10 each. Only £500,000 had to be spent on the concession from the French company and a further £155,000 to guarantee the planned bonds, the rest was intended for the development of the property (Papadopoulos 1993, 149). The £120,000 in ready money of the French company was thought to be enough to finish the work. The property, the CFC affirmed, was not less than 22,500,000 hectares in size.[96] In addition, Lee included in the first contract a safety mechanism in case the Greek government could after all demand the bond of 1.7 million drachmas from the company: shares of the new company equal to £60,000 were not granted to the CFC but were rather deposited elsewhere.[97]

After the preliminary contract was signed, Lee received the two reports and now tried to safeguard himself against the risks that they revealed. Firstly, he had to deal with the fact that Fraser had increased the cost estimate for construction from the £130,000 estimated by Pochet to £150,000. The British company therefore demanded a guarantee from the French company that the costs would not exceed £130,000. In April 1887, a compromise was found: Stephanos Skouloudis would be personally liable for compliance with the upper spending limit providing that Pochet remained the chief engineer. In return, he received a bonus of £20,000 out of the shares of the British company that were transferred to the CFC. If the guarantee should really fall due, then he would be entitled to a further £20,000 in shares of the LCC, which this time would be transferred directly from Lee.[98] Lee himself had thus limited his own risk with regard to the costs of the project to a maximum of £20,000.

Secondly, Lee wanted to safeguard himself in case further claims should be brought against the CFC. This was primarily due to the court case between the CFC and its first building contractor Lerat, in which the company faced high claims for damages. At the time that the contract was drawn up, the outcome of the proceedings was unclear.[99] The CFC was thus to keep the cash-in-hand of £120,000 until all the French court cases were concluded. In return, the British company kept a further £100,000 of the £500,000 (Papadopoulos 1993, 152).

Once the agreement had reached this stage, the French company held an extraordinary general meeting on 5 May 1887 and went into liquidation, whereby the former members of the supervisory board were named liquidators. Skouloudis and Elissen were permitted to act as administrators in the new company.[100] This generated an overlap of interests between the old company and the new one. The non-reserved shares of the new company were to be distributed among the shareholders of the old French company.

A month later, on 11 June 1887, the LCC was formed as a new British company.[101] It was a free-standing company, one of many such bodies that had only a secretariat and a supervisory board in London, whereby members were active on a number of boards. The aim of such companies was to do business abroad; they just had a British nameplate and acted under British law. Companies of this sort were very popular in Great Britain in the 1880s because the opportunities for profit abroad were much greater than those of companies which were active in Britain, although the risks were also higher.[102] The LCC first bought the concession and the Greek property from Lee for £655,000[103] of which Lee had already paid £500,000 to the CFC. He received the remainder (£155,000 in shares) in return for his guarantee to subscribe the debenture bonds still to be issued for £250,000 at an interest rate of 6% with 11% discount.[104] Lee was thus to pay only £89 for shares with a nominal value of £100. Here too, Lee managed the risk carefully by involving two additional investors: the London diaspora banker John Balli (Constantinides 1933) and the Dutchman Markus van Raalte,[105] a friend of Skouloudis.[106] The three investors were obliged to acquire any of the debenture bonds that could not immediately be sold, Lee 13%, van Raalte 42% and Balli 45%.[107] Lee remunerated the other two investors for their assumption of part of the risk with some of his block of shares of £155,000: £70,000 or 45% went to Balli, £50,000 or 32% to van Raalte, while only £35,000 or 23% remained with Lee (Papadopoulos 1993, 154). He thus reduced his risk of being left with the bonds to less than a quarter of the original amount. The issue of the bonds at the exchange was additionally safeguarded through the use of another intermediary, a trust company: the Plate Trust Loan and Agency Company[108] guaranteed to pay the interest on the bonds in the event of the company having difficulties[109] – a fairly common procedure for a free-standing company (Papadopoulos 1993, 145). In return, the LCC's Greek property was mortgaged in favour of the trust company (ibid., 153).[110] The additional guarantee of the Plate Trust Loan Company further increased the attractiveness of the bonds.

Despite the new British investors and the fact that they were governed by British law, the LCC was not actually British-dominated. As half of the British shares had been transferred to the former owners of the French company, these individuals now had a significant stake in the new enterprise. The largest shareholder remained Stefanos Skouloudis with 42% of the LCC shares. Overall, 53% of the share capital of the new company was in Greek hands, 23% in French hands and 24% held by the British. The situation with the bonds differed (the surplus of which the three large investors Lee, Raalte and Balli were obliged to buy up). Most of these were in British hands, also in diverse trusts.[111] The directors of the new company were neither shareholders nor bondholders, which was intended to favour the development of trust.

There was one exception to this rule: the negotiations between the two companies and between the partners were led by Charles Cheston, who later became the legal representative of the LCC, and he was also one of the principal holders of the newly issued bonds and a member of the board of directors (ibid., 155). He was listed as one of the shareholders even at the founding of the company.[112] In May 1887, Cheston had travelled to Athens to clarify all open questions with the Greek government.[113] On this trip, he had personally met Skouloudis, and a kind of friendship had developed between the two men. On 14 June 1887, the Greek consul in London was then able to approve the agreement between the two companies with the consent of the Greek government.[114]

Nonetheless, in October 1887, it looked as though the transfer was going to fail after all, because Leon Pochet had to adjust his cost forecast upwards. The CFC was unable to transfer the work to the LCC in the state that had been agreed (Skouloudis' guarantee was not relevant here because it only referred to the work to be undertaken later by the British company). The documentation fails to clarify whether mistakes in the calculations were to blame, whether it had become obvious that additional work was required or whether the CFC had not used its cash-in-hand of £120,000 to continue the work, as had been agreed. No matter the cause, Robert Castle threatened to withdraw his name from the prospectus if the figures used as a basis for his report were no longer valid, and Lee threatened to resign from the board. Cheston urgently advised Skouloudis to avoid confrontation with Lee as this would seriously damage the reputation of the company.[115] Skouloudis therefore agreed to the British demands to replace Pochet with a different chief engineer, but this did nothing to alter the fact that £26,000 were required to complete the work promised by the CFC. Cheston made various suggestions as to how a 'via media' could be found, because confrontation with Lee was of no avail. 'We shall begin with a law suit here which we may win, but which whether won or lost will destroy the prospects of success'.[116] A compromise was found: another £10,000 of the British shares were not paid out to the CFC but kept by the British company.[117]

A total of only £310,000 in shares was thus given to the CFC, and the remaining £190,000 was deposited at a bank as a guarantee for Lee and the British investors. Lee had carried out exemplary risk management – all eventualities seemed to be covered.

In spring 1888, the LCC applied to be admitted to the London exchange, where the bonds should be issued in the near future, and repeatedly emphasised the risk management of the investors,[118] particularly the guaranteed construction costs:

> Mr. Lee procured an agreement to be entered into between the French Company and Mr. Etienne Scouloudi of Athens a gentleman of high position and large fortune whereby Mr Scouloudi guaranteed

> that the works remaining to be done should not cost the English Company a greater sum than £130,000 thus giving the Company the advantage of a Contract for their completion at that sum.[119]

A map of the region was included in the application, and the prospected railway connection to Athens in the one direction and Larissa in the other direction was marked (see Figure II.7.3) – this new line would further improve the options for marketing agricultural goods.

The LCC did not want a public share issue because the shares had gone directly to the investors involved. But mortgage bonds were to be issued to the value of £300,000 – this sum was subsequently increased by £50,000.[120] The risk presented by this increase was also safeguarded: John Balli guaranteed the subscription of the additional bonds valued at £50,000 in return

Figure II.7.3 Map of the Lake Copais Company, 1888.

for a prerogative with regard to a further £30,000 of shares, which were additionally charged to the CFC.[121] In February 1888, the first half of the mortgage bonds were then issued, £150,000 of a total of £300,000. The issue price was 95, the interest was 6% and the papers were to be bought back at a price of £100 on 15 June 1907 or earlier at a price of £115. The mortgage of the Greek property of the company served as a guarantee.[122] The prospectus gave detailed information about the work planned for the next year and a half, and included maps, the results of the soil analyses and quotes from the expert reports.[123]

The actors

The investors' risk management was clearly exemplary. But why did they choose to do business in Greece? What links did they have to the country and what were their experiences? How did they make their contacts? An examination of the biographies of those involved helps shed light on these questions.

John Cockburn Francis Lee

John Cockburn Francis, the son of the plate glass manufacturer John Lee, was born in 1834 in St. Mary in Lancashire.[124] The origin of his fortune remains obscure but he was a major shareholder in various companies and, for instance, sat on the board of directors of the Electric Lighting Contract and Maintenance Company.[125] His investments seemed to have focused on the railways: he was a shareholder in the Chignecto Marine Transport Railway Company,[126] the Smyrna and Cabassa Railway Company,[127] the New York, Pennsylvania, and Ohio Railroad[128] and the Buenos Ayres Pacific Railway Company.[129] The fact that Lee presided or spoke at the various gatherings and general meetings of these companies shows that he was one of the major shareholders – it may well be that he had smaller holdings in other companies which left no trace in the press. He also invested in goldmines in Venezuela,[130] was a shareholder in the Santa Fe Land Company,[131] sat for a while on the Board of Directors of the Persian Investment Cooperation[132] and was one of the creditors of the Province Entre Rios.[133] There is at least one other case where Lee embarked on a high-risk project in Southern Europe: the building of the railway from Alcoi to Gandia near Valencia in Spain (Peiró I Pérez/Morales Ferrandis 2003). In 1889, he bought the Alcoi and Gandia Railway and Harbour Company Ltd and engaged in the construction of the line. His interest was due to his activities as the president of the Cargo Steam of Sea Royal Company which aimed to develop the transport routes in the region (Garrigós Sastre 2014, 894).[134] He was not only a shareholder of this company, but also the manager. Here too, Lee took over a pre-existing company that was in financial difficulties but had already obtained a concession and completed the necessary planning. In this case, the building work was completed quickly and largely unproblematically and in 1893 the railway line, also known as 'El Treno des Ingleses', was inaugurated.[135] However, the profits were not as high as expected because the railway was not sufficiently utilised.[136] In addition to his financial activities, Lee was also a fellow of the Royal Botanic Society of London.[137] He ensured the involvement of his relative, the engineer Henry Lee, in the LCC, taking him on board as the Chairman and Managing Director of the company, until Henry Lee died in March 1888.[138] It is not possible to reconstruct how John Cockburn Francis Lee came into contact with the CFC. Perhaps bankers of the Greek diaspora in London drew his attention to it, or perhaps he was actively looking for worthwhile projects on the European 'periphery'.

Stephanos Skouloudis

Stephanos Skouloudis (1838–1928) (Βάρδα [Varda] 1995, 1) seems to have played a key role here. In 1880, Skouloudis had negotiated with the Greek government for the potential investor Vouros and was one of the major shareholders of the CFC, which meant that he was also a major shareholder of the LCC. Skouloudis was the driving force behind the execution of the Copais project. He came from Constantinople where, after completion of a medical degree in Athens, he worked in the Greek trading house of Ralli. In 1871, he joined Andreas Syngros to found the Bank of Constantinople.[139] In 1876, he then moved to Athens. The establishment of the CFC was one of the last financial business deals that he organised before he turned to the sphere of politics. After representing Greece at the Congress of Berlin in 1878, he was elected an MP as a member of Charilaos Trikoupis' liberal party for the first time in 1881, and two years later went to Madrid as the Greek ambassador (1883–1886). Towards the end of his time in Spain, the aforementioned newspaper campaign was waged against him, leading to the boycott of the CFC by the Greek shareholders. After his return to Greece, he continued his political career. Under Trikoupis, he became the minister for education and religion in 1892, and was then responsible for naval affairs. He was at the same time involved in various companies active in public work in Greece, e.g. railway construction, and led international negotiations for the country in various contexts. In 1897, he was the foreign minister under the conservative government of Dimitrios Ralli and also continued his diplomatic career after 1910 under Eleftherios Venizelos. In 1915–1916, Skouloudis was the prime minister and unsuccessfully attempted to prevent the division of the country over the question of entering the war. In addition to political activities, he was an important art collector and was exceptionally well-connected in the business world and in political spheres both in Greece and in the rest of Europe. Skouloudis thus brought to the LCC precisely the kind of diplomatic and political reputation that fostered trust among British investors (Wilkins 1988, 260ff.). His political connections in Greece engendered hope of quick and unbureaucratic communication between the LCC and the Greek government.

Nonetheless, the documentation related to the negotiations suggests that Skouloudis and Lee only reached an agreement due to the involvement of an intermediary. The subsequent manager of the LCC, Charles Cheston, took on this role. He corresponded with Skouloudis and advised him on how to handle the French shareholders,[140] he put together the Board of Directors of the new company, he negotiated the conditions of the guarantee with Skouoloudis,[141] he kept the negotiations up and running, and he repeatedly interceded between those involved whenever problems arose.[142] Even before the negotiations were completed, Cheston and Lee reinforced their business links with family ties: on 24 November 1897, Cheston's eldest son Charles Franklin married Lee's eldest daughter, Louisa Maude.[143]

Charles Cheston

Lee's daughter married into a well-respected company: Charles Cheston was the owner of the law firm Cheston & Sons. Nothing is known about his family background although he is likely to have come from the educated and wealthy middle classes as he studied at King's College, where he won an award for outstanding achievements in mathematics.[144] He took his B.A. and M.A. at Merton College in Oxford.[145] Through his marriage to the daughter of a former mayor of Ipswich, Edward Packard, Cheston gained connections to political circles (Martin 2000, 343). He and his wife were also active philanthropists: Cheston supported the East London Hospital for Children from the early 1880s until his death, often holding the position of chairman.[146] Cheston & Sons was a flourishing company and when he died Cheston left his wife assets of £46,565.[147] As early as 1880, Cheston was described in the press as a 'powerful City solicitor'.[148] His reputation was 'above suspicion', and one of the 'most solid in his profession'. He was a member of the Council of the Incorporated Law Society.[149] Cheston furthermore represented the Nitrate Railways Company in Chile,[150] the River Plate Trust Loan and Agency Company (which also then acted for the LCC),[151] and he sat on the supervisory boards of the Law Union Fire and Life Insurance Company,[152] the Lower California Development Company Limited, the Mexican Land and Colonization Company Limited and the Transport, Trading, and Agency Company of West Australia. In addition, he was one of the pioneers involved in developing the small port town of Felixstowe to a harbour and railway hub with a railway line to Ipswich.[153] It is impossible to determine whether Cheston held shares in all these companies or only acted for them as a manager. However, a newspaper announcement sheds some light on his investment behaviour: in 1902, he possessed 1,000 shares at £84 each of the Klersdorp Gold Mining and Diamond Company.[154] This shows that Cheston not only administered the assets of others, but also speculated himself. From the beginning of the LCC, he was not only a legal advisor and manager, but also financially involved in the company as a co-founder and one of the major bondholders. Additional biographical information about Cheston emerged on the occasion of his death: on 8 May 1906, he committed suicide at the age of 63. Afterwards, it was established that he had lost all the assets entrusted to his management by Lord William Amhurst Tyssen-Amherst, Baron of Hackney, an important art collector (Bell 2004; Duggan 2009, 68). His suicide can be understood as a flight from 'dishonesty', the consequences of which he thus never experienced: 'More than a quarter of a million went, no one can say where, for this criminal carried much of his secret to his grave'.[155]

At the time of the establishment of the LCC, Cheston still enjoyed a spotless reputation. He developed the system of guarantees and securities, and ensured that they were contractually anchored. But why did he invest in this company himself? Why did he not limit his involvement in the Greek company to active legal advice rather than investing such a large sum of his own? How did he frame his decision and how did he legitimate it?

His correspondence with Skouloudis sheds some light on this issue. In a letter from summer 1887, he asked the Greek banker and politician to provide the most comprehensive statistical material about Greece possible. He was particularly interested in itemisations of food prices and wages, but also in reports about the mines of Lavrion, the Greek railways and government budgets,[156] and complained that reliable statistical material could not be found in London. Cheston did not disguise the reason for his request: he wanted to write something about Greece, not least in response to a very negative report on the country in the *Economist*.[157] Skouloudis sent the Englishman the material he sought. Cheston studied it attentively and asked for a number of specialist Greek terms to be translated:

> You will feel disposed at just to laugh at my ignorance, & wonder that I cannot understand plain Greek, but please remember that the Greek I learned was the Greek of Aischylus & Thukydides, & that I have not used even that for 25 years.[158]

Cheston had obviously attended an English public school and experienced Plato, Herodotus, Thucydides and Homer as 'the centrepiece of Oxford Hellenism' (Bowen 1989, 176). How did this contribute to his partiality for the Greek market?

> I am anxious if I could to get some few things on paper which shall do good to a country where I met with a reception, the warmest kindliness of which I shall never forget. To the glamour of the Greece that I read & wondered about as a boy, to the Greece that

> Byron pictured as Greece but living Greece no more, I want to add a third figure to the triad of Graces in the Greece which is a living Greece once more. Of course I want to help my friends with their financial venture. [...] What I want to do is to show, or at least to assert that the English ideas of Greece & Greeks at least of the country Greeks is quite erroneous. I want to show that it is a country which though it may have been nearly dead, is resuscitating. That its industries are waking up, that its finances show the statistics of a growing, not the relapse of a falling race.[159]

Cheston clearly aimed to improve the negative image of Greece that abounded in the 1880s. To this end, he wanted to show that the tax burden was not too great for the population and that the cost of living was very low, as revealed, for instance, by the lack of beggars in Athens. Cheston felt called to this task because, he claimed, nobody else seemed willing to undertake it, not even the diaspora Greeks in London, who talked about their homeland when the king was visiting but did not otherwise want to support it. Cheston wished to enlighten his compatriots about Greece, about Modern Greece in particular:

> I think it would be a good thing to teach English people what Greece is, they know more or less what it was. I would like to see it well done by a competent hand, but since no one does it, I feel that all the return that I can make for the kindness I met with in Athens & elsewhere, is to blow my penny whistle, since the great musicians will not play the tune – If I do any good, so much the better for England & possibly for Greece, if I do none it is on my head the fiasco will clash.[160]

When visiting the country, he had been shocked by the fact that the Greeks mostly spoke French as their first foreign language, while English remained an 'unknown tongue', although he believed that this was a connection that could only be profitable for Greece. This commentary was also an indication of the competitive situation with France, in both cultural and economic terms. Indeed, the two spheres overlapped. Cheston warmly recommended cooperation with England to his correspondent:

> England is a falling country, granted: but with all our faults, there is still at the bottom of the English nature a certain bigness & a certain generosity even without a great merit. We are only so ignorant. [...] Greece wants men & money. England has both & wants places to work in. I want to see Englishmen & money coming to Greece; I want to see a little competition for what you want done. Ponts et chaussées are very good, very fine, very theoretic, but very

> unpractical. I want to do what little I can in the undertow of a somewhat busy life to open the eyes to my countrymen to what I believe to be the facts about Greece. [...] People were so kind to me, I want to do or try to do something in return.[161]

Cheston also explicitly referred to the LCC:

> I would like to see that a success, I should like in 2 or 3 years to try my prentice hand at an appendix to your συννοια of the French & Greek nations, & to let in a fresh stone on the Karditza tunnel when the works are finished & the thing a fait accompli.[162]

Cheston felt connected to Greece not only because of the hospitality he had received there, but also due to his classical and literary education, which was at the heart of his identity. This was why he wanted to do something for the country, something that lay within his realm of expertise: economic promotion and investment. An additional motivation was competition with France, which Cheston, like many among the British educated classes, was quick to recognise (Bowen 1989, 176).[163] England should not allow the prize to be stolen away. The age-old struggle between the Grande Nation and the Empire concerning which of them was the true successor of Athens had made an impact on the classically educated Cheston and now influenced his economic behaviour in the 1880s. Cheston invested in Greece not only because of the chances of profit, but also as a Philhellene aiming to benefit the country.

In 1887, Cheston then really published his investment guide to Greece. He began with praising motherly love, which could provide hope in 'this money-cursed age' (Cheston 1887a, 5). He clearly wanted to create a counterweight to the dominance of the economic sphere in his life, 'ennobling' his business activities with the link to Greece. 'There is a magic in the very name of Greece, which instinctively carries the mind back to a remote antiquity' (ibid.). Greek art in its 'simple majesty and exquisite beauty' remained the 'delight, and the despair' of all artists of later times, he declared, and argued that the philosophy and poetry also set unattainable standards. British statesmen were said to praise Homer as having provided their most valuable education (ibid.). Byron was the one who connected this antiquity and the Greek struggle for independence with Great Britain, even when the Greeks of today were not as noble as those extolled in his verses. Although Greece was a poor country, Cheston believed it had interesting development opportunities. The French were taking advantage of these opportunities and becoming involved in railway construction and many other projects, while Great Britain was simply holding back (ibid., 10). In addition, he argued, the ancient heritage, the colours of the sea and the unforgettable light of the Greek sun offered great incentives for tourism. The Greeks still possessed 'the restless quickness of intelligence with which the national name has been identified for centuries' (ibid., 13); there was just a lack of capital and engineering expertise. 'English capital and skill may find employment, where they are now entirely unrepresented' (ibid., 13).[164] Cheston also mentioned negative characteristics such as rebelliousness, tax dishonesty, the way in which personalities rather than political programmes defined the political parties, the lack of continuity in the work of the ministries owing to the frequent changes of government. Nonetheless, his description was overwhelmingly positive and at times romantically idealised:

> About Lebadeia and the Copais plain, as evening falls, the traveller will see the ploughman unyoke his oxen, and, loading his plough and other implements on his patient donkey, mount on the top himself, and return slowly to his village, enjoying a silent cigarette, while the patient oxen pace solemnly by his side.
>
> (ibid., 19)

Cheston rhapsodised about spring meadows full of roses, poppies and anemones (ibid., 91). But he also reported on railway building, trade, the mines of Lavrion, the Canal of Corinth and, of course very positively, on the LCC, which he believed promised to be a triumph of engineering skill (ibid., 102–107). The Greeks were characterised by their love for the popular monarchy, their patriotism, unspoilt by any self-interested eying of offices and their hard work; this made the country an ideal place for the investment of British capital (ibid., 108f.). Cheston did what he had promised Skouloudis: he addressed both the clearly calculating investor and the romantic aesthete, both of which could often be found in the same person in the City of London.[165] With his book, Cheston presented himself as a specialist for the Greek economy. Indeed after the Greek bankruptcy of 1893, he was proposed as a member of a committee to be formed by holders of Greek bonds.[166] His book was also translated into French (Cheston 1887b; Shaw 1991, 345f.).[167]

Overlooked risks

Despite the very emotional and ideological framing of the decision-making situation, Cheston drew up an apparently ironclad system of guarantees and safeguards for the LCC that promised to cover every eventuality. Rhapsodies over Greece and elaborate risk management did not contradict one another in the slightest. In practice, the safeguards worked perfectly with regard to a number of risks. For instance, the court case against the building contractors went on and on, but the British company was safeguarded from any costs that might be incurred.[168] The expenditure for completing the planned drainage works also exceeded the budgeted £130,000, but Stephanos Skouloudis intervened and, as agreed, covered the additional costs himself.[169] He paid £12,000 in cash and £20,000 in shares.[170] This allowed the building programme from Moule's plan to be implemented. Nonetheless, new technical problems emerged repeatedly, e.g. the flammability of the soil in the hot summer months (exacerbated by the farmers clearing the land by burning off the undergrowth), subsidence which led to the drainage channels being higher than the fields and the heavy rainfalls which sometimes far exceeded the capacity of the drainage channels and caused flooding (Papadopoulos 1993, 159–167). Tackling all these problems cost money and despite the comprehensive contract, there were conflicts between the British company and the liquidators of the CFC about the way in which the rights and responsibilities were divided.[171] Improvements, extensions and repairs to the drainage system swallowed large sums of capital until the 1910s.[172] As the difficulties increased, so too did the tension between Skouloudis and Lee.[173]

Problems were not limited to the drainage work and associated technical difficulties. As early as 1889, it became clear that additional infrastructure was necessary for the land to be profitably developed. At the end of 1889, the second half of the bonds were issued (again to the value of £150,000), and the prospectus included a new report that recommended further investment for the cultivation of the reclaimed land. A sum of £17–20,000 was proposed.[174] The prospectus also forecast exceptional revenues, predicting annual profits of about 2.5 million francs, which after the deduction of all costs would have represented a payout of 27 or 28% for the bondholders.[175] Cheston remained correspondingly optimistic, despite the fact that the financial crisis of the early 1890s made issuing bonds on the London exchange extremely difficult.[176] As time passed, the profit expectations were successively reduced: by 1892, annual dividends of just 10% of the total capital were expected.[177] In 1893, there was a discussion about whether the estate was valuable enough for an additional mortgage.[178] Pochet (who was no longer the chief engineer but was still employed on the project) reported massive problems. Contrary to expectations, the farmers would not purchase any land because they lacked capital. It proved necessary to return to leasing, as was normal in Greece. To attract tenants,[179] the company was forced to provide not only the fertile land, but also infrastructure with houses, schools, storage facilities, irrigation canals and a credit system for the farmers. It was predicted that after completion of this work, the estate would be worth 40 million francs.[180] The plan to introduce modern agricultural methods, as promised to the Greek government, had only been implemented in part due to a lack of capital and the unwillingness of the farmers to adopt innovations.[181] Even the local staff started to lose enthusiasm for reform: 'We are among those who believe that agriculture is and must remain a simple art within reach of the people who practise it'. Improvements could only be introduced very gradually.[182] The confidence of potential investors was further undermined by the bankruptcy of the Greek state in 1893 and the fact that for a long time no agreement between the state and its creditors seemed possible. Two years later, Cheston was still searching desperately for new capital and even advanced the company money from his own private resources. Roses were again mentioned, but this time in a very different context:

> The Receivership of the Lake Copais is by no means a bed of roses. Personally, if it were not for my friends I should never have accepted it & I should not for one moment continue it; but I do not mean to be driven out if I can help it[.] [...] I should not myself mind leaving my £3500 if somebody finds the money as it comes due for the future.[183]

Cheston made his wish to leave the LCC ever clearer and regretted having to continue his involvement because of his friends.[184] The reputation of the company further suffered when it turned out to be impossible to pay any dividends.[185] The bondholders even won a court case, which led to the naming of a receiver-manager who was to represent their interests against those of the 'old' shareholders (Papadopoulos 1997, 367). In 1900, new bonds to the value of £70,000 were issued and in 1905 bonds for a further £30,000 were released, all of which took priority over the older debt securities (ibid., 300–304). The dividends paid remained meagre compared with expectations. Every year between 1900 and 1919, holders of the bonds from 1900 received 7% interest, while holders of the bonds from 1905 received 6%. However, there were many years when holders of the bonds from 1888 and 1889 received nothing at all and until 1914 they were never paid more than 4% (ibid., 308). The shareholders received no dividends until the end of the 1930s. In the long term, it was nonetheless possible to increase the net profits, as Sauvage had predicted in 1849: in 1900, the takings of the company did not exceed £5,800 but in 1938, they totalled over £59,000 and had thus increased more than tenfold. There were considerable fluctuations though: in 1918, net profits reached their highpoint of £79,000, but at the beginning of the world economic crisis in 1931/1932, the company had losses of £22,800 or £13,500. From the mid-1930s, things seem to have stabilised somewhat. Shareholders and bondholders who managed to prove their staying power (it was now almost 50 years since the first company had been established) benefited from these profits (ibid.).

The technical difficulties and capital required for the development of the property were two of the problems that had been underestimated. But there was another explosive issue that had been overlooked by Lee's experts: the question of the property rights of local residents all around Lake Copais. It had been contractually agreed that the Greek government would expropriate the local landowners and compensate them with parcels of the 15,000 stremmata relinquished by the company. However, the exact boundaries of the various properties had not been finally stipulated and there was still no cadastre (ibid., 370).[186] The unequivocal demarcation of boundaries was also hindered by pressure brought to bear on the political decision makers by their followers in the region, who urged that their interests should be defended against the foreigners. The Greek government, like all of those in Europe, was dependent on the support of the farming population.[187] The start of the auditing procedure was therefore repeatedly delayed (Papadopoulos 1993, 172). In 1888, Cheston complained to Skouloudis that most of the reclaimed land was now occupied by usurpers who refused to pay leases. The entirety of the rent collected by the company totalled only £40, most of which came from the leasing of fishing rights on the two small lakes. It was thus necessary for the company to file complaints as quickly as possible in order to establish property rights.[188] There was still hope that the Greek government would protect this 'great national enterprise'.[189] However, there were repeated riots leading to LCC tenants being expelled by local farmers or the farmers simply taking possession of LCC land and cultivating it on their own account. At times when Charilaos Trikoupis led the government, the investors could rely on a minimum of good will and help from the Greek state. But when the opposition led by Theodoros Delyannis was in power, the government support went to the local landowners. Delyannis showed no consideration for the LCC and its interests but simply referred the Englishmen to the relevant courts. By 1897, however, it was clear to Cheston that the courts were not a feasible option as the opponents of the LCC were influential and powerful enough to change the court decisions in their own favour (ibid., 195). Copais became an increasingly explosive political topic in Greece as the years passed. This was not eased when in 1890, on the occasion of a personal visit by Lee, the LCC sought and received support from the British Embassy in Athens. Papadopoulos provides detailed descriptions of how the frequent changes of government impacted negotiations between the company and the governments and the role played by the FO here (ibid., 172–206). For instance, one Greek government fined the company for not having completed the entire work on time, and the subsequent government rescinded the fine. At times, the company was provided with military protection against the riots; at times, they were left to their own devices. On occasion, the government pressed ahead with the compensation process, on occasion it delayed such activities. The Greek government thus swung from support to hindrance leaving no institutional security for the investors, no matter how much the British diplomats emphasised the catastrophic impression this made on potential foreign investors. The Greek government continually employed delaying tactics to avoid settling the politically sensitive question of Copais (Χρήστος [Christos] 2002). In the 1900s, the dispute continued its way through the courts and none of the agreements negotiated between the government and the LCC concerning the exact location of the LCC lands and the compensation were approved by the Greek parliament, hence nothing was settled (Papadopoulos 1993, 202). The tenants complained bitterly about the expensive leases and exploitation by the LCC, which fuelled the social conflicts. The LCC experimented with various forms of lease agreements, but none of these had the desired results and some even exacerbated the social unrest by increasing the lease rate to 20% depending on the crops in question (Papadopoulos 1997, 369). The use of waged labour to cultivate two model farms proved successful but it was impossible to extend this to the entire area.[190] When in 1907 numerous large landowners in Thessaly were expropriated by the government, the LCC reacted by exploring other forms of lease agreement (Papadopoulos 1993, 208–230). Furthermore, they tried to oblige their farmers to employ modern agricultural methods, e.g. to use combine harvesters, to regularly check their tools, to use copper sulphate to dress the seeds and to fertilise regularly (ibid., 311). None of these attempts were able to solve the social conflicts, however, which actually worsened when Eleftherios Venizelos took office in 1910. From the 1920s the threat of expropriation became more acute for the LCC. The British diplomats managed to arrange an agreement between the government and the LCC, which was then (after considerable modification) even passed by parliament. A decisive role was played here by Eric Hambro, the primary creditor of the Greek government who was now also one of the large shareholders of the LCC (Μέλιος [Melios] /Παπαδόπουλος [Papadopoulos] 1988, 1166).[191] The British were able to bring pressure to bear thanks to the new large loan that the Greek government wanted to issue to accommodate the refugees from Asia Minor (Papadopoulos 1993, 330–337). However, this preliminary solution was not stable, particularly as the LCC was now the last large landowner in the whole of Greece (ibid., 398). In the following years the focus of discussion was on the sale of the LCC property to the Greek government. The French shareholders in particular were in favour of this solution, while the bondholders tended to prefer the notion of the company continuing to manage the land itself (Μέλιος [Melios] 1996, 5). The sale never materialised, perhaps because Venizelos' government were well aware of the work involved in maintaining the drainage system that prevented the land from returning to its previous marshland state. In the early 1930s the LCC increased its leasing rates for certain field crops to 35%, triggering strikes and protests by the local population (Papadopoulos 1997, 376). Elsewhere in Greece work began on draining other marshes, in some cases to provide reclaimed land for the refugees from Asia Minor (Papayannis 1992b, 210). It was 1953 before the LCC was finally expropriated by the Greek government, not least in response to pressure from the US Americans who were keen to reduce British influence in Greece (Μέλιος [Melios] 1996, 5).[192]

Conclusion

The draining of Lake Copais was initiated in 1880 by a French company and after 1887 continued by a British one, as the initial company had run out of capital. The British investors prepared their investment decision on the basis of scientific expertise. This included reports by engineers and legal experts as well as chemical analyses of soil samples by well-reputed laboratories, and in some cases second opinions from other experts. When the decision was made to invest, a complicated contract ensured that all the risks were covered, mitigated by guarantees or spread across many shoulders.

The creator of this ingenious risk management was Charles Cheston, a London lawyer, manager and investor who had enjoyed a classical education. His decision to become involved in Greece was explicitly motivated by his Philhellenism: he felt a moral duty to help the country whose language and culture had so strongly influenced him and where he had enjoyed such hospitality on his travels. The Copais project did not represent the limit of his involvement in Greece. He also promoted the country in a romantic brochure offering investment advice in an attempt to attract British capital, particularly in response to French competition. The case study shows that an emotional decision need not be at variance with elaborate risk management: the preference for Greece was implemented using the most modern of practices.

Technical problems with the drainage system and conflicts about property rights appertaining to the reclaimed land nonetheless caused difficulties for the LCC. The resistance of the local residents troubled their activities until the mid-twentieth century, and the changes of Greek government meant that the investors sometimes received official support but sometimes found the government supporting the local population. The LCC did not succeed in installing itself as a win-win-situation both for foreign investors and local growers and therefore did not bring them in. The situation remained confrontational. The institutional parameters for investment proved to be highly unreliable, as had been the case with the Lavrion mines. At least the complicated contract ensured that the company was able to continue its activities for a number of decades. After a long lean period, the bondholders earned reasonable dividends in the first half of the twentieth century, before the LCC was finally expropriated by the Greek state in 1953.

Notes

1 A very short overview is found in Δερτιλής [Dertilis] (2009, 597–599).
2 On the discussion about the controversial term agricultural revolution, see, e.g. Osterhammel (2010, 317).
3 See the papers in Vivier (2008).
4 In the years between 1850 and 1880, the proportion of those employed in agriculture fell to under 50% in many countries in Northern and Western Europe (see Osterhammel 2010, 316).
5 On the discussion of increased productivity in British agriculture, see Beckett/Turner (2011). There is also an intensive discussion concerning the division of property rights and its impact on productivity and social structures worldwide in contemporary research (see Congost/Santos 2010). Berghoff also emphasises, with reference to Douglas North, the importance of property rights: 'The more

clearly the Property Rights are defined and protected, the lower the transaction costs' (Berghoff 2004, 63).

6 Unlike many of the researchers preceding him, Jones does not believe the third quarter of the nineteenth century to have been a 'Golden Age' of British agriculture and calls for better differentiation of the producers of the individual agricultural products.

7 The low profit margins changed little for a long time, as shown by a handbook for agricultural investors published by the Royal Bank of Scotland at the beginning of the 1980s (see Checkley 1983, XI).

8 In 1873–1888, the GDP per capita rose by 1.92% a year (see Petmezas 2013, 88). On the development of Greek agriculture, also see Progoulakis/Bournova (2001).

9 However in 1878–1881, Thessaly became part of the Greek state. Here, rich Greeks, especially from the diaspora, bought up the property of the former Ottoman owners. These large and influential landowners harboured hopes of autarky and were able to introduce certain customs barriers to protect their grain production. This meant that real wages failed to rise in all regions in the 1880s as they would probably have done without state regulation. Grain production was extended though (see Petmezas 2013, 95).

10 In 1853–1882, Greek exports did not cover more than 54–57% of imports, but these figures rose to 61% and 74% in the following two decades.

11 See Chapter II.9 in this book.

12 For a description of the utilisation of the wetlands in North and South America, see Meyer (2004, 89). Both authors mention the use of the marshes with regard to warfare.

13 On English land improvement in the eighteenth century, see Ciriacono (1995, 293–299).

14 For a description of various drainage methods, see Hoelscher (1963).

15 Between 1847 and 1872, in addition to private capital, £7,381,000 as government bonds was used for drainage (see Jones 1976, 23).

16 Jones mentions profits of 2.5% for the Duke of Northumberland's investments in the drainage of his lands (see Jones 1976, 30).

17 In 1950, the property was then expropriated by the Italian government, a remarkable parallel to Lake Copais (see Linoli 2005, 179, 184).

18 Reports are found in Homer, Hesiod and Strabo (who also reports on Lago Fucino; see Papayannis (1992a, 210)).

19 As early as the end of the nineteenth century, classical studies addressed Lake Copais, whereby modern undertakings were often mentioned as continuing the work of antiquity (see, e.g. Philippson 1894, 81–87). Philippson reports that the reclaimed land still lay fallow, primarily due to a lack of labour. He also deliberates on Burnouf's critical considerations about climate change.

20 See articles under the title: Bemerkungen und Nachrichten über die neuesten Begebenheiten im eigentlichen Griechenland, in: *Allgemeine Zeitung* No 91, 116, 122, 130, 133, 131, 154, 155 (1821, June–September).

21 Thiersch, Friedrich, to Thiersch, Amalie, 17.10.1831, in: Loewe/Thiersch (2010, 230), tr. by K.S. Thiersch was thrilled to hear that the digging over of these areas was undertaken not by human hands, but by black pigs that were herded onto the fields. 'The pigs of the Egyptians in Herodot crossed my mind, which instead of ploughing were driven across the fields after the Nile had retreated. Then the fields were sown' (Ibid., 234, tr. by K.S.).

22 The Wittelsbach family had some experience in land improvement; in 1790, they had founded the Donaumoos Kultursozietät to reclaim moorland in the Donaumoos north of Munich (see Ciriacono 1995, 286).

23 In 1835, a republican society named 'Aide-toi, le ciel t'aidera' was set up with the participation of one of the founders of the CEP Antoine-Laurent Pagnerre (see Stoskopf 2002b, 405).
24 The painting now hangs in the Neue Pinakothek in Munich.
25 Diary of Gustave d'Eichthals, 20.11.1834, in: Queux Saint-Hilaire (1887, 42).
26 Diary of Gustave d'Eichthals, 28.12./9.1.1835, in: ibid., 70.
27 As reported, without sources, by Papadopoulos (1993, 96).
28 Two years earlier at the age of 17, the engineer and geologist Sauvage (1814–1872) completed his PhD at the École polytechnique. He later worked as a mining expert and in railway construction (see N. N. 1897).
29 **125** in the book.
30 Sauvage (1868, 73), tr. by K.S.
31 From the beginning, voices opposed to this sort of project were heard, using religious or aesthetic arguments or predicting the serious consequences of change. From the 1860s, it is also possible to find mention of ecological considerations (see Blackbourn 2007, 16).
32 Burnouf (1850, 159f.), tr. by K.S.
33 There is speculation in the research that Webster may have been unable to find capital in London, that he may have insisted on a colony with only English settlers, which was rejected by the government, or that the foreigners believed the location to be unsafe and were afraid to come to the country (see Papadopoulos 1993, 99f.).
34 London, Thursday, December 18, 1862, in: *The Times*, 18.12.1862. 'A short canal would drain the Lake Copais, and restore Bœtia to fertility and salubrity'. Similarly: Greece, As It Is, and Might Have Been, in: *The Times*, 18.10.1873.
35 Yéméniz proposed providing labour by bringing the frugal Greeks of the diaspora to their homeland as farmers. His piece closes by predicting splendid future development for Greece: 'On the contrary, with all its energy it [Greece] will keep the principal attributes of its antique genius, its fervent patriotism, its lively faith, its warlike aptitudes and above all its ardent love of liberty' (Yéméniz 1865, 891, tr. by K.S.). Three years earlier, Yéméniz had published a book about Greece, also to counter Edmond About's comments (see Yéméniz 1862).
36 Papadopoulos reports on two other failed attempts.
37 Fraipont was born in 1849 in Brussels and lived mainly in Paris. He drafted lithographs and illustrations for newspapers like *Paris Illustré* and *Univers Illustré*, and cover drawings, posters, etc. (see N. N., s.t.).
38 On the question of whether the investments from Greeks abroad should be assessed as foreign investments, see Δερτιλής [Dertilis] (2009, 592). However, the reasons for the investment decisions of Greeks abroad are not the centre of research interest here. The sources do not reveal how it was possible to persuade the French investors to participate. The focus here is therefore on the English investors six years later.
39 A certain N. Coronio is mentioned. It is nonetheless unclear whether this is a reference to Skouloudis' brother-in-law and business partner Georgios Coronio.
40 This referred to modern ploughs and agricultural machinery. A stud and cattle farm were also planned to improve the local breeds.
41 Société Anonyme pour le dessèchement et l'exploitation du Lac Copaïs. Loi, Conventions, Documents relatifs au transfert de la concession, Paris Décembre 1880, GE Skou 35.1.
42 Greece. The Draining of Lake Copais, Monday 16 May 1881, GE Skou 35.2.
43 Such conflicts between residents who had to tolerate very different consequences of drainage work went on for centuries in some marshlands, e.g. in the marshes in Poitou (see Suire 2006).

44 Similarly, complicated legal conditions have been found in the nineteenth-century Hungarian marshland (see Vári 2013, 210–212).
45 CFC (1884c), tr. by K.S.
46 Karalis, P. M. (Avocat, ancien Député): Travaux publics en Grèce. Les scandales de Copaïs (1), in: *La Grèce*. Organe des intérêts francais et de la confédération des peuples orientaux, 12.6.1884, tr. by K.S.
47 Karalis, P. M. (Avocat, ancien Député): Travaux publics en Grèce. Les scandales de Copaïs (2), in: *La Grèce*, 15.6.1884.
48 Les Pantalons Scouloudis, in: *La Grèce*, 26.6.1884.
49 Βοκοτόπουλος, Δ. Κ. [Vokotopoulos, D. K.]: Κύριε Συντάκτα της Πατρίδος [To Mr. Author of the Fatherland], in: *Αλήθεια [Verity]*, 23.11.1885, GE Skou 44.3.
50 Much more positive: Τα έργα της Κωπαΐδος [The Works of Copais], in: *Ακρόπολη (Akropolis)*, 3.6.1886, GE Skou 44.4. *Έσπερος [Evening Star]*, 15/27.8.1886 published a report by Pochet and numerous drawings of the site, romantically presented with traditional costumes, water bearers, etc. (ibid.).
51 A photo with many pictures of the building work and the opening is found in the estate of Stephanos Skouloudis in the GE. One copy was presented to prime minister Trikoupis, another to the king; see CFC to Pochet, 21.3.1887, GE Skou 36.2.
52 Gautier, F. (Ingénieur civil des Mines, Ancien secrétaire du Comité des Forges): Travaux publics. Dessèchement du Lac Copaïs. Inauguration du canal émissaire de Karditza, in: *Le Génie civil*, 2.10.1886. The second part was published on 9.10.1886.
53 Richou, G.: Dessèchement du Lac Copaïs, in: *La Nature*, 10.11.1886. Ibid.
54 Ibid.
55 Ibid.
56 Bailly, B.: Le Lac Copaïs, in: *Cosmos*, 15.11.1886, 431–436.
57 Ibid.
58 Ibid.; Gautier, F. (Ingénieur civil des Mines, Ancien secrétaire du Comité des Forges): Travaux publics. Dessèchement du Lac Copaïs. Inauguration du canal émissaire de Karditza, in: *Le Génie civil,* 2.10.1886.
59 Richou, G.: Dessèchement du Lac Copaïs, in: *La Nature*, 10.11.1886. Similarly in Gautier, F.: Travaux publics: Dessèchement du Lac Copaïs. Inauguration du canal émissaire de Karditza, in: *Le Génie civil*, 9.10.1886.
60 Travaux publics: Les Travaux publics en Grèce, in: *Revue Industrielle*, No. 49, 2.10.1886.
61 Gautier, F.: Travaux publics: Dessèchement du Lac Copaïs. Inauguration du canal émissaire de Karditza, in: *Le Génie civil*, 9.10.1886, tr. by K.S.
62 Ibid.
63 Bailly, B., Le Lac Copaïs, in: *Cosmos*, 15.11.1886, 431–436, here 435f., tr. by K.S.
64 The classical sources actually report that the reeds from Lake Copais made the Thebans particularly good pipe players (see Verhoeven 1992, 95).
65 Our Athens Correspondent: Copaïs and Corinth, in: *The Times*, 23.7.1886.
66 Ibid.
67 Untitled, in: *The Times*, 26.7.1886.
68 Ibid. The project did not attract attention in the German press until somewhat later (see, e.g. Supan 1889): 'Improvement of nature is a catchword of our times. Countless works have been undertaken in service of this idea'. Tr. by K.S.
69 Lee to Skouloudis, Projet de conversion, Sep. 1886, GE Skou 35.4.
70 Ibid.
71 Prospectus of the Lake Copais Company, First Issue of £150,000, part of £300,000 First Mortgage Debentures, 1.2.1888, GE Skou 41.2 (see Carr 2004).

72 Castle, Report as to the general circumstances, present state and condition, and also as to the estimated probable value, when completely drained and fully reclaimed for cultivation, of the Estate known as the Dominion of Lake Copais, situated in the Province of Boeotia, in the Kingdom of Greece, and held, under a Concession from the Greek Government, by a French Company known as 'La Compagnie Francaise pour la Dessechement et Exploitation du Lac Copais', No 62 rue Provence, Paris, Oct. 1886, GE Skou 35.4.
73 On the conditions and tasks of the office of the British general consul in Greece, which was part of the 'Levant Service', see Platt (1971).
74 Castle, Report, 1.
75 Ibid., 2.
76 Ibid., 5.
77 Ibid., 6.
78 Castle, Question for the legal opinion and advice of Professor Damaschinos, Athens, 28.8.1886, GE Skou 35.4.
79 Castle, Report, 7.
80 Translation of Report of Professor Damaschino Lake Copais, 22.8./4.9.1886, GE Skou 35.4.
81 Castle, Report, 12f.
82 Ibid., 13f.
83 Ibid., 14f.
84 Ibid., 17.
85 'The result would probably be that the cultivators would suffer seriously in health, that the work done under very unfavourable conditions, would be imperfectly performed, and be found much less profitable to them than would be the case if all the necessary Engineering works were first completed in a proper manner – and the property might very likely therefore on this account get, undeservedly, a bad name, which might seriously hinder, and render much more difficult the future development or disposal of the Lands, and thus inflict upon the Growers a loss far exceeding any temporary gain which might be obtained' (Ibid., 10).
86 Ibid., 18.
87 Ibid., 21.
88 Ibid., 23.
89 A well-known and flourishing engineering company, founded in Manchester in about 1860 by James Livesey; see The Weald of Kent, Surrey & Sussex, 27.2.2014; Fraser, P. A., Livesey & Son: Report on the Drainage of Lake Copais, 1.11.1886, GE Skou 35.4. Also available GL 126 17B.
90 Ibid.
91 Ibid.
92 Ibid.
93 Advocat Lentés to CFC, 4.9.1886, GE Skou 35.4.
94 Ibid., 4.
95 An Agreement made the 16th day of October 1886 between La CFC [...] of the one part and John Cockburn Francis Lee [...] of the other part, in: LCC s.t., 66–70.
96 An Agreement, in ibid., 66–70, 68.
97 Ibid., 67. The English company actually demanded that the Greek government should waive this option. Minister Trikoupis did so (Tricoupis to CFC, 9.10.1887, in: LCC, s.t., 132). However, such an agreement required approval by the Greek parliament to take effect. Hence the safeguard; see Liquidators of the CFC to Skouloudis as liquidator, 29.10.1888, GE Skou 36.1.

98 An Agreement, in: LCC s.t., 71–84; Papadopoulos (1993, 151).
99 Directeur de la CFC to Skouloudis, 13.5.1887, GE Skou 36.2; Directeur de la CFC to Skouloudis, 27.5.1887, GE Skou 36.2.
100 They included: De Camondo, Athinogenes, Coronio, Elissen, De Louvencourt, Réniéri, Skouloudis (see CFC 1886/87, 8f.).
101 Articles of Association of the LCC, Limited, 11.6.1887, GL 712-79B.
102 Papadopoulos defines the Lake Copais Company as a free-standing company according to Wilkins (see Wilkins 1988).
103 An Agreement, in: LCC s.t., 61–65.
104 Articles of Association of the LCC, 11.6.1887, GL 712-79B.
105 Marcus Van Raalte (1833–1916) was a son of the Dutch business man Isaak Joseph van Raalte; see The Levi-Kanes Familiy Tree Collection, http://levie-kanes.com/humogen/family/humo_/F36291/I100839/ [10.2.20]. The Company da Costa, Raalte and Co, which he had run with his brother-in-law Jacob Mendes Da Costa and which had been active in Egypt, among other places, collapsed in 1875, but Marcus van Raalte seems to have survived this bankruptcy without impoverishment; see *The London Gazette*, 19.11.1875.
106 Cheston to Skouloudis, 10.4.1890, GE Skou 37.3.
107 An Agreement made the seventh day of December 1887 between the LCC [...] of the first part and John Cockburn Francis Lee [...] of the second part and Marcus Van Raalte [...] of the third part and John Balli of the fourth part, in: LCC s.t., 99–104.
108 The Plate Trust Loan and Agency Company Ltd (founded in 1881) became the River Plate and Mercantile Trust Ltd in 1961 (later the River and Mercantile Trust PLC). It specialised in the administration of companies in South America. See Archives in London and the M25 area, http://www.aim25.ac.uk/cgi-bin/vcdf/detail?coll_id=5032&inst_id=13 [10.2.2020].
109 This Indenture made the 15th day of June 1887 between the LCC [...] of the one part and the River Plate Trust Loan and Agency Company Limited [...] of the other part, in: LCC s.t., 115–118.
110 Also see LCC to the Committee of the London Stock Exchange, History of the Lake Copais C. from its Establishment to the present time, GL 126 17B.
111 Army and Navy Investment Trust, the Alliance Investment Company, the General and Commercial Trust, the Industrial and General Trust, and the Merchants' Trust (see Papadopoulos 1993, 155).
112 LCC, List of Shareholders, 6.6.1888, GL 126 17B.
113 Cheston to Skouloudis, 24.5.1887, GE Skou 37.2.
114 LCC to the Committee of the London Stock Exchange, History of the Lake Copais C. from its Establishment to the present time, GL 126 17B.
115 Cheston to Skouloudis, 12.10.1887, GE Skou 37.2.
116 Cheston to Skouloudis, 17.10.1887, GE Skou 37.2.
117 An Agreement made the seventh day of December 1887 between CFC [...] of the one part and the LCC [...] of the other part, in: LCC s.t., 89–92, 90; Papadopoulos (1993, 153).
118 LCC to the Committee of the London Stock Exchange, 18.5.1888, GL 126 17B.
119 LCC to the Committee of the London Stock Exchange, History of the Lake Copais C. from its Establishment to the present time, GL 126 17B.
120 Ibid.
121 An Agreement made the seventh day of December 1887 between CFC [...] of the one part and John Balli [...] of the other part, in: LCC s.t., 95–97.
122 Prospectus of the LCC, First Issue of £150,000, part of £300,000 First Mortgage Debentures, 1.2.1888, GE Skou 41.2. Exactly: £423,000, see LCC, GL 72 12B.

123 Prospectus of the LCC, First Issue of £150,000, part of £300,000 First Mortgage Debentures, 1.2.1888, GE Skou 41.2.
124 The Church of St. Helen (formerly St. Mary) in Lancashire: Baptisms recorded in the Register for the years 1833–1841, https://www.lan-opc.org.uk/St-Helens/St-Helens/sthelen/baptisms_1833-1834.html#TAIL [10.2.2020].
125 *The Times*, 6.4.1882.
126 *The Times*, 5.8.1897.
127 *The Times*, 23.6.1893.
128 *The Times*, 1.11.1882.
129 *The Times*, 8.10.1892.
130 In the Venezuelan Austin Gold Mining Company, in: *The Times*, 16.7.1892. Also in the Nacupai Gold Mining Company, *The Times*, 8.5.1886.
131 *The Times*, 5.6.1888.
132 *The Times*, 21.11.1890.
133 *The Times*, 24.5.1894.
134 The historical material is presented in the form of a novel here.
135 Homenaje al 'tren de los anglesos'. Una publicación recupera la historia del tren Gandia-Alcoi, que marcó una época entre los años 1893 y 1969, *El Pais*, 30.12.2003.
136 *The Times*, 20.8.1894. The livelihood of the region was based primarily on viticulture, which was failing to flourish. In 1894, further investment in infrastructure and harbours was found to be necessary to stimulate an economic upturn.
137 *The Times*, 5.5.1902.
138 LCC, Report to be presented at the Third General Meeting of the Company to be held [...] 19th December 1889, GL 13 26B. Cheston mentioned the energy with which Henry Lee engaged in Pochet's plans, see Cheston to Skouloudis, 28.7.1887, GE Skou 37.2.
139 **183 n.122** in this book.
140 Elissen to Skouloudis, 1.6.1887, GE Skou 36.2.
141 Cheston to Skouloudis, 31.12.1886, GE Skou 37.1.
142 Cheston to Pochet, 7.6.1887, as a copy, GE Skou 36.2.
143 Marriages, in: *The Times*, 26.11.1897.
144 University Intelligence, in: *The Times*, 9.6.1860.
145 University Intelligence, in: *The Times*, 9.12.1864; 8.3.1867.
146 The Prince of Wales and the East-end Children, in: *The Times*, 4.6.1887. This was about a bazaar held to benefit poor children. Cheston was the chairman of the bazaar committee and thus received the Prince of Wales when he visited. Cheston continued to be involved in the East London Hospital for Children and Dispensary for Women. He also supported the Royal Alfred Aged Seamen Institution, see *The Times*, 5.5.1888, and was active in the Grand Lodge of Freemasons, see *The Times*, 25.4.1889. His wife was also an active philanthropist (see Shaw 1991, 345f.).
147 Wills – Mr. Charles Cheston, in: *The Times*, 13.7.1906.
148 *East Anglian Daily Times*, 12 June 1880, cited from Martin (2000, 343).
149 Pathos of a peer's death, in: *Auckland Star*, Bd. XL, 56, 6.3.1909, 15.
150 Nikolson, M.: The Nitrate Industry, in: *The Economist*, 26.3.1892.
151 *The Times*, 2.8.1894.
152 *The Times*, 18.3.1890.
153 Wills – Mr. Charles Cheston, in: *The Times*, 13.7.1906.
154 Police, in: *The Times*, 11.9.1902. This was mentioned in the newspaper because a fraudster had forged shares.
155 Pathos of a peer's death, in: *Auckland Star*, Bd. XL, 56, 6.3.1909, 15.

156 Cheston to Skouloudis, 28.7.1887, GE Skou 37.2.
157 The Finances of Greece, in: *The Economist*, 23.7.1887.
158 Cheston to Skouloudis, 28.7.1887, GE Skou 37.2. This letter bears the same date as that named below but the date seems to be wrong because the two letters appear not to have been written on the same day.
159 Cheston to Skouloudis, 28.7.1887, GE Skou 37.2.
160 Ibid.
161 Ibid.
162 Ibid. (σύννοια meaning deliberations. It is not clear if this might refer to a work of Skouloudis.) Hence Cheston's annoyance that the financier Raphael, whom he had counted on, did not come on board because he believed the undertaking to be safe but not first class; in addition, it was too small for Raphael (see ibid.).
163 '[T]he history of the Peloponnesian and Persian wars, of the growth of small, maritime Athens to a powerful – and glorious – empire was read as a modern allegory: small maritime England in the nineteenth century triumphing over its continental neighbours, the French, seen in Persian dress, and building a great empire, governed by a noble class, born to rule' (Bowen 1989, 176).
164 Cheston defended the Greeks against prejudice, arguing that the equation of Greek with fraud in France, especially in the work of Edmond About, had nothing to do with reality (see Cheston 1887a, 14).
165 There was, however, criticism of his opinion: thus, the Athens correspondent of the *Economist* responded angrily that Greece state debts had grown greatly in recent years, that the tax burden was crushing, and that all this was just to strengthen one party; see Greek Finances, in: *The Economist*, 3.12.1887.
166 The Greek Debt, in: *The Times*, 22.12.1893.
167 Over a 100 years later, this was also translated into Greek: Τσέστων [Cheston] (1990).
168 Telegram from Richard to Skouloudis, 5.7.1894, GE Skou 36.4.
169 The liquidators to Skouloudis, 28.11.1892, GE Skou 36.4.
170 LCC 1892, Report to be presented at a General Meeting [...] 21st December, GL 712-79B.
171 LCC to the liquidators of the CLC, 6.7.1888, GE Skou 36.1.
172 An overview of the size of the cultivated area is provided by, e.g. Melios (1990, 41).
173 Cheston to Skouloudis, 25.7.1895, GE Skou 37.8; Lee to the directors of the LCC, 30.12.1889, GE Skou 43.1.
174 Cheston to Skouloudis, 24.6.1895, GE Skou 37.8.
175 Prospectus of the LCC, Second Issue of £150,000, balance of £300,000 First Mortgage Debentures, 3.12.1889, GE Skou 41.3 (including a report from Chirico dated 5.5.1890).
176 Cheston to Skouloudis, 10.4.1890, GE Skou 37.3.
177 LCC, Prospectus, after 1891, GE Skou 41.3.
178 CFC, Pochet, Note sur la valeur du domaine de Copaïs, Novembre 1893, GE Skou 34.18, 3.
179 Between 1889 and 1896, the population of the region increased greatly, but later many inhabitants left the region (again), because living conditions did not encourage them to stay. Papadopoulos links this to the fact that the LCC quickly increased the cost of the leases, which were initially very low (see Papadopoulos 1993, 52).
180 CFC, Pochet, Note sur la valeur du domaine de Copaïs, Novembre 1893, GE Skou 34.18, 11.
181 On the difficulties of introducing innovations into agriculture (see Jones 1963, 403).

182 CFC, Pochet, Note sur la valeur du domaine de Copaïs, Novembre 1893, GE Skou 34.18, 5, tr. by K.S.
183 Cheston to Skouloudis, 18.6.1895, GE Skou 37.8.
184 Cheston to Skouloudis, 28.6.1895, GE Skou 37.8; Cheston to Skouloudis, 25.10.1895, GE Skou 37.8.
185 Cheston to Skouloudis, 10.7.1895, GE Skou 37.8.
186 The development of cadastres in many European countries, although not in Spain or England, is presented by Vivier/Petmezas (2008, 18). As discussed, Gustave d'Eichthal proposed a cadastre in Greece in the early 1830s; **107** and **113f.** in this book.
187 This is investigated for Prussia in the 1880s by Harwood (2008).
188 Charles Cheston to Skouloudis, 12.6.1888, GE Skou 35.4, 7.
189 Ibid., 8.
190 Working conditions in agricultural production in Europe and their consequences are discussed by Landsteiner/Langthaler (2010). The edited volume that is introduced by this paper shows that the virulent problems experienced with organising working conditions at Lake Copais were typical of agricultural societies in Europe, a fact that Greek research has insufficiently acknowledged.
191 This refers to Eric Hambro, son of Everard, who joined the banking house in the mid-1890s (see Bramsen/Wain 1979, 326). However, there are no indications in the sources that C. J. Hambro & Son were involved in the founding or the early years of the company as is sometimes claimed in the literature.
192 Shortly before the company published a short monograph about its history and property: Ανώνυμος Εταιρεία της Λίμνης Κωπαΐδος [LCC] (1951). On the discussions of the inter-war period and the history of Copais after 1953, see the edited volume Μέλιος [Melios]/Παπαδόπουλος [Papadopoulos] (1988). Lago Fucino in Italy had been expropriated only two years earlier.

8

INCASSO INTERNATIONAL

Building up confidence by debt redemption?[1]

The state bankruptcy of 1893

The world economic crisis of the early 1890s was not at all beneficial for the LCC's business. It started in November 1890 with the collapse of the Baring Brothers Bank, which could only be rescued thanks to a large-scale initiative of the London City managed by the Bank of England. Baring's problems were triggered by the financial crisis in Argentina, where the bank was particularly active (Chapman 1984, 78–81).[2] The crisis also affected Greece, although the financial decline of the country had in any case been increasingly clear to financial experts in the preceding years. The level of state debt had become alarming: the country had accumulated 730 million francs of foreign debt, although its budget was just 80 million drachmas, about 65 million francs, in 1890 (Psalidopoulos/Schönhärl 2013; Ψαλιδόπουλος [Psalidopoulos] 2019). Greece thus had to spend about 33% of its budget on servicing foreign debts in this year, not including the bonds held by Greek residents in the country (Levandis 1944, 75). The public debt ratio had risen from 60% in 1876 to 230% in 1892, equivalent to 1,200% of the annual taxation revenue (Δερτιλής [Dertilis] 2009, 603). By way of comparison, in 1876, the Spanish public debt ratio was 160% (which led to the state bankruptcy of 1882), while the French debt ratio reached 100% in 1900 (Taylor s.t., 7, 15). The dramatic decline of the drachma, which fell to 1.81 francs in the course of 1893, meant that the Greek government found it increasingly difficult to service the debts in gold (Wynne 1951, 306).[3]

Despite his excellent reputation abroad, Greek prime minister Trikoupis found himself ever more on the defensive in domestic politics, particularly as work on the prestige project of the Piraeus-Larissa railway was delayed by disputes with the company carrying out the work,[4] like with the Corinth Canal. In 1891, the change of government and the transfer of responsibility to Theodoros Deyannis led to a decline in the rates of all Greek bonds in London, because the diaspora there had less trust in the new government than in that led by Trikoupis.[5] It was suddenly impossible for the Greeks to obtain new loans abroad, either in Paris or in London. The Deutsche Bank

DOI: 10.4324/9780429286537-11

was also uninterested in such business, despite enquiries by the governor of the ETE Stephan Streit,[6] who was of German origin and a close confidant of Crown Prince Constantine.[7] The foreign diplomats in Athens reacted with increasing coldness to the repeated requests for loans: 'If, instead of the wasteful financial administration of recent years with its dependence on ever more new loans, there had been a parsimonious financial policy at the helm that had wisely kept the budget within the country's available resources, the situation would probably differ to today's worryingly compromised state credit'.[8] The German press now displayed understanding for the reluctance of the investors to become further involved, suggesting 'that European capital was getting tired of always reaching into its pocket to enable the Greek government to make interest payments'.[9] The Greek bonds fell massively by up to 25%.[10] Hoping for an injection of new foreign capital, in 1892, Trikoupis invited the British government to send financial experts to audit the Greek finances. The diplomat and engineer Edward FitzGerald Law was therefore sent to Greece and compiled a detailed and positive report in which he attempted to show 'that, with temporary assistance, the present crisis may be tided over, and that proper care in the future may secure the continence of the hitherto normal development of the country'. But he also warned that 'without such care in the future no temporary assistance can avail to prevent final misfortune' (Morison 1911, 132–149).[11] The banks were extremely interested in this report, e.g. the Gibbs banking house.[12] The French followed suit and in 1893 their diplomat Roux also produced a report.[13] The objective of the French government was to persuade the French banks to issue a loan to Greece, thus allowing the country to continue to service its foreign debts without abandoning the Greek market to the British and the Germans: Hambro, Bleichröder and the Rothschilds were already negotiating a new Greek loan. In contrast, the French banks remained very sceptical and reserved, despite government attempts to promote a loan. For instance, the CL and the Banque de Paris & des Pays-Bas rejected plans for a loan presented by the ministry of finance.[14] The banking house Hoskier was the only one to display any interest in participating in an international consortium and attempted, unsuccessfully, to gain access to the Roux report from the French ministry of finance for Hambro, a potential partner in the consortium.[15] The banks were primarily concerned with ensuring that the country remained solvent and avoided bankruptcy. By 1893, negotiations were well advanced, the sub-holdings agreed and the promotional material for the bond issue printed,[16] but the demission of Trikoupis as the prime minister on 15 May prevented the loan from coming to fruition: 'the panic around the Greek securities in London explains it'.[17] In the press, e.g. in Germany, euphoria transformed into bitter criticism:

> When a Prussian princess married into Greece, many capitalists then bought Greek papers; those who allow themselves to be led

> into capital investments by such motives may not complain about the consequences, even though this does not mitigate the serious accusation levelled at the issuers of the Greek papers.[18]

In May 1893, under prime minister Sotirios Sotiropoulos, the Hambro banking house then proved willing to issue a so-called 'funding loan' of 100 million francs at 5%. All the interest due on Greek debts (with the exception of the monopoly loan of 1887), which should actually have been paid in gold, was to be paid in bonds from this funding loan for the next two-and-a-half years – a step that deeply shook the confidence of the financial markets (Levandis 1944, 77ff.). Only about a tenth of the foreseen sum of the new loan was actually issued.

In autumn 1893, the economic crisis then led to the sudden collapse in the price of raisins, Greece's main export,[19] and the country was no longer able to maintain its financial viability. On 10 December 1893, Trikoupis, who in November had replaced Sotiropoulos and been elected as the prime minister for the seventh time, declared the bankruptcy of the country in parliament.[20] The amortisation of foreign debts ceased and interest payments were reduced to 30% of the original rate. The guarantees for the various loans were seized. Years of negotiations with the creditors followed, but without any agreement being reached (Petersson 2009, 33–50).[21]

Very few voices spoke in defence of Greece in Western Europe at this time. It was rather the case that the 'extinguishment of the exotic through the banalisation' of Greece continued throughout the 1890s, not least thanks to the continued expansion of tourism, giving Greece the 'appearance of a colony' (Basch 1995, 240, 247, tr. by K.S.). The disappointment of the French with the country grew as its modernisation advanced. What remained was often just folklore and nostalgia. 'Greece, a country like no other, has no right to a *golden mean*: we immediately reproach it for not being the ideal homeland that we had imagined' (ibid., 494, tr. by K.S.). The Greeks were increasingly infantilised in public perceptions and seen as the spoilt children of Europe, which seemed to justify all kinds of interference in the country's politics (ibid., 495). Of course, the state bankruptcy further strengthened such perceptions. This decade was thus characterised by the 'constant indifference of Europe to Greece' (ibid., 295, tr. by K.S.), despite a few isolated positive comments, e.g. in the aftermath of the Greek-Turkish war, and the enthusiasm that met the first modern Olympic Games held in Athens in 1896. It was usually only when Greece found itself in an extremely negative situation that, for instance, France felt called upon to protect the country, and the name and 'idea' of Greece again became the focus of attention – naturally with references to antiquity (ibid., 493). While interest for modern Greece declined or indeed was transformed into contempt, the enthusiasm for antiquity continued its renaissance (ibid., 314). Many Europeans saw the ancient heritage of the Greeks as 'their only noble title, their only right to existence' (ibid., 301, tr. by K.S.).[22] In contrast, modern Greece was met with increasing 'mishéllenisme' or anti-Hellenism in Europe, and the word 'Philhellene' could be used as a term of abuse. Hatred of the Greeks was at times directed even more intensely towards the Philhellenes, who were portrayed as idealist adventurers (ibid., 249, 255). There were seldom any middle positions between the two camps of Greece haters and Greece lovers, both sides tended to extremes (Holland/Markides 2006, 2). This was the background against which an agreement needed to be reached between Greece and its creditors. Trikoupis, now again in office, stalled and delayed the negotiations until representatives of the creditors appealed to their governments for diplomatic support. The British and French governments were unyielding: the bankers and investors were themselves responsible for the risks they had taken and they would now have to bear the losses (Petersson 2009, 33–50). In contrast, the German diplomats (the German share of the foreign debts amounted to about 125 million francs (Schaefer 1995, 323[23])) were less dismissive and allowed creditors to hope for full repayment, which the diplomats believed could be achieved through bringing political pressure to bear. The German investors therefore firmly refused the compromises proposed by Trikoupis, who wanted to repay 30% or 35% of the capital (Petersson 2009, 39–46).

In fact, the Great Powers were soon given an opportunity to exercise leverage: in 1897, another armed conflict broke out between the Ottoman Empire and Greece, with Greece supporting a Cretan uprising (Holland/Markides 2006, 81–107). Within a few weeks, it was clear that the Ottomans had won an overwhelming victory.[24] They occupied Thessaly, which had only been granted to Greece as recently as 1881, and declared that they would only leave after the payment of high reparations; they originally demanded ten million Turkish £ but finally settled for four million (94.3 million francs). Bankrupt Greece was forced to turn to the international financial markets to find the necessary money. To make this possible at all, and especially at reasonably acceptable conditions, a guarantee from the Great Powers was required. Russia, Great Britain and France therefore provided a guarantee for Greece for a loan in 1898,[25] and the loan enjoyed great success at the exchanges.[26] During the preliminary peace of September 1897, the German diplomats also managed to gain agreement that, given the sum to be paid, the rights of the foreign creditors should be protected and a financial commission should monitor repayment of the Greek debts (Wynne 1951, 313). An international financial commission (IFC) was therefore installed in Athens with the task of organising repayment of the Greek foreign debts. There were only very isolated cases, for instance in France, of intellectuals who understood why the financial commission was so disliked in Greece and tried to defend the country (Basch 1995, 288). However, most decision makers continued to insist on intransigence. In the following years, much of the Greek population suffered in the very poor economic conditions and many viewed the situation as hopeless, which explains the large numbers of emigrants, most of whom headed for the USA.[27]

Trust in institutions?

Nonetheless, just a few years after the commission had been established, Greece was again able to independently borrow money on the international financial markets at the usual conditions. Thus, the loans for the railway from Piraeus to Larissa and Demerly on the Turkish border, issued in 1902, 1904 and 1906, were not guaranteed by the Great Powers, although the servicing of the loans was administered by the international commission (Παπαγιαννάκης [Papayiannakis] 1982, 132).[28] In 1910/1911, Greece was then able to issue a loan for 150 million drachmas, the servicing of which was solely the government's responsibility, even if the IFC surplus was among the guarantees. The financial markets thus regained confidence in Greece in just 12 years. How did the banks perceive the risks of these loans? What role did the IFC as a supra-national organisation play in the evaluation and management of risks?

According to institutional economics as propounded by Douglass North, state institutions such as a functioning legal system or police force are particularly important in the development of trust. 'Institutions constitute the rules of the game of human interaction in a world of social interdependence. [...] [They] stabilise expectations and thus reduce the subjective uncertainty with which an actor is confronted in social exchange relations' (Ripperger 2005, 24, tr. by K.S.). In increasingly complex societies, personal trust is ever more difficult, and institutions can create new impersonal trust and confidence.[29] The IFC can be understood as such an institution on an international level, in the context of increasing globalisation in the second half of the nineteenth century. In the terminology of Marek Korczynski, this involves governance/incentive trust, which is largely based on the fact that an enforcement agency can guarantee adherence to agreed rules (Korczynski 2000). Sharp and Maerean reach a similar conclusion in their empirical macro-economic investigation of financial commissions in Southern Europe (Sharp/Maerean 2015). However, at the end of the nineteenth century and beginning of the twentieth century, the international community of states had no instruments of power with which they could enforce the rules of the IFC, despite gunboat policy. The only sanction which could be inflicted on a defaulting state was the loss of trust and reputation on the international financial markets, an informal sanction – indeed, little has changed in this situation until today. So what role was played by the IFC in reconstituting trust on the market for Greek government bonds?

The installation of the IFC

The conditions enforced on Greece by the IFC were relatively mild. The country not only received the money necessary for the reparations, but also an 'economic loan' to cover the state deficit, all guaranteed by the Great Powers.[30] The Powers approved 170 million francs, of which 150 million were finally issued by a French banking group led by Alphonse de Rothschild, the Bank of England and the imperial Russian bank representing a Russian consortium.[31] Although the interest was only 2.5%, the guarantee from the Great Powers made it possible to issue the first instalment of £4,980,000 in Paris and London at a rate of 100.5, and the second of £961,500 at a rate of 104, considerably above par (Wynne 1951, 320). The loans were greatly oversubscribed on both exchanges.[32]

At the same time, the IFC was installed in Athens. By 1898, a certain amount of experience had already been gathered with such organisations, though previous attempts to administer Greece's debts externally had failed: as early as May 1843, a commission in London had called for the transfer of certain Greek state revenues to creditors, but this was prevented by the revolution of 1843; in 1845, Great Britain made a similar proposal but was forced to abandon it due to French resistance; from 1857, a commission then at least supervised budget planning and developed various proposals for repaying foreign debts, although none of these were implemented (Zelepos 2015, 68). However, other defaulting countries had successfully been subjected to a foreign administration of their debts. Thus, following the bankruptcy of the Ottoman Empire in 1876, the Council of the Administration for the Ottoman Public Debt was established in 1881 and diverted state revenues from the monopolies for tobacco and salt, certain custom duties and the silk tithe to creditors – in return for a reduction in total Ottoman debts to somewhat less than half (Blaisdell 1929; Birdal 2010; Tunçer 2011, 3). In 1876 in Egypt, formally a province of the Ottoman Empire, a financial commission was also established to meet the demands of foreign creditors. In this case, the authority of the commission was so great that the Khedive was de facto excluded from the financial administration of his country (Tunçer 2009, 2011, 2015). In both cases, the organisations of foreign creditors dispatched their representatives to the commissions.

At the end of 1897, an international working group met in Athens to set up the financial commission and it was quickly clear that Greece would not be subjected to strict conditions. As their representative, the British foreign office dispatched Edward Fitzgerald Law who, after his marriage to a Greek woman,[33] presented himself as a Philhellene and personally campaigned for Greek reparations to be reduced and the country to be treated leniently.[34] For their part, the Greeks named as the minister of finance the governor of the ETE Stephan Streit, who had studied in Germany and enjoyed an international reputation as a financial specialist; Streit led the working group (Ανδρεάδης [Andreadis] 2010, 306f.).[35] In January 1898, the group presented the Greek parliament with draft legislation which was then passed on 7 March.[36]

Greece's foreign debts, which were to be administered by the commission, amounted to 551.7 million francs in gold. Each of the six states that had acted as intermediaries in the conflict (the Protecting Powers France, Great Britain and Russia, and also Austria-Hungary, Italy and the German Empire) sent a representative to the commission.[37] In contrast to the situation in, e.g. Egypt, these delegates were not representatives of the creditors, but members of the diplomatic service. The intention was that the commission should administer the revenues from the state monopolies on salt, petroleum, matches, playing cards and cigarette papers, as well as revenue derived from the mining of emery on Naxos, from stamp and tobacco taxes and from the custom duties collected in Piraeus (Wynne 1951, 320): together 35% of total revenue in 1898 (Théry 1905, 56).[38] The foreigners were not responsible for collecting the revenue; this was undertaken by the Greek Monopolies Authority Corporation (Société de Régie des Monopoles de Grèce), which had been founded as a joint-stock company in 1887. Until 1893, this company had collected the revenue for the so-called monopoly loan (Wynne 1951, 321). Now, the institution was renamed the Hellenic Public Debt Servicing Revenue Agency Company (Société de Régie des revenus affectés au service de la dette publique hellénique).[39] The revenues collected were used to service the old debts from the years 1881 to 1893 as well as the new debt from 1898. The proposal that the commission should also administer Greek domestic debts was rejected by the government due to concerns about interference in domestic affairs.[40]

The bondholders had to accept losses. Their overall capital was preserved but they only received part of the originally agreed interest, between 43 and 32% (e.g. for the monopoly loan of 1887, this meant only 1.72% interest instead of 4%) (Wynne 1951, 329, 336). The sum to be paid annually to the creditors was fixed at nine million francs, equivalent to 14,850,000 drachmas at an exchange rate of 1.65.[41] If the Greek currency was to recover in the coming years, then fewer drachmas would be necessary to procure the necessary amount of gold francs. It was agreed that such a surplus would then be divided between the creditors and the government at a ratio of 60 to 40 (Wynne 1951, 330). The same procedure was to be followed if more revenue was forthcoming. In order to improve the exchange rates, the government was to reduce the amount of paper money in circulation from 94 million drachmas in 1900 by two million annually.[42] In summer 1898, the commission (this more neutral word was chosen rather than using the term control) began its work. It was able to successfully further the interests of the creditors, collecting more than the expected minimum sum. Overall, the revenues were increased from 47.4 million drachmas in 1899 to 79.1 in 1914 – this was equivalent to 40% of the state revenues (Tunçer 2011, 10).[43] The commission was also concerned to keep administrative costs as low as possible; in 1899, they totalled 6.34% of revenue, in 1904 only 5.7% (Théry 1905, 43).

The bankers' risk perception and risk management 1902–1910

The annual IFC reports were printed in a number of publications, including the Reports of the British Foreign Bondholders, and represented an important source of information for the bankers. Other information was drawn from diplomatic circles and the daily press.[44] For instance, the CL compiled a review on Greece that provided detailed evaluations of French, British and German newspaper reports, translating them into French and thus making them quickly accessible for decision makers in the bank.[45] What information did this source provide on the Greek financial market and how did the bankers interpret it?

The establishment of the IFC in 1898 attracted a great amount of international attention, but this was followed by a calmer period in Greek financial affairs and consequently less press reports. The few articles that were published struck a positive note and focused, for instance, on increases in the turnover of the Greek merchant navy, on the growing revenues of the commission and on the rising interest payments made to creditors.[46] For this reason, a number of newspapers even predicted a boom in Greek bonds.[47] Such positive evaluations referred to the annual reports of the commission and diplomatic opinions that attested to the surprisingly quick recovery of Greece's economy:

> The years which have elapsed since the Greco-Turkish war have been marked by a distinct improvement in the financial position of this country and by an increase in the receipts exceeding the most sanguine estimates.[48]

The role played by the commission in these positive developments was, however, judged to be much less substantial by the diplomats than by the press:

> [T]he improvement, such as it is, cannot, I fear, be ascribed directly to the influence of the Commission; it has in the main been automatic; the most we can claim is by straightforward dealing to have introduced into the administration an element of stability, and which has not been without its usefulness.[49]

At least the fear of public criticism by the commission prevented the government from making any further financial experiments.[50]

In addition to these positive assessments, however, the IFC reports also contained a great deal of criticism. The commission did not view its responsibilities as being restricted to the repayment of debts but also wanted to contribute to the economic recovery of the country and encourage the urgently required reforms of the Greek financial administration. This proved impossible. The annual reports constantly reiterated the mantra that it was not necessary to increase taxes in order to increase revenue; it would rather suffice to rigorously combat the high levels of fraud, the forgery of, e.g. stamp coupons, and surreptitious salt production (e.g. Corporation of Foreign Bondholders 1903, 160). There were repeated calls for a crackdown on smuggling, e.g. by establishing a well-equipped system of coastguards and customs stations – but without success.[51] No progress was made on this front (Corporation of Foreign Bondholders 1910, 194). The need for reform of the financial administration was abundantly clear. Reportedly, frauds were brazenly perpetrated in full view of the police and silently tolerated by the authorities, who boycotted any attempts at investigation. The commission attributed this to the very low salaries of the civil servants involved, many of whom were said to be corruptible (Wynne 1951, 344). State revenue totalled 90 million drachmas, and it was estimated that annually between two and six million were lost through tax evasion (Théry 1905, 210). It was pointless to complain about an unbalanced budget, commented the commission, when there were entire regions in which no taxes were collected and when parliament passed additional spending plans without providing any way of covering the costs.[52] Time and again, it was regretted that the Greek government failed to finalise or delayed the reforms proposed by the commission, or that the reforms were rejected by parliament (e.g. Corporation of Foreign Bondholders 1903, 151). The commission viewed itself as a 'true friend of Greece' (ibid.), but the Greeks seemed to disagree and the commission could do little but admonish. The IFC had a de jure veto against redundancies and transfers of personnel. Nonetheless, they were unable to prevent the government dismissing or transferring those whom the IFC viewed as the most able and replacing them with government supporters (Wynne 1951, 345).[53] Usually, the commission avoided conflict. The image of Greece portrayed in the IFC reports was clearly far from consistent but the press initially picked up on little of the criticism, focusing rather on the positive aspects.

This was the situation in 1901, just three years after the commission had been established when the Greeks wanted once again to take out a foreign loan for the construction of the Piraeus-Larissa-Demerly railway (Παπαγιαννάκης [Papayiannakis] 1982, 132).[54] The foreign diplomats, e.g. the Germans, were initially extremely sceptical about these plans.[55] The British also reacted with reserve, questioning the purpose of the loan and predicting that Greek credibility on the European exchanges would suffer considerably if the money was used for the purchase of armaments, as seemed likely.[56] Similarly, most of the newspapers warned against these new bonds, suggesting that the Greeks were so corrupt and sly that the Powers had to take control of their finances to protect them from themselves – the colonial view of the country was thus swiftly updated. It was suggested that ever since it had been established, the commission had struggled to save Greece from another bankruptcy, while the government once again put its money in its 'opera-comique warriors'. In the event of a large-scale war in the Balkans, the international commission would surely have to leave the country.[57] The German papers were also critical: Greece had once before used money intended for the Piraeus-Larissa railway for other purposes. 'But despite all the contracts how often has Greece violated its creditors; therefore *wallets closed*!'[58] Opinions like those of *The Times*, which judged the bonds to be a safe option,[59] remained an exception.

Despite the many critical comments, the Greeks managed to obtain permission to issue the loan. This was particularly thanks to the purpose to which the money was to be put, not only to finance the railway, but also to purchase coastal patrol vessels to tackle smuggling, and to construct an irrigation system in Thessaly and tobacco manufactories and customs buildings in Piraeus – all undertakings that the IFC had long demanded.[60] The commission therefore agreed to the loan and even agreed to administer it to ensure better conditions.[61] The banking houses Hambro, Erlanger and the ETE issued the first instalment in 1902 (Στεφανίδης [Stefanidis] 1930, 218f.; Παπαγιαννάκης [Papayiannakis] 1982, 132), with a term of 98 years and interest of 4%.[62] The sources available do not provide detailed insights into the risk perception or risk management of the bankers, although the splitting of the risk between three reliable partners with a great deal of experience in Greece seems to have been the key. However, given the unfavourable situation on the stock markets, it was not possible to speak of a successful issue or of reawakened confidence in Greece[63]: of the £880,000 required, only £8,000 were subscribed, primarily in England and France.[64]

The second instalment of the loan was planned for 1904. The press reports struck a much more friendly tone this time, suggesting that the new railway would offer great business opportunities, thanks to the link it provided to the Ottoman rail-network and the Suez Canal.[65] The soundness of the bonds was emphasised: 'The value of the guarantee is very great, in addition the guarantee is fixed in Greece to the benefit of the security holder, like otherwise nowhere in the world'.[66] The press failed to mention that this new loan was not intended to finance the construction of the railway, but rather to balance the budget of 1903 and to allow the abolition of the forced exchange.[67]

What was behind this change in the coverage of most of the newspapers? A decisive role was played by the development of the exchange rate between the drachma and the franc, which in September 1903 sank to 1.54 (compared to 1.60 the previous year). This was greeted positively by the financial press as it meant additional profits for the holders of the Greek bonds and a quicker amortisation.[68] As the exchange rate fell, the value of Greek state bonds rose and the comments in the European newspapers became increasingly positive – prospect theory would interpret this development as the effects of positive emotions resulting from market fluctuations (Barberis et al. 2001, 2). When the drachma fell to 1.40 in June 1904, just before the second instalment of the loan was issued, the *Cote européen* deliberately drew the attention of its readers to the bond issue, with reports of the large profits that could be expected.[69] The railway line was said to be sure to further increase state revenues and thus also to improve the position of creditors.[70] The newspapers intensively discussed the reasons for the sensational decline of the gold agio, attributing importance not only to the capital borrowed abroad, but also to the good harvest which meant that fewer imports were necessary, and to the money sent from the USA by emigrants.[71] There were few contrary opinions published, but the *Capitaliste* was extremely negative about Greece: the instability of the Greek 'spoilt finances' was said to be notorious and the political and economic situation in the region was such that further involvement was deemed inadvisable.[72] The guarantees offered investors were described as simply illusionary given the country's corrupt finances.[73]

This one-sided and negative view remained the exception. The majority of reports employed two different images of Greece: on the one hand, the work of the commission was fulsomely praised,[74] the soundness of the bonds was emphasised and Greece's general economic development was noted with approval; on the other hand, the ineffective, chaotic and corrupt financial administration was harshly criticised.[75] Positive and negative portrayals of Greece sometimes even appeared together in the same publication. Both could draw on the reports of the commission and information from diplomatic circles. The diplomats censured the chaotic financial administration but also wholeheartedly praised the economic development of the country, which, if only the state would straighten out its finances, stood 'on the eve of a definite recovery'.[76] However, the government passed more and more spending plans rather than tackling the necessary reforms.[77] The French envoy to the IFC therefore proposed that the financial reforms should be made a conditio sine qua non for acquiring foreign capital, in the hope that this would force the Greeks to act and avoid undermining the control legislation.[78] The French diplomat d'Ormesson produced a discerning analysis of the contradictory Western views, describing the two diverging images of Greece. The belief in 'the work of economic recovery of Greece' that could be recognised in the fields of trade, agriculture, railway construction and even banking was contrasted with the poor financial administration.[79] D'Ormesson criticised the foreign countries 'that separate the badly administered and badly positioned state finances from the growing economic strengths of the country'.[80] The contrasting but unconnected images of Greece were, he argued, also responsible for the extreme fluctuations on the exchanges: while two or three years ago nobody was at all interested in Greek securities, now everyone was suddenly fighting over them, leading to a boom in the bonds as all caution was forgotten.[81]

Such analyses did nothing to stem the positive mood. In the wake of the improving exchange rates, the issue of the second instalment of the

Piraeus-Larissa line proved a complete success, in turn, further strengthening the drachma which improved to 1.30 in August 1904.[82] The IFC declared the return of confidence in the Greek market:

> It was therefore natural that the past year should have been marked by a considerable improvement in the status of Greek Bonds on the European markets, on which confidence had been so seriously shaken by the crisis of 1893 that it was but slowly reviving, notwithstanding the guarantees by which the settlement of the old Debt had been surrounded.[83]

The government had no problems finding investors for the additional bonds issued in December to extend the railway.[84] At the same time, Edmond Théry, the director of the *Économiste européen*, published a large study of the Greek economy, commissioned by the Greek government, both as a series of articles in his newspaper and in the form of a book.[85] His conclusion was almost entirely positive and he pointed out that despite the new loans the overall amount of debt had scarcely increased (Théry 1905, 53). The commission had apparently managed to improve the position of the creditors in every way, in terms of both the interest and the value of their bonds. This happy result completely justified the confidence of the foreign investors in the excellent quality of the revenue sources of the commission and their perfect administration of the Greek loans, and this, in turn, very much benefited the credit of the state (ibid., 39, 205). In addition, Théry mentioned the commission's criticism of the Greek government and the government's unwillingness to execute reforms. He suggested a solution would be to greatly increase the share of the surplus that the Greeks received; as had been seen in Egypt, he argued, this was the only way to interest the state in increasing revenues and initiating the necessary reforms (ibid., 221f.).

The murder of the prime minister Theodoros Delyannis on 13 June 1905 triggered a government crisis in Athens that dominated the newspapers at the end of 1905 and the beginning of 1906 but did little to dampen the overwhelmingly positive attitude towards the Greek financial market (Tzermias 1986, 106). The rate of exchange continued to fall: in 1905 to 1.23, in 1906 to 1.10, and it was expected that the trend would continue towards par.[86] Assessments of the work of the IFC remained as positive as those of the general financial and economic development of the country,[87] despite the fact that the government could not even afford to pay the Greek soldiers.[88] The commission agreed to another bond issue for the extension of the Piraeus-Larissa railway to the Macedonian border in August 1906[89]; this issue was once again a success.

From 1905, negotiations were held about another loan, this time not for the purpose of railway construction but for, e.g. the purchase of weapons. Although other nations were somewhat critical of such a proposal, the

French were more open to the notion of a loan being issued for armaments – providing the contracts then went to France. If this seemed unlikely – in 1904, for instance, the Greeks negotiated with Krupp – then the French were not willing to support a new bond issue.[90] The French banks adopted the same attitude as the diplomats and were primarily concerned with ensuring that their clients from the armaments industry secured contracts.[91] The French papers commented in a similar vein.[92] Thus, the BUP was particularly concerned with ensuring that Greek contracts for armaments be won by their customer, the Société Anonyme des Ateliers & Chantiers de la Loire.[93] The BUP's local partner, the Greek BA, received corresponding instructions:

> I would like to remind you that this company [Anonyme des Ateliers & Chantiers de la Loire, K. S.] is our customer and that we have common administrative boards; this means that we are most interested in including them in the communication and that we wish to be agreeable to them.[94]

If successful, the manufacturers were willing to grant the BA 5% of the order value as commission. It seems likely that the French bank was also interested in competitive positioning vis-à-vis the Germans, who had founded the Banque d'Orient in 1905 and were just as keen to influence the arms contracts as the BUP.[95] Beyond the question of orders for weapons, the French diplomats agreed with most of Edmond Théry's positive evaluation and were inclined to look favourably on loans being issued for productive purposes.[96] Despite French opposition, in 1907, the Greek government then managed to gain approval for a bond issue for armaments that was not tied to contracts for French firms.[97] No French banks participated. The loan of £800,000 (20 million francs) at 5%, repayable in 36 years (Στεφανίδης [Stefanidis] 1930, 217f.), was issued by the ETE and Hambro[98] in London and was guaranteed by the revenues from the National Defence Fund and the surpluses of the commission, but without being under the commission's control.[99] Hambro was persuaded to participate in the loan, although 1907 was a poor year for the London City and the banking house had become less involved in government bonds, focusing increasingly on municipal loans (Oslo, Rome, Rosario, Goteborg and Copenhagen) (Bramsen/Wain 1979, 330f.; Chavagneux 2013, 63–82). Hambro's decision may well have been influenced by a commission of £2,000[100] and the good prices of the older Greek bonds caused by the favourable exchange rates.[101]

The issuers initially did not dare to offer the bonds to the public. It was 1908 before they brought £200,000 (five million francs) of this loan onto the market in London, Athens, Paris, Berlin and Cairo, while the rest remained in the hands of the syndicate.[102] The prospectus was entitled 'Principal and interest payable in gold' – a direct reference to the possibility of making exchange rate gains and the solidity of the bonds. The issue rate was 97, although the ETE had even proposed 98.[103] The issue of the bonds, which were duly subscribed, was greeted as a sign of Greece's credit recovery.[104] The exchange rates continued to fall, in 1908 to 108.76.[105] This trend was unaffected by the miserable economic situation of a large proportion of the Greek population, emigration to the USA, the continued decline of Greek metallic money and the continuation of the forced exchange rates which led to Greek silver coins being drained off into other countries of the Latin Monetary Union and in 1908 to the nationalisation of the one- and two-drachma coins.[106] Untouched by these problems, the path to a new, more comprehensive foreign loan seemed clear and Austrian, German and French banks correspondingly began negotiations with Greece.[107]

In spring 1909, the Greek government wanted to negotiate more concretely. Rather than using the ETE as an intermediary as usual, they asked the much smaller BA, which had only been founded in 1905, to organise a syndicate.[108] It was clear that the French 'sister bank' of the BA, the BUP, would also participate. French demands for a tied loan that involved commitments concerning armaments contracts were thus back on the agenda. The foreign office in Paris told the French ambassador to make it unmistakably clear to the Greek government:

> that our conduct in the question of granting credit will be determined by the attitude that they believe they must adopt towards the French industrialists who are called upon to compete with those of other countries in the restoration of armaments.[109]

The foreign minister instructed the press to remain silent about these links so as not to alienate the self-confident Greeks.[110] The BUP, which had strengthened its diverse business relations with the Greek BA in recent years,[111] continued to pursue the idea of a tied loan, in line with the wishes of the French government. At this time of financial difficulties, the Greek government, normally sceptical of agreements that limited its freedom, was willing to negotiate about a 'mixed combination'.[112] The BA and the BUP praised each other, suggesting that such a deal not only provided a 'nice profit' for them, but was 'morally also very profitable' in terms of supporting French industry against the German competition.[113] And in fact similar considerations played a role in Berlin.[114] The press also recognised that the Greeks were attempting to play off the French and German investors against one another.[115]

The BA director Matsas contacted not only potential French partners, but also Emil Erlanger in London.[116] Erlanger initially assessed the threat of war on the Balkans as too acute,[117] but he nonetheless sounded out Hambro, with whom he had cooperated for many years. Hambro was also reserved, especially because renewed support from the commission could not be expected after the project of 1907. He also believed such business to be impossible without the involvement of the ETE. Erlanger continued nonetheless to pursue the topic, urging that a productive purpose should be stipulated for the money because a loan intended only for armaments would not be well-received by the press in London.[118] He expressly asked that the completion of the Piraeus-Larissa railway should be specified as one of the objectives – his personal financial involvement in the construction of this line was significant,[119] making the path dependency of his decision clear.[120] In addition, he also emphasised that without binding arms contracts for England and France, it would be impossible to gain the agreement of the governments of these countries.[121] He demanded an unusually high 4.5% of the total sum as commission for the issue.[122] In their financial distress, the Greek government accepted these conditions and negotiations turned to possible guarantees. However, given the instability of foreign affairs, Erlanger did not want to make firm commitments and demanded a contractual clause which would release him from the obligation to issue the loan in the event of 'force majeure'.[123] It was typical that the risk perception of bankers of the time was dependent on the financial and political climate (Pohle-Fraser 1999, 112–117).[124]

The banking house of Hambro displayed no real enthusiasm for the loan. Everard Hambro advised his son and partner Eric, over whom he had great influence,[125] against the deal if the ETE, as an old and trusted partner, was not involved, especially as he mistrusted the demand that negotiations be confidential. It was somewhat typical that Hambro relied on the assessment of a dependable and familiar business partner to judge a new project instead of gathering information himself (Pohle-Fraser 1999, 268). If the trusted partner was not involved, or was deliberately excluded, then this was interpreted as an alarm signal. The ETE was, as was common for a regional bank, significant in procuring information for Hambro.[126] Eric Hambro's other partner Robert Heriot[127] also believed that the abstention of the ETE was a sign that it did not approve of further arms investment by the government; this second-order observation was more important than any primary information about the project. In addition, Heriot warned of the negative repercussions of a dubious issue on the reputation of the issuing house if the British press picked up on the rearmament plans.[128] The senior Hambro also viewed the need to tie the loan to the French armaments industry as extremely obstructive (Pohle-Fraser 1999, 268). Furthermore, he was concerned that the relationship between Hambro and the ETE could suffer if Hambro proceeded with the business without involving this bank. Eric Hambro clearly and succinctly summarised his position to Stephan Streit of the ETE: 'We have now been told that you did not wish to participate or take the lead, and therefore we also have declined to have anything to do with it'.[129]

But why did Erlanger agree to act despite all this opposition? Everard Hambro could only explain this by suggesting a lack of morality in his partner or competitor:

> I further think it would be wrong for us to use our influence to try and make it [the loan, K. S.] go, whatever the profit may be. As far as Erlanger is concerned he is simply trying to get commissions. His thoughts are only to make money. We have so far looked at business from another point of view, and that is probably why the two names stand in a different category.[130]

Defaming competitors who were prepared to take risks as irresponsible and interested only in quick profits is a semantic construction that Monika Pohle-Fraser views as typical of nineteenth-century banking (Pohle 1995, 33; Pohle-Fraser 1999, 9, 45–48, 63). A lower appetite for risk is justified by the suggestion that long-term reputation is much more important than short-term profits, and this behaviour is defined as a norm which should not be violated, evoking the notion of an 'honest merchant' (Olegario/McKenna 2013, 649f.).

Despite the misgivings in the Hambro banking house, Erlanger continued his negotiations through the spring of 1909 on his own initiative. He was keen to include the Banque de Paris, the BUP, the BA and the ETE in the syndicate. A co-founder of the BUP, Sauerbach Thalmann et Cie, acted as intermediary for the negotiations. 50 million francs were supposed to be issued as soon as the Balkan crisis was settled with the prospect of a further 50 million francs and the payment of an advance of ten million. The commission payment, now only 2.5%, was to be divided between the four partners, after a deduction of ½% for Erlanger.[131] The armaments contracts were to be divided proportionally between French and British firms. Furthermore, Erlanger insisted on the funding of the Piraeus-Larissa railway line being included in the contract as a conditio sine qua non.[132]

Once the negotiations were well advanced, Erlanger again asked Hambro to participate in the loan by issuing it in London, at least in the second row. He offered a fifth of the profits after the deduction of 1% for himself.[133] Eric Hambro now immediately agreed to take £800,000: 'We think we had better go ahead'.[134] Without any further concerns, Hambro plunged into negotiating details: Erlanger proposed an issue price of 88 but Hambro countered with the comment that they should not appear greedy in this difficult situation and suggested 82.5. Hambro explained this change of mind by arguing that his new decision was motivated by the wish to provide a means for the Greek government to service old debts – this can only have referred to the national debt and railway loan of 1902 as the international debts were serviced by the IFC. Was this really Hambro's main motivation? A letter from Everard Hambro, who grudgingly accepted his son's reassessment, to Streit (ETE) provides deeper insight into perceptions of the decision-making situation. Hambro senior explained the behaviour of his partners, suggesting 'that they think that in view of future Greek business not leaving us we had better consent to issue it, and that they have done so'.[135] It thus seems that fear of the competition was key to the decision – a very common justification for risky decisions in nineteenth-century banking (Pohle-Fraser 1999, 103). In order to additionally legitimate this decision, Hambro senior argued:

> I must confess that I am sorry that the Greek Government has been able to make the contract, and this in the interest of Greece herself, for it seems to me the security they now acquire is very nearly the last that they have to offer, and that the money could have been more profitably used than in the increase of their navy and army, which I suppose is the purpose of the Loan.[136]

Certainly, there had been changes in the perception of Greece as a financial market in the last 85 years, and the Hambro banking house can hardly be compared to the merchant bankers Ricardo who issued the first Greek state loans in London in 1824/1825. But the bankers were still using colonial images of Greece to justify decisions which they had made for other reasons. They declared that a sense of responsibility prevented them from wanting to allow Greece to use the borrowed money freely and led them instead to tie it to a particular purpose – officially in the interests of the debtor country which did not really know what was good for it, but unofficially in the interests of, e.g. the national arms industry, as in the case of the BUP. The relationship between Greece and its foreign bankers was still not a classical principal-agent relationship, no matter how much the country had learnt about dealing with international financiers.

Despite Hambro's change of heart, the deal did not materialise at this time. The BA was unable to persuade the Greek government to accept a tied loan with France, and the French government therefore refused consent.[137] Erlanger blustered that such Greek stubbornness was totally unrealistic – without armaments contracts of this sort, a loan was simply impossible in France and in England. Angrily, he threatened to break off business relations with the BA.[138] But nonetheless he then attempted to push through a scaled-down version for just 30 million drachmas in order to secure finance for his railway line.[139] The BUP indicated that it would participate in a smaller project from the second row, if necessary even without the official consent of the French government.[140]

These plans were never realised, as political events in Greece overtook them: on 15 August 1909, in the Goudi district of Athens, a Military League rose up in protest against shortcomings in the state and the army and against 'the old political world' (Tzermias 1986, 107, tr. by K.S.).[141] Among other things, those involved demanded the removal of Crown Prince Constantine from active military service because of dissatisfaction with his leadership; Constantine was seen as particularly pro-German due to his marriage to Sophie, sister of the German Emperor Wilhelm II (ibid., 108).[142] A major reason for the events in Goudi was, however, the striving of the middle class (even if it was smaller than in the rest of Europe) for a political voice in opposition to the privileged elites of the country (ibid., 110). The Young Turk Revolution of the previous year had led many to hope for an awakening in the region and also played a role here (Kennan 1993, 35–37). Political events in Greece were given a great deal of space in the European newspapers,[143] with reports about the agitation of the Military League against the monarchy, the demands for reform, the partial implementation of those demands in parliament in response to the threat of a coup and the resistance of the established politicians. In October 1909, the League turned to the Cretan politician Eleftherios Venizelos, who had been significantly involved in the de facto unification of Crete with Greece in the same year, and brought him to Athens (Tzermias 1986, 113).[144] He pushed through the formation of an interim government and obtained a resolution to hold an election to a constitutional assembly, which led to the disbanding of the League in March 1910. European commentators hoped that the revision of the constitution and the reforms would bring more stability.[145] In the elections in August 1910, Venizelos' Liberal Party won a broad majority, providing him with a basis from which to implement reform policies intended to benefit the lower middle class and farmers.

The turbulence of domestic politics did nothing to halt the growth in strength of the drachma: in 1910, it reached par with the franc (Wynne 1951, 338). The Greek economy suffered however. Imports declined and the discount rate for exchange increased to a high of 10–12%.[146] Nonetheless, the Military League demanded a far-reaching and expensive reorganisation of the military which urgently required new capital. In this highly unstable political situation, the interim Greek government, led by Stephanos Dragoumis, began negotiations about a large new foreign loan for 200 million francs in December 1909.[147] This was intended, firstly, to cover the deficits of the years 1898–1908, which amounted to a total of 40 million drachmas. Secondly, the money was to be used for the construction of the railway and infrastructure.[148] How should the Great Powers and the IFC respond to these wishes? Should the banks be given permission to issue the loan? Should the commission provide the guarantee for the new loan or be responsible for collecting it, should it offer its surplus as a guarantee or should it keep its distance? The British viewed the situation in Greece as being so unstable that anything from a war with the neighbouring countries to a new bankruptcy seemed possible.[149] They could scarcely believe that the German and French banks were interested in the business in this situation.[150] They were concerned about potential investors and the good reputation of the commission, which should on no account take on any moral responsibility:

> If any capitalists should be so ill-advised as to lend money to Greece for the maintenance of armaments disproportionate to her strength and resources they should surely do so at their own risk and without

> moral claim on the consideration of the commission in the performance of its sole duty – the execution of the law of control in the interest of the guaranteed debt and the holders of the old Greek stock alone.[151]

The MAE was equally aware of the precarious situation and bluntly declared that the budget for the present year 'never existed except on paper'. Its only aim was 'to demonstrate the possibility of a new loan and to inspire the foreigners to have sufficient confidence in the state of Greek finances to make this possible'.[152] The financial situation worsened so that staff from the ministry of finance found themselves personally pursued by creditors of the state.[153] Seeking further leverage, in December, the Greeks discussed the fate of the monarchy, which was supported by Great Britain. The British legate feared that in order to get 'the sweets she cries for', Greece could play off the various international interests against one another, given the concern of the Powers for the ruling dynasty, their desire to gain arms contracts for their own industries, the responsibility of the commission towards the bondholders, the fear of anarchy on the Balkans and the fear of a bankruptcy.[154] He believed the situation to be so grave that he told London that if violent unrest arose, only British troops would be able to protect the commission and the ETE.[155] The bankruptcy of numerous Greek trading houses and severe unrest among the farmers in Thessaly worsened the situation further.[156] The West European press compiled detailed reports. The *Frankfurter Zeitung* printed a letter from an anxious German bondholder to the AA. Officials assured him that the commission would protect the rights of the creditors and that there was no reason to be concerned.[157] Despite growing pressure to take action, in January 1910, the draft of a loan convention by the Greek government was negatively evaluated by the British diplomats,[158] particularly because the loan of 1898, which had been guaranteed by the Great Powers, was not safeguarded in this draft.[159] At this time, the British commissioner categorically rejected the notion of a new loan without extended powers of control by the commission, to prevent the assumption of moral responsibility vis-à-vis the investors.[160]

Not until March 1910, when Venizelos' interim government took over and the Military League was disbanded, was there any sign that the Powers were reconsidering their position. But the representatives of the foreign creditors had great hope in the new man at the top and his reform programme (Corporation of Foreign Bondholders 1910, 38). Venizelos made use of this leap of faith: in March 1910, a law was passed by the interim Greek government authorising a loan for 150 million francs at 4%. This was to be used to abolish the forced exchange, for railway construction, to balance the budget deficit from before 1909, and for 'other state spending'.[161] The sum could be increased up to 240 million and should be amortised within 50 years (Corporation of Foreign Bondholders 1910, 37).[162] The first negotiations were held with a banking group consisting of the BUP, the CEP, Hambro and Erlanger.[163] The Powers then needed to react to an official request from the Greek government in May. The British foreign minister saw this as a political decision rather than a financial one.

> The present Government is the best we have had; 40 million francs is all they need urgently, and it would be a pity if they were reduced to bankruptcy or to desperate measures such as an illegal issue of paper.[164]

The British therefore not only encouraged their banks,[165] but wanted the servicing of the loan to be made the responsibility of the IFC,[166] if indeed it was not possible for the commission to offer a guarantee.[167] The French would not agree however. Their demand for binding arms contracts for France represented the last hurdle to finalising the terms.[168] It was July before it emerged that the French agreed not to put any more insurmountable barriers in the way of the Greek plans if the old creditors were protected, even if there was to be no tied loan,[169] because this time the money was to be used productively for hydraulic engineering in Thessaly and the construction of railways, in line with Venizelos' reform programme.[170] The consent of the governments was now quickly given,[171] even though it was unofficial in the British case because, as the British legate emphasised, it was not usual 'for His Majesty's Government to take official cognizance of foreign loans'.[172] Only the German financiers withdrew their offer of participation at the final moment, 'owing to strong opposition of German Minister here'.[173]

The European newspapers used the opportunity to report in detail on the country and its finances, and again contradictory images of Greece were rife. Thus on 30 July 1910, the *Economist* reported on the progress made by trade and the economy, but complained that this was hindered by fickle politics and useless laws and taxation.[174] If only customs barriers and bureaucratic hurdles were removed and money no longer thrown down the throat of the incapable and much too influential army,

> there is no doubt that in a comparatively short space of time the small kingdom would become rich, prosperous, contented, and far more influential in Europe than it has ever been since its absorption in the Roman Empire.[175]

The *Economist* viewed the role of the commission as being most important: 'The only Greek loans which a prudent investor should purchase are those which are under the direct control of the International Financial Commission'.[176]

The decision to participate in the issue was easy for Hambro this time as both the ETE and the BA were charged with organising the consortium on the Greek side, despite the competition between the two. Emil Erlanger also participated again and continued his negotiations with the BUP.[177] In contrast to the previous year, in 1910, the issue of the involvement of the IFC was relevant. However, the banks were keen not to miss the favourable window of opportunity and believed that the IFC would need a good deal of time to come to an agreement due to the disparate objectives of its members.[178] Matsas therefore advised against appealing to the commission.[179] It was thus possible for the convention to be signed in London and Paris within a short space of time, allowing an advance of 40 million francs (£1,588,00) in the form of 80,000 treasury obligations for 500 francs and 5% (Παντελάκης [Pantelakis] 1995, 62),[180] with the option of issuing another 150 million by the end of 1911.[181] The banks earned a reasonable amount on the deal: 1.5% for granting the advance and another 3.5% for issuing the papers.[182] The price for the advance-papers was fixed at 99,[183] which was not surprising given that the papers for the 1902 loan, which the commission serviced, were at 88.75%.[184] The advance-papers were to be repaid by October 1915, but could be called in earlier. They were guaranteed by the surpluses of the finance commission, the profits of the railways yet to be built, an additional tax on tobacco and the revenues from the sugar monopoly, if it were really introduced. The customs revenues from Corfu, Patras, Lavrion and Volos acted as reserves.[185] The revenues were to be collected and administered by the ETE rather than by the commission (Wynne 1951, 347).

The newspapers reacted with caution. The *Frankfurter Zeitung*, for example, reported on the loan convention but without publishing any commentary at all.[186] *L'économiste d'orient* announced the new loan but also printed extracts of the commission's report that included not only the figures proving economic success but also criticism of the long-overdue reforms.[187] *The Economist* advised readers against the issue: 'Owing to the state of Greek finances it is hard to say what the security for this loan really is, and investors would be wise to seek something less involved'.[188] However, Venizelos was portrayed as a great source of hope in the foreign newspapers,[189] and detailed accounts of his social reforms were published.[190] The reports seemed to suggest that this was the person who could finally break through the ossified Greek structures and consequently modernise the country. The public certainly fell upon the new papers: the issue was fully subscribed in both Paris and London by 11 November and had to be closed.[191] In the same month, the syndicate could be disbanded.[192]

In 1911, attention turned to the issue of the actual loan for 150 million drachmas and the question of whether the commission was to be involved. If the commission participated, the bonds would be issued at 88.5 or 89 (with a handover price of 83.5%), if not then at one point less – clearly, the involvement of the IFC was seen as positive promotion but not as more than that. The syndicate's profit, after deducting the costs, was calculated to be between 2.9% and 3.4%.[193] Part of this was intended as reimbursement for the 40 million from 1910.[194] In the end, the bankers decided not to wait for the protracted decision of the commission, but agreed to issue the bonds at 87.5 with the surplus from the commission acting as the only guarantee.[195] The prospectus expressly pointed this out (see Figure II.8.1).

The press reported that the deficit for 1910 was smaller than had been expected, which had a positive effect on the sale.[196] Nonetheless, most newspapers limited their coverage to publishing a report of the loan conditions without any further commentary.[197] The *Revue économique* actually compared the price very favourably with that of the older Greek bonds.[198] In Paris, the issue was again a total success,[199] but in London it failed to really take off.[200] It seems clear that the newspaper coverage was not wholly responsible for the overall positive performance of the issue.[201]

The IFC continued its work after 1910 and organised the repayment of a large proportion of the old Greek debts. At the same time, Greece took out new loans, e.g. in 1914 £19,850,000 under the commission's control.[202] At the beginning of the First World War, Greek debts totalled about 1.25 billion francs, twice as much as in 1898 when the IFC was established (Feis 1974, 289). Robert Feis judges this to have overstretched the financial strength of the country, especially as only a small proportion of the money was used productively: 'Greece continued to push against the limitations of her size and wealth' (ibid., 287). The country still spent about 35% of its (now larger) budget on servicing its debts, although about 20% of the bonds were held in the country (ibid., 289). However, Greece significantly enlarged its territory in the Balkan War, and even during the war had managed to sustain the debt burden and meet its obligations. 'The holders of Greek bonds fared better than most purchasers of European government bonds' (ibid.). The trend was a long-term one: in the first 20 years of its existence, the commission was always able to satisfy the claims of the creditors and the interest rates were able to increase.[203] Only once, during the Balkan War of 1913, did the commission's revenues fall below the 28,900,000 drachma mark so that it was impossible to pay out a surplus. This positive trend was primarily due to the development of the exchange rates: in 1910, the drachma was for the first time again at par with the franc; in 1915, when France was already fighting in the First World War, the rate sank to 0.95, and in 1916 to 0.88. In 1920, the exchange rate reached its lowest point at 0.66, giving the creditors high exchange rate gains (Wynne 1951, 338). In the years 1920–1921, the interest rates even regained their original position (Wynne 1951, 336)[204] before the trend was reversed: the 'Asia Minor' crisis and the flood of refugees that consequently reached Greece were such a drain on public resources that the Greek government issued more paper money in an attempt to cover requirements; this led to strong inflation and a fall in exchange rates. In 1923, Greece had to request the League of Nations to broker a new large loan, which was put under the control of the commission, similarly in 1928, when pressure from abroad led to the founding of a Greek Central Bank, the Bank of Greece (ibid., 349).[205] Nonetheless, the payments by the

Figure II.8.1 Kingdom of Greece, National Loan 4% 1910.

commission continued uninterrupted. It was not until 1932 and the start of the world economic crisis that the first five-year moratorium occurred and convertibility was again suspended. In 1940, an agreement was reached with the creditors whereby 43% of the contracted interest should be paid. The creditors came off unusually well with this settlement, compared, for instance, to the creditors of Germany who lost all their assets in the hyperinflation of 1923. The commission continued its work unswervingly until 1941, when the German occupation forced the Greek government and the ETE into exile (Wynne 1951, 352–355). The IFC was not formally disbanded until 1978, although after 1945 it became practically irrelevant as the Greek government then serviced the foreign debts directly.[206]

Conclusion

This chapter has not been concerned with a concrete investment project, but rather with the role of an international institution, the IFC, in the development of the Greek market. From the perspective of institutional economics, it could be assumed that the establishment of the IFC in 1898 played a decisive role in re-establishing the confidence of the international financial markets in Greece five years after the country's bankruptcy. In fact, the IFC was judged overwhelmingly positively by the international financial press and viewed as a guarantee of stability and an important precondition for the recovery of the market. This optimistic image of Greece, which became more and more euphoric as the exchange rates improved and with them the opportunities for profit, was not, however, the only one. It contrasted with the image of a chaotic, insecure Greece that was used especially with reference to the corruptness of the Greek financial administration and its unwillingness to reform. These two images of Greece, in which the reception of antiquity played a subordinate role, were not considered in relation to one another in the press or in the reports of the diplomats, even if both at times reflected this dichotomy. The financial press hoped primarily for quick and – thanks to the IFC – apparently safe profits, but the diplomats were rarely seduced by this illusion. They rather considered a range of political and economic factors in decisions about whether to grant specific Greek governments a financial injection from abroad or not.

In the investment deliberations of the – extremely well-informed – bankers, the IFC played a somewhat subordinate role. It fostered confidence among the public and thus permitted higher issue prices. The risk perceptions of the bankers were, however, determined by other factors: the drive to ensure fixed contracts for their clients from the arms industry, the safeguarding of older investments in line with notions of path dependency, the wish to continue with familiar cooperations and the fear of losing market share to the competition. A further concern was the reputation of the issuing house. In order to justify decisions made for these reasons, the bankers liked to use colonial images of Greece that described the Greeks as dependent and unreasonable. It was said to be in the interests of the Greeks themselves that money should not be placed at their free disposal, but should either be kept from them or its expenditure controlled – this is undeniably reminiscent of the loan of 1825. In the context of this legitimation strategy, competitors who accepted higher risks were vilified as greedy, irresponsible speculators, and sharply contrasted with self-images of paternalist, caring bankers. If risks were taken, then it was seen as important to involve a reliable Greek partner. The abstention of such partners from projects was understood as an alarming sign.

The financial experts of the globalising banking world were not fooled by the illusion that the IFC could safeguard creditors from the risks of the Greek market, perceived as Oriental and thus chaotic. At most, the IFC restored confidence in the Greek state among investors, aided here by the improving exchange rates, and the bankers used this as a sales opportunity.

Notes

1 The following chapter has been published in an adapted and shortened form in German in Schönhärl (2014a).

2 More recent research suggests however that it was competition between the intermediaries involved that triggered the financial collapse of the country rather than the crisis in Argentina; see Decorzant/Flores (2012).

3 The regulations of the Latin monetary union, which Greece joined in December 1868, stipulated that the gold franc and the gold drachma were fixed at a rate of 1:1. However, this did not apply to paper drachmas. The Greek government printed too many of these and the subsequent inflation caused the rate of the paper drachma to fall, i.e. anyone who took drachma notes instead of the gold coins demanded a so-called agio. By 1893, this agio had risen to 81%, i.e. the rate of exchange between the franc and the paper drachma was at 1:1.81. The convertibility of the drachma was almost universally suspended; there was a forced exchange; see Thomadakis (1985).

4 There were continued disputes between the English construction company and the Greek government. The Germans believed that the Mission française was also responsible for the escalating problems. The French were said not to have been able to tolerate the fact that the contract had gone to an English company and not a French one; see German legate in Athens to Caprivi, 28.2.1892, BAR R 901-1540. **212 n.98** in this book.

5 Gibbs to Bleichröder, 30.7.1891, MA MS 11.113-2-166, 426.

6 Stefan Streit (1837–1920) was the son of a German Philhellene who had a military career in King Otto's army before settling in Patras. After being educated in Patras and studying law in Athens, Stefan Streit continued his studies in Germany and became a judge at the court of appeal in Athens. In 1872, he became head of the ETE branch in Lamia. In 1880, he was commissioned by the Greek government to settle Greece's debts with the house of Wittelsbach (see **213 n.108** in this book). In 1896, he was elected the governor of the ETE; in 1897–1899, he led negotiations abroad as the minister of finance before returning to his position at the ETE. See Ιστορικό Αρχείο [Historical Archives National Bank of Greece] (2001, 47f.).

7 A transcription of the letter is found in German legate to AA, 26.1.1893, in BAR 3101–701.
8 German legate, Lüders, to AA, 5.9.1891, BAR R 901–1540, tr. by K.S.
9 *Vossische Zeitung*, 14.10.1891, in BAR 901–1540, tr. by K.S.
10 Greek 5% loans from 1881 and 1884: 1.12.1890: 91.25; 1.2.1892: 66.20; Greek 4% gold monopoly loan from 1887: 1.12.1890: 74.40; 1.12.1892: 60.00; Greek gold loan of 1889: 1.12.1890: 70.80; 1.12.1892: 50.70; Greek 5% gold loan from 1890: 1.12.1890: 90.00; 1.12.1892: 59.20; see Börsen-Enquête-Kommission (1893, 24–29).
11 The detailed original report covering 108 pages: 1893–1894 [C. 6855–56] FO 1893. Annual Series. No. 1169. Diplomatic and Consular Reports on Trade and Finance. Greece. Report by Mr. E. F. G. Law on the Present Economical and Financial Position in Greece, https://parlipapers.proquest.com/parlipapers/result/pqpresultpage.previewtitle/0?pgId=6ad1ab19-1029-4ef3-b259-ce056ba32c04&rsId=16F4BA6C472 [27.1.2020], 2.
12 Gibbs to the Greek ambassador in London Ionides, 14.4.1893, MA MS1867. The French ministry received the report via Hoskier, who, in turn, had received it via Hambro from the FO; see Hoskier to MAE, 17.4.1893, CAEF B0031215-1.
13 The report by Roux and Montholon enclosed in a letter from them to the MEF, 1.8.1893, CAEF B0031215-1. On the reports by Law and Roux also, see Paulus (2014, 12).
14 CL, Mazerat, to MEF, 23.1.1893, CAEF B0031215-1. Vlasto (**221** in this book) was also involved in the negotiations. Banque de Paris & des Pays-Bas an MEF, 24.2.1893, ibid.
15 Hoskier to the MEF, 30.3.1893, CAEF B0031215-1.
16 The drafts of the convention and the correspondence between the interested banks are found in LMA, MS 19103.
17 Everard to Eric Hambro, undated, MA MS 19103, tr. by K.S.
18 *Der Deutsche Ökonomist*, 19.3.1892 , BAR R 901-1540, tr. by K.S.
19 On the raisin crisis, see Chapter II. 9 of this book.
20 Original in Greek: 'Δυστυχώς επτωχεύσαμεν', 'Unfortunately we are bankrupt'. As reported by the banker Andreas Syngros in his memoires: Συγγρός [Syngros] (1998, 170). Extracts from the corresponding speech in parliament translated into English in: The Greek Debt Proposals, in: *The Times*, 23.12.1893.
21 The first proposal from 1894 would have seen Greece paying 32% of the original interest, but it proved impossible to find a compromise on the use of any surplus that might accrue which led to rejection of the proposal by the German and French bondholders; the second proposal from 1896 saw the Greek government paying c. 27.5% of the original interest; this was thus even more disadvantageous for the bondholders; the Greek government rejected this proposal because they believed it allowed the bondholders to interfere in Greek domestic affairs; see Wynne (1951, 308–312).
22 Basch cites Gabriel Charmes here.
23 Schaefer believes the total Greek foreign debts to have amounted to 750–820 million francs.
24 Although the uprising was at least partially successful as in 1898 Crete achieved greater autonomy with the Greek Prince George as the High Commissioner; see Basch (1995, 272).
25 The guarantee was subject to some dispute among the Great Powers; see Wynne (1951, 315). Article 2 of the Preliminary Peace is cited on 316. The final legal text is found in Loi ΒΦΜΒ from 29.3.1898, in: Commission financière internationale (1916, 39f.). The effect of such guarantees on the development of prices is investigated using the Ottoman example in Al 2012.

26 There was a successful speculation taking advantage of price fluctuations between Paris, London and St. Petersburg, e.g. by the banking house of Baring; see BAL HC 10.62.

27 In 1897, only 571 emigrants left Greece (0.23 per 1,000 inhabitants), but in 1898, there were 2,339 (0.95). The numbers continued to rise: 1903 14,493 (5.66) and 1912 23,362 (8.59). A detailed table is found in Δερτιλής [Dertilis] (2009, 681–686), here 682. See also Tziobas (2009).

28 On the foreign loans of the following year, see Ηλιαδάκης [Iliadakis] (2011, 113–119).

29 Drawing on Max Weber: Berghoff (1999, 61).

30 This was intended to enable the country to balance the budget deficit from 1897, to convert the floating debt and to make special payments to the creditors in 1898; see Wynne (1951, 318).

31 Convention passée les 3 et 4 mai 1898 concernant l'emprunt garanti, in: Commission financière internationale (1916, 63–72); Théry (1905, 25). The Deutsche Bank was also interested

> with respect to the standing and prestige that the same acquires from the restoration of such a fouled up affair both politically and also especially in the interests of the German creditors/cf. the Rumanian proceedings/; further, because then economically it positions itself in first place for any possible future business that may arise in Greece when the country is then in an ordered financial state, and finally because in the financial transactions themselves it can secure pecuniary advantages either through the stipulation of a provision or through the cheaper acquisition of the loans or the acquisition of the servicing of the new loan and also in some other way.

Regelung der Griechischen Anleihen, undated, in DB S3829, tr. by K.S.

32 In London two times, in Paris 23.5 times; see Wynne (1951, 320), and also Théry (1905, 26).

33 More details on his wife Katharina Hadzopoulos in Holborn (1967, 168).

34 Law's biographer believes that he played a great role in ensuring that Greece was mildly treated; see Morison (1911, 32–45 and 175–226). 'He combined Philhellenic enthusiasm with true statesmanship and business ability'. Ibid., 224; Law was apparently very popular in Greece because of the pro-Greek position he took in 1892, his marriage to a Greek and the fact that he waived his salary. However, in the initial year, the Great Powers actually paid the salaries of all their representatives in the commission. When problems later emerged, Law also negotiated between foreign firms and the Greek government, e.g. with the construction of the Piraeus-Larissa railway; see British legate in Athens, Egerton, to FO, Rosebery, 17.4.1893, NA FO 32–674. In May 1906, Law was named one of the directors of the IOB located in London and again travelled to Greece to report in this capacity; see Court of Directors minutes no. 14/IOB 3/10. The biography by Μακρυμίχαλος [Makrimichalos] (1974) is in many parts a translation of the older work by Morison.

35 His correspondence with Law is found in ETE, private archive Streit (2011 not yet indexed).

36 Lois ΒΦΙΘ. Contrôle International from 26.2.1898, in: Commission financière internationale (1916, 1–31).

37 Very few bonds were held in Russia, Italy or Austria-Hungary; these countries were only represented in the IFC for political reasons; see Feis (1974, 289).

38 In 1898, 36.8 million of a total of 104.8 million drachmas. In 1903, the share of the IFC was 48% of total revenues (55.7 million of 114.8 million drachmas).

39 The capital was increased to four million francs; see Statuts de la société de régie des revenus affectés au service de la dette publique hellénique, Art. 4, in: Commission financière internationale (1916, 99).
40 These debts included 31.4 million francs of debt in gold, primarily held in Greece, and 177.2 million of debt in paper drachmas; see Wynne (1951, 324).
41 Reduced for the first five years to 14,437,500 drachmas; see Wynne (1951, 330).
42 On the question of convertibility and the gold premium, see **320 n.3** in this book.
43 Here is also a graphical illustration.
44 Generally on British reporting about Greece in the Trikoupis era: Δρίτσα [Dritsa] (2000).
45 All the following press reports are cited from this Grèce Bulletin, CL DEEF 73269/0001. The articles here are translated in full into French or summarised in that language. This explains the naming of French titles in German and English newspapers.
46 Douanes helléniques, in: *L'économiste européen*, 9.8.1901.
47 Le Marché des fonds grecs, in: *L'agence de presse Fournier*, 20.2.1901.
48 IFC, Corbett, to FO, Lansdowne, 7.7.1901, NA FO 32–742.
49 IFC, Corbett, to FO, Lansdowne, 5.6.1902, NA FO 32–742.
50 Ibid.
51 Report of the International financial Commission, in: Corporation of Foreign Bondholders (1904, 174).
52 Report of the International financial Commission, in: Corporation of Foreign Bondholders (1904, 182).
53 See also Accord intervenu entre le ministère royal des finances et la Commission financière internationale au sujet du mouvement du personnel des revenus affectés, in: Commission financière internationale (1916, 34f.).
54 See also **212 n.98** in this book.
55 German legate in Athens, Langwerth, to AA, von Bülow, 5.12.1901, BAR R 901–1542.
56 IFC, Corbett, to FO, Lansdowne, 5.6.1902, NA FO 32–742. Corbett related that it was only once the government was anxious to solicit the agreement of the commission for the Piraeus-Larissa railway that it was at all willing to discuss, e.g. the catastrophic personnel policy with the IFC. As soon as the guarantee had been settled, the situation worsened again, so he advised against repeating this approach.
57 Greek finances, in: *The Financier and Bullionist*, 22.3.1902, NA FO 32–742.
58 Griechische Finanzen, in: *Magdeburgische Zeitung*, No 146, 21.3.1902, BAR R 901–1542, tr. by K.S.
59 Le Chemin de fer piree-demerly, in: *The Times*, 14.6.1901.
60 IFC, D'Ormesson, to MAE, 10.5.1902, CAEF B0031219-1.
61 Ibid.
62 In 1902, £880,000 were issued at a rate of 83.5, in 1904 £870,000 at 84 (this time by C. J. Hambro & Son; Credit Algerien Paris; National Bank of Egypt, ETE). Further private issues followed to extend the railway to Larissa in December 1904 (£230,000) and in 1906 (£270,000); see Wynne (1951, 347). See Extrait de la convention pour la construction et l'exploitation d'un chemin de fer allant du Pirée à Démirly et la frontière ottomane from 9. /22.3.1900, in: Commission financière internationale (1916, 150–155). The guaranties were the surplus from the revenues of the commission, the revenue of the railway and a special tax on tobacco; see Corporation of Foreign Bondholders (1903, 141).
63 La situation financière de la Grèce, in: *L'agence des feuilles politiques*, 10.1.1903.

64 Ibid.
65 Finances helléniques, in: *Le Temps*, 28.9.1903.
66 Fonds hellénique, in: *L'Information financière économique et politique*, 15.12.1903, DEEF, tr. by K.S.
67 Loi ΑΧΜΒ sur un emprunt de drachmes or 240.000.000 au maximum, 19.3.1910, in: Commission financière internationale (1916, 189–201).
68 Finances helléniques, in: *L'économiste européen*, 25.9.1903.
69 Chemins de fer helléniques, in: *Cote européenne (Paris)*, 3.2.1904.
70 Chemin de fer Pirée-Larissa, in: *Le Temps*, 21.3.1904.
71 Le change hellénique, in: *La cote de la bourse et de la banque*, 5.8.1904. Feis names the reduction of the amount of money in circulation, the repatriation of foreign debt and the transfer of money by Greek emigrants to their homeland as reasons; see Feis (1974, 291). Other possible reasons are discussed by Δερτιλής [Dertilis] (2009, 608ff.).
72 L'emprunt hellénique des chemins de fer, in: *Le capitaliste* (Paris), 8.10.1903, tr. by K.S.
73 Finances helléniques, in: *Le capitaliste (Paris)*, 23.6.1904.
74 Finances helléniques, in: *L'économiste d'Orient*, 6.10.1904.
75 Finances helléniques, in: *Frankfurter Zeitung*, 6.4.1904; Le Change hellénique, in: *L'économiste européen*, 3.6.1904.
76 IFC, Allizé, to MAE, Delcassé, 9.1.1904, B0031219-1, tr. by K.S.
77 IFC, Allizé, to MAE, Delcassé, 10.1.1904, B0031219-1.
78 IFC, Allizé, to MAE, Delcassé, 10.1.1904, B0031219-1. It was said to be unacceptable that the Greek government shared in the additional revenues of the commission without reforming the financial administration, and that in the event of a conversion of the old debts, it would even buy a share of the surplus from the creditors, which must further increase if the exchange rates continued to recover, without displaying any true willingness to undertake reform on its part.
79 IFC, d'Ormesson, to MAE, as a copy, 22.6.1905, CAEF B0031219-1, tr. by K.S. The legate went so far as to suggest that the administrative chaos was not the responsibility of any individual politician or party, but was rather the logical consequence of the social structures and national character. It followed that it was not possible to hope for improvement despite the best of advice.
80 Ibid., tr. by K.S.
81 Ibid.
82 Les récoltes et le change en Grèce, in: *L'économiste d'Orient*, 30.6.1904.
83 Report of the IFC, in: Corporation of Foreign Bondholders (1905, 199). Wynne also attributes at least part of the success of the loans of 1902 and 1904 to the fact that the work of the commission had helped re-establish Greek credit: 'Investors no doubt tended to have an exaggerated concept of the commission's powers but they had also some tangible evidence of its success in the steady price rise in Greek securities'. Wynne (1951, 347).
84 Emprunt hellénique 4% 1902 des chemins de fer, in: *Le messager de Paris*, 14.4.1905. The government had been given the right to issue additional bonds to extend the railway line. This private issue occurred in December 1904 (£230,000) and again in 1906 (£270,000); see Wynne (1951, 347), FN 27.
85 MAE and MEF, 22.4.1905, CAEF B0031219-1.
86 Grèce, in: *L'économiste d'Orient*, 3.5.1906.
87 Finances helléniques, in: *L'information financière économique et politique*, 12.3.1906.
88 IFC, Pasteur, to MAE, 14.6.1905, CAEF B0031219-1.
89 L'emprunt hellénique des chemins de fer, in: *The Times*, 29.8.1906.

90 IFC, Allizé, to MAE, Delcassé, 4.4.1904, CAEF B0031219-1.

91 As early as 1902, the BUP's initial reflections were primarily concerned with their customers from the armaments industry, the Société de constructions navales; see Projet d'emprunt hellénique 4½%, undated, SG CN254. In this version, 70 million should be issued for 33 years.

92 The French press did not react to the expensive rearmament plans with criticism, but rather welcomed the involvement of French specialists in the hope that armaments contracts would then be awarded to the national industry; see Finances helléniques, in: *Le matin*, 21.5.1901.

93 BUP, Barbé to Moyse Dreyfus, 13.3.1907, SG CN254. The weapons manufacturers were most concerned to preserve a good relationship with the directors of the BUP. Thus, Dreyfuss not only sent a catalogue of the newest armament products to Barbé to be forwarded to Athens, but also included a second copy 'as required to entertain your children', Moyse Dreyfus to BUP, Barbé, 26.3.1907, SG CN254, tr. by K.S.

94 BUP, Barbé, to BA, Matsas, 11.2.1907, SG CN254, tr. by K.S.

95 French legate in Athens, Lefevre-Pontalis, to MAE, 26.12.1905, CAEF B0031220-1. Details on the competition between the Germans and French, the founding of the Orientbank by the Nationalbank für Deutschland in cooperation with the ETE and the involvement of the BUP in the BA are found in Κωστής [Kostis]/Τσοκόπουλος [Tsokopulos] (1988, 132–139).

96 MAE to MEF, 22.4.1905, CAEF B0031219-1.

97 Grèce, in: *L'économiste d'Orient*, 3.1.1907.

98 On Hambro's relationships to Greece, **340–344** in this book.

99 The Ionian Bank, the BA, the Bank of Anatolia, the CNEP and Hambro were involved in the syndicate; also see Παντελάκης [Pantelakis] (1995, 61, 95, 246ff.).

100 Hambro to ETE, Streit, 25.2.1908, MA MS 19107.

101 At the end of 1907, the bonds from 1881 to1893 were traded in London at between 47.5 and 50, those from 1902 in Paris even at 92.5%. Grèce Dette Publique 31.12.1907, SG CN254. The bonds from the 2½% loan of 1898 stood at 105; see ETE to Hambro, 29/13.3.1908, MA MS 19107.

102 Grèce, in: *L'agence de presse Fournier*, 26.3.1908.

103 The loan prospectus MA MS 19107.

104 L'emprunt pour la colonisation de la Thessalie, in: *Le messager de Paris*, 29.4.1907. That the Greeks in 1907 once more accessed money through a domestic bond made sense to these commentators as the money was intended to be used for Greek refugees from Bulgaria and Rumania. The situation was similar in summer 1909 when a new domestic bond for five million drachmas was issued at Greek banks for refugees from Macedonia; see Finances Helléniques, in: *L'économiste d'orient*, 28.5.1909.

105 Finances helléniques, in: *L'économiste européen*, 1.5.1908.

106 Due to the forced exchange, the Greek silver coins for one and two drachmas flooded the other countries of the Latin Monetary Union and there was a shortage of them in Greece. In 1908, Greece therefore applied for Greek coins to be nationalised, as had been the case for Italy since 1893. The other countries withdrew the Greek one- and two-drachma coins from circulation and sent them to Greece, receiving a compensatory payment in return. These coins replaced the one- and two-drachma paper notes in Greece and were no longer accepted as a legal method of payment in the other countries of the LMU, so as to prevent them from draining out of the country again. Greece was in no way expelled from the Union. The portrayal in Hoffritz (2015) is thus erroneous. Greece remained an

official member of the LMU until it was dissolved (see Greul 1926, 118, 120–126; Theurl 1992, 196; Koch-Mehrin 2001, 146).

107 Grèce, in: *Neue Frankfurter Presse*, 16.8.1909.

108 BUP, Wehrung, to BA, Matsas, 10.9.1909, SG CN254.

109 MAE to the French legate in Athens, Deville, 23.11.1909, as a copy, CAEF B-0031222-1, tr. by K.S.

110 Ibid.

111 On the relationship between BUP and BA, **339f.** in this book.

112 BA, Matsas, to BUP, Barbé, 10.10.1908, SG CN254, tr. by K.S.

113 BA, Matsas from Karlsbad to BUP, Barbé, 10.7.1908, SG CN254, tr. by K.S.

114 Germany, commented the French legate, wanted to extend its influence in the region without using any leverage other than financial: 'Will his financiers not attempt to do in Athens what the Austrian businessmen have just done in Sofia?' French legate in Athens, Deville, to MAE, Pichon, 15.1.1910, as a copy, CAEF B0031222-1, tr. by K.S.

115 Finances helléniques, in: *L'agence de presse Fournier*, 17.10.1904.

116 On the relationship of Erlanger to Greece, **344–347** in this book.

117 Erlanger to BA, Matsas, as a copy, 26.2.1909, MA MS 19108.

118 Ibid.

119 Telegram Erlanger to BA, Matsas, 25.2.1909, as a copy, MA MS 19108. This involvement was also contrived by Demetrius Georgiades, who is discussed in more detail below (**349f.** in this book); also see Βοβολίνης [Vovolinis] (1958–1963, B, 503f.).

120 Path dependencies can be dangerous when banks grant companies further loans in situations which are already hopeless because they do not want to finally accept the losses; see Battilossi (2008, 87). Behavioural finance would speak of a so-called 'sunk-cost-effect'; see Daxhammer/Facsar (2012, 226).

121 In the case of Argentina, the French government refused permission because the contracts went to Krupp. Erlanger to BA, Matsas, 26.2.1909, as a copy, MA MS 19108.

122 Ibid. Together with Matsas, Erlanger wanted to secure 1% of this as a fee for his work as an intermediary, Telegram Erlanger to BA, Matsas, 27.2.1909, as a copy, MA MS 19108.

123 Telegram Erlanger to BA, Matsas, 25.2.1909, as a copy, MA MS 19108.

124 'In *normal* times *irregularity* is the rule. In *abnormal* times regularity is *portrayed* as the rule'. Pohle-Fraser (1999, 117), emphasis in the original.

125 Bramsen/Wain emphasise that when Eric was a partner in C. J. Hambro & Son with his father for 30 years, he was very much under the influence of the latter and had almost no opportunity to act independently; see Bramsen/Wain (1979, 329).

126 With reference to the present day, see Nini (2004). Nini concludes 'that local banks, a particularly special type of official intermediary, provide value by considerably reducing financing costs, especially for riskier borrowers' (Ibid., abstract).

127 Heriot was one of four partners in C. J. Hambro & Son; see Bramsen/Wain (1979, 304).

128 Heriot to Eric Hambro, 4.3.1909, MA MS 19108. In the BUP, there was also speculation about why the ETE did not wish to participate in the project, although the conclusions drawn were quite different: Barbé believed that the ETE was 'a bit offended' that the BA had initiated negotiations with Erlanger and the government without it and that this was also the reason that they wanted to prevent the involvement of Hambro; see Note remis par E. Erlanger, 4.3.1909, SG CN254, tr. by K.S.

129 Hambro to ETE, Streit, 8.3.1909, MA MS 19108.
130 Everard to Eric Hambro, 29.2.1909, MA MS 19108.
131 Erlanger to BA, Matsas, 4.3.1909, as a copy, MA MS 19108.
132 Telegram Erlanger, from Paris, to BA, Matsas, 10.3.1909, as a copy, MA MS 19108.
133 This also included half a per cent 'of which no questions are to be asked, but it is chiefly for the papers, and in order to ensure getting a quotation in the Paris Exchange'. Eric to Everard Hambro, 11.3.1909, MA MS 19108.
134 Telegram draft from Eric Hambro, recipient not evident, 9.3.1909, MA MS 19108.
135 Everard Hambro to ETE, Streit, 12.3.1909, MA MS 19108.
136 Ibid.
137 Telegram Erlanger to BA, Matsas, 13.3.1909, as a copy, MA MS 19108.
138 Erlanger to BA, Matsas, 13.3.1909, SG CN254. He spoke of having had a great deal of good luck in his career. But in life 'the difference between those who are successful and those who are not successful is that the former know how to profit from the lucky circumstances while the latter do not know how' (Tr. by K.S.). The opportunity to do business should therefore be taken now.
139 Note from unknown person, undated, MA MS 19108.
140 Erlanger to BUP, 26.3.1909, SG CN254.
141 The research continues to debate whether the events in Goudi should be termed an uprising, military coup, revolt or revolution. Also see Zelepos (2014, 93f.).
142 Constantine's close links to Germany became increasingly problematic in Greece as the German Empire proved itself a supporter of the Ottoman Empire.
143 See, e.g. the long report: Greece. The Reassembling of the chamber, in: *The Times*, 15.2.1910.
144 De jure Crete only became part of the Greek state in 1913. Holland/Markides named the date of Venizelos' call to Athens as January 1910; see Holland/Markides (2006, 148).
145 The Situation in Greece, in: *The Times*, 5.5.1910. The significance of the king in the reform process was emphasised.
146 German legate in Athens, Riepenhausen, to AA, Bethmann Hollweg, 28.9.1909, BAR R 901-1543.
147 L'emprunt hellénique, in: *Berliner Tagblatt*, 16.12.1909.
148 L'emprunt hellénique, in: *Havas (Agence d'information et de publicité)*, 18.12.1909.
149 British legate in Athens, Young, to FO, Grey, 30.11.1909, NA FO T1-11244.
150 IFC, Young to FO, Grey, 30.11.1909, NA FO T1-11244. He believed that especially with the involvement of German financiers, there was a danger that they would secure priority for themselves ahead of the guaranteed loan of 1898, something which should be prevented if at all possible.
151 IFC, Young, to FO, Grey, 30.11.1909, NA FO T1-11244.
152 French legate, Deville, to French minister of foreign affairs, Pichon, 17.12.1909, CAEF-0031222-1, tr. by K.S. Deville was concerned however that the constantly changing tax and monopoly projects were more likely to unsettle foreign capital than to restore confidence.
153 IFC, Young, to FO, Grey, 8.12.1909, NA FO T1-11244.
154 IFC, Young, to FO, Grey, 15.12.1909, NA FO T1-11244. Young thought it extremely unlikely that the elderly and respected Streit from the ETE was actually a supporter of the League.
155 IFC, Young, to FO, Grey, 15.12.1909, NA FO T1-11244.
156 La représentation grecque à l'étranger, in: *Le matin*, 3.2.1910; La question agraire à Thessalie, in: *Le matin*, 4.3.1910. Some of the League's demands, e.g.

the recall of all Greek ambassadors in Europe, irritated the international newspapers extremely.

157 L'administration de la dette hellénique, in: *Frankfurter Zeitung*, 19.3.1910.

158 French legate in Athens, Deville, to French minister of foreign affairs Pichon, 15.1.1910, as a copy, CAEF B0031222-1.

159 Treasury chambers to FO, 18.1.1910, NA FO T1-11244.

160 IFC, Young, to FO, Grey, 20.4.1910, NA FO T1-11244.

161 Loi ΛΧΜΒ sur un emprunt de drachmes d'or 240.000.000 au maximum, in: Commission financière internationale (1916, 189–201).

162 Also see IFC, Young, to FO, Grey, 16.3.1910, NA FO T1-11244.

163 IFC, Young, to FO, Grey, 26.5.1910, NA FO T1-11244. It was important to the British that they not be pushed out of the business; see IFC, Young, to FO, Grey, 20.4.1910, NA FO T1-11244. On the role of the French banks, also see Bonin (2013, 86–91).

164 Telegram IFC, Young, to FO, Grey, 28.6.1910, NA FO T1-11244.

165 IFC, Young, to FO, Grey, 9.6.1910, NA FO T1-11244.

166 Note from Grey, 24.5.1910, NA FO T1-11244. The British bondholders were not thrilled about the plans because they saw their share of the surplus disappearing, but they nonetheless agreed; see Council of Foreign bondholders, Cooper, to FO, 13.4.1910, NA FO T1-11244.

167 Treasury Chamber to FO, 12.7.1910, NA FO T1-11244.

168 L'emprunt hellénique, in: *Financial News London*, 27.6.1910.

169 British legate in Athens, Carnegie, to FO, Grey, 1.7.1910, NA FO T1-11244.

170 BA, Matsas, to BUP, 22.4./5.5.1910, as a copy, SG CN255.

171 BUP, Syndicat Hellénique No. I, 22.7.1910, SG CN255. In August 1910, it again looked difficult: the French and English governments refused notice of the advance because the Greek government had failed to firmly assure them that no monopolies would be established, e.g. on sugar, for the guarantees. But the bankers now were willing to disregard this, if necessary. Syndicat Avance au gouvernement hellénique, réunion du 18.8.1910, SG CN255. It was September before the Greek government officially asked the British government to consent to the project: British legate in Athens to the Greek foreign minister Kalegri, 7.9.1910, as a copy, SG CN255, Subfolder letters of the CNE.

172 IFC, Young, to FO, Grey, 1.8.1910, NA FO T1-11244. The British representative still viewed the solvency of the Greeks critically. The Greeks were said to have used the Chinese convention for the Tientsin railway as a template for the draft of their convention; see Telegram IFC, Young, to FO, Grey, 29.7.1910, in: ibid.

173 IFC, Young, to FO, Grey, 18.7.1910, NA FO T1-11244. Initial reports suggested that the Bleichröder Bank was also in the consortium, a false report that was quickly recanted as no German banking house had shown interest in the loan; see L'emprunt hellénique, in: *Frankfurter Zeitung*, 9.7.1910. Others in Germany showed interest in Greek financial matters. Thus, a group of German investors, including Herrman Hilger, the editor of *Gegenwart*, examined agriculture in Thessaly and after an inspection came to the conclusion that it would be possible to make 'a splendid deal' (Tr. by K.S.) with the purchase and cultivation of the terrain in the hands of the large landowner (previously Tschifliks). The AA was reserved so as to avoid demonstrating 'official German interest'. German legate in Athens, Wangenheim, to AA, Bethmann-Hollweg, 7.4.1910, BAR R 901–1549, tr. by K.S. The foreign investors intended to buy the land with the aid of the expropriation legislation, sell part of it onto the farmers and keep the rest to cultivate themselves. They expected an annual profit of 20–25%, especially from the cultivation of cotton. The German legate in

Constantinople advised against the plan due to Turkish sensibilities; see imperial legate Constantinople, Marshall, to the AA, Bethmann-Hollweg, 3.5.1910, BAR R 901–1549. A French group also pursued competing plans to found an agricultural bank in Thessaly; see French embassy in Athens to MAE, 6.1.1911, CAEF B0031220-1.

174 The prospects and credits of Greece, in: *The Economist*, 30.7.1910.

175 Beauregard, Paul: La question financière en Grèce, in: *Le monde économique*, 13.10.1910.

176 Ibid. Beauregard also used this opportunity to promote his friend Georgiades' project (see **403** in this book) concerning the unification of Greek debts that intended to make the country debt free within 50 years. Opposition came from 'a group of fairly powerful financiers who exploit the state and its finances to their own exclusive benefit' (Tr. by K.S.). Beauregard emphasised that for some time the budget had been balanced and the organisation of the state respectable. He advised against rearmament as in the end all Greece needed to do with Crete was to wait and time would play into the country's hands.

177 Undated note of the BUP, Wehrung, apparently March 1910, SG CN255. Also see Le nouvel emprunt, in: *L'information financière économique et politique*, 8.7.1910, also Grèce, in: *Financial News Paris*, 11.18.1910.

178 BA, Matsas, to BUP, 5/18.4.1910, as a copy, SG CN255.

179 BA, Matsas, to BUP, 21.4.1910, as a copy, SG CN255.

180 Also see Report of the International Financial Commission, in: Corporation of Foreign Bondholders (1910, 198).

181 The convention in SG CN255. 12.5% were placed in London, while 37.5 went to the exchange in Athens and the lion's share with 50% was issued in France. Hambro (6.25%) and Erlanger (6.25%) were involved as British banks; the ETE (20%), the BA (12.5%) and the Banque d'Orient (5%) represented the Greek side, and in France, the CNE (17%), the SG (12%), the CEP (12%) and the BUP (9%) were involved. The invitation for the French participants in the syndicate and other French banks from 18/19.7.1910 and a list of participations is found in CEP 11-DFOM-221-846.

182 The CNE received 10% of the profits for the organisation of the syndicate, CEP 11-DFOM-221-908. Mallet, Hottinguer, Mirabaud and de Neuflize, among others, participated in the subscription. The directors of the joint-stock banks also purchased shares: Villars, Barbé, Wehrung, Lustgarten and Thalmann (through the BUP); see Avance de Frs. 40,000,000 au gouvernement hellénique, 21.7.1910, SG, CN255.

183 Avance au Gouvernement hellénique, Réunion du 3.11.1910, SG CN255; Grèce, in: *L'agence de presse Fournier*, 12.11.1910.

184 Notice d'Emprunt Grec 4% 1910, 23.5.1911, SG CN255.

185 Neue 5proz. Griechische Staatsanleihe, in: *Frankfurter Zeitung und Handelsblatt*, 10.11.1910.

186 Ibid. On German caution, also see Feis (1974, 287).

187 Commission financière internationale, Compte-Rendu pour l'année 1909, in: *L'économiste d'Orient*, 6.8.1910.

188 New Capital issues, in: *The Economist*, 21.10.1910.

189 Even more so once he, e.g. invited specialists from France to reorganise the military; see L'envoi d'une mission militaire française, in: *Le matin*, 28.10.1910.

190 So e.g. in La réforme des impôts, in: *L'économiste d'Orient*, 30.11.1910. Here a report on a project of the minister of finance Coromilas which involved using income tax to improve the situation of the working classes and increase the

burden on higher income groups. At the same time, the burden on trade and industry was to be reduced.

191 Grèce, in: *Financial News Paris*, 12.11.1910; Avance au Gouvernement hellénique, Réunion du 17.11.1910, SG CN255.

192 BUP, Délibérations du conseil d'administration Emprunt Grec 1910, 19.11.1910, SG CN255.

193 Notice d'Emprunt Grec 4% 1910, 23.5.1911, SG CN255.

194 Grèce, in: *L'agence de presse Fournier*, 10.6.1911, DEEF.

195 This time the bonds were distributed so that 18.1% were issued in Great Britain, 13.8% in Greece and again the lion's share of 68.1% in France; see Emprunt hellénique 4% 1910, réunion tenue au Comptoir le 20 Juin 1911, CEP 11-DFOM-221-908. Of this SG 60,000, CNE 60,000, CEP 15,000, BUP 10,000. The agents received 1.25% commission, the Chambre Syndicale a further 3.75%. The commission for intermediaries was limited to a maximum of 2.5%.

196 *La vie financière*, 14.1.1911.

197 E.g. New capital issues: The Greek Loan, in: *The Times*, 27.6.1911.

198 *Revue économique et financière*, 17.6.1911.

199 Réunion du Syndicat Emprunt hellénique 4% 1910, du 27 Juillet 1911, CEP 11-DFOM-221-908.

200 Emprunt hellénique 4% 1910, Réunion du 3.7.1911, SG CN255. The syndicate had to intervene so as not to endanger the success in Paris. Emprunt hellénique 4% 1910, Réunion du 29.6.1911, SG CN255.

201 The hopes seemed justified as the year progressed: Greece was not even particularly hit by the European financial crisis at the end of the year, and the ETE was able to act as a creditor for other European financial institutions, as the finance minister proudly declared. There seemed no reason to fear a slump in Greek bonds; see Grèce, in: *L'information financière économique et politique*, 2.12.1911.

202 £10,440,000 of this was successfully issued, primarily in Paris; the rest was lost in the beginnings of the First World War; see Wynne (1951, 348).

203 Until 1911, they were between 2.04 and 2.36% for the first group, 2.0–2.4% for the second and 1.7–2.3% for the third. In comparison, the new loan of 1898 yielded only 2.5% interest; see Wynne (1951, 335f.).

204 Also 1926 and 1929–1931.

205 On the loans of the League of Nations at this time, see Decorzant/Flores (2012).

206 A table with the year of each repayment of the nineteenth-century loans is found in Ηλιαδάκης [Iliadakis] (2011, 57). The last to be repaid (in 1989) is said to have been that of 1890.

9

CURRANT TRADE IN GREECE

'Monopoly or Death!'[1]

Currants as an important pillar of the Greek export economy

Confidence in the Greek economy began to return to the European financial markets after 1898, initially slowly but accelerating considerably by the start of the twentieth century (Dritsa 1999, 40f.). The negative image of Greece (Basch 1995, 27)[2] that was prevalent through much of Europe did little to hinder this process at a time when banking was expanding strongly and becoming increasingly international (Cassis 2007, 129–139). The newly developed confidence in Greece was in no way limited to state securities but also extended to embrace private direct investments – an additional argument in favour of the hypothesis that the IFC played only a minor role in this trend. How was confidence regained in the private economy? After the loss of institutional confidence, it seems probable that private networks and personal trust were particularly important in reactivating old business relationships or initiating new ones. Such trust in individuals should be distinguished from trust in institutions or 'abstract performance structures', even if an exact dividing line cannot always be defined in practice (Luhmann 2009, 34). This implies that the focus is once again on intermediaries, who play an important role in initiating new business and building trust and confidence (Berghoff 1999, 174). This hypothesis is considered in the following using a case study from one of the most important fields of the Greek economy: trade. Throughout the whole of the nineteenth century, trade, with the products of metallurgy and agriculture, was one of the most important pillars of the Greek economy. Naturally, trade and agriculture were closely interdependent, given the lack of industry in the country (Φραγκιάδης [Franghiadis] 2006).

Raisins and currants were one agricultural product for which Greece profited from comparative advantages. Along with wine and olive oil, they were the most important products of the country (Πετμεζάς [Petmezas] 2003, 233; Karouzou 2014).[3] They thrived in most regions of the kingdom and were excellently suited for cultivation on the small family farms that dominated

DOI: 10.4324/9780429286537-12

Greek agriculture. The very high taxes charged on grain further favoured the cultivation of raisins and currants (Franghiadis 1990, 11). In a number of regions, the weather and soil were especially suitable. Indeed, Greece had a monopoly on currants, which grew in the Corinth region and were characterised by their distinctive size, quality and sweetness that rendered them irreplaceable in the patisseries of Western Europe. There was nowhere else in the world where dried fruit of this quality was produced.[4]

The cultivation of currants expanded through the course of the nineteenth century: in 1830, 19 million Venetian pounds[5] (9,063 tonnes) of currants were produced on an area of 38,000 stremmata (3,800 hectares); by 1848, this had grown to 64.9 million Venetian pounds (30,857 tonnes) on 129,380 stremmata (12,938 hectares). On the Peloponnesus in particular, currants were the dominant arable crop. Despite the severe setback caused by a mildew epidemic that emerged in the mid-1850s, production in 1860 totalled 110,228 million Venetian pounds (52,578 tonnes) on 220,428 stremmata (22,042 hectares) (Tsiovaridou 1980, 129). In 1871, exports of currants accounted for 90.2% of all exports from the harbour of Patras (Frangakis-Syrett 1994, 12). A large proportion of the production was financed by credits that the traders granted the farmers (Franghiadis 1990, 299). In the 1870s and 1880s, production was further extended, a development encouraged by the 1871 law on land distribution for which the farmers had waited almost 40 years (ibid., 2, 11).[6] In 1871, 173,163 million Venetian pounds (82,598 tonnes) were produced on 346,326 stremmata (34,632 hectares), and in 1891, 334 million Venetian pounds (159,318 tonnes) were produced on 670,000 stremmata (67,000 hectares) (Tsiovaridou 1980, 129). Between 1887 and 1893, the value of the exported currants significantly exceeded that of all other export goods taken together (Φραγκιάδης [Franghiadis] 2006, 160). The long-term averages for exports also show the importance of the dried fruit: for the period 1851–1892, they accounted for 54% of total Greek exports (Franghiadis 1990, 29). This trend was encouraged by the devastating impact of the phylloxera epidemic on vineyards in Western Europe, especially in France (Meloni/Swinnen 2017). Due to their extremely poor domestic harvest, the French vintners increasingly used imported currants to press the popular sweet wines. This quite common technique caused a rapid increase in the market prices for dried grapes. The lion's share of Greek currants went nonetheless to Great Britain, where the growing middle class and the increasingly better-off working classes valued them as a well-loved food and baking ingredient. This allowed the Greeks to export the vast majority of the currant crop and made it profitable for farmers to further specialise in growing grapes.[7] Older historical studies suggest that this monoculture was the principal reason for the backwardness of Greek agriculture. More recent research offers a different perspective and understands the cultivation of currants rather as presenting an opportunity for the young Greek economy to move towards the industrial era and gain a foothold in the world economy, not only for the individual regions, but also for the country as a whole (Φραγκιάδης, A. [Franghiadis] 2006, 153f.). The reason for the lack of further industrial development in Greece was not the currant trade, but rather the social structures, e.g. typically Greek merchant capitalism (Franghiadis 1990, 19).

Although it clearly had advantages, such specialisation in currants made the economy vulnerable, as seen in 1893 when France introduced prohibitive tariffs on imports of currants to protect its own recovered production from foreign competition. Prices in the world market reacted promptly and fell dramatically: in 1890, up to 300 francs were paid per thousand Venetian pounds (477 kg) of currants, depending on the quality, but in 1893, the price fell to only 44 francs (Tsiovaridou 1980, 133). The Baring crisis, which shook the economy worldwide, contributed to this decrease in the prices and demand (Frangakis-Syrett 1994, 12ff.). Greece was unable to find buyers for its produce. For the Greek treasury, which drew a great part of its funds from export duties, this meant a disastrous decline in revenues which contributed decidedly to the bankruptcy of 1893 (Δερτιλής [Dertilis] 2009, 603ff.). The Greek state bankruptcy was accompanied by a severe currant crisis.

The crisis revealed the great need for reform in the organisation of the currant trade. Any attempts at reform had to involve finding purchasers for the annual surplus of about 60 million Venetian pounds and stabilising the prices. In 1895, the problems became even more urgent due to unrest in the areas of production, particularly on the Peloponnesus where a currant monoculture predominated at this time (Franghiadis 1990, 35). The prevailing methods of organisation meant that the risks of fluctuating prices and the weather were borne not by the traders, but rather entirely by the farmers, who were dependent on the credit granted to them by the traders. Franghiadis suggests that this system resembled neither capitalist agriculture where production was primarily for the market nor subsistence agriculture, but rather combined elements of both systems (ibid., 300–304). The currant farmers, who no longer even grew wheat for their own needs, fought for better prices for their products and were convinced that the only way to achieve this was through a trade monopoly, because the strong position of the traders meant that the farmers could not in any case profit from the advantages of free market participation. They coined the dramatic motto 'Monopoly or Death' (Βοβολίνης [Vovolinis]/ Βοβολίνης [Vovolinis] 1958–1963, E, 331, 337). Clearly, the Greek government needed to take urgent action.

In the same year, Greek parliament passed a law that stipulated that 15% of the crop was to be stored to reduce supplies and increase prices. In 1899, one year after Greece was put under international financial control, the so-called Currant Bank (Σταφιδική Τράπεζα) was founded to centralise the storage of currants and stabilise market prices. The bank received state capital for its work and its shareholders were farmers who were obliged to store a proportion of their crop, selling it later in the year (Πιζάνιας [Pizanias] 1988, 25; Franghiadis 1990, 166): this system functioned to a certain extent until the very rich crop of 1903 when the bank's capital proved insufficient to buy up the large surplus and the prices sank (Πιζάνιας [Pizanias] 1988, 26). Anarchistic unrest in Pylos increased the pressure on the government (ibid., 25). The protesters again demanded the introduction of a currant trade monopoly, and even set fire to the local branch of the ETE. However, the government found itself with few options: the desperate financial situation meant that they were unable to provide the necessary capital to set up a monopoly company and there was no prospect of obtaining an international loan for such a purpose. From the Greek perspective, the notion of involving private foreign capital was thus an obvious one.

A currant monopoly in times of free trade?

Interested parties were quickly found. The industrialist Edward Allen Brotherton and the banker Robert Solomon Backhouse from London[8] declared themselves willing to supply a large share of the proposed one million drachmas of capital and to float the company on the London Stock Exchange, where in 1893 the proportion of foreign securities was over 50% (Cassis 2007, 149). At the beginning of the twentieth century, it was clear that one bank could not cope with such an undertaking alone as it was necessary to share the risk among a number of partners. The ETE and Hambro were both interested,[9] and even Rothschilds apparently expressed an interest.[10] Why was the venture attractive to Brotherton and Backhouse and the other bankers? Writing to the ETE, Brotherton and Backhouse emphasised the good potential profits:

> If it be decided to adopt the scheme, and the Syndicate be finally formed, the Banks ought to help the scheme on to a successful issue; and, having regard to your and our shareholders' interests, we have every confidence that you will not be guided by the impulse of the Government alone, or by purely platonic motives; but will satisfy yourself that the terms of the Convention are of a workable character; and that those of the Syndicate are such as ultimately, if not immediately, to produce a reasonable profit to those who stake their money on the success of the scheme.[11]

The two British businessmen were not deterred by the fact that the idea of a monopoly company was diametrically opposed to the idea of free trade as propagated worldwide by Great Britain. They rather believed that it was perfectly legitimate for Britain to profit

> by establishing a preferential tariff for its colonies, and a tax on food, with a view to the extension of their prosperity by counteracting the effect of those gigantic trusts and syndicates of foreign

nations; and at the same time of binding the Empire together, and of making its own production selfsufficing.[12]

Was Greece thus to become part of the British Empire, at least informally? The Greek public would have been appalled at such a notion. An additional factor that encouraged the interest of the bankers was the rapid recovery of the exchange rate between the drachma and the franc: by September 1903, it had improved to 1.54.[13] This led, as discussed earlier, to a boom in Greek bonds. It was clearly a favourable moment to issue new Greek securities.

This initial attempt to organise the currant trade as a monopoly company failed nonetheless, apparently primarily due to the opposition of British trading houses. British currant traders,[14] the British Dried Fruit Trade Association and the Chamber of Commerce submitted complaints to the FO. They were concerned about the free trade of currants and about their profits.[15] The lobby groups argued that a monopoly would cause a considerable increase in the price of currants, a product that was well-loved by the British labour force.[16] The Board of Trade reacted correspondingly negatively. It suggested to the foreign office that the conditions granted to Greece in the 1890 trade agreement between Greece and the Empire were in any case too favourable in many points and that it was therefore impossible to discuss further concessions.[17] Greece declared that the changes would only impact the profits of the intermediaries and that prices for the consumers would not increase, but this was not regarded as plausible.[18] The objections expressed by the representatives of the various interests led to the intervention of the FO in Athens: the planned company was declared to be incompatible with the British-Greek trade agreement.[19] Holland, Italy and the German Empire also protested.[20]

Against this background of international opposition, the project was discussed in the Greek parliament where many negative opinions were also heard, although for quite different reasons. Mainly, there was fear that the foreign investors would take advantage of Greece. The MPs changed several points of the convention stipulating, for example, that the bankers should deposit a huge guarantee in advance.[21] Brotherton and Backhouse rejected the modifications to the convention and immediately withdrew their consent without initiating any further negotiations.[22] Backhouse believed that the new convention contained 'terms or conditions that in our opinion predoomed it to certain failure'. The modified agreement was apparently incompatible both with his desire for profit and with his sense of honour as a banker; the original conditions were 'a sine qua non from a strong sense of duty, not only to our friends on this side, but also to your Excellency and the Greek Government'. He was convinced that no other investors would be found 'to put their money into it, unless the blemishes we take exception to in the Convention are removed'.[23] Backhouse presented a very familiar explanation to justify this withdrawal: due to his sense of responsibility towards his partners, he, as a serious banker, could not accept any increased risks – otherwise, he would be behaving like a speculator. The relationship between the bankers and Greece was not a long-standing one and had not been tested in practice; it failed to survive the political disputes.

Prime minister Delyannis was forced to withdraw the proposed law, explicitly due to foreign opposition.[24] As an interim solution, he persuaded the ETE, the IOB and the BA to advance the Currant Bank 6.5 million drachmas to buy up the surplus from the 1903 crop.[25] This was enough to halt the unrest and uprisings on the Peloponnesus, at least for the time being.[26]

It became clear that before a solution for the Greek currant question could be found, a compromise had to be reached on the international level. Prolonged negotiations between the Greek government and the governments of the Great Powers followed. In the British case, the London branch of the IOB bank acted as an intermediary.[27] Great Britain was very interested in finding a solution because since 1898 the British diplomats in Greece had been extremely enthusiastic about the breathtaking speed of recovery of Greek trade and economic activity.[28] The new market looked very appealing for British merchants and investors, and there was a concern to secure the best conditions for British industries and trade. The British Board of Trade was therefore willing to give the Greeks a free hand in solving the currant question, if, in turn, the tariffs on certain British imports to Greece were reduced.[29] But on which? The negotiations were lengthy. Greece was, for instance, not prepared to reduce the dues on textile imports.[30] Talks continued and the next crop of 1904 was harvested. A reform bill was passed in July in an attempt to stabilise prices, but was unsuccessful.[31] In spring 1905, the British ambassador was still struggling with the Greek government about the reduction of duties on British products. Even the tariffs on Greek sweets like Halva and Loukum came under scrutiny.[32] Finally, an agreement was reached that the duties should be reduced on various British imports such as cod and stockfish, confectionary, biscuits and some cotton and jute products. The forecast loss for the Greek treasury was estimated at 247,000 drachmas per year, but, however, the United Kingdom agreed not to raise the import duties on currants for the next five years.[33] A promise was also made not to intervene in any reforms of the Greek currant trade.[34] In July 1905, a new Greek-British trade convention came into force. It was high time for this agreement: due to the very rich crop of 1905, the Currant Bank finally went bankrupt in the summer (Petmezas 2013, 17). A quick solution had to be found, despite the unusual scarcity of capital on the international markets at the time (Chavagneux 2013, 70f.).

A newcomer as intermediary in old networks

Surprisingly, it was not the time-honoured ETE which took the initiative in this situation, but the very young BA. The BA's director Ioannis Pesmazoglou presented a plan to establish an international 'Privileged Company to Protect Production and Trade in Currants' (Société privilégiée pour favoriser la production et le commerce du Raisin de Corinthe – SPRC), and was actually able to gain the support not only of the London banking houses Hambro and Erlanger, but also of the Paris BUP. All three banking houses have been mentioned on numerous occasions in this book and clearly had various relationships to Greece. But why and how did they allow themselves to be persuaded to enter into this highly risky venture? How did they perceive and manage the risks and what factors encouraged them to have confidence in a project that had already failed once in the past?

Ioannis Pesmazoglou and the BA

The initiator and intermediary of this venture was Ioannis Pesmazoglou, the director of the BA.[35] The Pesmazoglou family originated from Asia Minor. Ioannis' grandfather had moved to Smyrna, where he and his son Georgios were general consuls for France before Georgios moved on to Alexandria with its large community of Greek diaspora.[36] Here, Ioannis (1857–1906) was born as one of seven sons, most of whom became bankers and businessmen despite their father's bankruptcy in 1873. Ioannis attended the Protestant School in Alexandria, which he left in 1875. In this year, the impoverished, ambitious young man started his professional career at the local branch of the CL. Head of this branch was Georgios Averof, a business partner and friend of Ioannis' father (Βοβολίνης [Vovolinis]/Βοβολίνης [Vovolinis] 1958–1963, A, 326). Alongside his work, Ioannis wrote articles for Egyptian newspapers and he acquired a fortune by speculating on the stock exchange with some start capital that Averof gave him for financial transactions. In December 1876, he founded his own private bank, which he was able to enlarge through various affiliations with other banks. He earned a great deal of money in cotton trade with the USA and within just a few years was one of the most influent bankers in Alexandria, also specialising in the transfer of money from Greek businessmen in the diaspora to their homeland Greece.

Pesmazoglou thus became interested in Greece as a financial market and started to instigate his networks in Athens. In the house of the influent Constantinople banker Andreas Syngros,[37] who has already been discussed here as the purchaser of the Lavrion mines and the Corinth Canal,[38] he first met his later wife Irine, niece of Syngros and daughter of the famous Greek admiral Nikolaos Miaoulis. He married her in 1888.[39] During the economic crisis of 1893, King George asked the Greeks in Egypt to help their homeland, and in a patriotic gesture Pesmazoglou donated a huge sum to the Greek state. He thus attracted the attention of the king, who he finally met personally at Syngros' house. The king honoured him for his donation with the Silver Cross of the Knight. In the same year, Pesmazoglou published his thoughts on the possibilities of reform for the Greek financial system (Pesmazoglou 1893)

Outside Pesmazoglou's sphere of influence, the first joint-stock bank in Greece was founded in Athens in 1893 by a group of Greek bankers: the Bank of Athens (BA) (Κωστής [Kostis]/Τσοκόπουλος [Tsokopulos] 1988, 42f., 48–52). Its key objective was to grant commercial and industrial loans to Greek entrepreneurs in Greece, but also in the Ottoman Empire and in Egypt. When the BA opened a branch in Alexandria, Pesmazoglou affiliated his own bank with the BA, whereby the capital of the bank totalled four million drachmas. In 1895, after the BA's new building in Athens was inaugurated,[40] Pesmazoglou won a crucial vote against the former director Antonios Kallegris at the BA's annual stockholder meeting, and so became the bank's new director.[41] It should be noted that Andreas Syngros and Georgios Averof were also present at this meeting.

This remarkable career encourages us to believe contemporary descriptions of Pesmazoglou. He is said to have been a very charming and endearing character with great political ambitions and rhetorical talent.[42] As the director of the BA, he introduced modern French banking practices to Greece, learnt during his time at the CL.[43] Even the very traditional ETE, which had consistently rejected modernisation, found itself innovating in response to this competition. The BA was active in a wide range of fields: it invested in shipping companies, the construction of the Greek railway system, road building and the tobacco trade. The BA also earned a lot of money through speculation with Spanish bonds during the American-Spanish war in 1898. Pesmazoglou furthermore developed multifaceted philanthropic interests, not only becoming the vice-president of the Society of the Friends of Technical Development in Athens, but also giving donations for the building of churches in Athens, collecting donations for refugees from Asia Minor and giving 150,000 drachmas to the Society of Commercial Clerks to found a commercial school in Athens. With his bourgeois lifestyle, he clearly embodied typical middle-class virtues like competence, industriousness, reliability and responsibility, as well as virtues that would promote his reputation among the European bankers such as risk aversion, thrift and an aptitude for calculation (Pohle-Fraser 1999, 275). 'Trustworthy is he who stands by that which he has, consciously or unconsciously, disclosed about himself' (Luhmann 2009, 48, tr. by K.S.). Pesmazoglou was therefore regarded as part of a sworn and equal community within which, it was assumed, nobody would use information symmetries to the disadvantage of the others (Pohle-Fraser 1999, 362f.).

Pesmazoglou soon recognised the financial potential of the currant trade in his 'new' homeland, especially as a large proportion of the BA's customers were involved in trade. After only two years in Athens, he joined a congress for the discussion of the currant question and in this context published a memoir about a Greek Currant Bank (Πεσμαζόγλου [Pesmazoglou] 1898) – which, as mentioned earlier, was then indeed founded in 1899. In 1900, the BA founded a Society for Winegrowing and the Agriculture Industry with capital of 200,000 drachmas, which gave cheap credit to the farmers. The capital of the bank grew quickly to ten million drachmas in the same year, and it was able to open branches in Sofia (1902), London (1903), Constantinople (1904), Smyrna (1904) and Cairo (1905). In 1904, the capital of the bank increased to 20 million drachmas and shares were now offered on the Paris Stock Exchange with the help of the BUP. The BA rode on a wave of success as a classical modern deposit bank specialising in trade. Industrial finance played but a minor role here. The target group of the BA was not only Greeks in Greece, but also (Greek) business people in all other regions of the eastern Mediterranean where a dense network of correspondents developed.[44] The short-lived Orientbank, founded by the ETE and the Nationalbank für Deutschland in 1904, provided no real competition for the BA (Κωστής [Kostis] /Τσοκόπουλος [Tsokopulos] 1988, 132–139).[45]

In 1905, the Greek Currant Bank went bankrupt and the BA lost the capital invested thus far. In addition, unrest in the producer regions threatened the stability of the Greek state and its general economy. Pesmazoglou reacted by seizing the initiative and attempting to find foreign capital for a monopoly company for the Greek currant trade.

BUP, Paris

Hubert Bonin considers that the BA played a key role in putting Greece on the agenda of French financial interests in the Mediterranean. Although this suggestion minimises the importance of the business interactions that had long existed between Paris and Athens, it is undoubtedly the case that the close relationship between the BA and the BUP brought a new dimension to French-Greek capital interactions (Bonin 2001, 3). It was Ioannis Pesmazoglou who, as the director of the BA, first approached the BUP.

The BUP was a very young financial institute, founded in 1904 by various members of the Paris haute banque who were interested in profiting from opportunities provided by the internationalisation of banking (Bonin 2000, 18ff.). The bank was intended to pursue business that the bankers judged as too risky for their own banking houses but which they also did not wish to leave to the competition. There was hope that great opportunities would arise from venturing into many individual niche markets, e.g. on the Balkans (Bonin 2013, 112). The bank was explicitly founded for foreign business and Lucien Villars, formerly responsible for international relations at the Banque de Paris et Paribas, was appointed as the BUP's first director (Bonin 2000, 13). The founding of the bank showed that banking and its structures had fundamentally changed throughout Europe in the preceding decades: joint-stock banks had become just as indispensable as foreign business (Cassis 2007, 117–208). Important banking houses such as Michel Heine, Alphonse Mallet and Paul Mirabaud were among the founders of the new joint-stock bank. A number of them looked back on a long Philhellenic tradition.

For instance, in 1895, the Mirabaud banking house had incorporated the d'Eichthal bank with its particular links to Greece (discussed earlier).[46] The founder of Neuflize et Cie, Jean Abraham André Poupart de Neuflize II (1784–1836), also collected donations for Greece during the Greek War of Independence in 1821–1829.[47] Other founders were interested in the Mediterranean more widely, e.g. Rodolphe Hottinguer.[48] It is thus hardly surprising that Pesmazoglou approached the BUP in 1904 and that the bank proved very open to his suggestions of cooperation; with its predilection for specialising in niches, the BUP was most willing to add Greece to its fields of business (Bonin 2013, 112). Thanks to his activities with the CL in Alexandria, Pesmazoglou's name was familiar in French financial circles, which made instilling confidence even easier. In April 1904, the BA increased its capital from 10 to 20 million drachmas and the BUP used the occasion to acquire a share with 100,000 francs. The aim of the participation was 'to seize chunks of the trading finance that gathered momentum alongside the steady growth of Greek exports' (ibid.). Simultaneously, the BUP organised the introduction of the BA shares at the Paris Stock Exchange and delegated a representative to its advisory board (ibid., 115).[49] The close cooperation also penetrated the everyday business of banking (ibid., 127). It was specifically intended to strengthen the BA's reputation in the Paris market. Nonetheless, this only represented the initial steps of closer cooperation and did not mean that the French were willing to finance all and any of the BA's proposals. Some projects were rejected, e.g. Pesmazoglou's proposal for a new mining company in December 1904.[50] The fact that the cooperation between the two banks continued until the 1930s should not lead to any false conclusions being drawn about the robustness of the trust between them at the beginning of their collaboration in 1904/1905. The question about why the notion of founding a currant society was so attractive remains unanswered.

Hambro & Sons, London

This applies equally for the two British partners in the venture. One of them, C. J. Hambro & Son, has appeared in various places in this investigation due to his numerous relationships to Greece: Hambro was one of the main issuers of Greek state loans between 1878 and 1893 and indeed afterwards; the bank acted as an intermediary between Greece and the country's creditors in questions of state debts, and between Greece and the LCC right into the 1940s, in addition to many other activities. These special relationships deserve close attention.

The Hambro family can be traced back to Denmark. Calmer Joachim Levy, a Jewish merchant from Hamburg, founded the trading house in 1778 in Copenhagen, where the name 'Hamburg' seems to have been wrongly recorded by officials as 'Hambro' (Bramsen/Wain 1979, 11). The business flourished. His son Joseph joined the trading house in 1800 causing the name to be changed to C. J. Hambro & Son, and he progressed to become the house banker of Frederick VI of Denmark. Joseph's son Carl Joachim (1807–1877), a member of the third generation and baptised a Protestant, also joined the family business. After spending time in Le Havre, Antwerp, Bremen and North America, in 1832 he founded the trading house of C. J. Hambro & Son in London with capital of £50,000 (St. George 2004). In 1839, following disputes with his father, he moved permanently with his family to London. The London banking house was involved in the issuing of foreign securities, e.g. for the USA and Scandinavia (Denmark, Sweden, Norway), and in railway construction. After Carl Joachim had financed the war over Schleswig and Holstein (1848–1851), the Danish king rewarded him with a barony in 1851 (ibid.; Bramsen/Wain 1979, 238–246). In 1864, Hambro also financed the Danish-German war. His business was so successful that, shortly after the death of his first wife Caroline née Gostenhofer (1810–1852), Carl Joachim was able to purchase the estate of Milton Abbey in Dorset, which became the family seat (ibid., 250–256). After his second marriage in 1862, he lived there with his wife Eliza, née Turner, who he had met while she was nursing him.

Carl Joachim was close friends with the Sardinian finance minister Cavour, whom he supported with the issue of a four-million-pound state loan for Sardinia in 1852 (Bendix 1939, 15), despite Barings' refusal to become involved with the loan because Italy was known in the London City as the undisputed territory of the Rothschilds (Bramsen/Wain 1979, 264). The opposition from Rothschilds did not prevent the successful issue of the loan, which allowed Hambro to become firmly established in the Italian market (ibid., 272). He continued to support Cavour, and was described as a kingmaker with reference to Victor Emmanuel II, who was crowned King of Italy in 1861 (St. George 2004). Even after Cavour's death in 1861, Hambro remained active in Italy. The fact that he was also one of the most important financiers of Greece is another indication of the close links between the Italian Risorgimento and Greece in terms of acquiring foreign capital, a subject worthy of more investigation.[51] Carl Joachim also applied his kingmaker skills to Greece after King Otto was driven from the country in 1861. The Greeks were keen to offer the throne to Queen Victoria's second son, Alfred. Victoria spurned this suggestion so the Greek delegation that had travelled to London found it necessary to seek another candidate.[52] Hambro proposed the 17-year-old Danish Prince Wilhelm whose sister Alexandra was soon to marry the British heir to the throne Edward (VII). On 15 June, when the Danish prince was in London attending to wedding preparations, Hambro organised a church service in the Danish church of the city, and invited the Greeks. The carefully arranged service and the appearance of the prince made the necessary impression and in autumn 1863, Wilhelm was elected to be King George I of Greece (Bramsen/Wain 1979, 272–277).

This anecdote is extensively recorded in Bramsen and Wain's biography of the Hambro family but could not be verified from other sources. Nothing was found on the topic in the Hambro archive. The travel correspondence of C. F. Ricard, which Bramsen and Wain draw upon, describes the occasion organised by Hambro for the Danish delegation in London but does not mention the choice of George or the attendance of the Greeks at the event.[53] Neither could an episode of this sort be found in the FO correspondence. The files show only that the candidacy of the Danish prince was made public before either Victoria or the FO had commented on it – much to the displeasure of the queen.[54] Neither the research literature (Holland/Markides 2006, 66)[55] nor biographies of George I mention Hambro's influence on the choice of monarch (e.g. Christmas 1914, 40ff.; Καμπούρογλους [Kampouroglous] 1905). It is thus unclear where Bramsen and Wain found the anecdote. Perhaps it is a family story that had been passed on by word of mouth to explain and legitimate the special relationship between a country and a banking house, as is often the case with myths in banking history (Liedtke 2006). Be that as it may, there is evidence to show that Hambro supported the freshly elected king by advancing Wilhelm £10,000 for his enthronement in Athens,[56] a 'debt of honour' that was provided free of interest for four years. Hambro authorised Wilhelm Count of Sponneck to administer payment of the money. He had worked closely with Sponneck when the latter was the Danish minister of finance in 1848–1854. Sponneck accompanied Wilhelm to Greece where he was supposed to remain for five years but in 1865 his ill-health led him to curtail his stay (Rordam 1902). In his letters to Hambro, Sponneck reported on Greece's promising economic development under the new king, who wanted to finally ensure that the unused resources of the country were made fruitful.[57] However, Sponneck also complained about the corruption of the foreign press who had been bribed to stop them reporting negatively about Greece. Most of the loan, of which only £9,300 was actually claimed, was repaid by 1864.[58] Sponneck emphasised George's great gratitude towards Hambro and his willingness to do him any conceivable favour.[59] As the king's house banker, Hambro had clearly managed to firmly establish himself in Greece, a good 30 years after Simon von Eichthal's sobering experiences when holding this office. This explains why C. J. Hambro & Son was one of the first banks to take on the issuing of new loans for Greece after the country returned to the international exchanges in 1878. In the years leading up to 1893, Hambro participated in four of the seven Greek loans. And, once Greece's problematic financial situation was blatantly obvious to all observers, it was Hambro who in 1893 was again willing to issue a so-called Funding Loan for Greece despite the international financial crisis.[60] After the country nonetheless declared bankruptcy in 1893, Hambro was a key figure in negotiations with the bondholders[61] and, as we have seen, in 1902 was the first to be willing to issue Greek securities again.

By this time, however, Carl Joachim Hambro was no longer alive, having died in 1877. The business was now run by the youngest of his three sons Everard Alexander Hambro (known as Evy, 1842–1925), who had joined his father's bank in 1864 and now ran it with three other partners (St. George 2004). He had studied at Trinity College Cambridge with future colleagues such as Nathaniel Rothschild and Joseph Gibbs and was friends with the Prince of Wales, who later became Edward VII (Bramsen/Wain 1979, 298). In 1866, he married (Gertrude) Mary Stuart (1848–1905), a sister of his friend Martin Ridley Smith and a descendent of John Stuart, the third Earl of Bute, who had been the prime minster under George III; the couple had eight children, five of whom survived to adulthood.[62] Under Everard Hambro, the bank's capital grew from £650,000 when he became a senior partner in 1877 to £1.3 million in 1890. In the 1880s, Everard Hambro earned about £150,000 a year. '[I]t was one of London's largest and most prestigious houses' (St. George 2004). Unsurprisingly, he was elected to the Court of the Bank of England in 1879. In addition to its bills of exchange business, the bank focused firstly on trade, particularly with America and between North and South America, and secondly on issuing state loans. Following his father's example, Everard Hambro issued loans for a series of countries, e.g. Sweden, Norway, Denmark, Greece, Russia and Italy, often in cooperation with Morgan & Co, Barings or Hoskier in Paris, and in the case of Italy at times in bitter competition with Rothschilds.[63] Hambro was also active in the railway and telegraph business (Bramsen/Wain 1979, 307). When the Baring Bank required rescuing in 1890, Hambro stood up for his business partner and friend. C. J. Hambro & Son survived the crisis until the mid-1890s, suffering losses but never in serious danger (ibid., 319–323). Hambro was also known as a philanthropist, e.g. for his commitment to orphans and his generous support of a pension fund for nurses. In the case of Greece, Everard Hambro continued the family tradition so that C. J. Hambro & Son remained the country's most important foreign financier. In 1920, when Everard's son Eric (1872–1947) had been a partner in the bank for over 20 years, Hambro's commitment to Greece reached its peak (Minoglou 2002b).[64] The bank's assets had grown from £5 million in 1898 to £10 million by 1913 (Bramsen/Wain 1979, 330),[65] and its long tradition and great experience in foreign business were emphasised as being particularly important social capital.[66] In 1904/1905, when the establishment of a currant trading company was under discussion, C. J. Hambro & Son could thus look back on 40 years of intensive work with Greece and enjoyed the reputation of being a specialist for the Greek market. From the Greek perspective, there was no real alternative to Hambro in London and no way of bypassing the bank. Hambro was the undisputed gatekeeper of Greece on the 'hub of international financial traffic' of the time (Cassis 1990, 129). This makes it all the more interesting that Pesmazoglou chose not to first approach Hambro but went to Emil Erlanger, a much smaller private banker in the City of London. The very fact that Erlanger was asked *before* him must have given Hambro a reason to fear the loss of his position as Greece's gatekeeper in the City. The BA here pursued the same strategy that they would successfully use in

1909 for the planned state loan,[67] forcing Hambro's hand by activating his smaller competitor.

Emil Erlanger, London

Emil (or Émile) Erlanger was also far from inexperienced when it came to Greece. The Jewish Erlanger family came from Heddernheim near Frankfurt, and the grandfather Löb (1780–1857) worked as a bill broker in Frankfurt but was also a fund manager in the original house of the Rothschild family (Kirchholtes 1969, 33).[68] Emil Erlanger's father Raphael (1806–1878) continued the business and in 1829 converted to Christianity, apparently to Protestantism.[69] While consul in Portugal, he gained a baronial title in 1859 and was later made a member of the Sachsen-Meiningen nobility and also given the rank of Freiherr in the Austrian nobility (Kirchholtes 1969, 34; Stoskopf 2002a, 165). He additionally held the office of general consul of Sweden and Norway. Raphael's son Friedrich Emil von Erlanger (1832–1911) attended the Musterschule in Frankfurt, which had been founded in 1804 as a reform school. Here, he learnt English and French but no classics (Eiselen 1880, 36). Nevertheless, the young Erlanger soon displayed an interest in Greece: in 1855 at the early age of 23, when a broker on the Frankfurt exchange,[70] he became the general consul for Greece in Frankfurt.[71] This office was very popular in Frankfurt banking circles at the time and its significance in terms of actual cooperation should not be overestimated as there was a great deal of variation from case to case.[72] However, Emil Erlanger actively used his position to initiate business relations with Greece. Very shortly after his appointment, he visited Athens and met Georgios Stavros, the director of the Greek National Bank and confidant of Jean Gabriel Eynard. He also became acquainted with Stavros' sister-in-law and his niece. Once back in Germany, he wrote and thanked Stavros for the very pleasant meeting.[73] He also introduced his brother Raphael, who was interested in working with the ETE, to Stavros[74] and a year later the first business deals were initiated.[75]

In 1859, Erlanger moved to Paris where he founded his own banking house with capital of 500,000 francs (Stoskopf 2002a, 162ff.) – a rather modest undertaking in comparison to Hambro. In the same year, he married Florence Laffitte, the daughter of Charles Laffitte and granddaughter of the famous banker and politician Jacque Laffitte (ibid., 162). The marriage doubled Erlanger's capital but was dissolved with a great deal of scandal in 1862 (ibid.).[76] However, the banking house flourished even though the haute banque, e.g. James de Rothschild, kept Erlanger at a distance. Erlanger maintained his contacts to the ETE,[77] and even intensified them in the course of the 1860s.[78] In 1867, he became the general consul for Greece in Paris – the position that Adolphe d'Eichthal had vacated at the beginning of the 1860s[79] – and remained in this office for decades. He organised the contributions of Greece to the Parisian world exhibitions of 1867 and 1878 (Stoskopf

2002a, 162ff.).[80] In 1868, Erlanger became involved in the exploitation of the emery reserves in Naxos, for which an English firm had previously held the concession.[81] Anti-Semitic stereotypes probably contributed to his reputation as a particularly ruthless and greedy banker. In 1863, when Erlanger had just arranged the so-called Confederate Cotton Loan for the Southern states, an achievement that brought him great renown, a competitor wrote:

> This man Erlanger is a dangerous one; he has the quickest intelligence I have ever been thrown in contact with and he is well calculated to exercise great influence over other minds not so active, but I judge him to be ambitious, selfish, daring and unscrupulous.[82]

Richard Roberts bases his assessment of Erlanger on this description by a competitor: 'Erlanger was a gambler who took great risks and generally reaped spectacular rewards' (Roberts 1992, 63). His son, however, described Erlanger in retrospect as a poor judge of character who was easily blinded by intelligence and often put his trust in people who did not deserve it.[83] Erlanger was also well-known for his diverse philanthropic activities and as an art collector, especially of tapestries and musical instruments.[84] There was a great deal of music in his home and Erlanger himself played the violin. After the German-French war in 1871, Erlanger moved to London where he founded Emile Erlanger & Company. Perhaps he felt his German origins to be a disadvantage in Paris (Stoskopf 2002a, 162ff.).[85] He had excellent contacts in London, e.g. to the Schroeder banking house (Roberts 1992, 63), also due to his second marriage: in 1864, Erlanger had married Mathilde Slidell (1842–1927), a Catholic Englishwoman.[86] They had four sons together. Erlanger, himself a Protestant, allowed his sons to be educated in Catholic schools: in Paris, they attended the Jesuit school in rue de Madrid, and the younger Emile later attended a Dominican school in Arcachon before he completed his baccalauréat in Canterbury.[87] The sons also learnt classics in these traditional schools, and later the younger Émile Erlanger published his own epic poem about the poet Sappho.[88]

In London, the banking house was quickly established as a 'highly regarded and reputable merchant bank' (Roberts 1992, 86). The London office had only up to ten employees and undertook little more than 'bread and butter business'.[89] The core business was carried out at the exchange. The banking house was active in the USA, especially in railway construction, and worked with the Schroeder banking house in the cotton trade, as well as in Costa Rica[90] and Buenos Aires.[91] In the early 1890s, Erlanger was also involved in railway construction in South Africa, e.g. in the Beira Railway Company.[92] He also invested in completely different areas, providing, for instance, 7.5% of the capital for the news agency Havas (Stoskopf 2002a, 164). Another specialised field was tunnel construction: from the 1880s, the bank was involved in plans to build a tunnel between France and England

(Erlanger 1918).[93] Erlanger also held the concession for a tunnel between Galata and Pera in Constantinople.[94] This was one of the many projects he undertook in the Mediterranean, especially in Egypt[95] and Tunisia. In 1864, Heinrich Schliemann was Erlanger's agent in Tunis for a Tunisian loan (Roberts 1992, 69).[96] In 1869, Erlanger was involved in the provision of water supplies in Naples,[97] and a year later, he received a concession for the building of a telegraph link between France, Algeria and Malta.[98] A link between Sardinia and Italy then followed.[99] The two Erlanger sons, Émile Beaumont (1868–1941) and Frédéric Alfred, joined their father's business, Émile after extended travel in the USA and internships with several of his father's business partners. The relationship between Erlanger and the Greek ETE continued without interruption and, indeed, was intensified in the 1890s when Erlanger put the ETE in contact with French and Belgian banking houses.[100] This important connection continued into the next generation: in June 1901, Erlanger senior warmly thanked Stephan Streit, the governor of the ETE, for the time he had spent with his son in Florence.[101] In 1898/1899, Erlanger negotiated intensively with Streit about converting old ETE debts. Hambro and the SG similarly displayed interest in such a project.[102] Erlanger also maintained good contacts with the Greek monarchy: when in London, George I often visited him to play cards[103] or the theatre lover Erlanger[104] invited the royal family to his box at the opera, where they saw William Tell together.[105] In 1902, Erlanger then participated in the aforementioned railway loan for Greece, together with the ETE and Hambro (Bramsen/Wain 1979, 331).[106] Although the issue of the first instalment was a failure, the second and third instalments of 1904 and 1906 were extremely successful, which was generally interpreted as a sign of Greece's economic recovery after the establishment of the financial commission in 1898, in addition to the steady fall of the exchange rate of the drachma. Erlanger maintained diverse business links to the Hambro banking house. Everard Hambro tended to address the young Erlanger in his letters familiarly as 'mon cher Émile'. Nonetheless, the two banking houses also perceived one another as competitors in certain situations. After 1909, the relationship seems to have deteriorated, as demonstrated by Everard Hambro's description of Erlanger cited earlier and Erlanger's over-heightened appetite for risk in 1909 (although this did not prevent further cooperation).[107] In any case, in 1905 when the notion of a currant company was rife, it was natural for Erlanger to turn to Hambro. The sharing of risk with this banking house was tried and tested.

All three banks (BUP, Hambro and Erlanger) had clearly maintained a relationship to Greece over a number of years and had well-established networks in the country. These links went back to a time when banking involved quite different practices, when close personal relationships were the conditio sine qua non for the creation of trust, also on an official level. Such reciprocally trusting relationships had developed over a considerable period of time and tended to reduce the significance of the price mechanism and enhance that of values like reliability, confidence, loyalty, gratitude and an appreciation of well-established processes (Berghoff 2004, 67). The importance of these trusted links for the acquisition and generation of information for the bankers should not be underestimated: 'The existence of close, long-term relationships between banks and firms is generally regarded as a particularly valuable mechanism for overcoming asymmetries between insiders and outsiders' (Battilossi 2008, 82). However, this does not explain why the bankers chose to participate in the currant trade project. What was the core idea behind the currant company that attracted the foreign bankers? Was it intensively evaluated or did the bankers rely on the observations of their partners in the sense of 'reputation approaches'? What did the risk management of the investors look like?

The proposed project

In 1905, Ioannis Pesmazoglou described the situation in the Greek currant trade in a memorandum for Emil Erlanger as follows:

> The overproduction of currants and the consequent heavy loss to the currant growers preoccupies for many years now not only the Greek Government and people, but also those who have an interest in the article, and, in a general way, all people who desire the welfare of Greece.[108]

The law of June 1904 dictated that a payment in kind of 35% or 40% was required on the exported currants, but the dried fruit thus collected could only be used for industrial purposes and earned little income for the treasury. The hope was that world market prices would be stabilised by keeping back part of the harvest. However, the Currant Bank was required to buy the surplus revenue of the non-exported crop at a fixed and very low price. It was seldom able to do so because its capital cover was very poor and much of it was locked up in loans for the currant growers, who were not able to pay the money back because of the very low price they received for their crop.[109]

Pesmazoglou wanted to break this vicious circle, give the currant trade greater stability, restore lost confidence and increase the low prices.[110] He emphasised that the project was in the interests of a significant proportion of the farming population and avoided the dangers facing the Currant Bank at the time.[111] The plan was to found a Greek company with capital of 20 million gold drachmas (at the exchange rate of 1905, which stood at 1:1 between the drachma and the franc, this was equivalent to 20,000,000 francs or £800,000[112]), divided into 200,000 shares of 100 drachmas each. A proportion of five million drachmas was reserved for the state-owned Currant Bank, which was allowed to deposit the full amount within four years. The dividend per year was guaranteed at 6%.[113] But where were the possible profits for investors? Prior to 1 July of every year, the SPRC had to determine a price for the expected surplus crop, which was classified into three categories according to quality. The company was obliged to buy all currants that had not been sold abroad for higher prices by the growers before this date. It was not permitted to sell this part of the crop abroad so as to stabilise prices on the world market; the dried grapes had instead to be turned into alcohol, wines or other products within the country. In return, the company held the monopoly to sell alcohol in Greece, and it was forbidden to make alcohol from any materials other than currants anywhere in the country.[114] The company had to pay a set sum to the treasury as an export tariff on *all* exported currants, whether their own or those of others, so the treasury could count on fixed and punctual payment. In return, the company received from the farmers a fee of 19 drachmas per 1,000 Venetian pounds of currants exported earlier in the year, which was nearly double the sum it had to pay to the treasury. However, it had to provide warehouses to store all of the harvest for free. For this service, it received an additional seven drachmas per 1,000 Venetian pounds of currants produced. Pesmazoglou counted on an annual profit of about four million drachmas, equal to 5% of the invested capital. For the missing 1% of the dividend, Pesmazoglou seems to have depended on exchange rate profits or profits resulting from a possible growth in consumption – he did not explicitly discuss the issue. He only saw a risk for the company if more than 330 million Venetian pounds of currants were produced. His project therefore involved the prohibition of new vineyards for 15 years, the duration of the concession. Additionally, the company was encouraged to advertise currants in new markets to enlarge the consumption of this natural Greek monopoly abroad.[115] In his memorandum, Pesmazoglou did not mention the objections raised by the small Greek currant merchants to the monopoly nor the strong opposition in the Greek parliament. But his partners must have known about these problems, because they were not surprised when it proved difficult to pass the necessary legislation in the Greek parliament later on.

The privileged company to protect production and trade in currants (SPRC)[116]

As early as 1903, Ioannis Pesmazoglou started travelling frequently to London and Paris to conduct initial talks about the SPRC. But the first concrete pre-negotiations held in 1905 were obviously carried out by brokers. A commission of £500 for a Mr de Zoete is mentioned[117] and in addition the Parisian bank Sauerbach Thalmann & Cie charged commission fees of 1.5 francs per share for intermediation before Pesmazoglou sent the first draft of his project to the BUP.[118] These intermediaries were clearly necessary even though the BA and BUP were already in close contact. In his drafts, Pesmazoglou emphasised his long preparatory deliberations with members of the Greek

Cabinet.[119] In fact, he cared greatly for opinions in Greece and simultaneously published a memorandum in Greek (Πεσμαζόγλου [Pesmazoglou] 1905). Later on, Pesmazoglou managed to induce Edmond Théry, the director of de *L'Économiste Européen* and author of the book 'La Grèce actuelle au point de vue économique et financier' to write a scientific memorandum about the question of the currant trade. This report totally supported his plans and he forwarded it to those he hoped to win as partners.[120] Pesmazoglou clearly relied on specialist expertise to persuade investors. Contacts in Paris were made relatively easily but, after the failed attempt of 1903, the hurdles were greater in London. Talks with the Dried Fruit Trade Company in London were therefore particularly important to Pesmazoglou.[121] He managed to persuade them to join his project by guaranteeing them a voice in the administrative council of the company and promising the unusually large sum of between £5,000 and £20,000 a year for advertising currants in Great Britain.[122] In this way, he not only avoided further problems with the lobbying group, but even won its active support of the monopoly plans, persuading it to write a letter to the British FO. Indeed this time, the FO did not intervene, notwithstanding the protests of individual merchants against the planned monopoly.[123] After his return to Athens, Pesmazoglou explained his idea in great detail to the British ambassador and pointed out that the monopoly would not increase the price of currants for the British public.[124]

With these activities, Pesmazoglou reduced political opposition to a minimum but had not yet established contact to the financiers in London. Strikingly, he did not first approach Hambro, who in 1903 had already demonstrated interest in the currant project, but rather Erlanger. Was this a deliberate attempt to activate Hambro, who was afraid of Erlanger's competition? Perhaps relevant was the recommendation of Erlanger by another broker, the Greek Demetrios Georgiades who had been Erlanger's agent in Greece for several years. The Parisian financial journalist, who wrote especially for *L'Économiste Française* and *Le Monde Économique*,[125] had himself attempted to set up a currant company, but to no avail. He then suggested that Pesmazoglou should get Erlanger on board for the project. Obviously, it was not possible for Pesmazoglou to contact Erlanger without the detour via Georgiades, although the relationship between the two Greeks was poor. Georgiades was firmly established as the Greek expert on the Parisian market – a position that Pesmazoglou coveted for himself. Georgiades profited from excellent connections in French financial circles – and indeed through Erlanger also in the British financial world[126] – and reinforced his position with regular publications about the Greek economy in French newspapers (Georgiadès 1892, 1893, 1896, 1907). His position on the supervisory board of the Greek railway company was also viewed by Erlanger as an advantage (Κωστής [Kostis]/Τσοκόπουλος 1988, 136). In the critical years of the 1890s, Georgiades came to the fore with proposals for the repayment of Greek debts (Georgiadès 1894),[127] and after the turn of the century, he intensively promoted a project for the unification of Greek foreign debts.[128] These activities clearly made Georgiades a serious competitor for Pesmazoglou. The conflicts threatened to escalate during negotiations about the SPRC. In a letter to the BUP director Villars, Pesmazoglou painted an unusually unpleasant picture of Georgiades and slandered his reputation. He told Villars that Georgiades had been banished from the Ottoman Empire because of his attempts to blackmail the Ottoman government, and that he later had to leave Paris because of conflicts with the CEP and its influential vice-director Vlasto.[129] The motives behind Pesmazoglou's defamatory attack seem fairly obvious. When it became clear that the SPRC would be established, Georgiades demanded a position as an administrator, which Pesmazoglou decisively refused. The conflict continued for several months. Pesmazoglou even threatened to resign from the supervisory board himself if Georgiades should be given a seat.[130] He seems to have initially been successful with this strategy but then in 1910, after his death, Georgiades is found among the company directors.[131] In terms of Erlanger's risk management, it is revealing that his involvement in the project was facilitated by his 'own' intermediary who he knew personally from his time in Paris and who maintained his contacts to Greece. Pesmazoglou was thus unable to approach Erlanger without using Georgiades.

Once the contacts to the foreign bankers were in place, Pesmazoglou sent them his proposals. The reactions of the international partners were positive – and so swift that it is difficult to speak of careful project evaluation. Apparently, it was already clear that the company would be brought into existence, so this must have been agreed by the intermediaries in preliminary oral negotiations. Quite obviously, the issue of who would participate was much more controversial than the project itself. A letter from Everard Hambro to Emile Erlanger written from Paris on 23 May 1905 informed the latter that the hearing with the BUP had already successfully taken place. All the bankers were interested in a huge consortium to split the investment risk, and the British were willing to pay the costs for this shared risk management. The French made considerable demands, but Hambro explained that he was 'convinced that we will not be able to reduce them'.[132] In accordance with ordinary banking practice, all participants received commission: the BUP 200,000 francs, Erlanger and the BA 100,000 each.[133] The bankers agreed to issue the stocks of the SPRC on the Paris market and to do everything possible to prevent the business appearing too speculative.

In the following months, Pesmazoglou tried to win the support of the Greek government and parliament for the project and to coordinate the interests of the Greek side with those of the foreign capitalists. For example, the BUP attempted to push the Greek Currant Bank out of the new company and to minimise its share of the profits – unsurprisingly as the Greek Currant Bank with its miserable finances was the weakest of the partners. Pesmazoglou had to exercise all his powers of persuasion to convince the investors that the involvement of the Currant Bank was imperative to win over the majority of the Greek MPs and to increase the popularity of the project with the Greek public.[134] As so often, a large proportion of the Greeks were extremely critical of the involvement of foreign investors. This made it even more important that Pesmazoglou was able to persuade the BA's strongest competitor on the Greek market, the ETE, to participate with 2.5 million drachmas,[135] thus clearly refuting accusations of speculation as the ETE was known to be extremely reliable and risk-averse – and was also, as seen earlier, an old partner of Hambro and Erlanger.

During the parliamentary proceedings, Pesmazoglou had to negotiate even the smallest concession with the BUP in numerous telegrams and letters.[136] The foreign banks did not generally empower their Greek partner, but wanted to make all the decisions on their own. They explained their caution through mentioning their 'responsabilité morale' vis-à-vis their partners and clients.[137] But this was not the only reason why the proceedings were complicated. There was strong opposition to the monopoly company in the Greek parliament amid fears that it would destroy all the small currant trading businesses in the country. The SPRC was accused of enriching foreign capitalists at the cost of the successful currant growers who did not actually need any help.[138] The discussions were heated but after a session of 48 hours, Pesmazoglou was able to inform the BUP that the second reading of the law had been passed.[139] After further 'stormy debates', the law was finally passed on 29 July 1905 at five o'clock in the morning.[140]

There was now no time left to lose. In August, the members of the consortium collected the capital for the new company.[141] The BA was the largest shareholder with 27,000 shares at 250 francs each, while the British group took second place with 17,500 shares.[142] The French banks divided the shares: La Marseillaise took 5,000 and the BUP surprisingly only 3,000 despite the high commission it received.[143] However, the individual houses of the Parisian haute banque represented in the BUP also participated: de Neuflize with 1,200, Heine with 800, Mirabaud with 400, Vlasto as head of the CEP with 200 and Dreyfus with 100, to name but a few examples. Sauerbach Thalmann & Co, which had acted as a broker, took 1,000 shares. The managers of the BUP also participated as private individuals: Villars bought 250 shares, Wehrung 100, Barbé 100 and Lustgarten 50. Edmond Théry, author of the report and director of the L'Économiste Européen, took 200 shares.[144] These individual investments demonstrated that the financiers were personally convinced that the company would be profitable.

Thanks to the swiftness of this organisation, the SPRC could begin its activities in August 1905 and was able to market that year's crop. This was possible despite a number of unresolved conflicts, e.g. about whether the Greek Currant Bank should be obliged to pay a proportion of the brokers' commissions (which was in the end the case).[145] The composition of the administrative board was also a source of conflict for some time.[146] The BUP deliberated for a long time about who to send as a representative, and eventually decided upon Zarifios Matsas who was employed at the BA and would later follow Pesmazoglou as the director.[147] The company was floated on the Paris exchange in November but was not as successful as had been hoped. The BA complained bitterly about the downturn in the share prices, which Pesmazoglou believed was due to malicious rumours.[148] In order to avoid a slump by supporting the prices, the syndicate was continued until December 1906 and stabilised prices by targeted purchases.[149]

In the meanwhile, Pesmazoglou attempted to organise and improve the currant trade and valorisation. The BA founded a Société Vinicole to take care of the refinement of the dried grapes into alcohol and other products. This company started with capital of six million drachmas, 2.35 million of which was taken over by the BA.[150] Pesmazoglou resorted to his family network in these activities: one of the companies that was subsumed by the Société Vinicole was Zannos Roche and Cie, which belonged to his relative Aristoboulos Zannos.[151] The success of the SPRC was modest but stable. Although its shares never boomed on the stock exchange, in the following years, the company organised the currant trade efficiently and prevented any large-scale unrest in the currant-growing regions. The farmers were able to maintain their income.[152] International prices for currants were stabilised, though at a lower level than before 1893: in 1905–1914, the average price for 1,000 Venetian pounds (477 kg) on the world market was 172 francs, while the average in 1895–1904 had been only 97 (Tsiovaridou 1980, 141). The British traders seemed satisfied with the work of the SPRC[153]; and the shareholders received their dividend of 6% each year[154] until the outbreak of the Balkan Wars in 1912 dramatically complicated trading conditions. The company nonetheless continued its activities until 1924 (Tsiovaridou 1980, 142).

'Social brokerage'

The analysis has revealed a network of brokers who were necessary for the generation of the trust and confidence required for large-scale investments. For the BA, the SPRC not only provided an important position in the Greek export trade, but also a considerable gain in reputation with the government (Φραγκιάδης [Franghiadis] 2006, 167). For the initiator Ioannis Pesmazoglou, the successful founding of the company resulted in an enormous increase in personal prestige – it is possible to speak here of Pesmazoglou benefiting from 'social brokerage' in addition to the profits made by his bank. The successful establishment of the company seemed to open the door for his political career. The king honoured him with the order of the Knight of the Saviour and the newspapers outdid one another in praising him and lauding the benefits of his achievements for the Greek people. An article in the *Reforme Smyrne*, from Pesmazoglou's homeland, glorified his contribution to the modernisation of the Greek state: 'He is the one who has injected Greece with a new spirit; the spirit of political economy, the spirit of work, the spirit of creative initiative'.[155] In 1905, even before the negotiations had been completed, Pesmazoglou was elected to parliament as the deputy of Calamata, where he joined Theodoros Delyannis' party. After Delyannis' assassination in June 1905, he continued his political activities under Delyannis' successor Dimitrios Ralli. Pesmazoglou was suggested as a candidate for the position of minister of finance and a street in Athens was named after him.[156] He was obviously able to clearly communicate the benefits of the SPRC for Greece, both within the country and abroad. He presented himself as a competent and successful financial authority. In 1906, Pesmazoglou was elected as the deputy of Attica and was treated as the third most important man in Ralli's party. In parliament, he commented not only on banking subjects, but also on more general economic questions like the funding of the Greek army.[157] His political career was on the up and up when in November 1906 he suddenly fell ill with sepsis. Once the serious nature of his illness became clear, an excited discussion about a possible successor became rife in the BUP: 'Intrigues from all sides must be expected concerning the successor of Pesmazoglou'.[158] He died on 24 December. For several weeks, the Greek newspapers were full of obituaries. For the BA and its international partners, Pesmazoglou's death was a hard blow, depriving them of a figure who had inspired strong personal confidence. When his death was announced, the BA shares fell rapidly at the stock exchange in Athens, and the BUP and the ETE had to warn the shareholders not to panic (Βοβολίνης [Vovolinis]/ Βοβολίνης [Vovolinis] 1957–1963, A, 342). At least the affiliation of the BA with the Industrial Bank and the small Bank of Mythilene which was organised by Pesmazoglou in the last months of his life could be implemented, which increased the BA's capital to 40 million drachmas. The SPRC also survived the death of its founder.[159] But the other massive project that Pesmazoglou had initiated with Hambro, Erlanger and Rothschilds, the unification of Greek foreign debt and its conversion into drachmas (which Georgiades had so often called for), was aborted (Βοβολίνης [Vovolinis]/ Βοβολίνης [Vovolinis] 1957–1963, 341). The necessary trust and confidence for such an undertaking seems to have been closely associated with Pesmazoglou himself. His old competitor Georgiades was also unable to instigate the idea, although until the First World War he repeatedly attempted to do so. The BUP continued its cooperation with the BA, but the basis of trust deteriorated and the French bank tried to gain more control over its partner and intensified its monitoring activities (Ripperger 2005, 69): in 1906, Charles Wehrung joined the BA's supervisory board as the second administrator, and in 1910, André de Neuflize became the third administrator after serious problems with the bank's branches in Egypt had arisen after 1908 (Bonin 2001, 58).[160] In 1910–1913, the crisis heightened so that it was unclear whether the BA would survive. The BUP supported the BA but in the course of this process, the latter gradually shifted from being a 'sister bank' to resemble a subsidiary which the BUP wished to observe, control and direct (Bonin 2013, 130). The trust that had made the cooperation possible without an element of control could obviously not be sustained after the death of the charming broker Pesmazoglou.

Conclusion

Investment in the Greek currant trade was attractive for foreign bankers for a number of reasons. Firstly, the specific characteristics of the project were promising: on the one hand, the guaranteed dividend of 6%, on the other hand, the enormous significance of the project for the Greek market; after all, the aim was the fundamental reform of the crisis-ridden currant trade, the improvement of Greek state finances and the appeasement of Greek domestic politics. For investors who were already active in the Greek market like Hambro, Erlanger and the BUP partners, path dependency thus played an important role. It is striking that, with the exception of the BUP, the investors were private banks with a long tradition and much experience of merchant banking in trade, especially with Greece, a country to which they had long-standing links in diverse business fields.

In the end, the written project evaluation undertaken by Edmond Théry, a specialist in Greece, commissioned by the BA, was much less important than personal trust in the intermediary. The director of the BA Pesmazoglou successfully promoted the SPRC as a win-win project for all participants and was able to overcome the considerable opposition of Greek politicians and foreign lobbyists and thus harmonise the various interests. Without Pesmazoglou's rhetorical and organisational talents and winning personality, the project would probably never have got off the ground, just as the earlier venture undertaken by London bankers had failed without a trusted intermediary. Pesmazoglou focused specifically on family banks with a long tradition of maintaining and valuing personal relationships that could be traced back to the middle of the century, a time characterised only by traditional practices of risk perception. Here, Pesmazoglou could play to his strengths. Stereotypes of Greece, which the same actors, e.g. Hambro, applied in other contexts, were not activated in negotiations with Pesmazoglou.

Pesmazoglou presented himself to the foreign bankers as an innovative and successful self-made man, but also as a socially responsible banker with great political ambition and impressive networks. He was the embodiment of an ideal Greek businessman who could lead business ventures to success in the midst of chaotic state institutions, circumnavigating all institutional barriers. Pesmazoglou generated enough confidence among the foreign bankers to compensate for the lack of confidence in Greek politics and institutions. He jealously and vigorously defended his position as a specialised intermediary for the Greek market against competitors like the Paris broker Demetrios Georgiades. After his death, the lack of this personal trust meant that the French BUP felt it necessary to treat the BA as a subsidiary and control it more closely.

Notes

1 The following chapter has been published in an adapted form as Schönhärl (2013b).
2 Contrasting examples are Bickford-Smith (1893) and Sergeant (1897).
3 A map on Πετμεζάς [Petmezas] (2003, 239) gives an overview of the most important agricultural regions in the country. Also see Αρώνη-Τσίχλη [Aroni-Tsixlis] (2000).
4 In the following, the term currants is used to refer to both currants and raisins.
5 Currants were measured in Venetian pounds. One Venetian pound was the equivalent of 477 grams or 1.06 British pounds.
6 Franghiadis points out however that more recent investigations suggest the land became the property of local elites rather than that of small-scale farmers. See also Καρούζου [Karouzou] (2018).
7 The export figures were always over 90%; see Tsiovaridou (1980, 131).
8 They were Managing Director and Attorney of the Concessions and Monopolies limited. The company cannot have survived for long as very few traces of it can be found. It seems likely that Backhouse came from the Backhouse family; see Davis (2004). Baron Brotherton was active in the chemical industry and a philanthropist; see Donnelly (2004). It is not possible to determine how the two of them came into contact with business in Greece.
9 The convention for the planned company was published in *The Grocer*, 6.6.1903 (translated from a Greek publication in the *New City (Νέον Άστυ)* of 9./23.5.1903); see IOB 1/15. Half the capital was to be publicly raised on the London exchange. On the negotiations between Brotherton, Backhouse and the ETE, also see ETE A1S28Y2F10.
10 Brotherton and Backhouse to Streit, 26.5.1903, ETE A1S28Y2F10.
11 Brotherton and Backhouse to ETE, Streit, 15.6.1903, ETE A1S28Y2F10.
12 Ibid.
13 Finances helléniques, in: *Économiste européen*, 25.9.1903.
14 For example, George Wood to British FO, Lansdowne, 23.3.1903, NA FO 32/768. Wood declared that the nephew of the Greek prime minister Delyannis was the driving force behind the project and that he was trying to exploit the monopoly for his own benefit. The Greek state should only receive the very small sum of £100,000 annually from the monopoly company, he argued. The monopoly would ruin traditional British currant trading houses, e.g. like that of Wood's own family which his great uncle Samuel Barff had founded in Zante (Zakyntos) as early as 1816, and which was now run by his brother F. B. Wood in Patras, who was also the British general consul there. Wood asked the FO for support against the monopoly plans. The general consul himself added to his brother's letter, suggesting that the monopoly would concentrate the profits of the entire currant trade on a small group. The only sensible way of easing the situation was, he suggested, the diversification of agricultural production (Wood to Lansdowne, 6.4.1903, NA FO 32/768). In fact, Dimitrius John Deliyanni was designated the Managing Director and authorised representative of the planned company; see the translation of the convention of the planned company in IOB 1/15.
15 London Dried Fruit Trade Association to FO, 17. 4.1903, NA FO 32/768; Secretary of the London Chamber of Commerce to FO, 3.4.1903, NA FO 32/768.
16 London Dried Fruit Trade Association to FO, 17. 4.1903, NA FO 32/768.
17 Board of Trade to FO, 29.5.1903, NA FO 32/768. However, the British member of the IFC in Athens Hawey recommended the plan because he saw no other alternative in the long term; see Hawey to FO, Lansdowne, 9.6.1903, NA FO 32/768.

18 British legate, Egerton, to FO, Lansdowne, 10.4.1903, NA FO 32/768.
19 See correspondence between the British legate, Egerton and the FO, Lansdowne, in NA FO 32/768. Even the storing of 15–20% of the crop was interpreted as a violation of the Greek-British trade agreement; see London Chamber of Commerce to Lansdowne, 3.4.1903, NA FO 32/768.
20 Egerton to FO, Lansdowne 9.6.1903; Egerton to the Greek minister Skouses, 24.6.1903, NA FO 32/768. Egerton threatened to suspend the trade agreement of 1890.
21 Amendments required by Messrs. Brotherton and Backhouse. Submitted to Board at their meeting of June 22th 1903. Messrs. Brotherton and Backhouse being absent, ETE A1S28Y2F10.
22 Egerton to FO, Lansdowne, 2.7.1903, NA FO 32/768.
23 Backhouse to ETE, Streit, 25.6.1903, A1S28Y2F10.
24 Egerton to FO, Lansdowne, 16.7.1903, NA FO 32/768.
25 In a sense, this can be viewed as a first step towards including the BA in the 'Greek taskforce for the brokerage of State bonds', to which the ETE, the IOB and for a time the Orientbank also belonged; see Bonin (2013, 125). A list of the Greek state loans in which the BA later participated ibid., 126.
26 The correspondence of the IOB with the ETE: ETE A1S28Y2F8.
27 Falconer Larkworthy of the IOB to FO, Lansdowne, 16.7.1903, NA FO 32/768.
28 E.g. IFC, Corbett, to FO, Lansdowne, 7.7.1901, NA FO 32-742.
29 FO, Lansdowne to the British legate, Elliot, 21.7.1904, NA FO 32/769.
30 'To withdraw the protection of existing duties from that industry at the present moment would be to kill it at once, and thereby not only to throw a very large number of people out of employment, but to create much bitterness of feeling between the cotton and the currant industries, the latter of which the Government would be attacked for protecting at the expense of the former'. British legate, Elliot, to FO, Lansdowne, 30.8.1904, NA FO 32/769.
31 Currant reform bill, as passed by the Greek Chamber on June 17/30th 1904, translation 14.7.1904, IOB 1/15.
32 British legate, Elliot to FO, Lansdowne, letters from spring 1905, NA FO 32/770.
33 British legate, Elliot to FO, Lansdowne, 8.7.1905, NA FO 32-770.
34 An especially difficult question was the reduction of Greek custom duties for products from Newfoundland, especially stockfish. Newfoundland was willing to abolish customs on Greek currants; see the correspondence in NA FO 32/768.
35 If not otherwise indicated, the following biographical information is taken from Βοβολίνης [Vovolinis], Βοβολίνης [Vovolinis] (1958–1963, A, 324–344).
36 The large Greek diaspora in Egypt, especially in Alexandria, played a central role in the development of the Greek economy from the 1840s (see Exertzoglou 1999; Σουλογιάννης [Soulogiannis] 2000).
37 In his memoires, Andreas Syngros did not mention Pesmazoglou, although he reflected on the need for a joint-stock bank in Athens; see Συγγρός [Syngros] (1998, III., 40f.).
38 See Chapters II.4 and II.6 in this book.
39 Ioannis' cousin Olympia Pasmaglou married Constantin Zannos, member of the influential industrial Zannos family. In 1884, Constantin's brother Aristovoulos Zannos founded the Zannos Roche and Cie Company together with Emmanuel Roche. This company was transformed into the Société Vinicole et d'Industries Agricoles SA in 1900, with the financial support of the BA. In 1906, the Société Vinicole merged with the Société E. Charilaos to form the Société Hellenique de Vins et Spiritueux. I thank Nikos Pantelakis (Historical Archives of the ETE) for this information. The connections give an idea of how family and business relationships were intertwined. They also demonstrate the

oligarchic structures of Greek capitalism which Franghiadis writes about; see Franghiadis (1990, 296).

40 Banque d'Athènes, in: *Réforme Smyrne* 20.3.1905, BUP CN 253. The Metropolitan of Smyrna Vassilios blessed the new building of the bank: 'When the religious ceremony was finished, the prominent and sympathic general director of this banking house, Mister Pesmazoglou, spoke up and in his charming and poetic address he thanked the audience for the event'.

41 The crucial vote is mentioned in: Amira, N. G.: M. Pesmazoglou, in: *Réforme Smyrne* 20.7.1905, BUP CN 253; also see Bonin (2006, 18, FN 14). The first very positive report of Pesmazoglou after the first six months as a director in Πεσμαζόγλου [Pesmazoglou] (1897).

42 Banque d'Athènes, in: *Réforme Smyrne* 20.3.1905, BUP CN 253.

43 For example, the establishment of cashiers' desks; see Κωστής [Kostis]/Τσοκόπουλος [Tsokopulos] (1988, 48).

44 An overview of the figures is found in Bonin (2013, 116–120).

45 Κωστής [Kostis]/Τσοκόπουλος [Tsokopulos] (1988, 132–139); on the business relations between the BA and the BUP, also see the details in Bonin (2013, 111–132).

46 See Chapter II.3 in this book.

47 See Secours aux grecs révoltés. Prospectus, listes de souscriptions, ANMT, 44 AQ 10. Jean Abraham's grandson André de Neuflize trained in the André & Cottier house, which had close links to Jean-Gabriel Eynard, with whom the bank had made an offer for a loan to Greece in 1824; **57f**. in this book. André de Neuflize had also been the secretary of the cabinet of François Guizot, who was well-known for his Philhellene politics; see Stoskopf (2002a, 266f.). André joined the supervisory board of the BA in 1910.

48 Rodolphe Hottinguer followed his father as a member of the supervisory board of the Imperial Ottoman Bank. He was one of the founders of the BUP; see Stoskopf (2002a, 217f.).

49 Léon Zarifi was a well-respected Marseille diaspora banker. Also see **253 n.178** in this book.

50 BA, Pesmazoglou, to BUP, Villars 17/27.12.1904, BUP CN 252.

51 See Jean Battista Serpieri as an investor in Lavrion (**150–153** in this book) and István Türr as the promoter of the Canal of Corinth (**217–219** in this book).

52 The intensive search on the part of the British for a suitable candidate for the Greek throne, also while under the impression that French influence was growing, is described by Holland/Markides (2006, 59–69).

53 C.F. Ricard to his parents, 17.7.1862, in: Ricard (1954, 101–110).

54 FO, Grey to Russel, 16.3.1863, No 215, NA FO PRO 30-22-14E.

55 Here, George's candidacy clearly appears to be a proposal made by the British diplomats. Not even the older family history Bendix (1939, 8) reports on Hambro's particular role. Minoglou (2002b) seems to have taken the anecdote from Bramsen/Wain without any further verification.

56 Loan contract, MA MS 19181.

57 Sponneck to Hambro, 3./15.1.1864, MA MS 19063-2.

58 Sponneck to Hambro, 6/18.8.1864, MA MS 19063-2.

59 Sponneck to Hambro, 30.9./12.10.1864, LMA MS 19063-2.

60 See **298** in this book.

61 He was drawn into the negotiations in 1897 by, e.g. Edward Law, just like Bleichröder; see Law to Thomas Sanderson, 11.9.1897, NA FO 32-699.

62 After the death of his first wife, Everard Hambro married Ebba Whyte (1887–1961) in 1911. At his death in 1925, he left a fortune of £2,323,711; see Wain (1986, 18).

63 For example, in the case of the 1881 loan, see Bramsen/Wain (1979, 310–319).

64 As mentioned earlier, Eric Hambro joined his father's bank in the mid-1890s, after completing his schooling, his degree at Cambridge and extended travels in America; see Bramsen/Wain (1979, 326, 328). In 1879–1924, he was the director of the Bank of England, where he caused furore in the mid-1890s with his attempts at reform; see ibid., 332–335. In 1920, C. J. Hambro fused with the British Bank for Northern Commerce Ltd. to create Hambro Bank Ltd; see Wain (1986, 17f.).

65 As the 'bread and butter of banking', the bills of exchange business accounted for £5.5 million.

66 'We believe that the object of a Banking business such as ours is, to a large extent, to assist the international movement of goods and, by reason of our century-long foreign connections, we feel that we have special knowledge and experience in this direction. It must be obvious that owing to our long acquaintance with Scandinavia and the Continent we have acquired a fuller understanding of the mentality, customs and commercial practices of these countries and are therefore able to offer clients from those parts of the world a more effective service than Banks for whom they are only just "a new customer"'. This promotional brochure also referred proudly to technical equipment, foreign language abilities and travel activities, illustrating these assets with photographs; see Bendix (1939, 34f.).

67 See **309** in this book.

68 There is no monograph about the London Erlangers in existence; most archival materials seem to have been destroyed (I thank Richard Roberts for this information from family circles). An exhibition catalogue provides information on the Ingelheim branch of the family: Mendelssohn 2005. The family is only briefly mentioned in the handbooks on the financial history of Frankfurt. In 1862, the German branch is involved in founding the Frankfurt mortgage bank, the first of its kind (see Holtfrerich 1999, 164; Roth 2008a, 97). In his business affairs, Raphael Erlanger drew guidance from the ideas of Crédit Mobilier; see Kirchholtes (1969, 34).

69 Stoskopf (2002a, 162) mentions a conversion to Catholicism. However in his memoires, Émile Beaumont d´Erlanger writes that his father Emil was a Protestant (Erlanger 1978; my thanks go to Richard Roberts for his help in finding the manuscript in SchA). It thus seems that Stoskopf is mistaken, especially as the young Erlanger had a certificate from the minister of the Katharinenkirche, the main Protestant church in Frankfurt a. M.

70 Raphael Erlanger tried many times to transfer his stockbroker concession to his son before the latter reached his majority, apparently because he was ill. The exchange did not permit the transfer; see Institut für Stadtgeschichte Frankfurt (ISG), estate files 1851/1890. Among the application documents is a report on Emil from the Musterschule in Frankfurt (29.6.1851), which attests to his good achievements in all subjects, especially in history. The Protestant minister of St. Katharinen Church in Frankfurt certified the young man as being hardworking and intelligent. It was 1853 before the concession could be transferred to Emil (17.8.1853, ISG Rechnei nach 1816, 1907).

71 Emil Erlanger was made the Greek general consul in Frankfurt on 26.5.1855, (ISG Rechnei nach 1816, 252). In 1856, he officially appears for the first time as the Greek general consul in the Yearbook of the city: Frankfurt am Main 1847–1866.

72 Thus, Carl Mayer Baron von Rothschild was the general consul of Parma and Sicily, and Anselm Salomon Baron von Rothschild was the general consul of Austria; see Frankfurt am Main 1847–1866. Erlanger's reports to the Greek government on the politics, economic development and monetary system of Germany are in GA 1856/36-23. See in general Goey (2014).

73 Emil Erlanger to the governor of the ETE, received 8./20.7.1855, ETE, A1S23YIA'F53.
74 Raphael Erlanger to the governor of the ETE, received 24.6.1855, ETE, A1S23YIA'F53.
75 Emil Erlanger to the governor of the ETE, April 1856, ETE, A1S23YIA'F53.
76 Ibid. The scandal arose because it became widely known that Florence had a lover.
77 Emil Erlanger to the governor of the ETE, 1.9.1860, ETE A1S23YIA'F55.
78 Erlanger to Kanas, 12.2.1868, ETE A1S23YIA'F 53.
79 See **142 n.255** in this book.
80 Chatzis and Mavrogonatou emphasise the importance of the 1878 exhibition particularly in terms of Greece's attempts to present itself as part of Europe; see Chatzis/Mavrogonatou (2012, 11f.).
81 The start of Erlanger's involvement cannot be precisely dated; see MAE to the Greek foreign minister, 21.6.1870, AN F12 2670. In 1874, Erlanger surrendered his concession to John Mars Evans; see the records of the case that later developed between the two in NA FO J 55-3-192 1874. The conflicts between the concessionary and the company led to problems with the Greek government; see Court of Queen's Bench, in: *The Times*, 23.1.1875.
82 Charles Prioleau to Trenholm, 21.10.1863, cited in Chapman (1984, 85).
83 Erlanger (1978, 30).
84 Ibid.
85 Erlanger's wife Mathilde was particularly shocked by the Commune and the Republic; indeed, she had been on visiting terms with the Empress Eugénie; see Erlanger (1978, 15).
86 Mathilde's father John Slidell was the US ambassador in Mexico and senator of Louisiana before he returned to Europe to represent the Southern States at the court of Napoleon III and also at that of Queen Victoria; see ibid., 15. Erlanger met his wife in connection with the Confederate Cotton Loan for the Southern States of 1863. In 1856, her grandfather Commodore Perry had bombed the harbour of Yokohama as the US commander in order to force Japan to become more open to the world economy; see Roberts (1992, 69).
87 Erlanger (1978, 34f.).
88 Erlanger (1935).
89 Erlanger (1978, 117).
90 The Republic of Costa Rica v. Erlanger-Erlanger, in: *The Times*, 9.12.1875. *The Times* reported on a scandal concerning a Costa Rican loan which led to Erlanger being questioned in the House of Commons.
91 Progress of Buenos Ayres Province, in: *The Times*, 3.6.1910.
92 Erlanger (1978, 178–182).
93 On the further history of the tunnel in the twentieth century and its completion, see Gourvish (2008).
94 Turkey, in: *The Times*, 24.1.1898.
95 In 1862, Erlanger took part in a syndicate of Frankfurt banks for an Egyptian loan; see Roberts (1992, 63). In 1890, he also applied for a railway concession in Egypt; see Erlanger (1978, 178).
96 Erlanger advanced a total of almost five million francs to the Tunisian government in 1869; see Erlanger (1869). There was disagreement about the repayment, as the correspondence between the Tunisian government and Bismarck shows: Translation of Bey's letter to Prince de Bismarck with reference to the claims of Mess. Erlanger & Cie., NA FO 335-128-5. Other Tunisian business is mentioned by Stoskopf (2002a, 163). Erlanger's son Rodolphe later settled in Tunisia as a painter and historian; see Erlanger (1978, 162).

97 The Naples Waterworks, in: *The Times*, 10.9.1869.
98 France, in: *The Times*, 8.2.1870. Further involvement in telegraph companies is mentioned by Stoskopf (2002a), 164.
99 Italy, in: *The Times*, 22.3.1875.
100 Emil Erlanger to ETE, Streit, May and June 1899, ETE A1S10Y3F5.
101 Erlanger to ETE, Streit, 24.6.1901, ETE A1S25Y2F32.
102 Letters from Erlanger to ETE, Streit, 10.11.1898–28.6.1899, ETE A1S10YS3F5. This was about a loan from 1880.
103 Erlanger (1978).
104 Erlanger was involved in a project to set up an International Theatre Trust; see The International Theatre Trust, in: *The Times*, 18.7.1907.
105 France, in: *The Times*, 7.11.1886.
106 Also see **305** in this book.
107 See **311** in this book.
108 Memorandum 'A project for the formation of a company to regulate the currant trade', IOB 10/18. Not just this memorandum is found in the Ionian Bank Archives, but also the letter as a copy from Emile Erlanger to Pesmazoglou 18.5.1905, which is mentioned below. So the Ionian Bank was informed about all the plans and perhaps acted as an intermediary.
109 Ibid.
110 Emil Erlanger to BA, Pesmazoglou, 18.5.1905, MA MS 19106.
111 Pesmazoglou, Projet pour la formation d'une société pour combattre la crise du raisin de Corinthe, BUP CN 252.
112 These sums were calculated using the official exchange rate of 1:1 between drachma and franc. In fact in 1905, the franc was traded at 1.23 paper drachmas. This meant that the capital invested in paper drachmas could result in a much higher return.
113 Erlanger to BA, Pesmazoglou, 18.5.1905, MA MS 19106. As well as the regular shares, the aim was to introduce 800,000 founders' shares without any nominal value. The founders' shares would participate in 50% of the profits after 6% had been paid on the normal shares and a certain amount to the reserve.
114 So, in fact, the law gave a kind of monopoly to the company. Furthermore, Pesmazoglou planned to produce and export sweet and dry wines to all of Europe except France and Italy; see Pesmazoglou to BUP, 4.8.1905, Annexe indiquant le détail de l'utilisation du raisin sec à la disposition de la Société. He also intended to produce alcohol for lighting and automobiles; see BUP CN 252.
115 Erlanger to Pesmazoglou, 18.5.1905, MA MS 19106. In this letter, Erlanger agreed to participate and to buy 50,000 shares (£4) and 200,000 founders' shares if Pesmazoglou were able to find guarantors for the remaining shares by the following summer; further conditions were that the law was passed by the Greek parliament and that all shares were issued by first-class banking houses in Paris, Greece, Egypt and London.
116 Société privilégiée pour favoriser la production et le commerce du Raisin de Corinthe.
117 Hambro to Erlanger 23.5.1905, MA MS 19106. This was probably one of the brothers from the de Zoete family who were active as stockbrokers on the London exchange. In the twentieth century, the bank was incorporated into Barclays.
118 Sauerbach Thalmann Cie to BUP, 16.5.1905, BUP CN 253. Sauerbach wanted to give half of his commission to BUP, BUP CN 205.
119 Projet de création d'une société privilegiée d'industrie viticole, BUP CN 252.

120 Edmond Théry, Projet pour la formation d'une société pour combattre la crise du raisin de Corinthe, BUP, CN 252. Rapport de M. Edmond Théry, in ETE A1S28Y2F23. In his book published in 1905, Théry presented a project to set up a currant company that was very similar to Pesmazoglou's project; see Théry (1905).
121 The visit was even mentioned in the reports of the British legate; see Elliot to FO, Lansdowne, 18.5.1905 and 24.5.1905, NA FO 32/770.
122 Elliot to FO, Lansdowne, 18.5.1905, 24.5.1905, NA FO 32-770; London Dried Fruit Trade Association to FO, Lansdowne, 21.6.1905, NA FO 32-770.
123 Thus, e.g. the Vienna banking house of Sina (see **50 n.15, 87 n.90, 134 n.51** in this book) complained 'that a clique composed of several influential persons is endeavouring to obtain a kind of covert monopoly of the currant trade'. Sina to FO, Lansdowne 24.5.1905, NA FO 32-770. The Board of Trade nonetheless declared that they had no further objections to the Greek plans; see 31.5.1905, NA FO 32-770.
124 Elliot to FO, Lansdowne, June 1905, NA FO 32-770.
125 The Settlement of the Greek Debt. From Our Own Correspondent, in: *The Times*, 19.1.1895. The liberal newspaper *Le monde économique* was set up in 1890 by the lawyer Paul Beauregard and supported by the economist Leon Say.
126 See, e.g. Beauregard, Paul: La question financière en Grèce, in: *Le monde économique*, 13.10.1910.
127 His proposals were discussed in detail in *The Times*; see The settlement of the Greek debt, From Our Own Correspondent, in: *The Times*, 19.1.1895.
128 Projekte mit den griechischen Schulden, in: *Frankfurter Zeitung*, 20.2.1910.
129 Pesmazoglou to BUP, Villars 19/1.9.1905, BUP CN 252. There may have been a connection to a court case pending in London between Georgiades and the Persian General Trading Co; see *The Times*, 28.11.1904.
130 Georgiades was obviously attempting to damage Pesmazoglou's project by writing articles in Greek newspapers where he described the SPRC as an instrument that exploited the country. He simultaneously tried to persuade Erlanger that the venture which he had until recently promoted was now too risky; see Pesmazoglou to BUP, Villars 19/1.9.1905, BUP CN 252.
131 The Privileged Company, in: *The Times*, 15.6.1910.
132 Hambro to Erlanger, 23.5.1905, MA MS 19106, tr. by K.S.
133 Villars to Pesmazoglou, 26.5.1905, BUP CN 252. There was no mention of Hambro so it seems probable that he had to share with Erlanger.
134 Pesmazoglou to BUP, 7.7.1905, BUP CN 253.
135 Pesmazoglou to BUP, 12.7.1905, BUP CN 253.
136 Pesmazoglou to BUP 18.7.1905, BUP CN 253; BUP to Pesmazoglou, 12.7.1905, BUP CN 253.
137 Hambro to Erlanger, 23.5.1905, MA MS 19106.
138 For example, an article from an unnamed Greek financial journal which Elliot translated for Lansdowne on 4.7.1905; see NA FO 32-770.
139 Pesmazoglou to BUP, 27.7.1905, BUP CN 253.
140 Pesmazoglou to BUP, 29.7.1905, BUP CN 253, tr. by K.S.
141 The BA had to found the company within 30 days of the signing of the convention; see Convention, 13.–15.7.1905, NA FO 32/770.
142 The balance of the Hambro banking house was around £5,500,000 at this time; see Bramsen/Wain (1979, 330). The sum invested in Greece thus seems relatively small.
143 The Nationalbank für Deutschland also participated with 400 shares as the German bank with the closest links to Greece. See Overview over shareholders, ETE A1S28Y2F23.

144 Société privilégiée pour la protection et le commerce du raisin de Corinthe, 29.8.1905, BUP CN 252.
145 BUP to BA, 12.9.1905, BUP CN 253.
146 The Greek government was represented by a royal commission; see Memorandum Conseil d'administration, BUP CN 252.
147 Wehrung to Villars, 20.8.1905; Pesmazoglou to Wehrung, 1/14.8.1905, BUP CN 252. Matsas later fell foul of the law; see Bonin (2001, 19, FN 28); his attempts at justification are in Μάτσας [Matsas] (1914); Μάτσας [Matsas] (1915).
148 BA to BUP, 23.11.1905, BUP CN 253. Pesmazoglou probably suspected his competitor Georgiades; see Copie des telegrammes communiqués par MM. Erlanger & Co, BUP CN 252. The Greek minister Ralli was asked to act as an intermediary between the two Greek financiers because their conflict endangered the entire project, but he refused. The BUP instructed their Greek partner not to purchase any additional shares, but to leave supporting the market to the French; see BUP to BA, 21.12.1905, BUP CN 253.
149 Sauerbach Thalmann Cie to BUP, 14.5.1906, BUP CN 252; Acte syndicate, ibid.
150 Pesmazoglou to Villars 1/14.2.1906, BUP CN 252. The BUP was not enthusiastic about the plans to found another company which it believed was intended only to change the label but not the approach; see Pesmazoglou to Villars, 9.2.1906, BUP CN 253.
151 See **356 n.39** in this book.
152 See on the further price trend Φραγκιάδης [Franghiadis] (2006, 167).
153 IFC to FO 10.9.1906, NA FO 32/770.
154 On the currant trade after 1910, see Φραγκιάδης [Franghiadis] 2006, 167f. In 1913, it was very difficult for the company to pay the guaranteed dividend; see J. Courcelle to ETE, 21.6.1913, ETE A1S28Y2F23.
155 Les élections parlementaires et M. J. Pesmazoglou, in: *Réforme Smyrne*, 21.9.1905, BUP CN 253, tr. by K.S. The author reported that Pesmazoglou had already been spontaneously called upon to stand for parliament by popular acclamation but that he had rejected the idea because he believed he could better serve Greece in his position with the BA – an unusually patriotic and heroic sacrifice, in the author's view.
156 Amira, N. G.: M. Pesmazoglou, in: *Réforme Smyrne*, 20.7.1905, BUP CN 253.
157 He complained that the Greek army was the only one in the world that was primarily financed by lotteries; see Βοβολίνης [Vovolinis]/ Βοβολίνης [Vovolinis] (1958–1963, A, 340–343). In 1904, he had published a memorandum on questions concerning the Greek currency: Πεσμαζόγλου [Pesmazoglou] (1898).
158 Villars to Wehrung, 10.12.1906, BUP CN 253, tr. by K.S.
159 After his death, the Athens newspaper *City (Άστυ)* published a series of articles between 26.11. and 7.12.1906 entitled: 'About the Life of one of the Greats of Progress: The History of Pesmazoglou. His entire life and interesting details about the social and financial rise of a great self-made man, with authentic information from our newspaper'; see Βοβολίνης [Vovolinis]/ Βοβολίνης [Vovolinis] (1958–1963, A, 325).
160 Bonin describes in detail the continued cooperation between the BA and BUP until 1953, when the BA was incorporated into the ETE.

Part III

CONCLUSION

GREECE AS A NEW MARKET IN THE PERCEPTION OF EUROPEAN BANKERS (1821–1911)

Research questions

This investigation has considered the risk perception and risk management of European bankers with reference to their investments in Greece in the nineteenth century. The focus has been on change and continuity in dealing with the risks of this new market on the European periphery. How did bankers make their decisions about whether to engage in Greece or not? It has been necessary to consider factors beyond pure profit interests. In some instances, e.g. with the LCC or the Canal of Corinth, high profits were initially forecast but this does not apply generally. For instance, in the case of the Bleichröder loan of 1889, the expected profits for the issuing house were below average. Greece thus did not consistently attract investors by offering above-average prospects of profit nor was it viewed per se as an 'Eldorado'.

Drawing on Joseph A. Litterer's model, as cited at the outset, this research can be understood as inquiring into the mechanisms of decision making. How and via which paths did the banks obtain relevant information about the Greek market? What information did they actually use and what did they pay no attention to? How did they interpret the information and how did they perceive the decision-making situation? Which personal values, experiences and images of Greece were significant for this process of interpretation? Finally, how did the bankers attempt to manage the risks that they perceived? The aim of the research was also to analyse the development of the Greek financial market for European capital during the nineteenth century.

Procuring and selecting information

The quantity and quality of the information available to the bankers continuously improved during the 90-year research period. This was in part due to the development of press coverage. In the 1820s, press reporting was largely based on very one-sided information but over time news about the economic situation in Greece improved, broadening and diversifying significantly, partially

DOI: 10.4324/9780429286537-14

in response to new infrastructure (e.g. quicker shipping lines and new railway connections) and new technology (e.g. the telegraph). The bankers' treatment of this information was thorough: while in 1825 the Ricardo brothers relied on fragmented, extremely ideological information provided by the London Philhellenic Committee, in the second half of the century, banks like the CL maintained comprehensive collections of press cuttings in which they gathered, translated and sorted diverse information from home and abroad. This new way of handling information is also a reflection of the increasing differentiation of tasks within the quickly changing banking business. In some cases, as with the Canal of Corinth, the banks also tried to actively influence press reporting in order to promote their projects with the public.

However, published information was not enough. Banks that relied on it, such as the CEP, at times made disadvantageous investment decisions. Other bankers tried to obtain additional information – behaviour that is not included in Litterer's twentieth-century model which envisions information simply as making itself available to the actors. A tried and tested way of obtaining additional information was the development of networks, which could include travellers to Greece or local bankers and politicians. Such networks could be established and maintained through correspondence, personal meetings, sponsoring travel costs or taking on the role of general consul, and thus involved considerable transaction costs. Some bankers, such as the Eichthals and Eynard, even sent members of the family or other representatives to Greece to gain an exact impression of the investment conditions, or they travelled to the country themselves like Emil Erlanger, Charles Cheston and Jean Battista Serpieri. The private bankers and family banks demonstrated particular interest in such networks and invested greatly in their maintenance. Information obtained in this way could be most helpful: it seems, for instance, that Jean-Gabriel Eynard suffered no overall loss from his diverse investment projects in Greece.

Valuable information could also be gained through observing the competition. Thus after 1830, the Eichthal family scrutinised the property purchases of international investors in Greece, and the Hambro banking house kept a close eye on Emil Erlanger, who was both a partner and a competitor. Serpieri also only took action in Lavrion when he feared that a competitor could pre-empt him. The confident engagement or wary caution of others played an important role in decision making, quite in the sense of herding.

In addition, a new method of procuring information emerged in the research period: the use of scientific expertise. Greece's first president Kapodistrias and first king Otto I sent experts to local sites to assess the feasibility of projects. And the first banker to use such scientific expertise was Gustave d'Eichthal, who sent an engineer to Greece to use his state-of-the-art technical knowledge to draw up a plan for the draining of Lake Copais. The use of scientific expertise to calculate risks became increasingly common, and indeed indispensable, through the research period. Thus, it was a scientific report that attracted Serpieri to the silver mines of Lavrion in the 1860s, and in the 1880s, Cheston commissioned a whole series of reports from engineers, chemists and lawyers before deciding to invest in Lake Copais. The use of scientific expertise for large-scale infrastructure projects became a conditio sine qua non in the course of the nineteenth century. In some cases, such reports represented an important element of the decision-making process, e.g. in the case of Lake Copais. In other situations, the bankers used the reports to legitimate their decision to shareholders or customers without allowing the scientific expertise to particularly influence them, as in the case of the Canal of Corinth.

The interpretation of information

The second step of Litterer's model of risk perception is the interpretation of information based on personal values and experience. The investigation has shown that the bankers' interpretation of the available information was in many ways a bounded rational one.

Firstly, not all information was treated as equal. Throughout the research period, *who* provided certain information played an important role, i.e. the familiarity and trustworthiness of the source of information. The role of brokers and intermediaries from various social spheres was extremely important for the initiation of business: noteworthy names here include the Greek politicians Ioannis Kapodistrias, Charilaos Trikoupis and Stephanos Skouloudis, travellers to Greece like Gustave d'Eichthal, the Hungary entrepreneur István Türr and the Greek financiers Ioannis Pesmazoglou and Demetrios Georgiades. The intermediaries were decisive figures in developing and maintaining the confidence necessary for business transactions, especially at times when institutional trust was weak. In some cases, the trust in such intermediaries developed over decades, as with the relationship between Emil Erlanger and Demetrios Georgiades or that between Hambro and the ETE. The example of Pesmazoglou clearly shows that the sudden death of such an intermediary could permanently damage the relationship between business partners. In terms of trust in intermediaries, the behaviour of the bankers shows clear continuity throughout the period of investigation.

After 1898, the example of the international financial commission for Greece reveals that the bankers' personal trust in intermediaries played a more important role in their decision making than confidence in (international) institutions. The bankers were certainly aware that the IFC could not force Greece to repay its foreign debts. They therefore took a positive note of the growing public confidence in the Greek market when forecasting expected profits. They themselves, however, preferred to insist on the participation of familiar partners to control their risks. Confidence in Greek institutions, or institutions concerning Greece, was very limited, also due to numerous bad experiences in the past.

When evaluating informants or potential business partners, the bankers focused on their appearance and lifestyle: their reputation was their most important capital. The financial intermediaries therefore invested a great deal in optimising the impression they made. For instance, István Türr married a granddaughter of Napoleon and honed his image as a freedom fighter; Ioannis Pesmazoglou presented himself as an all-round philanthropist and, like Demetrios Georgiades, published memorandums and extensive articles in foreign papers. In several cases, the intermediaries extended their activities far beyond the field of finance and became cultural brokers and ambassadors of transculturation, like Gustave d´Eichthal. Throughout the research period, the individual intermediary or business partner was, as Monika Pohle-Fraser has also shown, often more important than the concrete project itself.

This second-order observation became problematic when the bankers employed it in relation to scientific experts. They were not able to judge the reliability of the technical details and therefore relied solely on the reputations of the experts concerned. This is amply demonstrated by the example of the Canal of Corinth where the promoter Türr presented the CEP with an expert report by the engineer Dauzat who had actually never travelled to Corinth in person. Thanks to his name being well-known from his involvement in planning the Suez Canal, the bankers believed his evaluation and did not even demand a second opinion. A similar vote of confidence was granted Andreas Kordellas, thanks to his training at the renowned mining academy in Freiberg. The bankers failed to consider the limited applicability of the knowledge that the experts had learnt elsewhere to the foreign and unfamiliar settings.[1] The case of Corinth in particular shows that the combination of the bankers' traditional risk assessment, the reputation approach and modern scientific expertise could indeed be counterproductive, as when the bankers assessed the expert in terms of his reputation and failed to evaluate the quality of his report according to scientific principles.

Another important factor in the perception of decision-making situations is path dependency: once involvement in Greece had been initiated, it was often continued despite difficult conditions so as to avoid losing the investments already made. Behavioural finance speaks here of a sunk-costs effect, which is explained by prospect theory: investors weigh loss much more strongly than profit so that they tend to cling to a problematic investment in order to make it a success after all. Emil Erlanger argued along these lines when he tried to issue a new loan for Greece in 1909 despite the high risks, with the aim of being able to continue his railway investments. It is not only in individual investment projects that such mechanisms can be recognised; they also apply generally to dominant market positions, which the bankers sought to defend against competition. Of critical importance for Hambro & Son, for instance, was the relationship between the banking house and the Greek monarchy which had developed over decades and was even substantiated by the myth concerning the central role played by C. J. Hambro in the election of the king. Similarly significant was the ongoing cooperation with the ETE. The fear of losing market share legitimated participation in risky projects, even ones of which the banker concerned did not really approve and where no trusted Greek partner was involved. A decisive role was played by the time and effort that had already been invested in the form of the longevity of cooperation with the monarchy, with the Greek banks and with other actors in Greece. Behavioural finance describes this as a familiarity bias, referring to the power of the familiar and well-known which leads actors to feel competent and experienced and thus generates a feeling of perceived control over a situation.

Politics could have an equally decisive influence over the perception of investment decisions. Thus, Gerson von Bleichröder undertook Greek business as a service for his patron Otto von Bismarck, who wanted to bring political pressure to bear through the loan in question. The banks' participation in a number of other cases, such as the re-admittance of Greece to the European exchanges in 1878 or the issue of the 1910 loan for Eleftherios Venizelos, was also due to political pressure, exercised through both formal and informal channels. Furthermore, the need to maintain relationships to political decision makers played a role when the governments withheld approval for Greek loans until the bankers had organised tied loans to ensure that armament and other industrial contracts were awarded to companies from their own countries. This phenomenon was clearly associated with the weak political and financial position of Greece and manifested itself repeatedly throughout the entire research period. National differences in the style of risk perception are most striking in terms of the way in which the governments attempted to influence the banks and how the bankers reacted to such intervention. In France, the pressure was official and unabashed, but in Great Britain and Germany, it tended to be exercised through more unofficial channels. In the case studies considered here, the French banks were then most likely to follow the demands of their government, e.g. in the failed plans for a loan in 1909. However, in none of the countries considered was it possible for a bank to publicly participate in a loan issue against the express or implied wishes of the government, as could be seen through the whole period of investigation. The political background of the projects always influenced the bankers' perceptions of the decision-making situation.

Images of Greece

No matter whether the decision to consider a project was swayed by a politician, confidence in an intermediary or reliance on an expert report, feelings always had a role to play. This was particularly true for the emotionally charged question of how Greece was understood. The image of Greece fundamentally influenced the decision-making situation.

Far from all the bankers investigated had a positive image of Greece or were convinced Philhellenes. This could only be demonstrated for Jean-Gabriel Eynard (in the sense of political, liberal Philhellenism) and Charles Cheston (in the sense of Philhellenism focused on antiquity), remarkably with a time lapse of about 30 years. In the case of Eynard in particular, it is possible to compare his behaviour with that of modern investors in green and ethical investment who project their convictions and values into their investment behaviour and thus aim to change the world in which they live.

Even though only two of them were Philhellenes, all the bankers were engaged in 'imagined markets' – even if they themselves were not always in raptures about Greece. No matter whether they were Greece lovers, were merely making use of the Philhellene enthusiasm of their customers (like the Ricardos or Bleichröder) or were dismissive of Greece (like, due to his negative experiences, Simon von Eichthal), they all had to deal with the images of Greece commonly held by their contemporaries. It was impossible for them to have a neutral, impartial attitude towards the Greek investment market.

Two contrasting images of Greece have been identified, both of which were very emotionally charged. There was the positive image of modern Greece which had its origins in the time of the enthusiastic Philhellenism that arose during the Greek struggle for independence. This image emphasised the rich tradition of Greece and Greek hospitality, the blossoming landscape and pleasant climate, rich resources, reliable business partners, political successes and economic progress. The market was said to have the potential to quickly catch up with West-European industrialisation. This positive narrative of Greece was encountered throughout the entire research period. Events of very different types could cause it to be activated in the press, in diplomacy or in the correspondence of the bankers: the gaining of state independence (1830), the crowning of a new monarch (1862), the successes of Greece and the bringing of peace to the Balkans at the Congress of Berlin (1878), the wedding of a Greek prince and a Prussian princess (1889) and the establishment of an international financial commission (1898). Although few of these events were of a financial nature, they all made Greece the centre of European attention and created the image of an up-and-coming, promising market in the heads of investors. The bankers used this positive image of Greece to justify positive investment decisions and for promotion.

Nonetheless, it is not possible to speak of uninterrupted 'bourgeois optimism' in relation to Greece.[2] Disappointment in modern Greece after the struggle for independence quickly led to the development of a negative image of the country, which was manifested, e.g. in the work of Fallmerayer and About in the 1830s and 1840s and consolidated by the negative experiences of certain investors. This development can be described as a 'history of disappointment'.[3] Greece was seldom directly categorised as part of the Orient but was often described as being on the periphery of the Occident and as greatly influenced by the Orient; its otherness was said not only to endanger itself, but also to threaten the centre. Correspondingly, stereotypes like corruption, inefficiency, nepotism and lawlessness abounded and there was a severe lack of trust in state institutions. In her investigation of the French reception of images of Greece, Sophie Basch speaks of a veritable hatred of Greece which emerged and grew in the course of the nineteenth century (Basch 1995). Such negative images of Greece were the perfect justification for rejecting an investment project, and competitors who participated in such projects could be defamed as unscrupulous speculators in contrast to risk-averse and responsible bankers. One example of this is the initial rejection of the Greek loan in 1909 by Hambro, who then described his competitor Erlanger as an unscrupulous gambler. However, the negative images of Greece could also justify assuming an imperial attitude and depriving the Greeks of the right to make their own decisions. In these cases, the bankers ignored the agent role assigned to them in the principal-agent relationship and attempted to direct the use of the borrowed money themselves, sometimes in line with their own interests, e.g. in the armament trade. This colonial attitude towards Greece is encountered in the early phase of the 1820s (the loans of 1825 issued by the Ricardo brothers) and at the beginning of the twentieth century (the loans of 1909 and the relevant commentary by Hambro & Son). In some cases, the investors also used the negative image of Greece to retrospectively deny responsibility for failed projects and to activate (diplomatic) support, but nonetheless continued their activities once they had obtained redress – Jean Battista Serpieri's mineral business in Greece after the Lavrion affair serves as an example of this.

These two images of Greece were inextricably linked to fictional imaginations of the future and could be updated in different contexts. Indeed, they even existed side by side, as, for instance, in the press reports about the Greek financial situation at the time of the international financial commission after 1898. In this case, thanks to the drachma's high exchange rate gains, praise was directed towards the country's general economic development and the work of the international financial commission but the Greek financial administration and Greek politics were vilified, without these two contrary narratives being brought into connection with one another.

Both images of Greece often drew on antiquity, especially when the subject under consideration was an investment project with an ancient prehistory like the mines of Lavrion, the Canal of Corinth or the LCC. Modern Greece was inextricably linked to the ancient frame of reference. The long prehistory of the country could thus represent a considerable competitive advantage over other similar ventures. This should not be underestimated, as seen in the case of the Canal of Corinth when the history and tradition of the project distinguished it from the other large-scale maritime canals. Such ancient prehistory could 'ennoble' risky ventures. The financial actors latched onto a fashionable trend here. The intensive interest in Greek antiquity is explained not least by the strong emphasis given to this epoch in the curricula of elite schools in Western and Central Europe in the nineteenth century, schools that were attended by some of the bankers. The Homeric myths and the history of the ancient polis of Athens were particularly suited to the discourses of national affirmation and positioning in Victorian Britain, in the Third Republic of France and in the German Empire. The transformation of antiquity, which modified the receiving culture while constituting the reference culture, was thus extended to include the field of economic and financial activities.

The comparison to antiquity could be applied to both negative images of Greece and positive ones. For the former, it was used to present the miserable financial and moral position as being even more miserable and hopeless, and to blame the country for its backwardness as there could be no doubt that it possessed all the natural prerequisites for prosperity. Mishaps such as the temporary failure of the Canal of Corinth project were explained in this way. However, the link to antiquity could be used to highlight the rich potential of the country and its inhabitants, to illustrate the goal of its hopeful development and to emphasise the responsibility of Western Europe towards the cradle of its own civilisation. This Philhellene image of Greece was dominant during the struggle for Greek independence but it was also found among investors of the 1880s like Charles Cheston, who explained his enthusiasm for Greece by referring to his youthful reading of the classics and the poetry of Lord Byron, and who published work in an attempt to attract investors to Greece.

One particular version of this positive image of Greece can be identified in the peak phase of informal imperialism. From the beginning of Greece's existence as an independent state, the country had been treated as a plaything by the European Great Powers, who strived to extend their political influence into the country throughout the entire research period. After the late 1870s, it was not only the diplomats but also increasingly the financial elites who perceived Greece as an object of 'industrial competition' for investment markets between the industrialised nations. The counterpart to this economic competition was the cultural history debate about which European country was the legitimate heir of Greek antiquity, a debate that had been virulently conducted since the eighteenth century. In the case of the Canal of Corinth and the LCC, it has been possible to demonstrate that the French investors, led by the CEP, were concerned to present the projects not only as a proof of French engineering skills and French cultural superiority, but also as claims to the legacy of Ancient Greece.

Overall, however, there was a decline in the allusions made to antiquity in the sources of the 1890s and 1900s investigated here, in contrast to Basch's findings: the reports and correspondence concerning the international financial commission or the currant trading company scarcely mention antiquity as a reference point, which could be understood as a sign of the increasing professionalisation of banking. However, this interpretation is contradicted not only by Basch's findings concerning the time up to the end of the Second World War, but also by consideration of the current crisis dating from 2009, when antiquity has again been repeatedly employed as an interpretative mirror for Greek finances, as discussed in the introduction to this book. The findings thus rather suggest that in the last case study, personal trust and direct cooperation with the intermediary were of such great importance that the stereotypes of Greece, whether linked to antiquity or not, could be given less weight and space, even though in other contexts, the same actors nevertheless continued to employ such images.

Closure of the risk perception

Litterer's model suggests that after completing the interpretation of the information, a process of closure occurs, i.e. the construction of a coherent, consistent image of the decision-making situation on the basis of which a decision can be reached. Contradictory information is ignored to simplify the situation as far as possible so that it is possible to take action. Such processes of closure could be identified repeatedly in this investigation. One example is Eynard, whose wife accused him of being so fixated on Greece that he refused to learn his lesson despite all the setbacks he suffered. Another example is provided by the Ricardo brothers who wanted to view the Greeks as dependent newcomers in need of guidance and therefore totally ignored the wish of the provisional government to be self-determining and independent. A further instance is the case of the CEP whose managers perceived the promoter of the Canal of Corinth Stefan Türr as a freedom fighter and successful canal builder and were so swayed by this that they disregarded the accusations of corruption made against him. The Eichthal family can also be cited: they so generalised their bad experiences with the Bavarian regency that Gustave's positive assessment had no chance of influencing their perceptions. In line with the home bias, they preferred to invest in familiar France. In all these cases, particular information was blended out to allow a consistent image of the decision-making situation to be constructed. The biased images of Greece were perfect for legitimating the decisions reached, whatever those decisions may have been.

Values, experiences and imaginations of Greece clearly determined the interpretation of the information available to the bankers, but emotionality and the omission of discrepant information did not represent an obstacle to elaborate risk management. Ideologically tainted decisions or those based on 'gut feeling' could be combined with a focus on expert knowledge, and the increasing recourse to scientific expertise did not preclude emotional decisions, as has at times been assumed in the history of science (Lane 1966; Reinecke 2010). Even if decisions were emotionally influenced by a preference for Greece, they could be provided with professional safeguards, as seen in the cases of Jean-Gabriel Eynard and Charles Cheston.

Risk management

Once the decision to invest had been made and the risks identified, attention turned to managing those risks. For bankers in the nineteenth century, the most important means of doing this was the unbundling of risks. This could involve splitting investment between various projects, as practised by Eynard, Hambro and Erlanger. It could also involve spreading the risks of one project among a number of strong and reliable partners. This approach was already seen in the 1820s when the Paris banking house of André & Cottier only agreed to participate in the Greek loan once Eynard or his nephew assumed leadership of the consortium. It also applied in the case of the Lavrion mines, the currant trade company and the LCC. As Anders Mikkelsen has shown, international underwriting groups, much frowned upon in the 1820s, became increasingly popular in the course of the research period (Mikkelsen 2014; idem 2017), as demonstrated, for instance, by the Bleichröder loan of 1889. The insistence of the Hambro banking house on the participation of the ETE in the state loan of 1909 can also be understood in this light.

Another important method of risk management was safeguarding through the use of contracts. This can be traced back to the attempts of the Rothschild family to ensure a watertight guarantee from the Great Powers for the 60-million loan of 1832, a proceeding which was without precedent but was later often practised in similar situations. The growing number of contract drafts and contracts in the files indicates the increasingly important role they played for investors attempting to safeguard themselves from legal difficulties. Such safeguards were particularly critical because the institutional framework for the investment of foreign capital was repeatedly subjected to severe disturbance in the course of the nineteenth century. The three state bankruptcies of 1827, 1843 and 1893 contributed to this lack of stability. In addition, there was considerable controversy between the investors and the often volatile Greek governments, especially in relation to property rights, e.g. concerning the scoriae of the silver and lead mines in Lavrion and the property around Lake Copais. Such controversies were also seized upon by the international press and fuelled the activation of negative Greek stereotypes.

It is necessary to speak here of a culture of mistrust between investors and the Greek politicians or population. Encouraged by the often biased reporting in the Greek press, many Greeks suspected the foreigners of enriching themselves unlawfully and of exploiting the country. For their part, the investors had little confidence in the stability of the institutional framework for their investments, neither in the Greek administration and legal system nor in the domestic and foreign political situation in the turbulent Balkans. When the investing bankers were referred to the Greek courts, they questioned the legitimacy of the legal system itself and turned instead to international diplomacy. Both parties often found their negative image of the other confirmed by the experiences they made. This then further encouraged later investors to organise legal safeguards in the form of contracts.

Overall, it can be seen that the bankers at the end of the nineteenth century had recourse to a wide range of mechanisms for risk assessment and risk management; some of these tools were traditional, such as the reputation approach and the unbundling of risks; others, like the utilisation of scientific expertise, were more novel. The old and new methods were not always compatible, which could lead to problems and mistakes being made in risk assessment, for instance in the case of the Canal of Corinth. Generally, however, the case studies show that the endeavours to gather as much information as possible and multi-layered, careful risk management contributed significantly to the success of projects. If the risks were correctly recognised and assessed, then it was possible to safeguard against them or at least to lessen their impact, even if a guarantee of success was impossible and it was necessary to react with flexibility to changes in the parameters.

It was not possible to identify the various heuristics described by behavioural finance in a pure form in the archive materials, certainly not as they have been seen in behavioural psychology experiments. It is rather the case that mixed motives have been uncovered, where heuristics overlapped or alternated with one another. Viewing the sources from the perspective of behavioural finance was nonetheless helpful in working out the issues and developing a coherent narrative. In certain places, additional impulses were drawn from new institutional economics, such as principal-agent theory. The mechanisms of the bankers' decision making could thus be situated in the cultural context of their own time and tied into the world in which they lived, allowing a combination of financial, political and cultural histories. However, the aim was not to underpin the models of behavioural finance with historical material or, indeed, to provide evidence to support them. It is rather that historical investigation can stimulate an interdisciplinary approach to forms of rationality, as Gigerenzer and Selten call for (Gigerenzer/Selten 2001b, 11).

Integration in the European financial market

The majority of the bankers who ventured into Greece despite the difficult conditions were successful: Eynard and Serpieri, Bleichröder, Erlanger and Hambro, and if a long-term perspective is selected, then also Cheston's successors at Lake Copais. Even if they failed to achieve their original goals, if everything took a great deal longer than planned and if profit expectations had to be significantly reduced, ultimately the bankers did profitable business in Greece. Even the Canal of Corinth was eventually completed, although the original investors did not profit from its earnings. In contrast, the state loan of 1825 issued by the Ricardos was an unadulterated failure – but even here it cannot be determined how much the brothers actually lost with the venture and whether they perhaps nonetheless earned a profit from the armament deals linked to the loans.

No matter whether these projects were perceived as successful by the investors or not, they all furthered the step-by-step integration of the Greek financial market in the European one – despite all the tensions, resistance and conflict. Before the First World War, Greece was part of intertwined global finance flows and international banking networks, there were diverse and sustained investment projects and branches of European banks in Greece, Western banking houses specialised in the country with corresponding knowhow, there were Greeks with knowledge of Western banking practices and brokers who specialised in Greece, and the country possessed technological knowledge from the West and established paths of knowledge transfer. Even just the existence of all these parameters ensured that further investment would follow: to a certain extent, the investment behaviour reproduced itself. The aim of this research is not, however, to evaluate the integration of Greece into the European financial market, which is still regarded critically by much Greek research; similarly, no attempt is made here to offer simple solutions to the current problems.

Nonetheless, the many apparent parallels and continuities between the past and present seem to demand a comparison. The question of whether parallels can be drawn between the occurrences of recent years and those of the past is frequently addressed to historians researching the financial history of Greece. Was not the hopeless financial position in which prime minister Tsipras found himself basically the same as that endured by king Otto? Can Greece's membership of the Latin Monetary Union be compared with its membership of the eurozone? Can the international financial commission not be interpreted as a kind of precursor to the European troika (Schönhärl 2019c)? For instance, with reference to the IFC, such questions are certainly legitimate and interesting, especially as they can help to explain the defensiveness of many Greeks in response to international intervention, something that has been much exploited for political advantage. This is particularly true if the developments of the twentieth century are taken into consideration.

The identification and analysis of such parallels is, beyond the scope of this book and, indeed, is not always helpful from a historical perspective. However, this research has clearly shown two things. Firstly, there are good reasons why some investment projects are successful and others are not. These reasons are usually related to insufficient information gathering and inadequate risk management. If information procurement and risk management are thorough and meticulous, there is no harm in decisions being motivated by non-economic factors or even by ideological and emotional aspects. And although the world of banking and financial markets has continued to change greatly in the last 100 years, it seems as though a certain continuity can be detected here, which underlines the responsibility borne by banking houses for the functioning of the financial markets.

Secondly, continuities with regard to images of Greece in Western Europe could be detected. The extremes portrayed by these images and their, at least at times, imperial attitude were remarkably stable from the beginning of the nineteenth century until the present day, despite changes in the educational background of many decision makers and bankers. Without the dominant belief in progress of the elites that characterised the nineteenth century, this undifferentiated perception of Greece is even graver.

Notes

1 Here, this research therefore contradicts the findings of Pohle-Fraser, who summarises: 'Bankers – among themselves – instead point to the illogicality of trying to estimate the effects of an innovation on the basis of data from the past!' (Pohle-Fraser 1999, 372).

2 'The unshakeable belief that things will get better can be interpreted as an expression of the purest fatalism, which in the form of optimism, the belief in progress, forms an essential core of the bourgeois world-view' (Pohle-Fraser 1999, 358–361, here 361).

3 See the research perspective of the Leibniz Graduate School of the IFZ and the Department for Modern and Contemporary History of LMU: Enttäuschung im 20. Jahrhundert. Utopieverlust – Verweigerung – Neuverhandlung, in: LMU, Neueste Geschichte und Zeitgeschichte, http://www.ngzg.geschichte.uni-muenchen.de/forschung/enttaeuschung/index.html [11.2.2020].

ACKNOWLEDGEMENTS

This book represents the reworking of a post-doctoral *Habilitation*, which I submitted in November 2015 at the University of Duisburg-Essen, thanks to a diverse range of support.

First, I thank Ute Schneider, as whose research assistant I still found time to research and write, despite all the other tasks that such a position entails. Professor Schneider's critical appraisal greatly helped improve my methodological approach. The work was similarly most constructively evaluated by Wilfried Loth, who made every effort to advise and support me during its preparation. Two other reports which were extremely helpful for the reworking of the manuscript were produced by Christian Kleinschmidt and Rainer Liedtke.

I also received support and benevolent feedback from the Essen professors Stefan Brakensiek, Christoph Marx and Frank Becker. My two 'mentors' Justus Cobet and Lucian Hölscher are due my heartfelt thanks for helping me through some of the perils of everyday university life and for always being ready to listen to my concerns. Among my colleagues, Hanna Sonkajärvi and Henning Türk in particular provided stimulating discussions and valuable ideas about my research. With Sonja Hillerich, an expert in deciphering nineteenth-century handwriting, I was permitted to share not only our specialist interests, but also travel experiences and accommodation in various places. Katharina Tugend's support with Italian sources and texts was indispensable.

Without the local Greek colleagues, I would not have made much progress in the Athens archives: Maria Christina Chatziioannou, Kostas Kostis, Margarita Dritsa, Dimitris Kamouzis and Giorgios N. Dermatis helped me trace relevant holdings. I particularly thank Lydia Tricha as I would have been lost without her advice on the important estate of Charilaos Trikoupis. In Paris, I received guidance for the investigation and valuable tips from Hervé Le Bret, in London from Ricards Roberts and Albrecht Ritschl. To represent the many archivists who supported me, I would like to thank Nikos Pantelakis and Gerasimos Notaras in the ETE archive in Athens,

Roger Nougaret in the Archives et Histoire de BNP Paribas in Paris and Claire-Amandine Soulié in the Rothschild archive in London.

My long-standing office-colleague and friend Leonie Treber undertook the critical reading of the manuscript. Johannes Bähr, who accompanied the project from the very beginning, also closely read and commented on the manuscript, as did Michalis Psalidopoulos. I furthermore thank my father Lothar Schönhärl, a passionate classicist who, quite apart from untiring correction work, helped me with translations of the difficult Katharevousa, the Greek commonly used in the nineteenth century. I also owe thanks to my enthusiastic and reliable student assistants in Essen and Athens: Hendrik Herbers, Sofia Anagnosti and Stathis Pavlopoulos.

I was able to carry out the extensive archive work, thanks to a generous travel grant from the Fritz Thyssen Foundation. Scholarships from the German Historical Institutes in London and Paris and from the Max Weber Foundation allowed further local research to be undertaken. The manuscript could finally be completed in Munich where I had the pleasure of spending a year as a Fellow of the Historisches Kolleg. I would also like to thank the Historical Commission for including the German version of the book in its publication series.

During the work on this research project, my two daughters Pauline and Ricarda were born, enriching and brightening my life. In our attempts to combine family and research, my husband and I have been supported by the best nanny ever Andrea Grönner, by my sisters Katja and Julia Schönhärl, and by my nieces Lucia and Justina Braun, who I thank from the bottom of my heart.

Munich, in May 2017, Korinna Schönhärl

ABBREVIATIONS

AA	Auswärtiges Amt, Berlin
AAE	Archives des affaires étrangères, La Courneuve
AEG	Archives d'Etat de Genève
ADB	Allgemeine Deutsche Biographie
AN	Archives nationales de France, Sites de Paris et de Pierrefitte-sur-Seine
ANMT	Archives nationales du monde du travail, Roubaix
BA	Banque d'Athènes
BAL	Barings Archives, London
BAR	Bundesarchiv, Berlin-Lichterfelde
BDA	Bibliothèque de l'Arsenal, Paris
BGE	Bibliothèque de Genève, Département des manuscrits et des archives privées
BHSA	Bayerisches Hauptstaatsarchiv, Munich
BL	British Library
BLKÖ	Biographisches Lexikon des Kaiserthums Oesterreich
BN	Banque de France, Paris, and its archive
BNP	Banque nationale de Paris et de Paribas
BUP	Banque de l'Union parisienne
CEP	Comptoir d'escompte de Paris and its archive in the Archives et Histoire de BNP Paribas, Paris
CFC	Compagnie française pour le dessèchement et l'exploitation du Lac Copaïs
CFML	Compagnie Française des Mines du Laurium
CL	Crédit Lyonnais and its archive in the Archives historiques du Groupe Crédit Agricole, Paris
DB	Deutsche Bank/ Historisches Archiv der Deutschen Bank, Frankfurt
DBF	Dictionnaire de Biographie Française
ELIA	Ελληνικό Λογοτεχνικό και Ιστορικό Αρχείο (Hellenic Literary and Historical Archive)

ETE	Εθνική Τράπεζα της Ελλάδος (National Bank of Greece and its archive)
FO	Foreign Office (Great Britain) and its archive in the National Archives, London
GA	Διπλωματικό και Ιστορικό Αρχείο (Service of Diplomatic & Historical Archives (Y.D.I.A.) of the Hellenic Ministry of Foreign Affairs)
GE	Γεννάδειος Βιβλιοθήκη (Gennadios Library, The American School of Classical Studies at Athens)
GHA	Geheimes Hausarchiv des Hauses Wittelsbach, Munich
GL	Archives of the Stock Exchange in the Guildhall Library, London
GNA	Γενικά Αρχεία του Κράτους (General State Archives of Greece), Athens
IOB	Ionische Bank and its archive in the London School of Economics (LSE)
KA	Historisches Archiv Krupp, Essen
K.S.	Note by Korinna Schönhärl
LGC	Estate of the London Greek Committee, in the Εθνική Βιβλιοθήκη της Ελλάδος (Greek National Library, Athen)
LCC	Lake Copais Company
MA	Metropolitain Archives, London
MAE	Ministère des Affaires étrangères
MEF	Ministère de l'Économie et des Finances
MP	Member of parliament
NA	National Archives, London
NBB	Bleichröder Collection in the Baker Library, Harvard Business School, Boston
NDB	Neue Deutsche Biographie
ODNB	Oxford Dictionary of National Biography
RAL	Rothschild Archive, London
ISG	Institut für Stadtgeschichte, Frankfurt a. M.
SchA	Schröder's Archive, London
SG	Archives de la Société Générale, Paris
SHCC	Société Hellénique Canal de Corinthe
SICC	Société internationale du Canal Maritime de Corinthe
SPRC	Société privilégiée pour favoriser la production et le commerce du Raisin de Corinthe
STABI	Staatsbibliothek München, Abteilung Handschriften und alte Drucke
Tr. by K.S.	Translation (from French or German to English) by Korinna Schönhärl/Katharine Thomas

WEIGHTS AND MEASURES

Stremma (plural: stremmata): Greek unit for measuring land. A stremma is equivalent to 1/10 hectare.

Venetian pound: Unit of measurement for weighing raisins and currants. A Venetian pound is equivalent to 477 grams or 1.06 imperial pounds.

DATES

Until 1923, Greece used the Julian calendar rather than the Gregorian calendar, which was usual in Western Europe. Dates in the sources are therefore sometimes given double entries (e.g. 14/26 October 1863). To aid readability, this book generally uses just the second, Gregorian date.

FIGURES AND TABLE

Figure I.I.1 Focus, Cover, 22.2.2010 (with kind permission of Focus Magazine, Berlin).

Figure II.1.1 Loan Prospectus: Greek Loan for Ten Million Spanish Dollars or £2,000,000 Sterling: MA CLC-B-060-MS-34714 (with kind permission of the London Metropolitan Archives).

Figure II.2.1 Horace Vernet: Portrait de Jean-Gabriel Eynard en 1831: Musée d'art et d'histoire, Genève, no inv., 1905–0067 (with kind permission of the Musée d'art et d'histoire, Genève).

Figure II.3.1 Joseph Heigel: Portrait de Louis d'Eichthal en 1824: privately owned (the publication was possible thanks to the kind support of Hervé Le Bret).

Figure II.3.2 Joseph Stieler: Portrait von Simon von Eichthal 1845: Archives of HypoVereinsbank, Munich (with kind permission of the Archives of HypoVereinsbank, Member of UniCredit, Division CEO/Corporate Office).

Figure II.3.3 Edmond Fechner: Portrait de Gustave d'Eichthal en 1827: privately owned (the publication was possible thanks to the kind support of Hervé Le Bret).

Figure II.3.4 Edmond Fechner: Portrait de Adolphe d'Eichthal en 1827: privately owned (the publication was possible thanks to the kind support of Hervé Le Bret).

Figure II.4.1 The smelting ovens of Lavrion, in: Cordella, Le Laurium, 1869, Cover: Held by the Bibliothèque Nationale de France (with kind permission of the Bibliothèque Nationale de France).

Figure II.4.2 The Laurium Mines in Greece. General View of the Town and Port; Ancient Furnaces; Ancient Washing Place, in: *The Illustrated London News*, 6.11.1880: Held by the Staatsbibliothek Munich (with kind permission of the Staatsbibliothek Munich).

Figure II.5.1 Emile Wauters: Porträt Gerson Bleichröder, Berlin 1888, oil on canvas, 38,5x35,5cm: Jüdisches Museum Berlin, bought by the Gesellschaft für ein Jüdisches Museum Berlin, Photo: Jens Ziehe (with kind permission of the Jüdische Museum Berlin).

Figure II.6.1 Bulletin de la Société Internationale du Canal Maritime de Corinthe, No. 1, 21.9.1882, Cover: CEP, 73 AH 322-1 (with kind permission of the Archives et Histoire de BNP Paribas, Paris).
Figure II.6.2 Société Internationale du Canal Maritime de Corinthe, Obligation au Porteur à cinq cents francs, 8.3.1888, in: CEP, 73 AH 321 (with kind permission of the Archives et Histoire de BNP Paribas, Paris).
Figure II.6.3 Comparaison entre les canaux de Suez de Panama et de Corinthe, in: Prospectus Canal Maritime de Corinthe, in: CEP, 73 AH 317 (with kind permission of the Archives et Histoire de BNP Paribas, Paris).
Figure II.6.4 Plan Général et croquis explicative de la méthode de percement de l'Isthme de Corinthe, Assemblée général du 28. Juin 1884, in: CEP, 73 AH 319 (with kind permission of the Archives et Histoire de BNP Paribas, Paris).
Figure II.6.5 Carte du Canal Corinthe, concédé au Gal Türr d'après les levés de B. Gerster Ingénieur en chef du Canal François dessinée par Ch[arles] Muret, Geomètre de la Ville Paris, Membre de la Société de Géographie, Echelle 1: 33.333, Ch. Delagrave, Editeur, Rue Soufflot 15, Paris, gravé chez L. Wuhrer: Held by British Library, Maps 45165.(1.) (with kind permission of the British Library).
Figure II.6.6 Acro-Corinthe et Ancienne Ville de Corinthe, in: Bulletin de la Société Internationale du Canal Maritime de Corinthe, No 2, 18.11.1882: CEP, 73 AH 322-2 (with kind permission of the Archives et Histoire de BNP Paribas, Paris).
Figure II.6.7 Durocher, Léon: Le Percement de L'Isthme de Corinthe, Paris 1893, Cover: held by the British Library, 012314.f.43 (with kind permission of the British Library).
Figure II.6.8 Building site of the Canal of Corinth (1): CEP, 10 fi 147 (with kind permission of the Archives et Histoire de BNP Paribas, Paris).
Figure II.6.9 Building site of the Canal of Corinth (2): CEP, 10 Fi 148 (with kind permission of the Archives et Histoire de BNP Paribas, Paris).
Figure II.7.1 Compagnie Française du Lac Copaïs. Action de cinq cents francs au porteur, 25.2.1881: privately owned.
Figure II.7.2 Compagnie Française du Lac Copaïs: Plan du lac Copaïs et de la région entre le lac et le détroit de Négrepont d'après les documents de l'Etat Major-français et les travaux de la Compagnie, Echelle 1: 50.000, Paris Monrocq 1882: held by Bibliothèque Nationale de France, FRBNF40727592 (with kind permission of the Bibliothèque Nationale de France)
Figure II.7.3 Lake Copais Company, Limited: Map 1888, in: MA Applications for Listing 13 26B Lake Copais 1891 (with kind permission of the London Metropolitan Archives).
Figure II.8.1 Kingdom of Greece, National Loan 4% 1910: privately owned.
Table II.5.1 Greece's new foreign debts, 1879–1893

ARCHIVES

Germany

BHSA *Bayerisches Hauptstaatsarchiv, Munich*

Bayerisches Hauptstaatsarchiv, Abt. I:
Bayerische Gesandtschaft Athen 443–453
Bayerische Gesandtschaft Athen 491–494
Bayerische Gesandtschaft Athen 496
Bayerische Gesandtschaft Athen 501–502
MA2179
MA2181
MA84431
Bayerisches Hauptstaatsarchiv, Abt. III:
Nachlass Armansperg35-20
Nachlass Armansperg50-36
Nachlass Armansperg51.1–3
Nachlass Armansperg52.1–4
Nachlass ArmanspergIV
Nachlass ArmanspergV
Nachlass Schinas7
Nachlass Schinas11

BAR *Bundesarchiv, Berlin-Lichterfelde*

R 1–128
R 1501–102031
R 3101–594
R 3101–7401
R 8034 II-3799
R 8127–11265
R 8127-3881
R 901–01536

R 901–05709
R 901–13621
R 901–15278–80
R 901–1537–38
R 901–1542–43
R 901–1546–50
R 901–18103
R 901–36210
R 901–36211
R 901–5710
R 901–76997
R 901–80106
R 901–81269
R 901–90134–5
R 901–9531
R 91–01539–41

***DB** Historisches Archiv der Deutschen Bank, Frankfurt*

B0078–9
P11623
P11625
P24158
S1283
S3582–3
S3829–30

***GHA** Geheimes Hausarchiv des Hauses Wittelsbach, Munich*

Kabinettsakten König Maximilians II.75c
Kabinettsakten König Maximilians II.76h
Kabinettsakten König Maximilians II.80g
Kabinettsakten König Maximilians II.80k
Kabinettsakten König Maximilians II.87a
Kabinettsakten König Maximilians II.348s-2
Kabinettsakten König Maximilians II.349-s-2
Kabinettsakten König Maximilians II.442b
Kabinettsakten König Maximilians II.371
Kabinettsakten König Maximilians II.281
Kabinettskasse Ludwigs I.51
Nachlass König Ludwig I.88-4-3
Nachlass König Ludwig I.ARO14
Nachlass König Ludwig I.ARO16

Nachlass König Ludwig I.ARO26
Nachlass König Ludwig I.ARO28
Nachlass König Ludwig I.ARO30
Nachlass König Ludwig I.ARO27
Nachlass König Ludwig I.I-XVI-444
Kabinettsakten Ludwigs II.-XVI, 444
Kabinettsakten Ludwigs II.-XVI, 484
Nachlass Prinz Leopold,147
Nachlass Prinz Ludwig Ferdinand06

ISG *Institut für Stadtgeschichte, Frankfurt a. M.*

Rechnei Bücher Signatur 214, Blatt 252
Rechnei nach 1816, Signatur 1434
Rechnei nach 1816, Signatur 1900
Nachlassakten, Signatur 1851/90
Rechnei nach 1816, Signatur 1907
Senatssublikationen 573/6

KA *Historisches Archiv Krupp, Essen*

WA 4/1031
WA 4/1066
WA 2/246
WA 2/249
WA 4/1484

STABI *Staatsbibliothek, Abteilung Handschriften und alte Drucke, Munich*

Heydeckiana I.3a
Heydeckiana II.1a
Heydeckiana II.1.b
Heydeckiana II.2b
Heydeckiana II.2.a11
Heydeckiana II.2.b
Heydeckiana II.3f
Heydeckiana II.a.1
Heydeckiana III.2.h
Klenzeana III.21
Maureriana III.1.1.b
Thierschiana I.86
Thierschiana I.87
Thierschiana I.90

France

AN Archives nationales de France, Sites de Paris et de Pierrefitte-sur-Seine:

F12–2670
F12–7126
F12–7127
F12–7128
F12–7254
F12–6280
F12–6540
F12–2670
F14–11480
F14–11603
F14–11504
F14–11554

AAE Archives des Affaires étrangères, La Courneuve

P10508
P10500
P10507–8
P10509
P10592–3
P18569
P105901

ANMT Archives nationales du monde du travail, Roubaix

CAEF B0031215
CAEF B0031216–1
CAEF B0031216–2
CAEF B0031217
CAEF B003120-1
CAEF B003121-2
CAEF B003122-1
CAEF B003123-1
CAEF B003123-2
CAEF B003123-3
CAEF B003124-2
CAEF B003124-3
CAEF B003124-7

CAEF B0031218-1
CAEF B0031219-1
CAEF B0031287-4
CAEF B0061864-1
CAEF B0066871

***BDA** Bibliothèque de l'Arsenal, Paris*

19TMS 13747-8
19TMS 13755
19TMS 13759
19TMS 14379-86
19TMS 14385
MS 14393–14396
MS 14405-9

***BN** Banque de France, Paris*

1035200401
1060200109, 1–3
1064199002
1069199305, 9–10
1069200901
1370199703, 1–2
1370199807
1060201118-14
10060200101, 1–14
1135201001

***CEP** Comptoir d'Escompte in den Archives et Histoire de BNP Paribas, Paris*

DS 37–40
DS068
DS069
DS070
DS073
DS1514
DS195
DS020
DS072
FIN 2054
FIN 2780

11-DFOM-221-149
11-DFOM-221–724
11-DFOM-221–846
11-DFOM-221–908
11-DFOM-221–717
11-DFOM-221–72-1
11-DFOM-221–74-16
11-DFOM-221–77-34
A359, 1, 4–5

CL Crédit Lyonnais in den Archives historiques du Groupe Crédit Agricole, Paris

62 AG 78
69 AH 71
62 AH 77–78
62 AH 142–146
62 AH 142–150
98 AH 62
138 AH 1
138 AH 3
138 AH 4
138 AH 6–9
DAF 0140 BE.5.60 3001
DAF 237-1
DAF 200001 BE.1.27 3003
DEEF 73268 BE.11.53 3001
DEEF 3269 0001 BE.11.53 3001
DEEF 73269-0002 BE.11.53 3001
DEEF 73268
DEEF 73269-2
DEEF 73269-2
DEEF25273 BE.11.60.3001
DEEF29134 BE.11.66.3001
DEEF29236 BE.11.66.3001
DEEF73269-1

SG Archives de la Société Générale, Paris

Assemblée générale, Conseil d'Administration (without shelf numbers)
B04871
B04881
B04882
CN252–258

Greece

Academy of Athens

Kolettis Papers,
online at http://psifiakaarxeia.academyofathens.gr/en/rec.asp?id=66548.

ELIA *Ελληνικό Λογοτεχνικό και Ιστορικό Αρχείο (Hellenic Literary and Historical Archive)*

Estate Charilaos Trikoupis:
F2–10, F13–18, F20–22, F27, F28, F30
Estate Familie Balaoritis:
14.2–4, 21.7
Estate Stefanos Streit:
F7, F8, F12, F24, F 25, F27, F30, F31, F35, F40, F42, F44

ETE *Εθνική Τράπεζα της Ελλάδος (National Bank of Greece and its archive)*

A1S10Y1F23, 42
A1S10Y3F5–6
A1S10Y68F87
A1S22Y23F48
A1S22Y8F53
A1S23YIAF53
A1S25Y2F31–32
A1S25YAF28–31
A1S28Y2F22–23
A1S28Y2F8–10
A1S2Y1F34
A1S2YSAF7YF
A1S6Y1F2YF2
A1S6Y1F2YF3
A1S6Y1F2YF4
A1S6Y1F2YF4
A1S6Y1F2YF6
A1SXXIIY8F38
A2S10Y1F2
A2S10Y1Fs
A60 Archeio Georgiou Streit. Mission à Berne Mars à Octobre 1900.
A60 Archeio Streit 2623. Mission à Bruxelles 31.7.1875 au 22 août 1900.
AIIA19Book35–43
AIS2Y1F25
AIS2Y1F33

AIS2Y29F16
AIS2Y29F17
AISSXXIYB′F9, 2–4, 9–10, 20
AISVIMYAF2
AISVIY1F1
AISVIYA′F2YF1
AISXXI YB′F3
AISXXIAYB
AISXXIB′F4
AISXXIIYF48
AISXXIYAF56- YF10–11
AISXXIYB′F10
AISXXIYB′F2
AISXXIYB′F20
AISXXIYB′F5
AISXXIYB′F9
AISXXIYB′F9
AISXXIYB′F9
AISXXIYB′F9
AISXXIYIAF57
AISXYSA′F1
AISXYSA′F2
AISXYSA′F3–F15

***GA** Διπλωματικό και Ιστορικό Αρχείο (Service of Diplomatic & Historical Archives (Y.D.I.A.) of the Hellenic Ministry of Foreign Affairs)*

1855-36-23, 24
1856-36-23
1858-36-23
1859-37-23
1864-36-23
1864-37-2
1865-37-2
1867-36-23
1867-37-2
1878-8-1
1878-11-6
1878 20–1
1879-20-1
1883-A5-3
1883-D59
1883-G-85-1a
1884-37-2
1884-59-2

1887-D59-1, 2
1889-B19-2

GE *Γεννάδειος Βιβλιοθήκη (Gennadios Library, The American School of Classical Studies at Athens)*

Estate Stefanos Skouloudis:
F34–F45
Estate Stephanos Dragoumis:
F81–83

GNA *Γενικά Αρχεία του Κράτους (General State Archives of Greece), Athens*

All holdings viewed are digitalised online at http://arxeiomnimon.gak.gr/

LGC *Estate of the London Greek Committee, in der Εθνική Βιβλιοθήκη της Ελλάδος (Greek National Library, Athens)*

Files 1–11

Great Britain

BAL *Barings Archives, London*

300431
HC2.169
HC17.326
HC17.346
HC17.420
HC3.52II.I
HC10.62
HC7.67
HC7.27, 28
HC16.19
HC16.19
HC7.23

BL *British Library*

Add 35153
Add 36460–3
Add 38295
Add 43234
Add 47271
Add 49113

Add 60421

NA National Archives, London

BT31–30040–226093
BT31–39314-14152
FO286–1094
FO286–1132
FO286–1145
FO286–380
FO286–386
FO286–387
FO286–393
FO32–312
FO32–313
FO32–314
FO32–357
FO32–422
FO32–443
FO32–486
FO32–488
FO32–605
FO32–606
FO32–607
FO32–61
FO32–658
FO32–666
FO32–674
FO32–683
FO32–699
FO32–742
FO32–767–70
FO335-128-5
FO372–180019
FO386-26
FO421-18
FO78–2794
FO78–2808
FO881–1164
FO881–6276
FO881-857
FO881–8973
FO881–93
FO93-38-109

J55-3-192
PRO22–51
PRO30-22-14
PRO30-22-24
PRO30-22-62
PRO30-22-65
PROB37–895
RAIL770-40-3–779
T1–11244
T113536
T1–16795

GL Archives of the Stock Exchange in the Guildhall Library, London

App 1200 23A Ionian Bank 1864
App 13 26B Lake Copais 1891
App 163 20B Piraeus Athens 1889
App 246 21 B Piraeus Athens Peloponnesus Railway
App 31 16B Lake Copais 1888
App 398 19B, Piraeus-Athens-Peloponnesus Railway Com 1888
App 493-69B
App 115–293B
MS 17.957-1
MS 17.957-5
MS 17957-23
MS18001-126-17B
MS18001-27-151B
MS18001-412-16B
MS18001-415-62B
MS18001-644-124B
MS18001-712-79B
MS18001-72-12B
Ms18001-80-30B

IOB *Ionian Bank in the London School of Economics (LSE)*

1-1
1–8
1–15
1–16
2–5
3-3
3–23
4-1

4–19
6–30
8-1
10–1
10–6
10–15
10–18, 19

MA Metropolitan Archives, London

Estate Hambro & Son:
CLC-B-002–10–01–13–009
CLC-B-060-MS-34713-4
CLC-B-060-MS-34712-21
MS15814
MS19032-33
MS19033-3
MS19036
MS19036-1
MS19038-386
MS19063-2
MS19063-3
MS19063-17-19
MS19063-21
MS19063-24
MS19063-27
MS19063-29-30
MS19064
MS19099-109
MS19181
MS19219
MS19220
MS19221
Estate Gibbs:
MS11,113: Vol 1–4: Reel 164–167
The entire estate of the bank Anthony Gibbs and Sons is also available on microfilm (e.g. in the German inter-library loan system): The Gibbs Archive. Papers of Anthony Gibbs and Sons 1744–1953. Guildhall Mss 11021-96, 11108–11140, 111467–111474, 16869–16904, 19802–19888. Microfilm, London 1984.

RAL Rothschild Archive, London

(Some of the materials used were originally in Yiddish and the Rothschild archive provided a translation into English that was undertaken in the

context of Niall Ferguson's work. The archive explicitly points out that mistakes have since been found in some of the translations; it cannot be ruled out that such mistakes occur here.)
XI/109J/J/30
XI/109/25/1/10
XI/109/27/3/24
XI/109J/J/32
XI/109/27/1/54
XI/109/27/1/60
XI/109/27/1/62
XI/109/27/3/24
XI/109J/J/32B&C
XI/109J/J/33
XI/109/30/2/3
XI/38-16A
XI-63-17
XI-109
XI/112-11 1831
XI/112 1828
XI/112 1829E
XI/109-7
000–401B-5

SchA Schröder's Archive, London

Erlanger, Émile Beaumont: Quelques souvenirs: My English souvenir, privately printed in 1978.

Switzerland

BGE Bibliothèque de Genève, Département des manuscrits et des archives privées

Estate Jean Gabriel Eynard
1840
1844–45
1848
1863
1865–66
1868–71
1882–91
1901
1902

***AEG** Archives d'Etat de Genève*

Mi B 591n sequence 2 (Journal d'Albert Hentsch)

USA

***NBB** Bleichröder Collection in the Baker Library, Harvard Business School, Boston*

(In some cases copies on microfilm in the Bundesarchiv Berlin)
I1 Bismarck
II MS 783.4, 5
XI Bleichröder Firm
XIII.V Imelmann
XIV.5 Rothschild
XIV.1 Rothschild London
XIX Artists
XV Goldschmidt
XVI.2 Rothschild
XVII Rothschild Paris
XX.1 Bayern
XXI Ministers
XXI Graf Herbert von Muenster
XXII Royalty, High officials, Generals
XXIV 7 Rangabe
XXIV 14 Caratheodory
XXV.2 Eichthal
XXVI Government loans
Loan Agreement 64
Loan Agreement 68

BIBLIOGRAPHY

The transcription of Greek characters is undertaken in line with the 'ISO 5428:1984 Greek alphabet coded character set for bibliographic information interchange'. The alphabetical listing of Greek literature is based on the Latin characters, e.g. Greek authors whose names begin with a Greek B (*Βικέλας, Δ. [Vikelas, D.]*) are listed according to the transcription into the Latin alphabet under the letter V.

About, E.: *La Grèce contemporaine*, Paris 1854.

Idem: *Le Roi des montagnes*, Paris 1857.

Idem: *L'affaire du Laurion*, Paris 1872.

Idem: Griechenland: "Das Land lebt seit seiner Geburt im totalen Bankrott". Ein Nachdruck aus gegebenem Anlass. Übersetzt von Philipp Reuter, in: *Frankfurter Allgemeine Zeitung*, 15.2.2012.

Adam, T.: *Buying Respectability. Philanthropy and Urban Society in Transnational Perspective, 1840s to 1930s*, Bloomington 2009 (= Philanthropic and Nonprofit Studies).

Idem/Lässig, S./Lingelbach, G. (eds.): *Stifter, Spender und Mäzene. USA und Deutschland im historischen Vergleich*, Stuttgart 2009 (= Transatlantische historische Studien, Vol. 38).

Agriantoni, C.: A Collective Portrait of Greek Industrials, in: *Entreprises et Histoire* 63 (2011), pp. 15–25.

Idem: Spaniolika et Kyprianos: deux petites cités ouvrières à Lavrion. Actes du colloque international au Familistère du Guise (16 17 octobre 1993), in: *L'archéologie industrielle en France* 24–25 (1994), pp. 1–9.

Idem: *Οι απαρχές της εκβιομηχάνισης στην Ελλάδα τον 19ο αιώνα [The Beginnings of Industrialization in Greece in the 19th Century]*, Athens 1986, 2nd ed. 2010.

Akerlof, G. A./Shiller, R. J.: *Animal Spirits. Wie Wirtschaft wirklich funktioniert*, Frankfurt/New York 2009.

Al, H.: Was There a Guarantee Effect for the Ottoman Loans in the 19th Century? in: *Australian Economic History Review* 52 (2012) 2, pp. 191 208.

Allingham, M.: *Choice Theory. A Very Short Introduction*, Oxford et al. 2002 (= Very short introductions, Vol. 71).

Altgeld, W.: Das Risorgimento (1815–1876), in: idem (ed.): *Kleine italienische Geschichte*, Stuttgart 2002, pp. 257–322.

Altman, M.: Prospect Theory and Behavioral Finance, in: H. K. Baker/J. R. Nofsinger (eds.): *Behavioral Finance. Investors, Corporations, and Markets*, Hoboken NJ 2010, pp. 191 210.

Alville: *Anna Eynard-Lullin et l'époque des congrès et des révolutions*, Lausanne 1955.

Amandry, A.: Le philhellénisme en France à travers les étiquettes commerciales, in: *Revue de la Bibliothèque nationale de France* 3 (1983) 9, pp. 12–21.

Anderson, B.: *Die Erfindung der Nation. Zur Karriere eines folgenreichen Konzepts*, Frankfurt et al. 2005.

Ανδρεάδης, A. [Andreadis, A. M.]: *Ιστορία των εθνικών δανείων [History of the National Loans]*, Athens 1904.

Idem: *Εθνικά δάνεια και ελληνική δημόσια οικονομία [National Debt and Greek Public Economy]*, Athens 1925, 2nd ed. 2010.

Angelomatis-Tsougarakis, H.: *The Eve of the Greek Revival. British Travellers' Perceptions of Early Nineteenth-century Greece*, London et al. 1990.

Αγγελόπουλος, Α. Θ. [Angelopoulos, A. Th.]: *Η άμεσος φορολογία εν Ελλάδι [The Direct Taxation in Greece]*, Athens 1933.

Ανώνυμος Εταιρεία της Λίμνης Κωπαΐδος [Lake Copaïs Company]: *Συνοπτική έκθεσις της ιστορίας και του έργου της ανωνύμου εταιρείας της λίμνης Κωπαΐδος [Short Review of the History and Work of the Lake Copais Co. Ltd.]*, Athens 1951.

Appel, B. J./Loyle, C. E.: The Economic Benefits of Justice: Post-conflict Justice and Foreign Direct Investment, in: *Journal of Peace Research* (2012), http://jpr.sagepub.com/content/49/5/685 [7.2.2014].

Aretin, K. O. Frhr v.: Clemens Graf von Metternich-Winneburg (1773–1859), in: *NDB*, 17 (1994), pp. 236–243: http://www.deutsche-biographie.de/ppn118581465.html [15.5.15].

Armansperg, G. R.: *Joseph Ludwig Graf Armansperg: ein Beitrag zur Regierungsgeschichte Ludwigs I. von Bayern*, Munich 1976 (= Miscellanea Bavarica Monacensia, New Series 67).

Αρώνη-Τσίχλη, Κ. [Aroni-Tsixli, K.]: Η κοινωνία της σταφίδας και ο Τρικούπης [The Raisin Company and Tricoupis], in: Κ. Αρώνη-Τσίχλη [K. Aroni-Tsixli]/Λ. Τρίχα [L. Tricha] (eds.): *Ο Χαρίλαος Τρικούπης και η εποχή του. Πολιτικές επιδιώξεις και κοινωνικές συνθήκες [Charilaos Trikoupis and His Time. Political Aims and Social Conditions]*, Athens 2000, pp. 349–378.

Ασανάκη, Ε. Ν. [Asanaki, E. N.]: *Arthemond Regny: Ο Γάλλος οικονομολόγος και η προσφορά του στην Ελλάδα 1831–1841 [Arthemond Regny: The French Economist and His Action in Greece 1831–1841]*, Athens 1989.

Asmussen, T./Krämer, D./Condorelli, S.: Risiko. Editorial, in: *Traverse. Zeitschrift für Geschichte* (2014) 3, pp. 14–19.

Attard, B./Dilley, A.: Finance, Empire and the British World, in: *The Journal of Imperial and Commonwealth History* 41 (2013) 1, pp. 1–10.

Austin, P.E.: *Baring Brothers and the Birth of Modern Finance*, London 2007.

Μπαμπούνης, Χ. [Babounis, Ch.]: Δύο αρχεία για την ιστορία της Λαυρεωτικής [Two Archives on the History of the Laurion Area], in: Π. Φιλίππου-Αγγέλου [P. Philippou-Angelou] (ed.): *Πρακτικά Γ' Επιστημονικής Συνάντησης Ν.Α. Αττικής 1987 [Conference Proceedings G of the Scientific Meeting of N. A. Attika 1987]*, Kalivia 1988, pp. 135–154.

Baecker, D.: *Womit handeln Banken? Eine Untersuchung zur Risikoverarbeitung in der Wirtschaft*, Frankfurt 2008.

Baer, M.: Burdett, Sir Francis, Fifth Baronet (1770–1844), Politician, in: *ODNB*, Oxford 2004, doi:10.1093/ref:odnb/3962.

Baigent, E.: Stanhope, Leicester Fitzgerald Charles, Fifth Earl of Harrington (1784–1862), in: *ODNB*, Oxford 2004, doi:10.1093/ref:odnb/26250.

Baker, H. K./Nofsinger, J. R.: Answers to Chapter Discussion Questions, in: idem (eds.): *Behavioral Finance. Investors, Corporations, and Markets*, Hoboken NJ 2010, pp. 681–726.

Μπάλογλου, Χ. Π. [Baloglou, Christos P.]: Η ίδρυση της Εταιρίας Μεταλλουργείων Λαυρίου και η προκύψασα κυβεία [The Foundation of the Metallurgical Company of Laurion and the Resulting Game], in: Π. Φιλίππου-Αγγέλου [P. Philippou-Angelou] (ed.): *Πρακτικά Γ' Επιστημονικής Συνάντησης Ν.Α. Αττικής 1987 [Conference Proceedings G of the Scientific Meeting of N. A. Attika 1987]*, Kalivia 1988a, pp. 197–217.

Idem: *Το Λαυρεωτικόν Ζήτημα και οι κοινωνικοοικονομικές του επιδράσεις [The Laurion Affaire and Its General Economic Effects]*, Athens 1988b.

Idem: The Diffusion of the Ideas of Saint-Simon in the Hellenic State and Their Reception Thereby (1825–1837), in: *History of economic ideas* 17 (2009) 2, pp. 155–179.

Bank of England, *Bank Charter Act 1844*, legislation.gov.uk, http://www.legislation.gov.uk/ukpga/Vict/7-8/32/enacted [31.1.2020].

Barau, D.: *La cause des Grecs. Une histoire du mouvement philhellène (1821–1829)*, Paris 2009 (= Histoire culturelle de l'Europe, Vol. 10).

Barberis, N./Huang, M./Santos, T.: Prospect Theory and Asset Prices, in: *Quaterly Journal of Economics* 116 (2001) 1, pp. 1 53.

Barceló, P. A./Schmidt, P.: *Kleine Geschichte Spaniens*, Bonn 2005.

Barnett, M. L./Pollock, T. G. (eds.): *The Oxford Handbook of Corporate Reputation*, Oxford 2012.

Barth, B.: Banken und Kapitalexport vor 1914. Anmerkungen zum Forschungsstand der politischen Ökonomie des Kaiserreichs, in: M. Köhler (ed.): *Banken, Konjunktur und Politik. Beiträge zur Geschichte deutscher Banken im 19. und 20. Jahrhundert*, Essen 1995a, pp. 42–54 (= Bochumer Schriften zur Unternehmens- und Industriegeschichte, Vol. 4).

Idem: *Die deutsche Hochfinanz und die Imperialismen: Banken und Außenpolitik vor 1914*, Stuttgart 1995b (= Beiträge zur Kolonial- und Überseegeschichte, Vol. 61).

Idem: Die Deutsche Bank und die Bagdadbahn seit 1888. Internationale Finanzbeziehungen in der Ära des Imperialismus, in: D. Lindenlaub/C. Burhop/J. Scholtyseck (eds.): *Schlüsselereignisse der deutschen Bankengeschichte*, Stuttgart 2014a, pp. 178–188.

Idem (ed.): *Globalgeschichten. Bestandsaufnahme und Perspektiven*, Frankfurt 2014b (= Series Globalgeschichte, Vol. 17).

Idem: Möglichkeiten einer Globalgeschichte der Finanzwirtschaft, in: idem (ed.): *Globalgeschichten. Bestandsaufnahme und Perspektiven*, Frankfurt 2014c, pp. 113–141 (= Series Globalgeschichte, Vol. 17).

Bartle, G. F.: Bowring and the Greek Loans of 1824 and 1825, in: *Balkan Studies* 3 (1962), pp. 61–74.

Idem: Jeremy Bentham and John Bowring: A Study of the Relationship between Bentham and the Editor of His Collected Works, in: *Bulletin of the Institute of Historical Research* 36 (1963) 93, pp. 27–35.

Barton, J. S.: *Policy Signals and Market Responses. A 50-Year History of Zambia's Relationship with Foreign Capital*, London 2016 (= Palgrave Studies in the History of Finance).

Basch, S.: *Le mirage grec. La Grèce moderne devant l'opinion française depuis la création de l'École d'Athènes jusqu'à la guerre civile grecque (1846–1946)*, Paris 1995 (= Collection Confluences).

Batardon, J.: *Le philhellène Jean-Gabriel Eynard: sa collaboration à la mise en place des systèmes éducatif et financier en Grèce (1828–1863)*, Genève 2006.

Battilossi, S.: 'Ephors' from Growth to Governance. How Modern Theories are Reshaping Historians′ Views of the Economic Functions of Bankers, in: E. Green/M. Pohle-Fraser (eds.): *The Human Factor in Banking History. Entrepreneurship, Organization, Management and Personnel*, Athens 2008, pp. 75–96.

Baumstark, R. (eds.): *Das neue Hellas. Griechen und Bayern zur Zeit Ludwigs I. Katalogbuch zur Ausstellung des Bayerischen Nationalmuseums München, 9. November 1999 bis 13. Februar 2000*, Munich 1999.

Bavaj, R./Steber, M. (eds.): *Germany and 'The West'. The History of a Modern Concept*, New York/Oxford 2016.

Bayerische Hypotheken- und Wechselbank: *Hundert Jahre Bayerische Hypotheken- und Wechselbank 1835–1935*, Munich 1935.

Beales, D.: Canning, George (1770–1827), in: *ODNB*, Oxford 2004, doi:10.1093/ref:odnb/4556.

Becker, F./Scheller, B./Schneider, U. (eds.): *Die Ungewissheit des Zukünftigen. Kontingenz in der Geschichte*, Frankfurt 2016 (= Kontingenzgeschichten, Vol. 1).

Beckert, J.: Imagined Futures: Fictional Expectations in the Economy, in: *Theory and Sociology* 42 (2013) 3, pp. 219–240.

Idem: *Imagined Futures. Fictional Expectations and Capitalist Dynamics*, Cambridge 2016.

Beckert, S: *King Cotton. Eine Geschichte des globalen Kapitalismus*, Munich, 2nd ed. 2015.

Beckett, J./Turner, M.: Agricultural Productivity in England, 1700–1914, in: M. Olsson/P. Svensson, P. (eds.): *Growth and Stagnation in European Historical Agriculture*, Turnhout 2011, pp. 35–56 (= Rural History in Europe, Vol. 6).

Bell, A.: Amherst, William Amhurst Tyssen-, First Baron Amherst of Hackney (1835–1909), in: *ODNB*, Oxford 2004, doi:10.1093/ref:odnb/30402.

Bellet, M.: *Saint-Simonism and Utilitarianism: the History of a Paradox. Bentham's Defence of Usury under Saint-Amand Bazard's Interpretation (Groupe d'analyse et de théorie économique Lyon – St. Étienne, P 1135*), 2011, Decembre, https://halshs.archives-ouvertes.fr/halshs-00654847 [20.1.19].

Μπελογιάννης, N. [Belogiannis, N.]: *Το ξένο κεφάλαιο στην Ελλάδα [The Foreign Capital in Greece]*, Athens 1998.

Bendix, O.: *Hambros Bank Ltd., London. 1839–1939*, London 1939.

Bergemann, L. et al.: Transformation. Ein Konzept zur Erforschung kulturellen Wandels, in: H. Böhme et al. (eds.): *Transformation. Ein Konzept zur Erforschung kulturellen Wandels*, Paderborn 2011, pp. 39–56.

Berghoff, H.: Transaktionskosten: Generalschlüssel zum Verständnis langfristiger Unternehmensentwicklung? Zum Verhältnis von neuer Institutionenökonomie und moderner Unternehmensgeschichte, in: *Jahrbuch für Wirtschaftsgeschichte* (1999) 2, pp. 159–176.

Idem: Vertrauen als ökonomische Schlüsselvariable. Zur Theorie des Vertrauens und der Geschichte seiner privatwirtschaftlichen Produktion, in: K.-P. Ellerbrock (ed.): *Die Wirtschaftsgeschichte vor der Herausforderung durch die New Institutional Economics*, Münster 2004, pp. 58–71 (= Untersuchungen zur Wirtschafts-, Sozial- und Technikgeschichte, Vol. 24).

Berndt, C./Pütz, R. (eds.): *Kulturelle Geographien: zur Beschäftigung mit Raum und Ort nach dem Cultural Turn: ausgewählte Beiträge der vierten Kulturgeographietagung in Frankfurt a. M.*, Bielefeld 2007.

Bernhardt, M./Brakensiek, S./Scheller, B. (eds.): *Ermöglichen und Verhindern. Vom Umgang mit Kontingenz*, Frankfurt/New York 2016 (= Kontingenzgeschichten, Vol. 2).

Eidem/ Blösel, W.;. (eds.): *Möglichkeitshorizonte. Zur Pluralität von Zukunftserwartungen und Handlungsoptionen in der Geschichte*, Frankfurt/New York 2017 (= Kontingenzgeschichten, Vol. 4).

Bickes, H./Otten, T./Weymann, L. C.: Die Rolle der Medien, in: U.-D. Klemm/W. Schultheiß (eds.): *Die Krise in Griechenland. Ursprünge, Verlauf, Folgen*, Frankfurt 2015, pp. 326–351.

Bickford-Smith, R. A. H.: *Greece under King George*, London 1893.

Biondich, M.: *The Balkans. Revolution, War, and Political Violence since 1878*, Oxford 2011 (= Zones of Violence).

Birdal, M.: *The Political Economy of Ottoman Public Debt. Insolvency and European Financial Control in the Late Nineteenth Century*, London/New York 2010 (= Library of Ottoman Studies, Vol. 18).

Birmingham, S.: *"Our Crowd". The Great Jewish Families of New York*, New York 1967.

Blackbourn, D.: *Die Eroberung der Natur. Eine Geschichte der deutschen Landschaft*, Munich 2007.

Blaisdell, D. C.: *European Financial Control in the Ottoman Empire. A Study of the Establishment, Activities, and Significance of the Administration of the Ottoman Public Debt*, New York 1929.

Blaquiere, E.: *Report on the Present State of the Greek Confederation, and on Its Claims to the Support of the Christian World*, London 1823.

Boaglio, G.: Auf der Suche nach nationaler Identität: Der Philhellenismus in Piemont, in: A. Noe (ed.): *Der Philhellenismus in der westeuropäischen Literatur, 1780–1830*, Amsterdam et al. 1994, pp. 133–163 (= Internationale Forschungen zur allgemeinen und vergleichenden Literaturwissenschaft, Vol. 6).

Boblaye, E. L. P. de/D'Aoust, P. T. V.: *Géologie et minéralogie Paris 1833* (= Expédition scientifique de Morée, Vol. 2.2).

Boldt, H.: Staat und Souveränität, in: O. Brunner/W. Conze/R. Koselleck (eds.): *Geschichtliche Grundbegriffe. Historisches Lexikon zur politisch-sozialen Sprache in Deutschland*, Stuttgart 1978, pp. 1–154.

Bonin, H.: *La Banque de l'union parisienne (1874/1904–1974). Histoire de la deuxième grande banque d'affaires française*, Paris 2000 (= Collection Ecoclio, Vol. 2).

Idem: La Banque d'Athènes, point de jonction entre deux outre-mers bancaires (1904–1953), in: *Outre-mers: revue d'histoire 330–331* (2001), pp. 53–70.

Idem: *Histoire de la Société générale*, Paris 2006.
Idem: *History of the Suez Canal Company 1858–1960. Between Controversy and Utility*, Genève 2010 (= Publications d'histoire économique et sociale internationale, Vol. 25).
Idem: *French Banks and the Greek "Niche Market" Mid-1880s–1950s*, Genève 2013.
Born, R./Lemmen, S. (eds.): *Orientalismen in Ostmitteleuropa. Diskurse, Akteure und Disziplinen vom 19. Jahrhundert bis zum Zweiten Weltkrieg*, Bielefeld/Berlin 2014 (= Postcolonial Studies, Vol. 19).
Börsen-Enquête-Kommission: *Uebersicht über die an der Berliner Börse von 1882 bis 1892 zur Einführung gelangten Werthpapiere. Zusammengestellt unter Benutzung der Akten der Börsen-Registratur und der Berliner Börsen-Zeitung, sowie der entsprechenden Ausgaben von Saling's Börsen-Jahrbuch*, Berlin 1893.
Borutta, M.: Braudel in Algier. Die kolonialen Wurzeln der "Méditerranée" und der "spatial turn", in: *Historische Zeitschrift* 303 (2016) 1, pp. 1–38.
Borutta, M./Lemmes, F.: Die Wiederkehr des Mittelmeerraumes: Stand und Perspektiven der neuhistorischen Mediterranistik, in: *Neue Politische Literatur* 58 (2013) 3, pp. 389–420.
Bourguet, M.-N./Panayotopoulos, V./Sinarellis, M. (eds.): *L'invention scientifique de la Méditerranée. Égypte, Morée, Algérie*, Paris 1998 (= Recherches d'histoire et de sciences sociales. Studies in History and the Social Sciences, Vol. 77).
Bourne, K./Preston, P./Stevenson, D. (eds.): *British Documents on Foreign Affairs: Greece, 1847–1914. Reports and Papers from the Foreign Office Confidential Print*, Frederick 1987.
Bouvier-Bron, M.: La mission de Capodistrias en Suisse (1813–1814), in: *Αρχείο Ιωάννη Καποδίστρια [Archive of Ioannis Kapodistrias]*, Vol. 4, Kerkyra 1984.
Bowen, J.: Education, Ideology and the Ruling Class: Hellenism and English Public Schools in the Nineteenth Century, in: W. C. Graeme (ed.): *Rediscovering Hellenism. The Hellenic Inheritance and the English Imagination*, Cambridge et al. 1989, pp. 161–186.
Bowring, J.: A Summary Account of the Steam-boats for Lord Cochrane's Expedition; With Some Few Words Upon the Two Frigates Ordered at New York for the Service of Greece, in: *Westminster Review* 6 (1826) 11, pp. 113–133.
Brakensiek, S./Marx, C./Scheller, B. (eds.): *Wagnisse. Risiken eingehen, Risiken analysieren, von Risiken erzählen*, Frankfurt/New York 2017 (= Kontingenzgeschichten, Vol. 3).
Bramsen, B./Wain, K.: *The Hambros: 1779–1979*, London 1979.
Braudel, F.: *La Méditerranée et le monde méditerranéen à l'époque de Philippe II*, Paris 1949.
Idem/Duby, G./Aymard, M.: *La Méditerranée. Arts et métiers graphiques*, Paris 1977/1978.
Μπρέγιαννη, Κ. [Bregianni, K.]: *Νεοελληνικό νόμισμα: Κράτος και ιδεολογία από την Επανάσταση έως το Μεσοπόλεμο [Modern Greek Currency. State and Ideology From the Revolution Until the Interwar Period]*, Athens 2011.
Brehl, M. et al. (eds.): *The Mediterranean Other – The Other Mediterranean*, Paderborn 2016.
Brennecke, C.: *Von Cádiz nach London. Spanischer Liberalismus im Spannungsfeld von nationaler Selbstbestimmung, Internationalität und Exil (1820–1833)*,

Göttingen 2010 (= Veröffentlichungen des Instituts für Europäische Geschichte Mainz; Abteilung für Universalgeschichte, Vol. 222).

Briffaud, S.: L'expédition scientifique de Morée et le paysage méditerranéen, in: M.-N. Bourguet/V. Panayotopoulos/M. Sinarellis (eds.): *L'invention scientifique de la Méditerranée. Égypte, Morée, Algérie*, Paris 1998, pp. 289–297 (= Recherches d'histoire et de sciences sociales. Studies in history and the social sciences, Vol. 77).

Brisse, A./Rotrou, L.: *Dessèchement du Lac Fucino, exécuté par S. E. le prince Alexandre Torlonia*, Rome 1876.

Brötel, D.: *Frankreich im fernen Osten: Imperialistische Expansion in Siam und Malaya, Laos und China*, 1880–1904, Stuttgart 1996.

Burhop, C.: Die Vergütung des Führungspersonals deutscher Großbanken: 1871–1913, in: *Vierteljahrschrift für Sozial- und Wirtschaftsgeschichte* 92 (2005) 3, pp. 281–300.

Idem: Banken, Aufsichtsräte und Corporate Governance im Deutschen Reich (1871–1913), in: *Bankhistorisches Archiv* 32 (2007), pp. 1–25.

Idem: *Wirtschaftsgeschichte des Kaiserreichs* 1871–1918, Göttingen 2011 (= UTB, Vol. 3454).

Idem: Ressourcenkonflikte bei Aktienerstemissionen im Deutschen Reich um 1900, in: *Bankhistorisches Archiv* 39 (2013) 1, pp. 1–19.

Burkhardt, S.: *Medienskandale. Zur moralischen Sprengkraft öffentlicher Diskurse*, Köln 2006.

Burnouf, É.: *Le Lac Copaïs*, Paris 1850 (= Archives de missions scientifiques, pub. Ministère de l'Instruction publique et des Cultes, IIIe cahier).

Idem: La Grèce en 1869, in: *Revue des deux mondes* 81 (1869), pp. 458–459.

Idem: La Grèce en 1886, in: *Revue des deux mondes* 79 (1887), p. 547.

Burton, A.: *Canal Mania. 200 Years of Britain's Waterways*, London 1993.

Büttner, F.: Ludwig I. Kunstförderung und Kunstpolitik, in: A. Schmid/K. Weigand (eds.): *Die Herrscher Bayerns. 25 Portraits von Tassilo III. bis Ludwig III.*, Munich 2001, pp. 310–329.

Cáceres/Wernicke: Nur eine halbe Umarmung, in: *Süddeutsche Zeitung*, 5.2.2015, p. 7.

Calapodis, M.: *La communauté grecque à Marseille. Genèse d'un paradigme identitaire (1793–1914)*, Paris 2010 (= Etudes grecques).

Cameron, R. E.: *France and the Economic Development of Europe, 1800–1914. Conquests of Peace and Seeds of War*, Princeton NJ 1961.

Capizucchi, L.: *Le mie relazioni con Commendatore G. B. Serpieri*, Rimini 1884.

Caron, F.: *An Economic History of Modern France*, New York 1979.

Carr, F. G. G.: Caird, Sir James, of Glenfarquhar (rev. Ann Savours), in: *ODNB*, Oxford 2004, doi:10.1093/ref:odnb/32240.

Cassis, Y.: Swiss International Banking, 1890–1950, in: G. Jones (ed.): *Banks as Multinationals*, London 1990, pp. 160–172.

Idem: Financial Elites in Three European Centres: London, Paris, Berlin, 1880s–1930s, in: G. Jones (ed.): *Banks and Money: International and Comparative Finance in History*, London 1991, pp. 53–71.

Idem: *City Bankers, 1890–1914*, Cambridge 1994.

Idem (ed.): *Finance and Financiers in European History 1880–1960*, Cambridge 2002.

Idem: *Metropolen des Kapitals. Die Geschichte der internationalen Finanzzentren 1780–2005*, Hamburg 2007.

Idem: Family Banks, Private Banks, Investment Banks: Wall Street and the City of London from the 19th to the 21st Century, in: A. Perlinge/H. Sjögren (eds.): *Biographies of the Financial World*, Möklinta 2012, pp. 69–84 (= Monograph Series EHF-EHFF).

Idem/Cottrell, P.: *Private Banking in Europe. Rise, Retreat, and Resurgence*, Oxford 2015.

Idem/Feldman, G. D./Olsson, U. (eds.): *The Evolution of Financial Institutions and Market in Twentieth-century Europe*, Aldershot 1995.

Chancellor, V. E.: Hume, Joseph (1777–1855), Radical and Politician, in: *ODNB*, Oxford 2004, doi:10.1093/ref:odnb/14148.

Chapman, S. D.: *The Rise of Merchant Banking*, Boston MA 1984.

Chaponnière Meyer, C. (ed.): *Nos deux cents premières années: Lombard Odier & Cie*, Genève 1998.

Chapuisat, É.: *La Restauration hellénique d'après la correspondance de Jean-Gabriel Eynard*, Genève 1924.

Idem: *Jean-Gabriel Eynard et son temps. 1775–1863*, Genève 1952.

Χαριτάκης, Γ. [Charitákis, G.]: *Ανάλυσις του δημοσίου χρέους της Ελλάδος [Analysis of the Greek Public Debt]*, Athens 1933.

Chastagnaret, G.: Espace industriel et stratégie personnelle: Hilarion Roux et la construction d'une Méditerranée du plomb, in: P. Aubert/G. Chastagnaret/O. Raveux (eds.): *Construire des mondes. Élites et espaces en Méditerranée, XVIe–XXe siècle*, Aix-en-Provence 2005, pp. 269–287 (= Le temps de l'histoire).

Chatziioannou, M. C./Harlaftis, G.: From the Levant to the City of London: Mercantile Credit in the Greek International Commercial Networks of the Eighteenth and Nineteenth Centuries, in: P. L. Cottrell/E. Lange/U. Olsson (eds.): *Centres and Peripheries in Banking*, Aldershot et al. 2002, pp. 13–40 (= Studies in Banking and Financial History).

Idem: Mediterranean Pathways of Greek Merchants to Victorian England, in: *The Historical Review/La Revue Historique* 7 (2010), pp. 213–237.

Idem: War, Crisis and Sovereign Loans: The Greek War of Independence and British Economic Expansion in the 1820s, in: *The Historical Review/La Revue Historique* 10 (2013), pp. 33–55.

Idem: Greek Sovereign Debt and Loans in the 19th-Century Public Discourse, in: *Journal of European Economic History* XLVIII, 2 (2019). pp. 21–55.

Chatzis, K./Mavrogonatou, G.: Greece at the Paris Universal Exhibition in 1878, in: *Quaderns d'Història de l'Enginyeria* 13 (2012), pp. 11–24.

Idem/Nikolaides, E. (eds.): *Science, Technology and the 19th Century State: The Role of the Armee. Conference Proceedings Syros*, 7–8 July 2000, Athens 2003.

Chavagneux, C.: *Kleine Geschichte der Finanzkrisen. Spekulation und Crash von 1637 bis heute*, Zürich 2013.

Checkley, K.: *Finance for Farming. A Guide for the Lending Banker*, London 1983.

Cheston, C.: *Greece in 1887*, London 1887a.

Idem: *La Grèce en 1887. Traduit de l'anglais par Hector France*, Paris 1887b.

Τσέστων, Κ. [Cheston, K.]: *Η Ελλάς τω 1887 [Greece in 1887]*, Athens 1990.

Chevalier, M.: *Système de la Méditerranée. La paix considérée sous le rapport des intérêts* (20.1.1832); *Impossibilité de fonder un équilibre européen par la guerre* (31.1.1832); *La paix définitive doit être fondée par l'association de l'Orient et de *l'Occident* (5.2.1832); *Système de la Méditerranée. Politique nouvelle* (12.2.1832), Paris 1832.

Chiapello, E./Walter, C.: The Three Ages of Financial Quantification: A Conventionalist Approach to the Financiers' Metrology, in: *Historical Social Research/ Historische Sozialforschung* 41 (2016) 2, pp. 155–177.

Christ, G. et al. (eds.): *Union in Separation. Diasporic Groups and Identities in the Eastern Mediterranean (1100–1800)*, Rome 2015.

Christmas, W.: *King George of Greece*, London 1914.

Christophorou, C.: *Die Entwicklung der Griechischen Nationalbank unter besonderer Berücksichtigung der griechischen Währung*, Leipzig 1926.

Χρήστος, Δ. Ο. [Christos, D. O.]: *Το Κωπαϊδικό ζήτημα και οι κοινωνικοί αγώνες για την επίλυση του (1865–1953): ο Γ. Παπασπύρου (1902–1987) και η συμβολή του στη διευθέτηση της κωπαϊδικής υπόθεσης [The Question of Lake Kopais and the Struggles for Its Solution. G. Papaspiros (1902–1987) and His Contribution to the Clearing of the Kopais Case*], Athens 2002.

Ciompi, L./Endert, E.: *Gefühle machen Geschichte. Die Wirkung kollektiver Emotionen – von Hitler bis Obama*, Göttingen 2011.

Ciriacono, S.: Land Reclamation. Dutch Windmills, Private Enterprises, and State Intervention, in: *Review: A Journal of the Fernand Braudel Center for the Study of Economies, Historical Systems and Civilizations* 18 (1995) 2, pp. 281–304.

Clarke, G. W. (ed.): *Rediscovering Hellenism. The Hellenic Inheritance and the English Imagination*, Cambridge et al. 1989.

Clavel, D.: *Fraude financière, dette souveraine et impérialisme d'affaires une micro-histoire de l'échec de Poyais 1820–1824*, Geneva 2018.

Clay, C. G. A.: *Gold for the Sultan: Western Bankers and Ottoman Finance 1856–1881*, London et al. 2000 (= International Library for Historical Studies, Vol. 20).

Cobbett, W. M.: London Tavern Humbug, "For affording assistance to the Spaniards", 18. June 1823, in: *Cobbett's Political Register* 46 (1823) 12, pp. 706–744.

Cochran, P.: Hobhouse, John Cam, Baron Broughton (1786–1869), Politician, in: *ODNB*, Oxford 2004, doi:10.1093/ref:odnb/13404.

Codman, F.: *Fitful Rebel. Sophie de Marbois, Duchesse de Plaisance*, Paris 1965.

Colvin, C. L.: *The Past, Present and Future of Banking History*, QUCEH Working Paper Series, No. 15-05, 2015, http://hdl.handle.net/10419/112786 [18.8.2015].

Comité de Genève en faveur des Grecs (ed.): *Documents officiels sur les secours envoyés en Grèce par Monsieur Eynard, et sur l'état de la Grèce à la fin de juillet 1826*, Genève 1826a.

Comité de Genève en faveur des Grecs (ed.): *Documents officiels sur les secours envoyés en Grèce par Monsieur Eynard, et sur l'état de la Grèce à la fin de juillet 1826*, No II, Genève 1826b.

Commission financière internationale (ed.): *Dette publique de la Grèce. Historique, lois, décrets, conventions, protocoles, règlements, etc.*, Athens 1916.

Commissione per la pubblicazione dei documenti diplomatici (ed.): *I documenti diplomatici italiani*. Prima serie (II), Roma 1959.

Compagnie française pour le dessèchement et l'exploitation du Lac Copaïs: *Statuts*, Paris 1880.

Idem (ed.): *Note sommaire sur le dernier projet de dessèchement. Approuvé par le Gouvernement hellénique, et sur l'état actuel des travaux*, Paris 1884a.

Idem (ed.): *Renseignements sur la marche des travaux du Lac Copaïs soumis à M. Léonce Vée*, Arbitre, Paris 1884b.

Idem (ed.): *Renseignements sur la situation actuelle des travaux (mai 1884)*, Paris 1884c.

Idem (ed.): *Rapport du Conseil d'administration. Assemblée Générale du 19 Juillet 1886*, Paris 1886.

Idem (ed.): *Rapport du Conseil d'administration. Assemblée générale extraordinaire du 5 Mai 1887*, Paris 1887.

Congost, R./Santos, R. (eds.): *Contexts of Property in Europe. The Social Embeddedness of Property Rights in Land in Historical Perspective*, Turnhout, Belgium 2010 (= Rural History in Europe, Vol. 5).

Consiglio, J. A./Martinez Oliva, J. C./ Tortella, G. (eds.): *Banking and Finance in the Mediterranean. A Historical Perspective*, Farnham et al. 2012 (= Studies in Banking and Financial History).

Constantinides, M.: *The Greek Orthodox Church in London*, Oxford 1933.

Corboz, A.: Le Palais Eynard à Genève: un "design" architectural en 1817, in: *Geneva* 23 (1975), pp. 195–275.

Cordella, A.: Ueber eine neue Gesteinbildung [sic!] oder alluviales Schlackenconglomerat, in: *Berg- und Huettenmaennische Zeitung* 23 (1864) 35, pp. 285f.

Idem: *Le Laurium*, Paris 1869.

Idem: *Le Laurium*, Marseille 1871.

Corporation of Foreign Bondholders (ed.): *Thirtieth Annual Report of the Council of Corporation of Foreign Bondholders for the Years 1902–03*, London 1903.

Idem (ed.): *Thirty-first Annual Report of the Council of the Corporation of Foreign Bondholders for the Years 1903–04*, London 1904.

Idem (ed.): *Thirty-second Annual Report of the Council of the Corporation of Foreign Bondholders for the Year 1904–05*, London 1905.

Idem (ed.): *Thirty-seventh Annual Report of the Council of the Corporation of Foreign Bondholders for the Years 1909–10*, London 1910.

Cottrell, P. L.: *Industrial Finance, 1830–1914. The Finance and Organization of English Manufacturing Industry*, London 1980.

Idem: *The Ionian Bank. An Imperial Institution 1839–1864*, Athens 2007.

Idem: *East Meets West: Banking, Commerce and Investment in the Ottoman Empire (Studies in Banking and Financial History)*, Aldershot et al. 2008a.

Idem (ed.): A Survey of European Investment in Turkey, 1854–1914: Banks and the Finance of the State and Railway Construction, in: idem (ed.): *East Meets West: Banking, Commerce and Investment in the Ottoman Empire*, Aldershot et al. 2008b, pp. 59–95 (= Studies in Banking and Financial History).

Coulson, M.: *The History of Mining. The Events, Technology and People Involved in the Industry That Forged the Modern World*, Petersfield, Hampshire 2012.

Crue, F. de/Brocher, J.: *Genève et la Société de lecture (1818–1918)*, Genève 1919.

Cullis, J. B./Lewis, A./Winnett, A.: Paying to Be Good? UK Ethical Investments, in: *Kyklos* 45 (1992) 1, pp. 3–24.

D'Aoust, V.: *Percement de l'isthme de Corinthe. Extrait du Bulletin de la Société de Géographie*, Paris 1881.

D'Eichthal, E. (ed.): *La langue grecque. Mémoires & notices 1864–1884; précédé d'une notice sur les services rendus, par M. G. d'Eichthal à la Grèce et aux études grecques par le Marquis de Queux de Saint-Hilaire*, Paris 1887.

Idem: *John Stuart Mill: Correspondance inédite avec Gustave d'Eichthal. 1828–1842 et 1864–1871*, Paris 1898 (= Bibliothèque de philosophie contemporaine).

D'Eichthal, G.: *Lettres à MM. les députés composant la commission du budget, sur la permanence du système de crédit public et sur la nécessité de renoncer à toute espèce de remboursement des créances sur l'État*, Paris 1829.

Idem: Lettre à un banquier, in: *L'Organisateur*, Paris, 23.10.1830.

Idem: Les Deux Mondes, in: D. Urquhart (ed.): *La Turquie, ses ressources, son organisation municipale, son commerce, suivis de considérations sur l'état du commerce anglais dans le Levant*, Paris 1836, pp. 3–105.

Idem: *Lettres sur la race noire et la race blanche*, Paris 1839.

Idem: *De l'unité européenne*, Paris 1840.

Idem: *Discours d'inauguration d'un nouveau local de la Société ethnologique de Paris*, Paris 1847.

Idem: La vie humaine ou les âges de la vie, in: *Le Magasin pittoresque*, mai 1852, pp. 148.

Idem: *Les Évangiles. Première partie, examen critique et comparatif des trois premiers Évangiles*, Paris 1863a.

Idem: Étude sur la philosophie de la justice: Platon, in: *Revue germanique et française*, 01.3.1863b.

Idem: *Notice sur la fondation et le développement de l'Association pour l'encouragement des études grecques en France (Avril 1867–avril 1877)*, Paris 1877.

Idem: *Socrate et notre temps: théologie de Socrate, dogme de la Providence*, Paris 1881.

Idem: Voltaire et la question grecque. Paru dans le journal Le Temps 9.3.1869, in: E. d'*Eichthal* (ed.): *La langue grecque. Mémoires & notices 1864–1884; précédé d'une notice sur les services rendus, par M. G. d'Eichthal à la Grèce et aux études grecques par le Marquis de Queux de Saint-Hilaire*, Paris 1887, pp. 321–331.

Idem: *Οικονομική και κοινωνική κατάσταση στην Ελλάδα μετά το 1821 [Economic and Social Circumstances in Greece after 1821]*, ed. by Παπαδόπουλος, Θ. Χ. [Papadopoulos, Th. Ch.], Athens 1974.

Idem: British Society in 1828. Gustave d'Eichthal's Journal and Notes, in: B. M. Ratcliffe (ed.): *A French Sociologist Looks at Britain. Gustave d'Eichthal and British Society in 1828*, Manchester 1977, pp. 13–108 (= University Manchester: Faculty of Arts, Publications, Vol. 22).

D'Ideville, H.: *Journal d'un diplomate en Allemagne et en Grèce. Notes intimes pouvant servir à l'histoire du second Empire. Dresden – Athènes 1867–1868*, Paris 2nd ed. 1875.

Dabag, M. et al. (eds.): *Handbuch der Mediterranistik. Systematische Mittelmeerforschung und disziplinäre Zugänge*, Paderborn 2014.

Dahlem, M.: *Die Professionalisierung des Bankbetriebs. Studien zur institutionellen Struktur deutscher Banken im Kaiserreich 1871–1914*, Essen 2009 (= Bochumer Schriften zur Unternehmens- und Industriegeschichte, Vol. 17).

Dakin, D.: *British and American Philhellenes during the War of Greek Independence, 1821–1833*, Salonica 1955.

Idem: British Intelligence of Events in Greece, 1824–1827: A Documentary Collection, in: *Δελτίον της Ιστορικής και Εθνολογικής Εταιρείας της Ελλάδος* [Bulletin of the Historical and Ethnological Society of Greece] 13 (1959), pp. 1–184.

Dale, R.: *'Napoleon is Dead'. Lord Cochrane and the Great Stock Exchange Scandal*, Stroud 2006.

Dalleggio, E.: *Les Philhellènes et la guerre de l'indépendance. 138 Lettres inédites de J. Orlando et A. Louriotis*, Athènes 1949 (= Collection de l'Institut français d'Athènes, Vol. 19).

Daskalov, R./Mishkova, D.: "Forms without Substance": Debates on the Transfer of Western Models to the Balkans, in: R. D. Daskalov/D. Miškova (eds.): *Transfers of Political Ideologies and Institutions*, Leiden 2014, pp. 1–97 (= Entangled Histories of the Balkans, Vol. 2).

Davis, L. E./Huttenback, R. A.: *Mammon and the Pursuit of Empire. The Political Economy of British Imperialism, 1860–1912*, Cambridge 1986 (= Interdisciplinary Perspectives on Modern History).

Davis, P.: Backhouse Family (per. c.1770–1945), in: *ODNB*, Oxford 2004, doi:10.1093/ref:odnb/56500.

Davis, R. W.: *The English Rothschilds*, Chapel Hill NC 1983.

Dawson, F. G.: *The First Latin American Debt Crisis. The City of London and the 1822–25 Loan Bubble*, New Haven CT 1990.

Daxhammer, R./Facsar, M.: *Behavioral Finance. Verhaltenswissenschaftliche Finanzmarktforschung im Lichte begrenzt rationaler Marktteilnehmer*, Konstanz/Munich 2012 (= UTB, Vol. 8504).

Decorzant, Y./Flores, J. H.: Public Borrowing in Harsh Times: The League of Nations Loans Revisited, *IFCS - Working Papers in Economic History, Universidad Carlos III de Madrid, Instituto Figuerola*, July 2012, https://ideas.repec.org/p/cte/whrepe/wp12-07.html [5.5.15].

Défourneaux, M.: Complot maçonnique et complot jésuitique, in: *Annales historiques de la Révolution française* 37 (1965), pp. 170–186.

Demont, V.: *Pourquoi oublier le profit? Cloisonnements de l'information et rationalité marchande dans le groupe Briers-Heusch-von Cassel (1620–1633)*, XVIe Journées d'histoire de la comptabilité et du management, Nantes, 23–25 mars 2011 (Unpublished Manuscript).

Derix, S.: Transnationale Familien, in: J. Dülffer/W. Loth (eds.): *Dimensionen internationaler Geschichte*, Munich 2012, pp. 335–352 (= Studien zur Internationalen Geschichte, Vol. 30).

Δερμάτης, Γ. Ν. [Dermatis, G. N.]: *Λαύρειο το μαύρο φως. Η μεταλλευτική και μεταλλουργική βιομηχανία στο Λαύρειο 1860–1917: Ελληνική και ευρωπαϊκή διάσταση* [Laurion the Black Light. The Metallic and Metallurgical Industry in Laurion 1860–1917. Greek and European Dimension], Athens 2003.

Idem: Η μεταλλευτική και μεταλλουργική βιομηχανία του Λαυρίου, 1865–1990. Το μαύρο φως [The Metallurgical and Metallic Industry of Laurion 1865–1990. The Black Light], in: Γ. Καραγιάννης [G. Karagiánnis] et al. (eds.): *Λαυρεωτικά 1869–1873: Η πρώτη αρπαγή δημόσιας περιουσίας. Το ναυάγιο του χρηματιστηριακού Ελντοράντο* [Laureotika 1869–1873. The First Deprivation of Public Property. The Shipwreck of the Stock Exchange Eldorado], Athens 2011, pp. 155–192.

Δερτιλής, Γ. Β. [Dertilis, G. B.]: *Το ζήτημα των τραπεζών (1871–1873). Οικονομική και πολιτική διαμάχη στην Ελλάδα του 19^{ου} αιώνα* [The Central Bank Question (1871–1873). Economic and Political Conflict in Nineteenth-Century Greece], Athens 1980.

Idem (ed.): *Banquiers, usuriers et paysans: réseaux de crédit et stratégies du capital en Grèce 1780–1930*, Paris 1988 (= Histoire contemporaine).
Idem: Entrepreneurs grecs: trois générations, 1770–1900, in: A. Franco/R. Daniel (eds.): *Cultures et formations négociantes*, Paris 1995, pp. 110–129.
Idem: Dette publique et dépenses militaires: la Grèce et la question d'Orient, in: J. Andreau/G. Béaur/J.-Y. Grenier (eds.): *La dette publique dans l'histoire. "Les journées du Centre de recherches historiques" des 26, 27 et 28 novembre 2001*, Paris 2006, pp. 395–422 (= Histoire économique et financière de la France. Animation de la recherche).
Idem: *Ιστορία του ελληνικού κράτους 1830–1920* [History of the Greek Government 1830–1920], Athens 5th ed. 2009.
Dessaux, N./Révillion, S./Delchambre, S.: Stratégies d'exploitation et mutations du paysage dans la vallée de la haute Deûle (Nord): l'exemple du marais de Seclin du XIIIe au XIXe siècle, in: *Revue du Nord: Nord de la France, Belgique, Pays-Bas* 80 (1998), pp. 326–327, 531–571.
Diesbach, G. de: *Ferdinand de Lesseps*, Paris 1998.
Dieterich, K.: *Aus Briefen und Tagebüchern zum deutschen Philhellenismus (1821–1828)*, Hamburg 1928 (= Historisch-literarische Schriftenreihe der deutsch-griechischen Gesellschaft, Vol. 2).
Dilley, A. R.: Empire and Risk: Edwardian Financiers, Australia, and Canada, c. 1899–1914, in: *Business and Economic History On-Line* 7 (2009), pp. 1–12.
Idem: *Finance, Politics, and Imperialism. Australia, Canada, and the City of London, c. 1896–1914*, Basingstoke/Hampshire 2012 (= Cambridge Imperial and Post-colonial Studies Series).
Idem: Financial Centres as Fields: Reflections on Habitus and Risk in the Nineteenth and Twenthieth Centuries, in: K. Schönhärl (ed.): *Decision Making, Confidence and Risk Management in Banks from Early Modernity to the 20th Century*, Basingstoke/Hampshire et al. 2017, pp. 125–145 (= Palgrave Studies in the History of Finance).
Dimakis, J.: La "Société de la morale chrétienne" de Paris et son action en faveur des Grecs lors de l'insurrection de 1821, in: *Balkan Studies* 7 (1966), pp. 27–48.
Idem: Le Philhellénisme en Europe pendant l'insurrection Grecque et le rôle de la presse, in: *Etudes slaves et est-européennes: revue universitaire* 13 (1968), pp. 46–53.
Dimou, N.: *Über das Unglück, ein Grieche zu sein*, Munich 2012.
Divall, C.: Railway Imperialisms, Railway Nationalisms, in: M. Burri/K. T. Elsasser/D. Gugerli (eds.): *Die Internationalität der Eisenbahn 1850–1970*, Zurich 2003, pp. 195–209 (= Interferenzen, Vol. 7).
Dolezal, H.: Heldreich, Theodor Heinrich Hermann von, in: *NDB*, 8 (1969), p. 467, http://www.deutsche biographie.de/sfz29463.html;jsessionid=EC7C519B-FA9654D823000EE72CB03284 [21.1.2020].
Donnelly, J.: Brotherton, Edward Allen, Baron Brotherton (1856–1930), in: *ODNB*, Oxford 2004, doi:10.1093/ref:odnb/46948.
Δραγούμης, Σ. Ν. [Dragoumis, S. N.]: *Οι ξένοι δανεισταί, η χώρα και το νόμισμα: Πολιτική μελέτη* [The Foreign Creditors, the Country and the Currency. Political Studies], Athens 1901.
Driault, É./Lhéritier, M.: *Histoire diplomatique de la Grèce de 1821 à nos jours. Tome II: Le Règne d'Othon – La Grande Idée (1830–1862)*, Paris 1925.

Δρίτσα, Μ. [Dritsa, M.]: Πολιτισμική ιδιαιτερότητα και επιχειρήσεις: Η περίπτωση των εβραϊκών δικτύων [Cultural Specialties and Businesses: The Case of the Jewish Networks], in: Εταιρεία Σπουδών Νεοελληνικού Πολιτισμού και Γενικής Παιδείας [Society for Modern Greek Culture and General Education] (ed.): *Ο ελληνικός εβραϊσμός* [The Greek Hebraism], Athens 1998, pp. 303–344.

Idem: Monetary Modernisation in Greece: Bimetallism or Gold Standard (1833–1920), in: *The Journal of European Economic History* 28 (1999), pp. 9–48.

Idem: Η Ελλάδα και ο ευρωπαϊκός οικονομικός τύπος κατά την Τρικουπική περίοδο: Απαρχές της πολιτικής επικοινωνίας [Greece and the European Financial Press in the Tricoupis Era: Beginnings of Political Communication], in: Κ. Αρώνη-Τσίχλη [K. Aroni-Tsixli]/Λ. Τρίχα [L. Tricha] (eds.): *Ο Χαρίλαος Τρικούπης και η εποχή του. Πολιτικές επιδιώξεις και κοινωνικές συνθήκες* [Charilaos Trikoupis and His Time. Political Aims and Social Conditions], Athens 2000, pp. 63–88.

Drucker, L.: *An Appeal to the Governments and Monarchs of Europe: A Letter to the Right Honourable J. Gennadius*, Leiden 1877.

Dücker, F. F.: *Die griechische Laurion-Angelegenheit. Auszug aus der Norddeutschen Allgemeinen Zeitung Nr. 251–253, 1872*, Kassel 1873.

Duggan, B. P.: *Saluki. The Desert Hound and the English Travelers Who Brought It to the West*, Jefferson NC 2009.

Dünki, R.: *Aspekte des Philhellenismus in der Schweiz 1821–1830*, Bern et al. 1984.

Düring-Ulmenstein, U. v.: Simon von Eichthal – Mitbegründer der Bayerischen Hypotheken- und Wechselbank, in: R. A. Müller (ed.): *Unternehmer – Arbeitnehmer. Lebensbilder aus der Frühzeit der Industrialisierung in Bayern*, Munich 2nd ed. 1987, pp. 116–122 (= Veröffentlichungen zur bayerischen Geschichte und Kultur, Vol. 7).

Durlauf, S. N.: Path Dependence, in: idem/L. E. Blume (eds.): *The New Palgrave Dictionary of Economics*, Basingstoke Hampshire 2008, p. 318ff.

Durocher, L.: *Le percement de l'isthme de Corinthe. Avec 64 dessins par A. Vignola*, Paris 1893.

Edelstein, M.: *Overseas Investment in the Age of High Imperialism. The United Kingdom, 1850–1914*, London 1982.

Edwards, R. D.: Wilson, James, in: *ODNB*, Oxford 2004, doi:10.1093/ref:odnb/29660.

Erler, M.: *Friedrich Lübker's Reallexikon des classischen Alterthums für Gymnasien*, Leipzig 1882.

Eiselen, F.: *Festschrift zur Eröffnung des neuen Gebäudes der Musterschule am 11. October 1880. Geschichte des deutschen Schulwesens in Frankfurt am Main bis zur Gründung der Musterschule; die ersten Jahre dieser Anstalt selbst und ihre beiden ersten Oberlehrer*, Frankfurt 1880.

Eldem, E.: Ottoman Financial Integration with Europe: Foreign Loans, the Ottoman Bank and the Ottoman Public Debt, in: *European Review* 13 (2005) 3, pp. 431–445.

Elo, M./ Minto-Coy, I. (eds.): *Diaspora Networks in International Business. Perspectives for Understanding and Managing Diaspora Business and Resources, Contributions to Management Science*, Cham 2019.

Engel, A.: Zank um Zwiebeln – Kontroversen um den agrarischen Börsenterminhandel in den USA (1954–72), in: *Bankhistorisches Archiv* 39 (2013) 1, pp. 40–58.

Engel, E.: *Griechische Frühlingstage*, Jena 2nd ed. 1887.

Engerman, S. L./Davis, L. E. (eds.): *Finance, Intermediaries, and Economic Development*, Cambrige/New York 2003.

Erlanger, É. B.: History, Benefits and Prospects of the Tunnel: Lecture to British Soldiers in Paris by Baron Emile d'Erlanger, Chairman, Channel Tunnel Company, Ltd., in: N. N. (ed.): *The Channel Tunnel. London and the Tunnel. International Parliamentary Commercial Conference – The Tunnel in Its Commercial Aspects. History, Benefits and Prospects of the Tunnel. From London to the Cape by Rail*, London 1918, pp. 65–82.

Idem: *Sappho ou Le Dernier Jour de l'Académie de Lesbos (Pièce en un acte, en vers)*, London 1935.

Idem: *Quelques souvenirs: My English souvenir*, privately printed in 1978, s.l. (available at Schröder's Archive, London).

Erlanger, É. de: *Mémoire sur la créance de M. M. Émile Erlanger und Cie envers le gouvernement Tunisien*, Paris 1869.

Esteves, R. P.: *The Belle Epoque of International Finance. French Capital Exports, 1880–1914*, 2011, doi:10.2139/ssrn.2024984.

Etzioni, A.: *The Moral Dimension. Toward a New Economics*, New York 1988.

Eulambio, M. S.: *The National Bank of Greece. A History of the Financial and Economic Evolution of Greece*, Athens 1924.

Exertzoglou, H.: The Development of a Greek Ottoman Bourgeoisie: Investment Patterns in the Ottoman Empire, 1850–1914, in: D. Gondicas/C. Issawi (eds.): *Ottoman Greeks in the Age of Nationalism. Politics, Economy, and Society in the Nineteenth Century*, Princeton, NJ 1999, pp. 89–114.

Eynard, J. G.: *Journal de Jean-Gabriel Eynard au Congrès de Vienne; publ. avec une introduction et des notes par Édouard Chapuisat*, Genève et Paris 1914a.

Idem: *Les Cent-Jours, avec une introduction et des notes par Édouard Chapuisat*, Genève et Paris 1914b.

Idem: *Der tanzende Kongreß. Tagebuch Jean Gabriel Eynards. Übersetzt aus dem Französischen von Karl Soll*, Berlin 1923.

Eynard, P.: *Le Palais Eynard*, Genève 1986.

Fahrmeir, A.: *Revolutionen und Reformen. Europa 1789–1850*, Munich 2010 (= Beck'sche Reihe, Vol. 1985).

Fallmerayer, J. P.: *Geschichte der Halbinsel Morea waehrend des Mittelalters. Ein historischer Versuch*, Stuttgart/Tubingen 1830.

Fargette, G.: *Émile et Isaac Pereire. L'esprit d'entreprise au XIXe siècle*, Paris 2013.

Farina, F.: Giovan Battista Serpieri (1832–1897). Un visionario riminese dell' Ottocento tra finanza e industria internazionali, in: *Romagna arte e storia: rivista quadrimestrale di cultura* 33 (2013) 97, pp. 23–60.

Faure, P.: Eichthal, Adolphe Seligman d', in: *DBF*, 12 (1970), Sp. 1162–1163.

Fehrenbach, E.: *Vom Ancien Régime zum Wiener Kongress*, Munich 4th ed. 2001 (= Oldenbourg Grundriss der Geschichte, Vol. 12).

Feis, H.: *Europe the World's Banker 1870–1914. An Account of European Foreign Investment and the Connection of World Finance With Diplomacy before the War*, Clifton NJ 1974 (1st ed. 1930) (= Reprints of Economic Classics).

Feldman, G. D.: Is the Sun Setting on Banking History as We Have Known and Practised It?, in: E. Green/M. Pohle-Fraser (eds.): *The Human Factor in Banking*

History. Entrepreneurship, Organization, Management and Personnel, Athens 2008, pp. 281–295.

Felisini, D.: *Alessandro Torlonia. The Pope's Banker*, Cambridge 2016 (= Palgrave Studies in the History of Finance).

Felis-Rota, M.: Un Paseo por la literatura sobre capital social desde una perspectiva económica, in: *Revista de Historia Económica. Journal of Iberian and Latin American Economic History* 29 (2011) 3, pp. 461–475.

Ferguson, N.: *Die Geschichte der Rothschilds: Propheten des* Geldes, Vol. 1: 1798–1848, Vol. 2: 1849–1999, Stuttgart 2nd ed. 2002.

Ferrari, E. D.: *In the Service of the Tsar: The Autobiography of Count John A. Capodistrias*, New York 1980.

Ferris, D. S.: *Silent Urns. Romanticism, Hellenism, Modernity*, Stanford CA 2000 (= Cultural Memory in the Present).

Fiedler, K. G.: *Reise durch alle Theile des Koenigreichs Griechenland im Auftrage der Königlichen Griechischen Regierung in den Jahren 1834–1837*, Leipzig 1840.

Finger, J.: Spekulation für Jedermann und Jedefrau. Kleinanleger, Frauen und der graue Kapitalmarkt in Paris in der zweiten Hälfte des 19. Jahrhunderts, in: *Archiv für Sozialgeschichte* 56 (2016), pp. 139–168.

Fisch, S./Rudloff, W. (eds.): *Experten und Politik: wissenschaftliche Politikberatung in geschichtlicher Perspektive*, Berlin 2004.

Flandreau, M./Flores, J. H.: Bonds and Brands: Foundations of Sovereign Debt Markets, 1820–1830, in: *The Journal of Economic History* 69 (2009) 3, pp. 646–684.

Fletcher, S.: Lead Mining in Spain in the 19th Century: Spanish Industry or British Adventure?, in: *Bulletin of the Peak District Mines Historical Society* 11 (1991) 4, pp. 195–202.

Foad, H.: Familiarity Bias, in: H. K. Baker/J. R. Nofsinger. (eds.): *Behavioral Finance. Investors, Corporations, and Markets*, Hoboken NJ 2010, pp. 277–294 (= The Robert W. Kolb Series in Finance).

Forbes, W.: *Behavioral Finance*, Chichester 2009.

Foreign Office: *Livre bleu: Further Communications Relating to the Souvereignty of Greece. I – Papers Deliverd to Lord Aberdeen on the 7th Juni 1830, by Order of His Royal Higness Prince Leopold. II – Despatch from his Majesty's Ambassador at Paris, Transmitting Communications from M. Eynard*, London 1830.

Fornaro, P.: *István Türr: una biografia politica*, Messina 2004.

Foucault, M.: *Essential Works of Foucault 1954–1984*, ed. by J. D. Faubion, trans. by R. Hurley et al., New York 2000.

Idem: *Schriften in vier Bänden. Dits et Ecrits. Vol. III: 1976–1979*, ed. by D. Defert/E. François, Frankfurt 2003.

Frangakis-Syrett, E.: Monoculture in Nineteenth-Century Greece and the Port City of Patras, in: *Journal of Hellenic Diaspora* 20 (1994) 2, pp. 9–34.

Franghiadis, A.: *Peasant Agriculture and Export Trade: Currant Viticulture in Southern Greece, 1830–1893*. Thesis Florence 1990 (Unpublished Manuscript).

Φραγκιάδης, A. [Franghiadis, A.]: Αγροτική οικονομία και εξωτερικό εμπόριο [Agriculture and International Trade], in: Κ. Π. Κωστής/Σ. Δ. Πετμεζάς [K. P. Kostis/S. D. Petmezas] (eds.): *Η ανάπτυξη της ελληνικής οικονομίας κατά τον 19ο αιώνα (1830–1914)* [The Development of the Greek Economy in the 19th Century (1830–1914)], Athens 2006, pp. 153–174.

Frankfurt am Main: *Staats- und Adreß-Handbuch der Freien Stadt Frankfurt*, Frankfurt 1847–1866.

Freris, A. F.: *The Greek Economy in the 20th Century*, London et al. 1986.

Frevert, U.: Vertrauen in historischer Perspektive, in: R. Schmalz-Bruns/R. Zintl (eds.): *Politisches Vertrauen. Soziale Grundlagen reflexiver Kooperation*, Baden-Baden 2002, pp. 39–59 (= Schriftenreihe der Sektion Politische Theorien und Ideengeschichte in der Deutschen Vereinigung für Politische Wissenschaft, Vol. 2).

Idem: Vertrauen - eine historische Spurensuche, in: Idem (ed.): *Vertrauen. Historische Annäherungen*, Göttingen 2003a, pp. 7–66.

Idem (ed.): *Vertrauen. Historische Annäherungen*, Göttingen 2003b.

Idem: *Vertrauensfragen. Eine Obsession der Moderne*, Munich 2013 (= Beck'sche Reihe, Vol. 6104).

Idem/Schmidt, A. (eds.): *Geschichte, Emotionen und visuelle Medien*, Göttingen 2011 (= Geschichte und Gesellschaft, Vol. 37).

Friedrich, R.: *König Otto von Griechenland. Die bayerische Regentenschaft in Nauplia 1833/34*, Munich 2015.

Fry, M.: George Canning (1770–1827), in: R. Eccleshall/G. Walker (eds.): *Biographical Dictionary of British Prime Ministers*, London 1998.

Fukuyama, F.: *Trust. The Social Virtues and the Creation of Prosperity*, New York 1995.

Idem: Differing Disciplinary Perspectives on the Origins of Trust, in: *Boston University Law Review* 81 (2001) 3, pp. 479–494.

Galassi, F. L./Newton, L.: *My Word Is My Bond: Reputation as Collateral in Nineteenth Century English Provincial Banking*, Warwick Economic Research Papers No 599, 2001, http://wrap.warwick.ac.uk/1583/ [21.1.2020].

Gall, L.: Die europäischen Mächte und der Balkan im 19. Jahrhundert, in: R. Melville (ed.): *Der Berliner Kongreß von 1878. Die Politik der Großmächte und die Probleme der Modernisierung in Südosteuropa in der zweiten Hälfte des 19. Jahrhunderts*, Wiesbaden 1982, pp. 1–16.

Garrigós Sastre, J. J.: *El tren de los ingleses*, Madrid 2014.

Gaschke, J.: *Hellas ... in One Living Picture. Britische Reisende und die visuelle Aneignung Griechenlands im frühen 19. Jahrhundert*, Frankfurt et al. 2006 (= Europäische Hochschulschriften/28, Vol. 422).

Geiger, L.: Geschichte der Juden in Berlin, Part II: Anmerkungen, Ausführungen und Urkundliche Beilagen, Berlin 1871, in: idem (ed.): *Geschichte der Juden in Berlin. Festschrift zur zweiten Säkular-Feier. Anmerkungen, Ausführungen, urkundliche Beilagen und zwei Nachträge (1871–1890)*, Nachdruck Leipzig 1988, pp. 1–207.

Geiss, I.: Der Berliner Kongress. 13. Juni – 13. Juli 1878, in: K. O. v. Aretin (ed.): *Bismarcks Außenpolitik und der Berliner Kongress*, Wiesbaden 1978, pp. 69–105.

Gennadios, I.: *The Greek Loans of 1824 and 1825: Their Conversion and Settlement and the Dutch Protest*, London 1880.

Georgiadès, D.: *Le développement économique de la Grèce contemporaine. Extrait de l'Économiste français du 6 février 1892*, Athènes 1892.

Idem: *La Grèce économique et financière en 1893 – Réponse à M. E. F. G. Law, délégué du gouvernement anglais*, Paris 1893.

Idem: *La Grèce et ses créanciers avec introduction de Paul Beauregard* (Articles publiés dans le Monde Economique les 22 et 29 septembre et les 6, 13 et 20 octobre 1894), Paris 1894.

Idem: *Les jeux olympiques à Athènes* (Extrait du Monde Economique des 9 et 16 mai 1896), Paris 1896.
Idem: *Les associations coopératives helléniques à la fin du XVIIIe siècle et les sociétés par actions modernes en Grèce* (Extrait du Monde Economique des 5, 12 et 19 octobre 1907), Paris 1907.
Gerschenkron, A.: Economic Backwardness in Historical Perspective, in: idem (ed.): *Economic Backwardness in Historical Perspective. A Book of Essays*, Cambridge 1966, pp. 5–30.
Gerster, B.: L'Isthme de Corinthe. Tentatives de percement dans l'Antiquité, in: *Bulletin de correspondance hellénique* 8 (1884) 1, pp. 225–232.
Idem: *L'Isthme de Corinthe et son percement*, Budapest 1896.
Geyikdağı, V. N.: *Foreign Investment in the Ottoman Empire. International Trade and Relations 1854–1914*, London/New York 2011 (= Library of Ottoman Studies, Vol. 27).
Γιαννίτσης, Α. Κ. [Giangitsis, A. K.]: Οι ξένες άμεσες επενδύσεις και η διαμόρφωση της νεοελληνικής οικονομίας (1830–1939) [The Foreign Direct Investments and the Formation of the Greek Economy (1830–1939)], in: *Επιθεώρηση Κοινωνικών Ερευνών* [The Greek Review of Social Research] 80 (1977), pp. 234–253.
Gibbs, H. H.: *Letter to the Most Honorable the Marquess of Salisbury on the Depreciation of Silver*, London 1876.
Gigerenzer, G./Selten, R. (eds.): *Bounded Rationality. The Adaptive Toolbox*, Cambridge 2001a.
Idem: Rethinking Rationality, in: Idem (eds.): *Bounded Rationality. The Adaptive Toolbox*, Cambridge 2001b, pp. 1–12.
Gille, B.: *La banque et le crédit en France de 1815 à 1848*, Paris 1959 (=Mémoires et documents, Vol. 14).
Gillespie, A.: The Intersubjective Dynamics of Trust, Distrust and Manipulation, in: I. Marková (ed.): *Trust and Distrust. Sociocultural Perspectives*, Charlotte NC 2008, pp. 273–289 (= Advances in Cultural Psychology).
Gironés, E. O./Viejobueno, C. D.: Spain's Almadén Mine: 2000 Years of Solitude, in: G. McMahon/F. Remy (eds.): *Large Mines and the Community. Socioeconomic and Environmental Effects in Latin America*, Canada/Spain/Washington, DC 2001, pp. 199–222.
Glasemann, H.-G.: *Die Finanzgeschichte des Kanals von Korinth. Historische Wertpapiere 1882–1977*, Norderstedt 2010.
Glaser, M./Weber, M.: Overconfidence, in: H. K. Baker/J. R. Nofsinger (eds.): *Behavioral Finance. Investors, Corporations, and Markets*, Hoboken NJ 2010, pp. 241–258 (= The Robert W. Kolb Series in Finance).
Goey, F. de: *Consuls and the Institutions of Global Capitalism, 1783–1914*, London 2014.
Gournaris, B. C.: Greco-Turkish Railway Connection: Illusions and Bargains in the Late Nineteenth Century Balkans, in: *Balkan Studies* 30 (1989), pp. 311–332.
Gourvish, T.: Project Finance and the Archives of Entrepreneurship. The Channel Tunnel, 1957–1975, in: E. Green/M. Pohle-Fraser (eds.): *The Human Factor in Banking History. Entrepreneurship, Organization, Management and Personnel*, Athens 2008, pp. 45–74.
Grass, G.: Europas Schande, in: *Süddeutsche Zeitung*, 26.5.2012.

Green, E./Pohle-Fraser, M. (eds.): *The Human Factor in Banking History. Entrepreneurship, Organization, Management and Personnel*, Athens 2008a.

Idem: Introduction, in: idem/M. Pohle-Fraser (eds.): *The Human Factor in Banking History. Entrepreneurship, Organization, Management and Personnel*, Athens 2008b, pp. 13–20.

Greene, J.: *The Canal Builders. Making America's Empire at the Panama Canal*, New York 2009 (= The Penguin History of American Life).

Gregory, C. E.: *A Concise History of Mining, Lisse*, Netherlands/Exton, PA 2001.

Greul, R.: *Die lateinische Münz-Union. Eine völkerrechtsgeschichtliche Studie*, Berlin 1926 (= Völkerrechtsfragen, Vol. 16).

Gross, S. G.: *Export Empire. German Soft Power in Southeastern Europe, 1890–1945*, Cambridge 2015.

Grunwald, K.: *"Türkenhirsch". A Study of Baron Maurice de Hirsch, Entrepreneur and Philanthropist*, Jerusalem 1966.

Gudermann, R.: *Morastwelt und Paradies. Ökonomie und Ökologie in der Landwirtschaft am Beispiel der Meliorationen in Westfalen und Brandenburg (1830–1880)*, Paderborn/Wien u.a 2000 (= Forschungen zur Regionalgeschichte, Vol. 35).

Guex, S./Mazbouri, M.: Historiographie des Banken- und Finanzplatzes Schweiz im 19. und 20. Jahrhundert, in: S. Bott/G. Hürlimann (eds.): *Wirtschaftsgeschichte in der Schweiz. Eine historiografische Skizze*, Zürich 2010, pp. 203–228.

Gunnar, H.: Der griechische Unabhängigkeitskrieg und der Philhellenismus, in: A. Noe (ed.): *Der Philhellenismus in der westeuropäischen Literatur. 1780–1830*, Amsterdam et al. 1994, pp. 17–72 (= Internationale Forschungen zur allgemeinen und vergleichenden Literaturwissenschaft, Vol. 6).

Hahn, A.: Risiko und Gefahr, in: G. v. Graevenitz/O. Marquard/M. Christen (eds.): *Kontingenz*, Munich 1998, pp. 49–54.

Hahn, Fr. von: Hahn, Johann Georg von, in: *ADB*, 10 (1879), pp. 366–369.

Hannell, D.: Lord Palmerston and the 'Don Pacifico Affair' of 1850: The Ionian Connection, in: *European History Quarterly* 19 (1989) 4, pp. 495–508.

Harlaftis, G.: Mapping the Greek Maritime Diaspora from the Early Eighteenth to the Late Twentieth Centuries, in: I. B. McCabe et al. (eds.): *Diaspora Entrepreneurial Networks: Four Centuries of History*, Oxford 2005, pp. 147–171.

Hartmann, A. V.: *Reflexive Politik im sozialen Raum. Politische Eliten in Genf zwischen 1760 und 1841*, Mainz 2003 (= Historische Beiträge zur Elitenforschung, Vol. 3).

Hartmann, M./Offe, C. (eds.): *Vertrauen. Die Grundlage des sozialen Zusammenhalts*, Frankfurt/Main 2001 (= Theorie und Gesellschaft, Vol. 50).

Harwood, J.: Research and Extension in Political Context: Rural Unrest and the Origins of the Prussian Chambers of Agriculture, in: N. Vivier (ed.): *The State and Rural Societies. Policy and Education in Europe, 1750–2000*, Turnhout 2008, pp. 135–157 (= Rural History in Europe, Vol. 4).

Haupert, M.: Panic of 1825, in: D. Glasner (ed.): *Business Cycles and Depressions. An Encyclopedia*, New York 1997, pp. 511–513 (= Garland Reference Library of Social Science, Vol. 505).

Haupt, H.-G./Hinrichs, E./Martens, S.: *Kleine Geschichte Frankreichs*, Stuttgart 2006.

Hauser, C.: *Anfänge bürgerlicher Organisation. Philhellenismus und Frühliberalismus in Südwestdeutschland*, Göttingen 1990 (= Kritische Studien zur Geschichtswissenschaft, Vol. 87).

Hautcoeur, P.-C./Riva, A./White, E. N.: Floating a "Lifeboat": The Banque de France and the Crisis of 1889, in: *Journal of Monetary Economics* 65 (2014), pp. 104–119.

Hegel, G. W. F.: *Grundlinien der Philosophie des Rechts*, Berlin 1821.

Heilbrunn, R.: Bismarcks blinder Hofjude, in: *Jahrbuch des Instituts für Deutsche Geschichte* 10 (1981), pp. 283–317.

Heine, J. G. (ed.): *Papers Relating to the Third Instalment of the Greek Loan 1835, 1836*, London 1836.

Henrich, J. et al.: Group Report: What Is the Role of Culture in Bounded Rationality?, in: G. Gigerenzer/R. Selten (eds.): *Bounded Rationality. The Adaptive Toolbox*, Cambridge 2001, pp. 343–359.

Herodot: *Historien*, ed. and trans. by Josef Feix, Düsseldorf 2001.

Hertner, P.: German Banks Abroad Before 1914, in: G. Jones (ed.): *Banks as Multinationals*, London 1990, pp. 99–119.

Idem: Foreign Capital in the Italian Banking Sector, in: R. Cameron/V. I. Bovykin (eds.): *International Banking, 1870–1914*, New York 1991, pp. 345–350.

Idem: The Balkan Railways. International Capital and Banking from the End of the Nineteenth Century until the Outbraek of the First World War, in: G. D. Feldman/idem (eds.): *Finance and Modernization. A Transnational and Transcontinental Perspective for the Nineteenth and Twenthieth Centuries*, Farnham 2008, pp. 125–154.

Heydenreuter, R. (ed.): *Die erträumte Nation: Griechenlands Wiedergeburt im 19. Jahrhundert. Begleitband zur Ausstellung „Die Erträumte Nation. Griechenlands Wiedergeburt im 19. Jahrhundert. Bilder und Dokumente zu den bayerisch-griechischen Beziehungen im 19. Jahrhundert"*, Munich 1995a.

Idem: Die erträumte Nation. Griechenlands Staatswerdung zwischen Philhellenismus und Militärintervention, in: idem (ed.): *Die erträumte Nation: Griechenlands Wiedergeburt im 19. Jahrhundert. Begleitband zur Ausstellung „Die Erträumte Nation. Griechenlands Wiedergeburt im 19. Jahrhundert. Bilder und Dokumente zu den bayerisch-griechischen Beziehungen im 19. Jahrhundert"*, Munich 1995b, pp. 47–78.

Hicks, G.: Don Pacifico, Democracy, and Danger: The Protectionist Party Critique of British Foreign Policy, 1850–1852, in: *International History Review* 26 (2004) 3, pp. 515–540.

Hildebrand, K.: *Das vergangene Reich. Deutsche Außenpolitik von Bismarck bis Hitler 1871–1945*, Stuttgart 2nd ed. 1996.

Hirschman, A. O.: *Exit, Voice and Loyalty. Responses to Decline in Firms, Organizations, and States*, Cambridge 1970.

Idem: *Entwicklung, Markt und Moral. Abweichende Betrachtungen*, Munich et al. 1989 (= Hanser Anthropologie).

Historical Archives National Bank of Greece (ed.): *Jean-Gabriel Eynard. Visionary and Architect of the Establishment of the National Bank of Greece*, German-Greek Edition, Athens 1999.

Ιστορικό Αρχείο της Εθνικής Τράπεζας [Historical Archives National Bank of Greece]: *Ιστορικό Χρονολόγιο ΕΤΕ (1841–2001), 160 Χρόνια*. [A Chronicle of the National Bank of Greece, 1841–2001. 160 Years of Banking], Athens 2001.

Ιστορικό Αρχείο της Εθνικής Τράπεζας [Historical Archives National Bank of Greece] (ed.): Εθνική Τράπεζα. Μια διαδρομή από το 1841 έως το μέλλον [National Bank. A Passage from 1841 to Future], Athens 2014.

Hobhouse, J. C.: *A Journey through Albania and Other Provinces of Turkey in Europe and Asia to Constantinople, During the Years 1809 to 1810*, London 2nd ed. 1813.

Hoelscher, LaVern: Improvements in Fencing and Drainage in Mid-nineteenth-Century England, in: *Agricultural History* 37 (1963), pp. 75–79.

Hoffritz, J.: Kein Glück mit Athen, in: *Die Zeit*, 12.2.2015.

Hohenlohe-Schillingsfürst, F.-J. z.: *Geneaologisches Handbuch des in Bayern immatrikulierten Adels*, Vol. 4, Neustadt/Aisch/Middle Franconia 1953.

Holborn, H. (ed.): *Aufzeichnungen und Erinnerungen aus dem Leben des Botschafters Joseph Maria von Radowitz*, Vol. 2 (1878–1890), Osnabrück 1967 (Reprint of first ed. 1925).

Holland, R./Markides, D.: *The British and the Hellenes. Struggles for Mastery in the Eastern Mediterranean 1850–1960*, Oxford et al. 2006.

Hollow, M.: Strategic Inertia, Financial Fragility and Organisational Failure: The Case of the Birkbeck Bank, 1870–1911, in: *Business History* (2013), pp. 1–19, doi:10.1080/00076791.2013.839660 [12.2.2014].

Idem: Investigating Attitudes to Risk in British Banking: A Case Study of Barclays' Branch Banking System, c. 1900–80, in: K. Schönhärl (ed.): *Decision Making, Confidence and Risk Management in Banks from Early Modernity to the 20th Century*, Basingstoke/Hampshire et al. 2017, pp. 173–188 (= Palgrave Studies in the History of Finance).

Holtfrerich, C.-L.: *Finanzplatz Frankfurt. Von der mittelalterlichen Messestadt zum europäischen Bankenzentrum*, Munich 1999.

Hooper, S. G.: *The Finance of Farming in Great Britain*, London 1955.

Hösslin, H. v.: *Hösslin. Daten aus 5 Jahrhunderten*, Augsburg 1990.

Hubler, L.: David Charles Odier, in: *Historisches Lexikon der Schweiz*, http://www.hls-dhs-dss.ch/textes/d/D20516.php [15.4.2011].

Huet, A.: Mémoire sur le Laurium, in: *Mémoires et comptes rendus de la Société des ingénieurs civils* 32 (1879), pp. 731–772.

Hughes, P.: Operational Risk: The Direct Measurement of Exposure and Risk in Bank Operations, in: *Risk Management in Financial Institutions* 1 (2007) 1, pp. 25–43.

Hummert, L.: *Die finanziellen Beziehungen jüdischer Bankiers und Heereslieferanten zum bayerischen Staat in der ersten Hälfte des 19. Jahrhunderts*, Munich 1927.

Iancu, C.: *Bleichröder and Crémieux: The Struggle for the Emancipation of Romanian Jews during the Congress of Berlin.* Unpublished correspondence, 1878–80, Montpellier 1987.

Ilbert, R.: *De Suez à Panama. L'articulation des mondes*, Arles 2010.

Ηλιαδάκης,Τ. [Iliadakis, T.]: *Ο εξωτερικός δανεισμός στη γένεση και εξέλιξη του Νέου Ελληνικού Κράτους 1824–2009* [The Foreign Loans and their Role in the Formation and Development of the Modern Greek State 1834–2009], Athens 2011.

Im Hof, U.: *Geschichte der Schweiz*, Stuttgart 8th ed. 2007 (= Urban-Taschenbücher)

Institute for Balkan Studies, Salonica (ed.): *Der Philhellenismus und die Modernisierung in Griechenland und Deutschland: Erstes Symposium organisiert in Thessaloniki und Volos (am 7. – 10. März 1985)*, Salonica 1986 (= Institute for Balkan Studies, Vol. 207).

Ioannides, S./Minoglou, I. P.: Market-Embedded Clans in Theory and History: Greek Diaspora Trading Companies in the Nineteenth Century, in: *Business and Economic History On-Line* (2004), pp. 1–26, https://thebhc.org/file-download/download/public/470 [10.06.2020].

Ioannidou-Bitsiadou, G.: The Bavarian Loans and Chancellor Bismarck's Intervention in the Greek-Turkish Dispute Over Greece's Borders (1878–81), in: *Balkan Studies* 34 (1993) 1, pp. 73–83.

Irmscher, J.: Das Antikebild des deutschen Philhellenismus, in: E. Konstantinou (ed.): *Die Rezeption der Antike und der europäische Philhellenismus*, Frankfurt 1998, pp. 121–138 (= Philhellenische Studien, Vol. 7).

Isabella, M.: *Risorgimento in Exile. Italian Émigrés and the Liberal International in the Post-Napoleonic Era*, Oxford 2009.

Itzen, P./Müller, S. M.: Risk as a Category of Analysis for a Social History of the Twentieth Century: An Introduction, in: *Historical Social Research* 41 (2016) 1, pp. 7–29.

Jacoud, G. (ed.): *Political Economy and Industrialism. Banks in Saint-Simonian Economic Thought*, London 2010.

Jäger, A. S. A. von: *Schweizerskizzen*, Leipzig 1838.

Jauffret, J.-C.: Chapitre Premier: L'épée, in: G. Pedroncini (ed.): *Histoire militaire de la France. De 1871 à 1940*, Paris 1992, pp. 3–27 (= Histoire militaire de la France, Vol. 3).

Jean, B.: *Premières études financières confidentielles sur le Canal de Corinthe. Pourquoi! Ses divers titres atteindront les cours suivants*, Paris 1890.

Jedwab, R./Kerby, E./Moradi, A.: History, Path Dependence and Development: Evidence from Colonial Railroads, Settlers and Cities in Kenya, in: *The Economic Journal* 127 (2015), 1467–1494, doi:10.1111/ecoj.12347.

Jelavich, C./Jelavich, B.: *The Establishment of the Balkan National States*, 1804–1920 (= A History of East Central Europe, Vol. 8), Seattle WA 1986.

Jenkins, R.: *The Dilessi Murders*, London 1998.

Jenks, L. H.: *The Migration of British Capital to 1975*, New York/London 1927 (= Borzoi Political Science Texts).

Jenkyns, R.: *The Victorians and Ancient Greece*, Oxford 1980.

Idem: Hellenism in Victorian Painting, in: G. W. Clarke (ed.): *Rediscovering Hellenism. The Hellenic Inheritance and the English Imagination*, Cambridge et al. 1989, pp. 83–119.

Jensen, J. H./Rosegger, G.: British Railway-Builders Along the Lower Danube, 1856–1869, in: *Slavonic and East European Review* 46 (1968), pp. 105–128.

Jobs, S./Mackenthun, G. (eds.): *Agents of Transculturation. Border-Crossers, Mediators, Go-Betweens*, Münster 2013a.

Idem: Introduction, in: idem (eds.): *Agents of Transculturation. Border-Crossers, Mediators, Go-Betweens*, Münster 2013b, pp. 8–22.

John, R.: Basevi, George (1794–1845), Architect, in: *ODNB*, Oxford 2004, doi:10.1093/ref:odnb/1615.

Johnson, C. H. (ed.): *Transregional and Transnational Families in Europe and Beyond. Experiences since the Middle Ages*, New York 2011.

Jones, C.: *Anthony Gibbs & Sons Limited. A Record of 150 Years of Merchant Banking, 1808–1958*, London 1958.

Jones, E. J.: *The Development of English Agriculture 1815–73*, London 1976 (Reprint of the Edition of 1936).

Jones, G. E.: The Diffusion of Agricultural Innovations, in: *Journal of Agricultural Economics* 15 (1963) 3, pp. 387–409.

Jureit, U.: *Generationenforschung*, Göttingen 2006 (= Grundkurs neue Geschichte, Vol. 2856).

Idem: *Generation, Generationalität, Generationenforschung*. Version 1.0, in: Dokupedia Zeitgeschichte, 11. 2.2010, http://docupedia.de/zg/Generation [6.5.2015].

Jüttner: Die orientalischen Eisenbahnen, in: *Archiv für Eisenbahnwesen* 5 (1882), pp. 187–212, 281–292.

Kahneman, D.: *Thinking, Fast and Slow*, New York 2011.

Κακαβογιάννης, Χ. Ε. [Kakavogiannis, Ch. E.]: Το Ορυκτολογικό Μουσείο Λαυρίου [The Mineralogical Museum of Laurion], in: Π. Φιλίππου-Αγγέλου [P. Philippou-Angelou] (ed.): *Πρακτικά Γ' Επιστημονικής Συνάντησης Ν.Α. Αττικής 1987* [Conference Proceedings G of the Scientific Meeting of N. A. Attika 1987], Καλύβια [Kalivia] 1988, pp. 345–374.

Idem: Το Λαύριο και ο Καποδίστριας [Laurion and Kapodistrias], in: Σ. Κόλλιας [S. Kollias]/Δ. Πρόφης [D. Profis] (eds.): *Πρακτικά Ζ'Επιστημονικής Συνάντησης Ν.Α. Αττικής 1995* [Conference Proceedings Z of the Scientific Meeting N. A. Attika 1995], Koropi 1998, pp. 440–458.

Καλαφάτης, Θ. [Kalafatis, Th.]/Πρόντζας, Ε. [Prontzas, E.]/Ασδραχάς, Σ. [Asdrachas, S.]: *Οικονομική ιστορία του ελληνικού κράτους* [Economic History of the Greek State], Vol. I–III, Athens 2011.

Καμπούρογλους, Δ. [Kampouroglous, D.]: *Η εκλογή και η άφιξις του βασιλέως Γεωργίου* [The Election and Arrival of King George], Athens 1905.

Καραγιάννης, Γ. [Karagiannis, G.]: Τα Λαυρεωτικά "καθρέφτης" της Ελλάδας στο δεύτερο μισό του 19ου αιώνα [The Laurion "Mirror" of Greece in the Second Half of the 19th Century], in: Γ. Καραγιάννης [G. Karagiannis] et al. (eds.): *Λαυρεωτικά 1869–1873: Η πρώτη αρπαγή δημόσιας περιουσίας. Το ναυάγιο του χρηματιστηριακού Ελντοράντο* [Laureotika 1869–1873. The First Deprivation of Public Property. The Shipwreck of the Stock Exchange Eldorado], Athens 2011, pp. 9–42.

Karouzou, E.: *Les jardins de la Méditerranée. Agriculture et Société dans la Grèce du Sud 1860–1910*, Athenes 2014.

Καρούζου, Ε. [Karouzou, E.]: Εθνικές γαίες, εθνικά δάνεια και εθνική κυριαρχία. Βρετανική διπλωματία και γαιοκτησία στο ελληνικό κράτος 1833–1843 [National Lands, National Loans and National Rule, British Diplomacy and Land Property in Greece 1833–1843], Athens 2018.

Kaser, K.: *Südosteuropäische Geschichte und Geschichtswissenschaft*, Wien et al. 2nd ed. 2002 (= Uni-Taschenbücher, Vol. 8224).

Κατηφόρη, Δ. [Katifori, D.]: Σχέσεις J.-G. Eynard – J. von Armansperg [Relationship between J.-G. Eynard and J. von Armansperg], in: *Δελτίον της Ιστορικής και Εθνολογικής Εταιρείας της Ελλάδος* [Bulletin of the Historical and Ethnological Society of Greece], 1984, pp. 134–153.

Κατσούλης, Γ. [Katsoulis, G.] et al. (eds.): *Οικονομική ιστορία της νεώτερης Ελλάδας [Economic History of Modern Greece]*, Athens 1985.

Keisinger, F.: *Unzivilisierte Kriege im zivilisierten Europa? Die Balkankriege und die öffentliche Meinung in Deutschland, England und Irland 1876–1913*, Paderborn/Munich 2008 (= Krieg in der Geschichte, Vol. 47).

Κεκροπούλου, Μ. Π. [Kekropoulou, M. P.]: Η ιστορική αλήθεια για το Λαύριο και ο Τύπος [The Historical Truth about Laurion and the Press], in: Αι. Πρεβενά [Ai

Prevena] (ed.): *Πρακτικά Γ' Επιστημονικής Συνάντησης Ν. Α. Αττικής* [Conference Proceedings I of the Scientific Meeting N. A. Attika 2002], Kalivia 2004, pp. 243–251.

Idem: *Η ιστορία του λαυρεωτικού ζητήματος: το λαυρεωτικό ζήτημα (1870–1873): ο ρόλος του κράτους και της διπλωματίας* [The History of the Laurion Affaire: The Laurion Affaire (1870–1873): The Role of the State and the Diplomacy], Athens 2007.

Kennan, G. F.: *The Other Balkan Wars. A 1913 Carnegie Endowment Inquiry in Retrospect*, Washington DC 1993.

Kerschbaumer, F./Schönhärl, K.: Der Wiener Kongress als "Kinderstube" des Philhellenismus: das Beispiel des Bankiers Jean-Gabriel Eynard, in: A.-R. Meyer-Eisenhut (ed.): *Vormärz und Philhellenismus*, Bielefeld 2013, pp. 99–127 (= Jahrbuch Forum Vormärz-Forschung, Vol. 18).

Kirchholtes, H.-D.: *Jüdische Privatbanken in Frankfurt am Main*, Frankfurt 1969.

Kirchner, H.-M.: *Der Aufbau eines Korrespondetennetzes für die Augsburger "Allgemeine Zeitung" in Südosteuropa durch Johann Friedrich und Johann Georg Cotta*, Vortrag (held in the Institut for Newspaper Research, Dortmund), 1991.

Κυρίτση, Ι./Μάλλης, Ι. [Kiritsis, I./Mallis, I.]: Καταγραφή ιστορικών μεταλλευτικών εγκαταστάσεων στη Μήλο [Registration of Historical Mining Installations in Milo], in: Εθνικό Μετσόβιο Πολυτεχνείο – Σχολή Αρχιτεκτόνων Μηχανικών, Πολιτιστικό Ίδρυμα Ομίλου Πειραιώς (ΠΙΟΠ). Οικονομική Βιομηχανική Επιθεώρηση/αρχείο Βοβολίνη [National Technical University of Athens (NTUA) – School of Architectional Engineering, Piraeus Bank Group Cultural Foundation, Economic and Industrial Review – Archives of Vovolinis] (ed.): *Ιστορικά μεταλλεία στο Αιγαίο, 19ος–20ός αιώνας: Επιστημονικό συνέδριο, Μήλος, 3–5 Οκτωβρίου 2003* [Historical Metallurgy in the Aegean, 19th –20th Century. Conference at Milos 3.–5. October 2003], Athens 2005, pp. 217–224.

Klein, M./Schöning, S.: Entwicklungsbanken, in: *Gabler Wirtschaftslexikon*, http://wirtschaftslexikon.gabler.de/Archiv/3658/entwicklungsbanken-v11.html [30.9.2015].

Klein, N.: *L'humanité, le christianisme, et la liberté. Die internationale philhellenische Vereinsbewegung der 1820er Jahre*, Mainz 2009.

Klemm, U.-D.: Deutsche und Griechen: Eine Beziehung mit Missverständnissen, in: idem/W. Schultheiß (eds.): *Die Krise in Griechenland. Ursprünge, Verlauf, Folgen*, Frankfurt 2015, pp. 352–370.

Knake, S.: The "Reputation Approach" and the Justificatory Function of Economic Calculation. Some Critical Reflections on Monika Pohle Fraser's Analysis of Risk Management Techniques in the Nineteenth Century, in: K. Schönhärl (ed.): *Decision Making, Confidence and Risk Management in Banks from Early Modernity to the 20th Century*, Basingstoke Hampshire et al. 2017, pp. 147–171 (= Palgrave Studies in the History of Finance).

Knight, F. H.: *Risk, Uncertainty and Profit*, Chicago 1971 (Originally published 1921).

Knight, G. A.: The Rothschild-Bleichröder Axis in Action. An Anglo-German Cooperative 1877–1878, in: *Yearbook of the Leo Baeck Institute* 28 (1983), pp. 43–57.

Knudsen, H.: Wolfgang Heribert Tobias Otto Maria Johann Nepomuk Dalberg, in: *NDB*, 3 (1987), p. 490 f.

Kobrak, C.: The Concept of Reputation in Business History, in: *Business History Review* 87 (2013), pp. 763–786.

Koch-Mehrin, S.: *Historische Währungsunion zwischen Wirtschaft und Politik* (Doctor's degree deprived in 2011), Baden-Baden/Heidelberg 2001.

Kocka, J./Gebhardt, B./Häfele, R.: *Das lange 19. Jahrhundert. Arbeit, Nation und bürgerliche Gesellschaft*, Stuttgart 10th ed. 2001 (= Handbuch der deutschen Geschichte/Gebhardt, Vol. 3).

Kofas, J. V.: *Financial Relations of Greece and the Great Powers. 1832–1862*, New York 1981 (= East European Monographs, Vol. 91).

Kohlrausch, M. et al. (eds.): *Expert Cultures in Central Eastern Europe. The Internationalization of Knowledge and the Transformation of Nation States since World War I*, Osnabrück 2010.

Koliopoulos, J. S./Veremis, T. M.: *Modern Greece. A History since 1821*, Malden MA 2010.

Konstantinou, E. (ed.): *Die Rezeption der Antike und der europäische Philhellenismus*, Frankfurt 1998 (= Philhellenische Studien, Vol. 7).

Idem (ed.): *Das Bild Griechenlands im Spiegel der Völker (17. bis 18. Jahrhundert) – The Image of Greece in the Mirror of Nations (17th–18th Century)*, Brussels 2008.

Korczynski, M.: The Political Economy of Trust, in: *Journal of Management Studies* 37 (2000) 1, pp. 1–21.

Κορδάτος, Γ. Κ. [Kordatos, G. K.]: *Ιστορία της νεώτερης Ελλάδας* [History of Modern Greece], Athens 1957–59 (= Μεγάλη ιστορία της Ελλάδας, Νεώτερη Β΄, Vol. 10 [Big History of Greece, New Serie B., Vol. 10]).

Κορδέλλας, Α. [Kordellas, A.]: *Περί των σκωριών και της μεταλλουργικής βιομηχανίας εν Ελλάδι* [About Soil Resources and Metal Industry in Greece], Athens 1865.

Idem: *Εγγραφα αφορώντα τας μολυβδούχους σκωρίας του Λαυρείου* [Documents Concerning the Silver-Lead Scories of Laurion], Athens 1866.

Idem: *Εγγραφα αφορώντα εις τας μολυβδούχους σκωρίας και τα μεταλλεία του Λαυρείου, από του 1860 μέχρι του 1865* [Documents Concerning the Lead Scories and the Metallics of Laurion, from 1860 to 1865], Athens 1870.

Kosev, K.: Die Orientpolitik Preussen-Deutschlands in den 60er und 70er Jahren des 19. Jahrhunderts und die Befreiung Bulgariens, in: R. Melville (ed.): *Der Berliner Kongreß von 1878. Die Politik der Großmächte und die Probleme der Modernisierung in Südosteuropa in der zweiten Hälfte des 19. Jahrhunderts*, Wiesbaden 1982, pp. 71–81.

Κωστής, Κ. Π. [Kostis, K. P.]/Τσοκόπουλος, Β. [Tsokopulos, B.]: *Οι τράπεζες στην Ελλάδα 1898–1928* [Banks in Greece 1898–1928], Athens 1988.

Kostis, K. P.: Banque et industrie, in: G. B. Dertilis (ed.): *Banquiers, usuriers et paysans: réseaux de crédit et stratégies du capital en Grèce 1780–1930*, Paris 1988, pp. 145–156 (= Histoire contemporaine).

Idem: *Ιστορία της Εθνικής Τράπεζας της Ελλάδος 1914–1940. Με τη συνεργασία του* Γιώργου Κωστελένου [The History of National Bank of Greece 1914–1940. In Collaboration with Georgios Kostelenos], Athens 2003.

Kotsowilis, K. S.: König Otto I. von Griechenland im Lichte neuer archivalischer Quellen. Zur Kritik der "Bavarokratie" in Griechenland in den Jahren 1832–1862, in: *Zeitschrift für Bayerische Landesgeschichte* 67 (2004), pp. 641–677.

Idem: *Die Griechenbegeisterung der Bayern unter König Otto I.*, Munich 2007.

Koukkou, H. E.: *John Kapodistrias. A Greek Europhile Diplomat*, Athens 1994a.
Idem: The Swiss Philhellenic Press and the Greek Revolution, in: A. Ruge/E. Konstantinou (eds.): *Europäischer Philhellenismus: die europäische philhellenische Presse bis zur ersten Hälfte des 19. Jahrhunderts*, Frankfurt et al. 1994b, pp. 109–114 (= Philhellenische Studien, Vol. 3).
Kraemer, H./Lux, H./Kroker, E.: *Die Ingenieurkunst auf der Pariser Weltausstellung 1900*, Düsseldorf 1985.
Kramper, P.: Warum Europa? Konturen einer globalgeschichtlichen Forschungskontroverse, in: *Neue Politische Literatur* 54 (2009), pp. 9–46.
Kraus, A. (ed.): *Signate König Ludwigs I.*, ausgewählt von Max Spindler, Vol. 4: 1839–1841, Munich 1992 (= Materialien zur Bayerischen Landesgeschichte).
Krauss, S.: *Die politischen Beziehungen zwischen Bayern und Frankreich 1814/15–1840*, Munich 1987 (= Schriftenreihe zur bayerischen Landesgeschichte, Vol. 87).
Krooss, H. E./Blyn, M. R.: *A History of Financial Intermediaries*, New York 1971.
Külow, D.: *Schalom und Alefbet. Die Geschichte des Jüdischen Gymnasiums in Berlin*, Berlin 2014.
Kurgan-van Hentenryk, G.: The Social Origins of Bank Managers, in: E. Green/M. Pohle-Fraser (eds.): *The Human Factor in Banking History. Entrepreneurship, Organization, Management and Personnel*, Athens 2008, pp. 171–188.
Kynaston, D.: *The City of London. Vol. I: A World of Its Own, 1815–90; Vol. II: Golden Years, 1890–1914*, London 1994.
Lainer-Vos, D.: *Sinews of the Nation. Constructing Irish and Zionist Bonds in the United States*, Cambridge et al. 2013.
Λάιος, Γ. [Laios, G.]: *Σίμων Σίνας* [Simon Sinas], Athens 1972.
Lake Copais Company, Limited: *Memorandum and Articles of Association and Agreements*, etc., London s.t.
Lambert, A.: Cochrane, Thomas, Tenth Earl of Dundonald (1775–1860), in: *ODNB*, Oxford 2004, doi:10.1093/ref:odnb/5757.
Lampe, J. R./Jackson, M. R.: *Balkan Economic History, 1550–1950. From Imperial Borderlands to Developing Nations*, Bloomington IND 1982 (= The Joint Committee on Eastern Europe Publication Series, Vol. 10).
Λάμπρος, Γ. Λ. [Lampros, G. L.]: *Η λίμνη της Κωπαΐδας: αφετηρία αγροτικής ανάπτυξης* [The Lake Copais: The Starting Point of Agricultural Development], Athens 2000.
Landes, D. S.: Das Bankhaus Bleichröder. Ein Zwischenbericht, in: R. Weltsch (ed.): *Deutsches Judentum. Aufstieg und Krise. Gestalten, Ideen, Werke. Vierzehn Monographien*, Stuttgart 1963, pp. 187–215.
Landfester, M./Lessenich, R.: Philhellenismus, in: H. Cancik et al. (eds.): Der Neue Pauly, 2006, doi:10.1163/1574-9347_dnp_e15201790.
Landmann, J.: Die Schweizerische Nationalbank, in: *Zeitschrift für Volkswirtschaft, Sozialpolitik und Verwaltung* 15 (1906), pp. 187–201.
Landsteiner, E./Langthaler, E.: Agrosystems and Labour Relations, in: eidem (eds.): *Agrosystems and Labour Relations in European Rural Societies* (Middle Ages – Twentieth Century), Turnhout 2010, pp. 13–29 (= Rural History in Europe, Vol. 3).
Lane, R. E.: The Decline of Politics and Ideology in a Knowledgeable Society, in: *American Sociological Review* 31 (1966), pp. 649–662.
Lanier, A.: *Die Geschichte des Bank- und Handelshauses Sina*, Frankfurt 1998.

Lässig, S.: *Jüdische Wege ins Bürgertum. Kulturelles Kapital und sozialer Aufstieg im 19. Jahrhundert*, Göttingen 2004 (= Bürgertum. Neue Folge, Vol. 1).

Idem: Zwischen Markt und Kultur? 'Weiche' Faktoren in der Wirtschafts- und Sozialgeschichte am Beispiel von Privatbanken und Privatbankiers, in: O. Hartung/K. Köhr/K. H. Pohl (eds.): *Geschichte und Geschichtsvermittlung. Festschrift für Karl Heinrich Pohl*, Bielefeld 2008, pp. 104–124.

Le Bret, H.: *Les frères d'Eichthal. Le saint-simonien et le financier au XIXe siècle*, Paris 2012 (= Collection Roland Mousnier, Vol. 63).

Le Comité établi à Genève en faveur des Grecs: *Souscription ouverte à Genève en faveur des Grecs, à trois sols par semaine, jusqu'à la fin de Mai 1827*, Genève 1826, 27 Novembre.

LeBoeuf, R. A./Shafir, E.: Decision Making, in: K. J. Holyoak/R. G. Morrison (eds.): *The Cambridge Handbook of Thinking and Reasoning*, Cambridge et al. 2012, pp. 301–321.

Leconte, C.: *Étude économique de la Grèce. De sa postion actuelle, de son avenir*, Paris 1847.

Lecoq, A.-M.: *La Querelle des Anciens et des Modernes. XVIIe – XVIIIe siècles: précédé de les abeilles et les araignées* (= Collection folio, Vol. 3414), Paris 2001.

Ledoux, C. (1837–1927): Le Laurium et les mines d'argent en Grèce, in: *Revue des deux mondes* (1872) 2, pp. 552–571.

Lehmann, S.: Die Bedeutung der Emissionsbanken auf dem deutschen Aktienmarkt 1896–1913, in: *Vierteljahrschrift für Sozial- und Wirtschaftsgeschichte* 98 (2011), pp. 331–338.

Leonhard, J.: *Liberalismus. Zur historischen Semantik eines europäischen Deutungsmusters*, Munich 2001.

Levandis, J. A.: *The Greek Foreign Debt and the Great Powers 1821–1898*, New York 1944.

Lewis, A./Mackenzie, C.: Morals, Money, Ethical Investing and Economic Psychology, in: *Human Relations* 53 (2000) 2, pp. 179–191.

Idem: *Morals, Markets and Money. Ethical, Green and Socially Responsible Investing*, London 2002.

Λιάτα, Ε. Δ. [Liata, E. D.]: *Γενικό Ευρετήριο του Ιστορικού Αρχείου της Εθνικής Τράπεζας* [General Catalogue of the Historical Archives of National Bank of Greece], Athens 1980.

Lichtenberger, A./Rüden, C. v. (eds.): *Multiple Mediterranean Realities. Current Approaches to Spaces, Resources, and Connectivities*, Paderborn 2014 (= Mittelmeerstudien).

Liedtke, R.: *N M Rothschild & Sons. Kommunikationswege im europäischen Bankenwesen im 19. Jahrhundert*, Köln/Weimar/Wien 2006.

Λιγνάδης, Α. [Lignadis, A.]: *Το πρώτον δάνειον της ανεξαρτησίας* [The First Loan of Independence], Athens 1970.

Lill, R.: Integrationspolitik oder Imperialismus? Von der Nation zum radikalen Nationalismus und zur Teilnahme am Ersten Weltkrieg (1876–1918), in: W. Altgeld (ed.): *Kleine italienische Geschichte*, Stuttgart 2002, pp. 325–369 (= Universal-Bibliothek, Vol. 17036).

Linoli, A.: The Fucino: The Drainage of a Major Lake in the Second Half of the XIXth Century, in: C. Ohlig (ed.): *Integrated Land and Water Resources*

Management in History, Norderstedt/Siegburg 2005, pp. 167–186 (= Schriften der Deutschen Wasserhistorischen Gesellschaft [DWEd] e.V. Sonderband, Vol. 2).

Litterer, J. A.: *The Analysis of Organizations*, New York 2nd ed. 1973.

Idem: *The Emergence of Systematic Management as Shown by the Literature of Management from 1870–1900*, New York 1986.

Littré, E.: De l'usage pratique de la langue grecque par M. Gustave d'Eichthal, in: *Journal des Débats* (1865), 13 mai.

Loewe, H./Thiersch, F.: *Friedrich Thiersch. Ein Humanistenleben im Rahmen der Geistesgeschichte seiner Zeit; Reisebriefe aus Griechenland*, ed. by E. Konstantinou/K. Maras/H. Scholler, Frankfurt 2010 (= Philhellenische Studien, Vol. 15).

Löffler, B.: Währungsgeschichte als Kulturgeschichte? Konzeptionelle Leitlinien und analytische Probleme kulturhistorischer Ansätze auf wirtschafts- und währungsgeschichtlichen Feld, in: *Die kulturelle Seite der Währung* (2010), pp. 3–35.

Loizillon, G. J.: *The Bunau-Varilla Brothers and the Panama Canal*, [s.l.] 2nd ed. 2013.

Loraux, N./Vidal-Naquet, P.: La formation de l'Athènes bourgeoise: Essai d'Historiographie 1750–1850, in: R. R. Bolgar (ed.): *Classical Influences on Western Thought A. D. 1650–1870. Proceedings of an International Conference Held at King's College*, Cambridge, March 1977, Cambridge et al. 1979, pp. 169–222.

Löschburg, W.: Karl Mendelssohn Bartholdys Reise nach Griechenland, in: E. Konstantinou (ed.): *Die Rezeption der Antike und der europäische Philhellenismus*, Frankfurt 1998, pp. 198–208.

Loukos, C: Dix ans de tentatives pour la création d'une banque en Grèce, in: D. Chambers (ed.): *Actes du IIe colloque international d'histoire (Athènes, 18–25 septembre 1983): Économies méditerranéennes: Équilibres et intercommunications, XIIIe–XIXe siècles*, Vol. II., Athènes 1986, pp. 437–449.

Loules, D.: Politique banquière et monétaire dans la Grèce d'après-guerre (1828–1832), in: D. Chambers (ed.): *Actes du IIe colloque international d'histoire (Athènes, 18–25 septembre 1983): Économies méditerranéennes. Équilibres et intercommunications, XIIIe–XIXe siècles*, Vol. II., Athènes 1986, pp. 409–420.

Loulos, K.: *Die deutsche Griechenlandpolitik von der Jahrhundertwende bis zum Ausbruch des Ersten Weltkrieges*, Frankfurt 1986.

Idem: Deutsch-griechische Beziehungen im Schatten des Ersten Weltkriegs, in: W. Schultheiß/E. Chrysos (eds.): *Meilensteine deutsch-griechischer Beziehungen. Beiträge eines Deutsch-Griechischen Symposiums am 16. und 17. April 2010 in Athen*, Athens/Berlin 2010, pp. 139–184.

Louriotis, A.: *Correspondence Respecting the Steam Vessels Which Were Intended to Form the Expedition to Greece, Under the Command of Lord Cochrane, Together with Copies of the Original Agreements Entered into with His Lordship and with Mr. Galloway, the Engineer*, London 1827.

Λουριώτης, A. [Louriotis, A.]/Ορλάνδος, I. [Orlandos, I.]: *Απολογία εις την κατ' αυτών απόφασιν του Ελεγκτικού Συνεδρίου περί των εν Λονδίνω διαπραγματευθέντων δύο ελληνικών δανείων κατά το 1824 και 1825, εκδοθείσαν εν Ναυπλίω την 29^η Οκτωβρίου 1834 και κοινοποιηθείσαν την 18^η Ιανουαρίου 1835* [Defence of Ioannis Orlandos and Andreas Louriotis Against the Decision Delivered Against them by the Committee of Auditors Regarding the Two Loans, Published in Nafplio on 29 October 1834 and Publicized on 18 January 1835], Athens 1839.

Lovett, C. M.: *The Democratic Movement in Italy*, 1830–1876, Cambridge 1982.
Luhmann, N.: *Vertrauen. Ein Mechanismus der Reduktion sozialer Komplexität*, Stuttgart 4th ed. 2009 (= UTB, Vol. 2185).
Luis, J.-Ph.: *L'ivresse de la fortune. A.M. Aguado, un génie des affaires*, Paris 2009.
Lyons, T./Mandaville, P. G.: *Politics From Afar. Transnational Diasporas and Networks*, London 2012.
MacGrew, W. W.: *Land and Revolution in Modern Greece, 1800–1881. The Transition in the Tenure and Exploitation of Land from Ottoman Rule to Independence*, Kent, Ohio 1985.
Mack, G.: *The Land Divided: A History of the Panama Canal and Other Isthmian Canal Projects*, New York 1944.
Maier, C. S.: *Leviathan 2.0. Inventing Modern Statehood*, Cambridge 2012.
Maissen, T.: *Geschichte der Schweiz*, Baden 2011.
Μακρυμίχαλος, Σ. Ι. [Makrimichalos, S. I.]: *Sir Edward Fitzgerald Law: ένας λησμονημένος Βρεττανός Φιλέλλην* [A Forgotten British Philhellene], Athens 1974.
Mariadis, S.: *Die Entwicklung der Agrarfrage in Griechenland seit Entstehung des neugriechischen Staates (1821) bis zum zweiten Weltkrieg und ihre Einflüsse auf das Wirtschafts- und Sozialleben*, Bonn 1966.
Marinov, T./Vezenkov, A.: The Concept of National Revival in Balkan Historiographies, in: R. Daskalov (ed.): *Shared Pasts, Disputed Legacies*, Leiden 2015, pp. 406–462 (= Entangled Histories of the Balkans, Vol. 3).
Μαρκουλή-Μποντιώνη, Α. [Markouli-Bontioni, A.]: *Γαλλική Εταιρεία Μεταλλείων Λαυρείου (Γ.Ε.Μ.Λ.): η εξέλιξη και η συμβολή της στην ανάπτυξη της ελληνικής οικονομίας κατά τον 19ο και 20ό αιώνα* [Compagnie Française des Mines du Laurium (C.F.M.L.): Its Development and Its Contribution to the Evolution of the Greek Economy in the 19th and 20th Century], Athens 2010.
Marková, I./Linell, P./Gillespie, A.: *Trust and Distrust in Society*, in: I. Marková (ed.): *Trust and Distrust. Sociocultural Perspectives*, Charlotte NC 2008, pp. 3–28 (=Advances in Cultural Psychology).
Martin, G.: John Cordy Jeaffreson (1831–1901) and the Ipswich Borough Records, in: C. Harper-Bill (ed.): *East Anglia's History. Studies in Honour of Norman Scarfe*, Woodbridge 2002, pp. 333–349.
Mathias, P.: *The First Industrial Nation. An Economic History of Britain, 1700–1914*, London 1969.
Μάτσας, Ζ. Κ. [Matsas, Z. K.]: *Η Αληθεία εν τη υποθέσει της Αθηναϊκής Τραπέζης* [The Truth in the Affaire of the Bank of Athens], Athens 1914.
Idem: *Η υπόθεσις της Αθηναϊκής Τραπέζης κρινομένη από τον κόσμον των εργασιών* [The Affaire of the Bank of Athens, Judged from the World of Works], Athens 1915.
Maufroy, S.: *Le philhellénisme franco-allemand (1815–1848)*, Paris 2011.
Maurer, G. L. v.: *Das griechische Volk in öffentlicher, kirchlicher und privatrechtlicher Beziehung vor und nach dem Freiheitskampfe bis zum 31. Juli 1834*, Vol. II, Osnabrück 1968 (Reprint of the First Edition 1835).
Mazurel, H.: *Vertiges de la guerre. Byron, les philhellènes et le mirage grec*, Paris 2013 (= Histoire, Vol. 124).
McCabe, I. B. et al. (eds.): *Diaspora Entrepreneurial Networks: Four Centuries of History*, Oxford 2005.

McCullough, D.: *The Path between the Seas: The Creation of the Panama Canal, 1870–1914*, New York 1977.

McErlean, J. M. P.: *Napoleon and Pozzo di Borgo in Corsica and after, 1764–1821. Not Quite a Vendetta*, Lewiston NY 1996 (= Studies in French civilization, Vol. 10).

Meid, C.: *Griechenland-Imaginationen. Reiseberichte im 20. Jahrhundert von Gerhart Hauptmann bis Wolfgang Koeppen*, Berlin 2012.

Μέλιος, N. [Melios, N.]/Παπαδόπουλος, A. [Papadopoulos, A.]: Το Κωπαϊδικό ζήτημα στον 19ο και 20ο αιωνα: Μια πρώτη προσέγγιση [The Lake Copais Question in the 19th and 20th Century. A First Historical Approach], in: *Επετηρίς της Εταιρείας Βοιωτικών Μελετών* [Yearbook of Boetian Studies] α (1988), β, pp. 1159–1179.

Idem: El lago Copaïs y la agricultura helenica, 1830–1911, in: *Areas* (Rivista de Ciencias Sociales) 12 (1990), pp. 37–42.

Idem: Επιχειρηματικές και επενδυτικές στρατηγικές στην Κωπαΐδα (1830/1953) [Business and Investment Strategies in Copais (1830–1953)], in: N. Μέλιος [N. Melios]/A. Παπαδόπουλος [A. Papadopoulos] (eds.): *Το Κωπαϊδικό ζήτημα* [The Question of Lake Copais], Athens 1996a, pp. 3–5.

Idem/Παπαδόπουλος, A. [Papadopoulos, A.] (eds.): *Το Κωπαϊδικό ζήτημα* [The Question of Lake Copais], Athens 1996b.

Meloni, G./Swinnen, J. F. M.: Standards, Tariffs and Trade. The Rise and Fall of the Raisin Trade between Greece and France in the Late 19th Century and the Definition of Wine, in: *SSRN Electronic Journal* (2017), LICOS Discussion Paper Series No. 386/2017, doi:10.2139/ssrn.2919311.

Mendelssohn, G.: *Die Familie Erlanger. Bankiers – Mäzene – Künstler*, Ingelheim 2005.

Mendelssohn-Bartholdy, C.: De l'usage pratique de la langue grecque, in: *Heidelberger Jahrbücher* 9 (1865).

Idem: *Geschichte Griechenlands von der Eroberung Konstantinopels durch die Türken im Jahre 1453 bis auf unsere Tage*, 2 Vol., Hildesheim et al. 2004 (Second Print of 1st ed. 1874).

Mengozzi, G. C.: Serpieri, Giambattista, in: *Dizionario del risorgimento nazionale*, Milano 1931–1937, Vol. IV, pp. 264.

Μεσσηνέζης, N. [Messinesis, N.]: *Γεώργιος Σταύρος και Εθνική Τράπεζα: έρευνα εις τα ανέκδοτα αρχεία του Βασιλέως Όθωνος, της Εθνικής Τραπέζης, του Γεωργίου Κουντουριώτη, του Λέοντος Μεσσηνέζη και άλλων [Georgios Stavros and the National Bank: Research in The Archives of King Otto, of the National Bank, of Georgios Kountouriotis, of Leon Messinezis and Others]*, Athens 1956.

Messinesis, D. M./Ritthaler, A.: *Der grösste Freund der Hellenen: König Ludwig I. von Bayern als Philhellene. Sein Beitrag zu Griechenlands Aufstieg und besonders zur Gründung der Nationalbank von Griechenland*, Munich 1966.

Meyer, W. B.: From Past to Present. A Historical Perspective on Wetlands, in: S. L. Spray et al. (eds.): *Wetlands*, Lanham 2004, pp. 84–100 (= Exploring Environmental Challenges).

Meyer-Eisenhut, A.-R. (ed.): *Vormärz und Philhellenismus*, Bielefeld 2013 (= Jahrbuch Forum Vormärz-Forschung, Vol. 18).

Mikkelsen, A.: Dealing with Risk: Underwriting Sovereign Bond Issues in London 1870–1914, eabh Working Papers, No. 14–06, 2014, pp. 1–26, http://hdl.handle.net/10419/97320 [21.1.2020].

Idem: Minimising Risk: Financial Intermediaries and Bond Issuing in London before the Great War, in: K. Schönhärl (ed.): *Decision Taking, Confidence and Risk Management in Banks From Early Modernity to the 20th Century*, Basingtoke 2017, pp. 105–124.

Millar, G. F.: Ellice, Edward (1783–1863), Merchant and Politician, in: *ODNB*, Oxford 2004, doi:10.1093/ref:odnb/8650.

Minoglou, I. P.: Ethnic Minority Groups in Internatinal Banking. Greek Diaspora Bankers of Constantinople and Ottoman State Finances, 1840–81, in: *Financial History Review* 9 (2002a), pp. 125–146.

Idem: The Rise and Fall of the House of Hambros in Greece, 1864–1940, in: H. Bonin (ed.): *Transnational Companies. 19th–20th Centuries*, Paris 2002b, pp. 401–417 (= Collection Ecoclio).

Idem: Toward a Typology of Greek-diaspora Entrepreneurship, in: I. B. McCabe et al. (eds.): *Diaspora Entrepreneurial Networks: Four Centuries of History*, Oxford 2005, pp. 173–189.

Mitsou, M.: Philhellenism and Colonialism in the 1830s. Presentation Held at the the Conference 'Perceptions of History in Germany and Greece' in Hamburg on 1.4.2016.

Mohun, A. P.: Constructing the History of Risk. Foundations, Tools, and Reasons Why, in: *Historical Social Research* 41 (2016) 1 (Special Issue: Risk as an Analytical Category: Selected Studies in the Social History of the Twentieth Century), pp. 30–47.

Mollier, J.-Y.: *Le scandale de Panama*, Paris 1991.

Monnier, V.: *Jacques Laffitte. Roi des banquiers et banquier des rois*, Brussels 2013.

Moraïtinis, P. A.: *La Grèce telle qu'elle est. Ancien consul de Grèce, chevalier de l'ordre du sauveur et de l'ordre de S. Anne de Russie, précédé d'une lettre de M. le Marquis de Queux de Saint-Hillare*, Paris 1877.

Morazé, C./Allen, G. (eds.): *History of Mankind. Cultural and Scientific Development (V, Parts One and Two: The Scientific Revolution. Industrial Revolution and Technical Developments)*, Chatham 1976.

Morera, R.: *L'assèchement des marais en France au XVIIe siècle*, Rennes 2011.

Morison, T.: *The Life of Sir Edward FitzGerald Law, K.C.S.I., K.C.M.G*, Edinburgh/London 1911.

Mosse, W. E.: Die Juden in Wirtschaft und Gesellschaft, in: idem (ed.): *Juden im Wilhelminischen Deutschland 1890–1914*, Tübingen 1976, pp. 57–113.

Idem: *Jews in German Economy. The German-Jewish Economic Élite 1820–1935*, Oxford 1987.

Müchler, G.: *Napoleons hundert Tage. Eine Geschichte von Versuchung und Verrat*, Darmstadt 2014.

Müller, S.: *Wiring the World. The Social and Cultural Creation of Global Telegraph Networks*, New York 2016.

Musset, A. de: *Rolla. Poésies nouvelles (1836–1852)*, Paris 1857.

Musset, A. de: *Rolla. Complete writings.* Ed. and trans. by K. Warren et al., New York 1908.

Musso, P.: *La religion du monde industriel. Analyse de la pensée de Saint-Simon*, La Tour d'Aigues 2006 (= Monde en cours).

Mylona, N.: *Griechenlands Gedenkorte der Antike in der deutschsprachigen Reiseliteratur des 19. und 20. Jahrhunderts*, Würzburg 2014.

N. N.: (Gennadios, I.): *The Greek Loans of 1824 & 1825. How They Were Handled, and What the World Thought of It; Opinions of the Day, Without Comment*, London 1878.

N. N.: Dauzats, Guillaume-Vincent — Société des anciens élèves des écoles nationales d'arts et métiers, *Bulletin administratif*, 1111, n°245, avril 1885, pp. XXI–XXVI.

N. N.: Biographie de Sauvage, in: *Livre du centenaire* (Ecole Polytechnique), Vol. III., 1897.

N. N.: *Société des ponts et travaux en fer*, Paris 1910.

N. N.: Société des ponts et travaux en fer, in: *Comité français des expositions* (ed.): *Exposition coloniale internationale. Section métropolitaine, groupe VI: génie civil et moyens de transports*, Paris 1931, pp. 582–589.

N. N.: Ferdinand, Erzherzog von Österreich, Großherzog von Toscana (1769–1824), in: *ÖBL* 1815–1950, I (Lfg. 4, 1956a), p. 300.

N. N.: Franz II. Joseph Karl von Österreich (1768–1835), in: *ÖBL* 1815–1950, I (Lfg. 4, 1956b), pp. 348f.

N. N.: Talleyrand-Périgord, Charles-Maurice de, in: B. Yvert (ed.): *Dictionnaire des ministres de 1789 à 1989*, Paris 1990.

N. N.: Laurium, in: *Brill's New Pauly*, Leiden et al. 2006, http://referenceworks.brillonline.com/cluster/New%20Pauly%20Online?s.num=0 [15.5.2015].

N. N.: Vom Ideal geblendet. Günter Grass übersieht in seinem Gedicht "Europas Schande", dass das antike Griechenland mit dem heutigen wenig zu tun hat, in: *Süddeutsche Zeitung*, 2.6.2012, p. 46.

N. N.: Antinori, Orazio, in: *Enciclopedia italiana*. Treccani.it, s.t.a, http://www.treccani.it/ [7.2.2020].

N. N.: Serpieri, in: *Enciclopedia italiana*. Treccani.it, s.t.b, http://www.treccani.it/ [7.2.2020].

N. N.: Serpièri, Enrico, in: *Enciclopedia italiana*. Treccani.it, s.t.c, http://www.treccani.it/ [7.2.2020].

N. N.: *Mémoire affaire du Laurium question des Ecvoladés*, s.l, s.t.d.

N. N.: Fraipont, Gustave, s.t.Wynne, in: *Dictionnaire des peintres belges*, http://balat.kikirpa.be/peintres/Detail_notice.php?id=2342 [29.3.2017].

Nagel, J.: *Zwischen Kapitalarmut und Kapitalexport. Zum Problem der Auslandsinvestitionen deutscher Grossbanken am Beispiel der Unternehmen der Deutschen Bank in Südosteuropa und dem Osmanischen Reich zwischen 1888 und 1914*, Frankfurt et al. 1996 (= Europäische Hochschulschriften: Series 3, Geschichte und ihre Hilfswissenschaften, Vol. 706).

Naldi, L. et al.: Entrepreneurial Orientation, Risk Taking, and Performance in Family Firms, in: *Family Business Review* 20 (2007) 1, pp. 33–47, doi:10.1111/j.1741-6248.2007.00082.

Εθνική Τράπεζα της Ελλάδος [National Bank of Greece]: *Επιστολαί Ι. Γ. Εϋνάρδου προς Γεώργιον Σταύρον 1841–1843* [Correspondence between I. G. Eynard and Georgios Stavros 1841–1843], Athens 1923.

National Bank of Greece: *125 χρόνια στην υπηρεσία του έθνους* [125 Years of Duty towards the Nation], Athens 1966.

Newton, L.: Trust and Virtue in English Banking: The Assessment of Borrowers by Bank Managements at the Turn of the Nineteenth Century, in: *Financial History Review* 7 (2000) 2, pp. 177–199.

Νικολοπούλου, Ε. Η. [Nikolopoulou, E. H.]: *Η Γερμανική εξωτερική πολιτική στην Ελλάδα 1871–1897* [The German Foreign Policy in Greece 1871–1897], Athens 2010 (Unpublished Manuscript).

Nini, G.: *The Value of Financial Intermediaries: Empirical Evidence from Syndicated Loans to Emerging Market Borrowers*, 2004 (International Finance Discussion Papers 820, Board of Governors of the Federal Reserve System U.S.), http://www.federalreserve.gov/pubs/ifdp/2004/820/ifdp820.pdf [21.1.2020].

Nipperdey, T.: *Deutsche Geschichte 1800–1918*, 3 Vol., Munich 1998.

Noe, A. (ed.): *Der Philhellenismus in der westeuropäischen Literatur, 1780–1830*, Amsterdam et al. 1994 (= Internationale Forschungen zur allgemeinen und vergleichenden Literaturwissenschaft, Vol. 6).

Obstfeld, M./Taylor, A. M.: *Global Capital Markets: Integration, Crisis and Growth*, New York 2004.

Olegario, R./McKenna, C.: Introduction: Corporate Reputation in Historical Perspective, in: *Business History Review* 87 (2013), pp. 643–654.

Ορλάνδος, Ι. [Orlandos, I.]: *Ο Ορλάνδος απολογούμενος. Ενώπιον του κοινού* [Orlandos Defending Himself in Public], Athens 1841.

O'Rourke, K. H./Williamson, J. G.: *Globalization and History. The Evolution of a Nineteenth-Century Atlantic Economy*, Cambridge 1999.

Ortiz, F.: *Contrapunteo cubano del tabaco y el azucar*, La Habana 1940 (= Nuevo plan de publicaciones/Universidad Central de Las Villas, Vol. 50).

Idem et al.: *Cuban Counterpoint. Tobacco and Sugar*, New York 1947.

Osterhammel, J. (ed.): *Das Kaiserreich transnational. Deutschland in der Welt*, 1871–1914, Göttingen 2004.

Idem: *Die Verwandlung der Welt. Eine Geschichte des 19. Jahrhunderts*, Munich 5th ed. 2010 (= Historische Bibliothek der Gerda Henkel Stiftung).

Ostrower, F.: *Why the Wealthy Give. The Culture of Elite Philanthropy*, Princeton NJ 1995.

Ouvaroff, S. S.: *Stein et Pozzo di Borgo*, St. Petersbourg 1846.

Παγουλάτος, Γ. [Pagoulatos, G.]: *Η Εθνική Τράπεζα της Ελλάδος, 1940–2000* [National Bank of Greece, 1940–2000], Athens 2006.

Pak, S. J.: Reputation and Social Ties: J. P. Morgan & Co. and Private Investment Banking, in: *Business History Review* 87 (2013a), pp. 703–728.

Idem: *Gentlemen Bankers. The World of J. P. Morgan*, Berlin, Cambridge 2013b.

Palma, C. A.: *Greece Vindicated; in Two Letters by Count Alerino Palma; to Which Are Added, by the Same Author, Critical Remarks on the Works Recently Published on the Same Subject, by Messrs. Bulwer, Emerson, Pecchio, Humphreys, Stanhope, Parry, & Blaquiere*, London 1826a.

Idem: *Summary Account of the Steam Boats for Lord Cochrane's Expedition; With Some Few Words Upon the Two Frigates Ordered at New York for the Service of Greece*, London 1826b.

Idem: *The Greek Steam Boats, and Mehemet ali's Firman, Being a Following Statement of the Pamphlet a Summary Account of the Steam-Boats for Lord Cochrane's Expedition*, London 1827.

Palmer, A. W.: *Alexander I.: der rätselhafte Zar*, Frankfurt 1994.

Pan-Montojo, J.: State Credit and Foreign Debt in the Early Nineteenth Century: Contradictory Representations of a Renovated Scenario, in: *Journal of Iberian and Latin American Studies* (2019), doi:10.1080/14701847.2019.1680004.

Πανδής, Τ. [Pandis, T.]: *Ιωάννης Καποδίστριας ο κυβερνήτης* [Ioannis Kapodistrias, the Governor], Corfu 2008.

Παντελάκης, Ν. Σ. [Pantelakis, N. S.]: *Δημόσια δάνεια (1847–1939)* [Catalogue of Public Loans (1847–1939)], Athens 1995.

Papadopoulos, A. G.: *The Drainage and Exploitation of Lake Copais (1908–1938). Socio-economic Implications of the Exploitation of Lake Copais, Greece. A History of the Lake Copais Question, 1908–1938, with Special Reference to the Relations between State, Company and the Peasant Communities of the Area*, Bradford 1993 (Unpublished Manuscript).

Idem: The Socio-economic Effects of the Drainage of Lake Copais, in: J. L. Bintliff (ed.): *Recent Developments in the History and Archaeology of Central Greece. Proceedings of the 6th International Boeotian Conference*, Oxford 1997, pp. 365–377 (= British Archaeological Reports, Vol. 666).

Παπαγιαννοπούλος, Ε. [Papagiannopoulos, E.]: *Η διώρυγα της Κορίνθου: τεχνικός άθλος και οικονομικό τόλμημα* [The Canal of Corinth: Technical Feat and Economic Adventure], Athens 1989.

Παπαθανασόπουλος, Κ. [Papathanasopoulos, K.]: *Ελληνική εμπορική ναυτιλία (1833–1856). Εξέλιξη και αναπροσαρμογή* [The Greek Merchant Marine (1833–1856). Development and Readjustment], Athens 1983.

Papayannis, T.: Greek Wetlands: Cultural Values and Tertiary Sector Activities, in: P. A. Gerakes (ed.): *Conservation and Management of Greek Wetlands: Proceedings of a Workshop on Greek Wetlands, Salonica, Greece, 17–21 April 1989*, Athens 1992a, pp. 157–174.

Idem: Greek Wetlands: Factors of Change, in: P. A. Gerakes (ed.): *Conservation and Management of Greek Wetlands: Proceedings of a Workshop on Greek Wetlands, Salonika, Greece, 17–21 April 1989*, Athens 1992b, pp. 207–227.

Παπαστεφανάκη, Λ. [Papastefanaki, L.]: Εξορυκτικές επιχειρήσεις και εργασία. Η περίπτωση του Αιγαίου (1860–1960) [Montan Industry and Work. The Aegean Region (1860–1960)], in: Εθνικό Μετσόβιο Πολυτεχνείο – Σχολή Αρχιτεκτόνων Μηχανικών Πολιτιστικό Ίδρυμα Ομίλου Πειραιώς (ΠΙΟΠ). Οικονομική Βιομηχανική Επιθεώρηση/αρχείο Βοβολίνη [National Technical University of Athens (NTUA) – School of Architectional Engineering Piraeus. Piraeus Bank Group Cultural Foundation Economic and Industrial Review – Archives of Vovolinis] (ed.): *Ιστορικά μεταλλεία στο Αιγαίο, 19ος–20ός αιώνας: Επιστημονικό συνέδριο, Μήλος, 3–5 Οκτωβρίου 2003* [Historical Metallurgy in the Aegean, 19th –20th century. Conference at Milos 3.–5. October 2003], Athens 2005, pp. 27–47.

Παπαγιαννάκης, Λ. [Papayiannakis, L.]: *Οι Ελληνικοί Σιδηρόδρομοι (1882–1910). Γεωπολιτικές, οικονομικές και κοινωνικές διαστάσεις* [Greek Railroads (1882–1910). Geopolitical, Economic and Social Perspectives], Athens 1982.

Pappé, H.O.: The English Utilitarians and Athenian Democray, in: *R. R. Bolgar* (ed.): *Classical Influences on Western Thought A. D. 1650–1870. Proceedings of an International Conference Held at King's College*, Cambridge, March 1977, Cambridge et al. 1979, pp. 295–307.

Πάρη, Ε. [Paris, E.]: Ο Ελληνισμός υπό το πρίσμα της Μασσαλίας (μέσα 19ου – αρχές 20ου αιώνα) [The Hellenism Seen through the Lens of Marseille (Mid 19th – Beginning of the 20th Century)], in: E. Konstantinou (ed.): *Das Bild Griechenlands im Spiegel der Völker (17. bis 18. Jahrhundert) – The Image of Greece in the Mirror of Nations (17th–18th Century)*, Brussels 2008, pp. 111–120.

Idem: Les Grecs de Marseille dans la deuxième moitié du XIXe siècle: une perspective nationale et transnationale, in: *Revue européenne des migrations internationales* 17 (2001) 3, pp. 23–42.

Paulus, C. G.: *A Debt Restructuring Mechanism for Sovereigns: Do We Need a Legal Procedure?* Munich 2014.

Payne, R.: *The Canal Builder. The Story of Canal Engineers through The Ages*, New York 1959.

Peiró i Pérez, J. L./Morales Ferrandis, J.: *El Tren Alcoi-Gandia. Alcoy and Gandia Railway and Harbour Company Limited*, València 2003.

Penn, V.: Philhellenism in England (1821–1827), in: *The Slavonic and East European Review* 14 (1936a) 41, pp. 363–371.

Idem: Philhellenism in England II, in: *The Slavonic and East European Review* 14 (1936b) 42, pp. 647–660.

Idem: Philhellenism in Europe, 1821–1828, in: *The Slavonic and East European Review* 16 (1938) 48, pp. 638–653.

Pepelasis, A. A.: The Legal System and Economic Development of Greece, in: *The Journal of Economic History* 19 (1959) 2, pp. 173–198.

Pepelasis, I. S.: Mapping Greek Banking Historiography, in: O. Feiertag/idem (eds.): *European Banking Historiography. Past and Present*, Athens 2009, pp. 135–154.

Idem: Joint Stock Company Births in Greece (1830–1909), in: *Entreprises et Histoire* 63 (2011), pp. 26–39.

Idem/Varvaritis, D.: An Unexplored Facet of International Business in Greece: Foreign and Diaspora Shareholders in Joint Stock Company Start-Ups, 1833–1920, in: *Journal of Evolutionary Studies in Business* 2 (2016), pp. 100–128.

Περάκης, Μ. [Perakis, M.]: Η αντικατάσταση της δεκάτης από το φόρο των αροτριώντων ζώων. Η πρώτη φορολογική αλλαγή του Χαρίλαου Τρικούπη [The Replacement of the Tithe by the Tax on Livestock. The First Tax Modification by Charilaos Tricoupis], in: Κ. Αρώνη-Τσίχλη [K. Aroni-Tsixli]/Λ. Τρίχα [L. Tricha] (eds.): *Ο Χαρίλαος Τρικούπης και η εποχή του. Πολιτικές επιδιώξεις και κοινωνικές συνθήκες* [Charilaos Trikoupis and His Time. Political Aims and Social Conditions], Athens 2000, pp. 275–292.

Perceval, M. Á. P. de/López-Morell, M. Á.: Hilarion Roux, 1819–1898. Auge y decacencia de un minero emprendedor, in: *Argentum* 1 (2009), pp. 10–20.

Pesendorfer, F.: *Die Habsburger in der Toskana*, Wien 1988.

Pesmazoglou, I.: *Projet de règlement des Finances helléniques*, Alexandrie 1893.

Πεσμαζόγλου, Ι. Γ. [Pesmazoglou, I. G.]: *Εκθεσις του γενικού διευθυντού της Τραπέζης Αθηνών κ. Ι. Γ. Πεσμαζόγλου προς το συμβούλιον της Τραπέζης, εισηγητήριος του ισολογισμού της Α΄ης εξαμηνίας 1897* [Report of the General Director of the Bank of Athens Mr. I. G. Pesmazoglou for the Administrative Council of the Bank, on the Occasion of the Balance Sheet 1897], Athens 1897.

Idem: *Υπόμνημα περί ιδρύσεως σταφιδικής τραπέζης* [Memoir about the Foundation of a Currant Bank], Athens 1898.

Idem: *Υπόμνημα περί του καταλληλοτέρου μέσου προς άρσιν και ριζικήν θεραπείαν της νομισματικής κρίσεως* [Memoir about Proper Measures for the Enhancement and the Root Therapy of the Currency Crisis], Athens 1904.

Idem: *Περί διαρρυθμίσεως του σταφιδικού ζητήματος: εισήγησις και επεξήγησις αυτού* [About the Solution of the Currant Question. Proposal and Explanations], Athens 1905.

Petersson, N. P.: *Anarchie und Weltrecht: das Deutsche Reich und die Institutionen der Weltwirtschaft 1890–1930*, Göttingen 2009.

Πετμεζάς, Σ. Δ. [Petmezas, S. D.]: *Η ελληνική αγροτική οικονομία κατά τον 19ο αιώνα: Η περιφερειακή διάσταση* [The Greek Agriculture Economy in the 19th Century. The Peripherial Dimension], Athens 2003.

Idem: L'économie agricole grecque face à la grande crise de la première globalisation, in: *The Historical Review/La Revue Historique* 10 (2013), pp. 85–105.

Petropulos, J. A.: *Politics and Statecraft in the Kingdom of Greece. 1833–1843*, Princeton NJ 1968.

Πετρόπουλος, Ι. Α. [Petropulos, J. A.]: *Πολιτική και συγκρότηση κράτους στο Ελληνικό Βασίλειο 1833–1843* [Politics and Statecraft in the Kingdom of Greece 1833–1843], Athens 1985/1986.

Philippson, A.: Der Kopais-See in Griechenland und seine Umgebung, in: *Zeitschrift der Gesellschaft für Erdkunde* 19 (1894), pp. 1–90.

Phillips, A. D. M: *The Underdraining of Farmland in England during the Nineteenth Century*, Cambridge/New York 1989 (= Cambridge Studies in Historical Geography, Vol. 15).

Picon, A.: *Les Saint-Simoniens. Raison, imaginaire et utopie*, Paris 2002.

Pictet, E. O.: *Biographie, travaux et correspondance diplomatique de C. Pictet de Rochemont. Député de Genève auprès du Congrès de Vienne, 1814, envoyé extraordinaire et ministre plénipotentiaire de la Suisse à Paris et Turin, 1815 et 1816, 1755–1824*, Genève 1892.

Pictet, R. de/Ivernois, F. d'/Cramer, L.: *Genève et les traités de 1815: correspondance diplomatique de Pictet de Rochemont et de François d'Ivernois, Paris, Vienne, Turin 1814–16*, Genève 1914.

Pittakïs, M.: Description faite par M. Pittakïs, conservateur des antiquités, dans son rapport adressé à M. Christopoulos, ministre de l'Instruction publique et des Cultes à Athènes (Journal l'Espérance, du 30 décembre 1856), in: *L'investigateur. Journal de l'institut historique* 24 (1857) VII/III, pp. 51–55.

Pizanias, P.: Rapports de prêt et domination économique. La Fondation de la Banque nationale de Grèce (1841–1847), in: D. Chambers (ed.): *Actes du IIe colloque international d'histoire (Athènes, 18–25 septembre 1983): Économies méditerranéennes: Équilibres et intercommunications, XIIIe–XIXe siècles, Vol. II.*, Athènes 1986, pp. 447–476.

Πιζάνιας, Π. [Pizanias, P.]: *Οικονομική ιστορία της ελληνικής σταφίδας 1851–1912. Παραγωγή, διεθνής αγορά, διαμόρφωση τιμών, κρίση* [Economic History of the Greek Raisin 1851–1912. Production, International Market, Price Development, Crisis], Athens 1988.

Plaschka, R. G./Drabek, A. M./Zaar, B. (eds.): *Eisenbahnbau und Kapitalinteressen in den Beziehungen der österreichischen mit den südslawischen Ländern*, Wien 1993 (= Veröffentlichungen der Kommission für die Geschichte Österreichs, Vol. 19).

Platt, D. C. M.: *The Cinderella Service. British Consuls since 1825*, London 1971.

Plumpe, W.: Wie entscheiden Unternehmen?, in: *Zeitschrift für Unternehmensgeschichte* 61 (2016) 2, pp. 141–159.

Plusieurs membres de l'ancien comité grec de Paris (eds.): *Lettres et Documents officiels relatifs aux derniers événements de la Grèce, qui ont précédé et suivi la mort du comte Capodistrias, jusqu'au 31 octobre 1831*, Paris 1831.

Pohle, M.: Risk, Information and Noise: Risk Perception and Risk Management of French and German Banks during the Nineteenth Century. Iain L. Fraser (trans.), in: *Financial History Review* 2 (1995) 1, pp. 25–39.

Pohle-Fraser, M.: *Noisy Optimists: Risk Management in French and German Banks in the 19th and Early 20th Centuries*, Florence 1999 (Unpublished Manuscript).

Πολυκανδριώτη, O. [Polikandrioti, O.]: Οψεις της Ελλάδας του 19ου αιώνα στο περιοδικό Revue des Deux Mondes [Aspects de la Grèce du XIXe siècle dans la Revue des Deux Mondes], in: E. Χρυσός [E. Chrysos]/C. Farnaud (eds.): *Ελλάδα και Γαλλία τον 19ο αιώνα. La France et la Grèce au XIXe siècle. Πρακτικά ελληνογαλλικού συνεδρίου. Αθήνα, 29 και 30 Μαρτίου 2011. Actes du colloque*, Athens 2012, pp. 301–312.

Pöls, W.: Bleichröder und die Arnim-Affäre, in: *Historische Zeitschrift* 211 (1970) 1, pp. 65–76.

Porter, T. M.: *Trust in Numbers. The Pursuit of Objectivity in Science and Public Life*, Princeton NJ 1995.

Potter, L.: British Philhellenism and the Historiography of Greece: A Case Study of George Finlay (1799–1875), in: *The Historical Review/La Revue Historique* 1 (2004), pp. 183–206.

Pozzo DiBorgo, C. A./Nesselrode, K. R. von: *Correspondance diplomatique du comte Pozzo di Borgo et du comte de Nesselrode depuis la restauration des Bourbons jusqu'au Congrès d'Aix-la-Chapelle, 1814–1818*, Paris 1890.

Idem: *Mémoires sur les Cent-Jours*, ed. by Benjamin de Constant Rebecque, Paris 1961.

Prévélakis, G.: Géopolitique du philhellénisme, in: C. Montandon (ed.): *Regards sur le philhellénisme. Mission permanente de la Grèce auprès de l'ONU: Consulat général de Grèce: Association gréco-suisse Jean-Gabriel Eynard*, Genève 2008, pp. 43–50.

Πρεβενά, A. [Prevena, A.]: Το Λαυρεωτικό ζήτημα στην ελληνική ιστοριογραφία [The Laurion Affaire in Greek Historiography], in: A. Πρεβενά [A. Prevena] (ed.): *Πρακτικά Γ' Επιστημονικής Συνάντησης Ν.Α. Αττικής* [Conference Proceedings I of the Scientific Meeting N. A. Attika 2002], Kalivia 2004, pp. 573–581.

Prevost, M.: Beulé, Charles-Ernest, in: *DBF*, 6 (1954), p. 362f.

Idem: Burnouf, Émile-Louis, in: *DBF*, 7 (1956), p. 702f.

Priemel, K.: Spekulation als Gegenstand historischer Forschung, in: *Jahrbuch für Wirtschaftsgeschichte* (2013) 2, pp. 9–26.

Progoulakis, G./Bournova, E.: Le monde rural grec, 1830–1912, in: *Ruralia* 8 (2001), http://ruralia.revues.org/214 [21.1.2020].

Ψαλιδόπουλος, M. [Psalidopoulos, M.]: Τα δάνεια της Ελλάδας [The Loans of Greece], Athens 2019.

Psalidopoulos, M./Mata, M. E. (eds.): *Economic Thought and Policy in Less Developed Europe: the Nineteenth Century*, London et al. 2002 (= Routledge Studies in the History of Economics, Vol. 53).

Psalidopoulos, M./Schönhärl, K.: Die griechische Staatsverschuldung in der zweiten Hälfte des 19. Jahrhunderts, in: T. Beigel/G. Eckert (eds.): *Vom Wohl und Wehe der Staatsverschuldung. Erscheinungsformen und Sichtweisen von der Antike bis zur Gegenwart*, Münster 2013, pp. 149–164.

Psalidopoulos, M./Theocarakis, N. J.: The Dissemination of Economic Thought in South-Eastern Europe in the Nineteenth Century, in: H. Kurz (ed.): *The Dissemination of Economic Ideas*, Cheltenham et al. 2011, pp. 161–191.

Puig, N./Castro, R.: Patterns of International Investment in Spain, 1850–2009, in: *Business History Review* 83 (2009), pp. 505–537.

Quack-Eustathiades, R.: *Der deutsche Philhellenismus während des griechischen Freiheitskampfes 1821–1827*, Munich 1984 (= Südosteuropäische Arbeiten, Vol. 79).

Queux Saint-Hilaire, L. (Marquis de): Notice sur les services rendus à la Grèce et aux études grecques par M. Gustave d'Eichthal, in: E. d'Eichthal (ed.): *La langue grecque. Mémoires & notices 1864–1884; précédé d'une notice sur les services rendus, par M. G. d'Eichthal à la Grèce et aux études grecques par le Marquis de Queux de Saint-Hilaire*, Paris 1887, pp. 1–103.

Radu, R.: *"Auguren des Geldes" – Eine Kulturgeschichte des Finanzjournalismus in Deutschland (1850–1914)*, Göttingen 2017.

Rae, G., alias Thomas Bullion: *The Internal Management of a Country Bank. In a Series of Letters on the Functions and Duties of a Branch Manager*, London 1850 (2nd ed. Toronto 1876).

Raff, T.: Die Münchner Propyläen – ein Denkmal des griechischen Freiheitskampfes, in: R. Heydenreuter (ed.): *Die erträumte Nation: Griechenlands Wiedergeburt im 19. Jahrhundert. Begleitband zur Ausstellung „Die Erträumte Nation. Griechenlands Wiedergeburt im 19. Jahrhundert. Bilder und Dokumente zu den bayerisch-griechischen Beziehungen im 19. Jahrhundert"*, Munich 1995, pp. 195–208.

Ratcliffe, B. M.: Saint-Simonism and Messianism: The Case of Gustave d'Eichthal, in: *French Historical Studies* (1976) 9, pp. 484–502.

Idem (ed.): *A French Sociologist Looks at Britain. Gustave d'Eichthal and British Society in 1828*, Manchester 1977a (= University Manchester: Faculty of Arts. Publications, Vol. 22).

Idem: Gustave d'Eichthal (1802–1886). An Intellectual Portrait, in: idem (ed.): *A French Sociologist Looks at Britain. Gustave d'Eichthal and British Society in 1828*, Manchester 1977b, pp. 109–161 (= University Manchester: Faculty of Arts. Publications, Vol. 22).

Idem: The Business Elite and the Development of Paris: Intervention in Ports and Entrepôts, 1814–1834, in: *Journal of European Economic History* 14 (1985) 1, pp. 95–142.

Rechberger, W.: Zur Geschichte der Orientbahnen, in: *Österreichische Osthefte* 2 (1960) 5, pp. 348–359.

Idem: Zur Geschichte der Orientbahnen II, in: *Österreichische Osthefte* 3 (1961) 2, pp. 102–112.

Recktenwald, N.: Enttäuschung im 20. Jahrhundert, Conference Report 21.12.2001, in: *Institut für Zeitgeschichte München – Berlin*, https://www.ifz-muenchen.de/das-institut/veranstaltungsrueckblick/veranstaltung/datum/21/12/2011/enttaeuschung-im-20-jahrhundert/ [30.9.2015].

Reese-Schäfer, W.: *Amitai Etzioni zur Einführung*, Hamburg 2001 (= Zur Einführung, Vol. 242).

Régnier, P.: Saint-Simon, les Saint-Simoniens et le Saint-Simonisme, in: *Cahier de l'Association culturelle du Razès* 82 (2010), pp. 11–40.

Reinecke, C.: Wissensgesellschaft und Informationsgesellschaft, Version: 1.0, in: *Docupedia-Zeitgeschichte*, 11.2.2010, http://docupedia.de/zg/Wissensgesellschaft [21.1.2020].

Reinhart, C. M./Rogoff, K. S.: *Dieses Mal ist alles anders. Acht Jahrhunderte Finanzkrisen*, Munich 3rd ed. 2010.

Reitmayer, M.: *Bankiers im Kaiserreich. Sozialprofil und Habitus der deutschen Hochfinanz*, Göttingen 1999 (= Kritische Studien zur Geschichtswissenschaft, Vol. 136).

Ρενιέρης, Μ. [Renieri, M.]/Γεννηματάς, Π. Ν. [Gennimatas, P. N.] (eds.): *Τι είναι η Ελλάς;* [What Is Greece?], Athens 1998 (Reprint of the 1st ed. of 1842 in the Journal Eranistis).

Revaux, G.: Mines. L'industrie minérale en Grèce, in: *Le Génie civil. Revue générale des industries françaises & étrangères* 3 (1882) 1, pp. 194–196.

Ricard, C. F.: *Reisebreve*, ed. by Jean Ricard, Kopenhagen 1954.

Ricardo, D.: *Biographical Miscellany*, ed. by Piero Sraffa, London 1973 (= The Works and Correspondence of David Ricardo, Vol. 10).

Ricciardi, V.: Risk: Traditional Finance versus Behavioral Finance, in: F. J. Fabozzi (ed.): *Handbook of Finance, Vol. 3: Valuation, Financial Modeling, and Quantitative Tools*, Hoboken NJ 2008a, pp. 11–38.

Idem: The Psychology of Risk: The Behavioral Finance Perspective, in: F. J. Fabozzi (ed.): *Handbook of Finance, Vol. 2: Investment Management and Financial Management*, Hoboken NJ 2008b, pp. 85–111.

Richard, E.: Hilarion Roux, in: R. Caty/E. Richard/P. Échinard (eds.): *Marseille*, Paris 1999, pp. 269–273 (= Les patrons du Second Empire, Vol. 5).

Richter, J. S.: *Die Orientreise Kaiser Wilhelms II. 1898*, Hamburg/Kiel 1997.

Riehl, K.: Freispruch und Ende, in: *Süddeutsche Zeitung*, 3.4.2012.

Ripperger, T.: *Ökonomik des Vertrauens. Analyse eines Organisationsprinzips*, Tübingen 5th ed. 2005 (= Die Einheit der Gesellschaftswissenschaften, Vol. 101).

Ritschl, A.: *Sustainability of High Public Debt: What the Historical Record Shows*, 1996, CEPR Discussion Paper No. 1357, https://ideas.repec.org/p/cpr/ceprdp/1357.html [21.1.2020].

Riz, A. de: *Le Laurium*, Paris 1872.

Roberts, R.: *Schroders. Merchants & Bankers*, Basingstoke/Hampshire 1992.

Röhl, J. C. G.: *Kaiser, Hof und Staat. Wilhelm II. und die deutsche Politik*, Munich 1987.

Rordam, H. F.: Wilhelm Sponneck, in: *Dansk Biografisk Leksikon*, 1902, Sp. 234–242.

Rosen, F.: *Bentham, Byron and Greece. Constitutionalism, Nationalism and Early Liberal Political Thought*, Oxford 1992.

Idem: *Greek Nationalism and British Liberalism*, Athens 1998.

Idem: Blaquiere, Edward (1779–1832), Author and Philhellene, in: *ODNB*, Oxford 2004a, doi:10.1093/ref:odnb/57497.

Idem: London Greek Committee (act. 1823–1826), in: *ODNB*, Oxford 2004b, doi:10.1093/ref:odnb/95072.

Roth, B.: Pictet [de Rochemont], Charles, in: *Historisches Lexikon der Schweiz*, http://www.hls-dhs-dss.ch/textes/d/D20517.php [21.1.2020].

Roth, R.: *Das Jahrhundert der Eisenbahn. Die Herrschaft über Raum und Zeit 1800–1914*, Ostfildern 2005.

Idem: Von der Zollvereinsgründung bis zur Annexion der Stadt 1834–1870, in: W. Plumpe/D. Rebentisch (eds.): *"Dem Flor der hiesigen Handlung". 200 Jahre Industrie- und Handelskammer Frankfurt am Main 1808–2008*, Frankfurt 2008a, pp. 80–103.

Idem (ed.): *Across the Borders. Financing the World's Railways in the Nineteenth and Twentieth Centuries*, Aldershot 2008b.

Rothpletz, E.: *Der Genfer Jean Gabriel Eynard als Philhellene 1821–1829*, Zürich 1899.

Ruge, A./Konstantinou, E.: *Europäischer Philhellenismus: die europäische philhellenische Presse bis zur ersten Hälfte des 19.* Jahrhunderts, Frankfurt et al. 1994 (= Philhellenische Studien, Vol. 3).

Russegger, J.: *Reise in der Levante und in Europa. Mit besonderer Rücksicht auf die naturwissenschaftlichen Verhältnisse der betreffenden Länder; unternommen in den Jahren 1839 bis 1841*, Stuttgart 1848 (= Reisen in Europa, Asien und Afrika, Vol. 4).

Sabean, D. W./Teuscher, S.: Rethinking European Kinship. Transregional and Transnational Families, in: C. H. Johnson (ed.): *Transregional and Transnational Families in Europe and Beyond. Experiences since the Middle Ages*, New York 2011, pp. 1–21.

Said, E. W.: *Orientalism*, New York 1978.

Σαλίμπα, Z. [Salimba, Z.]: Τα θέλγητρα των μεταλλευτικών εταιρειών και η κουλτούρα των μικρονοικοκυραίων μετόχων (1873–1893) [The Attraction of the Metallurgical Companies and the Culture of the Small Shareholders], in: Εθνικό Μετσόβιο Πολυτεχνείο – Σχολή αρχιτεκτόνων μηχανικών Πολιτιστικό Ίδρυμα Ομίλου Πειραιώς (ΠΙΟΠ), Οικονομική Βιομηχανική Επιθεώρηση/αρχείο Βοβολίνη [National Technical University of Athens (NTUA) – School of Architectional Engineering Piraeus. Piraeus Bank Group Cultural Foundation Economic and Industrial Review – Archives of Vovolinis] (ed.): *Ιστορικά μεταλλεία στο Αιγαίο, 19ος–20ός αιώνας: Επιστημονικό συνέδριο, Μήλος, 3–5 Οκτωβρίου 2003* [Historical Metallurgy in the Aegean, 19th–20th century. Conference at Milo 3.–5. October 2003], Athens 2005, pp. 49–56.

Salomon-Delatour, G.: *Die Lehre Saint-Simons.* Edited with an introduction by Gottfried Salomon-Delatour, Neuwied 1962 (= Politica, Vol. 7).

Salvucci, R.: *Politics, Markets, and Mexico's "London Debt". 1823–1887*, Cambridge 2009 (= Cambridge Latin American Studies, Vol. 93).

Samakovitis, G.: U. K. Banking Experts as Decision-Makers: A Historical View on Banking Technologies, in: *Journal of Technology Research* 3 (2012), pp. 1–20.

Sandys, J. E.: *An Easter Vacation in Greece with Lists of Books on Greek Travel and Topography and Time-Tables of Greek Steamers and Railways*, London 1887.

Sauvage, C.: *Projet de Dessèchement du Lac Copaïs, rédigé en 1849*, Athènes 1868.

Sauvigny, B. de: Charles X., in: *DBF*, 8 (1959), pp. 536–543.

Savoy, B./Potin, Y. (ed.): *Napoleon und Europa: Traum und Trauma; Kunst- und Ausstellungshalle der Bundesrepublik Deutschland*, Bonn 2010.

Schaefer, K. C.: *Deutsche Portfolioinvestitionen im Ausland 1870–1914. Banken, Kapitalmärkte und Wertpapierhandel im Zeitalter des Imperialismus*, Münster 1995.

Schaffer, S. et al. (eds.): *The Brokered World. Go-betweens and Global Intelligence, 1770–1820*, Sagamore Beach MA 2009 (= Uppsala Studies in History of Science, Vol. 35).

Schenk, F. B./Winkler, M. (eds.): *Der Süden. Neue Perspektiven auf eine europäische Geschichtsregion*, Frankfurt 2007a.

Idem: Einleitung, in: Idem (eds.): *Der Süden. Neue Perspektiven auf eine europäische Geschichtsregion*, Frankfurt 2007b, pp. 7–20.

Scherf, W.: *Öffentliche Finanzen. Einführung in die Finanzwissenschaft*, Konstanz et al. 2nd ed. 2011 (= UTB, Vol. 8313).

Schiif, H.: Jewish Bankers 1850–1914: Internationalization along Ethnic Lines, in: I. B. McCabe et al. (eds.): *Diaspora Entrepreneurial Networks: Four Centuries of History*, Oxford 2005, pp. 191–216.

Schleiff, H./Konečný, P. (eds.): *Staat, Bergbau und Bergakademie. Montanexperten im 18. und frühen 19. Jahrhundert*, Stuttgart 2013 (= Vierteljahrschrift für Sozial- und Wirtschaftsgeschichte Beiheft 223).

Schmale, W.: *Geschichte Frankreichs*, Stuttgart 2000 (= UTB 2145).

Schnee, H.: Bleichröder, Gerson von, in: *NDB*, 2 (1955), p. 299, http://www.deutsche-biographie.de/ppn11851167X.html [21.1.2020].

Schneider, U.: Die Farbe der Religion. Topografie und Topik der "Deux France", in: *Journal of Modern European History* 9 (2011) 1, pp. 117–139.

Idem: *Die Macht der Karten. Eine Geschichte der Kartographie vom Mittelalter bis heute*, Darmstadt 3rd ed. 2012.

Scholler, H.: Griechenland als Imago, Rezeption oder Perspektive: Das Bild Griechenlands bei Friedrich Thiersch im Kontrast zu dem Bild, das der bayerischen Regentschaft vorschwebte, in: E. Konstantinou (ed.): *Das Bild Griechenlands im Spiegel der Völker (17. bis 18. Jahrhundert) – The Image of Greece in the Mirror of Nations (17th–18th Century)*, Brussels 2008, pp. 237–252.

Schönhärl, K.: Warum Geld für Hellas? Die Verschuldung Griechenlands in den 1880er Jahren, in: *Bankenhistorisches Archiv* 39 (2013a) 1, pp. 20–39.

Idem: Fighting the Financial Crisis in Greece: The Privileged Company to Protect Production and Trade in Currants (1905) as International Bank Cooperation, in: *The Historical Review/La Revue Historique* 10 (2013b), pp. 107–134.

Idem: Vertrauensarbeit nach dem Bankrott: Die Internationale Finanzkommission für Griechenland zwischen 1898 und 1914, in: A. Hedwig (ed.): *Finanzpolitik und Schuldenkrisen 16.–20. Jahrhundert*, Marburg 2014a, pp. 173–196.

Idem: Review on: Bonin, Hubert: French Banks and the Greek "Niche Market" mid-1880s–1950s, in: *Financial History Review* 21 (2014b) 2, pp. 218–220.

Idem: 'Leider sind wir bankrott' – Zahlungsausfälle in der Geschichte Griechenlands im 19. und frühen 20. Jahrhundert, in: U.-D. Klemm/ W. Schultheiß, (eds.): *Die Krise in Griechenland Ursprünge, Verlauf, Folgen*, Frankfurt/New York 2015, pp. 182–197.

Idem (ed.): *Decision Making, Confidence and Risk Management in Banks from Early Modernity to the 20th Century*, Basingstoke/Hampshire et al. 2017a (= Palgrave Studies in the History of Finance).

Idem: Introduction, in: idem (ed.): *Decision Making, Confidence and Risk Management in Banks from Early Modernity to the 20th Century*, Basingstoke/Hampshire et al. 2017b, pp. 1–12 (= Palgrave Studies in the History of Finance).

Idem: Why Invest in Greece? Gerson von Bleichröder and the Greek Loan of 1889, in: *German-Greek Yearbook of Political Economy* 1 (2018), pp. 33–54.

Idem: Socially Responsible Investment in 19th Century Greexe: A Case Study of a Swiss Banker, in: *Vierteljahrschrift für Sozial- und Wirschaftsgeschichte* 106 (2019a), pp. 167–190.

Idem: Why Does a Prestigious Emission House Emit a Loan for a Peripheral State? The House of Rothschild and the Greek Guaranteed Loan of 1833 in: *Business History* (2019b), doi:10.1080/00076791.2019.1593373.

Idem: Geld zurück! Internationale Finanzkontrolle in Griechenland im 19. Jahrhundert und in der Gegenwart, in: C. Henrich-Franke et al. (eds.), *Grenzüberschreitende institutionalisierte Zusammenarbeit von der Antike bis zur Gegenwart*, Baden-Baden 2019c, pp. 269–300.

Idem: 'Wie tief der kern dieses Volkes dem antiken wesen verwandt ist'. 'Cultural brokers' und ihre Strategien zur Vermittlung des Unbekannten, in: *Historische Zeitschrift* 304 (2020), pp. 285–305.

Schönpflug, D.: *Die Heiraten der Hohenzollern. Verwandtschaft, Politik und Ritual in Europa 1640–1918*, Göttingen 2013.

Schulin, E.: Die Rathenaus – Zwei Generationen jüdischen Anteils an der industriellen Entwicklung Deutschlands, in: W. E. Mosse (ed.): *Juden im Wilhelminischen Deutschland 1890–1914*, Tübingen 1976, pp. 115–142.

Schulz, O.: *Ein Sieg der zivilisierten Welt?* Berlin/Düsseldorf 2011.

Schunck, P.: *Geschichte Frankreichs. Von Heinrich IV. bis zur Gegenwart*, Stuttgart 1994.

Schütz, A./Luckmann, T.: *Strukturen der Lebenswelt*, Stuttgart 2003 (= UTB, Vol. 2412).

Schwarz, H. J.: *Stefan Türr. Zeitgemälde aus Oesterreichs jüngster Vergangenheit*, Wien 1868.

Schwarz, S. L.: *Despoten – Barbaren – Wirtschaftspartner. Die Allgemeine Zeitung und der Diskurs über das Osmanische Reich 1821–1840*, Wien Köln Weimar 2016.

Seasholes, M. S.: Social Interactions and Investing, in: H. Kent Baker/John R. Nofsinger (eds.): *Behavioral Finance. Investors, Corporations, and Markets*, Hoboken NJ 2010, pp. 647–670 (= The Robert W. Kolb Series in Finance).

Seewald, B.: *Karl Wilhelm v. Heideck. Ein bayerischer General im befreiten Griechenland (1826–1835)* (Beiträge zur Militärgeschichte, Vol. 45), Munich 2009.

Seidl, W.: *Bayern in Griechenland: Die Geschichte eines Abenteuers*, Munich 1970.

Idem: *Bayern in Griechenland. Die Geburt des griechischen Nationalstaats unter der Regierung König Ottos*, Munich 1981.

Seni, A. et al.: *Jean Gabriel Eynard entre Genève et la Grèce: la vie, l'œuvre, le palais.* 1 vidéocassette [VHS] (30 min.), Genève 1994.

Sergeant, L.: *Greece in the Nineteenth Century. A Record of Hellenic Emancipation and Progress: 1821–1897*, London 1897.

Serpieri, J. B.: *Une spoliation. Aperçu général sur la question des minerais des terres du Laurium avec documents à l'appui et titre en grec*, Athènes 1871a.

Idem: *Encore quelques observations et documents sur la question du Laurium*, Rome 1871b.

Idem: *Réponse à l'exposé de M. le président du conseil des ministres sur la question du Laurium*, Athènes 1872.

Serpieri, P.: *I Serpieri di Rimini*. Memoria, Rimini 1982.

Sharp, P. R./Maerean, A.-A.: *Sovereign Debt and Supersanctions in Emerging Markets: Evidence from Four Southeast European Countries, 1878–1913, Vortrag am Ersten Deutschen Kongress für Wirtschaftsgeschichte*, Bonn, 12.3.2015 (Unpublished Manuscript).

Shaw, B.: *Bernard Shaw's Book Reviews. Originally Published in the Pall Mall Gazette from 1885 to 1888*, ed. by B. Tyson, Pennsylvania State University Park 1991.

Sifneos, E.: Diaspora Entrepreneurship in the Southern Russian Ports, in: *Entreprises et Histoire* 63 (2011), pp. 40–52.

Simal, J. L.: National Credit and the International Financial Market: The Spanish Debt and Its Foreign Bondholders, 1820–1834, in: *Journal of Iberian and Latin American Studies* (2019), pp. 381–402, doi: 10.1080/14701847.2019.1680005.

Simitis, K.: *The European Debt Crisis. The Greek Case*, Manchester 2014.

Simmel, G.: *Philosophie des Geldes*, Leipzig 1900.

Simmel, G.: *Sociology: Inquiries into the Construction of Social Forms*, translated by A. J. Blasi et al., Leiden, Boston MA 2009.

Idem: *Soziologie. Untersuchungen über die Formen der Vergesellschaftung*, Berlin 7th ed. 2013.

Simon, H.: Vorwort, in: L. Geiger (ed.): *Geschichte der Juden in Berlin. Festschrift zur zweiten Säkular-Feier. Anmerkungen, Ausführungen, urkundliche Beilagen und zwei Nachträge (1871–1890)*, Nachdruck Leipzig 1988, pp. VII–XLII.

Συρμαλόγλου, A. [Sirmaloglou, A.]: *Φορολογία ή χρεοκοπία: Η φορολογική πολιτική στη Βουλή των Ελλήνων, 1862–1910* [Taxation or Insolvency. The Tax Policy in the Greek Parliament 1862–1910], Athens 2007.

Smith, C. O.: The Longest Run: Public Engineers and Planning in France, in: *The American Historical Review* 95 (1990) 3, pp. 657–692.

Société genevoise d'utilité publique (ed.): *La Société genevoise d'utilité publique en son temps, 1828–1978. Contribution à l'histoire économique et sociale de Genève*, Genève 1978.

Sotiropoulos, S. (ed.): *Affaire du Laurium*, Athènes 1871.

Soulié, C.-A.: Financing the Railway in France: The Haute Banque between Collaboration and Competition, 1832–52, in: *Bankhistorisches Archiv* 39 (2013) 1, pp. 59–72.

Σουλογιάννης, Ευ. [Soulogiannis, Ev.]: Μερικά για τον ελληνισμό της Αιγύπτου και την Τρικουπική εποχή, με ειδική αναφορά στα έτη 1867, 1875, 1884 [Remarks Concerning the Hellenism in Egypt and the Period of Trikoupis, Especially in the Years 1867, 1875, 1884], in: K. Αρώνη-Τσίχλη [K. Aroni-Tsixli]/ Λ. Τρίχα [L. Tricha] (eds.): *Ο Χαρίλαος Τρικούπης και η εποχή του. Πολιτικές επιδιώξεις και κοινωνικές συνθήκες* [Charilaos Trikoupis and His Time. Political Aims and Social Conditions], Athens 2000, pp. 585–596.

Spaenle, L.: *Der Philhellenismus in Bayern: 1821–1832*, Munich 1990 (= Veröffentlichungen des Instituts für Geschichte Osteuropas und Südosteuropas der Universität München, Vol. 9).

Idem: Philhellenismus und Öffentlichkeit in Bayern: Die bayerische Griechenbewegung im Spiegel der Presse, in: A. Ruge/E. Konstantinou (eds.): *Europäischer*

Philhellenismus: die europäische philhellenische Presse bis zur ersten Hälfte des 19. Jahrhunderts, Frankfurt et al. 1994, pp. 171–221 (= Philhellenische Studien, Vol. 3).

Σπανιολάκης, Γ. [Spaniolakis, G.]: *Παρατηρήσεις επί της απολογίας Ι. Ορλάνδου και Α. Λουριώτου εις την κατ' αυτών απόφασιν του Ελεγκτικού Συνεδρίου* [Observations on the Defence of Ioannis Orlandos and Andreas Louriotis before the Committee of Auditors Regarding the Decision against Them], Athens 1839/1840.

Σπανός, Β. [Spanos, V.]: *Ιωάννης Καποδίστριας – Ο θεμελιωτής του ελληνικού κράτους* [Ionannis Kapodistrias – Founder of the Greek State], Athens 2008.

Spindler, M.: *Handbuch der bayerischen Geschichte*, Munich 1974.

St. Clair, W.: *That Greece Might Still Be Free. The Philhellenes in the War of Independence*, Cambridge 2008 (1th ed. 1972).

St. George, A.: Hambro, Baron Carl Joachim (1807–1877), in: *ODNB*, Oxford 2004, doi:10.1093/ref:odnb/48884.

St. George, A.: Hambro, Sir Everard Alexander, in: *ODNB*, Oxford 2004, doi:10.1093/ref:odnb/47596.

Στασινόπουλος, Ε. Κ. [Stasinopoulos, E. K.]: *Η ιστορία της Εθνικής Τραπέζης της Ελλάδος: 1841–1966* [The History of the Bank of Greece: 1841–1966], Athens 1966.

Statistical Society of London: *Journal of the Statistical Society of London*, London 1878 (June).

Στεφανίδης, Δ. [Stefanidis, D.]: Η εισροή ξένων κεφαλαίων και αί οικονομικαί και πολιτικαί της συνέπειαι [The Invasion of Foreign Capital and Its Economic and Political Consequences], in: *Επιστημονική επετηρίς Αριστοτέλειου Πανεπιστήμιου Θεσσαλονίκης εκδιδόμενη υπό της Σχολής των Νομικών και Οικονομικών Επιστημών* [Scientific Yearbook of the Aristoteles University Salonica edited by the School of Law and Economics] 1 (1930), pp. 25–335.

Stern, A.: Stein, Heinrich Friedrich Karl Freiherr vom und zum, in: *ADB*, 35 (1893), pp. 614–641.

Stern, F. R.: *Gold und Eisen: Bismarck und sein Bankier Bleichröder*, Munich 1988.

Stewart, R.: Viscount Castlereagh, Second Marquis of Londonderry (1769–1822), in: H. Boylan (ed.): *Dictionary of Irish Biography*, Dublin 3rd ed. 1998, B612.

Stoskopf, N.: *Banquiers et financiers parisiens* Paris 2002a (= Les patrons du Second Empire, Vol. 7).

Idem: La fondation du Comptoir national d'escompte de Paris, banque révolutionnaire (1848), in: *Histoire, économie et société* 21 (2002b) 3, pp. 395–411, https://www.persee.fr/doc/hes_0752-5702_2002_num_21_3_2310 [21.1.2020].

Suire, Y.: *Le Marais poitevin. Une écohistoire du XVIe à l'aube du XXe siècle*, La Roche-sur-Yon 2006.

Sunderland, D.: *Social Capital, Trust and the Industrial Revolution, 1780–1880*, London 2007 (= Routledge Explorations in Economic History, Vol. 34).

Supan: Die Trockenlegung des Kopaissees, in: *Dr. A. Petermann's Mitteilungen aus Justus Perthes' Geographischer Anstalt* 35 (1889), pp. 71–73.

Συγγρός, Α. [Syngros, A.]: *Απομνημονεύματα [Souvenirs]. Επιμέλεια: Ά. Αγγέλου/Μ. Χ. Χατζηιωάννου [Ed. by A. Angelos/M. C. Chatziioannou]*, Athens 1998.

Taffler, R. J.: The Representativeness Heuristic, in: H. K. Baker/J. R. Nofsinger (eds.): *Behavioral Finance. Investors, Corporations, and Markets*, Hoboken NJ 2010, pp. 259–276 (= The Robert W. Kolb Series in Finance).

Tanner, J.: Der diskrete Charme der Gnomen: Entwicklung und Perspektiven des Finanzplatzes Schweiz, in: C. M. Merki (ed.): *Europas Finanzzentren. Geschichte und Bedeutung im 20. Jahrhundert*, Frankfurt et al. 2005, pp. 127–165.

Idem: "Die Währung der Finanzmärkte ist Vertrauen": Nachhaltigkeit und Hinterhältigkeit eines mentalen Phänomens in historischer Perspektive, in: J. Baberowski (ed.): *Was ist Vertrauen? Ein interdisziplinäres Gespräch*, Frankfurt/New York 2014, pp. 73–100 (= Eigene und fremde Welten, Vol. 30).

Tarrade, H.: *Cross-Border Venture Capital Investments. Why Do Venture Capital Firms Invest at a Distance?* Wiesbaden 2012.

Tauger, M. B.: *Agriculture in World History*, London 2011.

Taylor, B.: Paying Off Government Debt (GFD White Paper), in: *Global Financial Data*, s.t., http://globalfinancialdata.com/paying-off-government-debt/, [10.2.2020].

Taylor, D.: *Don Pacifico. The Acceptable Face of Gunboat Diplomacy*, London 2008.

Taylor, J.: Privacy, Publicity, and Reputation: How the Press Regulated the Market in Nineteenth-Century England, in: *Business History Review* 87 (2013), pp. 679–701.

Tchernoff, J.: *Les Syndicats Financiers. Syndicats d'Émission et de Placement; Syndicats de Bloquage; Syndicats de Résistance; Syndicats de Bourse; Investment Trust; et Holding*, Paris 1930.

Tesar, L. L./Werner, I. M.: Home Bias and High Turnover, in: *Journal of International Money and Finance* 14 (1995) 4, pp. 467–492.

The Gibbs Archive: *Papers of Anthony Gibbs and Sons 1744 1953. Guildhall Mss 11021–96, 11108–11140, 111467–111474, 16869–16904, 19802–19888*. Microfilm, London 1984.

Theile, G.: Verteufelte Humanität. Weltbürger und Weimaraner in gutmeinender Absicht, in: N. Bolz (ed.): *Weltbürgertum und Globalisierung*, Munich 2000, pp. 29–41 (= Weimarer Editionen).

Θεοτόκης, Σ. Μ. [Theotokis, S. M.]: *Αλληλογραφία Ι. Α. Καποδίστρια – Ι. Γ. Εϋνάρδου, 1826–1831 [Correspondence I. A. Kapodistrias – J. G. Eynard, 1826–1831]*, Athens 1929.

Théry, E. (Directeur L'économiste européen): *La Grèce actuelle au point de vue économique et financier, études économiques et financières*, Paris 1905.

Theurl, T.: *Eine gemeinsame Währung für Europa. 12 Lehren aus der Geschichte*, Innsbruck 1992 (= Geschichte & Ökonomie, Vol. 1).

Thiersch, F.: Bemerkungen und Nachrichten über die neuesten Begebenheiten im eigentlichen Griechenland, in: *Allgemeine Zeitung* No 91, 116, 122, 130, 133, 131, 154, 155 (1821, Juni–September).

Idem: *De l'État actuel de la Grèce, et des moyens d'arriver à sa restauration*, Leipzig 1833.

Thomadakis, S.: Monetary Arrangements and Economic Power in the Nineteenth-Century Greece: The National-Bank in the Period of Convertibility (1841–77), in: *Journal of the Hellenic Diaspora* 12 (1985) 3, pp. 55–90.

Thomas, M.: *Mental Maps of Empire and Colonial Encounters*, Lincoln 2011 (= The French Colonial Mind, Vol. 1).

Tocqueville, A. de: *Voyages en Angleterre et en Irlande*, Paris 1835 (= Collection Idées Sciences humaines, Vol. 462).

Todorova, M. N.: *Imagining the Balkans*, New York 1997.

Tönnies, F.: *Gemeinschaft und Gesellschaft. Abhandlung des Communismus und des Socialismus als empirischer Culturformen*, Leipzig 1887.

Tornow, I.: *Das Münchner Vereinswesen in der ersten Hälfte des 19. Jahrhunderts, mit einem Ausblick auf die zweite Jahrhunderthälfte*, Munich 1977 (= Neue Schriftenreihe des Stadtarchivs München, Vol. 95).

Torp, C.: Weltwirtschaft vor dem Weltkrieg. Die erste Welle ökonomischer Globalisierung vor 1914, in: *Historische Zeitschrift* 279 (2004), pp. 561–606.

Τούντα-Φεργάδη, Α. [Tounta-Fergadi, A.]: *Ο Ιωάννης Καποδίστριας ως διπλωμάτης* [Ioannis Kapodistrias as Diplomat], Athens 2009.

Tourraix, A.: *Le mirage grec. L'Orient du mythe et de l'épopée*, Besançon 2000.

Trepp, A.-C.: Code contra Gefühl? Emotionen in der Geschichte, in: *Sozialwissenschaftliche Informationen: Sowi* 30 (2001), pp. 44–52.

Τρίχα, Λ. [Tricha, L.] (ed.): *Διπλωματία και πολιτική. Χαρίλαος Τρικούπης, Ιωάννης Γεννάδιος, Αλληλογραφία 1863–1894* [Diplomacy and Politics. Charilaos Trikoupis, Ioannis Gennadios, Correspondence 1863–1894], Athens 1991.

Idem: *Χαρίλαος Τρικούπης: Μία βιογραφική περιήγηση* [Charilaos Trikoupis: A Biographical Introduction], Athens 2009.

Idem: *Χαρίλαος Τρικούπης. Ο πολιτικός του «Τις πταίει» και του «Δυστυχώς επτωχεύσαμεν»* [Charilaos Trikoupis. The Politician of "Who Sins?" and "Unfortunately We Are Bankrupt"], Athens 2016.

Tricoupis, C.: *The Finances of Greece*. Speech Delivered on Introducting to the Hellenic Chamber the Budget for 1888 on November 2nd (November 14th) 1887, London 1887.

Troebst, S.: Vom spatial turn zum regional turn? Geschichtsregionale Konzeptionen in den Kulturwissenschaften, in: M. Middell (ed.): *Dimensionen der Kultur- und Gesellschaftsgeschichte. Festschrift für Hannes Siegrist zum 60. Geburtstag*, Leipzig 2007, pp. 143–159.

Τσακίρης, Δ. [Tsakiris, D.]: Η στάση της γερμανικής πολιτικής στο Ανατολικό ζήτημα και ειδικότερα σε σχέση με την Ελλάδα [The Position of German Politics in the Oriental Question and Especially the Relationship with Greece], in: K. Αρώνη-Τσίχλη [K. Aroni-Tsixlis]/Λ. Τρίχα [L. Tricha] (eds.): *Ο Χαρίλαος Τρικούπης και η εποχή του. Πολιτικές επιδιώξεις και κοινωνικές συνθήκες* [Charilaos Trikoupis and His Time. Political Aims and Social Conditions], Athens 2000, pp. 89–98.

Tsiovaridou, T.: La Répercussion en Grèce à la fin du XIXe siècle de la crise du raisin sec, in: *Balkan Studies* 21 (1980), pp. 128–145.

Τσουκαλάς, Κ. [Tsoukalas, K.]: *Κοινωνική ανάπτυξη και κράτος: Η συγκρότηση του δημοσίου χώρου στην Ελλάδα* [Social Development and State: the Building of a Public Space in Greece], Athens 1981.

Τσουλφίδης, Λ. [Tsoulfidis, L.]: *Οικονομική ιστορία της Ελλάδας* [Economic History of Greece], Θεσσαλονίκη 2009.

Tsoulfidis, L./ Zouboulakis, M.: Greek Sovereign Defaults in Retrospect and Prospect, in: *South Eastern Europe Journal of Economics* 27 (2016), pp. 141–157.

Tunçer, A. C.: *International Financial Control and Sovereign Risk in the Peripheries of the Gold Standard: A Comparison of Greece and the Ottoman Empire*, 2009, http://graduateinstitute.ch/files/live/sites/iheid/files/sites/international_history_politics/users/stefano_ugolini/public/papers/Tuncer.pdf [5.6.2015].

Idem: *How Did Creditors Enforce Sovereign Debt Contracts? International Financial Control during the Classical Gold Standard Era*, 2011, https://www.semanticscholar.org/paper/How-Did-Creditors-Enforce-Sovereign-Debt-Contracts-Tuncer/3d13048e70e0f3629fe38e6953666a4d5edb9095 [6.5.2015].

Idem: *Sovereign Debt and International Financial Control. The Middle East and the Balkans, 1870–1914*, Basingstoke 2015.

Turczynski, E.: *Sozial- und Kulturgeschichte Griechenlands im 19. Jahrhundert. Von der Hinwendung zu Europa bis zu den ersten Olympischen Spielen der Neuzeit*, Mannheim et al. 2003 (= Peleus, Vol. 16).

Turner, F. M.: Why the Greeks and Not the Romans in Victorian Britain? in: G. W. Clarke (ed.): *Rediscovering Hellenism. The Hellenic Inheritance and the English Imagination*, Cambridge et al. 1989, pp. 61–81.

Türr, I.: *Die Nationalitätenfrage in ihrem Zusammenhange mit der Wehrfrage*, Wien 1868.

Idem: Observations sur la guerre. Publié dans le Journal des débats à Paris le 7 octobre 1870, in: idem (ed.): *Solution pacifique de la question d'Orient*, Paris 1878a, pp. 25–30.

Idem: Question d'Orient. Le 15 décembre 1867, publié dans le Journal des débats à Paris en décembre 1867, in: idem (ed.): *Solution pacifique de la question d'Orient*, Paris 1878b, pp. 5–18.

Idem: Question des nationalités. Publié dans le Journal des débats à Paris en décembre 1867, in: idem (ed.): *Solution pacifique de la question d'Orient*, Paris 1878c, pp. 19–24.

Idem: *Bismarck et Garibaldi*, Paris 1887.

Tzermias, P. N.: *Neugriechische Geschichte: Eine Einführung*, Tübingen 1986.

Tziobas, D. (ed.): *Greek Diaspora and Migration since 1700. Society, Politics and Culture*, Farnham 2009.

Tzogopoulos, G.: *The Greek Crisis in the Media. Stereotyping in the International Press*, Farnham 2013.

Urquhart D.: (ed.): *La Turquie, ses ressources, son organisation municipale, son commerce, suivis de considérations sur l'état du commerce anglais dans le Levant*, Paris 1836.

Vacalopoulos, C. A.: *L'économiste français Arthemond de Regny et son rôle dans l'histoire financière de la Grèce (1831–1841): Recherches sur la période de la monarchie*, Salonica 1977.

Idem: Lemaitre et la crise financière de la Grèce (1842–1843), Salonica 1979.

Βακαλόπουλος, Α. Ε. [Vakalopoulos, A. E.]: *Ο κυβερνήτης Ιωάννης Καποδίστριας και το πρώτο ελληνικό κράτος (1828–1831)* [Govenor Ioannis Kapodistrias and the First Greek State (1828–1831)], Θεσσαλονίκη 2009.

Vakalopolos, K.: Der Beitrag der Schweizer Zeitung "Journal de Genève" zu den philhellenischen Aktivitäten im griechischen Freiheitskampf, in: A. Ruge/E. Konstantinou (eds.): *Europäischer Philhellenismus: die europäische philhellenische Presse bis zur ersten Hälfte des 19. Jahrhunderts*, Frankfurt et al. 1994, pp. 241–248 (= Philhellenische Studien, Vol. 3).

Βακαλόπουλος, Κ. Α. [Vakalopoulos, K. A.]: *Ευρωπαίοι φιλέλληνες, παρατηρητές και τεχνοκράτες στην επαναστατημένη Ελλάδα και στο ελλαδικό βασίλειο* (1821–1843) [European Philhellenes, Observers and Technocrats in Revolutionary Greece and in the Greek Kingdom (1821–1843)], Salonica 2008.

Βαλαωρίτης, I. A. [Valaoritis, I. A.]: *Ιστορία της Εθνικής Τραπέζης της Ελλάδος 1842–1902* [History of the National Bank of Greece 1842–1902], Athens 1902.

Vandendriessche, J. et al. (ed.): *Scientists' Expertise as Performance. Between State and Society*, 1860–1960, London 2015.

Βάρδα, X. [Varda, C.]: *Αρχείο Στέφανου Σκουλούδη και οικογένειας Αθηνογένη: Ευρετήριο* [Archive Stephanos Skouloudis and Familiy Athinogeni: Finding Aid]. ΕΛΙΑ (Ελληνικό Λογοτεχνικό και Ιστορικό Αρχείο) [Society of the Literary and Historical Archives], Athens 1995.

Vári, A.: River Regulation, Land Use, Property and Rural Society in Hungary from the Eighteenth Century to 1914, in: B. J. P. van Bavel (ed.): *Rural Societies and Environments at Risk. Ecology, Property Rights and Social Organisation in Fragile Areas (Middle Ages – Twentieth Century)*, Turnhout 2013, pp. 209–238 (= Rural History in Europe, Vol. 9).

Vaucelles, P.: Brunet de Presle, in: *DBF*, 7 (1956), pp. 550.

Βαβαρέτος, Γ. A. [Vavaretos, G. A.]: *Ο Γεώργιος Σταύρου και η Εθνική Τράπεζα* [Georgios Stavros and the National Bank], Athens 1967.

Vlachopoulou, A. S.: *Revolution auf der Morea. Die Peloponnes während der zweiten Turkokratie (1715–1821)*, Berlin 2017.

Βελεστινλής, P. [Velestinlis, R.]: Νέος Ανάχαρσις [New Anarchises], Vienna 1797 (new ed. Athens 2006).

Verhoeven, J. T. A.: Vegetation as a Resource in Wetlands with Special Reference to the Wetlands in Greece, in: P. A. Gerakes (ed.): *Conservation and Management of Greek Wetlands: Proceedings of a Workshop on Greek Wetlands*, Salonica, Greece, 17–21 April, 1989, Athens 1992, pp. 79–108.

Vidal-Naquet, P.: *Paris – Athen und zurück. Die griechische Demokratie von außen gesehen*, Munich 1996.

Vierhaus, R.: Liberalismus, in: O. Brunner/W. Conze/R. Koselleck (eds.): *Geschichtliche Grundbegriffe. Historisches Lexikon zur politisch-sozialen Sprache in Deutschland*, Stuttgart 1978, pp. 243–289.

Βικέλας, Δ. [Vikelas, D.]: Ο Γουσταύος Εϊχτάλ εν Ελλάδι [Gustav Eichthal in Greece], in: *Εστία* 21–22 (1886), pp. 337–242, 353–357, 369–372, 385–389, 401–403, 417–419.

Idem (ed.): Επιστολή Γουσταύου Εϊχτάλ [Letters of Gustav Eichthal], in: *Δελτίον της Ιστορικής και Εθνολογικής Εταιρείας της Ελλάδος* [Bulletin of the Historical and Ethnological Society of Greece] II (1887), pp. 515–520; IV (1892), pp. 331–343.

Vivier, N. (ed.): *The State and Rural Societies. Policy and Education in Europe, 1750–2000*, Turnhout 2008 (= Rural History in Europe, Vol. 4).

Vivier, N./Petmezas, S. D.: The State and Rural Societies, in: N. Vivier (ed.): *The State and Rural Societies. Policy and Education in Europe, 1750–2000*, Turnhout 2008, pp. 11–33 (= Rural History in Europe, Vol. 4).

Vlachopoulou, A.: Revolution auf der Morea. Die Peleponnes während der zweiten Turkokratie (1715–1821), in: *Südosteuropäische Arbeiten*, Vol. 157, Berlin 2017.

Vlasto, A. D.: La Grèce en 1884, in: *Nouvelle Revue* 34 (1885), pp. 263–289.

Βοβολίνης, K. A. [Vovolinis, K. A.]/Βοβολίνης, Σ. A. [Vovolinis, S. A.]: *Μέγα ελληνικόν βιογραφικόν λεξικόν* [Big Greek Biographical Dictionary], Vol. A-E, Athens 1958–1963.

Wain, K. M.: Hambro, Everard Alexander, in: *Dictionary of Business Biography*, Vol. 3, Butterworths 1986, pp. 16–18.

Watbled, E.: *Exploitation des mines du Laurium* (Grèce), Paris 1883.

Weatherall, D.: *David Ricardo. A Biography*, The Hague 1976.

Weckerle, F.: Die pfalzbayerische Sechs-Mio.-Anleihe bei den Häusern Schmaltz und Seeligman vom Jahre 1796. Ein Beitrag zur Finanzpolitik Pfalz-Bayerns unter Karl Theodor und Max I., zugleich zur Geschichte der Familie Seeligman-Eichthal, in: *Zeitschrift für Bayerische Landesgeschichte* 13 (1941/1942), pp. 297–329.

Wehler, H.-U.: *Bismarck und der Imperialismus*, Köln/Berlin 1969.

Weiss, J. H.: *The Making of Technological Man. The Social Origins of French Engineering Education*, Cambridge MA 1982.

Werner, W.: *Der Kanal von Korinth und seine Vorläufer*, Brilon-Gudenhagen 1993 (= Das Logbuch: Sonderheft).

Wiczlinski, V. von: *Im Zeichen der Weltwirtschaft. Das Frankfurter Privatbankhaus Gebr. Bethmann in der Zeit des deutschen Kaiserreichs 1870–1914*, Würzburg 2011.

Wilkins, M.: The Free-Standing Company, 1870–1914: An Important Type of British Foreign Direct Investment, in: *Economic History Review* 41 (1988) 2, pp. 259–282.

Williamson, R.: The Role of Culture in Finance, in: H. K. Baker/J. R. Nofsinger (eds.): *Behavioral Finance. Investors, Corporations, and Markets*, Hoboken NJ 2010, pp. 631–646 (= The Robert W. Kolb Series in Finance).

Willinger, M./Keser, C./Lohmann, C./Usunier, J.-C.: A Comparison of Trust and Reciprocity Between France and Germany: Experimental Investigation Based on the Investment Game, in: *Journal of Economic Psychologic* 24 (2003) 4, pp. 447–466.

Wilms, J.: *Talleyrand: Virtuose der Macht 1754–1838*, Munich 2011.

Wurzbach, C. v.: Türr, Stephan, in: *BLKÖ*, 48, 1883, pp. 91ff.

Wylegala, D.: Top Careers as a Means of Risk Management in Organisations, in: K. Schönhärl (ed.): *Decision Making, Confidence and Risk Management in Banks from Early Modernity to the 20th Century*. Basingstoke/Hampshire et al. 2017, pp. 57–79 (= Palgrave Studies in the History of Finance).

Wynne, W. H.: *State Insolvency and Foreign Bondholders, Vol II: Selected Case Histories of Governmental Foreign Bond Defaults and Debt Readjustments*, New Haven CT 1951 (= Yale Law School studies, Vol. 2).

Yannoulopoulos, Y.: Greek Society on the Eve of Independence, in: R. Clogg (ed.): *Balkan Society in the Age of Greek Independence*, Totowa NJ 1981, pp. 18–39.

Yéméniz, E.: *La Grèce moderne, héros et poètes*, Paris 1862 (= Bibliothèque contemporaine).

Idem: L'agriculture et les travaux publics en Grèce, in: *Revue des deux mondes* 57 (1865), pp. 858–891.

Zabel, C.: *Polis und Politesse. Der Diskurs über das antike Athen in England und Frankreich, 1630–1760*, Berlin/Boston MA 2016 (= Ancien Régime, Aufklärung und Revolution, Vol. 41).

Zahra, S. A.: Entrepreneurial Risk Taking in Family Firms, in: *Family Business Review* 18 (2005) 1, pp. 23–40, doi:10.1177/0894486518776871.

Ζακυνθινού-Ξάνθη, Μ. [Zakinthinou-Xanthi, M.]/Μυλωνά, Έ. [Milona, E.]/Τζουνίδου Ζ. [Tsounidou, Z.] (eds.): *Γεφυρώνοντας το παρελθόν με το μέλλον. Η διώρυγα της Κορίνθου. Όταν η Ελλάδα τολμούσε και θα ξανατολμήσει! Έκθεση Ιστορικό Αρχείο της Εθνικής Τράπεζας και την ομάδα διπλωματικής εργασίας της Σχολης Αρχιτεκτόνων*

Μηχανικών ΕΜΠ [Bridging past with future. The Canal of Korinth. When Greece Dared and Will Dare Again. Exhibition of the Historical Archives oft the National Bank of Greece and the School for Architects and Engineers EMP], Athens 2018.

Zelepos, I.: *Die Ethnisierung griechischer Identität 1870–1912. Staat und private Akteure vor dem Hintergrund der "Megali Idea"*, Munich 2002.

Idem: *Kleine Geschichte Griechenlands. Von der Staatsgründung bis heute*, Munich 2014 (= Beck'sche Reihe, Vol. 6121).

Idem: Griechenlands Krisenzyklen seit der Unabhängigkeit: Gründe und Erklärungsansätze, in: *Südosteuropa Mitteilungen* 55 (2015), pp. 65–81.

Ζωγράφος, Δ. Λ. [Zografos, D. L.]: *Ιστορία της ιδρύσεως της Εθνικής Τραπέζης: (1833–1843)* [History of the Foundation of the National Bank], Athens 1925.

Zons, R.: Weltbürgertum als Kampfbegriff, in: N. Bolz (ed.): *Weltbürgertum und Globalisierung*, Munich 2000, pp. 9–28 (= Weimarer Editionen).

PERSONS INDEX

Note: Page numbers followed by "EN" denote endnotes.

PLACES INDEX

Note: Page numbers followed by "EN" denote endnotes.

SUBJECTS INDEX

Note: Page numbers followed by "EN" denote endnotes.

For Product Safety Concerns and Information please contact our EU representative GPSR@taylorandfrancis.com Taylor & Francis Verlag GmbH, Kaufingerstraße 24, 80331 München, Germany

Printed and bound by CPI Group (UK) Ltd, Croydon, CR0 4YY
30/09/2026
02225126-0010